Russian Subjects

Russian Subjects

Empire, Nation, and the Culture of the Golden Age

Edited by
Monika Greenleaf
and
Stephen Moeller-Sally

NORTHWESTERN UNIVERSITY PRESS / EVANSTON, ILLINOIS

Northwestern University Press
Evanston, Illinois 60208-4210

Printed in the United States of America

ISBN 0-8101-1524-7 (cloth)
ISBN 0-8101-1525-5 (paper)

Library of Congress Cataloging-in-Publication Data

Russian subjects : empire, nation, and the culture of the Golden Age / edited by Monika Greenleaf and Stephen Moeller-Sally.
p. cm.—(Studies in Russian literature and theory)
Includes index.
ISBN 0-8101-1524-7 (cloth : alk. paper).—ISBN 0-8101-1525-5 (paper : alk. paper)
1. Russian literature—19th century—History and criticism. 2. Group identity in literature. 3. Nationalism in literature. 4. Imperialism in literature. 5. Russia—Civilization—19th century. I. Greenleaf, Monika, 1952– . II. Moeller-Sally, Stephen. III. Series.
PG3011.R74 1998
891.709'003—dc21 97-50445
CIP

The paper used in this publication meets the minimum requirements of the American National Standard for Information Sciences—Permanence of Paper for Printed Library Materials, ANSI Z39.48–1984.

Contents

Acknowledgments

From its conception a collaboration, this volume has depended on the painstaking labors and goodwill of many people on its journey into print. First of all, we would like to thank our contributors, who responded to our call for papers with unexpected enthusiasm and not a little amazement that we had actually volunteered to undertake such an enterprise. The conversation that emerges among them here did not proceed from a conference: no rubrics were set, no forms prescribed. Rather than create the conditions for a hasty command performance in an airless auditorium, we hoped to bring together parts of substantive, long-term projects that had been gestating in the individual studies and garrets of our colleagues.

We owe our deepest debt of gratitude to Caryl Emerson, who not only recognized the value of the project and the strength of its contributions, but also played our Virgil in the inferno of contemporary academic publishing. With her help, we emerged into the *paradiso* of Northwestern University Press, where we have enjoyed rare understanding and support for a kind of intellectual venture that is becoming ever more endangered. We could not have asked for more knowledgeable, meticulous, and penetrating readers than William Mills Todd III and Caryl Emerson herself. Their comments helped each paper reach its full potential and persuaded Northwestern University Press to publish a volume of uncommon and heroic girth. Our introductory essay also benefited from the experience and insight of our Stanford colleagues Lazar Fleishman and Gregory Freidin. We are grateful to Susan Harris, editor-in-chief at Northwestern University Press, whose energy and enthusiasm helped sustain us during the inevitable periods of waiting and who was always available to answer our questions. We would also like to thank Ellen Feldman, who ushered the manuscript smoothly through production.

Finally, let us celebrate the sheer luck of our conjunction at Stanford. Had we not pooled our inspiration, as well as our mutually complementary knowledge, skills, and intuitions, this book would not have materialized. Pushkin captures the exhilaration of such moments best: "Поздравим / Друг друга с верегом. Ура! / Давно в (не правда ли?) пора!"

Notes on Contributors

David M. Bethea is Vilas Research Professor of Russian Literature at the University of Wisconsin-Madison. He is the author of various books on modern Russian literature and culture, including *Khodasevich: His Life and Art* (Princeton, 1983), *The Shape of Apocalypse in Modern Russian Fiction* (Princeton, 1989), *Joseph Brodsky and the Creation of Exile* (Princeton, 1994), and *Realizing Metaphors: Pushkin, Derzhavin, and the Life of the Poet* (Wisconsin, forthcoming).

Melissa Frazier received her Ph.D. from the University of California at Berkeley and is on the faculty at Sarah Lawrence College. She has written on Pushkin, Tolstoy, and Senkovsky, and is currently working on a book entitled *Frames of the Imagination: Gogol's "Arabesques" and the Romantic Question of Genre*.

Monika Greenleaf is associate professor of Slavic and comparative literatures at Stanford University. She is author of *Pushkin and Romantic Fashion: Fragment, Elegy, Orient, Irony* (Stanford, 1994), and is presently deciding which of several projects on Gogol, Catherine the Great, and Tsvetaeva to finish first.

Jennifer J. Hixon is a doctoral student in the Department of Slavic Languages and Literatures at Yale University. She is completing her dissertation on Karamzin's historical fictions and his *History of the Russian State*.

Katya Hokanson is assistant professor in the Comparative Literature Program at the University of Oregon, where she teaches courses on Russian and European literature, travel literature, and literary theory. She is preparing for publication a book entitled *Russia Between East and West: A Genealogy of Russian Orientalism*, and has published and given conference papers on issues of Orientalism in nineteenth-century Russian literature and culture.

Judith Deutsch Kornblatt is associate professor of Slavic Languages and Literature at the University of Wisconsin-Madison. Although she continues to publish on Gogol (see the forthcoming *N. V. Gogol': Materialy i issledovaniia*, ed. Iu. V. Mann), her main research interests are now in Russian religious thought, particularly V. S. Solov'ev. She is the author of *The Cossack Hero in Russian Literature* (Wisconsin, 1992) and coeditor with Richard Gustafson of *Russian Religious Thought* (Wisconsin, 1996).

Sally Kux holds degrees from the University of Chicago and Stanford University. She is currently a program specialist at the United States Information Agency, where she administers educational reform programs in the NIS and Central Europe.

Ronald D. LeBlanc is an associate professor of Russian and humanities at the University of New Hampshire and a research associate at the Davis Center for Russian Studies at Harvard University. The author of *The Russianization of Gil Blas: A Study in Literary Appropriation* (Slavica, 1986) and several articles on Russian prose writers from the first half of the nineteenth century, he is presently at work on an annotated translation of what is arguably Russia's "first" novel, Vasily Narezhny's *Rossiiskii Zhilblaz*.

Stephen Moeller-Sally, assistant professor of Slavic languages and literatures at Stanford University, is soon to complete a book entitled *Gogol's Afterlife: The Evolution of a Classic in Imperial and Soviet Russia*.

Leslie O'Bell is associate professor of Slavic languages and literatures at the University of Texas at Austin. She is the author of a book and a number of essays on Pushkin as well as articles on other aspects of nineteenth- and twentieth-century Russian literature. Among her particular interests is Franco-Russian literary relations, which she has pursued in published pieces about Annensky's reception of Mallarmé and the reception of the nineteenth-century Russian novel in *Vogue*.

David Powelstock is assistant professor of Russian and Czech literatures at the University of Chicago. His book, *The Framing of Mikhail Lermontov*, will appear soon.

Harsha Ram is assistant professor in the Department of Slavic Languages and Literatures at the University of California at Berkeley. He is currently working on a book-length study of the literary expressions of Russian imperial culture from the eighteenth century to the revolutionary avant-garde, concentrating primarily on the poetry inspired by Russia's southern borderlands.

Irina Reyfman is associate professor of Slavic languages and literatures at Columbia University. She is the author of *Vasilii Trediakovsky: The Fool of the 'New' Russian Literature* (Stanford, 1990) and is currently completing a book on dueling in Russia.

Stephanie Sandler, professor of Russian and women's and gender studies, Amherst College, is author of *Distant Pleasures: Alexander Pushkin and the Writing of Exile* (Stanford, 1989), co-editor of *Sexuality and the Body in Russian Culture* (Stanford, 1993), and the editor of a collection of essays about Russian poetry (Yale, forthcoming in 1998).

Judith Vowles is an independent scholar. She is co-editor of *Sexuality and the Body in Russian Culture* (Stanford, 1993) and *Russia Through Women's Eyes. Autobiographies from Tsarist Russia* (Yale, 1996). She is also a contributor to *Women Writers in Russian Literature* and *The History of Russian Women's Writing* (Cambridge, forthcoming in 1998).

Monika Greenleaf and Stephen Moeller-Sally

Introduction

TO EVOKE THE Golden Age is to do more than designate a discrete period in Russian cultural history: it is to unroll a palimpsest of myths. Broadly defined, the Golden Age extends from the reign of Catherine the Great to the death of Nicholas I (that is, from 1762 to 1855); more narrowly it denotes the "Age of Pushkin." In either case, it was an era of mythic consciousness, permeated by a broad interest in classical antiquity and the deliberate cultivation of a style of empire modeled on the reign of Augustus.[1] Perceived as part of an imperial series originating in Rome and extending through France to Russia, the Golden Age was, in a real sense, made to be revived. During the second half of the nineteenth century, survivors of the Golden Age like Petr Viazemsky transformed it into an emblem of mourning: along with its defining personalities, characteristic ideologies, and institutional formations, its spirit seemed irretrievably lost. However, as the recent *Cultural Mythologies of Russian Modernism* so richly demonstrates, both the modernists at the turn of the twentieth century and the Soviet cultural elite would look to the period not only as a summit of cultural achievement, but also as a model for self-renewal.[2] In an effort to reanimate the genius of the period, the modernists channeled their energies into its distinctive cultural forms—for example, the salon and the poetic almanac—and cultivated their own mythic sensibilities. Subsequently, the Soviet cultural elite played on the Golden Age myth of a unique historical destiny. When we address the Golden Age, then, we must pay heed to the numerous abrasions left on it by the thumbnails and penknives of each succeeding historical generation.

The goal of the current volume is to reexamine Russia's Golden Age through the lenses of empire and nation. The historical relevance of these concepts to the Golden Age cannot be gainsaid: Russia was at this time a self-proclaimed empire—an absolutist multinational state subordinated to a military ruler and dedicated to its own territorial expansion. At the same time it was an increasingly self-conscious nation—a people bound together by a common language and cultural discourse. The essays gathered here thus return to the roots of a crisis of identity that has plagued Russia in the post-Soviet period. They remind us, however, that empire and nation not only represent different paradigms for the constitution of states and political institutions, but also exert a profound influence on subjective experience and its cultural representations. Three interlocking stages in Golden Age culture emerge: the invention of cultural analogues for imperial power and the translation of competition between imperial states to the realm of letters; the cultivation of national consciousness segregated from the state along lines of class, geography, and gender; the co-optation of nationhood by the state through control of the means for its imagining—print culture.[3] By retelling this story, the current volume breaks through the scrim of Russia's Golden Age myth to recapture a fundamental irony: if the rapid cultural development of the period was undertaken to substantiate Catherine and Alexander's *imperial* pretensions, it survives instead as the moment when a great *national* culture was born.

TRANSLATIO POETAE: POETICS OF EMPIRE

> Did the old classical whore . . . really exist here in Russia?
> —Pushkin, letter to P. A. Viazemsky, April 1824

The very uncertainty about the Golden Age's parameters in Russia reflects the underlying interference of two different paradigms: what one might call the "imperial" (French/Roman) paradigm of cultural transmission, as opposed to the "national" (English/German/"Greek") myth of organic original generation. Imitation and translation became a means for, not the opposite of, the fashioning of a modern national identity. By reproducing the forms (and the rules for production of those forms) of antiquity's Golden Age culture, a modern nation produced proofs of its own direct and august lineage, the fact of its inheritance. In contrast, Herder's apparently modest formulation, "If we do not become Greeks, we will remain barbarians,"[4] offered Germans a way of bypassing the gauntlet of neoclassical imitation and perpetual cultural adolescence by making their very "lateness" (newness) and "barbarity" (vigor) the basis for a truly original, national cultural flowering ("creation in the *spirit* of the ancients").[5]

The genealogy of the Catherinian-Alexandrine Golden Age reveals other important hybridizations as well. Russian ideologies of empire, for example, stemmed from two different sources. Up until the reign of Peter the Great, Byzantium served as the primary model for empire; only thereafter did Russian autocrats turn their sights to Rome.[6] As Stephen Baehr describes it in his *The Paradise Myth in Eighteenth-Century Russia*, with her "inheritance" (conquest) of formerly Byzantine territories, Russia annexed the physical and imaginary space for creating paradise on earth. The Golden Age was conceived as a return to Eden after the Fall: not as a modern progression forward, but as a return to perfection.[7] When Peter the Great introduced Russia into the forward relay of the Roman Golden Age tradition, a narrative of renewal, or *renovatio*, replaced the Byzantine image of a return to paradise. Richard Wortman's recent *Scenarios of Power* shows that each successive eighteenth-century ruler acceded to power by a real or symbolic act of violence that both imposed new conditions on the elite and bound it to the state by inaugurating a new spectacle of shared power and privilege. The empresses who succeeded Peter inherited the role established for his wife Catherine, a lowly peasant girl whom he had sculpted into a symbol of both Western culture and taste, and imperial aggression.[8]

If the ideal state had its roots in the culture of Byzantium and every eighteenth-century ruler laid claim to a Golden Age, how is it possible to consider Catherine II's reign the moment when Russia's age of gold was invented? First, more than any other Russian monarch, Catherine realized the political achievements that are associated with the originary Augustan model: the territorial acquisitions of Catherine's reign were unrivaled by any of her predecessors and finally brought Russia to geographic, not just rhetorical, parity with the Roman Empire, into which the old domains and spiritual mission of the Byzantine-Orthodox Empire were now incorporated. Second, it was in Catherine's reign that the spectacle of the Russian monarchy was projected, via Catherine's extensive, well-publicized travels and establishment of institutions of court life in the provinces, beyond the ruling elite to a broader national and European audience.

When Catherine II, the favorite monarch of enlightened *philosophes*, commissioned from the French sculptor Falconet the equestrian statue of Peter I, she inscribed Peter in the line of Europe's city- and nation-builders traditionally commemorated by equestrian statues;[9] in turn, she received from the statue's hands, as it were, legitimation for her own usurped crown. The statue had a double addressee and a double message: we belong to the European tradition, and I belong to Peter the Great's tradition. The erection of the statue together with its laconic inscriptive plaque brackets a Golden Age project that her own name and reign implicitly bring to fruition: military conquest yields to peacefully encompassing empire; visible, violent transformation to the slower-ripening fruits of inner civilization and "self-conquest"—literary art, the classical statue itself, imperial "subjecthood." By demonstrating Russia's engagement in the sign-system of European history, Catherine radically changed her empire's Golden Age ideal. No longer was Russia the hermetically enclosed mythological paradise of the East; instead, it became an active—if still exotic—participant in a political and cultural *entretien* with other imperial powers, most notably, France.

Catherine's Golden Age emerged as both the figurative form of legitimate, divinely and rationally ordained social organization and as a means for transforming Russia's geographical inhabitants into participants in a cultural endeavor from which they, in turn, received their new "identity."[10] Royal spectacle mediated between power and culture by establishing exemplary topics of discourse and acting as a catalyst for the development of a native Russian literary and cultural idiom. As an example, one might note the conversion of the image of *rai myslei* ("paradise of thought") associated with the divinity of eighteenth-century empresses first into an eclogic mini-kingdom of the Russian gentry estate, and then into a model for the interior world of the gentry subject.[11] Thus, the gentry's own "spectacles," which it undertook in a kind of oblique contest with the autocrat, were increasingly translated into writing. Gentry writers attempted to replicate in their own domain the discourse of power exercised by the monarch: in the nineteenth century, representations of the landscape would continue to echo the territorial conquests of the imperial army and fiction would become the locus of narratives intended to compete with the history of the state.

For finally, of course, each Golden Age asserts and stimulates rivalry. Thus in the years following her death, Catherine's Golden Age would be contested on two fronts. Alexander I was as eager to demote his foreign grandmother's political and cultural leadership (and blur the issue of his own bloodlines) as Pushkin was to dismiss Derzhavin's literary paternity as a monument "one quarter gold, three quarters lead," inscribed "not in Russian, but in Tartar."[12] Pushkin intimates a connection between Derzhavin's unorthodox grammar and the shameful taint of Russia's Mongol history: a suspected hereditary condition of foreign admixture, political subjection, and cultural and psychological "minority" that are located not safely outside—on the peripheries of the Russian empire—but inside the Russian mind and language. Catherine II's court was, in the eyes of Alexander I's lycée-educated, humanistic elite, a continuation of Russia's heritage of Eastern servitude, thinly disguised; and any poetry that issued from it was contaminated at the source. To borrow the era's own metaphorics, the spurious feminine realm of her despotism stood in relation to Alexander I's Europe-wide "Pax Russica" as Cleopatra's voluptuous Egypt had to Augustus's Rome. By contrast, Alexander came to the peace tables of Versailles (1814) and Vienna (1816) not as an Eastern potentate, but as the savior of the European nations from promiscuous fusion in Napoleon's empire. Russia's imperial might thus served, paradoxically, to guarantee the privilege of nationality to Europeans, while absorbing into her own body any incipient non-European struggles for self-determination.

That the object of our critical inquiry has been traditionally equated with the age of the two Alexanders tells us whose version won. If the Catherine period awaits further reassessment,[13] here we simply open the subject to further debate by beginning our Golden Age volume with Harsha Ram's "Russian Poetry and the Imperial Sublime." Ram locates the invention of modern Russian poetry and a potential discourse of the individual self precisely in the Catherine era, in the challenges of celebrating, perpetuating, justifying, and internalizing the space and cultural faces of empire. Catherine put into practice the "displacement and absorption" mechanism by which the improvisational/imperial "Western self" rapidly penetrated and exploited archaic cultures' more fixed belief systems.[14] In her *Nakaz* (*Instruction*), her allegorical "Tale of the Tsarevich Khlor," and her role as addressee of both panegyric odes and playful *entretiens*, she grafted a philosophical nomenclature of lawful monarchy onto the structures of "autocracy." The poets shaped by her court's culture perforce evince this same faculty of "displacement and absorption" in their own domains. Ram identifies the components of Lomonosov's remarkable synthesis: the revival of Longinus's "sublime" aesthetic of power and terror at precisely the moment when the concept of monarchy was being refounded on rational and legal grounds; and the fusion of a high religious lexicon, mountainous imperial landscape, and "rising" iambic meter that allow the Pindaric panegyrist's absorption of the tyrant's persona into his own. How that "imperial sublime" style gets translated into a new psychology of both grandiose identification and inward-turned subjectivity is then illuminated through the lens of Derzhavin's poetic development. In effect, Ram concludes, neither the Russian autocratic state nor the Russian subject exist, but are "endlessly produced and reaffirmed in the violent encounter" with the East.

Equally important for the forging of a flexible, improvisational Russian subjectivity was Derzhavin's importation of his comical oriental Murza persona into his "Odes to Felitsa." Murza's quasi-obsequious panegyric formulas may have the effect of "rendering Russia an oriental despotism precisely at the moment when the monarch's Western Enlightenment virtues are being lauded"; but they also turn courtly panegyric into King-and-Fool repartee, whose flickering irony and intimacy continually test the borders of the monarch's self-rule. For underlying the "liberties" taken with artistic form (familiarity of address, mixture of stylistic levels, crude physicality) was the often danger-fraught reality of the writer's changing legal status. Defined as slaves of the autocrat at the beginning of Catherine's reign, both gentry and nongentry writers were enabled, by her superimposition of "enlightened" standards of conduct upon an autocratic base, to negotiate—as representative and articulate imperial subjects—a new relationship with power, at first unofficial, then customary and eventually legal. Each of Derzhavin's epistle-odes to Catherine not only describes or exemplifies his unusual relations with the monarch, it changes them. As soon as she steps into the role he has designed and baited for her, that of philosophizing conversationalist, he has realigned the emperor-subject relationship. Derzhavin's most distinctive recurrent phrase—"*A ia* . . ." (While I . . .)—conveys his individualistic/Russian divergence from accepted cultural models, and also traces his wily negotiation for every inch of legroom in a situation of patronage where benevolence and despotism could alternate almost freely.

What made this eclectic palimpsest of rituals possible was eighteenth-century culture's affinity for spectacle, carnival, and all manner of dress-up and role-reversal: vertiginous glimpses of the contingency of both worldly identity and social law.[15] Lyric poetry conveyed a culture's power not merely to reshape geographical boundaries and the movements of its subjects, but to imprint the structures of the imaginary on the sensibility, the "I" of subjectivity itself.[16] Both as an officer in the major Napoleonic campaigns and as the poet of Russia's wartime experience and "Roman" civility, Konstantin Batiushkov was deeply identified with Alexander I's *translatio imperii* myth. Monika Greenleaf's "Found in Translation: The Subject of Batiushkov's Poetry," suggests that even as Batiushkov clothes himself in the poems he selects for translation or imitation, they tell ventriloquistically of the lyrical and cultural predicament of the Alexandrine subject, striving to hold together Golden Age, total war, and budding national spirituality in a durable form. Through an international and self-less phantasmagoria of voices and costumes, involving a persistent metaphorical play with fluttering draperies and imminent unclothing, erotic interruption and "raising" of dead cultures, Batiushkov dramatizes the Russian subject's disappearance precisely as he materializes in language. Thus, we can now see that his grandly culture-encompassing collection, *Essays in Verse and Prose*, which chimed perfectly with Alexander's imposition of a characteristically Russian peace on Europe in 1816, was also to be the epitaph of the "Augustan Age."

The essays in the first part, "*Translatio Poetae*," thus explore individual instances of this characteristic stage of cultural apprenticeship, whose aim may have been initially to pay tribute to the cultural "forefather" and to appropriate his skills, but instead ended up indenting his text with marks of the son's incorrigible difference, his irreducible Russian identity. It is conceivable, for example, that Derzhavin might simultaneously recall Western imperial forms (Pindaric and Horatian ode, Anacreontic and pastoral), and not reproduce them purely; his very protrusion beyond the mode's confines, his "barbaric" roughness of language, the syncretic contamination of Western by oriental forms would then manifest the irreducible originality and excess of Russia's young, vigorous culture, just beginning its trajectory as the surrounding European *and* Eastern cultures waned.

We can begin to detect a collaboration, rather than opposition, between Russian "translation and imitation," on the one hand, and "self-fashioning and national identity" on the other. Reread in this light by Leslie O'Bell, for example, Krylov's fables no longer emerge as clumsy approximations of La Fontaine's sophisticated anecdotes, but as far more daring explorations of the expressive potential of popular humor, nonliterary, peasant, and dialectal strata of the spoken language, and authentic "native" narrative forms than his French model ever dreamed of. Once Krylov undertook to write fables, comparisons with La Fontaine were inevitable; indeed, Krylov's career as a fabulist began in 1806 with several translations of La Fontaine. Despite the persistence of the comparison between the two, O'Bell shows that the Russian's path to the fable was quite different from the Frenchman's, not least of all because Krylov consciously fashioned his own fabulist's persona on the model of Aesop. The result is a role-reversal: the French "original" pales in comparison with its earthy Russian "copy." Russian culture thus emerges as intrinsically more vigorous, original, closer to "the spirit of the ancients" and the sources of poetic language, and more "internally free," as Fonvizin liked to insist,[17] than the elegant and exsanguinated salon-cultures of modern Europe.

Variations on this French-Russian role-reversal resound throughout the culture of the Golden Age. Ronald D. LeBlanc's article argues that Nikolai Gogol achieved in the novel what Krylov had earlier accomplished in the fable. If Russia had produced superior poetry during the first two decades of the nineteenth century, its original prose fiction, particularly the novel, was only embryonic. Russian readers contented themselves, therefore, primarily with translated novels. The earliest attempts to initiate a native novelistic tradition (for example, Vasily Narezhny's *A Russian Gil Blas*) drew openly on foreign models, from the Continental picaresque novel to the English social comedy. Although Lesage's *Gil Blas de Santillane* enjoyed great vogue in the early nineteenth century, in fact Fielding's *Joseph Andrews* had been the most frequently translated and excerpted English novel in eighteenth-century Russian periodical literature.[18] Against this background, LeBlanc re-poses the question of intertextual dialogue between *Dead Souls* and *Tom Jones*. As it turns out, Gogol could have had access to Fielding's novel only in a ruthlessly abridged French translation by Pierre-Antoine de la Place. Drawing on Bakhtin's notion of genre memory, LeBlanc contends that Gogol "read through" La Place's bowdlerization to recapture the digressive lyricism and comic spirit of *Tom Jones* in his own *Dead Souls*. In this reading, then, Gogol's novel represents a double victory over French literature, subverting both its reigning influence on the Russian novel and its pale translation of the English style.

No one was so thoroughly yet ambiguously associated with the enterprise of cultural translation as Pushkin. To be sure, he referred to himself nonchalantly as the Russian Tiberius or the Russian Ovid as often as he impersonated Byron, represented his exile on the southern periphery of the Russian empire as an enviable immersion in the land of classicism's origins, and shared jokes with his friends at the enlightened emperor's expense ("Our Augustus looks like September"). Yet the continual efforts by Pushkin's contemporaries to groom him into a national genius were meant to counter anxiety about the changeably fashionable, minor, and derivative aspects of his works even as he wrote—for who, as Wilhelm Kiukhel'beker reminded him and his elegiacally redundant colleagues, "translates translators?"[19] The unspoken fear was that even Pushkin was still part of the old collective imperial culture, with its witty or melancholy reproduction of civilized forms and its fatal lack of creative originality. This may partly account for Pushkin's exultant feeling of breakthrough as he wrote *Boris Godunov*: "I can create!"[20]

Pushkin's Southern Poems have traditionally been treated as his "translation" of the European trope of the Orient. In a bold revisionary reading of "The Fountain of Bakhchisarai" (which should be read in dialogue with Ram's essay on the imperial sublime), Katya Hokanson shows how Pushkin takes back the Tatar Crimea as a subject creatable only by Russian poetry. The poem's complex time frame displays a long history of Russian-Tatar relations unmediated by Europe, just as its epigraph from the Persian poet Saadi and its quasi-qaasida form identify the Russian poet as inheritor of an ancient Arabic line of love and nature poetry. The Russian poet-traveler thus inherits the Tavrida directly from Russian-Tatar history and ancient poetic tradition, bypassing the mediation of tsar, imperial/Western culture, Byron and Moore, and the bastardized "Tatar-Russian" of Derzhavin's panegyrics. Pushkin asserts his right to build on the ruins of a defunct culture his more permanent Russian "empire of the imagination."

FEMININE LANDSCAPES

If the neoclassical/humanistic mirror was cracking—no longer able to differentiate the "fairest" of the moderns, much less to organize the complex cultural vectors bearing down on nineteenth-century Russian society into a unified image—what would take its place? In particular, what "self-story" would the gentry, soundly punished for its attempted coup in 1825 and increasingly disempowered in the still further bureaucratizing state of Nicholas I, find to tell? It is quite possible to view the proliferation of literary genres in the literature of the 1820s not simply as a Golden Age flowering stimulated by the military prestige, prosperity, and cosmopolitan contacts of the Russian Empire, but as the product of the threatened gentry-elite's intensifying search for self-expression and a new basis of influence.[21]

As their relationship with the state apparatus became more complex, gentry writers increasingly favored the land-based identity of the European nobility to the service ethos of the tsarist court.[22] This turn found its literary expression in an affiliation with the more ancient voices of nature and archaic-pastoral art, mute and buried under the crust of modern life until they were heard and resuscitated by the Russian poet's meditative inspiration. What differentiates the Russian version from other Romantic landscape poetry is its frequent association not with Wordsworthian valleys and language "common to all," nor with foreign Byronic places open to any traveler's view and poetic associations, but with the country estate of the gentry family, poetically hallowed by the inherited language of pastoral. Pushkin himself pointed out the affinity of this genre of landscape poetry with the Flemish genre paintings of local country-scenes and water- or ice-scapes with which Dutch city-dwellers decorated their homes: in each case the devotion to country values is compensatory or symbolic. Unlike in England, Germany, or even France, landed estates changed hands frequently in Russia and were treated as rarely visited sources of income and occasional retreat. Country traditions, much like the imaginary bridge Manilov flings across his pond, were invented in the nineteenth century to flesh out the Russian gentry's precarious "identity."[23]

It was Pushkin's house arrest at the family estate of Mikhailovskoe that, despite his loud complaints of terminal boredom, endowed the trope of country inspiration with a modicum of reality. Symbolic of this tactical gilding of the gentry's own forced rustication or marginalization, is Tatiana's emergence from her beloved Russian countryside to preside with "natural elegance" over the Petersburg "world." The story of her "Napoleonic" conquest of Moscow and then Petersburg can be seen as an allegory both of the poet's literary ascendance, and of its cost. The dwindling patrimony of gentry prerogatives (ramshackle country houses, inner refinement nourished by reading and compensatory imagination, which in turn engender love of local nature and attention to "native" superstitions and customs and family lore) is projected onto the charismatic figure of Tatiana, "deva russkaia dushoiu," in whom weakness and disadvantage are alchemically transmuted into strength, and whose specific incarnation of "Russian identity" would exercise precisely the symbolic power over the national imagination that the nobleman had in practical terms lost.[24]

The frequent donning by Russian authors of "transvestite" narrative disguise can also be viewed as the telltale sign of their disempowerment, with its attendant tactical necessity of constructing a Russian identity—*faute de mieux*—out of the feminine, childlike, or bourgeois virtues of silence, nature, and spirituality. Tatiana is rewarded with recognition she does not seek or desire for what she *is* or involuntarily images, rather than for what she does or wants (indeed the noble stillness of her image is predicated on the sacrifice of her desire and volition). Thus Russian identity is defined as an essence already contained within, to be seen and recognized by the world, not made.[25] Tatiana has in consequence been naturalized as a revelation of true Russian womanhood, rather than as Pushkin's willful act and artifact—his own reconquest of the right to fashion and refashion "Russian identity," the very categories through which a Russian subjectivity thought its relation to the world.

Tatiana figures not only the growing sublimation of the gentry's social status into inner values, but also the available roles for women within Golden Age culture. The examples of Evgeny Baratynsky and Karolina Pavlova show, in fact, how these two trajectories converged. As a proponent of what is called in Russian criticism the "poetry of thought," Baratynsky cultivated images of solitude that, as Stephanie Sandler and Judith Vowles write in this volume, seemed the site of thought itself, but also characterized the poet's experience in society. Pavlova found in Baratynsky's pose of isolation a perfect model for her own experience as a woman poet on the margins of a male-dominated poetic culture. With Baratynsky as her interlocutor, Pavlova would circumvent the gender-specific conventions of occasional poetry and transform light verse into the stage of her poetic debut. However, as her variations on the familiar epistle suggest, the poet nonetheless found herself in a position of seclusion. She addresses not her equals in a network of familiar associations, but either herself or an expansive natural world that extends beyond the civilized boundaries of the aristocratic country house. She images this position as a state of "virgin wildness" that, because its power could not be contained within a recognizable form, is destined to remain inarticulate.

If the form and pressure of Nicholas I's growing bureaucratic state caused the gentry to retreat into splendid, if sometimes mute, isolation, it also gave impetus to the compensatory myth of the Russian Cossack. As Judith Deutsch Kornblatt's essay illustrates, in works like Gogol's *Taras Bul'ba*, the notion of virgin wildness, that force which lay beyond the bounds of state and civilization, is transposed from a lyric into a heroic key. The Cossack runs roughshod over the domestic boundaries within which the gentry increasingly invested its identity and self-esteem. To his wife or lover, he prefers the brotherhood of the *sech'*, the damp mother earth, the boundless steppe. Indeed, the Cossack's very freedom depends on the exclusion of women, as if the feminine were the objective correlative of the state. Thus, with its recurrent motif of nonreproductive regeneration, *Taras Bul'ba* both rescues for Russians a space liberated from the restrictions of autocratic rule and enacts the possibility of a narrative unencumbered by the discourse of the state.

ALTERNATIVE HISTORIES

The very fact that Russia was recycling the Golden Age model at the beginning of the nineteenth century, precisely when concepts of national identity were coalescing around notions of a unique history shaped by and engraved on the people's "spirit" or national character, made it an exercise in historical irony. By this time it was a sine qua non for any European state to legitimate its existence historically. The most powerful narrative for an elite to gain control of was, therefore, the nation's history. Needless to say, quite different versions could be told, not only in fiction, but in historiography itself. Between Karamzin's monarchist-providential history of the Russian state and Polevoi's Romantic history of the Russian people[26] the political history of the gentry had been elided, a story that by its loss of power it had forfeited the right to tell—at least in the overt form of historiography.

One of the legacies of eighteenth-century skeptical thought was the blurring of the border between historical documentation and historical fiction. This rested on a recognition of authorial interestedness, the inevitable embedding of a metahistorical and ideological perspective in every assembling and narration of "facts," copying of documents, and even the perceptual process itself. Walter Scott's use of a "peripheral hero,"[27] who participates in and narrates historical events he cannot comprehend, or comprehends quite differently at various physical and temporal removes, was among other things a shrewd demonstration of this eighteenth-century philosophy of history—popularized at precisely the time that Russian national histories began to be written.

Karamzin's several historical versions of the Time of Troubles (so masterfully analyzed by Caryl Emerson),[28] as well as his two radically different representations of the subduing of Novgorod by the centralizing Muscovite state, illuminated in this volume by Jennifer Hixon, further expand the hermeneutic potential of historical representation. If in "Marfa Posadnitsa" the heroine and her city's unique civic culture are invested with a legendary and Russian resonance, these are treated by the state historiographer Karamzin as "unwomanly" acts of leadership and excessive individualism presaging a French Revolution-like disorder that can only be averted by the coalescence of national monarchy. Hixon demonstrates, however, that the overt story of the founding, legitimacy, and ultimate providentiality of the existing state power is fugally intertwined with a covert story of suppressed losses on which the authority of the state—together with the author's identity as its historiographer—have been built.[29]

Karamzin's representation of archaic values as a feminine force in "Marfa Posadnitsa" establishes a crucial topos in the Russian historical imagination. The most obvious pair of stories, around which opposing myths of Russian identity would cluster for the next two hundred years, were the alternate myths of eternal *matushka-Moskva* and history-making Petersburg. Stephen Baehr's essay shows that Griboedov's *Woe from Wit* may represent the first sustained attempt to construct an image of Russian identity around a covert myth of Moscow's death and resurrection. Under the surface of Griboedov's slightly archaic comedy of manners, encrypted in a network of paronomastic allusions to fire, lies an allegory of Moscow's recent history: her apocalyptic immolation at the hands of Napoleon, the restoration of the city's buildings and its dead crust of social and intellectual forms—such as the reified comedy of manners we are watching—while the live sparks of change continue to smolder in the spiritual life of its secret societies. Read in this light, *Woe from Wit* emerges as a highly suggestive model for Tolstoy's later, thorough mythologization of Moscow as the heart of Russian identity in *War and Peace*, complete with the planting of the seeds in the great Moscow fire of Pierre's spiritual renewal and future Decembrist involvement.

In answer to the Decembrists' attempted coup and desire to establish a constitutional monarchy in Russia, Nicholas severely curtailed certain distinctive privileges of the gentry class. The executions and brutal physical punishment of "six hundred" Decembrist sons of the old gentry, violated this estate's immunity, gradually won during the Catherine age, from corporal punishment, and thus eliminated one of its defining boundaries. What is more, now not only public action and published language, but also private life, communication—even thought—would be liable to routine governmental scrutiny and regulation. For example, when before 1825 Pushkin had been subjected to extraordinary measures of surveillance and punishment (the long exile under police jurisdiction, as well as humiliating personal surveillance by bureaucratic superiors, his father, mistress, a local priest), these measures were a mark of his special standing.[30] After 1825 he would perceive the abrogation of his right to passport-free travel (according to the *Complete Collection of Russian Imperial Laws* then a prerogative granted exclusively to the gentry, not to the urban trading or peasant classes) as an intolerable infringement of his identity as a *gentleman*. "Citizenship" was thus transformed from a status that guaranteed a certain degree of legal protection and dignity, into an encroachment by the legal and public domains on the aristocracy's privileged freedoms or exemptions from common law.

Hotly contested between the centralized state and the service-nobility was the domain of personal conduct. In the absence of a legal code that would adjudicate civil grievances, Russian nobles, like their European counterparts, settled their differences "out of court" in duels governed by an arbitrary etiquette and enforced by notions of social honor and shame. This autonomous set of rules marked a violent challenge to the monarch's authority over the nobleman's body and honor. Represented as "historic traditions" of the nobility, these practices were, as Irina Reyfman observes, recently imported and highly contemporary, reaching their apogee in the decades preceding and following the Decembrist rebellion. In her article on Alexander

Bestuzhev-Marlinsky as practitioner and theorist of the duel, she uses specific dueling incidents to establish both the formal structure and the consciously held political resonance of these rituals, often represented as acts of public protest and civil self-defense by a "middle" or "democratic" class under siege by the state. Reyfman's analysis of the *self*-defining function of the duel in Russian culture explains why Bestuzhev's dueling tales and personal legend played a key role in shaping the tastes of the expanding popular reading public of the 1830s. If Pushkin polemicized to some degree with Bestuzhev in his depiction of the Onegin-Lensky duel, he conducted his own fatal duel in 1837 in strict accordance with the tragic ethos formulated by his contemporary.

No less than they demanded control of their own bodies, the gentry defended their right to tell their own story, despite the incursions of the state. If the monarchy relied on subsidized writers like Bulgarin to deface the historical narratives of aristocratic writers, the latter, as William Mills Todd III has shown, were equally determined to guard the borders of literary genre and diction against interlopers of dubious breeding and taste. As Sally Kux reveals in her contribution to this collection, the gentry did not find a grand historical narrative that could compete with Karamzin's and Polevoi's necessary or even desirable. Petr Viazemsky, for one, defended the anecdote, still redolent of oral wit and the salon's theater of symbolic power, as the only appropriate and accurate form for a history of the gentry. Pushkin, too, toyed with a similar model of auto-historiography in his "Table-talk," but ultimately settled on another solution. It is no accident that, as Tatiana moves from provincial periphery to her central role as "law-giver" of the Petersburg salon, the narrator also promises to leave *Eugene Onegin* behind and devote himself to a "family chronicle" or historical novel—the only form, Pushkin had come to feel, in which the history of his class could be preserved.

Even as he enmeshed himself in the inexorable series of moves that would lead to his death by duel in 1837, Pushkin completed his last masterpiece, the historical novel *The Captain's Daughter*. David Bethea allows us to perceive anew the boldness and philosophical originality with which Pushkin fuses his fictionalized portrait of a beleaguered gentry family's participation in history, with a powerful evocation of the uniqueness of the Russian psyche. The improvisational exchange of life-and-death gifts binds Pugachev and Grinev ever more closely in a drama of mutual generosity and honor that overrides the purported political conflict between two classes despoiled by the throne. It is also this gift exchange outside bureaucratic and social law that brings Grinev to an immovable consciousness of his own honor, even if expressed only in silence. In Bethea's reading, Pushkin leaves the image of the gifted, historically recurring and renewing pretender as his last word on Russian identity—and as his own last gift to Russia.

ENCROACHING MODERNITY: THE PUBLIC AND THE SUBJECT

As literary life turned, along with Pushkin, from poetry to prose, literature was gradually transformed into the domain of the publicly owned "author." The stimulus to this change was the development of literary commerce; characteristically for Russia, the story is one of late arrival and compressed development. Private printing presses were not generally permitted in Russia until 1783, several centuries after they appeared in England and France.[31] Catherine's liberation of the printing press from exclusive service to the practical and political demands of the state encouraged the development of a limited, but by no means inconsequential, forum of public opinion. Despite periodic retrenchments during the French Revolution, Paul's reign, the Napoleonic Wars, and following the Decembrist rebellion, the book trade and the incipient public sphere it nourished grew rapidly and brought into relief the question of the relationship between literature and society. Indeed, if we juxtapose those poems of Pushkin that bound him to a network of intimate aristocratic associations with such metapoetic works as "Conversation of The Bookseller and the Poet" or "The Poet and the Crowd," we can see that the very terms of the relationship were undergoing a metamorphosis.[32] What was literature? Who belonged to society?

These questions stood at the forefront of Russian cultural consciousness in the 1830s, when the book trade had become fully established and the Pushkin period ceded to what Belinsky called, after the leading publisher and bookseller of the decade, the Smirdin period. The professionalization of literature, which began in the 1820s and rapidly coalesced into an established system during the 1830s, drew the man of letters out of the closed circle of aristocratic equals into a public sphere circumscribed by technology, laws, contracts, and the profit motive. At once the driving force behind the book trade and a prize in the struggles between literary factions, the Russian reading public of the 1830s—not only larger, but also geographically and socially more diverse than in the previous decade—entered into a relationship of collaborative self-fashioning with the writers of the time. The task of engaging this new audience was complicated for the gentleman-amateur by the appearance of such author-publishers as Faddei Bulgarin and Osip Senkovsky, who catered doggedly to established tastes and for whom commercial ingenuity meant more than literary craft and aesthetic innovation. Indeed, the brief lives of Pushkin's *Literary Gazette* and Kireevsky's *European* revealed that, as the forum for literature shifted from the salon to the periodical press, business acumen would be as important as new modes of artistic expression to the success of the new gentleman-professional.[33]

The commodification of literature induced a certain anxiety of authorship among Russia's literary elite, for the printing press threatened to drown the originality they associated with literature in a potentially infinite reproduction of texts. Earlier the German Romantics of the Jena circle had also perceived this threat and conceived in response an ideal modern genre that could hold formally diverse parts together in a state of irresolution. This dynamic structure resisted the ossification of reproduction as its resolution into a whole varied with each individual reader. Nikolai Gogol's *Arabesques*, a collection of essays, prose tales, and critical articles, asserted an affinity for this concept of genre in its very title and miscellaneous contents. However, as Melissa Frazier's analysis of this work shows, the tension between part and whole extends directly from the question of literary genre to the formation of a public sphere. While Gogol did not, as did some of his contemporaries, reject the development of literary commerce in Russia, he did harbor reservations about the impact of the printing press on modern society. Specifically, Gogol saw in it the demise of architecture as the primary force shaping public life: lost to the chaos of infinitely multiplying literary texts was the grandeur, order, and unity symbolized by religious architecture. Communities that were once collectively elevated by the sheer ascent of a Gothic spire could now congregate only incompletely under the fragmentary arches of the letter.

If the printing press shattered the unified community of the Middle Ages, it ultimately fractured the Golden Age as well. Poetry, which had been intimately identified with the Golden Age project, now found itself in a state of crisis: pushed to the margins by the contingencies of literary journalism, bereft of the ludic space that had formerly vitalized its language, pressed by demands to match the ideational content and cultural relevance of prose.[34] Perhaps most important, the relationship between the poet and his audience had changed. In a literary environment dominated by the periodical press, the poet addressed his audience increasingly as a *public* figure. David Powelstock examines this phenomenon in his essay on Lermontov's aesthetic mythology of the poet. As an initial response to the "crisis" of poetry, Lermontov determined that his primary poetic task was to realize his unique self in the image of a poet-hero, which he projected to the reading public in his verse. Events in his own life, especially the scandal surrounding his poem on the death of Pushkin, would later overtake this image and would cause Lermontov to comprehend his poetic persona as a product of negotiation and co-production with his audience. In an ironic reversal, his poetic self was becoming ever more important to his reception just as the self-referentiality of his poetry was decreasing. Lermontov's self-fashioning proceeded, then, not by his manipulation and projection of selected cultural codes, but by the creation of a subject's space into which his readers interpolated their own image of the poet.

The collaborative self-fashioning of author and public manifested itself even more visibly in the career of Nikolai Gogol.[35] Unlike Lermontov in poetry, Gogol did not have the safeguard of a well-cultivated native tradition. And unlike Pushkin, whose multiple public guises—as historian, lyric poet, author of folk tales, critic, publisher, historical novelist—could all somehow be predicated on his aristocratic privilege not to coincide with his "self," Gogol's social status had little buttress outside the contemporary institutions of literature. As Stephen Moeller-Sally's contribution to this volume shows, Gogol exploited these institutions to create for himself a freer and more mobile subjectivity. Masquerading behind a series of pseudonyms in the early 1830s, Gogol sought refuge from the reifying force of Petersburg's constituent (and constitutive) sign systems—economic, bureaucratic, social, cultural—which marked him as an outsider. Subsequently, his stories "Nevsky Prospect," "Diary of a Madman," and "The Nose" show him translating the crisis of subjectivity he himself had experienced as a Petersburg ingenu into a series of ironic, hypothetical selves. However, popular literary journalism—particularly in the person of Osip Senkovsky—brought to Gogol's attention the perils of the literary masquerade and the provisional subjectivity that attended it. Finally, in 1835, he committed himself to a relationship with the Russian reading public under his own name and in the identifiable role of "author."

By the beginning of the 1840s authorship had coalesced into a single system of entrapment for the creative and free "aristocratic" spirit.[36] Ironically, it was not the gentleman Pushkin who would be ensnared in this web, although it is possible, especially during the final years of his life, to discern in him the figure of his hero Don Juan, hounded by society and the law. Instead it was Gogol, the eccentric, dubiously educated son of a petty Ukrainian landowner and poor cousin to the urban salons, who under the public's weighty anticipation of the second volume of *Dead Souls* would struggle—and fail—to find a form adequate to his perceived authorial mission.

Although Pushkin remained vigorously productive even during the mid-1830s, the years of his perceived decline, in death he would himself finally be overtaken by the logic of the printing press. As a means for representing a vivid and unified image of national identity Pushkin was appointed cultural forefather and the public was subsequently "imprinted" with his image and cult. The increasingly efficient and profitable printing and publicity industries clearly facilitated the simultaneous multiplication of a national author's texts, in their now official and critically "authorized" editions, and of reader-consumers eager for their product. Marcus C. Levitt has persuasively documented the ways in which literary, educational, and social institutions were mobilized by the Russian state to purvey an expurgated, noncontroversial figure of national unity: "*Pushkin-klassik*," visibly incarnated in the Pushkin statuary sprinkled across the city squares of the sprawling empire, and in the periodic state-run celebrations that sought to bind time to a historical and soothingly rhythmic narrative.[37] At the same time, precisely those things that were omitted or suppressed from an easily legible, monolithic image of the national poet could constitute secret spiritual identities that invited recovery by oppositional groups. National self-definition, the major preoccupation of both the Russian state and the Russian intelligentsia for the next century and a half, would continue with remarkable tenacity to write itself on Pushkin's texts.

If we set aside, for the moment, its religious-prophetic dimension, Dostoevsky's Pushkin speech of 1880 may provide the most successful and suggestive mediation between the two Golden Age poles of emblematic "translation and imitation" and national originality. Dostoevsky locates Pushkin's distinctive Russian identity precisely in his talent for multiple impersonation, eclectic kleptomania and instant "displacement and absorption" of diverse cultural strands in a synthetic new form. In this way, Dostoevsky echoes the reversal of the host/guest relationship that Pushkin's Peter had announced in "The Bronze Horseman":

Все флаги в гости будут к нам,
И запируем на просторе!

(All flags will be our guest,
and we'll throw a feast in the expanse!)

It is so customary to position Russia with the archaic, fixed, or "reactive" cultures vis-à-vis the conceptually advanced and exploitative West, that it might be refreshing to turn the schematic tables: to view "imitation" not as a passive, reverent, emasculated, or otherwise uncreative cultural activity, but as a necessary component of impersonation and improvisation, the fastest possible way for a cultural "latecomer" to break and enter, pilfer, and utterly transform a thickly settled cultural field. The authors of Russia's Golden Age might see an irreverent emblem of their subjectivity in the illimitable figure of Gogol's imaginary imperialist Nozdrev who exceeds the borders of his estate while in the very act of displaying them to Chichikov: "There's the boundary! . . . Everything you can see on this side, all this is mine, and even on the other side, that's mine too, that whole forest that shows blue, and everything beyond that forest, it's all mine."

Much like Nozdrev, we have tried in this introduction to map the expansive domain of Russia's Golden Age culture. Each essay, however, has an independent conceptual direction and material that can be pursued further in the larger projects from which they are excerpted. Taking them together, the readers of this volume will share in the discovery of an energetic ferment in scholarship on Russia's Golden Age.

Translatio Poetae: *Poetics of Empire*

Harsha Ram

Russian Poetry and the Imperial Sublime

THE LITERATURE OF EMPIRE

If asked whether Russia's writers have ever pondered the question of empire, a reader familiar with the Russian tradition would readily point to the "Caucasian theme" in Russian letters. From Pushkin's Byronic poem *Prisoner of the Caucasus* (*Kavkazskii plennik*, 1822) to the poetry and fiction of Lermontov and Tolstoy, Russia's nineteenth-century engagement in the Caucasus and Transcaucasia steadily evolved from a topical theme into a literary tradition, spanning at least the heyday of Russian Romanticism, and culminating somewhat belatedly in Tolstoy's realist novella *Hadji Murat* (1896–1904).

Following a historical trajectory whose beginnings this essay will seek to delineate more precisely, a prolonged and still incomplete chapter in Russian imperial history has thus acquired a singular literary prestige. The charismatic names already cited corroborate the extent to which the Caucasian theme marked the consolidation and development of a classical Russian tradition: where literature and territory seem to have expanded in tandem, a juxtaposition of the aesthetic and historical dimensions of Russian imperial conquest appears possible.

Precedents for this juxtaposition can, of course, be found in Russian history: in the paradigmatic cases of Pushkin, Lermontov, and the Decembrists, Russian Romantic culture was itself able to reconcile imperial adventure and literary innovation in the form of poetic biography. The operative model linking the poet's life to the imperial domain was *exile*. Literally or metaphorically, whether imposed by the tsar or pursued as an escape from the monarch's watchful gaze, the experience of exile functioned for two generations of Romantics, from Pushkin to Griboedov to Bestuzhev-Marlinsky to Lermontov, as a measure of the poet's evolving relationship to the mutually implicating spaces of nation and empire.

The dénouement to Pushkin's *Prisoner of the Caucasus* suggests a temptingly simple resolution to this exilic paradigm: the hero escapes captivity at the hands of the Circassians and returns to Russia. By analogy, the same scenario could be applied by critics to the writer and his work: the poet's repatriation has been traditionally reenacted as the fact of his posthumously entering the national patrimony. In this way, the difficulties of negotiating colonial terrain are reduced to a distance from the Russian motherland that appears only as far or as perilous as the successful journey home: "V Rossiiu dal'nii put' vedet" (The distant path leads to Russia), the prisoner of the Caucasus observes, although more in nostalgia than in hope.[1] Despite—and often because of—the frequently antagonistic relations between poet and tsar in the nineteenth century, one is tempted to suggest that the exilic paradigm in Russian letters is often a deeply alienated literary correlative to imperial expansion, and a hasty reading of both risks fortifying the concept of nationhood at the very moment when it appears most problematic.

Interestingly, Pushkin's *Prisoner of the Caucasus* itself provides a more allegorical reading of the spatial dynamic underlying the experience of exile:

Отступник света, друг природы,
Покинул он родной предел
И в край далекий полетел
С веселым призраком свободы.[2]

(An apostate of worldly society, a friend of nature,
He left the confines of his native land
And flew to a far-off place
With the merry phantom of freedom.)

In these lines, Russia and its imperial periphery are distinguished as two borderlands (*predel, krai*), that are then equated with a nature-culture dichotomy. This dichotomy serves to allegorize the descriptive detail of the Caucasus that Pushkin provides, creating a natural foil (*priroda*) to Russian culture (*svet*).

Inevitably, the resulting profusion of physical and ethnographic detail calls for an explanatory apparatus: in a series of twelve footnotes to *Prisoner of the Caucasus*, Pushkin makes "nature" legible to "culture" by translating the foreign terms into Russian, locating toponyms and, most important, by acknowledging his precursors, Derzhavin and Zhukovsky, in Russia's Caucasian tradition.

These glosses, I suggest, constitute an alternative approach to the difficulties of Caucasian terrain, and to the drama of Russia's literature of empire. Intertextual and genealogical rather than biographical, citational rather than simply descriptive or thematic, they also point to the constitutive role of the early Romantic and pre-Romantic poets in constituting the Caucasus as a literary topos.

This essay is a response to the challenge of Pushkin's footnotes: it will seek to elaborate and extend Pushkin's genealogy of eighteenth-century antecedents for the Caucasian tradition, and to flesh out the richly allegorical detail that marks a great deal of Russian literary orientalism. In quoting Derzhavin's ode "On Count Zubov's Return from Persia through the Caucasian Mountains" ("Na vozvrashchenie iz Persii cherez kavkazskie gory Grafa V.A. Zubova," 1797), Pushkin himself points to the rhetorical features of the tradition I propose to trace:

> О юный вождь! —сверша походы,
> Прошел ты с воинством Кавказ,
> *Зрел ужасы, красы природы* . . . (3:118; emphasis added)
>
> (O young leader!—in waging your campaigns,
> You have marched through the Caucasus with your soldiery,
> *You have gazed upon the horrors, the beauties of nature* . . .)

In these lines (to which we shall be returning later), imperial aggression is made graphically visible through an allegorization of Caucasian nature, whereby *horror* and *beauty* are seen as compatible and finally equivalent. Significantly, Zhukovsky's lines, also quoted by Pushkin in his notes, invoke precisely the same topos: "*Uzhasnoiu* i *velichavoi* / Tam vsë blistaet *krasotoi*" [Everything there gleams with a horrible and grandiose beauty] (3:118, emphasis added). The above allegory, whereby beauty and horror are reconciled as grandeur, is in fact one expression of a larger and remarkably consistent poetic mode, which we first discern in the eighteenth-century victory odes of poets such as Lomonosov and Derzhavin, and which is revived, almost as an anachronism, at different junctures in the history of Russian poetry.

This mode, which Russian poetry elaborates during the first hundred years of its modern existence, I shall call the *imperial sublime*. Closely linked to the poetics of eighteenth-century Russian classicism, the imperial sublime will establish Russian poetry as a national patrimony only by projecting it onto the scene of Russia's imperial exploits. The complex relation of Russia to its newly colonized southern peripheries will provide the occasion and even the idiom through which a range of issues, both poetic and historical, will be pondered. From the figuration of lyric subjectivity to the nature of Russian autocracy, from questions of lexical choice and genre to the geopolitics of empire, the sublime will function repeatedly as a rhetorical stepping-stone from literary form to political content.

Born in the eighteenth century, the imperial sublime significantly predates the systematic conquest of the Caucasus and hence the celebrated Caucasian adventures of Pushkin and his contemporaries, establishing a precedent to which they were in effect compelled to respond. Such a hypothesis would serve as a corrective to some of the received assumptions of literary history: it compels us to look beyond Russian Romanticism to the eighteenth century, and beyond the geographical (and biographical) locus of the Caucasus toward an examination of Russian imperial culture as an aesthetic phenomenon. (Both assumptions, of chronology and geography, are summarily reasserted by the subtitle to Susan Layton's pathbreaking book *Russian Literature and Empire: Conquest of the Caucasus from Pushkin to Tolstoi.*)[3] In going back beyond Pushkin to the eighteenth century, we discover an idiom developed enough to have seemed archaic by Pushkin's time, and whose terms, while modified by each generation, would provide an aesthetic form to the quest for Russian imperial nationhood over nearly two centuries.

GEOGRAPHIES OF THE SUBLIME

The discourse of the sublime, of course, predates even the eighteenth century, going back to a tract of late antiquity, Longinus's *On The Sublime*, whose modern currency is due to the immense influence of Boileau's French translation of 1674. Longinus explains the sublime as a form of elevation, a loftiness or excellence of diction that forces the reader beyond aesthetic appreciation to a sense of wonderment, an apprehension of grandeur. The sublime in Greek is *hypsos*, height itself, whose proportions can be gauged only by the emotional turbulence it provokes. The fascination Longinus held for the eighteenth century and beyond lies perhaps in his anticipating a shift in contemporary aesthetics. His treatise functions essentially to psychologize rhetoric, translating questions of style and diction into a problem of the subject whose psychic responses are no longer gauged by purely normative terms.

The sublime, in the first instance, suggests less a taxonomy of art than a cluster of affective reactions through which the subject registers the pathos of transport or uplift, an experience that is both empowering and radically privative: "with its stunning power," the sublime has "a capability and force which, unable to be fought, take a position high over every member of the audience."[4] The sublime, in fact, involves a mobile structure of possession, which entails at least one and often two displacements of force. The speaker is first absorbed involuntarily into his or her own utterance; the listener, where there is one, is in turn overwhelmed by what he or she hears, elevated by its force to the point of identifying with its speaker.

How does this psychology of the sublime evolve as a geography? Can we speak of a specifically Russian sublime? A brief juxtaposition of western European debates as they evolved and their Russian equivalents becomes necessary.[5] In western Europe the sublime evolves primarily in polemical opposition to beauty as an aesthetic norm. Where beauty provides an object of contemplative pleasure, the sublime is the experience of pain inflicted and mediated, a kind of aesthetically cushioned blow. This will be the thesis of Edmund Burke's *A Philosophical Enquiry into the Origin of our Ideas of the Sublime and the Beautiful* (1757). Burke lists the possible sources of the sublime—the positive excesses of infinity, vastness or magnificence, and the negative privations of darkness or difficulty—to conclude: "In short, wherever we find strength, and in what light soever we look upon power, we shall all along observe the sublime as the concomitant of terror."[6] Burke's astonishing legacy is the reduction of the sublime to *fear* as the affective response to strength. Where power is wielded, it does not register in being inflicted but in being received. The sublime is this instance of authority, as it is lived in the terror it provokes.

It is Hegel, however, who definitively establishes the sublime as a cultural marker: in his *Aesthetics* (delivered as a series of lectures during the 1820s), the sublime is canonized as a distinguishing feature of *oriental* art. Within Hegel's art-historical trajectory, the sublime is seen as the aesthetic correlative of a wider failure in Asiatic civilization. Hegel assimilates the mystical experiences of several Eastern religions—Hinduism, Islam, and Judaism—under the rubric of the sublime. These traditions (Hegel will place a special emphasis on the Jewish faith) are similar in contemplating the Absolute according to the flawed theology of a remote and omnipitent god. Such a god, like the sovereign who is his earthly will, is limitless, and hence in excess of any verbal embodiment. God's grandeur eclipses humanity: the oneness of the universe can be acknowledged only through an erasure of the individual—a fact experienced, in verbal art, as the ineffable. The resulting cleavage, in any human expression of the divine, between form and content generates the sublime as a mystical moment. Here the "Divine can come to consciousness only through the vanishing of the particular individuals in which the Divine is expressed as present."

Whereas Christian mysticism realizes the "unification of . . . God with human subjectivity," the "strictly Eastern" forms such as Hindu pantheism as well as the Hebrew Bible depict a world in which "the creature, held over against God, is what is perishing and powerless, so that in the creator's goodness his justice has to be manifested at the same time." The sublime is an experience of divine law as purely privative: "man views himself in his unworthiness before God," and submits to a greater force, in the spiritual and finally in the secular realms.[7]

Hegel's great predecessor in this debate is Kant. In *The Critique of Judgment* (1790), Kant had located the sublime in the mind itself, away from the object that had precipitated the experience. Dwarfed by the vastness or power of the object confronting it, the mind initially feels inadequate, and yet "this inadequacy itself is the arousal in us of the feeling that we have within us a supersensible power." The very ineffability of the object is thus embraced by Kant as evidence of the mind's superiority in finally being able to conceive of the *idea* of the infinite, even if—indeed precisely because—the mind cannot conceive its sensuous form. Kant concludes, "Sublime is what even to be able to think proves that the mind has a power surpassing any standard of sense."[8] The Kantian sublime, then, differs from Hegel's on at least two counts. First, it appears to lack geographical or historical specificity; second, it hypostatizes the mind, hailing its cognitive efficacy at precisely the moment when Hegel insists it has been overshadowed by its object. How are we to understand these divergences? Between Kant and Hegel, we should remember, lies the tumult of European Romantic culture, fueled in no small part by the scholarly enthusiasm of what Raymond Schwab has called the "oriental renaissance." The European philologist's exaltation of the East as the spiritual birthplace of Europe is the polemical context of Hegel's critique. What Romantic philology hailed as origin, Hegel would dismiss as a flawed beginning, an early and transient episode in the history of art.

Yet this broad intellectual history can be verified by the most concrete precedent for Hegel's own orientalization of the sublime in the *Aesthetics*—Kant himself. In the same section of the *Critique of Judgment*, Kant muses:

> Perhaps the most sublime passage of the Jewish Law is the commandment: Thou shalt not make unto thee any graven image, or any likeness of any thing that is in heaven or on earth, etc. This commandment can explain the enthusiasm that the Jewish people in its civilized era felt for its religion when it compared itself with other peoples, or can explain the pride that Islam inspires. The same holds also for our presentation of the moral law, and for the predisposition within us for morality.[9]

For Hegel as even for Kant, the Eastern monotheisms exemplify the sublime by bringing together the aesthetic and the ethical under the aegis of law. Where the spirit is articulated as a divine command, its coercive force is sublimated in art as transcending representation. Heard but not seen, the disembodied imperative of God's word extracts obedience to the precise extent that its formlessness inspires an aesthetic sense of awe.

In locating the sublime exclusively in the Orient, Hegel isolates the example of Jewish law from Kant's general claim about morality. Hegel's innovation is to generate instead a series of cultural equivalences of which the sublime is the aesthetic moment. Where religion is divine commandment, we experience politics as tyranny and art as sublime: these analogies constitute the static pattern of Asiatic cultures. Hegel's *Aesthetics* clarifies the conceptual basis for the conflation of the artistic sublime with the despotisms and theocracies of the East, which now become its political and spiritual equivalents. Schematizing this complex path, it might be said that the European sublime moves largely within the margins of Kant's and Hegel's formulations, between a deepening subjective inwardness and the persistent phantom of the oriental despot and his realm.

To what extent is this trajectory of the sublime (*vozvyshennoe,* or alternatively, *vysokoe* in Russian) reproduced in Russia itself? Like the Hegelian sublime, which can be said to render artistically the radical imbalance in power that obtains between sovereign and subject, the Russian sublime will also mark an analogy between the aesthetic and the political. Specifically Russian, however, is the literary-historical moment in which the imperial sublime appears, coinciding as it does with the beginnings of a secular literary institution. This moment embraces a rich context of literary polemic and political debate that implicates Russia, to a far greater extent than Europe, in a ramified relationship to the Orient, as a political paradigm and as an allegory of power.

LOMONOSOV'S REVOLUTION

Longinus's treatise on the sublime was known through Boileau's French translation to Mikhail Lomonosov, the said founder of modern Russian poetry, who read it along with other influential texts of eighteenth-century European poetics in 1738 during his sojourn in Marburg as a student. Lomonosov's own notes from Boileau have survived in manuscript form along with his précis of a manual by the German rhetorician Gottsched: together these notes point to the immediate Franco-German precedents for a mid-eighteenth-century polemic over Russian prosody that took place between Lomonosov and his older rival Vasily Trediakovsky. Lomonosov's notes suggest a reader for whom the sublime is first and foremost a stylistics: he finds in Longinus a rhetorician who can select and appraise pieces of verse or prose for their merit and whose conclusions are always grounded in ready citations.[10]

Boileau's Longinus came to function for Lomonosov as part of a powerful normative poetics, derived from European debates but never coinciding with them. Boileau himself, for example, had insisted on the need to distinguish the sublime as an aesthetic *effect* from the materialities of style such as ornament or lofty diction; for him, then, there was no contradiction between the sublime and the simple. Lomonosov was to break with Boileau precisely over this question, absorbing the classical Pindaric and Franco-German genealogy of the sublime for the sake of a specifically Russian poetic model that he was in effect himself inventing.

Lomonosov adapted the ode as a genre to the needs of a new Russian prosody and stylistics. The Russian sublime, through Lomonosov and somewhat in contrast to Boileau's precepts, came to be marked by a close link to a specific lexical register, the *vysokii shtil'* that Lomonosov later defined within the taxonomy of discourses elaborated in the "Foreword on the Usefulness of Ecclesiastical Books in the Russian Language" ("Predislovie o pol'ze knig tser'kovnykh v rossiiskom iazyke," 1758): "Heroic poems, odes, prosaic speeches on important matters should be composed in this style, by which they are raised [*vozvyshaiutsia*] from ordinary simplicity to a lofty grandeur. This style gives Russian an advantage over many modern European languages, in making use of the Slavonic language from our books of liturgy."[11]

Lomonosov's linkage of the sublime to the ecclesiastical language of Eastern Orthodoxy was to prove a defining moment in the early history of Russian poetics. The panegyric and spiritual odes that constitute his own poetic opus are no more than an elaboration of this principle; they survived as a legacy over which the literary battles of Pushkin's day were fought. Championed as a perennial norm by the reactionaries of the Collegium of Amateurs of the Russian Word as well as the Decembrist poets such as Wilhelm Kiukhel'beker, they would appear dangerously outmoded to Pushkin and his allies. As late as 1824, in his preface to Pushkin's *Fountain of Bakhchisarai*, Prince Viazemsky felt obliged to critique the norms of classical rhetoric, which he saw as embodied by Aristotle and Longinus: after Lomonosov and Derzhavin, the Longinian sublime would be perceived as an archaism, although one destined to persist.[12]

The first battle-cry of this prolonged literary war was Lomonosov's "Ode on the Taking of Khotin" ("Oda na vziatie Khotina 1739 goda") hailed by Belinsky as the earliest poem in modern Russian. The poem, written in Germany to mark a Russian victory over the Turks, was sent by Lomonosov to Russia along with his seminal "Letter on the Rules of Russian Versification" ("Pis'mo o pravilakh rossiiskogo stikhotvorstva," 1739) and circulated as a practical example of Lomonosov's intended revolution in prosody. The letter's burden is to locate a formal specificity within the language upon which a uniquely Russian system of versification may be founded. This specificity, for Lomonosov, was the Russian accentual system, distinct from the older mode of syllabic scansion that had been introduced into Russia through Poland and only recently undermined by Trediakovsky.

Boileau's version of Longinus, which Lomonosov had read barely a year before, maintains a large if subtle presence in these deliberations. In Lomonosov's letter on prosody Longinus himself is never mentioned. Instead Lomonosov chooses to quote Boileau's "Ode on the Taking of Namur" ("Ode sur la prise de Namur," 1693) which, along with the prose text it in turn had accompanied, the brief "Discourse on the Ode," becomes one of several crucial if largely implicit prior voices authorizing Lomonosov's own polemic, both in its terms of reference and in its coupling of a theoretical intervention with a sample of poetic practice. Boileau's "Discourse on the Ode" is an attempt at reviving the Pindaric victory ode as a model of the sublime held to be still valid for the modern world. (Interestingly, here Boileau insists far less on simplicity, speaking even of a "magnificence of words"—Lomonosov's formula precisely.)[13]

Yet Lomonosov's polemical choices—of the victory ode as a genre, of the accentual system of versification, and of Boileau's work over Longinus himself—have another precedent, Russian and hence more weighty than any authority the poet may have encountered abroad. In 1734, four years before Lomonosov's intervention, Trediakovsky had published his "Solemn Ode on the Surrender of Gdansk" ("Oda torzhestvennaia o sdache goroda Gdanska"), the first ode, its author would later claim, to be written in Russian, and accompanied, like Boileau's poem, by a brief disquisition on the ode's virtues. The following year saw the publication of Trediakovsky's "New and Brief Method for Composing Russian Verse" ("Novyi i kratkii sposob k slozheniiu rossiiskikh stikhov") the first Russian text to establish theoretically the principle of accentual versification.

How then can we speak of Lomonosov's revolution? Lomonosov's "Letter on the Rules of Russian Versification" is undeniably a critical extension of Trediakovsky's recent "Method," and his ode on Khotin is equally a response to the ode on Gdansk. Yet only in Lomonosov's interventions of 1739 do we find the three elements of what would come to be the imperial sublime: the complete adoption of the syllabo-tonic metrical system (Trediakovsky's ode is purely syllabic), the lexical choice of the *vysokii shtil'*, and the oriental-imperial theme. Trediakovsky was not indifferent to the nature or breadth of this challenge: his subsequent decision to revise each of the three texts that had served as Lomonosov's immediate Russian context reads like a sophisticated acknowledgment of defeat. The gap between these two redactions illustrates the impact of the Lomonosovian revolution over a decade: the 1752 edition of Trediakovsky's works accepts Lomonosov's reforms in most of their ramifications and provides a new rendering of the ode on Gdansk in trochaic tetrameters. Significantly, it is far more insistent on the centrality of Boileau: Trediakovsky's *Works* offer a complete translation of Boileau's *Art poétique*, which the author explicitly invokes, along with the ode on Namur, as his chief inspiration for the ode on Gdansk (thereby also exposing, if implicitly, the genealogy of Lomonosov's own choices). As with Lomonosov, the stylistic and psychological dimensions of the odic sublime are instantiated by the celebration of a military victory:

> Son style impétueux souvent marche au hazard,
> Chés elle, un beau désordre est un effet de l'art.
>
> This rule, it seems, has been put to use in the French language by none better than the Author [Boileau] Despréaux himself, as he demonstrated indeed to absolutely everyone in his exceptional ode composed on the occasion of the taking of the city of Namur by French troops . . . of which my ode is an Imitation.[14]

These broader contexts, Russian and European, are necessarily muted in Lomonosov's intervention of 1739, which is above all a flourish of authorial independence and national pride. Lomonosov himself praises Boileau in passing, and only for his fidelity to the nature of his *own* language, a premise that frees Lomonosov to evolve his own Russian rendering of the sublime against and beyond Boileau's example. Embedded in a discussion of meter and genre, the sublime functions as the moment of *transition* in the argument from formal categories to the ideological premise of imperial victory: "Pure iambic verse, although rather difficult to compose, does augment, in its silent upward rise, the nobility, grandeur and sublimity [*velikolepie i vysotu*] of the material. Nowhere is it better employed than in victory odes, as I have done in the present one."[15]

Lomonosov's revolution, which naturalized the four-foot iamb as a meter somehow inherent in the Russian language, is of interest here as an ideology of form. The letter, along with the "Ode on the Taking of Khotin," which illustrates its proposed reforms, together offer a formal and ideological basis for a poetics of imperial nationhood.

In its theory as well as its poetic implementation, this ensemble of formal and ideological premises constitutes the earliest rendering in modern Russian literature of the *imperial sublime*. Emerging with the eighteenth-century ode, the imperial sublime allows a new prosody, grounded, it is claimed, in the nature of the Russian language, to be instantiated by an ideology of imperial conquest. The sublime, we should note, cannot be schematically reduced to either a purely formal construct or an ideological category. It functions rather as a moment of *mediation,* serving to negotiate between such formal problems as genre, lyric voice, lexical choice, even prosody and the ideology of national specificity that Russia will vindicate, yet also complicate, through conquest.

In the poetry of Lomonosov and Derzhavin, the sublime as a mediation between form and ideology can be sketched more vividly: it is registered firstly as an abstract psychic force and then elaborated spatially as a topography. An initial experience of lyric afflatus is found to anticipate the negotiation of nationhood through empire that will provide the poem's eventual theme. An experience of poetic inspiration is thus presented as analogous to the political power it then describes. This sublime force, at once aesthetic and political, is then projected onto the space of empire.

In this complex negotiation between European poetics and Eastern (Ottoman and then Caucasian) territory, Russian poetry is conceived as a national patrimony. Well after the ode as a genre loses its relevance and Lomonosov's metrical revolution has been assimilated, the sublime will persist as a trope of imperial authority, and of the poet's responses to it.

THE POETRY OF LOMONOSOV AND THE IMPERIAL SUBLIME

The "Ode on the Taking of Khotin" puts Lomonosov's innovations into practice. The very first lines of the poem establish the sublime as the privileged idiom of the new poetics:

Восторг внезапный ум пленил,
Ведет на верьх горы высокой,
Где ветр в лесах шуметь забыл;
В долине тишина глубокой.
Внимая нечто, ключ молчит,
Которой завсегда журчит
И с шумом вниз с холмов стремится.
Лавровы вьются там венцы,
Там слух спешит во все концы;
Далече дым в полях курится.[16]

(A sudden rapture has captivated the mind
And leads it up a lofty mountain,
Where the wind in the forests has forgotten to roar;
In the deep valley there is silence.
The noise, hearkening to something, falls silent,
The noise that forever gurgles
And courses noisily down from the hills.
There wreaths of laurel wind about,
There rumor rushes in all directions;
Further out smoke curls along the fields.)

The ode's first two stanzas, identically structured and very close to Boileau's model, characterize the sublime as a purely lyrical afflatus, a dialectic of poet and nature that appears prior to any history. Vertical uplift is its quintessential axis: the mind is here thrust upward to the top of Mount Parnassus by the sudden onset of poetic rapture over which it has no control. The authority that the mind yields to poetry it then reestablishes over nature. Where the difficulty of height consumes the first seven lines, the final period provides a compensatory horizontal axis of extension. The mind's elevation grants it a panoramic view: potentially infinite, this horizontal space will nonetheless become localized as the historical occasion that is the poem's real object.

Horizontality is the site of conflict; its field of attraction is territorial aggression, the surge of battle, the line of advance, victory or retreat. Poetry encounters history at the intersection of two axes, the point at which the terror of lyric afflatus is resolved in a compensatory and transformative identification with imperial power. The uplifted poet, slave to his vision, becomes Russia's heraldic eagle surveying the horizontal spread of the retreating Ottoman forces:

За холмы, где паляща хлябь
Дым, пепел, пламень, смерть рыгает,
За Тигр, Стамбул, своих заграбь,
Что камни с берегов сдирает;
Но чтоб орлов сдержать полет,
Таких препон на свете нет.

(19–20)

(Beyond the hills where a fiery abyss
Belches smoke, flame and death
Retreat with your men, Istanbul, beyond the Tigris
That rips the rocks off its own shoreline;
But to restrain the eagles' flight
There is no hindrance left on earth.)

The sublime, which had seemed at first to be outside any history, thus emerges as an allegory of poetic possession that anticipates a manifestation of imperial might. This power is finally shared, by poet and Russian monarch, in a scenario of territorial aggression, such as the capture of the Turkish fortress of Khotin by Russian troops in 1739.

Much of Lomonosov's poetry functions according to the same displacements of force. Intimately tied to the rhythms of court life, the Lomonosovian ode generally commemorates a victory, anniversary, or an ascension to the throne. In it the *poetic* moment of sublime rapture is made homologous with the poet's abject relation to the monarch as an embodiment of *political* power. The poet's fear is then muted through an identification with the sovereign's achievements in the imperial arena. Alongside the fact of empire, the relationship of poet and monarch will become a determining factor in the evolution of the imperial sublime. In the same ode on Khotin, the poet's description of the battle is soon interrupted by another vision:

Что так теснит боязнь мой дух?
Хладнеют жилы, сердце ноет!
Что бьет за странной шум в мой слух?
. . . .
Блеснул горящим вдруг лицем,
Умытым кровию мечем
Гоня врагов, Герой открылся.

(22)

(Why does fear so weigh upon my spirit?
My veins go cold, my heart aches!
What strange noise strikes at my ears?
. . . .
A burning face suddenly flashed,
With a sword bathed in blood
Scattering his enemies, the Hero appeared.)

The hero who appears here is Peter the Great, who then begins to converse with Ivan the Terrible about the course of Russian history:

«Чрез нас предел наш стал широк
На север, запад и восток.
На юге Анна торжествует,
Покрыв своих победой сей».

Свилася мгла, Герои в ней;
Не зрит их око, слух не чует.
(23)

("Through us our boundaries have grown wide
To the north, west and east.
In the south Anna is triumphant,
Sheltering her subjects with this victory,"
The gloom coiled round, the Heroes (dissolved) into it;
The eye no longer sees them, and the ear hears them not.)

In these lines Lomonosov abstracts from the battle scene to stage a visionary encounter between a series of Russian tsars. Barely individuated, Peter and Ivan are here little more than the sum of their military victories, which they recount in order to insert Russia's most recent triumph into a ready sequence of historical milestones. Long dead, these monarchs appear as phantoms, abstract dramatizations of Russian expansion. Yet even where Lomonosov addresses Russia's living monarchs—and most of his odes hail a given ruler on the occasion of this or that event or its anniversary—the ensuing representation is anything but tactile or particular:

Надежда, свет России всей
В Тебе щедрота Божья зрится,
Хоть внешней красоты Твоей
Довольно всяк, кто зрит, дивится.
Душевных лик Твоих доброт
Краснее внешних всех красот,
Где всяки совершенства явны,
Любезны всем, во всем преславны.
(Poem 23, p. 55)

(Hope and light of all Russia
In You God's generosity can be seen,
Although Your external beauty,
Is marveled at enough by any who gaze upon it.
The image of your inner virtues
Is more beautiful than all external charms,
Where all forms of perfection are evident
Pleasing to all, and glorious in every way.

These lines, entirely formulaic but dedicated in fact to the Empress Elizabeth, perform the cliché that governs Lomonosov's rendering of Russia's ruling monarchs. The poet's flattery acts to empty the figure of the monarch of all specificity: an idealized but fleshless vision of perfection, the sovereign body is necessarily diaphanous, so that the seeing eye can pass unimpeded from its outer beauty to its inner virtues, rendering them equally visible and hyperbolically equivalent.

The eighteenth-century sublime will repeatedly elaborate imperial history through successive embodiments of power, highly abstract but essentially mobile. These allegorical bodies are the tsars themselves who coexist in the space of empire and are coextensive with it, displaying their face and limbs as attributes of might or retributive justice. Lomonosov's panegyric ode is an exercise in sublime abjection: it survives the crushing power to which it bears witness only by identifying with it in the shared space of empire.

DERZHAVIN AND THE IMPERIAL SUBLIME

In Lomonosov's odes, then, a parallel dynamic of poetic and political power come together as the imperial sublime. This idiom we have seen ramify into at least two facets of concern: (a) an imperial geography linking the Russian metropolis to a southern periphery evolving in competition with the Ottoman and Persian empires, but also—if differently—with the now neutralized remnants of the old Tatar Khanates as well as the mountain peoples of the Caucasus itself; (b) the creation of a new lyric subjectivity born out of the dynamic of supplication that enjoins the poet to the tsar.

In the poetry of Lomonosov's greatest successor Derzhavin, as in the intellectual debates of his time, these two elements are brought crucially together. A new lyric voice, in part the monarch and in part his or her subject, evolves spatially in tandem with Russia's southward expansion. By this I do not mean to suggest that the poetic subject continues to function as a crudely celebratory mouthpiece, hailing a victory won or a treaty signed. The poetry of Derzhavin is already a radical transformation of the Lomonosovian sublime. The great Formalist critic Iurii Tynianov has taught us to see Derzhavin's new path as "the destruction of the ode as a closed, canonical genre."[17] The collapse of Lomonosov's hierarchy of registers—the high, middle, and low styles—is for Tynianov the principal feature of the Derzhavinian ode, but the place of the sublime in Derzhavin's new poetics remains to be examined.

We should first note that the sublime is not omnipresent in Derzhavin and is thus no longer coextensive with the ode as such. At the widest level of generality, it is, for Derzhavin, the erasive force of time itself. In such classic pieces as "On the Death of Prince Meshchersky" ("Na smert' kniazia Meshcherskogo," 1779), "Waterfall" ("Vodopad," 1791), or Derzhavin's last poem "The river of time in its coursing" ("Reka vremen v svoem stremlen'i," 1816), time figures as a current of water that is spatialized as a precipitous fall:

Алмазна сыплется гора
С высот четыремя скалами,
Жемчугу бездна и сребра
Кипит внизу, бьет вверх буграми;

От брызгов синий холм стоит,
Далече рев в лесу шумит.[18]

(A diamond mountain is scattering
[Plunging] from the heights like four cliffs,
A chasm [or multitude] of pearls and silver
Seethes below and thrusts up mounds;
From the jets of water a dark-blue hill stands,
Farther away a roar reverberates in the forest.)

Figured as a mountain, Derzhavin's waterfall generates the vertical sublime with which we are already familiar: indeed, this first stanza of "Waterfall," and the poem as a whole, must be read as a parody of Lomonosov's ode on Khotin. "Farther away a roar reverberates in the forest" ("Daleche rev v lesu shumit"), says Derzhavin at the end of his first stanza; "Farther away smoke curls along the fields" ("Daleche dym v poliakh kuritsia"), reads Lomonosov's equivalent line. Both *incipits* are based on a contamination of visual and auditory detail; both lead to a sustained reflection on the vicissitudes of Russo-Ottoman imperial conflict.

Unlike Lomonosov's poem, however, "Waterfall" does not mark a single military victory. Its allegorical premise, the waterfall as the all-consuming vortex of time, is quickly narrowed to a more human dimension: "Ne *zhizn' li chelovekov* nam / Sei vodopad izobrazhaet?—" (Is not *the life of men* / Depicted by this waterfall?—[164]). "Waterfall," like many of Derzhavin's poems, attempts to map the effects of time on the scale of life as it is lived by individuals. What results are lyric biographies: where Lomonosov gauged events in terms of the benefits accruing to the emperor *qua* empire, Derzhavin will particularize these events as watersheds in the political life of the noblemen of his day.

Lomonosov's "Heroes," we recall, were Tsars Ivan and Peter; Derzhavin's are Count Rumiantsev and Prince Potemkin, prominent statesmen whose conflicting ambitions marked the course of Catherine the Great's second Russo-Turkish war of 1787–92. Unlike Lomonosov's ode, the imperial theme in "Waterfall" does not simply glorify Russian expansion; it establishes the possibility of a military-diplomatic career that might be pursued for its own sake, beyond its value to the sovereign and the state. The poet identifies Potemkin as the hero whose life and death are now coterminous with Russia's gains in the Turkish war, but whose own goals significantly transcended the nation's:

Не ты ль, который взвесить смел
Мощь Росса, дух Екатерины,
И *опершись на них*, хотел
Вознесть твой гром на те стремнины,

> На коих древний Рим стоял,
> И всей вселенной колебал!
> (170; emphasis added)
>
> (Is it not you who dared to weigh
> The might of the Russian and the spirit of Catherine,
> And *leaning on them*, wanted
> to let your thunder reach those cliffs
> On which ancient Rome had stood
> And swayed the entire universe?)

Derzhavin's poetry bears witness to the individuation of a modern lyric voice, for which the exuberance of lived experience, the vicissitudes of ambition, the struggle for dignity and conscience become an intrinsic object of poetic interest. The crushing sublimity of vertical time must be confronted on a human level, and the ode that Pushkin cites in *Prisoner of the Caucasus* as having inaugurated the Caucasian problematic attempts precisely to measure the imperial sublime along the axis of a lifespan.

In "On Count Zubov's Return from Persia through the Caucasian Mountains," Derzhavin addresses Catherine's favorite, the military commander Zubov, upon his return from an interrupted and effectively abortive campaign against Persia. The poet muses on life as a sequence of sceneries to be traversed, each success or failure figured as a topographical rise or a descent: "Sei s kholma v propast' upadaet, / A tot vzoiti speshit na kholm" (This man falls from a hill into an abyss, / And that one races to climb the hill).

The Caucasus figures in this sequence as a sublime landscape of extraordinary power:

> О юный вождь! —сверша походы,
> Прошел ты с воинством Кавказ,
> Зрел ужасы, красы природы:
> Как с ребр там страшных гор лиясь
> Ревут в мрак бездн сердиты реки:
> Как с чел их с грохотом снега
> Падут, лежавши целы веки;
> Как серны, вниз склонив рога,
> Зрят в мгле спокойно под собою
> Рожденье молний и громов.
> (234)
>
> (O young leader! —in waging your campaigns,
> You have marched through the Caucasus with your soldiery,
> You have gazed upon the horrors, the beauties of nature:
> The angry rivers, as they pour forth there from the ribs of terrifying mountains
> As they roar into the gloom of abysses:

The snows as from their brows [of the hills] thunderously
They fall, after having lain there for whole centuries;
The chamois, their horns bent down,
View calmly in the gloom below them
The birth of lightning and thunder.)

This stanza and those that follow it contain the germ of Russian Romanticism's Caucasian problematic, with which we began. Derzhavin signals the beginning of what is a more specifically sensuous or natural sublime, with its refractory visual excess, anticipating the nature-culture dialectic that is fleshed out, for the Caucasus, in Zhukovsky's "To Voeikov" and Pushkin's southern verse. The luxuriant profusion of local detail here is no longer abstractly symbolic (as with Lomonosov) and not yet simply picturesque or enumerative (as often with Pushkin); it is strictly organized according to the visual criteria of horror and beauty ("uzhasy, krasy prirody"), which the sublime will juxtapose and then conflate. Descriptive detail proliferates up and down a sheer vertical drop that is contrasted with the horizontal perspective of the itinerant eye.

Derzhavin's poem is a series of glances ("vnizu, vverkhu ty videl vse" [below, above you have seen everything]), arrested and then displaced, providing a series of southern vignettes that are recounted through the poem's articulation of life as a career. Within this lifespan the sublime, like Janus-faced time, has two aspects. Derzhavin himself in a later essay wrote: "But there are two kinds of sublimity [*vysokost'*], one is *sensuous* and consists of the lively representation of material substances [*veshchestv*]," "the incessant representation of a multitude of brilliant pictures and feelings in a sonorous, grandiloquent, flowery diction that induces rapture and astonishment." The other sublime is "*intellectual*, and consists of showing the actions of a lofty spirit," "the silent and calm actions of a great soul."[19]

In the poem to Count Zubov this dual sublime acquires a spatial dimension, in reproducing the polar relationship of the metropolis and its colonial periphery. The *sensuous* or natural sublime celebrates the physical grandeur of the Caucasus and complements, as its peripheral correlative, the sheer vertigo of political power concentrated in the Petersburg court, which the poem identifies as the *intellectual* sublime. Both are experienced as a series of vicissitudes, but are structured asymmetrically. The poem begins and ends with a meditation on the intellectual sublime, which becomes a gauge of the individual's capacity to negotiate and survive the ruses of power:

Кого же разум почитает
Из всех, идущих сим путем,
По самой истине счастливым?
Не тех ли, что, челом к звездам
Превознесяся горделивым,

Мечтают быть равны богам,
Что в пурпуре и на престоле
Превыше смертных восседят?
(233)

(Whom does reason consider
Of all those who tread this path,
To be truly lucky?
Surely it is those who, with their brows
Raised proudly to the stars,
Dream of being equal to the gods;
Those who dressed in purple and seated upon a throne
Will be seated above mortals?)

The sensuous sublime of the Caucasus is framed by a meditation on power's futility, and the metropolis and colonial periphery are linked in this bifurcation of the sublime that defines the geography of the poem even as it is dismissed as episodic in lived experience.

In Derzhavin, it must be said, the sublime is often philosophically subordinated to the poet's search for a reflective equilibrium, just as it is rhetorically the privileged mode of expressing that very search. Derzhavin's great poetic quest is for a contemplative peace that would emerge *at the other end* of both natural and intellectual sublimities, in the irreducibility of the individual's "great soul" as a partner in the poem's dialogue: "Siian'e vkrug tebia zasnulo, / Proshlo, —ostalsia tol'ko ty. / Ostalsia ty! —i ta prekrasna / Dusha pochtenna budet vvek" (The luster about you has faded, / It has passed, —you alone remain. / You remain! —and that splendid / Soul will be esteemed forever [235]). The individual is like the poem itself, a residue that survives the experience of sublimity to measure its rise and fall.

RUSSIA AND THE ORIENTAL DESPOT

Derzhavin's poetry must be read as a remarkable attempt to initiate a subjective dimension within the depersonalized idiom of the sublime. This tentative autonomy, however, involves more than the dignity of a military career, or even the rewards of rustication that Derzhavin will fondly celebrate as an alternative to life in the city. It remains wedded to the figure of the sovereign, and to a wider Russian and European debate on the nature and limits of monarchical power. It is this debate that we must now finally address.

As with Lomonosov, many of Derzhavin's best known odes address Russia's ruling tsars. Unique in their strange juxtaposition of the lofty and the chatty, in their contradictory gestures of sycophancy and didactic presumption, these poems stand out as much for their odd sense of location. In the poem "To the Tsarevich Khlor" the world depicted is a generalized and generically indeterminate Orient: the poet, masquerading as a brahmin from Kashmir, is unable to distinguish among the Hindu, Zoroastrian, and Islamic faiths, and blithely calls Russia a "Tatar land." At this point, not only is the lyric voice oriental; the entire world it encounters and addresses, Russia included, appears equally Asiatic. As the Kashmiri says to Alexander I:

> И подлинно, весьма чудесный
> Бывал ли где такой султан?
> Да Оромаз блюдет небесный
> Тебя, гарем, седой диван,
> И всю твою орду татарску![20]
>
> (And verily has there ever been so wondrous
> A sultan anywhere?
> May celestial Oromaz keep
> You, your harem, your venerable court [*divan*],
> And your entire Tatar horde!)

Such oriental masquerades were not unprecedented in the European eighteenth century: Voltaire's tales and, to a still greater extent, Montesquieu's *Persian Letters* had established the allegorical tradition of the Asiatic protagonist whose observations of the West defamiliarized the assumptions of European politics. The playfully orientalized Russia we find in these poems was in fact crucial to contemporary debates on European absolutism, the political discourse through which eighteenth-century Russia was attempting to assert its imperial role and national destiny.

Sandwiched between Europe and Asia but undefinable in the civilizational terms of either continent, Russia sought to assert her uniqueness in the specificity of tsarist autocracy with respect to the evolving constitutional monarchies of Europe on the one hand and the supposed despotisms of the East on the other. Lomonosov's celebration of the monarchy summarizes nearly a century of shrill polemic with foreign detractors of Russia:

> through the freedom to diverge in opinion [*raznomyslennoiu vol'nostiiu*] Russia came to the brink of complete destruction, [while] through autocracy [*samoderzhavstvom*] she first gained in strength, then after some unhappy times grew larger, stronger and became covered in glory. We are reliably assured of our fatherland's well-being, seeing in monarchical rule [*edinonachal'nom vladenii*] the guarantee of our bliss.[21]

The eighteenth century was the dawn of monarchical historiography in Russia: preparing the way for the histories of Karamzin and others was an incipient narrative paradigm that repeatedly identified autocracy with the specificities of Russian nationhood itself. This specifying discourse was in fact polemical: it sought to dissociate Russia from the status of oriental despotism, a concept recently revived by the European Enlightenment.

Despotism was whatever the European monarchies were not, or should not be: this definition, apparently restrictive yet in fact open-endedly polemical, was Montesquieu's. His *Spirit of the Laws* (1748) established despotism as a purely negative category, functioning only to clarify the ideal nature of European monarchy. Operating outwardly as a theorization of Asia where it is "so to speak naturally domiciled," despotism designates the reign of a tyrant who governs through the force of fear alone. Whereas the monarch is the sole ruler, but governs "by fixed and established laws" the despot "*is* the law, the state and the prince." The transition from sheer, undifferentiated power to a law-based monarchy was, for Montesquieu, Russia itself:

> Observe, I beg of you, how industriously the government of Muscovy is seeking to move out of despotism [*sortir du despotisme*], which weighs upon it more than on the people themselves. The large bodies of armed men have been broken up, the penalties for crimes diminished, tribunals have been established, laws have begun to be acknowledged, and the people instructed. But there are particular reasons which will perhaps lead it [Russia's government] back to the ill fate it sought to flee.[22]

Russia, for Montesquieu's Europe, is this spatial oscillation: "moving out" yet relapsing into despotism, almost Europe but never arriving. Montesquieu's works circulated widely in Russia: befriended by Kantemir who translated *Spirit of the Laws* into Russian, Montesquieu was most importantly Catherine the Great's chief interlocutor in her celebrated "Nakaz" (Instruction) of 1767. A blueprint for Russian statecraft destined never to be realized, the "Nakaz" acknowledged the principle of law as limiting and defining authority without renouncing the absolutist model of power that Montesquieu had so vigorously condemned. The "Nakaz" discursively repeats the oscillation that Montesquieu had discerned in the Petrine reforms: it collapses the distinction, crucial to Montesquieu, between European monarchy and oriental despotism by terming Russia a European power and then supporting this definition by invoking precisely those attributes of the East that Montesquieu had defined as despotic.

A central trait—and justification—of despotism, in Montesquieu's eyes, was the fact of empire. *Despotism occurs when a nation acquires a colony*, a shift that Montesquieu contemplates spatially: "A monarchical state must be of a mediocre size," while "*a large empire supposes a despotic authority in him who governs*. The swiftness of decisions must compensate for the distance of the places to which they are conveyed, fear must hinder the negligence of the governor or magistrate far-away; the law must reside in one head alone [*que la loi soit dans une seule tête*]." Imperial space, with its extended distances and peculiar concentration of authority, finds its rationale and correlative in the *body* of the despot, its guardian and ultimate personification. Let us see how Catherine's "Nakaz" retains the terms of Montesquieu's geography while reshaping its limits:

> 6. Russia is a European power [*derzhava*] . . .
> 8. The possessions of the Russian state extend upon the terrestrial globe to 32 degrees of latitude and 165 of longitude.
> 9. The sovereign is autocratic [*Gosudar' est' samoderzhavnyi*]; for no other power [*vlast'*] save that which is united in his person [*v ego osobe*] can act in a manner commensurable with the space [*prostranstvom*] of so great a state.
> 10. An extended dominion [*Prostrannoe gosudarstvo*] presupposes autocratic power [*samoderzhavnuiu vlast'*] in the person who rules it. A swiftness in resolving affairs dispatched from distant parts must compensate for the delay caused by the distance of these places.[23]

Catherine's debt to Montesquieu has often been exposed, but no accusation of plagiarism should ignore the displacements effected by her mimicry: Montesquieu's definition of oriental despotism is deployed to assert Russia's place as a *European* nation. The term *despotism* is here crucially elided. Autocracy (*samoderzhavie*) replaces despotism at each point as the defining feature of Russia, claiming the contours and privileges of despotic space while asserting Russia's place in the European theater.

In the discourse of the Enlightenment and its characteristic Russian mutations, despotism functions as this imaginary geography, folding East into West and empire into nation. Yet these conflations are not effortless, and their residues mark the figure of the absolutist monarch. It is the equation of territorial expanse with the figural body of the despot ("dans une seule tête" in Montesquieu's words) that marks the attempted transition from imperial to national space. In the voice and body of the despot we find inscribed what Benedict Anderson has called the "inner incompatibility of nation and empire."

DERZHAVIN AND THE BODY OF THE DESPOT

In Derzhavin's work, the imperial sublime links the geography of Russia's shifting southern peripheries to an emergent lyric voice that speaks to address the oriental despot. It remains for us to read Derzhavin's other poems that elaborate the poet's personalized dialogue with power. More than do his traditional victory odes (such as "On the Peaceful Union of the Tauride and Caucasian Regions with Russian Power" ["Na prisoedinenie bez voennykh deistvii k rossiiskoi derzhave tavricheskikh i kavkazskikh oblastei," 1784], "Autumn during the Siege of Ochakov" ["Osen' vo vremia osady Ochakova," 1788], and even the important "Song on the Taking of Izmail" ["Pesn' po vziatii Izmaila," 1791])—all of which reproduce many of the stock features of the Lomonosovian sublime—Derzhavin's other poems, with their individuation of the human persona through and against the discourse of absolute power, constitute his contribution to, and modification of, the imperial sublime.

Derzhavin's poetry reads as the struggle of a poet enmeshed in the dominant paradigm of enlightened absolutism to redefine his place and voice within the ode as a genre. Gregory Nagy has recently argued that the authorial sensibility of the Pindaric ode is closely tied to the emergence in antiquity of the Greek tyrant: the concentration of power in the hands of one individual in effect shaped, through patronage, the poet's persona.[24] This dilemma, to the extent that it finds a parallel in eighteenth-century Russia, interests us as an allegorical geography of power.

In the poetry of Derzhavin this geography is made manifest in the numerous figures of address that invoke the sovereign body. "Bogopodobnaia tsarevna / Kirgiz-Kaisatskiia ordy!" (O God-like Princess / of the Kirgiz-Kaisak horde!), the poet exclaims in the poem "Felitsa" (1782), the first to win him public acclaim. This apostrophe to the monarch in fact marks a twofold orientalization: not only is the Empress Catherine figured as an oriental despot; the poet himself assumes the persona of a Tatar nobleman or "Murza." At the same time this and other poems such as "The Murza's Vision" ("Videnie Murzy," 1783–84) and "The Depiction of Felitsa" ("Izobrazhenie Felitsy," 1789) equally hail Catherine as an emblem of Enlightenment civic virtue. Ideologically straddling East and West, the sovereign's image is revealed in a series of sublime visitations in which she appears, in contrast to the all too human poet, as an "angel incarnate": a body, to be sure, but one abstracted to the level of a didactic and transcendental imperative. Her sovereign might is manifested in a vision that first rarefies her enthroned body and then allegorically projects it onto the space of empire:

Престол ее на скандинавских,
Камчатских и златых горах,
От стран Таймурских до Кубанских
Поставь на сорок двух столпах;
Как восемь бы зерцал стояли
Ее великие моря;
С полнеба звезды освещали,
Вокруг—багряная заря.

Средь дивного сего чертога
И велелепной высоты
В величестве, в сияньи Бога
Ее изобрази мне ты;
Чтоб, сшед с престола, подавала

Скрижаль заповедей святых;
Чтобы вселенна принимала
Глас Божий, глас природы в них.

Чтоб дики люди, отдаленны,
Покрыты шерстью, чешуей,
Пернатых перьем испещренны,
Одеты листьем и корой,
Сошедшися к ее престолу
И кроткий вняв законов глас
По желто-смуглым лицам долу
Струили токи слез из глаз.

Струили б слезы и, блаженство
Своих проразумея дней,
Забыли бы свое равенство
И были все подвластны ей:
Фин в море бледный, рыжевласый,
Не разбивал бы кораблей,
И узкоглазый Гунн жал класы
Среди седых, сухих зыбей.
("Izobrazhenie Felitsy," 75–76)

(Place her throne on the hills of Scandinavia,
Kamchatka and the Golden Hills,
From the countries of Timur to the Kuban
On forty-two columns;
Like eight mirrors
Her great seas would stand;
Stars from half the sky would illuminate [them],
All round—a purple dawn.

In the midst of this splendid palace
And magnificent elevation
In her grandeur and divine luster
Depict her for me;
So that, descending from her throne, she might offer
The tablet of sacred commandments;
So that the universe might accept
The voice of God and the voice of nature in them.

So that distant and savage people,
Covered in furs and scales,
Speckled with feathers,
Clothed in leaf and bark,
Converging on her throne

And hearing the voice of gentle laws,
Might shed streams of tears
Down their swarthily yellow faces.

They would shed tears, —and foreseeing the bliss
Of their [future] days,
Would forget their own equality
And all submit to her:
The pale and red-haired Finn,
Would not destroy ships at sea,
And the slant-eyed Hunn would reap the ears of grain
Among the dry, grey rippling [fields].)

These lines bear a remarkable resemblance to the discussion of the sublime we found in Hegel and even Kant: emanating from a phantasmatic source, a transcendental imperative descends to unify the profane and the religious into a Law that demands total submission. This Law is none other than Catherine's "Nakaz," the "tablet of sacred commandments" that together form the contractual basis of enlightened absolutism. The Nakaz enjoins the allegorical body of the despot to the racially marked bodies she has vanquished: exuberantly physical in contrast to the inorganic sovereign body, these subject peoples are territorially reorganized into a space—the forty-two *gubernii*—that is coextensive with the monarch's throne. The conquered Finn and "Hunn" (Turk?) are here evoked according to the classic assumptions of the European civilizing mission, willingly abandoning their primitive liberties to submit to the legal and territorial constraints of empire.

In a poem whose very title—"The Depiction of Felitsa"—thematizes the depiction of the monarch, the empress appears in her own way to be no less exotically foreign than the peoples over whom she rules. Oscillating between phantom and flesh, Catherine hovers at the edge of representability just as her throne looms over the empire she rules. Throughout this and other like poems she will remain abstractly *above* and *outside* the imperial unity she embraces, a unity negotiated, as we shall see, *from abroad*.

Derzhavin's allegorization of Catherine the Great as Felitsa derives from a text written by Catherine herself, a didactic fairy tale composed for her grandson. Her "Tale of the Tsarevich Khlor" is a search for moral virtue. The crown prince's quest for a "thornless rose that does not prick" gives the story its plotline: a journey marked by symbolic encounters with numerous virtues and vices that is finally crowned with success. The story is also about territorial conflict, disputed boundaries and bodies. While the Tsar of Russia is away from his palace attending, we are told, to a border dispute, his son Khlor, a young prince of rare intelligence and beauty, is kidnapped by the Khan of a nomadic Kirgiz tribe. Khlor emerges as a kind of royal fetish: his body, in being stolen, establishes theft as the medium of the tale's encounter between the Russian Tsar and the Kirgiz Khan. Felitsa herself is a transient if crucial figure in this exchange; Khlor's benign patron and guide, she is, most notably, not Russian at all but rather the Khan's daughter and her didactic presence is thus orientally coloured.

The final restoration of the prince to his family and kingdom is the tale's necessarily happy ending. Almost too easily achieved, the story's final equilibrium also imparts a more disquieting parable. The Russian autocratic state, the fairy tale suggests, never exists as a prior given. Rather, it is endlessly produced and reaffirmed *in* the violent encounter with an alien and eastern force—a war, a skirmish, a theft—an encounter from which the very principle of Russian statehood is derived. Khlor is not fully a prince until he is kidnapped and restored: he must go to the East to return, enlightened but already quasi-oriental. The Russian state is thus figured primordially ("before the time of the Kiev Prince Kii," says the story) in this identification with empire that transforms the tsar into the very despot he opposes. What is despotic is not the east as such, it seems, but rather the theft, concretely territorial and symbolically imaged, that transforms nation into empire.

The geography of the despot marks Derzhavin's poems most clearly as a highly charged contradiction between their professed ideology and its rhetorical form. The poems' panegyric description and honorific formulae of address have the paradoxical effect of rendering Russia an oriental despotism precisely at the moment when the monarch's Western Enlightenment virtues are being lauded. The Empress Catherine is shown taking the poet to task for his self-abasement in life and art (and it is the humorous listing of his frailties, as well as the slightly grotesque dynamic of the dialogue itself, that constitutes these poems' thematic novelty); yet the Enlightenment ideals of human dignity and civic merit that she espouses are expressed in the formal apparatus itself, the panegyric ode, which renders them untenable. Thus the poet will insist:

Татарски песни из-под спуду,
Как луч, потомству сообщу;
Как солнце, как луну, поставлю
Твой образ будущим векам
Превознесу тебя, прославлю;
Тобой бессмертен буду сам.
("Videnie Murzy," 73)

(From a hidden place I will convey Tartar songs
Like a ray, to posterity;
Like the sun, like the moon, I shall present
Your image to future ages;
I will elevate and praise you;
Through you I shall myself be immortal.)

Derzhavin's Tatar alter ego Mirza, presented here as a dialogic counterpoint to Catherine as Felitsa, is still more transparently historical than the persona of the empress. Derzhavin himself hailed from Kazan', the old Tatar capital annexed by Ivan the Terrible in 1552. The Pugachev uprising, as well as Catherine's territorial ambitions, had refocused attention upon these regions: in Derzhavin's time, prolonged military campaigns against Ottoman Turkey coincided with a rare period of tolerance toward Russia's Muslim subject populations. Official policy toward the colonial peripheries abandoned overt coercion for bureaucratic assimilation; the borderlands were to be stabilized through the absorption of the Muslim clergy and nobility into the state apparatus. The Tatars of Kazan', as the most assimilated non-Russian community, were to play a significant role as intermediaries in this new dispensation.[25] Derzhavin's lyric persona Mirza could be seen as a lyric refraction of this historical moment, when the civilizational discourse of the European Enlightenment, adopted and modified for the Russian autocratic tradition, created a new kind of pacified colonial subject. Mirza's voice locates enlightened absolutism as the contradictory idiom in which the discourses of nation and empire-building will circulate and coalesce.

The Russian eighteenth-century ode thus evolved an engagement in the dominant paradigms of Russian statehood that was profound yet subtly dissenting. The traditional panegyric form was certainly appropriate for celebrating the autocratic state, but at the price of translating its imperial achievements into the paradigm of despotism. What despotism as a *literary* construct defines, we have seen, is less a rigid political structure than a discursive space, liminal, allegorical, shifting.

The shifts of which I speak are the lyric poem's discursive adaptations to the spaces of nation and empire as geographical and conceptual limits. It is the ode's attempts to make these spaces coincide that renders its rhetoric so complex. The ode orientalizes Russia as a despotic land, yet calls also for the annexation of the east (or south) for a Russia that is consequently no longer, or not yet, oriental. Despotism is what, for western Europe, renders Russia Asiatic, yet is also the occasion that permits Russia's subjugation of its own orient in the name of a European civilizing mission. These are the necessarily blurred contours of a political allegory that will haunt Russian literature, from Pushkin's *Prisoner of the Caucasus* to Tolstoy's *Hadji Murat*. As Dostoevsky phrased the dilemma a century later: "In Europe we were hangers-on and slaves, whereas to Asia we shall go as masters. In Europe we were Tartars, whereas in Asia we too are Europeans. Our mission, our civilizing mission in Asia will bribe our spirit and drive us thither."[26]

The Russian imperial sublime, then, significantly predates the better-known Caucasian adventures of the Russian Romantics and Tolstoy. It begins, historically speaking, with Russia's eighteenth-century campaigns against

Ottoman Turkey, that constitute a shifting southern periphery into which the Caucasus will quickly be drawn. As a literary idiom, the imperial sublime coincides with the birth of modern Russian poetry, constituting an essential if neglected chapter in the literary ideologies of the eighteenth century.

Implicitly assimilating questions of territory to poetics, Lomonosov had sought to establish an idiom equal to the experience of imperial nationhood. To be sure, the Lomonosovian sublime remains relatively skeletal, an exclamation of praise and wonderment, and its rendering of landscape and subjectivity does not intimate the real complexities of court life and imperial policy characteristic of the poet's time.

It was Derzhavin's task to personalize the abstract limitations of the Lomonosovian sublime. While the monarch remains, as in Lomonosov, an allegorical figure, the despot is countered by the growth of the human personality. The Derzhavinian sublime thus antipicates the *career orientalist* (and its alienated counterpart, the exile) as a biographical paradigm. Derzhavin's poems repeatedly celebrate the concrete achievements of the soldier-diplomat, whose life story is now seen as a necessary foil to the abstractions of empire. The figure of the orientalist, destined to have a profound impact on the next literary generation (namely Griboedov, the Decembrists, Pushkin, and then Lermontov), viewed the challenge of imperial adventure as a vocation whose implications were as much literary as military. In poetry as in battle, the orientalist will write his own life story, as the roles of writer and biographer, still distinct in Derzhavin, merge for his successors.

Derzhavin's other legacy to the nineteenth century is to have offered the sublime encounter of the oriental despot and her subject as the symbolic matrix for the topos of the *prophet* that was so enthusiastically adopted by Pushkin and Lermontov:

«*Вос*трепещи, мурза несчастный!
И страшны истины *внемли*,
Которым стихотворцы страстны
Едва ли верят на *земли*».

("Tremble, unfortunate Mirza!
And hearken to terrible truths,
Which passionate poets
On Earth scarcely believe.")

So says Derzhavin's Empress in "The Mirza's Vision," and in "Prophet" Pushkin's God will exclaim:

«*Вос*стань, пророк, и виждь и *внемли*,
Исполнись волею моей,
И, обходя моря и *земли*,
Глаголом жги сердца людей».

("Arise, o prophet, both see and hearken
Be filled with my will
And, traversing sea and land
Burn the hearts of men with the word.")

In these literary echoes, we can already see how the so-called Caucasian or southern theme quickly ramifies beyond the picturesque exoticism of "scenery" to embrace a range of questions, poetic and political. In the eighteenth century, with Lomonosov and Derzhavin, the poet's voice, alternatively obsequious or subtly dissenting, develops the sublime as a literary corollary to the political landscape of despotism. With the nineteenth century, in the grandiose claims of the Decembrists, in Pushkin's subtler dissent, and in Lermontov's profound alienation, we see the imperial sublime collapse inward, its authority wrested from the sovereign and usurped by the poet. The subsequent fate of the imperial sublime, which I sketch here in the barest outline, might finally throw some light on one of the more puzzling features of Puskin's *Prisoner of the Caucasus*, the text with which we began. I am referring to the oddly dissonant note struck by the poem's epilogue, whose triumphant prediction of Russia's final conquest of the Caucasus has struck most readers as aesthetically aberrant if not ideologically abhorrent: "No se—Vostok pod'emlet voi! / Ponikshi snezhnoiu glavoi, / Smiris' Kavkaz: idet Ermolov!" [But lo—the East raises a howl! / Bending your snowy head, / Humble yourself, o Caucasus: Ermolov is coming!] (3:118). We might recall Prince Viazemsky's shocked insistence, on reading these lines, that poetry should never stoop to becoming the "ally of butchers," a "celebration of carnage." Strikingly, Viazemsky linked his viscerally expressed *political* rejection of Pushkin's apparent embrace of imperialist ideology to his perception of the epilogue's *aesthetic* dissonance: "Such rapture (*vostorg*)," he wrote, "is a real anachronism."[27] This "anachronistic rapture" was more precisely formulated by a later critic. "The tone of the epilogue," writes Tomashevskii, "is purely odic," "almost Lomonosovian."[28]

Yet if Pushkin's epilogue is clearly a revival of the odic sublime, it is surely more citational (like the notes invoking his predecessors) than actually performed. Let us not forget that Pushkin repeatedly defers Russia's final victory, as well as his poetic celebration of it, to a strangely receding future tense—"I vospoiu tot slavnyi chas . . ." [And I will celebrate that glorious hour . . ."] (3:118)—whence it finally resonates, like the Lomonosovian sublime for Viazemsky, as a powerful but already remote anachronism: "I vozvestiat o vashei kazni / Predaniia temnye molvy" [and the obscure rumors of legend / Will proclaim your sentence of death].[29] Having relegated the triumphalism of odic discourse to a time frame radically outside its own narrative, *The Prisoner of the Caucasus* in fact performs a subtler task: it citationally invokes the eighteenth-century sublime in order to absorb it within the operations of elegiac memory.[30]

This internalization of the sublime, Pushkin's true innovation within the imperial literary tradition, would determine the fate of more than one generation of Russia's literary protagonists: from Pushkin's Aleko to Lermontov's Pechorin to Tolstoy's Olenin, the grandeur of empire served to energize the *Wanderlust* and melancholy affinity of the romantic hero. Restless heirs to the imperial sublime, these "heroes of our time" constitute the next chapter of its history.

Monika Greenleaf

Found in Translation: The Subject of Batiushkov's Poetry

Что ж, поднимай удивленные брови,
Ты, горожанин и друг горожан,
Вечные сны, как образчики крови,
Переливай из стакана в стакан . . .

(Well then, raise your brows in amazement,
You urbanite, and urbanite's friend,
Pour eternal dreams, like templates of blood,
Back and forth from glass to glass . . .)
—Mandel'shtam, "Batiushkov," 1932

I am like a man who did not reach his goal; he was carrying on his head a beautiful vessel filled with something. The vessel slipped from his head, fell, and broke into fragments. Who can tell now what was in it?
—Batiushkov to Viazemsky, 1823

KONSTANTIN BATIUSHKOV's active literary career was encompassed by the reign of Alexander I (1801–25) and its cultural imperative: *translatio imperii,* or the nineteenth-century realization of the Golden Age of Augustus Caesar. The boundary between exact and "free" translation, between translation and "imitation," between "imitation" and "poetry in the spirit of the ancients" in this period was still fluid;[1] and even Batiushkov's original poems speak from within this continuum of forms and borrowed subjects. There are very few poems in which the lyrical "I" of the poem does not refer the reader past Batiushkov to an explicit foreign original—Tibullus, Parny, Petrarch, Tasso—or to a rarefied world of neoclassical nomenclature. The poet speaks—but not his own words. He is merely the translator, the transparent manipulator of words, draperies, other men's seductions and losses. There is no individual "self" to be found amid the rococo paraphernalia. Writing his critical epitaph on the Alexandrine Age's elegiac poetic legacy, Wilhelm Kiukhel'beker focused on the disparity between Russia's established power and prestige, and her poetry's colonial derivativeness and dependency on Europe. Who, in a world dominated by the "world-historical spirits" of rising nations, would "translate translators?"[2]

Perhaps because Batiushkov's poetry is characterized by such an excess, to our taste, of neoclassical signifier to signified meaning, modern critics have also been unable to read the two levels as interconnected. A sophisticated formal criticism has focused on Batiushkov's contribution to "the formation of the literary language," on the rules for poetic euphony and semantic conjunction that Lidiia Ginzburg calls "the school of harmonic exactitude" and Boris Tomashevsky, more dismissively, Batiushkov's "Empire style."[3] Dismembered into elegant solutions to linguistic problems, regarded *a priori* as derivative and formulaic, his individual poems forfeit any claim to our attention as lyrical expression. As a result, Batiushkov criticism has generally kept the tragedy of his growing disorientation and mental illness rigorously separate from the choices he made in his poetry or in his essays on aesthetics. Irina Semenko first allowed that Batiushkov's determined classicism might be a passionate lyrical position. In her view, the existential vertigo and antipathy to modern history that afflicted him after his long participation in the campaigns against Napoleon and the fall of Moscow fueled Batiushkov's attraction to an ahistorical epicurean world woven out of unchanging classical topoi.[4] The translator's and imitator's task to which Batiushkov dedicated his poetry amounted to an exclusion of both the historical and the personal dimensions of existence from language. Walter Benjamin's segregation of poet and translator would then seem perfectly apt:

> Of the differences between the situation of the translator and that of the poet, the first that comes to mind is that the poet has some relation to meaning. . . . The relation of the translator to the original is the relation between language and language, wherein the problem of meaning or the desire to say something, the need to make a statement, is entirely absent.[5]

It is possible, however, to take a more dynamic view of the role of classical poetry and translation in Batiushkov's career and his culture. In his imaginative article on "Pushkin and Antiquity," D. P. Iakubovich asked his readers to picture the impact on impressionable youths, in a culture that was just coming of age, of growing up amid the phantasmagorical stage set of Petersburg classicism, where the emperor played Augustus, and where one's very sense of self and gentlemanly status depended on one's participation in a system of signs that was deliberately foreign.[6] In his recent book *Scenarios of Power,* Richard Wortman has shown that Alexander's Augustan scenario was no novelty, but an obligatory post-Petrine rite of inheritance and maintenance of power: "Royalty was a foreigner." Each monarch represented his accession as a conquest and a reform; while the constant spectacular enactment of a foreign and privileged "Golden Age" mythology bound each new court elite to the throne.[7] Whereas Russia's eighteenth-century empresses had organized their spectacles around classical mythological figures like Minerva and Astraea, however, Alexander's model was historical: his announced mission was to re-create the *pax Romana* of Augustus's empire, together with its brilliant civic and cultural life. Detaching his reign from the image of Russia as an "eastern despotism," Alexander conflated a traditional neoclassical scenario, which valorized the reproduction of Roman imperial forms, with his court's admiration for the "philosophical" culture of pre-Revolutionary France.

It was the Napoleonic Wars that brought France and Russia, empire and its mythology, face to face. Whose was the despot's, whose the civilized "liberator" 's face? When Alexander I's armies entered Paris in 1814, they came as the guardians and restorers of Western civilization. This is the second aspect of Batiushkov's biographical context that I shall connect with his poetic practice. For Batiushkov was the only major poet of his generation to participate actively in the decade of Napoleonic campaigns by which Russia made itself known to Europe: the marches into Prussia and Finland, his wounding at Heilsberg, the Russian army's epochal crossing of the Niemen, the destruction of Moscow, the Russian army's pursuit of Napoleon across Europe, the "Battle of Nations" at Leipzig and Alexander I's glorious "liberation" of Paris in 1814—all were part of Batiushkov's personal experience.[8] His poems, published one by one in journals over the whole course of the Napoleonic Wars, offered a series of glimpses, some at close range, others in long-shot, of a Russian officer's experience of war.[9] Epic-tinged "pesni" represented in the mode of historical painting panoramic scenes like the crossing of the Niemen or a bivouac in Finland; elegies and epistles bound the loss of heroic friends and longing for homeland to the reader's crystallizing sense of national purpose and identity. Meanwhile, the interspersed classical erotic poems modeled the image of a Russian officer devoting his rare free moments to an interior world of poetry and free literary labor. They were—as Batiushkov's translations from Tibullus made clear—oases of pastoral domesticity and erotic bliss recalled through, and made precious by, the surrounding haze of war.

In short, Batiushkov's conquest for Russian literature of the forms of previous European "Golden Ages" reflected in miniature Alexandrine culture's self-definition. Paris, as we shall see, marked its peak and its demise. Once the improbable palimpsest had fractured, its products became as illegible as the shards of any lost culture. Kiukhel'beker, preoccupied in 1824 with the "republican" logic and national advances of Alexander's reign, could no longer fathom what had prompted Batiushkov to raise the ghost of "that pigmy Parny" while Russia was marching toward historical greatness.[10] It is therefore to that most ephemeral of Batiushkov's "light poems," his translation of Parny's 1778 erotic lyric "Le Revenant" in the Napoleonic year of 1810, that I shall turn to first.

Whether panoramic or intimate, Batiushkov's poems conveyed only the canonical images and rhetoric of war, never an individual's violent, fearful, or simply confused experiences. These, as we shall see, were excluded from the published portrait, emerging instead in Batiushkov's diary account of Moscow in ruins. The esentially Tibullan image of the warrior in battle and "at rest" would frame his collected works, *Opyty v stikhakh i proze* (*Essays in Verse and Prose*), in 1817. The entire structure of the collection projected an image of Russia's inner civilization that chimed perfectly with Alexander I and the Russian army's restoration of peace, order, and her old civilization to a Europe ravaged by three decades of "barbarism." The reader at home and the cultivated soldier at the front were united in this representation of a shared Russian mission and inner life.

Just when Napoleon's encroachment on European civilization had been successfully fought off, Batiushkov's own cultural identity—that is, the Russian-French neoclassical hybrid that had organized gentry culture since the eighteenth century—ceased to serve him. Critics have generally followed Batiushkov in attributing his "spiritual crisis" to his disillusionment and rage over the destruction of Moscow in 1812. Yet as long as Batiushkov's course of action was firmly dictated by the army, and his cultural activities firmly bound to a patriotic collective, he continued to write and to function. It was in postwar leisure that the loss of these two "uniforms" precipitated him into a critical depression. I shall, then, examine the rift that developed between an increasingly voluminous, compensatory cultural self, which one can identify with the patriotic cultural "spectacle" of Batiushkov's *Essays in Verse and Prose,* and the "small and weak mind" that cowered unpublished and formless in his diaries and the endless revisions of his book. I shall show exactly where, in the cultural fortress of his very un-Montaigne–like *Essays,* the empty self is secreted. Meanwhile, the agonizing disparity between Batiushkov's epic personal experiences and proclaimed vocation and his inner "subjectlessness" found voice in his exquisite translation of Schiller's tiny lyric, "Odysseus."

With the final publication of his collection of *Essays,* Batiushkov lost his work and the possibility of controlling or preempting its reception, and fell into still deeper alienation from the products of his own pen. Only one genre escaped his Tolstoyan curse on literature: the Greek anthological fragment. I shall show why this genre of classical translation continued to serve Batiushkov as a lyrical form even after his disintegrating sanity had ceased to find refuge in Russia's collective literary enterprise.

A better analytical grasp of the changing import of Batiushkov's classicizing gestures and choices as translator will, therefore, allow us greater imaginative access to his poetic development. What Batiushkov criticism has not quite registered is the degree to which the cult of antiquity was itself a modern obsession and construct, the product of an acute awareness of "modernity" as a historical and spiritual divide.[11] I suggest that far from being "ahistorical," Batiushkov's elusive translator represents precisely the form of subjectivity called into being by the unstable and overlapping scenarios of Alexandrine culture. By cross-cutting from Tsar to subject, I shall show that Alexander I and Batiushkov enact parallel trajectories, from the *translatio imperii* civilizing mission they inherited from Russia's eighteenth-century emperors, through the identity-conferring and -questioning encounter with Napoleon and total war, to the "selfless" repetition of icons of metaphysical order (the ancient epigram, the parade-formation) in the last years of Alexander's reign: "not for us, not for us, but for Thy name."[12] Finally, in my readings of individual poems I shall demonstrate that even as Batiushkov lends his voice to the poems he selects for translation, they tell "ventriloquistically" of the lyrical and cultural predicament of their translator.

EMPIRE IN THE LOOKING-GLASS

When Alexander I and Napoleon faced each other and their respective armies from opposite banks of the Niemen River in 1807, it was as if the European map, fragmented into so many little bargaining chips, had been elided between them. The ensuing Treaty of Tilsit proclaimed the rival emperors' sudden "friendship" and the exposure of Napoleon's true designs. Until 1807 Napoleon had managed to maintain the reputation of a "liberator" of captive nations from their ancien régime oppressors—and used a spare "republican" taste in architecture, art, and uniforms to advertise it. According to Robert Gildea, it was the "illusion of nationalism" that Napoleon manipulated while creating a system of buffer-states and a police and prison apparatus equipped to forestall any re-igniting of popular Revolutionary sentiment. Following the savage guerrilla war mounted against his brother Joseph in Spain in 1808, Napoleon finally sacrificed Josephine to the empire's need for an heir. His marriage in March 1810 to the Hapsburg emperor's daughter Marie-Louise rather than to Alexander's sister Anna effectively ended the alliance inaugurated at Tilsit. With this dynastic marriage, Napoleon restored the ghost, as it were, of pre-Revolutionary monarchy to the throne of France. "Dominating the whole world from horseback," as Hegel admiringly put it, Napoleon expressed his unprecedented modern ambition in his abduction of ancien régime culture—artworks, bloodlines, and regalia—to decorate his imperial court.[13]

Bloodbaths, political regimes, and their cultural displays had succeeded each other with the vertiginous rapidity of a magic-lantern show—a common contemporary metaphor that Terry Castle has richly documented.[14] Athanius Kircher's seventeenth-century invention, the origin of our slide and movie projector, had been used to entertain the court at Versailles with the ghostly spectacle of "Ombres Chinoises"—past and exotic royalty—throughout the 1770s. In the 1780s and 1790s Crabb Robertson's phenomenally popular seance-entertainments known as "Phantasmagorias" incorporated graveyard and Gothic imagery into the mythological and historical "fantômes artificiels" that he made to appear and vanish, swarm and overlap, and even race ever larger toward the terrified viewer. By 1802 the Seine and the Thames were lined with phantasmagoric "raisings of the dead" open to the boulevard public, although in Paris the resurrection of Louis XVI was strictly forbidden! And the metaphor led no less lively a literary life; to Byron, for example, the mad king George III was "a phantasmagoria in himself."[15] The effect must have been similar when, half a decade after "Brumaire," Napoleon dressed himself in imperial robes, had Josephine painted in late Empire-pastoral style by Prudhon, then sculpted as a reclining nude Venus by Canova, and finally replaced by a Hapsburg empress altogether.

In his *Addresses to the German Nation,* delivered in the wake of the devastating losses of Austerlitz, Jena, and Auerstadt and the occupation of Berlin in 1807–8, Fichte differentiated the rigid state "machine" France had become, together with its neoclassical cloning of dead forms, from a spirit-bearing nation that was identified with neither its state nor its territory, but with its language and culture.[16] Although in the eyes of philosophers like Fichte, Schlegel, and eventually Hegel, it was the young German nation that would liberate the European mind into new forms of consciousness, the role was theoretically open to any nation with a budding linguistic culture. It is tempting to look at the face-off of the two emperors on the Niemen as not only a symbolic mirroring of imperial cultures—which was the original, which the impostor-imitator?—but also as a turning point, the beginning of a reversal of roles. As Napoleon devoured the borders of Europe and any lingering illusions of national liberation, Alexander I took over the role of civilized liberator, moving westward not to conquer but to restore Europe's pre-Revolutionary borders. His right to dictate the terms of peace and resurrect the old body of Europe in 1816 would depend in part on the dissipation of Russia's barbaric image and on her claim to a refined cultural authority.

Batiushkov's "Discourse on the Influence of Light Poetry," delivered in 1816 before the archaist and saber-rattling Collegium of Amateurs of the Russian Word in Moscow, perfectly reflects Russia's imperial cultural mission.[17] He inserts Russia into a historical series of great cultural flowerings that have "translated" both the military glory and the centralized, civilizing culture of Rome, including its intimate poetry, to modern history. Light poetry, he says surprisingly, serves to develop the skills necessary for existence in a complex imperial culture. It teaches the subjects of empire "to decipher the secret play of passions, observe customs, preserve all of the social conventions and relations and speak clearly, effortlessly, and pleasantly" in the unforeseen and socially charged situations of life in a European capital. The interpretive skills, seductive linguistic surface, and elusiveness of content honed by erotic poetry are homologous with the skills used by the postbattle negotiator of provisional alliances or the modern military man or civil servant seeking to advance his career. Far from being the place where the unruly passionate subject appears, erotic poetry is the place where he *dis*appears into convention, leaving only a secret trace behind the undisturbed surface of social language. Light poetry has, in other words, more to do with the conduct of modern imperial life than does epic or panegyric.

In his letters Batiushkov used a still more militant vocabulary to describe his poetic work. Intimate poetry became the locus of a hard-won spirituality, even heroism, where the Russian poet-warrior waged hand-to-hand combat with the "barbarism" of the Russian language.

> The language smells of Tatarism (*pakhnet . . . tatarshchinoi*). What kind of sounds are *y, shch, sh, shii, shchii, pri, try?* O barbarians! And how about the writers? Never mind them! Excuse me for being angry at the Russian people and its language. I was just this minute reading Ariosto, breathing the clean air of Florence, delighting in the musical sounds of the Ausonian language, and conversing with the shades of Dante, Tasso, and sweet Petrarch, from whose lips each word is bliss.[18]

In a curious way, Batiushkov seems to believe that the greatness of his favorite Renaissance poets inheres metonymically in the phonetic qualities of the Italian language. If he can excise from the Russian language the barbaric phonetic-psychological precipitate of its history, isolate a sonic simulacrum of the Italian language within Russian, then a Renaissance will surely follow.[19] Russia's religious literature, historically oriented toward oratory, exhortation, and state ceremony, its phonetics distorted by what Batiushkov called "slavenshchina" (Church Slavic) or the slavish "Serbian dialect," could not serve as the flexible linguistic medium for modern spiritual cultivation. Instead, as Batiushkov put it to N. I. Gnedich in 1810, he was "conquering" for the Russian language and psyche the subtle interiority of the European erotic tradition. In the process, Batiushkov would liberate in the apparently shallow sensuality of a Parny lyric like "The Revenant," its modern "waft of melancholy, a love mystical and platonic."[20] It was this triple levitation—of physical body into interiorized image, of barbaric Russian into civilized language, and of a delicate late Empire sensibility in the midst of Napoleon's takeover—that made Batiushkov call his seemingly anachronistic tour de force, "The Apparition," an "original idea."

In "The Revenant" (1778) Vicomte Evariste de Parny seems indeed to have passed Edward Young's metaphysical *Night Thoughts* through the projector of a fashionable lantern show, and wittily gallicized them. John Locke had already co-opted the optical machine as a metaphor for the mind's power to "revive" or project on the screen of the mind things "that are actually nowhere." The modernized eighteenth-century theory, Castle has shown, defined ghosts as "hallucinations" projected outward by the haunted mind; the obsessed "lover is always a revenant."[21] Parny's ghostly lover flitting around the body of his beloved can be seen as a figure for the mnemonic "raising" of the erotic body in the mind—that is, the shared mind of the writer and reader. It is a typical rococo space, in which, as Norman Bryson puts it, the "pleasure in looking is broken between . . . woman as Image, and male as bearer of the Look." Just as in the rococo painting the palpable texture of the drapery fabric "escaping from the figure toward the picture-plane displays itself to the viewer as the displaced locus of eroticism,"[22] in Parny's poem that eroticism becomes focused on the playful surface of the language. Language itself is fetishized as the wispy veil that needs only to be stripped away to yield ecstatic vision. Yet when the veils do fall away, it is to reveal an abstract fleshy *embonpoint;* a fall into solid flesh terminates the poem's imaginative flight.

Batiushkov uses the Parny poem to dramatize his own position as translator or medium for its ghostly eroticism. Entering the theatrical rococo space of the French poet, Batiushkov reiterates the phrase that defines the speaker as forgotten, essentially self-less: *"i ia zabyt! / Ia zabyt"* (And I am forgotten!) It is precisely his entry into the foreign poem's "body" that allows him his apparitional being as lover. A notable feature of Batiushkov's lexicon, quite absent from Parny's, is his fusion of neoclassical nomenclature with a religious vocabulary: *voskresat', iarkimi luchami, ochi, glas, arfy golos, blazhenstvo* (resurrect, brilliant rays, orbs, harp's voice, blessedness). Having given up selfhood, he defines himself instead as the hidden but ubiquitous spiritual presence in the poem:

Стану всюду развевать
Легким уст прикосновеньем,
Как зефира дуновеньем,
От каштановых волос
Тонкий запах свежих роз . . .
Если лилия листами
Ко груди твоей прильнет,
Если яркими лучами
В камельке огонь блеснет,
Если пламень потаенный
По ланитам пробежал,
. . . Если пояс сокровенный
Развязался и упал—
Улыбнися, друг бесценный,
Это—я!

(1:98–100)

(I shall flutter everywhere
Like the light touch of lips,
Like a zephyr's breath,
Or from chestnut hair
The fine scent of fresh roses . . .
If a lily with its leaves
Clings to your breast,
If with brilliant rays
The fire flashes in the hearth,
If a covert flame
Raced across your cheeks,
. . . If the sacred sash
Came untied and fell—
Smile, my priceless love—
It is I!)

His spirit has been transubstantiated into the poem's language, with its airy, tendril-like proliferation of similes, its neoclassical draperies constantly postponing the moment of unveiling. Batiushkov resurrects the aesthetics of a Watteau painting like *The Swing*, which discloses not "embonpoint" but the momentary shared perspective of the young voyeur within the painting and the viewer outside as the skirts fly up. Both create the shared spiritual tension and "brotherhood" of desire, not the spectacle of consummation.

There is a structural relationship between *not* seeing or experiencing, and gaining a voice in poetry; between unveiling and muteness or death; between a "veil of words" and survival. Even as the moment of disclosure approaches, the speaker continues to fling neoclassical phrases over its nakedness:

Ты проснешься . . . о блаженство!
Я увижу совершенство . . .
Тайну прелести красот,
Где сам пламенный Эрот
Оттенил рукой своею
Розой девственну лилею;
Все опять в моих глазах,
Все покровы исчезают;
Час блаженнейший! . . . Но, ах!
Мертвые не воскресают.

(You'll awaken . . . o bliss!
I will see perfection . . .
The mystery of beauty's charms,
Where with his hand
Fiery Eros himself
Shaded with rose the virginal lily;

All is in my eyes again,
The veils all disappear;
Most blessed hour! . . . But, ah!
The dead cannot be resurrected.)

The neoclassical fabric of the poem in which he has clothed himself has come to an end; the text runs out. For Batiushkov, the translator, there is no sensual world to return to: "the dead cannot be resurrected." The translator lives only in the language of his borrowed poem, for the duration of a reading.

Writing—re-creating, resurrecting—other men's objects of desire was to become Batiushkov's principal mode of self-delineation, of writing a path to the distant object of his own desire: cultural glory (*slava*). Might this not be one possible meaning of Batiushkov's fading lover, repeatedly resurrected by the incantation of a classical formula? When Viazemsky pointed out Batiushkov's contentment with celebrating "other men's Eleonoras,"[23] he astutely identified the displaced role of the erotic in Batiushkov's poetry. His desire is not for the primary objects screened from him by "a veil of words," but for the fabric of the words to clothe his own "selflessness." The clothing and unclothing of the feminine body appear in his poetry as the exact correlates of his own excited clothing of himself in language: the body drops its veils and rushes toward the reader at the moment that he, the invisible translator, is fully clothed, "bodied forth," spirit made incarnate in language.[24]

I suggest, finally, that the Russian translation's exquisite "raising" of the Parny poem, rococo vestige of a now wistfully playful culture, is polemically aimed at the anachronism and crudity of Napoleon's "Empire style" revival in 1810. Written while Batiushkov was on leave from the battlefront, it is an act of mourning for the refined neoclassical French culture that was disappearing into the maw of Napoleon's total war even as he wrote. Batiushkov intercepts the lyrical legacy of the ancien régime and gives it a new occasion. The roles of "lover" and of "translator," not ordinarily linked, coincide within the specific cultural moment of a Russian officer's leave from the ongoing historical ordeal of the Napoleonic Wars. The precious interlude of intimate life is intensified and hallowed by the surrounding male context and proportions of war. This is reflected in the pleasurable prolongation of each moment, each sensory nuance, the "trouvaille" (lucky find) of each found phrase. Batiushkov abducts for the Russian language not only that missing strand of rococo grace, but what Terry Castle calls the modern "deep preference for the phantoms of the mind."[25] For Batiushkov, the ability to call up the ghosts of past Golden Ages is the highest proof of the Russian poet's imaginative power: a poetic feat on a par with Alexander's resurrection of the political bodies of Old Europe.

WAR BOOTY

> Moscow is gone! Irredeemable losses! . . . all has been besmirched by this band of barbarians! Behold the fruits of enlightenment. . . . The terrible events of our times, events which happened as though intentionally right before my eyes . . . have struck me with such force that I can barely collect my thoughts and often ask myself: Where am I? What am I? . . . The terrible actions of vandals or Frenchmen in Moscow and her environs, actions unmatched in all history, have completely disrupted my little philosophy and have made me quarrel with humanity. . . . Barbarians, vandals![26]

So lamented Batiushkov in a letter to Viazemsky in 1812. Batiushkov had been on leave from the army during the Grande Armée's invasion of Russia, participating instead in the lively, contentious, and somewhat oblivious literary life of Petersburg as Napoleon neared Moscow. Galvanized into action by rumors of the capital's imminent fall, he set off to join the fight for its defense, but was rerouted to Nizhny Novgorod and arrived only in time to witness Moscow's ruins. In letters to his Petersburg friends Batiushkov rehearsed the debates that were raging among the French-educated Moscow refugees, who now perceived in the depredations of modern war the logical consequence of the pernicious Enlightenment civilization that had seduced and then betrayed them. With the French in the role of "barbarians" and the Russians carrying the standard of "civilization," Batiushkov's Enlightenment conception of his vocation was put under strain.

His first reaction was to don his army uniform. His thirteen months as adjutant to the eminent general N. N. Raevsky during the fast-paced pursuit of Napoleon through Germany, the "Battle of Nations" at Leipzig, the embattled march through France, and sudden laying down of arms and effusive welcome by the people of Paris "passed before his eyes" in a spectacular kaleidoscope of scenes that, Batiushkov wrote from the front, he felt lucky to witness. Even the death of his closest comrade Petin at Leipzig did not dampen the euphoria of the Russian liberation of Paris in 1814, nor the civilized pleasures of the three-month occupation that ensued. Running from play to play, eagerly discussing the merits of the capital's two favorite actresses at gatherings that sparkled with the kind of conversation he and his friends had striven to re-create in Moscow, confronted for the first time in his life with the unparallelled concentration of European artworks plundered for Napoleon's imperial collection and now made available for public view, Batiushkov found himself in the cultural paradise of his dreams.

> Will you believe it? We who participated in all the major events, we who to this moment can scarcely believe that Napoleon has disappeared, Paris is ours, Louis on the throne, the mad countrymen of Montesquieu, Racine, Fénelon, Robespierre, Danton, and Napoleon are singing in the streets: "Vive Henri

Quatre, vive ce roi vaillant!" Such miracles exceed all understanding. And in such a short time, and with such strange details, and with such bloodshed, and with such lightness and frivolity! Miraculous are your works, Lord![27]

The sudden translation of enmity into friendship at Tilsit also marked the beginning of a decade of transformations for Alexander I. Appearing before the crowd in matching uniforms on matched steeds, the two emperors stood and clasped each other's hands in the dress circle while onstage the actor Talma pronounced an appropriate speech. That same year the Russian army's Austrian-style uniforms were replaced by the fashionable new Napoleonic cut. Where did theater end and reality begin? Riding into Paris in 1814 at the end of a year of military victories, Alexander spoke the words he felt his massive popular audience wanted to hear: he would not, he declared, quit France until Louis XVIII had signed a constitutional contract; in London he snubbed the regent and flirted with the Whig opposition, requesting its advice for installing an opposition movement in his own country. In Warsaw he donned his Polish uniform to announce a constitutional monarchy with himself its modern king—an experiment he promised to transplant to Russia.[28] Yet Napoleon's return from the political grave, Waterloo, and the sterner settlement in Metternich's Vienna demanded a further renovation of costume and rhetoric: encouraged by Alexander's spiritualist adviser, Julie von Krudener, the tsar conceived his divine mission to "raise" and protect the old divine-right monarchies from their own internal enemy: first Napoleon, then any revolutionary conspiracy, and finally the people's disorder (or "barbarism") itself. Metternich's secular "quadruple alliance" was translated into Alexander's "Holy Alliance," in which the revolutionary formula "fraternité et égalité," abducted and rebaptized as biblical language, served to justify not only balance of power politics but a network of internal surveillance and repression.

Emblematic of this shift, Wortman has shown, was the celebratory spectacle performed in 1815 by the Russian army at Vertus, on the very spot outside Paris where the Roman general Aetius had repelled Attila the Hun. Not only did the 150,000-man Russian army execute flawless geometrical formations before the assembled hilltop audience of "all of Europe," but during a climactic smoke-filled cannonade it vanished miraculously into thin air, leaving the field empty and peaceful when the smoke had cleared. The display was received as an icon for a kind of superhuman orderliness achievable only by Russia: the choreography of the people's wills and bodies into a gigantic ballet produced, as it were, for God's eye alone.[29] The "liberator" Alexander returned to Petersburg in January 1816 a reforming Luther, ordered the published text of his "Holy Alliance" posted on church walls, and proceeded to try to make the icon of Russianness he had invented for Vertus a reality. "Augustus" had abandoned his Golden Age.

The appetite after 1814 for an epic, victory ode, national saga, or some unprecedented Russian statement was high. Even the apolitical Zhukovsky joined the chorus of celebratory voices with his verse-epistle "To Alexander I," a poem that by its non-panegyric tone confirmed the increasingly pacifist and Christian representation of the Russian emperor. Meanwhile, in 1816 Batiushkov translated another elegy from Tibullus.

Was Batiushkov ducking the responsibility of the contemporary moment by pursuing his "timeless" philological labors? A look at his "free translation" of Tibullus's elegy (book I, 3) suggests the opposite.[30] The trademark juxtapositions of Tibullus's poetry—the contrast of war and domestic hearth, the poet's separation from homeland and erotic love—clearly speak for Batiushkov's situation, while translating the Russian army's experience of modern war into the customary Augustan public discourse. What is accentuated in Batiushkov's version is the speaker's sheer terror and almost childlike lamentation at having been left behind by his commander in a foreign land to face an unconsecrated, unmourned, *meaningless* death alone.

> Мессала! Без меня ты мчишься по волнам
> С орлами римскими к восточным берегам;
> А я, в Феакии оставленный друзьями
> Их заклинаю всем, и дружбой и богами,
> Тибулла не забыть в далекой стороне!
> (1:194–98)

> (Messala! Without me you speed over the waves
> With Roman eagles to eastern shores;
> While I, left behind in Phaeacia by my friends
> Conjure them by everything, by friendship and the gods,
> Not to forget Tibullus in a distant land!)
> (book I, 3, lines 1–5)

In Batiushkov's version the speaker mourns his own absence: "*Bez menia* ty mchish'sia" (without me you speed) . . . "*Ia sam, lishennyi* skorb'iu sil" (I myself, deprived by grief of strength) . . . "Vse tshchetno, milaia, *Tibulla net* s toboiu" (All's in vain, my sweet, there is no Tibullus with you). The army and national mission of which he was a part have abandoned him onshore and accelerate away from him; no national rite of mourning will translate his death into meaningful sacrifice and cultural memory. He will be forgotten.

By abandoning the Augustan metaphor just when Russia attained the pinnacle of her secular European glory, Alexander I had left his poets vocationless: "Bez menia ty mchishsia." Russia's acceleration into an era of pragmatic and historical contact with Europe, on the one hand, and a national theory of suprapersonal religious predestination, on the other, had deprived Batiushkov of the sign-system that had guaranteed the significance of his labors.

. . . к чему Изиде приношения,
Сии в ночи протяжны песнопенья
И волхвованье жриц, меди звучный стон.
(1:195)

(. . . what for these tributes to Izida,
These psalms long drawn-out in the night
And sorcery of priests, and bronze's resonant moan.)

Reading literally, one might say that it is indeed the absence of Tibullus that the abandoned poet mourns; that is, the obsolescence of the *translatio imperii* culture that bound the expressive discoveries Batiushkov was making in this very poem and the Russian conquest of Paris together in a mutually reinforcing system of meaning. With an almost petulant intonation, the speaker begs the goddess of war to "give back" what she has stolen: the idyllic fields of his homeland, the Golden Age itself, the innocently classical image of Delia:

В прелестной наготе явись моим очам:
Власы развеяны небрежно по плечам,
Вся грудь лилейная и ноги обнаженны . . .
(1:198)

(Appear in lovely nakedness before my eyes:
Hair windstrewn careless upon your shoulders,
The whole of your lily breast and legs bared . . .)

While Tibullus pictures Delia as simply barefoot, Batiushkov's Delia is the familiar phantasmagorical apparition "raised" by the magic lantern of translation, shedding her draperies as she runs toward him into the poem. Turning toward his audience, Batiushkov ends his translation in the first person plural ("to us") and with an urgent future interrogative:

Когда ж Аврора нам, когда сей день блаженный
На розовых конях в блистаньи принесет,
И Делию Тибулл в восторге обоймет?

(When will Aurora bear this blessed day
On rosy horses in radiance to us,
And Tibullus in ecstasy his Delia embrace?)

The object of his desire is the Golden Age, Tibullus-and-Delia as the lost paradise of images that, for the duration of his translation, he has successfully "raised." One might say that its urgency is addressed to the receding eutopic myth that has left him stranded, perhaps forgotten, on the shores of modernity.

Meanwhile, however, Batiushkov has woven a gorgeous, sensuously vivid, and lexically and rhythmically ceremonious language of mourning: a Russian language that could serve not only to praise and celebrate, but also to incorporate the tragic losses of the war into the nation's history and psyche, carry out the responsibility of the postwar process that has been called "nationalizing death."[31] Batiushkov turns an apparently old-fashioned classical translation into a complexly ironic piece of "double voicing" that reflects more accurately than the festive restoration of Europe's prewar borders and political regimes did, the disappearance of a whole world.

Alexander I was, Wortman shows, equally paralyzed by the shock of war to his system of available identities. Having forfeited the role of military conqueror that had traditionally been implied by the Petrine-Roman scenario, the emperor fell back on the older Byzantine role of Basileus, or chief worshiper of an emphatically Christian kingdom. The text of the Holy Alliance, published in Russia in 1816, deliberately deflected attention away from the Muscovite and Russian people's actions onto the city's buildings and immutable religious tradition. The erection of the world's biggest cathedral, Vitberg's unrealizably mammoth project, would have served as the ultimate "nationalization of death" precisely in its substitution of a grandiose wordless monument and ritual for individuals' memories and stories.[32] In the context of such a deliberately mandated historical gap, Batiushkov's difficulty in producing a coherent public narrative about his personal experience of war and loss is doubly revealing. It may, indeed, account for the persistence with which he traced his own postwar malaise to the sight of Moscow's ruins and their homeless inhabitants. It was as if Moscow had completed her Roman trajectory and crossed the line into ancient history, while the living survivors of her culture constituted a ghostly phantasmagoria.

> We have lived two centuries since that beneficent time. . . . I entered Paris with sword in hand. . . . From Paris to London, from London to Gottenburg, to Stockholm . . . to Petersburg. That has been my Odyssey, truly my Odyssey! Now we resemble Homeric warriors, scattered over the face of the earth. Each one of us is pursued by some god of vengeance.[33]

One translation written in 1816 allowed Batiushkov to reconcile the public appetite for a national epic with his need to speak of his own trauma. Not in Homer, but in Schiller's small lyric "Odysseus" (1796), written a few years after the French Revolution, Batiushkov found a text to name his experience. Compare:

Odysseus

Alle Gewässer durchkreuzt' Odysseus, die Heimat zu finden,
Durch der Scylla Gebell, durch der Charybde Gefahr,
Durch die Schrecken des feindlichen Meers, durch die Schrecken des
  Landes,
Selbst in des Aides Reich führt ihn die irrende Fahrt.
Endlich tragt das Geschick ihn schlafend an Ithakas Küste,
Er erwacht, und erkennt jammernd das Vaterland nicht![34]

(All the waters crossed Odysseus, his homeland to find,
Through the baying of Scylla, through Charybdis's perils,
Through the terrors of hostile gulfs, through the terrors of land,
To the very kingdom of Hades his wandering journey led.
At last Fate bore him sleeping upon Ithaca's coast,
He awoke, and wailing knew the Fatherland not!)

Судьба Одиссея
Средь ужасов земли и ужасов морей
Блуждая, бедствуя, искал своей Итаки
Богобоязненный страдалец Одиссей;
Стопой безтрепетной сходил Аида в мраки;
Харибды яростной, подводной Сциллы стон
 Не потрясли души высокой.
Казалось, победил терпеньем рок жестокой
И чашу горести до капли выпил он;
Казалось, небеса карать его устали,
 И тихо сонного домчали
До милых родины давножеланных скал.
Проснулся он: и что ж? отчизны не познал.
(1:193)

(The Fate of Odysseus
Among the terrors of the earth and the terrors of the sea
Wandering, imperiled, searched for his Ithaca
The godfearing sufferer Odysseus;
With intrepid foot he descended into Hades' darkness;
Charybdis's ferocious, Scylla's underwater moan
 Did not shake his high soul.
It seemed, with patience he had vanquished cruel fate
And drained the cup of bitterness to its last drop;
It seemed, the heavens of punishing him had tired,
 And quietly the sleeping one delivered
To the homeland's dear long-desired cliffs.
He awakened: and what? His fatherland he did not know.)

Schiller's poem narrates in elliptically foreshortened fashion the obstacles overcome by Odysseus on his determined way home to Ithaca. The modern poet retells the story of the *Odyssey,* yet it inevitably comes out differently, bears the imprint of his sensibility. Its lyrical tone is one not of leisurely epic certainty, but of accelerated modern compression; typically for the modern epigram, it reserves its most significant change for the surprise ending, or *pointe:* the *lack* of fit between the worldviews of classical epic and modernity. In the *Odyssey* the problem of time and change was solved by the famous recognition scene, in which Odysseus's nanny recognizes her drastically changed master by an old scar—an external sign of his essential, changeless identity and their common history. The single half-line with which "Odysseus" ends brilliantly transposes the static, comic-epic conclusion of the *Odyssey* to the age of modern historical change, in which a few years could render one's "fatherland" tragically unrecognizable, the homecoming forever postponed. The poem's subject is thus not Odysseus's epic story, but the impossibility of return: Schiller's own theory about the unrecoverability of "the naive" rendered in poetry.[35]

The translation looks at first glance remarkably accurate, yet Batiushkov has introduced most of its figurative language. Schiller's poem is dry and spare, quickly enumerating the famous travails of Odysseus's journey without descriptive elaboration. Batiushkov's elaborate epithets and paraphrases attach a dimension of internal suffering to Odysseus's heroic exploits, transforming him from an epic to a metaphysical hero. The mythological horrors of the journey, which for Schiller are purely textual, are for Batiushkov the metaphoric equivalents of his own, unmentioned experiences. Schiller's text offers him exactly the counterpoint he needs, between an ancient, "original" text that captures and depersonalizes his experience of war, and a modern lyric that renders his sense of displacement. The modern Russian's paradoxical experience can only be named indirectly, as the point of intersection between extroverted epic action and modern introspection, between Greek and German, Homer and Schiller.

The poem is constructed on the tension between untranslatable and phonetically foreign names (*Itaki, Odissei, Aida, Kharibdy, Stsilly*) and the Russian grammatical constructions and assonances that they create in their wake. There is no comparable interplay between the sounds of Greek and German in Schiller. The features of Greek that were particularly admired in the eighteenth century—the compound adjective, inflection and inversion[36]—are rendered by Batiushkov's flamboyant, but grammatically Russian neologisms (*bogoboiaznennyi, beztrepetnoi, davnozhelannykh*) and outlandish inversions (*skhodil Aida v mraki; do milykh rodiny davnozhelannykh skal*) that leave the reader in semantic suspense until the syntactic resolution of the sentence: the reader's equivalent of "skhozhdenie v mraki" (descent into darkness). What is left out of the repertoire of Russian expressive possibilities is equally noteworthy: there are no "Slavonic" participles or roots, none of the coiling embedded participial phrases typical of Church Slavic, and none of the "barbaric" consonantal clusters Batiushkov associated with "Slavenshchizna."[37] Batiushkov is clearly proposing his own modern simulacrum of archaic style, including his signature tight fabric of alliterative repetitions, as a replacement for what he regarded as the spurious revival by the archaists of Church Slavic diction. "The Fate of Odysseus" thus links an elegiac treatment of Greek—not Roman—epic with an equally sharp and innovative activation of the Russian language's hidden strengths.

Odysseus's overcoming of geographical obstacles on his way home is analogous to the fate of Odysseus's image in time. "Bluzhdaia, bedstvuia, iskal svoei Itaki" echoes the search of the modern translator, attempting to navigate a recognizable path toward Greece (and "the language of humanity") in a vertiginous ocean of linguistic possibilities and traps. The soldier's arrival at the longed-for cliffs of Ithaca coincides with the end of the poem's journey in search of its own classical language—and a renewed heroic image of the translator. Instead of a happy homecoming, however, there is an anticlimactic drop into terse, colloquial diction: "I chto zh—otchizny ne poznal" (And what?—he did not know his fatherland). *Itaka* and *otchizna* belong to different cultural realms; the parallel journeys of translation and of war have isolated the poet in his own time zone. In Benjamin's words, "the gates of a language thus expanded and modified may slam shut and enclose the translator with silence."[38]

A recurrent source of Batiushkov's embitterment on his return home was his inability to establish a reliable conversion-table for words, actions, reputation or character, and material rewards. Zubkov has documented how persistently Batiushkov's attempts to separate himself from his moniker "The Russian Parny" and his early "Gallic" erotics were ignored by the friends who constituted his public. Frustrated, perhaps, by his inability to convert his army experiences into a richer public persona, he spent two fruitless years pursuing the extra military decoration and accompanying rise in rank and salary he had heard were due him. In a similar vein, when friends and relatives attempted to mediate between Batiushkov and the object of his unrequited passion, Batiushkov was indignant that his selfless, Petrarchan act of renunciation was not taken at face value. He himself did not "translate well." Zubkov has shown by meticulous study of the revisions and reorderings of *Essays in Verse and Prose,* how deliberately Batiushkov worked to refashion the public's image of his poetic and intellectual development up to the moment of publication. A book must be constructed like a batallion, he advised his editor, the better soldiers leading off, the weakest secreted in the middle, and the best defending the rear.[39] Zubkov's precise textological work allows me to step back and consider the strangeness of Batiushkov's internalized military imagery.[40]

The book is girded round with signposts that direct the reader in different directions at once. On the one hand, they seek to re-create an atmosphere of improvisation and fortuitousness, even the old Alexandrine culture of "friendship"; the dedication urges friends to decipher in the book the ongoing "diary of the poet's passions" and ephemeral enthusiasms. Meanwhile, a note from the editor creates a more public persona of the poet as warrior-at-rest, united with his readers by their common patriotic experience of war.

Much like Alexander at the peacetables in Paris and Vienna, Batiushkov points beyond himself in the first poem to a transcendental origin for his poetic vision: "On! On! Ego vse dar blagoi!" (He! He! His still the blessed gift). The collection's apparently classical ordering by genres nevertheless implies a developmental portrait of Batiushkov's vocation, culminating in the long, philosophical-historical meditative poems that are clearly meant to look beyond the present book toward a new, more serious horizon. Pleasing and appeasing everyone, the framing texts seem designed to preempt the fear, experienced quite often as Batiushkov labored over his prose-essays and poems in the unaccustomed solitude of the Russian countryside, that he had been/would be forgotten.

How, then, are we to respond to the collection's Montaignesque title and epigraph: "Et quand personne ne me lira, ay je perdu mon temps, de m'estre entretenu tant d'heures oysifves a pensements utiles ou agréables?" (And when no one reads me, have I wasted my time, for having spent so many leisurely hours in useful or agreeable thoughts?). On the one hand, they promised two volumes filled with the individualistic thoughts and poetic experiments of a cultivated man in his "heures oysifves"—taking solitary pleasure in the process of thought itself. Montaigne's calm indifference to public opinion becomes in Batiushkov's version a somewhat resentful display of the "inner riches" of high culture. He quotes approvingly: "They cannot read in my heart, but they will read my book, Montaigne said; and in the most tempestuous times of France, to the sound of weapons, the blaze of pyres lit by superstition, he wrote his *Essays* and, conversing with good hearts of all ages, forgot his unworthy contemporaries."[41] For Batiushkov, the important thing is not Montaigne's turn toward himself as subject, but his compensatory turn away from contemporaneity toward "timeless" culture. The very word *essay* acquires a different meaning in Russian translation: the reasoned exploration by a single Renaissance mind of its inner domain becomes, in Batiushkov's hands, the spectacle of a Russian cultural Renaissance.

The experimental side of Batiushkov's *Essays in Prose* lies in his evident effort to display Russian cultural life in an array of eighteenth-century philosophical/aesthetic genres: the philosophical letter, the Diderotian *entretien* or philosophical dialogue, the peripatetic *Salon*-style art commentary, the Winckelmannian "rhapsody" or "reverie" on antique and modern sculpture.[42] Thus Kantemir argues the pros and cons of writing poetry for a Russian audience in an informal salon setting with no less than Montesquieu, and proves more than a match for his witty French interlocutors. In "Strolls in the Academy of Arts" Batiushkov impersonates an elderly Muscovite undertaking a visit to the art gallery "with Winckelmann in hand." The lively discussion that ensues about the relative merits of antique and modern sculpture (for example, the *eques* of Marcus Aurelius is compared unfavorably to Falconet's dramatic *vsadnik*) is clearly a polemic with Winckelmann's famous views—and paints a favorable picture both of the gallery's holdings, and of the level of Russian aesthetic discourse.[43] Thus the prose essays create a portrait of a Russian "Golden Age" that serves as a frame for Batiushkov's experiments (*opyty*) in poetry.

These are, as Zubkov has shown, organized in such an order as to display the greatest cultural sweep together with an accelerating developmental momentum. The erotic "bezdelki" (trifles) and translations of light poetry of which Batiushkov was the acknowledged master were secreted in the middle section, "Smes' " (miscellany), flanked and justified by epic glimpses of river-fordings and mourned warriors, pastoral elegies to peace and the homeland, a Petrarchan cycle of spiritualized love poetry, and extended moral allegories on mortality, vocation, and fate. Ending with his most recent and most ambitious historical elegy, "The Dying Tasso," the volume pointed simultaneously to the Renaissance as its inspiration, and to the poet's own opening poetic horizon. In this way Batiushkov's early narrow reputation as the "Russian Parny" was not deleted but woven into a much grander portrayal of his own poetic range and Russia's stature as standard-bearer of civilization. The entire structure of the collection projected an image of Russia's inner and outer civilization that chimed perfectly with Alexander I and the Russian army's restoration of peace, order, and her old civilization to a Europe ravaged by three decades of "barbarism."

In short, Batiushkov represents Russia's "Golden Age" as a series of cultural conquests. Much like Napoleon ordering his minister Colbert to amass "tout ce qu'il y a de beau en Italie" (all there is of beauty in Italy) and each conquered country of Europe for his imperial collection,[44] the Russian poet's imagination produced as proof of Russia's rich inner life that same many-roomed and well-labeled museum.

Even as he translates Buffon's famous line, "Po slogu mozhni uznat' cheloveka" (by the style one knows the man), Batiushkov's own style betrays the museum label's habit of cultural apposition. Great names become the gold coin of a system of identification and exchange. Lomonosov is ludicrously bracketed with Raphael: "on the bed of his agony and death Raphael lamented his unfinished paintings—our northern genius his uncompleted works."[45] M. N. Murav'ev's sentimental philosophizing elicits comparisons with Montaigne, Matthison, Fénelon, Cicero: name-brand labels that are meant, clearly, to raise his value. Quoting Montaigne himself—"Si on me presse de dire, pourquoi je l'aimais, je sents que cela ne se peut exprimer qu'en répondant: parceque c'était lui, parceque c'était moi" (if one presses me to say why I loved him, I feel that this can be expressed only by responding: because it was he, because it was I)—Batiushkov is deaf to the disparity between Montaigne's vigorous assertion of irreducible individuality and the

Russian philosopher's colorless generalizations about friendship, virtue, and so forth. Even as Batiushkov attempts to focus on the features that make his Russian subject an original man, he reflexively reaches for a comparison: "It was long ago said that the style is the mirror of the soul, and in reference to our author, this is completely just. His style can be compared to Fénelon's. . . . The same thing can be said about it that Schiller said about Matthison." Apparently unaware of the allusive *mise en abyme* he has created, he summarizes optimistically, "Here we find our author himself, we enter into intimate acquaintance with him. Human art can imitate everything, except the movements of a good heart. That is the true originality of our author!"[46]

A diary entry written in May 1817, shortly before his *Essays* went to press, shows, however, that Batiushkov was quite aware of the difference:

> My illness has not passed, but slightly quieted down. All around is gloomy muteness (*molchanie*). . . . So let me write without a draft, impromptu, without self-love, and let's see what pours out; write as quickly as few authors write, for self-love always tugs at one's lapel and makes one substitute for the first word a different one. But Montaigne wrote whatever came to his mind. I believe that. But Montaigne was a truly unusual man. With a small mind, feeble and unquick, like mine, to write straight off is very hard. . . . Think! I've tried to think several times, but it doesn't come out. . . . This hurts. Why can't I think . . . I don't know how to help the grief. Let me think. By the way, I recall someone else's words—Voltaire's, I remember: so that's how one writes history.[47]

The foreign quotation at last breaks the heavy muteness around him and inside him, and a stylish military anecdote, no worse than the ones published in magazines, fills the empty page. On the one hand, lack of self and ominous muteness, on the other, an entry into language always unlocked by *chuzhoe slovo*—the self-confident, already uttered phrase of another, in which Batiushkov's small mind can clothe its nakedness: this is the creative process that is constantly dramatized, even eroticized, in his poetry; and that stands nakedly exposed in his prose.

Batiushkov was essentially trapped in the binary fixity of his own categories: cultured or barbarian, immortal or forgotten, intelligent or mad. *Essays in Verse and Prose* was built to shore up these distinctions, and his own position. To displace Russia's—and his own—narrow French ancestry, his book forged alliances with world cultures of the ages (Germany, Greek and Roman antiquity, pre-eighteenth-century France, Russia's own eighteenth-century Golden Age, and above all Renaissance Italy); it displayed a Golden Age of prose and poetry ventriloquized by himself alone. It recuperated his light poetry as a classical, rather than "Gallic," phase that, followed by a spiritualized Petrarchan love poetry, would lead finally to his ultimate conquest for Russian literature: a "lyrical epic" of the stature of Tasso's *Jerusalem Delivered.* The historical elegy on Tasso's death with which the collection ended was a promissory note, a proof of vocational commitment and readiness that looked beyond the border of the book.

Batiushkov wrote proudly to Gnedich: "The plot, and everything—is mine. My own simplicity." And indeed, the plot of the elegy is frighteningly revealing; Tasso, imprisoned and insane, dies at unbearable length, unaware of the crown of laurels on his head or the applauding crowd. In this figure meet several of the polar opposites between which Batiushkov's imagination hung suspended: mad *and* cultured, ostracized *and* idolized, dead to the world *and* alive; having completed his masterpiece *and* freed at last from the tyranny of vocation. Even as *Essays in Verse and Prose* enlarged its cultural domain, it incarcerated Batiushkov still more unforgivingly in its internal hierarchy of "great works" and great expectations. The grandiosity of the culturally constructed "I" implied by the collection also created its guilty ghost, the "small and weak mind" dwarfed by its own battalion.

THE NAKED AND THE DEAD

The literary glory that Batiushkov pictured for Tasso surely resembles the mass demonstrations that had greeted Alexander (and Batiushkov in his suite) on their entry into Paris more than it does any conceivable scene of literary reception. Notice, for example, that the scene entirely omits the book, which was the focus of Batiushkov's passionate hope and dread. In a letter to Zhukovsky he quavered, "What do you say about my prose? With horror I pose this question. . . . Why did I take it into my head to publish? I feel, I know there's a lot of nonsense. . . . Three wars, always on horseback, and on the open road in peacetime. . . . So why publish? It's no loss, of course: they'll scold it and forget it. But this thought is killing to me, killing! . . . If God lets me undertake a second edition, I will make everything over; maybe I'll write something new."[48]

If Alexander had trouble readjusting to a Petersburg culture that he had essentially fathered, and that had remained untouched by the intervening wars and their religious revelation, so did Batiushkov. "Otdelavshis'" (having separated himself) in his book from the earlier half of Alexander's reign, he urgently wanted to move beyond it, while Petersburg's literary society Arzamas continued the same prewar culture of "friendship," epicurean play, irresponsible language, and inaction. "Praises and unrestrained friends lead one into the woods, the fog. I love each Arzamasian on his own, but together in a bunch, like all societies, they babble, twist and turn, and cause harm."[49] Batiushkov was eager for Arzamas to found an English-style periodical that would regularly publish the members' literary works, but also provide a forum for political and critical discussion, replace the informal and ephemeral babble of the "circle" with books in print. In his recent essay "A Word on Poets and

Poetry" he had renounced "the modern art of titillating the senses while concealing the nakedness of truth." Rephrasing Karamzin's famous line "Speak as you write, write as you speak," Batiushkov made a stand for authenticity: "Live as you write, write as you live, otherwise the echoes of your lyre will be false."[50] Why then did his search for the "naked truth" lead him in 1817 not to an abandonment of classical models, nor to a more empirical, autobiographical poetry, but to yet another translation project? In what way was Batiushkov's collaborative effort with S. S. Uvarov on a Greek-to-French-to-Russian translation of selected epitaphs from *The Greek Anthology*—a tenth-century compilation of epitaph verses from ancient Greece, the Roman Empire, and Byzantium, rediscovered in the mid-eighteenth century and translated into all the major modern European languages[51]—a step in a new direction?

The *Greek Anthology* represented one solution to the cultural impasse debated in Nizhny Novgorod: how to reconcile an intensifying desire to express national identity with a widening of the cultural net. With the sudden evanescence of their French-Roman cultural framework, educated Russians became aware of the new historical interpretation of the classical legacy by which German writers proposed to break out of the binary deadlock of "culture" and "barbarism." Schlegel interpreted Herder's famous exhortation, "We must become Greeks, otherwise we will remain barbarians," to mean: the Greeks were the Germans of their time in their youth and vitality. To become "classical," one must first be "modern." The stigma of being a cultural latecomer was transformed into an advantage: only at the beginning of its history did a nation generate rather than reproduce cultural forms. If these forms did not resemble anything a neoclassicist would recognize, so much the better. Only in retrospect, Schlegel explained in "On Incomprehensibility," would modernity discover its own identity in the strange, "incomprehensible" new forms it had spawned.[52] In practice, however, certain ancient lyrical genres could provide the model for a modern poetics that sought a surprising, unmediated, original relationship between experience and language: the ruptured, "accidental" forms of Sappho's fragments and the surviving epitaphic fragments of the *Greek Anthology.* As Schlegel put it, "Many works of the ancients have become fragments. Many works of the moderns are so at their genesis."[53]

In the preface to the project undertaken by him and Batiushkov jointly, S. S. Uvarov adapted the new German Grecophilia to the Russian situation. His commentary gives a very clear indication of the differences between the ancient/modern poetics of the *Greek Anthology* and the habitual Russian poetics of neoclassicism.

> By epigram we mean short verses with a satirical content, terminating on a witticism, a reproach, or a joke. The ancients gave this word a different meaning.

For them any small piece, written in elegiac meter (that is, a hexameter followed by a pentameter) was called an epigram. Anything can serve as its subject: now it instructs, now it jests, and almost always it exudes love. Often it is nothing but an instantaneous thought or a fleeting feeling, inspired by the beauties of nature or the monuments of art. Sometimes the Greek epigram is complete and perfect, sometimes careless and unfinished . . . like a sound, fading in the distance. It almost never concludes with a sharp, striking idea, and the more ancient it is, the simpler. This genre of poetry embellished both feasts and graves. Reminding them of the insignificance of life passing by, the epigram said, "Mortal, catch the fleeting moment!" . . . A true Proteus, it adopts all forms.[54]

Not intended for contemporary society, but for some future archaeological dig, the anthological fragment eliminated the distorting lens an effeminate society interposed between the poet's direct, masculine experience of life and his language.[55] Fragments of poetry accidentally preserved bore the most authentic witness to a great people's history and way of life. Paradoxically, then, the form of the epitaph could "liberate" contemporary "moments" of inspired perception from the dictatorship of contemporaries.[56] Uvarov and Batiushkov's selection of epigrams represents utterances clearly belonging to different speakers, caught in a cross-section of the present. An assignation with a prostitute falls through for lack of cash, a love affair is hidden from people's envy, the seduction of a modest young girl breaks off abruptly with her admission of her fear of men; a tribute to the experienced passion of an older mistress, an old man's self-destructive attachment to a cruel young mistress, a conspiracy against a dull-witted husband flash by. Between each voice and the next, jostling in their secular pursuits, lies a silence; like the Herculaneum dancers petrified in motion, their speech is frozen into epitaphs. The scenic fragments thus illustrate Uvarov's contrast of the "naive" Greek sensibility, "concentrating the measureless strength of their genius on the transient sphere of the present," with modern introspection and historical consciousness.

Yet Batiushkov's figurative language tells a slightly different story. There is no moment of experience that is not already haunted by its transition into the next historical moment or the next psychological mood. The first lament could be spoken by any subject orphaned by the loss of his culture and its definition of "glory," "beauty," "citizenship":

Где слава, где краса, источник зол твоих?
Где стогны шумные и граждане счастливы? . . .
Увы! погиб навек Коринф столповенчанный!
И самый пепел твой развеян по полям.
Все пусто: мы одни взываем здесь к богам,
И стонет Алкион один в дали туманной!

(1:286)

(Where is the glory, where is the beauty, the source of your evils?
Where are the noisy squares and happy citizens? . . .
Alas! perished for eternity is column-wreathed Corinth!
And your very ash windstrewn over the fields.
All is empty: we alone cry out here to the gods,
And Alcion alone moans in the cloudy distance!)

Even the hot erotic pursuit of the third epigram, "Svershilos': Nikagor i plamennyi Erot" (It is accomplished: Nicagorus and fiery Eros) echoes the volume's epitaphic language:

Вы видите: кругом рассеяны небрежно
Одежды пышные надменной красоты;
Покровы легкие из дымки белоснежной,
И обувь стройная, и свежие цветы:
Здесь всё—развалины роскошного убора,
(1:285)

(You see: carelessly scattered all around
The luxuriant garb of arrogant beauty;
Light veils of snow-white vapor,
And elegant footwear, and fresh flowers:
Everything here—ruins of sumptuous arrayment)

The diaphanous garments falling away do not reveal human bodies or desires, but are themselves revealed, in an unexpected metaphor (the original Greek had simply "debris"), as cultural "ruins." If the message of neoclassicism was repeatability, the possibility of an eternal return to an ahistorical realm of value, the separate voices of Uvarov and Batiushkov's *Greek Anthology* convey the opposite message of historical irreversibility. Their selection of epigrams offers a distinctly modern image of a Golden Age passing into nonbeing, wrapped in the gauzy draperies of a language that is its shroud. What is captured by Batiushkov's translation is not so much the vitality of Greek or "naive" life, as the vanishing act of the present: a portrait of antiquity penetrated by the narrative desires of an alienated modern sensibility.[57]

The *Greek Anthology* also suggested a different "model of authorship": instead of "I" or Tibullus, anonymity; instead of whole texts, carefully transmitted from age to age, striking fragments accidentally rescued from destruction. Writing from a position outside his published oeuvre and his name, Batiushkov could feel safely concealed and modestly justified by his work as restorer of damaged archaeological artifacts. Anonymously translating anonymous poets, he was freed from the relay of great names and great works, the burden of their "slava i krasa," reputation and size. The anthological fragment authorized dimensions that were tailored for the single flash of verbal inspiration or interval of lucidity, the single work-session. I would even suggest that

Batiushkov's ignorance of the Greek language enabled the detachment of self-standing images. In all his other translations, his acutely musical ear was preoccupied with trying to reproduce the missing sounds of French, Italian, or Latin in a selectively purified Russian phonetics, in dramatic combat with "the barbarism" of the Russian language, itself personified as the enemy that might block Batiushkov's entry into immortality. Working with an interlinear translation, and in an intellectual partnership with a Russian man of confident culture and authority, Batiushkov was freer to invent his images of the Greek psyche in a Russian language at peace with its own linguistic potential: "Every language has its syntactic flow, its harmony. Manly harmony does not always express itself in fluidity."[58] He no longer had to disguise the discontinuity of his mental and linguistic energy, nor the roughness of the Russian language; they had found perfect incarnation in the ancient ruptured text.

Batiushkov's urgent proposal for an Arzamas publication that would have framed his *Greek Anthology* in an anthology of contemporary Russian voices, caught in turn in the midst of their Petersburg pursuits, failed to materialize. When the manuscript was finally published in 1820 in the form of a brochure, a deadpan foreword framed it quite differently as the obsolete scribblings of two obscure provincials, accidentally found among the possessions of the Arzamas innkeeper.[59] Increasingly estranged from literature in which he saw "a system of evil, an infallible means of harming me, for it is disguised," Batiushkov translated his life back into a war record. This document reached the desk of Alexander I and earned for Batiushkov his dreamed-of escape to Italy, the land of his poetic origins. But in Naples Batiushkov found that "waves of people" pressed on him too thickly from the street, indistinguishable from the morbid fertility and fatality of matter nourished on the ash of Vesuvius.[60] To his erstwhile collaborator Uvarov he reported in dismay: "the mind, requiring nourishment in the present, the active mind, would soon wither and perish here. . . . I am astonished at the change which has taken place in me: I cannot write poetry at all."[61] In a final attempt, perhaps, to liberate himself from the weight of the cultural past, Batiushkov burned his entire library, books and manuscripts.

If a few of Batiushkov's last original poems survived the final encroachment of his mental illness and the immolations it dictated, this may be because the form of the epitaphic fragment allowed the cultural identity he revered to coexist with the intermittent products of his poetic talent.

Ты пробуждаешься, о Байя, из гробницы
При появлении Аврориных лучей,
Но не отдаст тебе багряная денница
    Сияния протекших дней,
Не возвратит убежищей прохлады,
    Где нежились рои кросот,

И никогда твои порфирны колоннады
    Со дна не встанут синих вод.
        (1819) (1:294)[62]

(You awaken, O Baiae, from the tomb
With the appearence of Auroran rays,
But the crimson daybreak will not give back to you
    The confluence of days flowed by.
It will not return the refuge of coolness,
    Where beauty luxuriated in swarms,
And never will your porphyry collonades
    Stand up from the bottom of blue waters.)

Batiushkov's poem symmetrically inverts Horace's ode to the builder of Baiae (book II, xviii).

> Not ivory or gilded panel gleams in my home, nor do beams of Hymetian marble rest on pillars quarried in farthest Africa, nor have I, as heir of Attalus, become unwittingly the owner of a palace, nor for me do highborn dames trail robes of Laconian purple. But I have loyalty and a kindly vein of genius. . . . Day treads upon the heel of day, and new moons haste to wane; yet thou on the grave's verge dost contract for the cutting of marble slabs, and, forgetful of the tomb, dost rear a palace, eager to build out the coast of the sea that thunders by Baiae, not rich enough in the mainland shore.[63]

Whereas Horace discounts the present and an ambitious nobleman's attempts to remake nature, in favor of a future when only his own verbal monument will survive and be heard, in Batiushkov's time (that future), it is precisely the ruin of Baiae that is still eloquent, and devalues the present in favor of an imagined past. Hence the anthropomorphic vitality of the ruin: it has a name, and therefore a gender; it awakens (indeed audibly yawns [Fr. *baille*]); it is addressed as "ty." The poem's speaker, by contrast, is nameless and disembodied. Baiae awakens to exactly the same degree that the name Baiae awakens language in him; it will return to "the tomb" of its objecthood precisely when his language stops. Yet the spectacle of the ruin lit up by the rays of the morning sun is presented not as a visual epiphany but as a drama of deprivation. Within the repeated, even angry negations (*ne otdast, ne vozvratit*), the glamour of the past survives as a distant radiance painted in rough, Turneresque brushstrokes—"gde nezhilis' roi krasot"—not, as in Batiushkov's translations, a beautiful nude coming toward us into full phantasmagorical focus. The automatic sinuous linkage of classical names will *not give back* the imaginary shining of the past, on which the *translator's* sense of his own creative power depends.

It is only when the poem closes off the possibility of imaginary restoration that the brilliantly colored image of Baiae as it looks in the present enters the poem: the porphyry colonnades that will never again be raised by the power of human imagination from the bottom of the ocean, nor from the depths of time. The four anchored stresses of the last line (and its complexly symmetrical, mirroring phonetic structure) signal the emphatic closure of a suddenly vivid epitaph on the poem's inability or even *refusal* to "raise" the past. It is precisely the emptying of the visual world of its historical meaning that makes it available not to the translator, but to the lyrical poet, as an original and tragic metaphor for his mind's death. Without a text to translate, indeed, without a belief in "the task of the translator," there is no "I" at all, only the reflexes and ruins of the language, addressing itself. The stranded Roman ruin Baiae becomes a rich "objective correlative" for linguistic artifacts excluded from the human world of meaning. The ringing silence signals the climax of the poem's negations, the end of the translator's vocation—but the beginning of the lyrical poet's?

Having handed over the ordering of the empire to Arakcheev, and its spiritual dominion to an eclectic group of mystics, from imported Quakers and the Bible Society to home-grown Dukhobors, Khlysty, and Archimandrite Photius, Alexander spent the remainder of his life fleeing his capital in feverish, empire-wide travels. Indeed, as province after province was absorbed into the draconian regime of Arakcheev's military colonies (in a peculiar throwback to Napoleonic rhetoric, Alexander rebuked a despairing peasant: "The military colonies will continue to exist, even if I had to cover the route from Petersburg to Chudovo with corpses"),[64] Alexander had to travel ever further in search of "naive" audiences before which he could display his "simple humanity." At regular intervals he re-created for each new provincial audience the original charismatic vision of Vertus: the miraculous transformation of tsar and serf-subjects into a uniformly selfless parade of Christian souls.[65]

Alexander I's and Batiushkov's trajectories criss-crossed one more time. Touched by the poet's story and present helplessness—so different from that of Pushkin, the troublemaker he held at bay in exile, so similar, perhaps, to his own—Alexander I granted Batiushkov a lifelong leave with pay from the foreign service, as well as a generous royal subsidy for his psychiatric treatment in Germany. The tsar met a pious death on the southern edge of his empire in 1825, not long after Batiushkov composed what seems to have been his last poem.[66]

The poem buttonholes its listener confidentially—"Ty znaesh', chto izrek" (Do you know what he spake)—and then proceeds to quote the speech of a certain biblical sage Mel'khisedek. Colloquial speech and high style, Slavic phonetics and Hebrew phonetics, contemporary occasion and millennia casually overlap. Conspicuously absent are any differentiating cultural structures, classical landmarks, Judeo-Christian wisdom, or a grammatical "I." The quotation itself seems to be invented, though the *mise-en-abyme* apparatus of quotation is in place. If, as scholars conjecture, the poem's form most closely resembles Herder's translations of epigrams from the early Christian *Palatine Anthology*,[67] and Batiushkov's Mel'khisedek is a composite of two biblical figures from the Old and the New Testaments, the poem could reflect the kind of pietist and mystical discourse that had gained currency in the last years of Alexander's reign. Among the words attributed to Mel'khisedek, the twice-repeated instrumental *rabom* (slave)—stands out starkly: the forbidden word, uttered aloud? The authority and permanence with which a biblical text is usually invested dissolve instead in an open-ended series of oral utterances, each left unanswered: the speaker's question to a silent listener; Mel'khisedek's farewell to life; death's withheld word to him about the purpose of life; the sound of a man's unanswered sob; and finally the last sounds of the poem vanishing into the vast, unpopulated silence of time.

Ты знаешь, что изрек,
Прощаясь с жизнию, седой Мельхиседек?
Рабом родится человек,
Рабом в могилу ляжет,
И смерть ему едва ли скажет,
Зачем он шел долиной чудной слез,
Страдал, рыдал, терпел, исчез.
(1:298)

(Do you know what he spake,
Parting from life, grey-haired Mel'khisedek?
A slave man is born,
A slave he will lie down in his grave,
And death will scarcely tell him
Why he walked along a marvelous vale of tears,
Suffered, sobbed, endured, disappeared.)

The subject's disappearance was complete.

Leslie O'Bell

Krylov, La Fontaine, and Aesop

I

La Fontaine and Krylov occupy similar places in the literary pantheons of French and Russian literatures. Despite the fact that they both produced much more than fables, each has been canonized as the national fable writer. In light of this rough cultural approximation, Krylov has naturally come to be called the Russian La Fontaine. This parlance was already a cliché by the 1840s,[1] and it persisted in the scholarship of many comparatists, whose commentaries invariably included long excerpts from La Fontaine.[2] The comparison is grounded in the fact that Krylov launched his career as a fable writer after rereading La Fontaine and translating several of the French fables into Russian. The first group of Krylov's fables, which appeared in 1806, was composed of "The Oak and the Reed," "The Choosy Bride," and "The Old Man and the Three Youths" ("Dub i trost'," "Razborchivaia nevesta," and "Starik i troe molodykh"[3] which represent Russian versions of "Le chêne et le roseau," "La fille," and "Le vieillard et les trois jeunes hommes"). Several dozen of Krylov's most successful fables are based on the French,[4] and his entire enterprise of publishing a series of fables organized into books suggests that Krylov did, in fact, take La Fontaine as a model. Moreover, several of the keynote fables that open Krylov's books are imitations or translations of La Fontaine.

The comparison between the two writers is ultimately misleading, however, as I shall show.[5] It was disputed from the very start by Krylov's contemporaries, and those old arguments form a convenient point of departure. But after analyzing their often astute stylistic perceptions, I shall go on to take a broader view, to outline the place of the fable in the creation of La Fontaine and Krylov respectively, in order to show how that locus of the fable had been prepared by the history of their respective cultures. By so doing, I shall make clearer just why our more recent cultural approximations tend to conceal that Krylov's fables belong to another literary world and another cultural context from La Fontaine's. Even those fables of Krylov that are directly descended from La Fontaine function in a very different ecosystem, so to speak.[6] La

Fontaine had brilliantly reinvented the fable as poetry, culminating a rich and long tradition, while Krylov's role as fable writer was to take part in the very foundation of a literature.

It should be clear that what underlies the question is more than the old Romantic distinction of national identities—the "Gallic" essence of La Fontaine or the "Russianness" of Krylov. The *samobytnost'* or uniqueness at issue here is not an ideological imperative; it is a simple fact of life. It is not that Krylov should have been different, but that it was impossible for him not to be different. He may well have been a proto-slavophile.[7] He may have gloried in the appellation of "the national fable writer." But let us first consider what could not have been otherwise.

In Krylov's lifetime, although it was obligatory to compare him to La Fontaine, Krylov was declared either to have surpassed him or else, indeed, not to be up to him. But the two writers were by no means casually equated. Pushkin, writing to Bestuzhev, remarked that Krylov was as far above La Fontaine in the fable as Derzhavin was above Jean-Baptiste Rousseau [in the ode] (K, 326). He expressed himself more diplomatically, but in the same vein, in his review of Lemontey's preface to a translation of Krylov into French. "Of course, no Frenchman would be so bold as to place anyone at all above La Fontaine, but we, I think, may prefer Krylov" (K, 40).[8] Pushkin distinguished two kinds of humor in their work, which he saw as characteristic of the spirits of their two nations, La Fontaine's *naïveté* and *bonhomie,* versus the *veseloe lukavstvo uma* and *nasmeshlivost'* of Krylov (K, 40)—his cheerful slyness of mind and propensity to make fun of things. In the 1840s Gogol would carry the nationalist sentiment still further (without motivating it any longer by a difference in the quality of the comic element). Gogol wrote, "He who would call Krylov a fable writer in the sense that La Fontaine . . . was one, would be making a big mistake. . . . Krylov's fables are a national treasure and constitute the people's own book of wisdom" (K, 295). But there were those who, while agreeing with Pushkin's characterization of Krylov's humor, were not attracted to it and frankly preferred La Fontaine. There is the interesting set of remarks by the predictably acerbic Vigel writing in the 1830s and 1840s:

> Krylov is called the Russian La Fontaine; each is the premier fable writer of his country, but as a poet, I think, the Frenchman stands higher. How touching and spontaneous he can sometimes be. . . . While reading him no one would ask, was he a kind man? Anyone can feel it [the famous *bonhomie*]. If I were asked the same question about Krylov, I would have to answer in the negative. . . . In his verse there is purity, grace and harmony; intelligence abounds everywhere, but feeling never shows through, and intelligence without feeling is like light without warmth. (K, 94)

Krylov was a notorious glutton, and Vigel cannot resist the gibe "apparently his heart was in his stomach" (K, 94). Vigel was actually seconding the opinion of

Pushkin's friend (but in this an opponent), the poet Viazemsky, who had always championed their confrère Dmitriev as the subtlest and most sophisticated fable writer that Russia had produced, and a better counterpart to La Fontaine.

> Krylov was by no means the carefree, absent-minded and childishly simple-hearted La Fontaine that he passes for with us. He was rather, if I may say so, unkempt, but in everything he was what is called *sebe na ume* [a Russian idiom that means something like "one who keeps his own counsel," "one who holds his cards close to the vest"]. Which he was perfectly right to do, since his counsel was extraordinarily deep. . . . The fable was his true calling . . . here he could totally keep his own counsel (*byt' sebe na ume*); here he could say a lot without giving himself away. (K, 174)

This was Viazemsky at his most diplomatic, however. Turning to his letters we find him writing to Bestuzhev in 1824:

> I respect and love Krylov as a writer of wit, but in the aesthetic, literary regard I will always place Dmitriev above him. . . . I will say more: I value Krylov higher than the standard opinion of his so-called admirers. What do most of them so marvel at in him? . . . Banalities, vulgarisms (*ploskosti, poshlosti*) which detract from his true qualities. Everyone goes around repeating "The philosopher can't grow any cucumbers," "Oh, the lapdog is a mighty beast to bark at an elephant" and such-like jokes, that's all ("A filosof bez ogurtsov!" "Ai, mos'ka! Znat', ona sil'na, chto laet na slona!"). While, of course, it isn't those chapbook jingles (*lubochnye pribautki*) which are the mark of his talent. (K, 322)

The next year he wrote the following to Pushkin about the review of Lemontey:

> Your article on Lemontey is very good for its clear, mature style and for many brilliant ideas. But what kind of image of Krylov is this? . . . Say what you will, but there is something of the lackey in Krylov: that slyness (*lukavstvo),* the curses out of earshot (*bran' iz-za ugla*), the cowering before the masters. Maybe there is something characteristically Russian about all of this but . . . it is hardly suitable for us to boast about it to foreigners. . . . Call Derzhavin or Potemkin representatives of the Russian people, that is something different; in them you can find both our gold and our dross *par excellence,* but to make Krylov into our representative even in the literary sense is a mistake. (K, 322–23)

To his wife, Viazemsky wrote, "You can't talk to Krylov about poetry or anything elevated, because he is positively prose, but in his character as prose he is very charming" (K, 324). Griboedov, too, saw Krylov as utterly prosaic: "He sleeps and eats inordinately. Oh, these Poets of ours! And yet such rotund bodies beget such puny ideas: for example, that Poetry should have an *aim*" (K, 321). Pushkin's reply to Viazemsky was one of amusement: "Your critique of Krylov is hilarious; but stop it," and here he quotes a Krylov fable: "To znaiu ia sama, da èta krysa mne kuma" (in other words: I can't be too hard on the rat; after all, we're pals).[9] "I called him a representative of the spirit [*dukh*] of the Russian people [a pun on spirit and smell]—I can't guarantee that he doesn't partly stink" (K, 325).[10] In another part of the correspondence, though, Pushkin ribbed Viazemsky about making Dmitriev into a literary hero, "le poète de notre civilisation." "Some civilization!" was Pushkin's retort (*khorosha nasha civilisation!*).[11]

Pushkin had many reasons to be interested in Krylov at this time and even to identify with him in certain ways. But we should discard questions of personality and vague national spirit and turn to the literary and cultural history that laid the grounds for the debate about Krylov. As so often, it is Pushkin who points the way with his ironic reference to "civilization" where Russia was concerned and his zeroing in on what we would call today the archaic Russian comedic culture or *smekhovaia kul'tura* to define Krylov.[12] What Viazemsky and others held against Krylov was essentially that he was not a lyric poet in his fables, while La Fontaine was. As one of Dmitriev's admirers wrote to him in 1816, "I have learned from La Fontaine and from you that a fable writer should be a true poet" (K, 316). This is a key observation, but the reasons for Krylov's lack of "poetry" were not personal, I think ("his heart was in his stomach") but cultural.

It is time to make a broad comparison of La Fontaine's path to the fable with Krylov's in order to show just what the fable meant to each. Although two centuries separate them, their situations were not entirely dissimilar. If we approach the question of the tradition of the fable, we find that Greek and Latin literary models were relevant for both of them, though in very different ways. La Fontaine had had an excellent humanistic education and was cognizant of the quarrel between the ancients and the moderns and the arguments to be made for both sides (S, 121–23). Krylov, though largely self-taught, was part of the neoclassicizing circle that had formed around Olenin, a disciple of Winckelmann. Olenin was the influential director of the Imperial Library and a patron of culture.[13] Krylov's closest friend and literary confidant was perhaps Gnedich, the Russian translator of Homer. The conservative Collegium of Amateurs of the Russian Word laid claim to Krylov as their own (that is, the party of the classicists rather than the Romantics), though the fable writer nevertheless consorted with all manner of literary heretics and moderns.[14]

What did a classical orientation mean for the fable? In the West, ever since the Renaissance the revival of classical learning had carried with it a complex of philosophical or cosmological questions about the place of man in the scheme of things, somewhere between the bestial and the divine. Science had begun to vie with speculative thought as to which could better know nature. The natural as an artistic aim tried to assert its prestige against the fashion for *préciosité* or *galanterie*. Perhaps the fable had acquired a new potency for La Fontaine's world because it represented a kind of animal mythology of the earthly realm. There, human nature is represented by similitude with the animals, and animals are charmingly anthropomorphized. There, the animal aspects of man are also viewed and dramatized by the higher man, the writer of fables and composer of morals. You have both mythos (a world narrated), and logos (its explanation). The style of the fable should be "natural" but also preserve a place for the rhetorical and even the sententious.

The fable like so many Western genres bequeathed by the ancient world, is a development out of folkloric material used in a philosophically and aesthetically self-conscious way.[15] We are far from the time when animals might speak, and when one could encounter the totem ancestors if one were appropriately masked.[16] Metamorphosis—the literal interchangeability of the human and the animal—has been replaced by the imaginary world of the fable. Concepts of what is natural to man and beast and an analysis of the particular nature of each species and type underlie the fable. The tone and stance of the fable writer, or in general the presence or absence of a higher viewpoint on the "natural" world, are equally important to the style and message of the fable.

This has been my theoretical preamble. We know that La Fontaine was quite well read philosophically. It has been argued, for instance, that the fables are informed by the classic epicurean outlook of Lucretius's *On the Nature of Things,* with its philosophy of prudence, detachment, simplicity, and repose.[17] One can also assume that La Fontaine was aware that he was a reworker of mythologies. His path to the fable demonstrates that quite clearly. Scholars of La Fontaine's development have focused attention on the larger allegories that he wrote containing separate animal episodes as the predecessors of his fables. The first instance of this was the poem "Adonis" in which the hero descends from his aspiration to a divine love, to be achieved through union with his goddess, to the world of the hunt below (S, 18). As one scholar has commented, "the hunt gave La Fontaine the opportunity of introducing elements that are essential in the fables, animals, war, destruction and death" (S, 18). The hunt scene, in which the hero must do combat against monsters, forms a bridge in the poetic whole between the introductory idyll and the elegiac lament that closes the poem (S, 21). La Fontaine also explored the idea of the human versus the bestial or the monster in his version of the story of Psyche. Loving the god without being able to see his divine person, Psyche fears that he is a monster and resolves to confront him, which leads to all her trials but eventually to the soul's understanding of love. There is also La Fontaine's extended poem, the *Songe de Vaux,* created for his patron Fouquet. This dreamscape contains the adventures of the squirrel, the swan, the salmon, and the sturgeon as a lighthearted contrast to the poem's more serious allegories (S, 27, 29). One fragment even uses the *vers libre* of the fables. Free verse was also the idiom of La Fontaine's *Tales*, those bawdy and jocular but still poetic versions of the stock in trade of European popular fiction, the fables of the bedroom. The *Contes* are perhaps the nearest thing in La Fontaine's creation to the fables. In them he adopts an artfully folksy tone, but uses the traditional scabrous material as the point of departure for his own treatment (S, 37–39). His culture is one of broad-minded tolerance of human foibles and the physicality of the human animal.

What is most striking about La Fontaine's animal mythologies, however, is that they are only part of his cosmos. He has a vision of the whole where the lower realm is ordinarily balanced by a higher realm. The iconography of his artistic universe is complete from gods to beasts, and his poetic voice is capable of a wide range of expression. In the fables the higher realm remains accessible to the poet, who preserves his lyrical powers even in proximity to the animals. La Fontaine obviously thought deeply about classical myths concerning man and beast. He opened his twelfth and last book of fables with the programmatic piece, "The Companions of Ulysses," a metafable recounting how Ulysses' men drank Circe's potion, were turned into beasts, and remained happily in that condition "to follow their appetites," while Ulysses alone mistrusted the enchantress, interceded to restore their humanity, but was left to continue his heroic journey alone.[18] La Fontaine's fable-poet has the higher perspective of Ulysses: he has seen men embrace bestiality but he can still give voice to the nobler alternative.

La Fontaine always provides a larger context of *écriture* or self-conscious writing around the little oral narratives that are the fables. His collections of fables have prefaces, the Life of Aesop, and addresses to various patrons that consciously explain their aims. The collections themselves contain such compositional devices as "double-fables" for the pleasure of writing variations on a theme, like "Le Héron" and "La Fille." Krylov's books of fables are bare of such apparatus and contain nothing but the fables themselves.

There are also ways in which the general culture in which La Fontaine wrote provided a large context for the fables. In the world of the graphic arts he could rely on the emblem books that had been popular since the Renaissance (S, 50). The fables of Aesop were used in schools as the basis for rhetorical exercises in "amplification." French vernacular fables known as the *ysopets* had existed side by side with the learned fables of the schools since the Middle Ages (S, 49), as had animal epics like the *Roman de Renart*. We can observe the activity of the fable over the entire range of French culture, top to bottom. La Fontaine's own fables called up a stream of artistic response: some of France's most talented artists were to vie in illustrating them.[19] Another selection of fables had already become the subject of a series of fantastical animal fountains created by Le Nôtre for the maze at Versailles, fables "positioned so as to emphasize their role as a guide through the maze and through life itself."[20] But La Fontaine was also aware that the fable was still more universal than all its manifestations in European culture. In his last book of fables he moved away from classical sources to take subjects from exotic Indian fables and the Lives of the Desert Fathers.

When we turn to Krylov, our first response is: how different his path to the fable was and how different the context that his culture provided for it. Krylov certainly had a concept of the natural or the inherent nature of things.[21] He is supposed to have used the French saying, "chassez le naturel, il revient au galop" (banish the natural, and it will return at a gallop) (K, 118). Characteristically, this quotation comes from the French comedy,[22] and it was through his comedies and his satires that Krylov prepared for his metamorphosis into a writer of fables. According to the genre hierarchy that was accepted in Russia in the eighteenth century, comedy was located in the realm of middle diction and everyday subjects. Low language—*prostorechie* and colloquialisms—might be admitted into comedy, but not elevated parlance, except for purposes of burlesque. The young Krylov almost never aspired to the higher genres or noble diction. If the comedy of morals was one school for his fables,[23] the satirical journal was another. In fact, it is in *The Spirits' Mailbox* (*Pochta dukhov*) that we find a rudimentary sort of mythology in Krylov: the cosmic satirical concept of the sylphs and the gnomes, those unmaskers and secret spies who can be summoned by the author to tell tales of the foolish doings of the earthlings. The figure of the misanthrope in *The Spirits' Mailbox* may be a predecessor of the fabulist in that he rejects direct moralizing and recommends ridicule as the best corrector of mankind.[24] The critical consensus is that "Krylov's fables reproduce much of the thematic repertoire of his journalistic satires . . . for example, the comparison of the *petit-maître* with a monkey in *The Spirits' Mailbox* and in the fable "Monkeys."[25]

What Krylov made of La Fontaine was, of course, conditioned by the path that he had followed in reaching his famous moment of attraction to the French fables in 1805. It is obvious from this discussion that Krylov's fables emerged from a personal literary world that lacked a higher sphere and a true lyric voice, unlike La Fontaine's. Krylov's comedies and satires had indeed had the higher "philosophic" goal of making an irrational world see reason. But by the time he reached the point of writing fables Krylov had become disenchanted with Enlightenment philosophy. He was looking for new masters, and new ways to "nature." At this point Krylov tried philosophical poetry: pantheism, stoicism, the role of the passions in human life. But all this heady material only led him to be skeptical of all philosophical systems, modern or ancient. "Pust' mudretsy sistemy schast'ia ischut" (Let wise men seek for systems of happiness), he sighed.[26] The only sages he now wanted to emulate were the possessors of practical wisdom, and at this point he launched his new career as a fable writer. Not for nothing was the savage dig "a filosof bez ogurtsov" one of Krylov's most quoted lines: the philosopher-farmer can produce no cucumbers.[27]

What is fascinating to note is that just before encountering La Fontaine and finding himself as a fable writer Krylov also tried his wings for the first and last time as a lyric poet. This is a rather neglected part of his creative history, treated only in one article by Gukovsky.[28] But if Krylov had not at least sat in the school of sentimentalism and Rousseau, if he had not attempted to find the voice of feeling and a range of poetic pathos, he would have lacked the equipment to handle La Fontaine. Never mind that Krylov's attempts often break tone in midpoem and are more often droll and self-deprecating than convincing. "Odna mechta rodit druguiu / I vse—odna drugoi glupei. / No chto s prirodoi delat' stanesh?" (One dream gives birth to another—each more foolish than the last / But what can you do with human nature?)[29] Gukovsky emphasizes Krylov's newfound interest in Derzhavin, who figures as a concrete protorealist and the creator of a private lyrical persona, but even Gukovsky's own material makes apparent that pre-Romantic trends were just as important. This cross-fertilization of classicism with sentimentalism is part of what Il'ia Serman has called their "mutual exchange of literary experience."[30] Derzhavin, too, was evolving during this period and choosing a new classical model, Anacreon. One might say that both late Derzhavin and the later Krylov ended up as writers of what the early nineteenth century termed "light poetry" (mainly short pieces) without becoming lyric poets in the strict sense of the word.[31] Indeed, to find a breeding place for lyrical poetry in Russia we have to turn to the school of the Karamzinian "new style," to which neither of our eighteenth-century holdovers would convert. This is why Viazemsky nominated the Karamzinian Dmitriev to be the Russian La Fontaine. But it was not only *Krylov's* aesthetic world that was lacking. Dmitriev himself was much too narrow to rival La Fontaine. There *was*, in fact, no Russian La Fontaine. Only Pushkin, over the course of the 1820s and 1830s, would create a lyrical range to compare with that master.[32]

La Fontaine had been able to "inscribe himself" into a very rich, one might say complete, culture of the fable where popular and erudite versions had interacted for a long time, where there was a natural exchange of information between high culture and popular culture. Perhaps this does something to explain the facility with which he could modulate his voice. The Russian situation was very different. Popular culture had received insufficient early exposure to classical fable tradition, and for a long time a barrier existed between the two cultures of *knizhnost'* (scribal book literature), and *slovesnost'* (oral folk composition). First of all, although Russia might have taken the Aesopian fables, as well as the Life of Aesop directly from Byzantine manuscript tradition, where they were abundant,[33] as with so many other aspects of classical civilization, the evidence is that Russia chose not to. One would have thought that at least the Life of Aesop would be attested to, since it has been called the "younger brother" of the Alexander legend, which was very popular in old Russia. The most that we find is the "Tale of Akir the Wise," a legend of oriental origins that became incorporated into the standard life of Aesop.[34] Medieval Russia also knew the *Physiologus,* which described traditional animal characteristics and created Christian allegories from them, but these manuscripts were not widespread and were not elaborated into "bestiaries" as happened in the West.[35] We assume that Old Russia had the folklore later collected as animal folktales. It had the *medvezh'ia potekha,* or bear entertainment. It knew the Apocalyptic beasts. The Russian language contains expressions like "l'vinaia dolia" (the lion's share), which reflect an acquaintance with fable tradition,[36] although it is hard to tell when they entered the lexicon. By the seventeenth century when westernization was well under way, the new "democratic satirical literature" introduced parodies on aspects of high or official culture like court proceedings and ecclesiastical legends in the form of animal tales, "The Tale of Ersh Ershovich" (the carp), and the "Legend of the Cock and the Fox" (which derives from the *Roman de Renart*).[37] These relatively late animal travesties of human folly have something in common with the fable. The new mentality now permitted the written word to be used for fictions and these fictions to serve not so much for edification as for amusement. And it finally permitted folk material to be reworked in written form. Thus the appearance of the translated collections of *facetiae* (funny stories or witty sayings) known as *zharty pol'skie* (Polish jests), containing motifs from Aesop that soon made their way into the *lubki* or popular woodcuts that circulated into the eighteenth century.[38] Nevertheless, there had been no Russian translations of Aesop and no tradition of native vernacular fables.

The first manuscript translation of Aesop in Russia occurred in 1607 in the chancery milieu, apparently via a West Slavic intermediary.[39] Although its opening verse epistle to the reader was the first example of learned poetry in Russia, its aims were ethical rather than aesthetic. The main text was in laconic prose and the language was a dignified Russian Church Slavic. The Russian Aesop was part of the new learning reaching Russia via Poland and the Ukraine and functioned within the baroque culture of sermons and parables and the new interest in statecraft. (Fables were part of the education of the monarch.) Yet the resonance of the manuscript collection in the seventeenth century was limited; these echoes of the Renaissance humanists' interest in Aesop were not truly developed in Russia until the eighteenth century and the first printed editions of the fables, based on new translations.[40] Only then did Russia really become current in the realm of the fable, with Lomonosov and Sumarokov taking opposite sides in the contemporary debate about the moral versus the aesthetic uses of the form.[41] The fable then became a much-cultivated part of literature.

When he turned to La Fontaine about 1805, Krylov was gaining access to the genre that he needed in the language most open to him, French. What Krylov learned from him was far from all that the French poet had to offer. Whether we lament the fact or celebrate the difference, he is not a Russian La Fontaine. Not for Krylov the range of poetic pathos from the comic to hints of the sublime. But he learned to create freedom of discourse behind his mask. And for Krylov the fable was not so much an object of aesthetic play and philosophical reinterpretation; it preserved more of a raw connection to the topical. Hence the *nasmeshka* or satiric tone rather than La Fontaine's *naïveté* and *bonhomie,* which are not just the products of his natural disposition but of the detachment proper to an observer and narrator who has no particular stake in the outcome of the fable. And here we come to the other side of the coin: for all his excellence, La Fontaine had not written original fables; the point was in the reworking of the mythologies and the savoring of the poetic temperament. Krylov did write a good many original fables.[42] What a typical situation for Russian literature! In the absence of a culture take an accomplished model but then reinvent the genre on the basis of nature. Unsatisfied by philosophy and uncomfortable with aesthetics, bring art into direct contact with its origins. Not fable becomes fable, but life becomes fable. Numerous textual commentaries have been written to explicate the topical basis of particular Krylov fables,[43] and studies exist that use the fables to analyze Krylov's model of the world. But the typological principle of life into fable goes further than that. In fact, Krylov's own later life was stylized after the manner of a fable; it was as if he became one of his own characters and enacted the life of Aesop.

He might have chosen La Fontaine, the dreamer, the voracious reader of popular fiction, and the writer who despite all his high culture could still declare himself to be "gros Jean comme avant," (the same old big John). But Batiushkov and Zhukovsky had laid claim to the dreamer, and with every right. Batiushkov rivaled La Fontaine in poetic power with a translation of the famous fable "Songe d'un habitant du Mogol," "Son Mogol'tsa"("The Mughal's Dream," 1806) where he had to find an equivalent for La Fontaine's haunting praise of solitude and his final elegiac cadences: "Solitude, où je trouve une douceur secrète, / Lieux que j'aimai toujours. . . . Quand le moment viendra d'aller trouver les morts, / J'aurai vécu sans soins, et mourrai sans remords" (Solitary places where I find a secret sweetness, / Places I have always loved. . . . When the moment comes to go and join the dead, / I will have lived without care and shall die without remorse).[44] In 1809 Zhukovsky paid tribute to La Fontaine as the one who had, in fact, transferred the genre of the fable from the realm of rhetoric to the sphere of poetry[45] and thus defined the "true character of the perfect fable."[46] His portrait of the soul of La Fontaine radiates Romantic genius. La Fontaine possesses "the artless sensibility of an innocent heart which draws him to all the creatures of nature without exception." "You hear the dear child, full of high wisdom . . . and imperceptibly find everything around you beautiful."[47] It is this model poet, La Fontaine, who is able "without the slightest apparent effort to adorn his simple narration with elevated expressions, poetic tropes and tableaux. . . . No one can pass so spontaneously from a simple subject to an elevated one, from ordinary narration to poetic discourse."[48] There is no better statement of the reason that Krylov is not the Russian La Fontaine, despite the fact that Zhukovsky, ever the dreamer himself, wanted to force him into the Procrustean bed of La Fontaine's perfection. La Fontaine had written the "Epitaph of an Idler," "Epitaphe d'un parreseux." But what in La Fontaine was poetic indolence was closer to prosaic sloth in Krylov's case. As for Krylov himself, after some of his fables had been translated into French with a biographical sketch of their author, he commented dryly, "The French, too, know that I am lazy" (K, 239). He knew what the French expected from their fable writer, but he could not really model himself on La Fontaine. Instead he chose to reinvent himself more in the image of the Russian Aesop.

II

Aesop and La Fontaine have been contrasted as the two great opposites, the two great poles, of the world of fable writing ever since Lessing's influential eighteenth-century essay "Studies on the Fable" ("Abhandlungen über die Fabel," 1759). For Lessing, La Fontaine's extended verse fables emphasized the pleasures of narrative and of poetic effect, while Aesop's pithy prose fables trained the reader's attention on the situations being discussed and their morals. For the Enlightenment philosopher, La Fontaine's fables were little more than playthings, while Aesop was the proper kind of study for the thinking man. We might note that Lessing's austere neoclassical attitude was unhistorical, like so many other forms of the idealization of antiquity. The Aesopian fables as they have come down to us are indeed brief and simple. But they were intended to be merely schemata that the able pupil of rhetoric could elaborate, adapt and ornament as the occasion demanded. This, in fact, was their role in traditional education.[49] Nevertheless, we moderns like our Greek sculpture unpainted and our Aesopian fables unadorned.

It must be evident from this discussion that as far as his texts are concerned Krylov belongs more in Lessing's La Fontainian school than he does with Aesop. Krylov is a master of inventive narrative, spirited dialogue and sparkling verse. However, the persona of Krylov's fable writer, the voice behind his fables, is considerably more folksy and less urbane than

La Fontaine's. The same is true for Krylov's intended audience; it is also considerably more folksy and less urbane. Pushkin laughed at Viazemsky for asking the ideal Russian fable writer to be the "poet of our civilization," in other words, to be a poet like La Fontaine. I would suggest that despite a form that seems to bespeak "La Fontainian" civilization, Krylov has actually created his fable poet more in the image of Aesop. This does not mean that he imitated the text of Aesop's fables, or Aesop's manner. Or that he had in mind Lessing's Aesop. Rather, in a nonphilosophical or prephilosophical society with a more archaic comedic culture than La Fontaine's, Krylov was bound to reconnect himself with the originator of the fable tradition, a figure who had also operated in a far less "civilized" setting. For Krylov, the Aesopian fable was perhaps less important than what we might call the Aesopian poet.

Of course, it is possible to show that Krylov was indeed familiar with the text of Aesop's fables. Whatever we think of the legend that Krylov taught himself Greek in order to read Aesop in the original, or the other legend that he then simply threw his volumes of Aesop under the bed to gather dust (K, 77–78), there is evidence that Krylov was in the habit of comparing later versions of fables that derived from Aesop with the original and sometimes taking details of his treatment from the Aesopian collection.[50] What is more important for my purposes, Aesop's fables were ordinarily published together with the equally fabulous life of Aesop that served as their preface. So if Krylov knew the one he certainly knew the other as well.

The fables were always closely identified with the figure of their creator, although the life of Aesop in its modern redactions was firmly attached to the texts of the thirteenth century, just before the newly edited corpus of Aesop passed to the West and was taken up by the Renaissance.[51] It has been said that in the medieval Byzantine world, unlike the West, Aesop's life was more popular than his fables.[52] The first translation of Aesop's fables into Russian, done in 1607, was prefaced by the Life and entitled "Kniga, glagolemaia Ezop," or "The Book Called Aesop."[53] We still speak of "Aesop's fables" as a single concept.

What, then, was Aesop like, and what was his life, according to the legend? Here I quote from the introduction to Lloyd Daly's *Aesop Without Morals:*

> He was a slave born in Phrygia. He was dwarfish and had a swarthy skin, a pot-belly, a pointed head, a snub nose, bandy legs, short arms, squint eyes. . . . His keen wit and ingenuity are pictured in strong contrast not only to the grotesqueness of his body but also to the obtuseness and stupidity of those about him. This superiority does not, of course, endear him to those whom he outwits, and he soon becomes the property of a slave dealer who promptly unloads him on the philosopher Xanthus of the island of Samos . . . efforts to find an excuse to punish him invariably backfire and eventually Xanthus grants

> his freedom. His reputation for wisdom has now grown to such a degree that he is consulted by the Samians on their relationships with Croesus. . . . Although he is treacherously surrendered to Croesus, he dissuades the king from attacking the islanders and upon his return to Samos is richly rewarded. . . . After many prosperous years in Samos he sets off to see the world. At Babylon his sagacity wins for him the position of minister to the king. . . . After many adventures he takes leave of the king to visit Delphi. . . . But although he was well received everywhere else, at Delphi the throngs fail to show themselves properly appreciative. Incensed at this treatment, Aesop publicly castigates the Delphians and prepares to take his departure. . . . The Delphians then lay a trap for Aesop. By stealth they secrete a golden bowl from the temple in his baggage . . . they overtake him, search his baggage and find the bowl. Hauled back to Delphi, Aesop is found guilty of sacrilege against Apollo for the theft of the bowl and is condemned to death by being hurled over a cliff.[54]

Though Aesop cut a comic figure, he could also be a serious model for the philosophically minded Greeks. Otherwise Socrates would not have occupied himself during his last hours in versifying Aesop's fables, if we rely on Plato's accounts (*Phaedo,* 60–61). Like Aesop, Socrates also had a scolding wife, an ugly face but a keen mind, and a bone to pick with the civic authorities. In fact, classical scholars have argued that the legendary trial of Aesop by unappreciative compatriots who accused him of sacrilege may well have served as a prototype for the trial of Socrates himself, the "trial of the satirist," as the larger phenomenon has been termed.[55] The Aesopian legend does indeed move toward this conclusion, but it certainly does everything possible to stave it off. Aesop is a prototype for the hero of the picaresque novel who lives by his wits and by matching wits with the powerful of the world.[56] He rises to a position of freedom and eminence, but often is poised on the brink of some disaster or other. At crucial moments his clever "apologues" please the masters and save Aesop's skin. Aesop uses the Aesopian tactic from the very start. As Krylov would write, "the truth is more tolerable when only half disclosed" (*istina snosnee vpolotkryta*).[57] By speaking in fables, Aesop masks his social criticism and avoids the trial of the satirist as long he can. But underneath it all, Aesop "takes the figure and words of the cynics to punish society."[58] As one critic has written, "He has a specific animus against the claims of the educated elite to have proprietary rights over wisdom and shrewdness"; he fulfills the traditional role of the "grotesque outsider."[59]

According to the legend, Aesop's relationship with Apollo was complex.[60] Aesop resembles the satyr Marsyas, who had the audacity to pit his uncouth music against Apollo's; and thus Apollo nurses anger against Aesop. Yet the Muses have given Aesop of their gifts, and in the end the Delphians must be punished for calumniating Aesop and must create a hero-cult around him. So Aesop is the original model of a poet without a "poetic" style. Perhaps in creating a lyrical voice in the fable a writer like La Fontaine is trying to forestall the wrath of Apollo. It is interesting that La Fontaine edited the version of the Life of Aesop that opens his own fable collection to make it serve his personal purposes. La Fontaine was far from believing wholeheartedly in the veracity of the legendary material, but he thought that Aesop's life had been handed down as a message about the "power of fables" (*le pouvoir des fables*). Thus, though he wanted an Aesop to reinforce the authority and seriousness of fable writing, La Fontaine removed much that was characteristic of the genre for the Life, such as its deliberate grossness and its cynical outlook.[61]

By the time that Krylov had turned to fable writing, his biography had definite Aesopian potential. Through the exercise of the pen he had risen from humble origins to sit at the tables of the elite. Painful personal experience had taught him not to give direct offense to the powerful, no matter what unjust fools they might be. He had witnessed his generation's version of the trial of the satirist in the cautionary fates of Novikov and Radishchev—upon which he had closed up literary shop and sunk for some murky years into what we can guess was the life of a provincial *pícaro* and cardsharper. When he surfaced again in Petersburg in a better political climate he was ready to make himself an Aesopian figure, to reinvent himself in that image.

Krylov's contemporaries do not seem to realize that they might be describing Aesop when they picture Krylov during this period. "Negligent in his dress, awkward in his physical movements, he was extraordinarily amusing in his speech which unexpectedly burst forth in the form of aphorisms" (K, 269). He was always "dropping proverbs and sayings" (K, 277). If Aesop's life was the stuff of legend, "fabulous" in itself, Krylov went one further and seemed to become a character out of his own creation. For one thing, he apparently existed as the human embodiment of the vices of sloth and gluttony.[62] As we remember, Vigel lamented wickedly, "His heart was in his stomach." Vigel also called Krylov "that shaggy poet" and was inspired to compare him to a bear. "In his gait, in his build and in his portliness, as well as in his style there is something bearlike. The same power, the same calm moroseness, and for all his clumsiness the same cleverness, ingenuity and deftness" (K, 93). Perhaps the reason was that Aesop had become part of Krylov's own experiment in the life-and-works amalgam that we call *zhiznetvorchestvo.* Like Aesop, Krylov lived with his fables and even died with them.

Pletnev writes of Krylov that in speaking he constantly explained his thoughts by means of apologues; he found material for them in every subject and in every person whom he happened to see from his window (K, 201). This specimen from one of Krylov's few letters illustrates his manner of speech quite well. It is in truth full of apt similitudes, proverbs, and allusions: life is constantly being transformed into fable. Krylov writes:

> Greetings, dear and esteemed Varvara Alekseevna. . . . Why don't I have wings to fly to Moscow! What a cute little bird I would be! . . . I would have been in Moscow long ago *ma per arivar bisogna caminar* [but to arrive one has to travel]. A simple enough proverb but very accurate. Nevertheless, if I had known that you would stay longer in Moscow I would have appeared before you no matter what "kak list pered travoi" [an expression taken from a Russian charm that conjures up the appearance of something "like a leaf before the grass"]. . . . I have to post this letter, and my thoughts (thousands of them) are jostling like a crowd of common folk coming out of church on a holiday. One blocks the other's way, one stops the other, and because of all this not one of them can get out.

Later in the letter Krylov asks his correspondent to tell him honestly if his current fables of 1829 are as good as his earlier ones. He says, "I am afraid to become the archbishop of Grenada [from *Gil-Blas*] and have people say to me 'point d'homélies, Monseigneur!' ['no homilies, your Grace!']" (K, 83). When Krylov was asked why he had ventured out near Senate Square during the Decembrist uprising, he put it this way: "Mne krepko zakhotelos' vzglianut' na ikh rozhi" (I was aching to get a look at their mugs) (K, 72). Of course he uses the Russian word for the face of an animal. To give another example of Krylov's pursuit of the fable in life, one day as he was walking towards the English Club in Petersburg he stopped along the way to observe the following folk scene. We can probably take the language and style of the account as deriving from Krylov's own words.

> A carriage was driving down the street, and something in the horses' harness went awry. The coachman who was driving them shouted out, "Hey there, you [to a passing peasant], come 'ere, fix that there, you see?" The fellow obligingly went up and started to fix the thing as best he could, but he went at it somehow clumsily. The coachman, seeing this, unceremoniously cursed him out. "Oh, you so and so," he says. "You don't even know how to do *that,* you dolt!"

However, the adjustment came out fine, and the coachman drove off without even a word of thanks to his helper. All this struck Krylov. "What a good-natured people we have! He called over a stranger, made him do his business, cursed him out and drove off without saying thanks! Now the German is not like that." Krylov concluded, "*He* wouldn't even have gone up to fix it" (K, 263). If Krylov didn't write this up into a fable, he should have. What rich layers of irony it contained for him.

Collections of fables were sometimes subtitled "The Theater of the Animals,"[63] and Krylov seems always to have been conscious that he was a spectator at that theater. But he went still further, when he compared his own body to a world or theater. With Rabelaisian naturalism he made his own physical being his fable. Eroshkin's account of Krylov's epic feasting quotes Krylov's graphic references to the geography of his digestive system where ships sail full tilt through the straits into the Mediterranean (at this point Krylov slapped himself just below the chest). The question arose after dinner whether he could find the space in his stomach to fit an enormous pâté. Krylov used the theater metaphor. "Every seat is filled," he lamented. "A spot will be found but what kind? The front rows are all taken, the whole floor, the parquet-circle and all the balconies too. Only the gallery is left. To put such a famous chef in the gallery, it's a sin." The other guests played out the image, "Never mind, he'll make his way down to the floor" (K, 273). Drawing the moral from his fabulous feasting, Krylov was in the habit of rising from the table with the comically inappropriate motto, "How much does a man really need?" ("Mnogo li nado cheloveku?") (K, 209). General mirth ensued.

By the time in his career that Krylov turned to fables, his relations with the powerful and the court were smooth, though they had been rough enough earlier under the reigns of Catherine and Paul. Krylov now attended masquerade balls at the palace, enjoyed the favor of the dowager empress, had the imperial librarian Olenin as his chief patron and dined with the Stroganovs (K, 267). But, like Aesop, Krylov had the gift of sassing the great so that they loved him even for that. The story is told how Nicholas I espied Krylov walking down the Nevsky Prospect and hailed in familiar terms, "How now, Krylov, we haven't seen each other for quite a while!" And Krylov shot back just as familiarly, "I was thinking the same thing myself, Sire, we seem to live rather close but we don't see much of each other" (K, 144). The tsar only laughed at Krylov's repartee, and went on his way, just as out of touch with his subjects' lives as he had been before. Like Aesop, Krylov was also expected to recite fables before the royal household on state occasions. And like Aesop, when he did so, the message was not really the flattering one that the tsar and his entourage expected. Krylov could not resist making the classic real-life use of the fable, as a comic lesson to tsars. For days before the court masquerade ball of 1836 Krylov was uncharacteristically worried about what he would wear (Krylov, whose slovenliness was legendary and who had once shocked his hosts at the dacha by imitating the dress of Adam in the Garden of Eden). The tragic actor Karatygin found the solution by sending Krylov in the costume of a *kravchii,* or royal carver, one of the tsar's servants at table. At the festivities, dressed as a servant, Krylov again covertly addressed the tsar as an equal. He recited a fable composed specially for the occasion. In it, he seemed to commend to the tsar the life of sloth and gluttony which had made Krylov himself a living fable. Tongue in cheek, Krylov advised, "Give us carvers something to do, forget about your business."

Желаю, наш отец, тебе я аппетита,
Чтоб на день раз хоть пять ты кушал бы досыта.

И там бы спал, да почивал,
Да снова кушать бы вставал,
Вот жить здоровая манера!
С ней к году, —и за то я, кравчий твой, берусь—
Ты будешь уж не боб, а будешь царь-арбуз!
Отец наш! не бери ты с тех царей примера,
Которые не лакомо едят,
За подданых не спят . . .
. . . .
Я всякий день молюсь тепло,
Чтобы тебе, отец, пилось бы лишь да елось,
А дело бы на ум не шло.
(K, 307–8)

(I wish you, Sire, a hearty appetite,
That you should eat your fill at least five times a day.
And then should sleep and take your ease,
And then again arise to dine.
Now that's a healthy way of life!
That way this time next year—and I your carver swear it—
You won't be crowned King Bean—you'll be King-Watermelon!
[a reference to the good-luck bean whose finder is King of the revels]
Oh Sire! do not take after
The kind of tsars who choose lean pickings,
Lose sleep over their subjects . . .
. . . .
And every day I pray in earnest
That you, o Sire, should only eat and drink,
And never turn your mind to business.)

One cannot help recalling Pushkin's sardonic golden cockerel crowing (only a year before), "Tsarstvui, lezha na boku!" (Reign, Tsar, lolling on your side!).[64] Perhaps Nicholas understood the irony about the "bad" tsar who took too good care of his realm. He allowed Krylov to go on and recite another, related fable, "The Grandee" ("Vel'mozha"). Its hero, a lazy Persian Satrap, goes to heaven when he dies because—in an ironic twist—with *his* power he could have done so much harm if he had really ruled instead of delegating everything to his secretary. "Pil, el i spal, da vse podpisyval chto on ni podaval." "Skorei zhe v rai ego! Kak, gde zhe spravedlivost'?" (He drank, he ate and slept / And signed just everything the flunkey set before him. Quick, pack him off to heaven! What, now! That's not fair!):

Не видишь разве ты? Покойник—был дурак!
Что если бы с такою властью
Взялся он за дела, к несчастью, —

Ведь погубил бы целый край.
Затем-то и попал он в рай,
Что за дела не принимался.[65]

(Well, can't you see, the dear departed was a fool!
What if, with power such as he had,
He'd tackled his affairs, alas,
He'd have done in the country.
But that's just why he went to heaven.
Because he never got to working.)

In the topsy-turvy world of the masquerade, Krylov could momentarily become the center of the revels and restore right order to the world with his ironic fables.

Fables could spring from any occasion in Krylov's life, and they were for the most serious occasions in life. Even for the deathbed. Aristophanes' comedy, *The Wasps,* reports that Aesop, before he died, told the fable of the Eagle and the Beetle.[66] This was an interesting choice of subject; for in this fable the eagle is forced to reckon with the lowly dung-beetle, and the moral is that we would be well advised not to scorn anyone, no matter how humble. In the traditional life of Aesop, "The Eagle and the Beetle" is only the first of several fables that Aesop recited in the face of the implacable Delphians who were demanding his death. The point of the remaining fables was: any fate but death at *your* hands! Upon which Aesop fulfilled his moral by leaping over the sacrificial cliff himself, thus in fact refusing to meet death at their hands. The fables that Aesop told before his death reaffirm the paradoxical privilege of his lowly status: he drops a dung-ball in the eagle's nest and calls the ones who impel him toward his death donkeys and incestuous rapists. This is strong stuff. Krylov could not equal it with his one deathbed fable, but its message is characteristic for him. Aesop's last fables were told as much "on them," on his repugnant society, as "on him." Krylov castigated only himself; he was alone with his last fable. Lobanov reported that "a few hours before his death Krylov compared himself to a peasant who, having thrown on his cart an immoderately large load of fish, had no idea that he would overburden his weak horse, because, after all, the load was only *dried* fish"[67] (K, 89). Thus Krylov tried to make light of the heaviness of impending death that was weighing him down. "Tiazhko mne," he complained, "It's hard on me." He made himself out to be just as puzzled as the foolish peasant. Claiming no privilege for his life, he only looked forward to dying in harness, like the poor horse. The self-deprecation did not extend to the fables themselves, however. For on his deathbed Krylov arranged to send all his friends a copy of the last edition of his fables to remember him by (K, 89). If Aesop had lived in the age of print, he certainly would have done the same. For the Aesopian poet, his life and his fables are coterminous.

The foregoing may help to explain why Krylov's legend has proved almost impossible to replace with a genuine biography. At the origins of a new literature, we see not only the conception of the different genres with their model works but also the invention of the various kinds of writers with the necessary exempla of their lives. Moreover, as the great linguist and philologist Potebnia long ago pointed out, the fable generates literary thinking at its most basic level. Each brief text, with its story and its moral, models for us what it means to make an interpretation on the basis of a narrative. The reader becomes involved in the act of realizing the question to which the fable is the answer.[68] It is a playful process, a game for children and grown-ups, and one in which the moral provided cannot be binding. As Potebnia wrote, it is useless to say to the child, "You must play with the toy this way."[69] Krylov worked at a time when Russian literature was still being formed and the reader was still being educated. It was only natural for him to identify himself with the fable's legendary originator.

Ronald D. LeBlanc

A la recherche du genre perdu: Fielding, Gogol, and Bakhtin's Genre Memory

> We have neither literature nor books.
> —Pushkin

> Our literature is so poor, that there is nothing I can appropriate from it.
> —Lermontov

> Gogol had no model and no precursors, either in Russian or in foreign literatures.
> —Belinsky

ALTHOUGH IT IS DEBATABLE whether Mikhail Bakhtin ever suceeded in formulating a coherent, systematic theory of genre, there is little disputing the claim that he attached enormous significance to genres, which for him—as "form-shaping ideologies"—constitute fundamental ways by which we visualize and conceptualize the world.[1] Indeed, given the essentially sociological approach to literature articulated by Bakhtin and the members of his circle, it is not surprising that literary genres—those so-called drive belts from social to literary history that help to carry and shape experience for us as individuals—are central to his theory of literature.[2] In his writings, Bakhtin even goes so far as to invest genres with a life of their own, often resorting to organic metaphors to describe them: he speaks of how they grow in meaning over time, how they develop their own organic logic. The life of a genre, according to Bakhtin, consists in its constant rebirths and renewals through original works that tap some of the rich potential hidden within this resilient transporter of creative resources from the past. "A genre lives in the present," Bakhtin notes, "but always remembers its past, its beginning."[3] Like human beings, therefore, genres for Bakhtin possess a memory.

In this essay I shall show how Bakhtin's anthropomorphic notion of "genre memory" is a useful conceptual tool for understanding what seems to be a rather problematic relationship of influence between Nikolai Gogol's nineteenth-century novel, *Dead Souls* (*Mertvye dushi,* 1842), and one of its more prominent eighteenth-century literary models, Henry Fielding's *Tom Jones* (1749). Influence studies fell into disrepute long ago, of course, largely because such studies did little more than enumerate the parallels that could be said to exist between the work of one author and that of a putative model. While they were able to draw broad typological affinities between the works of two different writers, these influence studies usually failed to explore the specific "generic contacts" that link one literary work to another. Indeed, I challenge here two of the better known studies of Fielding's influence on Gogol—one by Vasily Gippius, the other by Anna Elistratova—precisely on those grounds: both of them fail to consider *Tom Jones* as the literary artifact that actually existed during Gogol's lifetime. I shall attempt to remedy this situation by exploring the mediation of Fielding's style and narrative manner through eighteenth-century French and Russian translations that seriously distorted the nature and ethos of the original text of *Tom Jones.* In order to unearth the real text of Fielding's novel, Gogol had to penetrate through these pirate intermediaries. Before we launch into an examination of the French transmission of Fielding's English novel into early nineteenth-century Russia, however, it might prove helpful to look briefly at the literary and cultural context within which this twofold transmission took place—to review the status of prose fiction (and the novel in particular) in Russia during its Golden Age.

RESSENTIMENT, NARODNOST', AND THE NOVEL IN EARLY NINETEENTH-CENTURY RUSSIA

Although the novel would subsequently attain true greatness on Russian soil and eventually come to represent that nation's principal contribution to world literature, it was a genre that seems to have been largely neglected during the Golden Age of Russian literature, which remained very much an era of poetry. The "golden age" of the Russian novel would ensue only during the second half of the nineteenth century: during the reign of Alexander II (1855–81), rather than either Alexander I (1801–25) or Nicholas I (1825–55). One student of the Russian Formalists has even argued that the sentimentalist tale, the predominant prose genre during the early "Karamzinian" years of Russia's Golden Age, itself arose mainly as a stylistic and structural reaction to the long and rambling adventure novels—with their convoluted syntax, coarse language, and complicated plots—that had enjoyed such great popularity during the eighteenth century.[4] "It is significant," K. Skipina writes, "that the novel, one of the most popular genres of the eighteenth century, disappears almost completely at the beginning of the nineteenth century. For all practical purposes, Narezhny alone still continued the old line of the novel."[5] Other critics as well have argued that, with the salient exception of Vasily Narezhny's largely ignored contributions to the genre, not a single Russian novel of any kind appeared during the first two decades of the nineteenth century.[6] Moreover, as John Garrard observes, the very fact that Narezhny's finest novel, *A Russian Gil Blas* (*Rossiiskii Zhilblaz,* 1814), appeared almost exactly one hundred years after publication began of its putative French model, A. R. Lesage's *Gil Blas de Santillane* (1715–35), reflects just how backward was the state of prose fiction—particularly the novel—in early nineteenth-century Russia.[7]

During the late 1820s and early 1830s, however, the literary-historical situation changed dramatically. The audience for prose fiction in Russia had now developed and expanded to such a point that Faddei Bulgarin, the literary hack who was dubbed the "Apollo" of the St. Petersburg bookstalls, could publish a potboiling "moral-satirical" novel in 1829 that became a bestseller in the very same year that saw Pushkin's narrative poem *Poltava* prove to be an almost complete public failure. "With the appearance of *Ivan Vyzhigin,*" Belinsky wrote in describing this historical development, "our literature made a sharp turn from verse to prose."[8] The turn to prose was probably not quite as sharp so Belinsky would have us believe, but there can be little doubt that the huge commercial success of Bulgarin's artistically mediocre novel signaled that prose fiction had now managed to attain a position of dominance over poetry within the hierarchial system of Russian literature at the time. As the institution of letters in Russia continued to become increasingly commercialized, democratized, and professionalized during the 1830s, an aristocratic system of patronage yielded more and more to a mercantile system of book publishing and book trade. The Age of Pushkin, in short, was now giving way to the Age of Smirdin.[9] Even the great national poet himself would feel compelled to turn away from verse genres during the waning years of his brief career and condescend to write literary works in prose.[10] "The age impels toward stern prose," the author of *Eugene Onegin* (*Evgenii Onegin,* 1825–33) notes sadly in the sixth chapter of his famous "novel in verse."[11] It would be left to Pushkin's younger friend and colleague, Nikolai Gogol, however, to take full advantage of this shift to prose fiction in Russian letters. Following a line of development that Narezhny, a fellow Ukrainian, had tried to pursue a generation earlier, Gogol in *Dead Souls* would depict contemporary life in the provinces in a frank, unvarnished manner and thus prepare the ground for the flowering of the Russian novel that would take place during the subsequent Age of Realism. Although he may have been inspired by Dante's *Divine Comedy* and Cervantes's *Don Quixote* to write his "epic poem," Gogol's novel was also prompted in large part by a desire to counter the popular success of Bulgarin and other second-rate imitators of Lesage in Russia, seeking to challenge the poetics of these literary philistines as well as to repudiate the social and philosophical values espoused in their "moral-satirical" novels.[12]

It might strike one as rather odd to have the immortal names of Pushkin and Gogol mentioned alongside such decidedly lesser talents as Narezhny and Bulgarin in a discussion of how the novel initially developed on Russian soil during the first half of the nineteenth century. After all, it has now become a rather widely accepted critical commonplace to associate the rise of the novel in Russia with a trio of canonical works of fiction—none of which, however, neatly fits the formal definition of a novel—written by the three creative giants who dominated the literary scene during the reign of Nicholas I. Although Pushkin's *Eugene Onegin* was a narrative written in verse form, Lermontov's *Hero of Our Time* (*Geroi nashego vremeni,* 1841) was structured as a cycle of tales, and Gogol's *Dead Souls* was called an epic poem, these three literary masterpieces are commonly regarded as having laid the foundation for the classic Russian novels written by Turgenev, Goncharov, Dostoevsky, Tolstoy, and others during the second half of the nineteenth century. Whether it is Pushkin and Gogol—rather than Narezhny and Bulgarin—who ultimately deserve to be considered the true progenitors of the Russian novel, the fact remains that all four of these authors, although they may have been greatly unequal in terms of both talent and stature, faced a similar challenge: they had to find a way to liberate the fledgling Russian novel from the hegemony of European models in the genre. Each was faced with the daunting task of overcoming an established tradition in his country and, especially where the novel was concerned, of slavishly imitating foreign models. Interesting studies have been written recently about the origins of Russia's own literary and cultural imperialism, exploring how nineteenth-century Russian writers, in their works of fiction about the Caucasus, helped to underwrite their country's imperialistic ambitions and empire-building mentality.[13] What should not be overlooked in such discussions, however, is the extent to which writers and readers of novels in Russia during the first half of the nineteenth century themselves continued to feel constrained by a literary and cultural hegemony they assigned to Europe.[14] Russia's Golden Age was still very much a period of apprenticeship with regard to the novel, a genre in which Russian writers remained heavily indebted to—in some cases, even intimidated by—European literary achievements. The first few decades of the nineteenth century, as noted earlier, were essentially void of any indigenous attempts to write original novels; the eighteenth-century Russian novel, meanwhile, languished under the French neoclassical paradigm of imitation and translation. "The history of the novel in Russia in the eighteenth century," one scholar observes, "both begins and ends with the overwhelming predominance of the translated novel."[15] The authors of *Literature and Commerce* (*Slovesnost' i kommertsiia,* 1929), using terminology that seems to anticipate our own current critical idiom, echo this view, asserting that

"Russian literature during the second half of the eighteenth century was a country enduring foreign colonization."[16]

Even by the second quarter of the nineteenth century, when advocates of Romanticism were sounding the clarion call for *narodnost'* in art and when Russian readers seem to have become keenly interested at last in reading depictions of contemporary native (rather than foreign) life, the situation with regard to this literary colonialism had not changed substantially. It was primarily European writers such as Richardson, Fielding, Lesage, Rousseau, and Sterne—along with the relative newcomer, Sir Walter Scott—who continued to provide the most nourishing novelistic fare served up to the reading public in Russia. In the midst of the so-called decade of Smirdin, Bulgarin could still complain, just as Novikov had done some fifty years earlier, that a passion for foreign literary works prevented the sale of native ones in Russian bookstalls. The naturalization of the novel on Russian soil—its nationalization or "Russianization"—could proceed apace only when native writers and readers alike learned to overcome their subservience to Europe in literary and cultural matters: when they succeeded in emancipating themselves from their enslavement to European sensibilities and in establishing at last a measure of aesthetic autonomy. To make the Russian novel truly "Russian," writers needed, above all else, to develop much greater skill and sophistication in their use of foreign models: they needed to learn how to adapt these models in an appropriate and creative manner to Russian circumstances—to their country's own cultural values and sociopolitical conditions. Pushkin, of course, is widely recognized as the first Russian writer to have mastered this fine art of literary appropriation, marking in the minds of many critics a watershed between literary apprenticeship and artistic independence.[17] His skillful adaptations (stylistic as well as structural) of popular European literary models—from Lord Byron and Shakespeare to Benjamin Constant and Walter Scott—stand out amid the numerous indiscriminate and uncritical borrowings that characterized the works of so many of his contemporaries, most of whom suffered chronically from an eighteenth-century Russian malady: the "imitation syndrome."

In *Culture and Imperialism* (1993), Edward Said acknowledges that "the history of all cultures is the history of cultural borrowings."[18] Liberation from cultural imperialism can only occur, however, when colonials rise up and resist subjugation by reacting in a patriotic manner to the wholesale importation of foreign influence. Writing about nationalism during the modern period, Liah Greenfeld advances the Nietzschean concept of *ressentiment*—a psychological state resulting from suppressed feelings of envy and hatred—as a way to explain how Russian intellectuals were impelled to establish a sense of national identity and overcome feelings of inferiority vis-à-vis the West.[19] The hostility aroused by this *ressentiment* (or "existential envy" of the West) was often directed not at the foreign influences themselves, but at those fellow countrymen in Russia who persisted in their unabashed admiration of—and preference for—things Western. Deploring the pseudo-cosmopolitanism displayed by members of the educated classes in Russia, Aleksandr Bestuzhev-Marlinsky, for instance, would complain during the 1820s that "we have been brought up by foreigners and have drunk in with our mother's milk non-Russianness (*beznarodnost'*) and an admiration only for what is foreign."[20] Already by the second half of the eighteenth century a number of literary patriots of non-noble birth—"democratic" writers such as Denis Fonvizin, Mikhail Chulkov, and Matvei Komarov—were beginning to respond to the perceived threat of a growing Europeanization of Russia's literature and culture. They did so not only by turning to folktales and other popular narrative forms as native sources for their prose works, but also by satirizing and parodying those of their literary brethren who continued unconscionably to ape European (especially French) ways.[21] This sort of nativist reaction against foreign influence in general—and against the uncritical absorption of European tastes, values, and sensibilities by fellow Russians in particular—persisted during the first half of the nineteenth century as well. We can see with particular clarity how such nativist *ressentiment* and literary patriotism manifest themselves during this period in the type of writing that has come to be called *nravoopisatel'naia proza:* those works of prose fiction that seek to describe everyday Russian life—and thus native mores and manners—in a realistic fashion. As I have argued elsewhere, the model for native *nravoopisanie* provided by Lesage's paradigm—the quasi-picaresque *roman de moeurs*—attracted many of Russia's earliest novelists (including Narezhny and Bulgarin as well as Pushkin and Gogol) principally by its narrative structure, which provided a particularly useful framework for depicting contemporary Russian life.[22] In their attempts to appropriate *Gil Blas* and adapt it to fit Russia's unique social, political, and artistic realities, however, these writers were not only confronted with the challenge of responding to Lesage's novel as a model of writing; they also found themselves drawn into an intertextual dialogue within the genre, conversing with each other about the nature of Russian national identity and how best to represent it on the pages of an indigenous novel.

THE PROSE EPICS OF FIELDING AND GOGOL

What I shall explore primarily in this essay is the contribution to the Russian novel made not by Lesage, but by another eighteenth-century European novelist: Henry Fielding. Much like Lesage, Fielding was held in very high regard in late eighteenth-century and early nineteenth-century Russia, where he was considered one of the forefathers of formal realism. The so-called

English novel, which was associated primarily with Richardson, Fielding, and Sterne, was greatly admired by readers in Russia for its faithful depiction of contemporary social reality and its frank portrayal of human beings "as they really are."[23] Unlike the seventeenth-century French *roman d'aventures*, which told tales of love and adventure totally unrelated to real life, the eighteenth-century English novel could claim to be presenting "a clear and realistic picture of modern life and modern man with all his faults, vices, absurdities, and fancies."[24] As a result of this greater psychological verisimilitude and social relevance, English novels such as Fielding's *Tom Jones* helped to establish a measure of legitimacy for prose fiction in eighteenth-century Russia, a country where neoclassical critics long persisted in railing about the dangers inherent in reading *romany*, condemning these works as largely escapist fare that related a number of impossible feats accomplished by implausible heroes who travel across purely imaginary landscapes. Fielding's hero, by contrast, was seen as a psychologically individualized character endowed with a mixture of both vices and virtues; his travels, moreover, take him through the very real world of contemporary society and not merely the make-believe world of the author's own imagination. Contemporary defenders of the modern novel in eighteenth-century Russia repeatedly pointed out that the hero's adventures in works such as Lesage's *Gil Blas* and Fielding's *Tom Jones* could be seen to serve both as windows exposing the human heart within and as mirrors reflecting realities in the social world without.

As a number of reception studies have shown, Fielding's *Tom Jones* found itself included among the handful of European novels that enjoyed tremendous popular and critical success in late eighteenth-century and early nineteenth-century Russia.[25] Numerous editions of Fielding's novel were published in Russian translation during this period and *Tom Jones* was even adapted for the Russian stage.[26] Given the huge popularity of Fielding's novel in Russia at this time, it should not surprise us to find that quite a few of Russia's earliest novelists looked to *Tom Jones* as a model for their own attempts to describe contemporary social life in a manner at once satiric and realistic.[27] Thus D. S. Mirsky characterizes Aleksei Perovsky's *The Convent Girl* (*Monastyrka*, 1828), for instance, as a novel "obviously influenced by Fielding" and heavily dependent upon *Tom Jones*.[28] The protagonist of Narezhny's *The Seminarian* (*Bursak*, 1824), although he was hailed by contemporary critics as a "Russian Gil Blas," betrays a number of similarities with Tom Jones as well: Neon Khlopotinsky is a young man who is essentially good by nature but also inexperienced and weak-willed (particularly where his appetite for food, drink, and sex is concerned), and thus easily led astray by temptation and bad example.[29] Likewise, the fate of the eponymous protagonist in Bulgarin's *Ivan Vyzhigin* (1829) closely replicates the life pattern established by Fielding's hero: like Tom Jones, Ivan Vyzhigin is a lower-class orphan—a commoner and a bastard—who sets off upon a chain of picaresque adventures, precipitated by his efforts to pursue a beloved young lady, only to discover by journey's end his truly noble parentage and wealthy social status.[30] Even Chichikov, the main character in Gogol's *Dead Souls,* has been considered a Russian rogue whose literary lineage can be traced back, through Fielding's *Tom Jones,* Smollett's *Roderick Random,* and Lesage's *Gil Blas,* to the Spanish prototype in the picaresque genre, *Lazarillo de Tormes.*[31]

If Gogol was indeed attracted to Tom Jones as a genre model for his *Dead Souls,* however, it was probably due less to the picaresque features of Fielding's robust young hero, than to the stylistic manner and artistic method of his creator. As had been the case with Fielding, Gogol would be criticized by some of his contemporaries for the coarseness of language, vulgarity of expression, and grotesqueness of imagery that occur at times in his narrative—for the "Flemish" tendencies revealed in the pictures he painted of native life.[32] Moreover, both *Tom Jones* and *Dead Souls* have regularly been associated with a parodic novelistic tradition that Bakhtin, in an attempt at a historical poetics, has designated as the "second" stylistic line in the development of the modern novel: that is, the type of novel that incorporates into its narrative structure the heteroglossia—the rich diversity of voices and various speech types—that exists within contemporary social discourse.[33] Unlike novels of the first stylistic line, which seek instead to resist and repress such heteroglossia, the eighteenth-century English comic novel, infused with the playful, parodic spirit of Rabelais and Cervantes, unleashes those centrifugal forces that seek to decentralize, invert, and carnivalize the ideological discourse of official culture. In addition, the genre distinction that Gogol draws between the traditional novel and what he calls the "minor epic" (*men'shii rod epopei*) as a way to categorize his own *Dead Souls* closely parallels Fielding's definition of his new brand of novel as a "comic epic in prose."[34] Indeed, Gogol explicitly acknowledged that Fielding was one of only a handful of literary figures who served as an inspiration to him as a verbal artist. "The author is not in the habit of looking about himself when he writes," Gogol confesses in an early draft for part 1, chapter 11 of *Dead Souls,* "and it is only by their own volition that his eyes occasionally light on the portraits hanging on the wall before him, of Shakespeare, Ariosto, Fielding, Cervantes and Pushkin, men who reflected nature as it was, and not as it suited someone or other that it should be."[35] Gogol's literary talent clearly seems to have been linked very closely with Fielding's comic genius in the mind of Pushkin; upon hearing the anecdote about how the print compositors roared with laughter while typesetting the first volume of Gogol's *Evenings on a Farm Near Dikanka,* the poet noted that "Molière and Fielding would doubtless have been glad to have amused their compositors."[36]

Belinsky's sweeping claim that Gogol "had no model or precursors" is, therefore, greatly exaggerated. "Cervantes, Fielding, Sterne may, loosely speaking, be regarded as precursors in foreign literatures," Richard Freeborn observes, "Narezhny in Russian literature."[37] Indeed, Donald Fanger has characterized Gogol as a "literary magpie," a writer who borrowed freely throughout his career and from a wide variety of sources, both native and foreign.[38] What has been consistently overlooked in charting the exact extent of Fielding's influence on Gogol, however, is the particular form—what we might consider the specific literary-historical concretization—that the novel *Tom Jones* took for those early nineteenth-century Russian writers who were likely to have read Fielding's prose masterpiece. They were engaged dialogically by it, and responded to it in accord with the intertextual nature of narrative discourse: that is, through imitation, parody, stylization, or some other form of double-voiced reaccentuation. If writers such as Narezhny, Bulgarin, and Gogol did, in fact, read *Tom Jones* (and, given that novel's tremendous popularity in Russia, it is quite likely that they did), then they read it either in the French translation provided by Pierre-Antoine de La Place in 1750 or in the subsequent Russian translation from the French made by Evsignei Kharlamov in 1770. This seems a reasonable assumption as hardly any men of letters in early nineteenth-century Russia knew the English language well enough to be able to read a novel like *Tom Jones* in the original.[39] Gogol himself, for example, is reputed to have had a very poor knowledge of foreign languages and did not know any English, a subject that was not even taught at the Nezhin Lyceum, the gymnasium that provided him with the only formal schooling he ever received.[40] Moreover, direct translations of novels from English into Russian did not begin to appear with any regularity until later in the nineteenth century. The first Russian translation of *Tom Jones* to be made directly from the English original, for instance, without any intermediary French or German translation, was Andrei Kroneberg's 1848 version, which appeared some six years after Gogol published the first part of *Dead Souls*.[41]

If Fielding truly did exert an influence upon Gogol and other early novelists in Russia, therefore, he did so through the filter provided by French and Russian versions of his novel. The influence exerted upon nascent Russian prose fiction by a slew of English writers—from Shakespeare and Sterne to Byron and Walter Scott—was channeled in precisely this same manner: that is, through the mediation of translation.[42] Literary historians, curiously enough, have generally failed to consider the position and function of foreign translations within Russia's national literature.[43] Modern studies on the picaresque novel have shown, however, that translations were crucial in shaping that genre throughout Europe. In *The Picaresque* (1977), for instance, Harry Sieber writes that "the translations of Spanish picaresque novels are the key to an understanding of the European history of the genre. Translators were 'readers' who not only injected their own tastes and attitudes in their translations, but also assessed and attempted to include the sensibilities of a wider 'invisible' reading public."[44] In an article entitled "Translation and Literary Genre: The European Picaresque Novel in the Seventeenth and Eighteenth Centuries" (1985), Hendrik van Gorp demonstrates convincingly that seventeenth-century French translations of Spanish picaresque novels "were instrumental in orienting and directing subsequent versions and thus contributed substantially to the development of the picaresque genre in several national literatures of Western Europe."[45] This was certainly the case in late eighteenth-century and early nineteenth-century Russia as well, as readers and writers there were familiar with picaresque fiction exclusively through French translations and adaptations of the Spanish originals.[46] Fielding's famous novel would likewise make itself known to the Russian literary imagination throughout most of the nineteenth century exclusively by means of a French translation that dated back to the middle of the eighteenth century. As one critic notes, Russian readers would become fully acquainted with the "real" Fielding only in the twentieth century, during the Soviet period, when direct translations from the English at last became readily available.[47] As a result, Gogol, like other readers in early nineteenth-century Russia, was likely to have been acquainted not with Fielding's *History of Tom Jones, A Foundling* (1749), but rather with counterfeit versions: La Place's *Histoire de Tom Jones, ou L'Enfant trouvé* (1750), or even Kharlamov's *Povest' o Tomase Ionese, ili Naidenyshe* (1770).

BOWDLERIZING *TOM JONES: BIENSÉANCE* AND LA PLACE'S *"BELLE INFIDÈLE"*

I use the word "counterfeit" to characterize La Place's translation because even a cursory textual analysis reveals that the French version of *Tom Jones* (and Kharlamov's later Russian version, patterned with scrupulous fidelity on that French translation)[48] inflicts serious damage—both stylistically and thematically—upon Fielding's original text. Although the extreme distortions that were authorized by the liberal translation theory regnant in eighteenth-century France have been examined elsewhere, we should recall briefly the extreme liberties that were regularly committed during this period. These liberties were largely authorized by the neoclassicist theory of *bienséance,* an aesthetic notion that allowed translations into French to become, in essence, adaptations, as its governing principle was to preserve the proprieties of artistic decorum.[49] In order to spare highly civilized French readers the need to expose themselves to the literary "barbarism" perpetrated by "vulgar" novels imported from Spain and England, translators in eighteenth-century

France felt justified in adapting foreign works to suit the sophisticated tastes and refined sensibilities of their native reading audience. "The French have a monopoly on good taste at this period," Harold Streeter writes concerning these eighteenth-century neoclassicists, "and their constant preoccupation with it is nowhere better evidenced than in the apologetic prefaces of the translators, who commit so many crimes and indiscretions in its name."[50] The process of modifying Spanish and English works in order to have them please Gallic literary palates generally entailed two main operations: first, a foreshortening of the work, by eliminating unnecessary digressions, lengthy descriptions, or moral commentaries; and, second, its refinement, by expurgating vulgar imagery, unsavory details, or inelegant language. The eighteenth-century practice of *bienséance* resulted in bowdlerized French editions of such seminal works of modern European literature as Defoe's *Robinson Crusoe,* Swift's *Gulliver's Travels,* and Fielding's *Tom Jones,* foreign novels that were considered too virile and too primitive to be read in France in their original form.

Eighteenth-century French translators shamelessly eliminated most of the local color from these works of English prose fiction, expurgating narrative digressions and authorial commentaries, abridging lengthy descriptions, sometimes even opting to paraphrase entire sections of the original text. By removing anything that might possibly offend, shock, or, worse yet, bore French readers, and by making those textual emendations that were deemed necessary to "improve" the original, translators in eighteenth-century France succeeded in creating a whole series of so-called *belles infidèles:* beautiful but highly inaccurate texts that departed significantly—in some cases, radically—from the foreign original.[51] Some of the more egregious examples of this practice can be found in the French translations of Samuel Richardson's novels performed by l'abbé Prévost, who substantially shortened and embellished *Sir Charles Grandison, Pamela,* and *Clarissa,* on the grounds that English literature has need of such alterations (what he called "*petites réparations*") in order for it to become appropriately and effectively naturalized in Paris. In the preface to his translation of *Sir Charles Grandison* (1756), for instance, Prévost writes,

> I have given a new look to his work by removing languid digressions, exaggerated pictures, useless conversations, and inappropriate reflections. The principal reproach that critics have made of Richardson is that he occasionally loses sight of the dimensions of his subject and forgets himself in details; I have waged a constant battle against this defect in proportion.[52]

Another outspoken defender of the aesthetics of *bienséance* was l'abbé Desfontaines, who, in his translations from the English, severely bowdlerized, abridged, and adapted novels by both Swift and Fielding.[53] Commenting upon his 1727 translation of *Gulliver's Travels,* Desfontaines warned a correspondent: "You will find, Sir, a translation that is hardly faithful in many passages; but all that pleases in England does not have the same charm here, either because the mores are different . . . or because the taste of nations is not the same."[54] Astonishingly, Desfontaines's 1743 translation of Fielding's *Joseph Andrews* continues to be published in France even today.

Given this state of liberal translation practice in eighteenth-century France, what exactly is the extent of the textual damage—the stylistic and narrative injury—that La Place inflicted upon Fielding's original text in his *Histoire de Tom Jones, ou L'Enfant trouvé?* To begin with, the French translator abridged *Tom Jones* considerably, reducing it from six volumes to four and thus eliminating much of Fielding's colorful language and style. Apparently, however, even this drastic abridgment was not radical enough for some French critics. Pierre Clément, for instance, observed sardonically that reducing *Tom Jones* from six volumes to four merely meant that the novel was now only two volumes too long.[55] Elie Fréron likewise complained that the translator did not go far enough in shortening Fielding's text; to Fréron's mind, La Place should have eliminated the "annoying" character Partridge altogether.[56] Although La Place's textual abridgments are indeed extensive and substantial, worse yet is the manner in which the French translator goes about shortening Fielding's comic prose masterpiece. For one thing, he deletes nearly all instances of the mock-heroic description of fisticuffs that one frequently encounters in the novel, apparently because he finds these low scenes inappropriately vulgar parodies of classical models such as Homer and Virgil. In addition, La Place freely changes chapter headings. Book 5, chapter 9 of Fielding's novel, "Which, among other Things, may serve as a Comment on that saying of Æschines, that Drunkenness shews the Mind of a Man, as a Mirrour reflects his Person," is retitled in the French version "The Interrupted Feast."[57] La Place, moreover, often abridges, summarizes, or paraphrases scenes that Fielding has described at some length. In book 8, chapter 8, for instance, La Place observes curtly, "The English author, after having led Tom Jones and Partridge as far as Gloucester, without any adventure worthy of being transmitted to posterity, has them dine in a famous inn, whose hostess, as amiable as she is polite, gives a very warm welcome to Mister Jones, who even has the pleasure of dining with her" (2:35). As another means of abridging the original *Tom Jones,* La Place everywhere eliminates the comic periphrasis provided by Fielding's ironic narrator. In book 8, chapter 9 of the original, for example, we encounter the following passage, "The Shadows began now to descend larger from the high Mountains: The feather'd Creation had betaken themselves to their Rest. Now the highest Order of Mortals were sitting down to their Dinners, and the lowest Order to their Suppers. In a Word, the Clock struck five just as Mr. Jones took his

Leave of Gloucester" (331). This becomes, in the French translation: "The clock had struck five, says the eloquent English author, in a much more florid style, as our two adventurers left Gloucester" (2:37). In book 10, chapter 2 of the original we encounter a similar passage,

> Now the little trembling Hare, whom the Dread of all her numerous Enemies, and chiefly of that cunning, cruel, carnivorous Animal Man, had confined all the Day to her Lurking-place, sports wantonly o'er the Lawns: Now on some hollow Tree the Owl, shrill Chorister of the Night, hoots forth Notes which might charm the Ears of some modern Connoisseurs in Music: Now in the Imagination of the halfdrunk Clown, as he staggers through the Church-yard, or rather Charnel-yard, to his Home, Fear paints the bloody Hobgoblin: Now Thieves and Ruffians are awake, and honest Watchmen fast asleep: In plain English, it was now Midnight. (400)

This colorful and highly sardonic passage becomes, in La Place's reductive French translation, simply "The clock had struck twelve" (2:107).

Far more serious than the deletion of mock-heroic depictions of fisticuffs, the changed chapter headings, the summarizing and paraphrasing, the elimination of comic periphrasis, or the abridgment of lengthy narrative descriptions is La Place's expurgation of the introductory chapters for each of the eighteen books of *Tom Jones.* Entirely gone from the French translation of Fielding's novel are such memorable chapters as "The Introduction to the Work, or Bill of Fare to the Feast" (book 1), "Shewing what Kind of a History this is; what it is like, and what it is not like" (book 2), "Of the SERIOUS in Writing, and for what Purpose it is introduced" (book 5), "A Comparison between the World and the Stage" (book 7), "A wonderful long Chapter concerning the Marvellous; being much the longest of all our introductory Chapters" (book 8), "Containing Instructions very necessary to be perused by modern Critics" (book 10), "A Crust for the Critics" (book 11), "Shewing what is to be deemed Plagiarism in a modern Author, and what is to be considered as lawful Prize" (book 12), "An Essay to prove that an Author will write better, for having some Knowledge of the Subject on which he writes" (book 14), "Of Prologues" (book 16), and "A Farewell to the Reader" (book 18). The importance, as well as the problematical structural status, of these introductory chapters has long been the subject of the critical discourse that surrounds Fielding's novel.[58] Even Sir Walter Scott, while noting that these intercalary chapters interrupt the flow of the narrative (and thus the oft-mentioned Aristotelian "action" or plot of *Tom Jones*), admitted that upon rereading the novel he found them the most entertaining sections of the entire work.[59] In our own century, critics have recognized that these introductory chapters are more than finely ornamental (but intrusive) digressions or pleasurable (but irrelevant) entertainments served up rather whimsically by the author.[60] Instead these chapters have come to be seen as part of an important concurrent level of discourse in the text, a discourse that links literary theory with mimetic practice; as one critic observes, such chapters help to establish "terms for conduct, interpretation, and judgment in the literary realm that comment upon episodes in the social and moral realm."[61] To paraphrase the view promulgated by the Russian Formalists, Fielding's introductory chapters may be said to constitute not an intrusion upon the work, but the very essence of the work itself. Or, as one contemporary critic puts it, "the ultimate meaning in Tom Jones is found in the frame, not in its tale."[62]

A MAP OF MISREADING (AND MISTRANSLATING)

This formalist type of reading, which emphasizes the importance of the intercalary chapters to the overall meaning of Fielding's *Tom Jones,* finds its analogue in the current critical judgment that Gogol's *Dead Souls* is a text more concerned with the metaliterary than the literary. "Almost all of Gogol's writing," Donald Fanger notes, "is in some important sense about literature."[63] This is especially true of *Dead Souls,* where narrative digressions grant Gogol a large amount of authorial freedom: "the freedom to move from the level of presentation to the levels of reminiscence, confession, literary and social commentary, prophecy—setting against the soulless world he depicts an image of his own soulful and passionate concerns."[64] Although Fanger insists that it is Pushkin's *Eugene Onegin*—rather than *Tom Jones* or *Tristram Shandy*—that provided Gogol with the model for a "free" novel of this sort, a number of other Gogol scholars have traced the "freedom" of form in *Dead Souls* to the English comic novels written by Fielding and Sterne.[65] Vasily Gippius, for example, observes that close parallels exist between Fielding's *Tom Jones* and Gogol's *Dead Souls* precisely because of the presence in both texts of continuous authorial commentary, comic digressions, and lyrical interjections.[66] Anna Elistratova extends this connection even further in her comparative study of these two writers. "The role of the author in the works we have been comparing has another similarity, too," she writes:

> Both Fielding and Gogol are not merely "present" throughout the action alongside their characters, reminding the reader of their presence with the ironic touches in the descriptions, and with what we might call their authorial comments, which constitute an inherent part of the narrative. In addition, they both arrogate to themselves, in bold violation of the apparent "objectivity" of the exposition, the right to engage the reader in direct conversation—conversation that is by no means confined to the described events, but ranges over everything that strikes them as of vital importance. In *The History of Tom Jones* Fielding contrives, through the structure of the work, to motivate these digressions. To each of the eighteen books of his "comic epic poem" he prefaces a special

> introductory chapter, usually with a deliberately comic title and discussing with light-hearted irony but often great inner seriousness questions of morality and aesthetics which particularly concern him.[67]

"Both writers," Elistratova observes with respect to Fielding and Gogol, "recognize and exercise the right to converse aloud with the reader, to take issue with their more unscrupulous critics and to defend their ideal of truthful and honest art."[68]

The main problem with comparative analyses such as the ones proffered here by Gippius and Elistratova, however, is that when they discuss the stylistic and thematic similarities between *Tom Jones* and *Dead Souls,* they fail to consider Fielding's text as it actually existed during Gogol's lifetime. As we have seen, the *Tom Jones* that an early nineteenth-century Russian novelist such as Gogol is likely to have read (in French or Russian translation) was radically different from the *Tom Jones* that Fielding originally wrote and that we, as modern readers and literary critics, are familiar with today. Indeed, La Place managed to expunge from his version of *Tom Jones* precisely those stylistic features—the mock-heroic accounts, the authorial addresses to the reader, the narrative digressions—that are considered by Gippius, Elistratova and others to have exerted the strongest influence upon Gogol's narrative manner in his novel. Yet most critics, even those who are well aware that bowdlerized versions of Fielding's novel circulated in Russia, continue to downplay the effect that the intermediate French translation by La Place had upon Russian readers of *Tom Jones.* The renowned comparatist, M. P. Alekseev, for instance, writes: "Although many of Fielding's books were first translated from the French and German, these early versions gave the Russian reader a good idea of the author's rich language and of his distinctive stylistic manner."[69] Likewise, Iurii Levin, in a study with the promising title, "Translations of Henry Fielding's Works in Eighteenth-Century Russia," seriously understates the extent of the damage done to *Tom Jones* by foreign translations. "But still there was so much strength and merit in the 'comic epic' in prose which Fielding had created," Levin asserts, "that even the arbitrariness of the translators could not destroy them. And the Russian readers duly appreciated the socio-ethical and artistic significance of his works."[70] Edward Daniel Clarke, a Cambridge don who traveled in late eighteenth-century Russia, assesses more accurately the highly distortive effect of La Place's translation on Fielding's text when he states that in the Russian versions of *Tom Jones,* "Squire Western becomes a French Philosopher."[71]

Considerable hermeneutic space was thus opened up by the eighteenth-century French and Russian versions of Fielding's English novel, creating a gap between *Tom Jones* as *lecture* and as *écriture,* a gap that has interesting ramifications for influence studies, reception history, and genre theory.

Among other things, this gap should lead us to question the rather facile connections that Gippius and Elistratova construct in their comparative studies of Fielding and Gogol, analyses that at best show us the broad typological affinities that might exist between the works of these two great comic writers. But their failure to explore the actual generic or contact relations between *Tom Jones* and *Dead Souls*—in other words, the "French connection" established by La Place's intermediary text—effectively invalidates their contention that Gogol most likely adopted his digressive and intrusive narrative manner under the direct influence not only of Sterne, but also of Fielding.[72] In addition, this historical episode involving the French bowdlerization of Fielding's *Tom Jones* should prompt us to reconsider Harold Bloom's increasingly popular scheme for conceptualizing the dynamics of the relationship that exists between a writer and his putative model. Although Bloom himself tends to write exclusively about poets working within the monolingual culture of Anglo-American literature, his theories have nonetheless been applied to bilingual contexts in comparative studies that examine the influence of writers from different national literatures.[73] In works such as *The Anxiety of Influence* (1973) and *A Map of Misreading* (1975), Bloom has advanced a Freudian view of artistic creation, portraying an Oedipal relationship of hostility between a literary father and his literary son, both of whom compete agonistically with each other for verbal supremacy. The sense of belonging to a poetic tradition allegedly produces anxiety in the literary son who feels oppressed by what Bloom considers the "burden" of the literary past; that is, the perceived strength or greatness of poetic precursors.[74] This ego anxiety, Bloom contends, in turn leads the younger poets, in their struggle against artistic determinism, to "misread" their ancestors so as to clear some imaginative space for themselves. "A poet interpreting his precursors, and any strong subsequent interpreter reading either poet," Bloom writes, "must falsify by his reading."[75]

With respect to the French connection (or "correction") that we have been exploring, however, La Place's falsifying bowdlerization of *Tom Jones* mediates our reconstruction of Gogol's relationship to this English author and the concomitant debt that *Dead Souls* is said to owe to Fielding's novel. Where Lesage's influence on Gogol's novel was modulated largely by literary intermediaries, by second-rate Russian imitators (such as Bulgarin) who prompted a counter-example and thus provided, in effect, a reverse influence (*influence de rebours*),[76] Fielding's influence on *Dead Souls* made itself felt along an even more circuitous route that traveled through the distortive filter provided by French and Russian translators. The "map of misreading" that Bloom's theory would have us posit is thus charted, in this instance, more by Fielding's French translator, who distorted and destroyed *Tom Jones,* than by his young Russian literary disciple, whose challenge here is not to overcome an anxiety of influence, but rather to recuperate the comic spirit of the original English text—a text, unknown to Gogol, that lies hidden beneath the opaque varnish of its French and Russian mistranslations. These intermediary mistranslations that stand between Fielding and Gogol should also encourage us to rethink the notion of *ressentiment* as the stimulus for the nationalist sentiment and patriotic fervor that led to the emancipation of the Russian novel from the hegemony of foreign models. After all, Gogol's reaction to *Tom Jones* does not seem to have been to challenge or repudiate Fielding's artistic achievement; if anything, his work seeks to duplicate the formal freedom that characterizes this comic epic. Moreover, Gogol's intertextual response to the genre was prompted not directly by the famous English novel itself, but rather by a poor Russian translation of its French adaptation.

BAKHTINIAN THEORY: REMEMBERING GENRES, LIBERATING AUTHORS

It seems to me that Bakhtin's notion of "genre memory" provides us with a much more useful and productive conceptual model than does Bloom's ego-anxiety theory to account for the influence that Fielding exerted upon Gogol.[77] Bakhtin, in his scheme for explaining literary evolution and the dynamics of historical change in literature, shifts the emphasis away from the artists themselves and places it on the generic tradition in which those artists work; his concern lies less with the influence between two individual writers than with the generic contacts through which a literary tradition transmits itself to a particular author.[78] Since genre for Bakhtin serves as the central organ of creative memory, it carries within itself potential—indeed, a veritable "surplus" of potential—that great writers are able to sense intuitively. Although Dostoevsky, for example, may have known very little about ancient Menippean satire itself, he was able to see the rich resources and creative possibilities within carnivalistic forms generally and thus to realize the potential of a genre he barely knew. Dostoevsky looked "through" nineteenth-century works (such as the superficially carnivalized French boulevard novels of Eugène Sue) and sensed the rich generic tradition to which they once belonged; he sensed as well the artistic thinking, visualization, and representation endemic to the logic of Menippean satire. As Gary Saul Morson and Caryl Emerson explain in their recent study of Bakhtin's theories, "after understanding the genre's logic, a great writer can guess the uses to which it must have been put by someone or other at some time or other; and the writer can also imagine how the resources of his own age or experience might better realize the genre's potential."[79] In the case of Dostoevsky, he did not have to remember very much of the past, because the genre remembered it for him: in Bakhtin's words, "it was not Dostoevsky's subjective memory, but the objective memory of the very genre in which he worked, that preserved the peculiar features of the ancient menippea."[80] Just as the function of the literary critic is to use his or her "outsidedness" (*vnenakhodimost'*) in time and space to help liberate the artistic text from being a "captive of its own epoch," so too is it the role of the great writer—as a perspicacious reader blessed with the gift of creative understanding—to unearth the valuable semantic treasures that lie embedded not only in individual literary texts, but also in the narrative genres that inform and shape them.[81]

If we switch from Dostoevsky to Gogol, we can understand Bakhtin's notion of genre memory to mean that the author of *Dead Souls,* armed with a surplus of intuitive knowledge and creative insight, was able to uncover the potential meanings hidden within La Place's and Kharmalov's distortions of the original *Tom Jones.* According to Bakhtin's model, Gogol reconstituted the genre of the comic novel by supplying in *Dead Souls* many of the same Fieldingesque features (for example, authorial commentary, narrative digressions, lyrical interjections) that had been scrubbed out in the French and Russian translations of *Tom Jones.* Thus we encounter frequent instances in *Dead Souls* where Gogol, like Fielding, speaks directly to his reader. In chapter 4 of part 1, for example, we find the following passage:

> The author must confess that he is quite envious of the appetites and stomachs of this sort of people. All the top-notch people living in St. Petersburg and Moscow mean absolutely nothing to him—people who spend their time thoughtfully planning what they may eat tomorrow, and what sort of dinner to contrive for the day after, and who sit down to this dinner not otherwise than after having popped some pills into their mouths; people who gulp down oysters, sea spiders, and other such wondrous viands and eventually wind up with having to go to the baths at Karlsbad or to take the medicinal waters in the Caucasus. No, these gentry have never aroused any envy in me. But you take some of these fair-to-middlin' gentlemen, who will call for ham at one stage post, a suckling pig at a second, and at the third for a slice of sturgeon, or some sort of sausage baked with onions, and then, as if they hadn't eaten a thing all day, will sit down at a full table, at any hour you like, and tackle sterlet chowder, with eelpouts and soft roe, so hot it hisses and burbles as they take it into their mouths, followed, as a sort of chaser, by a fish pie with millet porridge, or cabbage dumplings, or a pie baked of young catfish, so that even an onlooker must needs work up an appetite—now, these gentlemen really are enjoying an enviable gift from Heaven! (6:61; 56)[82]

In book 1, chapter 2 of the original *Tom Jones,* Fielding warns his audience early on that he is prone—if not determined—to stray from the straightforward account of his hero's life story to provide the reader with authorial commentary on a wide variety of subjects. "Reader, I think proper, before we proceed any farther together, to acquaint thee, that I intend to digress, through this whole History, as often as I see occasion" (28). These frequent digressions so offended the aesthetic sensibilities of La Place that he felt compelled to omit them in his French translation of *Tom Jones.* "If Mr. Fielding had written for the French," La Place said by way of explanation (and justification), "he would probably have suppressed a multitude of passages, excellent in themselves, but which would appear to a Frenchman, unseasonable or misplaced."[83] To Gogol's mind, however, Fielding's narrative digressions seemed neither "unseasonable" nor "misplaced" for Russian readers. Thus the author of *Dead Souls* likewise digresses quite frequently, interrupting the narrative account of his hero's story—the so-called "adventures of Chichikov" (a title imposed upon Gogol by the censors)—to comment not only upon the prodigious capacity of the Russian stomach, but also on such matters as the fate of the writer in Russia, the beauty of the Russian word, and the destiny of the Russian people.

Gogol also saw fit in his "epic poem" (*poema*) to restore to the genre of the "comic epic in prose" the mock-heroic depiction of fisticuffs that the author of *Tom Jones* masterfully presents in scenes such as the one described in book 4, chapter 8 ("A Battle Sung by the Muse in the Homerican stile, and which none but the classical Reader can taste"), where the gallant young hero protects Molly Seagrim from the angry mob that has attacked her (134–38). We witness a similar scene in part 1, chapter 4 of Gogol's *Dead Souls,* where the author provides a mock-heroic account of the fight that breaks out between Nozdrev and Chichikov when the latter refuses to finish a game of draughts with his cheating host:

> "Beat him up!" Nozdrev kept yelling, all ablaze and sweating, straining forward with his cherrywood chibouk, as though he were storming an impregnable fortress. "Beat him up!" he kept yelling in the same sort of voice that some desperate lieutenant, whose harebrained bravery has already gained such a reputation that a specific order is issued to hold him back by his arms during the heat of battle, uses to yell, "Forward, lads!" to his platoon during a great assault. But the lieutenant has already felt the martial fervor, everything has begun going round and round in his head: Suvorov, that great general, soars in a vision before him; the lieutenant strains forward to perform a great deed. "Forward, lads!" he yells, dashing forward, without reflecting that he is jeopardizing the plan of attack already decided upon, that countless gun muzzles are thrust out of the embrasures of the fortress, that his impotent platoon will be blown up into the air like so much swan's-down, and that the bullet with his name on it is already whizzing through the air, just about to shut off his vociferous throat. (6:86–87; 82)

In part 1, chapter 7 of the novel Gogol seems to toy with the aesthetic expectations of what Fielding calls "the classical Reader" when he refers to the government bureaucrats in town as the incorruptible "priests of Themis" (6:141; 136), portraying one of them as a "new Virgil" who offers up his services to the Russian Dante (6:144; 139–40).

Another of the distinctively Fieldingesque stylistic features absent in the La Place and Kharlamov translations of *Tom Jones* that Gogol restores to the genre of comic epopeia is a down-to-earth concern with corporeality, which expresses itself largely in the robust appetite for food and drink revealed by many of their fictional characters. In the introductory chapter to book 1 of *Tom Jones,* Fielding likens himself to a cook at an inn and provides the reader with a "Bill of Fare to the Feast," promising in the novel that follows that he will "represent Human Nature at first to the keen Appetite of our Reader, in that more plain and simple Manner in which it is found in the Country, and shall hereafter hash and ragoo it with all the high French and Italian Seasoning of Affectation and Vice which Courts and Cities afford" (27). Throughout the text—and especially during the Upton Inn scenes (books 9 and 10) that Tony Richardson orchestrated so memorably in his 1964 film *Tom Jones*—Fielding presents his characters very often seated at table eating and drinking with great gusto.[84] Indeed, he even provides a mock invocation to the "God of Eating" and apologizes for the "good stomach" of his young hero in book 9, chapter 5, noting that "it may be doubted whether Ulysses, who by the Way seems to have had the best Stomach of all the Heroes in that eating Poem of the Odyssey, ever made a better Meal" (387). The hearty appetite of Fielding's hero, who lays upon the steak offered him at the Upton Inn with "immoderate Ardour," finds its Gogolian incarnation in the gargantuan gorging of gluttonous characters such as Sobakevich, who, in Nabokov's words, "works in the food line with great slabs and mighty hacks."[85] The abundance of food imagery and frequency of meal scenes in Gogol's novel led Andrei Bely to assert that the true hero of *Dead Souls* is not Chichikov nor the narrator, but rather the belly; indeed, Bely suggested that we might well call this comic epic not a modern *Iliad,* but a rather a *Gobble-iad* ("*ne* Iliada, *a* Zhratviada").[86] Gogol, a renowned gourmet and gourmand who entertained serious culinary aspirations himself, seems like Fielding to conflate the roles of poet and cook, looking upon both of them as artists who seek to feed their audience tasty yet nourishing fare.[87] This culinary analogy between poet and cook was reinforced by the contemporary critic Stepan Shevyrev, who compared *Dead Souls* to a large pie that had been overstuffed by an ingenious gastronome "who does not spare the filling."[88] Gogol himself, while struggling to finish the ill-fated part 2 of his novel, complained to one correspondent that "*Dead Souls* are not like pancakes, which can be prepared in an instant" (12:187).

Like the authorial commentary, narrative digressions, and mock-heroic descriptions, the gastronomic gusto that characterizes Fielding's robust novel was entirely removed in the sanitized translations of *Tom Jones* provided by La Place and Kharlamov. By restoring these Fieldingesque features to the genre in his *Dead Souls,* Gogol was thus liberating a comic epic that in his day was being held captive: *Tom Jones* was the prisoner mainly of a foreign adaptation that sought to impoverish its rich semantic resources and stylistic possibilities by enclosing the original text within the straitjacket of eighteenth-century French neoclassical aesthetics. To paraphrase what Bakhtin has said about the original "word" (*slovo*), we might say that in late eighteenth-century and early nineteenth-century Russia the original text of Fielding's *Tom Jones* had become populated—if not overpopulated—by the intentions of other people.[89] Through his bowdlerization of Fielding's robust comic novel, La Place attempted, in effect, to reverse the process of liberation that Bakhtin encourages us to associate with the novel as a highly carnivalized (and carnivalizing) literary genre. Recasting some of Bakhtin's own favorite terms, we might say that Fielding's French translator attempted to "denovelize" (or "decarnivalize") *Tom Jones* by removing its narrative discourse and artistic representations from the zone of familiar contact in which the English comic novelist had originally placed them. Fielding's seriocomic masterpiece, in its original form, epitomizes Bakhtin's delineation of the novel as a "subversive" genre, one that mocks other poetic or rhetorical forms, exposing the conventionality of their style and language, and reaccentuating them through parody, travesty, and burlesque.[90] The French neoclassicist La Place, however, in taking *Tom Jones* hostage, tried to convert Fielding's novel from the second to the first stylistic line of development, where centripetal forces of order, respectability, and decorum predominate within the discourse of the text.[91]

La Place may well have been able to bowdlerize Fielding's novel, but he could not lobotomize the genre to which it belonged: he could not erase the genre memory that continued to live through it. Indeed, this historical episode, in which genre memory enabled Gogol to penetrate the French falsification of *Tom Jones* and rediscover a "lost" genre, shares some close similarities, it seems to me, with the way Narezhny had earlier managed to look "through" French translations and adaptations of Spanish picaresque fiction.[92] Just as Narezhny was able to see the Spanish picaresque roots in Lesage's *Gil Blas* and reorient the genre in Russia back in the direction of baroque pessimism and grotesque realism from which it had originally come, so too was Gogol able to recognize, retrieve, and restore many of the features of the English comic novel that had been expurgated in the French and Russian versions of Fielding's famous novel.[93] By liberating *Tom Jones* at last from his eighteenth-century French captivity and reviving the lost genre of the comic novel, the author of *Dead Souls* helped to loosen the shackles of a foreign imperialism and cultural colonialism that—under the guise of literary translation, adaptation, imitation, and influence—threatened to enslave native prose fiction in early nineteenth-century Russia. This threat was especially palpable during the Age of Smirdin, when prose fiction began to be written by literary hacks who catered to the pedestrian tastes of the crowd rather than responding to the inspiration of a poetic muse, and when the commercial success of a novel far outweighed any concern for its intrinsic moral value or artistic quality. In such a climate, the crude and formulaic appropriation of successful foreign literary models—which served merely as external templates of the genre—was implicitly encouraged. To his great credit, Gogol helped to establish a tradition of original and independent national literature in his country. He did so in part by recuperating a prose genre that, had it been left in the hands of less creative (and more mercenary) talents, such as Bulgarin and Senkovsky, might otherwise have been irretrievably lost.

Katya Hokanson

Pushkin's Captive Crimea: Imperialism in *The Fountain of Bakhchisarai*

THE EDITORS of this volume point out in the Introduction that it was characteristic of the Russian Golden Age to overlap legitimizing cultural paradigms in an effort to establish proofs of lineage and to fashion a national identity. They and other contributors point out as well that the Russian identity of the Golden Age was perceived as malleable, accommodating, able to encompass every inhabitant of an increasingly diverse and far-reaching empire.[1] To imitate others and their culture was not a sign of weakness but of strength, of the ability to master and assimilate, to catch up and to make up for lost time, to exhaust all available possibilities.

Here I shall show how Pushkin, in *The Fountain of Bakhchisarai*, established diverse poetic and political lineages for his poetry and for his identity as a Russian poet, links of legitimation and of cultural affiliation. These lines of affiliation and filiation make way for the establishment of an identity that combines the cultural sophistication of both East and West as well as the brute strength of Eastern and Western manifestations of military might.

The Fountain of Bakhchisarai, written in the years 1821–23 and published in 1824, was Pushkin's next published narrative poem after *The Prisoner of the Caucasus.* In contrast to *Prisoner,* which was also an oriental/southern poem, Pushkin's third published poem was geographically situated not in the Caucasus but in the Crimea, and temporally situated not in the present but in the past. Pushkin set the narrative poem during the time of the Tatar khanate, which held sway over the Crimea from 1427 until the late fifteenth century. From the late fifteenth century until 1783, when the Crimea became part of the Russian empire, it was controlled by the Ottoman empire; Pushkin, however, does not refer to Turkish rule in his poem.

The Fountain of Bakhchisarai is even more clearly foregrounded and circumscribed by the notion of *narodnost'* than is *The Prisoner of the Caucasus. Narodnost',* a term coined by Prince Viazemsky, had been intended to glorify and promote literature on Russian life and history; instead, the discourse of *narodnost'* came to define the ability to write on any topic whatsoever—but in a Russian manner. This theoretical shift allowed Pushkin's *Prisoner,* which was mostly about a Caucasian people, the Circassians, as well as about the awesome mountains of the Caucasus, to be hailed as a great work of Russian literature.[2]

Beginning with its first edition, *The Fountain of Bakhchisarai* was introduced by an article by Viazemsky, "A Conversation between a Publisher and a Classicist from the Vyborg Side or Vasilievsky Island," and followed by a travel writer's description of the Bakhchisarai Palace, which will be discussed shortly. The telltale names of the participants in Viazemsky's introductory article indicated that it was intended to join the ongoing dialogue about Romanticism and classicism in the journals. The gist of the article is that the Publisher upholds the worth of the latest Romantic poetry (including *The Fountain of Bakhchisarai*), while the Classicist argues against his view.[3]

In his article Viazemsky proclaims the importance of the *narodnost'* of literature and indirectly asserts that *The Fountain of Bakchisarai,* as a representative of Romantic poetry in Russia, exhibits *narodnost'*. Viazemsky firmly dismisses the notion that Russian themes or names alone make a work Russian. He writes, in the guise of the Publisher:

> We still do not have a Russian cut in literature; perhaps there will never be one, because one does not exist; but, in any case, the newest poetry, the so-called romantic, is no less akin to us than the poetry of Lomonosov or Kheraskov, which you attempt to advance as classical. What is there in the "Petriada" and "Rossiada" that is national (*narodnyi*) except for the names?[4]

In other words, Viazemsky acknowledges the fact that *narodnost'* and the question of "nationality" are discursive constructs, susceptible to definition and change, and exerts his own powers to mold their definition. He exerts his energies toward further defining *narodnost'* in poetry: not only need the poetry not be about Russians, its subject matter need not be true in a historical sense:

> [Whether it is true or not], —this [Bakhchisarai] legend is worthy of poetry. . . . History must not be gullible; poetry the opposite. It often treasures that which the former repudiates with disdain, and our poet did very well, appropriating for poetry the Bakhchisarai legend and enriching it with plausible fancies; even better than that, he used both one and the other with excellent art. The local color is preserved in the storytelling with all possible freshness and brightness. There is an oriental stamp in the pictures, in the very feelings, in the style. In the opinion of judges, whose verdict can be considered final in our literature, the poet showed in his new work the sign of a talent that is maturing more and more.[5]

Viazemsky thus forcefully dismisses any possibility of "testing" the poet's merit through examining the "truth" or verisimilitude of the subject of his work. In fact, Viazemsky is far more concerned with the "plausible fancies" that display the imaginative skill of the poet, that enhance or "enrich" (as Viazemsky puts it) the story that the poet has inherited. The poet holds all the power, as it is up to him to put the "oriental stamp" on the work.

Viazemsky speaks of "local color" being *preserved* in Pushkin's storytelling, but in fact the poet engenders his own "local color," defines it from the beginning. This is the Orient as the Russian writer sees it and establishes it for his readers. It did not exist before he created it; as one critic noted:

> Bakhchisarai became famous only from 1824 on, when the poem about Maria and Zarema appeared in print. Until that time very few remembered that provincial little town of the Simferopol' district of the Tauride province, whose name did not yet sound with the captivating music of a Pushkinian title.[6]

Viazemsky's introductory article stressed the appropriateness of the Bakhchisarai legend for poetry, no matter its lack of historical "truth." Murav'-ev-Apostol's excerpt about the Bakhchisarai Palace, taken from "nonfictional" travel notes and appearing after the poem, emphasized on the contrary the prosaic and everyday qualities of the ruined palace. It underscored the fact that, in spite of the information given in Pushkin's poem, the memorial was a mausoleum and not a fountain, and was built not for the woman Pushkin designates, the Polish kidnap victim, but rather for a beloved Georgian beauty. Murav'ev notes, in a moment of criticism, that "in the second half of the eighteenth century it was not that easy for Tatars to kidnap Polish girls."[7] It is, however, part of historical record that the Crimean khan Mengli-Girei attacked Lithuania and Poland in the late fifteenth century, when Pushkin's poem is set. Karamzin's sources state that fifty thousand captives were taken when a number of cities were burned by the sons of Mengli-Girei.[8]

The major effect of Murav'ev-Apostol's version of the story, besides providing a strong contrast to the "plausible fancies" of the foregoing poem, is to remind the reader that Bakhchisarai is indeed a ruined remnant of a culture whose remains now belong solidly to the Russian Empire. Murav'ev-Apostol's whole manner of address—he speaks to the reader in the second person—is that of a guide who revels in exposing the already unveiled secrets of a former seat of power. Murav'ev-Apostol refers as well to the intervening years of Turkish rule, making note of the "iron doors, gaily decorated in Arabic taste, with a double-headed eagle over them, taking the place of the Ottoman moon" (146), thus alluding to the Turkish rule but also reminding the reader that the double-headed eagle now rules the Bakhchisarai roost. Murav'ev's description takes the reader from the world of the elegant, somewhat ethereal poem, to the quotidian, decaying palace itself, with its dirt, rust, and imperfections.

Nor does Murav'ev attempt to downplay the power of the Russian empire. When he describes the palace rooms that had been redecorated for the visit of Catherine II, he refers directly to the moment when the Russian empire acquired the Crimea. Murav'ev-Apostol's tone is also distinctly European, and orientalizing, when he mentions that the high tables installed for Catherine's use are especially valuable "for us baptized ones" (147). Finally, he refers repeatedly to the ruinous state of the palace, for good measure attributing this same "ruined" quality to any remaining historical structures in the Crimea. He declares that although the gardens might have been marvelous at one time, they now had a degenerate look "like all monuments in the Tauride" (148).

It was between these two framing pieces that *The Fountain of Bakhchisarai* first appeared; later, an excerpt from a letter by Pushkin was added, after the Murav'ev-Apostol quotation. In some ways, the original two frame pieces canceled each other: Murav'ev-Apostol spoke of the "real story" behind the monument, while Viazemsky declared historical truth to be unimportant in poetry. But each writer, in his own way, underscores a Pushkinian point: Viazemsky emphasizes that the poem is, above all else, a work of Russian Romantic literature, which is free to adopt any and every fancy it chooses, and Murav'ev-Apostol emphasizes the fact that the Crimea is a land firmly in Russian control, whose former foreignness, in spite of any poetic longings to the contrary, must now be relegated to the province of the imagination.[9] As the travel writer notes: "It did not bother me to rush along the towers and courts of the Tauride *Alhambra;* and the less visible the objects became, the more vivid became the play of my imagination, filling itself with the rainbow colors of Oriental poetry" (146).

With *The Fountain of Bakhchisarai,* Pushkin creates entirely new possibilities for Russian literature and for the topics Russian literature can address. For in *The Fountain of Bakhchisarai* itself, excluding the frame pieces, the only overt Russian presence in the poem is that of the figure of the traveler-poet, whose elegiacally oriented remarks appear toward the end of the piece. This is in direct contrast to *The Prisoner of the Caucasus,* in which a Russian is the main character of the narrative poem, and whose impressions remain always at the center of the piece. In *The Fountain of Bakhchisarai,* Pushkin appears to remove Russians from center stage, and indeed from the stage altogether. Moreover, that the plot of the later narrative poem revolves around the tension between two captive *women,* a Pole and a Georgian, rather than focusing on the ostensible main character, Khan Girei, is a dramatic shift of focus from the earlier tale. This "woman-oriented" specificity of *Bakhchisarai* has been analyzed from the point of view of gender issues,[10] but it is useful as well to analyze the shift in terms of politics.[11]

Before doing so, however, let us examine the plot of the narrative poem. It has been often noted that *The Fountain of Bakhchisarai* is heavily influenced by Byron's Turkish tales[12] (for example, the image of the oriental potentate smoking his chibouk). Thomas Moore's *Lalla Rookh* was also an important source for Pushkin's poem.[13]

As the poem, introduced by Saadi's epigraph, opens, the khan ruler Girei sits downcast; none of his aides can determine what bothers him. A list of his "accomplishments" is given: he has attacked Rus' and Poland, and has tangled with the Genoese. Now, however, he is "bored of martial glory" (132). The question is raised as to whether one of his wives has betrayed him; in a lengthy description of their lives, which are colorful, luxurious, and yet also monotonous, it is determined that Girei's watchful eunuch guard has not allowed any of the wives to stray.

> Его ревнивый взор и слух
> За всеми следует всечасно.
> Его стараньем заведен
> Порядок вечный.
>
> (132–33)

> (His jealous eye and ear
> Follow after everyone at all times.
> His efforts maintain
> The eternal order.)

As the narrator continues to describe the women of the harem, their baths, the way in which they drop earrings down to fish in a fountain, the answer to the question of why the khan is unhappy continues to be deferred. The women sing a song in praise of Zarema, "the star of love, the beauty of the harem" (134); the reader learns, however, that Girei no longer loves her. In spite of Zarema's beauty, it is revealed, Girei now feels unrequited love for a captured Polish princess, Maria. And so an answer is given as to the cause of his gloominess: though powerful, he is powerless over Maria's affections.

An encomium to young Maria now follows, a description of her happy, serene girlhood in Poland:

> Всё в ней пленяло: тихий нрав,
> Движенья стройные, живые
> И очи томно-голубые.
> Природы милые дары
> Она искусством украшала;
> Она домашние пиры
> Волшебной арфой оживляла
>
> (135–36)

> (Everything in her captivated: the quiet manner,
> The harmonious and lively movements,
> And the languorous blue eyes.
> The sweet gifts of nature
> She adorned with art;

She enlivened domestic feasts
With her enchanting harp)

Alas, however, the Tatars attacked Poland, killed her father, and took her prisoner, and she now pines in Girei's harem. The khan is afraid to disturb her and accedes to her every wish: she bathes alone and lives alone, and even the severe eunuch guard is forbidden to come near her. Her room is an island of impenetrability in an otherwise panoptically observed harem.[14]

Descriptions of the Crimean surroundings, given in a different register and from a different point of view, are interspersed with accounts of the quiet harem watched over by the guard. Then the Georgian girl, Zarema, creeps at night into the Polish princess's quarters, decorated with an image of the Virgin Mary. Zarema describes to the startled Polish girl the way in which she was herself kidnapped from her native Georgia, and her later happiness with the khan. But this happiness is now lost:

Мария! ты пред ним явилась . . .
Увы, с тех пор его душа
Преступной думой омрачилась!
. . . .
Оставь Гирея мне: он мой;
На мне горят его лобзанья,
Он клятвы страшные мне дал,
Давно все думы, все желанья
Гирей с моими сочетал;
Меня убьет его измена . . .
Я плачу, видишь, я колена
Теперь склоняю пред тобой,
Молю, винить тебе не смея,
Отдай мне радость и покой,
Отдай мне прежнего Гирея
(140–41)

(Maria, you appeared before him . . .
Alas, since that time his soul
Has clouded with criminal thoughts!
. . . .
Leave Girei to me: he is mine;
On me his kisses burn,
He gave me terrible oaths,
Long ago all his thoughts, all wishes
Girei combined with mine;
His treachery kills me . . .
I cry; you see, my knees
I now bend before you,
I pray, I dare not blame you,

Give me happiness and peace,
Give me my former Girei)

Zarema pleads with Maria to reject Girei, so that he will return to Zarema, and then threatens her: "I can use a dagger / I was born near the Caucasus" (141). Maria disappears and Girei, more bloodthirsty than ever, goes off on another round of attacks. The harem is forgotten, and it is revealed that Zarema was drowned by the harem guards on the same night that the Polish girl died. The khan then returns to the palace "Having ravaged by the fire of war / The countries near the Caucasus / And the peaceful villages of Russia" (143). Girei erects a marble fountain from which constantly fall tearlike drops and which the people name "the fountain of tears" (143). Thus the narrative returns full circle to Saadi's epigraph, "Many, just like myself, have visited this fountain; but some are already gone, others travel farther still" (131).

At this point the narrative abruptly shifts to focus on the narrator, who for the first time declares that he is from Russia, and who describes his visit to the now-ruined Bakhchisarai Palace. He visits the graveyard, "The final dwelling-place of sovereigns" (144), and remarks on how dismal the ruins are. Suddenly, he sees a ghost, and wonders if it was Maria or Zarema. This reverie leads the narrator-traveler to ponder upon his own lost love, for whom he longs in exile. The narrative ends with a paean to the beauty of the Crimean landscape, to which the narrator is drawn as if to a lover. The final stanza is addressed to the reader not from the grounds of the ruined palace, but from Russia, whence the narrator hopes to return to the "enchanted land" of the Crimea.

How should one read the poem politically? Many scholars have remarked that the poem is a study of contrasts between women of two utterly different cultures, one European and one "oriental." Although the Georgian Zarema is figured as the archetypically oriental woman, sexually experienced and sexually jealous, while Polish Maria is figured as the archetypically "pure" Western woman, virginal and averse to sexuality, the two are not necessarily polarized in the reader's sympathies. Indeed, I argue that their rival characterizations can be read as part of the two parallel filiations Pushkin draws in the poem, between Russians as Europeans and Russians as heirs to the Tatars. Maria, whose Catholic Christianity and Polish homeland ally her with Europe, contrasts with Zarema, whose passion for Girei, birth "near the Caucasus," and adoption of Islam align her with the Tatar Orient.[15] Zarema's murder of Maria further enhances her similarity to the sanguinary khans, but not before it has been established that Maria, though pious and pure, does not understand love (Zarema calls her a "cold beauty" [141]), while Zarema's recitations of her sorrow at losing Girei and pleas to Maria to reject him show that she is capable of real love, not merely blind passion. Even Zarema's heartfelt remembrance of her native, though nearly forgotten, Christian religion is a factor in the reader's sympathies. And while Maria is killed, the reader knows very well that she wanted to die and that her pure soul is assured of a place in heaven. Zarema's death by drowning, on the other hand, is horrifying retribution for her sin: "Kakaia b ni byla vina, uzhasno bylo nakazan'e!" (Whatever the guilt may have been, the punishment was terrible!) (143). The two women, though drawn as opposites, are nonetheless not mere caricatures; the reader's sympathies do not fully gravitate to Maria. This undecidability, as it were, between the two women, leaves the second male figure of the poem, the poet-traveler, with the possibility of aligning himself with either, or both women at the same time. For it is the poet-traveler who narrates the poem, as the reader discovers, and his own attraction to the two women is no less evident than the khan's. The harem women, too, are subject to his admiring and lascivious gaze:

Раскинув легкие власы,
Как идут пленницы младые
Купаться в жаркие часы,
И льются волны ключевые
На их волшебные красы
(133)

(Having let loose the light tresses,
Thus go the young captive maidens
To bathe in the hot hours,
And the waves of the spring pour themselves
On their enchanting beauties)

Nor is the poet's attraction to the Crimean landscape, figured always as the feminine "Tavrida" (rather than the masculine "Krym") any less politically or poetically significant.[16] The poet has his own harem, as it were, whose chief beauty/muse is the Tauride itself. This metaphorics of affiliation or attraction, given the politically marked nationalities of the figures and landscapes in question, can be seen as politically encoding the interpretation of the poem.

PUSHKIN'S POETIC ALIGNMENTS

To enact his construction of a poetic link between Russian and "oriental" poetry of great venerability and distinction, Pushkin starts his poem with an epigraph from the "Bustan" (garden, orchard) of the famous thirteenth-century Persian poet Saadi:

Многие, так же как и я, посещали
сей фонтан; но иных уже нет, другие
странствуют далече.
(131)[17]

(Many, just like myself, have visited this
fountain; but some are already gone,
others travel farther still.)

By using this epigraph, Pushkin self-consciously places his poem within a long and venerable line of "oriental" poetry, or to be precise, love poetry of the Arabic language or Arabic-inspired tradition.[18] In the double-voiced epigraph, spoken by both Saadi and Pushkin, the two poets become, for a moment, one and the same. Each writes, centuries apart, about the same subject: a much-visited fountain that outlasts its visitors, including the poets who sing of it. We know, historically speaking, that Saadi's fountain was not that of Bakhchisarai, but by itself the epigraph, with its dual attribution, implies that the speaker of the poem visits the same fountain that Saadi did. Moreover, the epigraph, metonymically linked to the title of the narrative poem, *The Fountain of Bakhchisarai* (indeed set on the page in such proximity to that title), could hardly be more strongly linked to the Bakhchisarai fountain.

Some scholars believe that Pushkin took the epigraph quotation from a French translation of Thomas Moore's *Lalla Rookh.*[19] In Moore's original text the quotation appears as follows:

> It was while they [Lalla Rookh and Feramorz, the poet] rested during the heat of noon near a fountain, on which some hand had rudely traced those well-known words from the Garden of Sadi—"Many, like me, have viewed this fountain, but they are gone, and their eyes are closed forever!"—that she took occasion, from the melancholy beauty of this passage, to dwell upon the charms of poetry in general.[20]

The French translation is somewhat different: the French translator substitutes "they are far away" ("ils sont loin") for "they are gone": "Plusieurs ont vu, comme moi, cette fontaine: mais ils sont loin et leurs yeux sont fermés à jamais" (Many have seen, like me, this fountain: but they are far away and their eyes are closed forever).[21]

Pushkin's own version of the epigraph underscores his emphasis on travel and on the poet as a traveler with a difference, one who not only visits the fountain but also, in some sense, immortalizes it. Pushkin alters the emphasis of the French version of the quotation: he writes "visited" rather than "viewed," and further underscores the notion of journeying by speaking of those who "travel still farther" rather than those whose eyes are "closed forever." While "traveling farther" retains the possibility of being a euphemism for death, Pushkin's quotation is less straightforward about that possibility.[22]

Importantly, the quotation from Saadi lends an aura of venerability to *The Fountain of Bakhchisarai.* Though the plot of "Bakhchisarai" takes place sometime in the fifteenth century, when the khanate ruled the Crimea, the

Saadi quotation draws the events back to an even earlier time. Therefore by implication, Russian literature can also be seen to have roots that go back far into the past. Pushkin avails himself of the opportunity to take his place, at least in terms of inspiration, at the contemporary end of a long genealogy of oriental poets.

If, however, Pushkin did not in fact take his quotation from Moore, but directly from Saadi's own "Bustan," a translation of which appeared in 1796, then this would only heighten the connections the Russian poet draws between himself and the Persian poet in *The Fountain of Bakhchisarai.*[23] The relevant stanza from Saadi, which appears toward the end of the first tale of "Bustan," entitled "A dervish becomes vizier and is vilified by his predecessor," is as follows:

> When territory can be taken by gentle means,
> Shed not blood by your strivings in conflict:
> By your manhood! All earth's rule
> Is not worth one blood-drop's trickling to earth!
> *I've heard that Jamshid of blessed constitution*
> *Wrote thus upon a stone above a wellspring:*
> *"At this spring many like us have drawn breath,*
> *Then gone on as they closed their eyes:*
> *We've taken the world in manliness and force,*
> *But carried it not with us into the tomb!"*[24]

Saadi's stanza is critical of war, which causes suffering for short-lived earthly might. Moore and Saadi both make an important point: power does not last beyond life, but poetry does. Moore's entire *Lalla Rookh* tells the story of an Indian princess who is to wed a rich and powerful prince; on the long journey to her wedding she is accompanied by the poet Feramorz, whose poetry charms her into falling in love with him. She is relieved to discover, at the end of her journey, that her betrothed was really Feramorz all along, a poet as well as a prince, and a man who wanted to gain his bride's love in the guise of a poor and humble poet.

A third important aspect of Pushkin's version of the Saadi quotation is its own emphasis on the passage of time: Saadi places himself (in Pushkin's version) as a visitor who comes after many other visitors, visitors who are long dead. Thus he emphasizes that the fountain itself remains, while its visitors pass away. This, of course, is also Pushkin's point in the poem: the fountain, the monument to Maria, remains, whereas the khan and his retinue have passed on, and the poet himself is also destined to pass on even as the fountain remains. More important, however, the fountain stands as a substitute for the poetic work: in the end, not the fountain but the poem about the fountain will persevere, and perhaps, even the name of the poet. The true affiliation between the Russian poet and the Persian poet consists in their joint appreciation of the passage of time and the strength of poetry (not military might) as a bulwark against the onslaught of change. And Saadi's poetry, already six hundred years old by Pushkin's era, was proof that poetry could withstand time.

Not insignificant in light of Pushkin's devising of this poetic lineage with Saadi is the fact that *Bakhchisarai* follows an old formula of Arabic poetry, the *qaasida,* which is told from the point of view of a poet on a journey who stops at deserted places, which remind him of love and the sorrow of parting, and include many descriptions of nature, of the poet riding on his horse or camel, and of gallantry.[25] Pushkin clearly utilizes the notion of stopping at ruins, the contemplation of which brings about remembrances of a past passion (in this case, both his own and that of Girei and Zarema). Though they appear briefly, the "natural descriptions" are important and make up some of the most lyrical parts of the poem, while the poem ends with an image of the poet riding his "accustomed horse." Whatever differences exist between Pushkin's poem and the ancient pre-Islamic Arabic model, whatever filters (Byronic or otherwise) the model may have been passed through, Pushkin follows an example that puts him squarely in the footsteps of the great poets of the Arabic tradition. In this poetic form, the concatenation of motifs of travel, poetry, and, by implication, warfare, reinforce the links that Pushkin makes throughout the poem, links that strengthen the bond between the Russian poet and his illustrious Persian forebear, and between Russian and oriental poetry. Saadi spent many years traveling, in a kind of exile, which may have been another reason that Pushkin chose to create the link with his work—to emphasize their common status as exiles.[26]

By demonstrating his affinity to Saadi, Pushkin attempts to bridge an otherwise unbridgeable distance. By means of the epigraph, Pushkin declares that he, a Russian poet, will tell a tale that in some sense would properly have been told by an "oriental" poet such as Saadi. The khan's story is told by a Russian poet, in the Russian language, and Pushkin, a Russian poet, puts himself in the position of being worthy to follow in Saadi's footsteps.[27]

PUSHKIN'S GEOGRAPHIC ALIGNMENTS

As Iurii Lotman has pointed out, in *The Fountain of Bakhchisarai* Pushkin establishes the three "corners of the world" as the Crimea/Caucasus (south), Poland (west), and Russia (north).[28] This geographic alignment, along with that of Russia and the Caucasus in *The Prisoner of the Caucasus,* assured the Crimea/Caucasus region its place as Russia's Orient. Historically and geographically, there has been a strong, continuous connection between Russia and her Orient.[29] Moreover, Russians and "orientals" have historically interacted and have consistently been within reach of each other. Thus the

Russian notion of the Orient has always differed most profoundly from the European notion of the "Orient." While European countries were separated by large bodies of water and great distances from their Orient and their colonies, Russia was close by, contiguous with her Orient, sometimes in fact indistinguishable from it.

There exists a long genealogy of the attempts to differentiate "Europe" from "Asia"; many different borders have been put forward and adopted or rejected at different times. Geographically speaking, "Europe" and "Asia" are of course not separate; only history and convention have conferred their separate status upon them, and even then they have not been continuously considered separate entities. The fragility and ambiguity of this differentiation between Asia and Europe was emphasized by Russian writers; the artificial constructedness of the border has long been important to them.[30]

The flexibility of Russia's borders, her ability to be a nation either close to or far away from the "Orient," is of great poetic advantage. This flexibility was demonstrated by Pushkin, as he altered Russia's proximity to the Caucasus/Crimea from one poem to the next. In *The Prisoner of the Caucasus,* Russia seemed to be a distant place, removed from the scene of action. To the eponymous Russian captive, his native land seemed far away, metonymized by a gloomy path leading into the distance. In *The Prisoner of the Caucasus* Russia also seemed to offer a potential safe haven to both the Russian and his Circassian lover. Although the Circassian girl did not choose to run away with the Russian captive, the possibility of their setting up household in faraway Russia was always implied. In the poem, danger existed only in the Caucasus. Russia itself was always removed, safe from conflict, indeed, guaranteed eventual hegemony over the Caucasus.

In *The Fountain of Bakhchisarai,* on the other hand, Pushkin uses the complex time frames in the narrative poem to show a Russia both vulnerable to the Tatars (in the time of the khanate) and at the same time, a present-day conqueror of the Crimea. Because of the way in which the narrator moves back and forth in this many-faceted time frame, for a long stretch of the narrative poem, it is as if Russia were holding both positions at once: that of conqueror and that of country in danger of being conquered.[31] Certainly Pushkin's contemporary reader would be well informed as to the status of Russia. Why, then, does Pushkin emphasize Russia's past (though "present," in terms of much of the poem) vulnerability to the Tatar khanate?

In much of the poem, Russia is figured entirely differently from the way it was in *The Prisoner of the Caucasus.* Russia is seen as vulnerable to the Tatars, not a refuge but a land with decidedly permeable borders. Indeed, *The Fountain of Bakhchisarai* reminds the reader that Girei actually did attack Russia:

Что движет гордою душою?
Какою мыслью занят он?
На Русь ли вновь идет войною,
Несет ли Польше свой закон
(143; emphasis added)

(What moves the proud soul?
With what thought is he occupied?
Does he attack Rus' anew with war,
Does he bring Poland his law)

Some commentators have said that Pushkin, in these lines, merely conflates various episodes in history, referring to the time when the khans were embattled with the Genoese and a later time when one khan reached into Russia as far as Tula.[32] But the threat to Russia was evident. As one source notes:

> Never had the Lithuanian state suffered such horrible blows as from Mengli Girei, in whose day the Crimean Horde received that robber character which for three hundred years made it famous. It tormented specially Russian regions connected with Poland, by seizing great numbers of captives, who, forced into slavery, were taken as living wares to the markets of the Osmanli.[33]

Other, less melodramatically inclined historians also attest to the frequent slave raids that were mounted into Russia and Poland; in fact, the Muscovite government had to spend heavily in order to ransom victims.[34] Pushkin emphasizes what a threat the Tatars posed to both Russia and Western countries. Had matters gone differently, they might have ruled the known world. For the purposes of indicating how much at risk the West might have been (and thus, in the time frame of the poem itself, might still be), it is not surprising that Pushkin takes special care to emphasize over and over how treacherous and sanguinary the khan is:

Дворец угрюмый опустел;
Его Гирей опять оставил;
С толпой татар в чужой предел
Он злой набег опять направил;
Он снова в бурях боевых
Несется мрачный, кровожадный . . .
(142)

(The dismal palace is empty;
Girei has left it again;
With a crowd of Tatars to a foreign land
He has once again sent a wicked raid;
Once again into battle storms
He rushes, gloomy, bloodthirsty . . .)

In the poem, the most detailed description of a Tatar attack is that of the raid on Poland which results in Maria's capture and her father's death. The attack is portrayed as a vicious, even animalistic event, a terrible incursion into an idyllically innocent Arcadia. The description establishes, for the purposes of the poem, a very strong dividing line between the peaceful, productive West and the warlike, ruinous Orient. Poland is unwary, undeserving; the Tatars merciless:

. . . Тьмы татар
На Польшу хлынули рекою:
Не столь ужасной быстротою
По жатве стелется пожар.
Обезображенной войною,
Цветущий край осиротел;
Исчезли мирные забавы;
Уныли села и дубравы,
И пышный замок опустел.
(136)

(. . . Hosts of Tatars
Gushed in a river to Poland:
Not even with such terrible swiftness
Does a fire spread along the harvest.
Disfigured by war,
The blossoming land was orphaned;
The peaceful amusements disappeared;
The villages and groves are despondent,
And the splendid castle is empty.)

A moral judgment is clearly indicated in the above lines; the Tatar attack is said to be worse than a fire destroying a harvest, it "disfigures" and "orphans" the land. Just as Girei takes captive an innocent, virginal girl, Maria, so the Tatars rape the virginal Polish countryside, disfiguring it and destroying its innocence. A superior land has been ruined, destroyed by an "uncivilized" force. There can be no question that the Tatar threat to the Polish West is also a threat to Russia, and that Russia is essentially in the same relation to the Tatars as is Poland. Pushkin's lines,

Опустошив огнем войны
Кавказу близкие страны
И села мирные России
В Тавриду возвратится хан
(143; emphasis added)

(Having ravaged by the fire of war
The countries near the Caucasus

> *And the peaceful villages of Russia,*
> The khan returned to the Tauride)

are very similar to the lines about Poland. In particular, the words *mirnye* (peaceful) and *sela* (villages) are repeated, which emphasizes the tranquillity and the peaceful pastoral quality of the lands under attack by the Tatars. Within the poetically established world of the first part of the poem, Russia *is* vulnerable—as those who had read their Karamzin knew Russia once had been. The evocation of Russia's wholly pastoral past thus obscures her recent imperial might and proffers a legitimate reason for Russia to be in control of the south.

Another way in which Russia is accorded the status of "subject" and "civilized nation" as against the objectified and "uncivilized" status of the Crimean Orient is by means of the feminized and sexualized descriptions of the Tauride landscape. That the Orient does not necessarily have to be objectified as "feminine" is abundantly clear from *The Prisoner of the Caucasus,* in which the landscape takes on distinctly "masculine" attributes, but the feminization of the Crimea serves a distinct purpose: it strengthens the dominance of the masculine Russian narrative presence and identifies the Crimea as a place that has already been "conquered," in both the political and sexual meanings of the term.

To read *The Fountain of Bakhchisarai* after *The Prisoner of the Caucasus* is to be presented with a continuing narrative of Russian conquest in the Caucasus and the Crimea. While *Prisoner* places events in the present and proffers a rather formidable landscape and a challenging foe, all of which requires a ringing call to arms in its epilogue, *Bakhchisarai* is a completely different narrative poem in terms of immediate Russian military concerns. While the Tatars are especially bloodthirsty, the action takes place in the distant past and the Tatars' power mainly threatens Poland. In part for that reason, the landscape of *Bakhchisarai* is a completely different one from that of *Prisoner:* warm and welcoming, rather than menacing and overwhelming.

It is especially interesting that although Khan Girei takes a far more hostile and aggressive stance toward Russia than do Pushkin's Circassians of the earlier narrative poem, the epilogue of the earlier narrative poem displays an uncompromisingly violent attitude toward the Caucasian peoples, while the ending of *Bakhchisarai* is emphatically nonmilitary. The conquest it hints at is sexual, not martial. The rocky, "manly" landscape that so closely mirrored both captive and Circassians in the earlier poem has no trace in *Bakhchisarai:* in accordance with the tradition of Pushkin's Crimean poetry, the Tauride landscape carries connotations of love, and is characterized as "feminine," yielding.[35] The harsh, snowy Caucasian crags harbored free, if doomed people. Crimea's warmth is deceptive: it promises luxury and comfort, but in reality harbors only captives. Only the narrator is free to come and go as he chooses, a denizen, we recall, of the harsh northern climate.

THE NARRATED LANDSCAPE

It is most important, in terms of defining the lines of affiliation drawn among Europe, the Crimea, and Russia in the poem, to determine where the narrating poet-traveler figure locates himself in the poem. How does the narrator situate himself vis-à-vis the characters, the landscape, and the overall structure of the narrative poem? As the only overtly Russian presence in the poem, his stances must be examined.

In *Bakhchisarai,* it is significant that descriptions of the landscape appear only when the narrator, who is presumably Russian and male (and, we discover, a poet), chooses to describe it. Setting aside the obvious facts that they are written in the Russian language and in Russian metrical style, the lines: "Kak sladko l'iutsia ikh chasy / dlia obozhatelei Proroka!" (How sweetly do their hours flow / For the adorers of the Prophet!) (138) reveal most strikingly the outsider's or European's viewpoint: the writer is himself clearly not an "adorer of the Prophet."

It is indeed in the first landscape description of the poem that we find the first overt mention of the narrator's "I":

Настала ночь; покрылась тенью
Тавриды сладостной поля;
Вдали, под тихой лавров сенью
Я слышу пенье соловья

(137)

(Night fell; with shadow were covered
The fields of the delightful Tauride;
In the distance, under the quiet canopy of laurels
I hear the singing of the nightingale)

It is notable that the narrator here speaks in the present tense, recalling himself in the present rather than in the distant past. From the location of this passage in the poem (between the description of Maria in her quarters in the harem and the eunuch's patrolling of the palace) the passage *should* be contemporaneous with the distant past. The narrator's interpolation of his own observations, however, creates a doubling effect, both bringing himself into the past, into the plot of the poem, and bringing the action of the poem into the "present," as it were.

The second overt mention of the narrating "I" comes in the last section of the poem, which is given over explicitly to the traveler-poet's point of view:

Покинув север наконец,
Пиры надолго забывая,
Я посетил Бахчисарая
В забвеньи дремлющий дворец.
(143–44)

(Having left the north at last,
Forgetting for a long time the feasts,
I visited the dozing, forgotten,
Palace of Bakhchisarai.)

By using the word "north,"[36] the narrator for the first time explicitly reveals that he is from Russia. In these lines, the narrator, far from being involved, seems to view the Tauride only well after the events of the story. A transition between the two levels of the poem takes place. The narrator shifts from the generally present-tense narration of the Maria-Zarema story, in which he has a nearly omniscient view of the action and at moments takes part in the experience of the landscape, to a rather different narrative viewpoint: that of a Russian traveler visiting Bakhchisarai, narrating for the most part in the past tense, and viewing the palace as it stands in ruins hundreds of years after the story of Maria and Zarema. In fact, this narrative shift occurs even earlier, during the description of the marble fountain Girei erected to Maria:

В Тавриду возвратился хан
И в память горестной Марии
Воздвигнул мраморный фонтан,
В углу дворца уединенный.
Над ним крестом осенена
Магометанская луна
(Символ конечно дерзновенный,
Незнанья жалкая вина).
Есть надпись: едкими годами
Еще не сгладилась она.
За чуждыми ее чертами
Журчит во мраморе вода
И каплет хладными слезами,
Не умолкая никогда,
Так плачет мать во дни печали
О сыне, падшем на войне.
Младые девы в той стране
Преданье старины узнали,
И мрачный памятник оне
Фонтаном слез именовали.
(143)

(The khan returned to the Tauride
And in memory of mournful Maria

Erected a marble fountain,
By itself in the corner of the palace.
Overshadowing it as a cross
Was the Mohammedan moon
[A daring symbol, of course,
The unfortunate fault of ignorance].
There is an inscription: with the caustic years
It has not yet been smoothed away.
Behind its foreign lines
The water babbles in the marble
And drops in cold tears,
Never ever falling silent.
Thus a mother weeps in days of sorrow
Over her son, fallen in war.
Young maidens in that land
Found out about the legends of old,
And they named the gloomy monument
"The fountain of tears.")

In the quotation above, rather than being a participating figure in the narration, the narrator stands away from what he speaks about. This is in direct contrast to the earlier, "loving" description of the nightingale's song and the moon's radiance, in which the narrator viewed events from close at hand, and from a more sympathetic point of view. But here, the narrator distances himself, speaking of the "fault of ignorance" of using an Islamic emblem to commemorate the Christian Maria, and referring to the "foreign lines" of the inscription. The mention of the "caustic years" and "legends of old" also point to the fact that the narrator now stands many years distant from his earlier subject, as well. The later time and emotionally removed perspective of the narrator are made quite clear in the stanza.

The narrator then launches into a description of the long-empty palace:

Я посетил Бахчисарая
В забвеньи дремлющий дворец.
Среди безмолвных переходов
Бродил я там, где, бич народов,
Татарин буйный пировал
И после ужасов набега
В роскошной лени утопал.
(144)

(I visited the dozing, forgotten,
Palace of Bakhchisarai.
Among the wordless passages
I wandered to where that scourge of peoples,
The violent Tatar, feasted

And after the horrors of the raid
Wallowed in luxurious ease.)

Perhaps the most striking aspect of the quotation above is its revelation that, among the ruins, the Russian poet-traveler is in control. He "wanders" where the "scourge of peoples" once reigned. In the guise of tourist-invader, he reveals that he has all along been the mouthpiece of the "oriental tale," and that he has bestowed life on what is in actuality a dead palace. He has provided the voice for what are now revealed to be "wordless passages." Khan Girei now no longer has a name, but has become, from the narrator's now-distant perspective, "that scourge of peoples, the violent Tatar." Even so, the narrator refrains from destroying the magic completely; he allows some of the former glory of the palace to remain:

Еще поныне дышит нега
В пустых покоях и садах;
Играют волны, рдеют розы,
И вьются виноградны лозы,
И злато блещет на стенах.
(144)

(Even now the sweet bliss breathes
In the empty rooms and gardens;
The waters play, the roses glow,
And the grapevines climb,
And gold glitters on the walls.)

But such life as still remains in the palace relies greatly on the imagination of the narrator, and the narration quickly returns to the subject of the decrepitude and deadness of the palace:

Я видел ветхие решетки,
За коими, в своей весне,
Янтарны разбирая четки,
Вздыхали жены в тишине.
Я видел ханское кладбище,
Владык последнее жилище.
Сии надгробные столбы,
Венчанны мраморной чалмою,
Казалось мне, завет судьбы
Гласили внятною молвою.
(144)

(I saw the tumbledown gratings,
Behind which, in their spring,
Counting amber beads,
The wives sighed in quiet.
I saw the khans' graveyard,

The final dwelling place of sovereigns.
These grave pillars,
Crowned with marble turbans,
It seemed to me, spoke a legacy
Of fate with a distinct prayer.)

Fittingly, the narrator ends his description with a Saadi-like description of the graveyard, "the final dwelling place of sovereigns." The line between earthly power and poetic power is being drawn; without the poem itself, the graveyard would not even "exist." The narrator completes the thought, as it were, by remarking that everything is now completely different from what it was during the pinnacle of the khanate rule:

Где скрылись ханы? Где гарем?
Кругом все тихо, все уныло,
Все изменилось . . .

(144)

(Where were the khans hiding? Where is the harem?
All around everything is quiet, everything is dismal,
Everything has changed . . .)

The implication, not difficult to understand, is that while the power of the khans is long gone, that of Russia has come into its own. Pushkin's introduction of the traveler-poet at the end of his poem seems at first to emphasize the great distance between the time of Khan Girei and the time of the Russian poet's visit to his now-ruined palace. The vast power of the khan seems also to have been far superior to the meager power of the poet. But it soon becomes clear that the mighty khan owes his memorialization to the poet, who now alone has the power to evoke him. As Saadi's lines intimate, power and glory cannot pass with one into the grave, but poetry can survive. Because of the geographical proximity and involvement in history of Tatars with Russians, the fact that only ruins and graveyards remain of the former "scourge of peoples" has a significance for the Russian reader that, for example, Byron's mentions of turbaned headstones did not have for the British reader:

A turban carved in coarsest stone,
A pillar with rank weeds o'ergrown,
Whereon can now be scarcely read
The Koran verse that mourns the dead,
Point out the spot where Hassan fell
A victim in that lonely dell.[37]

For Byron, the headstone and almost illegible inscription indicate the way in which the story barely has been rescued from oblivion; as the tale ends, this is emphasized again:

He pass'd—nor of his name and race
Hath left a token or a trace,
Save what the father must not say
Who shrived him on his dying day:
This broken tale was all we knew
Of her he loved, or him he slew.[38]

The irrevocable "pastness" of Byron's tale, the missing information, has poetic but not necessarily political importance for Byron. The tale does not necessarily impinge on the daily life of the reader; in fact, its strength may well lie in the fact that it does not. The poet relies on his powers as interpreter and teller of exotic and otherwise "lost" or incomprehensible stories. He holds sway with his privileged knowledge and expertise.

Pushkin, on the other hand, utilizes these same tropes of the barely readable inscription, the old graveyard with headstones, missing information and "pastness," but these tropes have become symbols for an entire past culture, an extinguished threat. The fact that the khanate existed and was powerful is of direct importance and relevance to the Russian reader; the narrator, a Russian poet, visits the ruined palace and tells his tale precisely *because* the khanate no longer exists. As Somov had hinted, the poet has become the surrogate conqueror, the ruler of the empire of the imagination.[39] Pushkin's presence, his poem, establishes to the Russian reader the supremacy of the Russian state. If Pushkin's *Prisoner of the Caucasus* had assured the reader of Russia's future victory in the Caucasus, his *Fountain of Bakhchisarai* emphasized Russia's already realized conquest of the Crimea.

At this point in the poem, the narrator turns to his own thoughts about his far-off love, which are suddenly interrupted by the appearance of a ghost, which in turn entails a return to the story that has already been told. Thus a sudden conflation occurs, of the narrator's now-distanced time frame with the immediacy of the earlier Maria-Zarema story.

Given the common contemporary interpretation that the lyrical "I" of a poem could be read as the "I" of the author of a text, and that Pushkin apparently did indeed wish the poem to be read as autobiographical (if only in order to garner more readers)[40] the contemporary reader could interpret the narrator's sudden vision of the flying shadow as a conflation of "art" and "life": the narrator (that is, the poet Pushkin) encounters in "real life" a character he has created:

И по дворцу летучей тенью
Мелькала дева предо мной!
. . . .
Чью тень, о други, видел я?
Скажите мне: чей образ нежный

Тогда преследовал меня,
Неотразимый, неизбежный?
Марии ль чистая душа
Являлась мне, или Зарема
Носилась, ревностью дыша,
Средь опустелого гарема?

(144)

(And along the palace with a flying shadow
Flashed a maiden before me!
. . . .
Whose shade, oh friends, did I see?
Tell me: whose tender image
Then followed me,
Irresistible, inescapable?
Was it the pure soul of Maria
That appeared to me, or did Zarema
Rush about, breathing with jealousy,
Amid the empty harem?)

At this moment of seeing the ghost, then, the narrative levels combine: past and present, history and fiction, art and life. The past of the Maria-Zarema story and the present of the "contemporary" narration combine; the fictional Zarema and Maria "come to life" as "truthful" "autobiographical" narration, and "art" in the guise of the poet's characters meets Pushkin, the poet, in "life." The effective insertion of the Russian poet into the place formerly occupied by Khan Girei (that is, the ruler of the Tauride, and the pivotal male figure for Maria and Zarema) establishes the Russian poet as a successor to the khan. It is the Russian poet, not an heir of the Tatars, who is privileged to see the ghost. In this way the reader of Pushkin's poem becomes the appropriate interpreter of the story of Maria and Zarema, of the pathos of murderer and murdered.

The vision of the mysterious shade leads immediately to the narrator's own, similar vision, of a living woman for whom he "longs in exile":

Я помню столь же милый взгляд
И красоту еще земную,
Все думы сердца к ней летят,
Об ней в изгнании тоскую . . .

(145)

(I remember such a sweet glance
And beauty still earthly,
All the thoughts of my heart fly to her,
For her I long in exile . . .)

The narrator thus places himself in the role of Girei, who longed for Maria, although she would not have him. The narrator's longing is similarly unrequited:

> Безумец! полно! перестань,
> Не оживляй тоски напрасной,
> Мятежным снам любви несчастной
> Заплачена тобою дань—
> Опомнись; долго ль, узник томный,
> Тебе оковы лобызать
> И в свете лирою нескромной
> Свое безумство разглашать?
>
> (145)

> (Madman! enough! Stop it,
> Do not revive longing in vain,
> You have paid your tribute
> To troubled dreams of unhappy love—
> Come to your senses; will it be for long, languorous prisoner,
> That you will kiss your fetters
> And in the world with immodest lyre
> Trumpet your madness?)

The poet's "lyre," his poem, is a counterpart to Girei's "fountain of tears"—a monument erected to unrequited love. The poet declares himself to be a prisoner who kisses his fetters, glad to be captive to his love. Here again is an implied comparison to Girei, who loved two captives, Zarema and Maria, but who was himself a captive to unrequited love. Pushkin's use of the ghost and of references to the narrator's own "lost love" construct for *The Fountain of Bakhchisarai* a quality of immediacy and an implication of continuation. Pushkin was quite successful in this regard; the references to the narrator's longed-for love proved so tantalizing to Russian readers and critics of the poem that they regarded her as the addressee of the poem and as a real woman, and have argued in endless detail about who that woman actually was.[41] The narrator of the poem thus in a very real way "succeeds" Girei to the position of the scorned lover; the speaker succeeds Girei both in luckless love and in a position of power over what he surveys (and narrates).

The final move the narrator makes is to shift the reader's attention away from the two stories; that is, the story of the khan and his two captives, and the story of the traveler-poet's own "lost love," to the viewpoint of a narrator who, unlike the earlier one, is now away from the Tauride, presumably in Russia, and is longing to return. In this final, crowning stanza of the narrative poem, the poet's true love is revealed to be not his far-away mistress, but the Tauride itself. The final stanza seems to stand by itself, as the poet emphasizes the revivifying and Elysian aspects of the Tauride scenery, and enters a new level of narration, from a new vantage point distant from the Tauride. The landscape of this stanza is, as some critics have also pointed out, the ultimate seductress of the story,[42] but it is a different kind of seductress than the mournful, unwilling Maria or the vengeful Zarema: it is both willing and also under the control of the traveler-poet, an ideal combination of Maria and Zarema:

> Поклонник муз, поклонник мира,
> Забыв и славу и любовь,
> О, скоро вас увижу вновь,
> Брега веселые Салгира!
> Приду на склон примирских гор,
> Воспоминаний тайных полный,
> И вновь таврические волны
> Обрадуют мой жадный взор.
> Волшебный край, очей отрада!
> Все живо там: холмы, леса,
> Янтарь и яхонт винограда,
> Долин приютная краса,
> И струй и тополей прохлада—
> Все чувство путника манит,
> Когда, в час утра безмятежный,
> В горах, дорогою прибрежной,
> Привычный конь его бежит
> И зеленеющая влага
> Пред ним и блещет, и шумит
> Вокруг утесов Аю-дага
>
> (145)

> (Worshiper of the muses, worshiper of the world,
> Having forgotten both glory and love,
> O, soon I will see you anew,
> Merry banks of Salgir!
> I will come to the slope of the seaside mountains,
> Full of secret memories,
> And anew the Tauride waves
> Will gladden my greedy gaze.
> Enchanted land, a comfort to the eyes!
> Everything is alive there: hills, woods,
> The amber and ruby of grapes,
> The sheltering beauty of the valleys,
> And the cool of streams and poplars—
> All feeling beckons to the traveler,
> When, in the serene hour of morning,
> In the mountains, along a coastal road,
> His accustomed horse rushes

And the greening moisture
Glitters and murmurs before him
Around the crags of Aiu-dag)

The landscape's charms are the only ones that do not fade, the poet-traveler's fascination with them is the only one that does not diminish. This is the love story that has actually given rise to the others.

Yet at the same time, the balance of power has not altered. The landscape is there for the pleasure of the male traveler, to "gladden [his] greedy gaze," to shelter him, cool him, beckon to him. He holds the landscape as securely in his power as the khan held Zarema or Maria; a female prisoner, the Crimean Tauride held captive to a Russian poet. The poet, as conqueror, secure in his dominance, is both seduced and renewed by the feminized landscape, in control of it and yet dependent upon it for inspiration. Interestingly, the poet's relationship to the landscape is left as something that will continue into the future, even as the poem itself trails off into an ellipsis. Russia's relationship to the Crimea is also in an ongoing state, Pushkin seems to be declaring. Its future has yet to be decided. Yet one might also interpret this stance as an illusion of eternal recurrence, as the many returns, repeats, revisits, recyclings, all lead inexorably to one conclusion: the poet has become sovereign of all he surveys. Powerful as the khanate once was, now only art can create the illusion of the khans' former power. As real as that power was, it is now possible only in poetry—indeed, in the poetry of the conquerors. Much as there is an emphasis on returns—as the travelers visit the fountain and the palace of Bakhchisarai, Girei returns to the harem and then to war, the ghost of Maria or Zarema returns to the palace, and the poet-lover to the Crimea—these returns are staged by the conquering poet, who makes of them his poetry. Indeed, in the final stanza the poet reveals that he does not even have to be in Crimea in order to evoke it.

While *Prisoner* strongly associated Russians with Europeans and northerners, making Russia a supposedly "civilized" intruder into "uncivilized" space, in *Bakhchisarai* Russians are allied with Poles as the Tatars' potential victims. At the same time, however, the poem also aligns the Russians with the Tatars, as well as with the whole Arabic-oriental strain of poets and warriors, presenting the Russians as the inevitable and proper heirs of the Tatars in both military might and poetry. While the Tatars were speakers of a Turkic language, whereas Saadi represents Arabia and Persia, their common link is the Islamic religion, the use of the Arabic script, and of course the common proximity to the Crimea. Beginning with the epigraph and ending with the poet's rejuvenation by the landscape of the Crimea, Pushkin indicates that Russians are worthy enough poets to take on the mantle of Saadi, and that they are the rightful military successors to the khans. Russians, the poem indicates, are European, but have absorbed the strength and poetic prowess of the Orient—putting them in an enviable position of superiority over both East and West. And the Crimean landscape, with all of its powers and delights, now exists only for the purposes of Russian poetry.

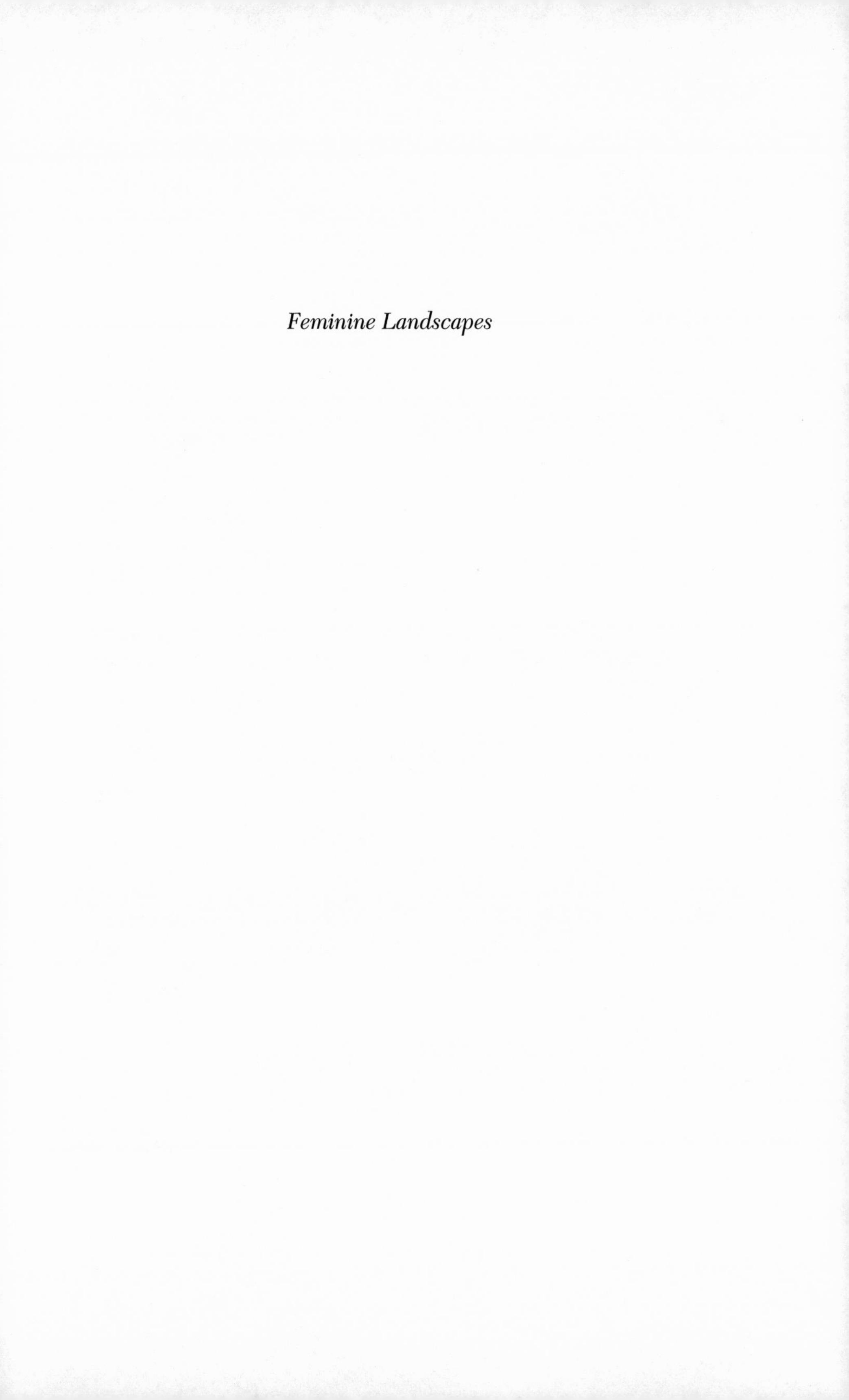

Feminine Landscapes

Stephanie Sandler and Judith Vowles

Beginning to Be a Poet: Baratynsky and Pavlova

ONE MYTH of Russia's Golden Age is that it was itself a beginning, the point of origin for all that is great in modern literature. The myth endures in part because of Pushkin's rapid emergence as Russia's national poet, but even before the culture was shaped so dramatically by the Pushkin myth, talented poets found their own ways to test their identities as poets. Our concern is to study this sense of poetic debut, particularly the qualities of speech and self required by a poet's earliest efforts. It is not a straightforward matter, of course, to establish the precise moment or way in which someone grows from writing poems to being a poet, nor is it uniformly true that poets confer this status on themselves. In the rituals of poetic initiation we know best, poets are designated by their predecessors, and tales about these rituals often take on the cultural status of myth, as in Pushkin's recitation of "Remembrance in Tsarskoe Selo" (Vospominanie v Tsarskom Sele," 1814) before the aging Gavriel Derzhavin.[1] Equally well known is the portrait inscription from Vasily Zhukovsky on the occasion of Pushkin's having completed *Ruslan and Liudmila* (*Ruslan i Liudmila*) ("To the conqueror-student from the conquered teacher on that solemn day when he finished his poem," 1820).[2] These examples show us how poets created rituals of debut among themselves, often following on the completion of a "major" poem.[3]

Such self-consciously important poems ought not to push less formal and occasional poetry from view. Informal, fledgling, often tentative verse can be penned before any publicly acknowledged status as poet has stabilized; it also lets poets experiment with personal mythologies for relationships with their audiences. For many poets, rather than a ritual of momentous emergence into fame, there was a slowly graded ascent from juvenile experimentation, like the composition of madrigals for a salon hostess or verse epistles for friends, to publication in almanacs edited by those same friends.[4]

We treat three genres in which these early experiments most often appeared—the familiar epistle (*druzheskoe poslanie*), the album inscription, and the self-reflective short poem about poetry itself—in the work of two poets, Evgeny Baratynsky (1800–1844) and Karolina Pavlova (1807–93). While they are divided by many differences, Pavlova and Baratynsky share an innovative use of poetic genres, a distinctive flair for unusual verbal formulations and psychological portraiture, and, most important, an affinity for a certain kind of meditative poetry and thus for the pose of poet as thinker. Both viewed this pose as central to their project as poets. Pavlova imagined herself as a poet according to the model Baratynsky first created: lyrics compare tender emotions with powerful thoughts, and poetry is measured by the quality of its thinking. In this sense, they are both poets of thought.

Because Pavlova was one of Russia's first serious women poets, her career also offers material for asking how gendered differences shaped poetic beginnings. In this period, changing concepts of gender, identity, and desire circulated in ways that shaped cultural processes and the social organization of polite relations. This social context exerted visible pressure on the poetic texts we examine. We suggest that poetic identity was typically achieved in poems that established relationships with other poets, relationships themselves marked by assumptions about gender differences. Baratynsky's earliest poems projected strikingly different identities for women and men in ways that were typical of the period; such views affected Pavlova's sensibilities and ambitions when she set about becoming a poet in the late 1830s.

Both Pavlova and Baratynsky wrote self-defining lyrics that were shaped by forms of address to others (and to each other, as we shall see); these turns to important others existed in some tension with the Romantic predisposition, particularly strong in their work, to value solitude. In the imagery and intonation of isolation Baratynsky and Pavlova comment on the value and the cost of solitude for any poet. Solitude seemed the site of thought itself, but increasingly it characterized the poets' experience in society and seemed imposed rather than chosen. Baratynsky and Pavlova wrote their mature work at a time when the cultural position of the poet was waning, and some measure of loneliness came to define their later work. In their beginnings, however, they think about poetic identity in terms of those around them. Baratynsky found the means of optimistic connection and of testing his similarity to poet-friends, but Pavlova quickly reached toward others who were like her in their utter difference from their surrounding world. Her greater difficulties connecting to others appears in her more hesitant use of two forms, the familiar epistle and the album poem, that were important to Baratynsky and other (male) poets.

SELF-DEFINITION IN THE FAMILIAR EPISTLE

The familiar epistle played an important role in the early work of Pushkin, Baratynsky, Delvig, Iazykov, among others.[5] A classic example of the form by

Baratynsky is "To Krenitsyn" ("K Krenitsynu," 1819), which ends in a self-conscious celebration of friendship: "O gentle friendship! Be thou true! / Let all else become a dream!" ("O druzhba nezhnaia! ostan'sia neizmennoi! / Pust' budet prochee mechtoi!")[6] But Baratynsky's early poetic epistles betrayed some nervousness about friendship and about the poetic vocation, especially after he reentered government service as a soldier.[7] In a poem to Baron Anton Delvig, for example, written in 1819, he juxtaposes his impending military service with the more attractive but faraway pleasures of being a poet. "How can I think of couplets?" ("Mne li dumat' o kupletakh?") he wonders, and then says:

Вам свободные пииты,
Петь, любить; меня же вряд
Иль камены, иль хариты
В карауле навестят.

(59)

(Free poets, you
Can sing and love; as for me,
Neither the Camenae nor the Charites
Are likely to come calling when I stand guard duty.)

Delvig responded with a poem about his own inability to write on martial or epic themes, as if reassuring Baratynsky that they can write on other topics.[8] He reiterates his own pose as a poet of pleasure and love and thus, indirectly, reaffirms Baratynsky's similar early poetic identity as consummate epicurean and master of erotic verse; his poem also confirms Baratynsky's continued participation in the fraternity of poets.[9] Elsewhere Baratynsky also stresses this side of his poetic personality, for example in a poem to Ivan Krylov on the pleasures of women and wine, "To K[rylo]v" ("K[rylo]vu," 1820; 67).

Baratynsky chose among several poses depending on his addressee. The pleasure-seeking poem to Krylov differs sharply from the lovely lyric to Wilhelm Kiukhelbeker written at precisely the same time (early January 1820), where Baratynsky presents himself as an involuntary wanderer, and where the muse is now associated with purest love and loyalty. The twenty-line poem begins:

Прости, поэт! Судьбина вновь
Мне посох странника вручила,
Но к музам чистая любовь
Уж нас навек соединила!

(70)

(Farewell, poet! Dame Fortune has once again
Handed me a wanderer's staff,
But a pure love for the Muses
Has already united us forever!)

Baratynsky bids Kiukhelbeker farewell by reaffirming their shared loyalty to the Muses. A longer lyric to Delvig that begins "Where are you, carefree friend?" ("Gde ty, bespechnyi drug?" 1820) includes detailed narrative evocations of their friendship and of Petersburg, the city that has been the scene for all these close bonds; it also reveals poignantly Baratynsky's fear of being forgotten by his friend.

Delvig was perhaps Baratynsky's most intimate addressee for familiar epistles. He was two years older and already situated among Petersburg's emerging poets, having been a lycée student with Pushkin and Kiukhelbeker. He saw Baratynsky's first poems to publication and introduced him to the literary salons of the city. And it was in the context of his epistles to Delvig and others that Baratynsky was first publicly attacked as a poet,[10] which was a further kind of initiation as a poet, one that strengthened the bonds of friendship and epistolary poetic conversation that themselves had provoked the polemic.

In the familiar epistle, then, we find poetic conventions and forms of address that enabled self-definitions based on similarity to one's addressee and often on a shared sense of identity as a poet. For Pushkin, Delvig, Baratynsky, Iazykov, and Kiukhelbeker, epistles circulated as frequent testimony to their having shared in an evolving project of refining literary taste;[11] as Lydia Ginzburg has noted, the verse epistle was a "transitional" genre, and thus was also chosen for experimental self-expression because it was malleable.[12] Epistolary verse was, however, largely a gentleman's genre. Karolina Pavlova emerged as a poet at a time when she knew many poets in Moscow, but she did not make similar use of this genre. To some extent, that was due to a changed cultural atmosphere: with the exception of one or two isolated poems, Pavlova's first Russian poems appeared at the end of the 1830s, when the cult of friendship had waned, indeed the ground note of cultural relations was contentious and more easily charged with anger, especially in the 1840s. But we should not put the familiar epistle aside so quickly, since poets continued to write these relatively informal but psychologically important poems to each other. Pavlova did work in this genre, although not at the very start of her career, and thus we need to return to the question of psychology: Why didn't she begin, as Baratynsky did, with poems that used the familiar epistle to experiment in poetic personae? The hidden assumptions about gender in the familiar epistle are not peripheral here: exchanged among men and frequently referring to amorous relationships with women, the familiar epistle imagined a specifically manly world of friendship and loyalty. For Pavlova, the genre had none of the instant ease that marked its use among men.[13] What, then, stood in its stead in her first poems?

PAVLOVA'S ALTERNATIVES TO THE FAMILIAR EPISTLE

We begin with an untitled poem in which Pavlova speaks of women's friendships without speaking to any particular woman friend. The poem thus repeats a major theme of the familiar epistle without its tone or rhetorical posture. Dated December 1839, it is one of Pavlova's earliest poems written in Russian:

Да, много было нас, младенческих подруг;
На детском празднике сойдемся мы, бывало,
И нашей радостью гремела долго зала,
И с звонким хохотом наш расставался круг.

И мы не верили ни грусти, ни годам,
Навстречу жизни шли толпою светлоокой;
Блистал пред нами мир роскошный и широкой,
И все, что было в нем, принадлежало нам.

Да, много было нас,—и где тот светлый рой? . . .
О, каждая из нас узнала жизни бремя,
И небылицею то называет время,
И помнит о себе, как будто о чужой.[14]

(Yes, we were many, young girlhood friends,
Once we gathered at childhood revels,
The rooms rang loud and long with our joy,
Amidst peals of laughter our circle dispersed.

We did not believe in sadness or misfortune,
We flocked to meet life bright of eye.
A world sumptuous and wide glittered before us,
And everything in it belonged to us.

Yes, we were many, and where is that bright throng now . . . ?
Oh, each girl among us learned the burden of life,
And now calls those days a fabled time,
And remembers herself as someone other.)

Scholars have suggested that Pavlova is recollecting her young girlhood, when she lived in the house of the Odoevsky family, but there is more than a familial memory here: the repeated use of first-person *plural* pronouns, unusual in her early verse, suggests that this is not an individualizing recollection of personal experience but rather a set of images that links the speaker to others like her.

Can Pavlova remain comfortably within this similarity among young girls, as Baratynsky stayed in his male circle? Pavlova carves out, with few of the "word-signals" Ginzburg would associate with the familiar letter,[15] a fabled memory of childhood friendship, a time when sadness and misfortune were unbelievable, and when the rooms of the remembered past rang out with joyous laughter. If the "word-signals" are present, they point in an unexpected direction: for example, "krug" (line 4), which suggests literally a circle of laughing girls holding hands, rather than the figurative literary circle found in familiar epistles. Even that reference proves ephemeral, in that the circle is already dispersing ("rasstavalsia krug").

The final line of the poem, "And remembers herself as someone other," seems to describe each young girl in the circle, yet it also aptly describes Pavlova herself, in part because the grammatical subject "each girl" is isolating, turning the unifying experience of remembered girlhood into a recollection that differentiates one from the other and each within herself. It is the poem's final formulation, its *pointe,* quite unlike the familiar epistle's joining forms of address—indeed, in the absence of others like her, Pavlova speaks to herself alone in a manner that came to characterize much of her mature verse. In the final emphatic word, "chuzhaia," a word found in so many of her poems, the speaker emphasizes her "otherness."[16] In many of her later self-reflective poems an inner estrangement becomes the ground that makes self-analysis possible.[17]

In other early poems, Pavlova explores a poetic identity based on isolation and estrangement from others. In "Poet" ("Poet," 1839), we find a similar artlessness:

Он вселенной гость, ему всюду пир,
Всюду край чудес;
Ему дан в удел весь подлунный мир,
Весь объем небес;

Все живит его, ему все кругом
Для мечты магнит:
Зажурчит ручей—вот и хор с ручьем
Его стих журчит;

Заревет ли лес при борьбе с грозой,
Как сердитый тигр,—
Ему бури вой лишь предмет живой
Сладкозвучных игр.
(77–78)

(He is a guest in the universe, everywhere is a feast for him,
Everywhere a land of wonders;
The earth entire is given him as his kingdom,
The vast embrace of the heavens is his,

Everything excites him, for him everything around
Is a magnet for a dream:

A stream starts to murmur, and right away in chorus with the stream
His poem murmurs.

Should the forest roar in battle with the storm
Like an angry tiger,
To him the howl of the storm is only the living subject
Of mellifluous wordplay.)

Here Pavlova places the poet in an expansive natural cosmos that seems particularly attractive when compared to the "burden of life" that shrank the wide, sumptuous world that the young girls had hoped to enter. She confers great powers of response on the poet, who has the inner resources to hear harmonious, playful melodies in an angry roar. Yet the poet is isolated,[18] and interaction occurs not between poets, as in familiar epistles, but between the poet and the natural world. The poem's use of the third-person pronouns suggests Pavlova's distanced identification with the keenly attentive poet, and there is a powerful and gathering sense of unease in all the poem's imagery. If there is comfort in the first stanza's embrace of the heavens, then there is also a kind of nervous excitability in the second stanza's picture of a poet as subject to the sensations of every single thing in the natural world. Small wonder that Pavlova keeps some rhetorical distance between herself and this particular image of the poet, since this is a poet on whom forests seem ready to spring like an "angry tiger." The tiger is a wonderful image for this early poem, pointing to a "wildness" that Pavlova was drawn to, although she ultimately found more important a "civilized" view of poetry, where reading and writing take place among educated men and women, and with other poets. Brief as it is, this poem's metrical experiment that mixes anapest with iamb in every line, and its risk-taking rhyme ("tigr" / "igr") show the skill and craftsmanship that made Pavlova from the beginning a "poet's poet."

In another 1839 poem the idea of wildness recurs,[19] again with an envelope of taming imagery: Pavlova writes of poets whose thought "is maiden wild" ("Mysl' ikh devstvenno dika"; 79).[20] In this poem, "There are favorites of inspiration" ("Est' liubimtsy vdokhnovenii," 1839), Pavlova considers the kind of poet who has no audience, who may not even speak. Here are the first three of the poem's six stanzas:

Есть любимцы вдохновений,
Есть могучие певцы;
Их победоносен гений,
Им восторги поколений,
Им награды, им венцы.

Но проходит между нами
Не один поэт немой,
С бесполезными мечтами,

С молчаливыми очами,
С сокровенною душой.

Этих манит свет напрасно,
Мысль их девственно дика;
Лишь порой, им неподвластна,
Их слеза заблещет ясно,
Вспыхнет жарко их щека.

(79)

(There are favorites of inspiration,
There are mighty bards;
Their genius is all-conquering.
To them go the adulation of generations,
To them the rewards, to them the laurel wreaths.

But among us passes
More than one mute poet,
With useless dreams,
Unspeaking eyes,
A guarded soul.

The world tempts them in vain,
Their thought is maiden wild;
But sometimes a disobedient
Tear shines bright and clear,
Their cheeks hotly flame.)

The epithet "devstvenno dika" is all the more striking after Pavlova's descriptions of those who succeed in the public eye: words like "moguchii" and "pobedonosnyi" attribute a martial quality to this accomplishment, as opposed to the vocabulary of the natural world which, in the final three stanzas, will characterize a different kind of poet. Only the adverb "devstvenno" mixes explicit femininity in with the nature descriptions (though something of a woman's face is also conjured up in the third stanza, where a shining tear or flaming cheek betrays the mute poet's depth of emotion). To the extent that Pavlova sets herself against a more readily successful, laurel-bearing masculine world, then, she does so with admirable subtlety.[21] The lasting impression of this poem, as of "Poet," rests in a Romantic conception of the poet as rarely inspired, intimately connected to the natural world, attractively awkward in social settings, and bearing a kind of involuntary chosenness that is as much burden as blessing.[22] As with "Poet," Pavlova feels kinship with the "mute poet" but does not fully identify with him. The "wildness" of the state within which the "mute poet" lives implies the same lack of civilization. The last line, "There are people without craft" ("Liudi est' bez remesla"), with its final emphasis on the "craft" central to Pavlova's mature conception of her work, suggests that she will ultimately not wish to embrace the particular poetic identity presented in this poem.

Pavlova relied on these same ideas of the poet in what appears to be her first published lyric, one that is less a definition of the poet (as in "Poet" and "There are favorites of inspiration") than a narrative about one man's encounter with these norms. Here, Pavlova speaks powerfully of the social norms and barriers that poets could face; rather than the typically Romantic assault on the ignorant throng of uncomprehending multitudes, however, she points to obstacles within the supposedly elite intellectual circles. "To E. Milkeev" ("E. Mil'keevu," 1838) addresses the painful experiences of E. L. Milkeev (1815–46 or 1847), a Siberian self-taught poet "discovered" by Zhukovsky, brought into Moscow society, and then cast off to his own fate (a tragic fate, as it turned out; Milkeev later killed himself).[23] Pavlova wrote a poem that urged him back to the natural sounds of his Siberian wilderness. It begins:

Да, возвратись в приют свой скудный:
Ответ там даст на глас певца
Гранит скалы и дол безлюдный,—
Здесь не откликнутся сердца.
(75)

(Yes, return to your mean abode:
There the poet's song will find an answer
In the granite crag and uninhabited glen;
Here hearts do not respond to one another.)

The stress laid on the way there will be no response "here" to the poet's words looks ahead to poems where Pavlova will listen keenly for a response to her own words, prizing the answers that come while noting their rarity. This poem instead locates the ideal response in natural sounds, far from the bored and uncomprehending chatter of Moscow society; Pavlova hopefully believes that Milkeev can remain a poet once he is far away. She identifies with Milkeev, and uses this early occasion to record her sense of intrusion and self-conscious oddity by analogy to another's much more dramatic difference.[24] Ironically, we here find her speaking to *someone whom she resembles,* as Baratynsky and others did in verse epistles. At the same time, however, she identifies with the world that rejects Milkeev; the second stanza in particular emphasizes the "we" of society among whom she places herself. Once again, Pavlova is reluctant to discard civilized society for a "natural" universe.

When the poem appeared in *Notes of the Fatherland* (*Otechestvennye zapiski*) in 1839, an answering verse by A. S. Khomiakov was on the facing page. It speaks to Milkeev as well as to Pavlova, contradicting the repudiation she had chronicled and declaring Milkeev in fact to be "one of us." His poem ends:

Ты наш, ты наш. По сердцу братья
Тебе нашлись. Тебя зовут
И дружбы теплые объятья,
И музам сладостный приют.[25]

(You are ours, you are ours. Brothers after your own heart
You have found. You are called by
The warm embraces of friendship
And an abode delightful to the Muses.)

The repetition that "you are ours" might disclose Khomiakov's own suspicion that Milkeev had not found a uniformly warm reception among Moscow's intellectual elite, belying his assertion that the encounter sparked mutual affection and mutual attachment. Addressed to Milkeev, the poem also spoke directly to Pavlova, given its placement in the journal. Khomiakov's rhetoric of brotherhood and friendship draws the Siberian poet into the poet's circle, but it rejects Pavlova by narrowing the "we" of her poem to a fraternity of poets. If she was writing allegorically about her culture's hesitating embrace of a poet marked by his difference, then her "readers" (those same poets who constituted a circle of poets bound by common experience and friendship) should have easily understood the response as throwing the allegory back at her. In this direct contradiction, Khomiakov pointedly reminds Pavlova of the boundaries of friendship, brotherhood, and the sweet embrace of the muse. Retrospectively, we might read his poem as a forewarning of the criticism that was to come,[26] or merely as a confirmation that her poetic debut challenged unspoken but crucial social and cultural norms. More important, we can see in "To E. Milkeev" and in "Poet" the ways in which Pavlova explored a poetic identity in which one's "wildness" led to a solitude where the wildness of language itself might be comprehended.[27] In her more measured mature verse, Pavlova adopted a different poetic identity, but a streak of rule-breaking and resistance remained visible to the end. Some sense of her ambivalent conformity to convention also emerges in her belated and unusual use of the verse epistle.[28] In 1842 she wrote one to Baratynsky, thanking him for sending his last volume of poetry, *Twilight* (*Sumerki*, 1842). We turn now to this poem, to clarify her relationship to Baratynsky and to establish her particular way of using the genre of the verse epistle to speak of herself as a poet.

PAVLOVA'S VERSE EPISTLE TO BARATYNSKY

Baratynsky and Pavlova met in the fall of 1825 in Moscow.[29] They frequented the same salons (although Pavlova of course did not share in all-male gatherings, and thus not in his world of wine, women, and song). We have little documentation of their friendship. Pavlova admired his work sufficiently to include five of his poems in her book of translations into German,[30] and

Baratynsky charmingly claimed to regret not knowing the language in order to read her translations.[31] Her admiration lasted through the end of his life in 1844, when she dedicated to him her narrative poem *Quadrille* (*Kadril'*, 1844); she also spoke fondly to him in "Life calls us" ("Zovet nas zhizn'," 1846), a longer, philosophical lyric that shows the substantive traces of his influence as well.

Her 1842 verse epistle to Baratynsky suggests that he remained her symbol of the ideal meditative poet. After three stanzas that conventionally recall how refreshing the sight and scent of a native flower can be to a wanderer, Pavlova writes of the similar effect on her of Baratynsky's volume of verse:

Так эти, посланные вами,
Сладкоречивые листы
Живили, будто бы вы сами,
Мои заснувшие мечты.

Последней, мимоходной встречи
Припомнила беседу я:
Все вдохновительные речи
Минут тех, полных бытия!

За мыслей мысль неслась, играя,
Слова, катясь, звучали в лад:
Как лед с реки от солнца мая,
Стекал с души весь светский хлад.

Меня вы назвали поэтом,
Мой стих небрежный полюбя,
И я, согрета вашим светом,
Тогда поверила в себя.
(112–13)

(Just so these sweet-tongued leaves
Sent by you
Quickened to life, as you yourself would,
My slumbering dreams,

I recalled the conversation
Of our last, fleeting meeting;
All the inspiring talk
Of those minutes, full of life's essence.

Playing, thought led to thought,
Words tumbling out rang in harmony:
Like ice on the river in May sunshine
All society coldness melted from my soul.

You named me a poet,
Liking my careless verse,
And I, warmed by your light,
Began to believe in myself.)

These lines (four stanzas from the poem's total of eleven) demonstrate the enabling poetic presence that Baratynsky represented in Pavlova's work. That is not to say that she never wrote with similar gratitude to others (in three poems to Nikolai Iazykov [1840, 1842, 1844], for example, Pavlova casts him as a reminder of earlier, more harmonious days for poets).[32] But Pavlova places Baratynsky in a separate category because of the quality of his writing, and because, as was noted by Munir Sendich, he "was the first to 'discover' her."[33]

She thus reminds Baratynsky that he "named" her a poet and gave her new faith in herself. These facts are reported straightforwardly in the poem, and our gaze rightly wanders to the more interesting narrative that contextualizes them. Baratynsky's recognition of her gifts, for example, happens in a salonlike setting: it is described as a conversation in which the coldness of typical social chatter melts away. Pavlova had seemed to come out of the salon milieu in the late 1820s and to occupy it centrally after her marriage. She valued the salon as a place of civilized discourse in the tradition of serious versions in eighteenth-century France: there, a woman could engage in intellectual conversation and literary work. In her salon, Pavlova worked to encourage the Enlightenment tradition, and her gatherings were known for their seriousness of conversation and pursuits.[34] At the same time, her writings frequently criticize more frivolous versions of the salon, particularly salon discourse: she finds it a site for false flattery, dangerously misleading impressions, and hostility toward the poet, as in *A Double Life* (*Dvoinaia zhizn'*, 1848).[35] Such views of the salon became increasingly common in the 1830s and 1840s, as literary life shifted to the commercial world and that disparagement of the salon is reflected in her epistle to Baratynsky. Her encounter with the older poet is not frivolous salon talk, but words that bespeak intense thinking.

The central stanza of the poem is thus the one that begins "Playing, thought led to thought" ("Za myslei mysl' neslas', igraia"), and it is also literally at the poem's center, falling sixth of eleven. The stanza has many virtues, not least its imagery of words eagerly flowing like ice being carried away by the sun's warmth (and in the next stanza, Pavlova will claim that his encouragement similarly warmed her with its radiant light). Pavlova may have had in mind Baratynsky's own stunning use of water frozen in apparent movement in his poem "Look on this cold countenance" ("Vzgliani na lik kholodnyi sei"), which we consider in a moment. But her emphasis is on warmth: elsewhere in the poem Baratynsky seems almost life-giving (the word "zhivitel'nyi" appears twice, stressing how his words animated her talent).

Indeed, their connection is built around his beneficent presence in her emergence as a poet. Clearly, the capacity of conferring identity and status was one that only he had; it was not reversible. Pavlova rather uncomfortably writes in "Life calls us" of the oddity that it is she who speaks his name: "Must I then name you, Evgeny / Do I alone pay you the tribute of verse?" ("I mne prishlos' tebia nazvat', Evgenii, / I dan' stikha ia dam tebe odna?" 130). If her self-questioning reflects her own uncertainty about her right to name him a poet, the context within which she does so—in the absence of other poets—suggests the ways in which literary life was changing. The singularity of her naming him reflects not only the deaths of leading Russian poets but also her larger sense of the decline of poetic circles during the dawning age of prose, a decline she describes in "Meditations" ("Dumy," 1847) as "Gone the chorus of poets" ("Ischez poetov khorovod," 135). The absence of response that troubles Pavlova in her earlier verse now helps her. She can urge Evgeny to accept her poetic tribute when there are no longer poets to address him as their equal, "Take it, then, when they are silent" ("Voz'mi zh ee [dan'], kogda molchat oni," 130). In the last stanza of "Meditations" she reflects on the difficulty of speaking as a poet under such circumstances:

Пришлось молчать мечтам заветным;
Зачем тому, кто духом нищ,
Тревожить ныне словом тщетным
Безмолвный мир святых кладбищ!
(135)

(Cherished dreams must fall silent;
Why should a beggar in spirit
Trouble now with a futile word
The quiet repose of sacred graveyards!)

In many respects, the silence within which she now writes is familiar. As we have seen, Pavlova's first poems strikingly asked whether the poet's words will reach any audience.[36] It had mattered deeply to her identity as a poet that her words reach Baratynsky. The final stanza of "Meditations" echoes another of his poems, an album verse that Baratynsky addressed to her.

We thus turn to a third genre, album verse. It plays an important role in Pavlova's relationship with Baratynsky; it also figures crucially in the process through which he announced himself a poet. His erotic album poems figure in the process of poetic initiation we are observing, taking their place next to his early verse epistles.

ALBUM VERSE AND ITS GAMES OF SELF-EXPRESSION

Like familiar epistles, album poems concentrate assumptions about the social positions and forms of knowledge available to men and to women, although in a more complex way. Album poems were a fact of social life and thus vividly bear the imprint of the relations they fortified. In them, roles were assigned to women and men that seemed to flow so naturally from the norms of the genre that few scholars have mentioned the gender arrangements of these poems. The history of album ownership and album inscription complicates quick judgments. Not all album owners were women, nor were inscriptions always by men, but the assumption that albums were prized by women and that album verse was a masculine tribute addressed to the woman owner of the album was powerful.[37]

Pavlova left very few album poems, although she was familiar with their conventions.[38] There were fewer ways in which she could turn the genre around to her own advantage (as she did brilliantly with narrative verse, for example, in *Quadrille*, and with some success in her work with the verse epistle, as the poem to Baratynsky bears out).[39] One difficulty seems to have arisen from the genre's usual address to a beautiful woman. As the oddity of her later poem "To A. D. B." ("A. D. B. . . . oi," 1858) suggests, poets' poems to beautiful women were traditionally written by men, not by other women.[40]

Baratynsky, however, wrote many album poems, some with stunning portrayals of women quite consonant with the norms of Western Romanticism.[41] His album poems associate women with thoughtlessness or cruelty, inconstancy or danger, and beauty that can be frighteningly erotic or sweetly lovely. Whereas, in familiar epistles, the speaker can take on the shared values of loyal friendship he attributes to his male addressee, flirtatious album poems to women pose a problem for poetic self-characterization. Is the poet to characterize himself as loyal and rejected? Some do, relying on a contrast between speaker and listener, which also lets the poet constitute himself as a locus for thinking and reflection in comparison to his empty-headed addressee. Women become objects to the masculine subject, the imagined "other" through whom he comes to comprehend his own feelings and ideas. For example, Baratynsky wrote an album poem in 1827 that associates its female addressee with the playful antics of a child (Romantic poetry commonly linked the feminine to the childlike on the basis of shared simplicity, happy innocence, and empty-headedness).

Перелетай к веселью от веселья,
Как от цветка бежит к цветку дитя;
Не успевай, за суетой безделья,
Задуматься, подумать и шутя.

Пускай тебя к Кориннам не причислят,
Играй, мой друг, играй и верь мне в том,
Что многие о милой Лизе мыслят,
Когда она не мыслит ни о чем.
(136–37)

(Flit from pleasure to pleasure,
As a child runs from flower to flower;
Don't hasten, pursuing idle vanities,
To reflect seriously, or to think when you are joking.
Don't let yourself be counted among the Corinnes,
Play, my friend, play and believe me:
Many think of dear Liza
When she is thinking of nothing.)

The poet, moreover, finds that the woman who herself thinks of nothing (as he describes her in the poem's final line) is most likely to be the object of attentive thought. Composing this kind of poetry, like thinking itself, is the province of those who contemplate her; thus the description of "lovely Liza" as a flighty, empty-headed child enables Baratynsky's self-characterization as a poet.

He also left us poems in which it is the poet who is, if not flighty, then changeable and uncertain, and in these poems his addressee is often all too knowing. As in other genres, most women in album poems are either ideal visions of purity or infernal nightmares of sexual temptation, so that the latter becomes a perfect foil for a poet who appears to founder on his own innocence. Baratynsky's 1821 poem "In an album" ("V al'bom," 1821) offers a good example:

Вы слишком многими любимы,
Чтобы возможно было вам
Знать, помнить всех по именам;
Сии листки необходимы;
Они ненужны были встарь:
Тогда не знали дружбы модной,
Тодга, Бог весть! иной дикарь
Сердечный адрес-календарь
Почел бы выдумкой негодной.
Что токловать о старине!
Стихи готовы. Может статься,
Они для справки обо мне
Вам очень скоро пригодятся.
(84–85)

(You are loved by too many
For you possibly to know or
To recall all by name;
These pages are essential.

They were not needed in days of old,
Then fashionable friendship was unknown,
Then, God knows, any savage
Would have thought the heart's day book
A worthless invention.
But why talk of the good old days!
The verses are ready. Perchance
They will very soon provide you
With all necessary information about me.)

The poet contends with excessive attention already lavished on the lady, as evidenced in the multitude of album inscriptions she has collected. He playfully notes his insignificance by suggesting that the lady will soon forget him; although the move to self-reference has a certain admirable deftness, the ending conforms to another cliché in pointing to the readiness of the verse. The poet expects he has provided "information," but he imparts precious little about himself. In the face of this woman's ability to choose among many men, Baratynsky stumbles into speechlessness. Without being able to evoke something more definite in the addressee, he seems to fall into comparative if ironic anonymity.

The poem's history provides a further twist on the themes of loyalty and identity. It is not just the lady who has quickly changing admirers; Baratynsky offered the poem to more than one lady, originally writing it to Sofiia Ponomareva but finally inscribing it in the album of A. V. Lutkovskaia. This was not the only occasion on which he let his poems do double duty—an apparent advantage of his habit of rewriting verse and, while he was at it, reconsidering the context of its creation.[42] Some have argued that this readiness to re-address poems reveals how little of the original inspiration came from the lady in question,[43] but Baratynsky's involvement with Ponomareva was deeply affecting.[44] Re-addressing poems once inscribed in her album let him turn dramatically away from a woman he found seductive and frightening.

Baratynsky's poems to Ponomareva test the elegiac reflections on erotic disillusion that stand out in his early poetry. In writing to her, he created his first version of the femme fatale whose snares men rarely resisted; a vivid example is the poem that begins "The lure of fond words" ("Primankoi laskovykh rechei," 1821), which he first read in the literary society Ponomareva created in her Petersburg salon. This lyric, with its images of entrapment, insanity, risky jokes, and passionate confession, may have been inspired by Ponomareva, but its audience was a larger circle of men—poets and intellectuals, friends and bare acquaintances—for whom Baratynsky sought to characterize himself as a shrewd analyst of women's wiles. In other poems to and about Ponomareva, Baratynsky develops the vocabulary of danger, combat, hot passion, and icy revenge that he was to use to brilliant effect in poems about other women or imagined heroines and in his lyrics of self-description. Of these, the following untitled poem from 1825 is one of the most interesting, in part because scholars originally claimed that the poem describes the great beauty Agrafena Zakrevskaia (on whom Baratynsky modeled the heroine of his narrative poem *The Ball* [*Bal,* 1828]).[45] In recent decades, an assertion that Baratynsky was writing about himself has gained sufficient credence to appear in commentaries to his work.[46]

Взгляни на лик холодный сей,
 Взгляни: в нем жизни нет;
Но как на нем былых страстей
 Еще заметен след!
Так ярый ток, оледенев,
 Над бездною висит,
Утратив прежний грозный рев,
 Храня движения вид.
(129)

(Look on this cold countenance,
 Look: there is no life in it;
Yet how perceptible still
 The trace of former passions!
Just as the raging torrent, ice-bound,
 Hangs over the abyss,
Its former threatening roar now spent,
 Its appearance of movement—preserved.)

The extraordinary image of water frozen in apparent movement makes this one of Baratynsky's most memorable short poems. It is a conceit worthy of the English metaphysical poets, which is unusual for Baratynsky, who rarely grounds philosophical reflections in intricate metaphorical patterns. The Orthodox tradition is invoked by his usage of the Old Church Slavic word "lik" for face. However, he preserves nothing that is identifying in the face he describes, although the face in the Western and Orthodox tradition is imagined as a locus of identity.

What are we to make of the suggestion that this poem, once thought to speak a woman's dangerousness, actually reflects on the poet's own enigmatic face? An apparent meditation on another's face is transformed into self-portraiture. That shifts cuts across many of the assumptions of gender assymmetry that have been at work in this essay, particularly in the discussion of album poems, in that it imagines an equivalency between the face of a woman (with whom one has an erotic relationship) and the face one presents to the world.[47] Baratynsky was more likely to establish an equivalency between himself and a male addressee, as in the familiar epistles discussed above, or in his occasional album poems to men.[48]

Such questions of equivalency, self-inscription, and description of one's addressee are rearranged slightly but startingly in the final example we want to consider. Addressed to a woman, it too is an album poem ("V al'bom," 1829).

Альбом походит на кладбище:
Для всех открытое жилище,
Он также множеством имен
Самолюбиво испещрен.
Увы! народ добросердечный
Равно туда или сюда
Несет надежду жизни вечной
И трепет Страшного суда.
Но я, смиренно признаюся,
Я не надеюсь, не страшуся,
Я в ваших памятных листах
Спокойно имя помещаю.
Философ я: у вас в глазах
Мое ничтожество я знаю.
(148–49)

(An album is like a graveyard:
A dwelling place open to all,
Strewn self-regardingly
With a multitude of names.
Alas! just so do good-hearted people
Bring there and here
Hope of life eternal
And fear of Judgment Day.
But I, I humbly own,
I neither hope nor fear.
In your memorial pages
I calmly place my name.
I am a philosopher: I know
My insignificance in your eyes.)

This poem has some features typical of album verse; self-consciousness about the act of inscription, awareness of others whose contributions will frame one's own. The latter topos allows the poet to invoke his modest claims on the lady's attention by comparison to others whose superiority is measured by their more successful album poems. The reference also gently attributes sexual availability to the lady in whose album so many others have already flatteringly made their mark.

This poem's overarching imagery of the graveyard, however, undercuts this sexual play, as does the lyric's curiously obsessive delineation of the poet from the "good-hearted people" who waver between hope for eternal life and fear of the Last Judgment. The first two sentences are about the album and about people, but the final sentences are about the self, repeating the pronoun "I" five times. What, the poet asks, is the relationship of his name, mentioned in line 12, to the multitude of names in line 3? He tries to take a stoical view, writing his name with insistent calm, but he can take little comfort from having dispatched the threats of competing album writers or inevitable mortality by concluding that he recognizes his insignificance in the eyes of his addressee.

Even given the very broad range of album inscriptions we have surveyed here, these are strange jottings. One reason for the oddity is Baratynsky's relationship with the owner of this particular album: the poem was addressed to Pavlova.[49] She would have been twenty-two years old at the time, and while it might seem that she was hardly the poet we recognize her becoming less than a decade later, these years are in fact the precise time when her identity as a poet was being formed.[50] Baratynsky writes with full knowledge of her intense engagement with words, ideas, and images. He addresses Pavlova as one poet to another. The light tone of his poem catches the atmosphere of the gentry world of salon culture, although the diction and the intonation do not entirely match. Genres almost seem to mix, as if Baratynsky knows that the familiar epistle would be a more appropriate form to speak to another poet but insistently models his poem differently; indeed, he begins with the word "album," as if the word can prompt him to think in terms of the genre. One senses his constraint: designed to be sent to an absent poet, the verse epistle's conventions of flattering nostalgia will not work when the act of composition and inscription must take place before the very person one writes to and about.

Baratynsky blends embarrassment at this proximity with ironic distancing from it, largely by means of two surprising bits of diction. First, the comparison of album to graveyard permits a rather deprecating but humorous gesture as Baratynsky regards the act of writing in the album to be as inevitable as dying. Death being one of his great themes in the mature philosophical lyrics, we could justifiably suspect him of substituting a self-identifying signature for the social ritual of album inscription that takes away all individuality—as he notes. The second important word here is *filosof*, also a moment of Baratynsky's identifying himself quite recognizably. As with the imagery of death, the usage seems at first humorous. It suggests the resignation of one who takes life's little rejections ironically, rather than the profound engagement with ideas that would define Baratynsky's emergence as a poet of thought. But like the idea of the album as a graveyard, the word *filosof* resounds with irony, which is to say that in both cases the meanings are doubled. Baratynsky's final sentence affirms his knowledge of this irony; he "knows" about his insignificance in the eyes of the album owner.

In spite of that knowledge, or perhaps thanks to it, the poem is not a study in failure, but rather a cautious assertion of success: success at overcoming the daunting situation of writing verse in the presence of the addressee (writing where her eyes can see him, as he suggests), and success at overturning the conventions of album verse by converting a meditation on one's sameness to all others into an individuating mark of difference. Baratynsky exudes, even speaks about, his calm response to these challenges,. Naming has none of the disruptiveness that, in other poets, contemporary to him and more frequently since, can cause a dizzying acknowledgment of how uncertain identity actually is.

Pavlova tried hard to match his calm. In a poem she dated June 1844, the month of his death, Pavlova assembled the pieces of identity we have tracked through this essay—solitude, self-address, a self-consciousness about the process of thinking (the poem is entitled "Meditation" ["Duma"]—to write about loss. It is a beautiful poem, whose last stanza reaches for a stoical posture:

И я встречаю, с ним не споря,
Спокойно ныне бытие;
И горестней младого горя
Мне равнодушие мое.
(122)

(And now, without disputing, I calmly
Meet life's essence;
And to me more sorrowful than youthful sorrow
Is my indifference.)

The indifference in the last line does not convince, particularly since the poem is only one in a series of "duma" poems that variously revise these same emotions. Thus the calm becomes excessive, something of a pose. But Pavlova pays tribute here to a way of being a poet, and to a way of describing that idea of the poet in her verse. She may not have known about Baratynsky's death when she wrote the poem (he died at the end of the month), but the dateline was added in her 1863 collection, and can be read as echoing the impression of Baratynsky's presence in the poem in the word *spokoino.*

His album poem has brought us right up to the moment when Pavlova was a mature poet, a point at which this essay must stop. But it also brings us back to the rituals of initiation with which we began. Baratynsky's album poem to Pavlova recalls Zhukovsky's portrait inscription to Pushkin, particularly in the way that an intense form of self-reference (Zhukovsky, after all, was inscribing a picture of himself) and a scenario of the moment of writing combine to confer the status of poet on the addressee. Zhukovsky's was after the fact, as we suggested earlier, and in a way Baratynsky's was a bit early.

But the gesture was powerfully felt by both recipients: Pushkin, for whom Zhukovsky was always a mentor and a difficult substitute-father, and Pavlova, who tried to keep writing long after Baratynsky was dead, and after the Golden Age of Russian poetry had ended.

Baratynsky's album poem thus characterizes Pavlova as significantly as it acts as a poem of self-description. Although the forms of address are lightly flirtatious and although there are similarities, as we have noted, to the erotic collections in women's albums, this poem seems knowingly to have been penned in the album of a woman for whom each inscription was prized *as a poem,* and a woman who was herself imagined in the album *as a poet.*[51] The possession of an album might have made Pavlova seem a typical woman, but her actual album distinguished her (this follows the same logic as Baratynsky's self-description in the poem).

The word that Baratynsky's album poem uses to name the dry self-regard that he and Pavlova shared is *filosof.* He seems to mean a person who accepts life, bears its burdens, withstands its privations. The other usage that would have been current in Baratynsky's lifetime would have been a person inclined toward meditation, thoughtfulness.[52] Such an inclination was part of Pavlova's and Baratynsky's conception of poetic identity, we have argued, and it was the basis for their laying claim to a position of centrality in cultural debates in their day. But even in the 1820s the many ironic instances of the term *filosof* in Pushkin's poetry readily attest to the way it was slipping in prestige as a form of social identity.[53] The person of philosophical demeanor was being displaced by a more activist, practical representative of the intelligentsia.

Pavlova went on to try out other ideas about herself as a poet, but in some ways the outmodedness of the philosophical temperament would have been no more limiting to her than the indisputable fact that poetry was going out of fashion. The salon settings for playful versions of these poems or for serious discourse were to fade from view by the mid-1840s, which by all rights should have been Pavlova's mature period as a poet. Instead, she seems almost to start over again (quite successfully in *A Double Life*),[54] only to repeat the process of beginning anew in the early 1850s (again, with some success, in the cycle of poems to Boris Utin), and then to try it one more time in the 1860s (now with very little success), as her life receded into emigration, translation, and isolation.

Baratynsky emerged from his early experiments in self-presentation to become a powerful poet of thought, writing some of the finest Russian lyric poems of the nineteenth century. But he was also a victim of the growing unfashionability of poetry, and for all the impressive achievements of his later work it still struck contemporaries as peripheral to the central tasks facing Russian literature in the 1840s. Fated to marginality, Baratynsky became an unexpectedly appropriate figure through whom a woman poet could see herself. It is a final paradox that both poetic debuts, although they successfully taught each poet a wonderful facility with reworking received literary precedent and with reconceiving a relationship to an audience and to oneself, should have led to poetic careers strangely tinged with a sense of failure. The stoical attitudes of both poets served them well as they wrote their ways through their respective lives: short and intense, in Baratynsky's case, cut off by death in Naples at the early age of forty-four; long and filled with drastic changes, for Pavlova, leading in the end to decades of poverty in Germany and self-imposed exile from Russia. After 1863, no poems of hers in Russian have survived.

Judith Deutsch Kornblatt

Cossacks and Women: Creation without Reproduction in Gogol's Cossack Myth

IN A DRAWING by the popular cartoonist Gary Larson, a saber-wielding horseman addresses a small group of warriors: "Listen up, my Cossack brethren! We'll ride into the valley like the wind, the thunder of our horses and the lightning of our steel striking fear in the hearts of our enemies! . . . And remember—stay out of Mrs. Caldwell's garden!" The success of the joke depends on several factors: the reader must hold a coherent mental picture to correspond to the word COSSACK; the rhetoric of thundering horses and lightning steel must reinforce that picture, exclamation points and all; and, finally, it must seem obvious that the Cossack of that mental picture, would never, ever care a hoot about Mrs. Caldwell.

The Cossack's gender is a vital element of the picture. He participates in a brotherhood ("Listen up, my Cossack brethren!"), a military cohort of men bonded to each other and their horses who evoke, but do not experience fear. It is to the exclusive maleness of our Cossack picture that this essay will attend. Other aspects of that mental picture—the Cossack's "Russianness," his association with freedom and the boundless steppe, his communal and organic connection to the Russian earth—will play a role in our analysis insofar as they relate to Cossack male exclusivity and their violent birth by and collective marriage to a free and expansive nonhuman female partner.

UNDERSTANDING THE COSSACK MYTH

To begin our analysis of the Cossack, we must ask whence comes the picture against which we read the cartoon described above. The answer depends on who the reader is. Americans have Yul Brenner to thank, in the 1962 film of Nikolai Gogol's *Taras Bul'ba* (1835; rev. 1842), or perhaps a translation of the nineteenth-century novel itself (although the seemingly jingoistic story has never been popular with Western audiences), or of Mikhail Sholokhov's *And Quiet Flows the Don* (*Tikhii Don,* 1928–40), or Isaak Babel's *Red Cavalry*

(*Konarmiia,* 1926) from the twentieth century. Contact with a Cossack might come only from a youthful reading of Byron's narrative poem about the seventeenth-century Polish/Ukrainian Cossack, *Mazeppa.* Or, those interested in current affairs might have read about the rebirth of the Cossack nation as the Soviet empire imploded, loudly trumpeted in the *New York Times Magazine* (31 October 1993) and the paper's international section (25 July 1992). Less likely, a reader might have seen "The Return of the Cossacks" in the dual language newspaper, *We/My,* a frightening article that could be subtitled: "Proof that Myths Never Die." The piece ends with a Cossack truism right out of *Taras Bul'ba,* uttered by Cossack leader Boris Gusev with no apparent self-irony: "A Cossack without a horse is not a Cossack." He continues: "Wherever Russian blood is spilled, we will come to fight" (in response to Cossack fighters in Moldova and, potentially, to the defenders of "Slavic blood" in Bosnia), and "If we have to kill someone, then that means we have to. If we have to kill women and children, we will" (*We/My* [31 May–13 June 1993], p. 8).[1]

How do these pictures, collected from such diverse genres and media, relate, so that Gary Larson can count on a standard response to his cartoon? Do Gusev's militant Cossacks of the post-Soviet 1990s recapitulate those of the nineteenth or early twentieth centuries, glorified in film, novel, and story? Indeed, does fiction, much less joke, recapitulate "reality"? If so, which reality? If we take a sober look, we must acknowledge that the actual Cossacks known to Gogol and Sholokhov and Babel, not to mention Gusev, were from very different historical groups, by no means homogeneous in temporal setting, habitat, language, dress, social structure, or most other marks of culture. (All, most likely, would profess Russian Orthodoxy, although this cultural marker, while often repeated in the literature about them, does not help support our picture of a saber-wielding warrior prepared to murder women and children.) We have clearly gathered our picture from somewhere other than historical reality. Few Americans have actually met a Cossack, and those who have no doubt saw him through the scrim of the picture that I here call the Cossack myth.[2]

By myth I imply not the opposite of fact, but, rather, a cultural construct in many ways more real than fact. One way to understand this statement is to realize that Americans' picture of the Russian Cossack is aided by a similar, but not identical picture of the gunslinging cowboy, a male warrior who lives on the ever-expanding frontier and wields his manly power in the community of other cowboys. That cowboy is clearly not fact, if for no other reason than that our mental picture leaves out many contradictory aspects of the "real" one, from deaths due to syphilis to battles with bedbugs.[3] He is also not fact insofar as he is never a she, nor is he, with precious few exceptions, of non-European descent. But he is also more than fact, for the brave cowboy has become a way in which we understand ourselves as Americans—powerful, self-sufficient, and ever-prepared to extend American borders through the wilderness. Tom Hanks of the Academy Award winning movie *Apollo 13* is but one more tough but wholesome cowboy, pushing the frontier upward.

A cowboy is not exactly a Cossack, however. One significant way in which the cowboy of the American myth differs from the Cossack is precisely in his attitude toward women. In countless stories of the American frontier, the cowboy, himself precariously close to the feral brink, nonetheless subdues the wild West, deriving strength and stability for his civilizing task from a lady-love. Off in the sunset lie ever more space to tame and more women in whose enduring arms the restless hero can find temporary (if easily spurned) calm and hope. These stories at once grow from and perpetuate America's self-definition as a land of limitless opportunities, inhabited by men who become civilized as they civilize, and women who, albeit passively, aid the advancement. Russia's frontier myth, although equally pervasive in its literature, and equally crucial for the self-definition of its people, differs decisively on two points, the second of which is the topic of this essay. Unlike the cowboys, the Cossacks become wild themselves in their contact with the uncivilized frontier; second, as will be explored, they aggressively reject all contact, even nominal, with "lady-loves."

Differences between historical cowboy and Cossack aside, the picture of the Cossack must be somewhat different for Russians than for us, precisely because he is their own, and because Russian culture and history, which intersect with Cossack history, differ from American.[4] Many of the writers who glorified the Cossack in nineteenth-century Russian literature did historical research themselves, knew Cossacks, or even traced Cossack blood in their own families. Yet their heroes, like ours, in every case rely more on myth than historical reality. Myth reduces or purifies the multifarious and often contradictory elements of that reality.[5] To associate with the Cossack as myth need not mean to condone missions of rape and pillage. Rather, it is to accept the material of the myth as a structuring mechanism of inherently chaotic reality. Myth, as the the critic Roland Barthes has said, "transforms history into nature";[6] it levels reality by erasing contradictions, purifying, freezing, and eternalizing the hero. In fact, as early as Pushkin's time, when folklorists and historians began gathering information on the "native" people of "Great" and "Little" Russia, the Cossacks became the COSSACK.[7]

We might ask whether writers are unconscious or conscious bearers, indeed creators, of the myth. The question is particulary important in regard to a myth of self that concerns politically volatile issues of empire, geography, and national destiny. An answer can be found in the fact that writers are also readers or, in more popular terminology, consumers and "native speakers" of the dominant culture. "Better" writers are never wholly subservient nor wholly divorced from their "patrons," meaning the ideology of both the authorities and the reading public. Some Cossack literature includes parody, irony, or, at the very least, ambivalence regarding the Cossack hero. Nonetheless, significant elements of stories even by Pushkin, Tolstoy, and certainly by Gogol look inward to determine the Russian "self," and backward to remember, recover, and sometimes invent a unique national personality.[8] Inspired by the Romantic obsession with the soul—individual and cultural—the Cossacks were reclaimed as a wondrous, yet essential Russian phenomenon.

Of course, historical Cossacks, like cowboys, were men like any others, with differing backgrounds and personalities. The word "Cossack" itself is ill-defined, and has been applied to groups as varied as fifteenth-century Tatar soldiers, nineteenth-century tsarist cavalrymen, Soviet collective farm workers, and the newly revitalized hosts. Historically, these men are linked by their home on the physical and cultural edge of Russian society, and by their ambiguous role as defenders of and rebels against the order they presumably brought to the frontier. The first Cossacks were probably drawn from Eastern nomadic tribes; the Cossacks most influential for the Cossack myth were Ukrainian (Zaporozhian) Cossacks; and even the more specifically *Russian* Cossacks of the Don, Ural, and other hosts frequently intermarried with women from the steppes, and accepted into their ranks Europeans, Poles, and even Jews (despite their reputation for anti-Semitism). Yet the Cossack hero in Russian literature is homogenized into a representative of Russia, a figure at once exotic, and, of utmost significance, essentially native.[9]

In 1870, Tolstoy claimed that "Cossacks have made the entire history of Russia. Not for nothing do the Europeans call us Cossacks. All Russians wish to be Cossacks."[10] Tolstoy asserts here that both Europeans and his own countrymen somehow equate the inner essence of the Russians with Cossacks. The Russian man wants to define himself as sharing vital qualities with the Cossacks. One hopes that Tolstoy was not referring, or not referring *only* to Cossack murder and debauchery. If his comment is any indication, there must be other aspects of the Cossacks that attract the reader, and allow for a dismissal or, perhaps, transformation of the Cossacks' violence together with an acceptance of their essence. These aspects not only enter into an individual Russian's self-definition, but become, in some way, coterminous with the history of all of Russia.

Cossacks did not "make" the entire history of Russia any more than cowboys "made" America. Despite any concrete role the Cossacks may have played in Russia's past, their mythic service has been greater. The Russians had no Trojan War upon which to base a positive image of themselves as victors. There were no militant Crusaders who valiantly fought a holy war. No brave pioneers battled savage Indians to make way for civilization, having successfully rebelled against their mother government. Instead, *The Lay of*

Igor's Campaign, considered by many a national epic, is the tale of a defeat.[11] And the first two national saints, Boris and Gleb, preferred to lay down their lives passively rather than fight for their rights. The Cossacks, by contrast, provide the Russians with an aggressive and colorful portrait of part of their past and of themselves.

By most criteria, the recovered Cossack was an exotic character, living a life separated from civilized Russia by more than geographic distance. His clothes, his hairstyle (the traditional forelock), his way of life, even his colloquial language departed drastically from that known to nineteenth-century Russians. In this regard, our, and nineteenth-century pictures of the Cossack do not differ substantially from our mental images of Pushkin's gypsies, of the mountain dwellers of writers like Marlinsky or Lermontov, or even of the original "noble savages," the cannibals of Montaigne. Certainly works by the western European poets Byron and Victor Hugo about the Cossack Mazepa, as well as many writings about Cossacks by Russians themselves, fit securely into the literary tradition of the Romantic and pre-Romantic noble savage.[12]

Yet the literary Cossacks ultimately are not interchangeable with those exotic characters, any more than they are with the cowboys. The noble savages of literature exist somewhere totally removed from our civilization, so that the city-dwelling hero can travel to their habitat, glorify them, perhaps learn from them, but ultimately cannot remain among them. The savage, no matter how noble, lives across an unbridgeable abyss from the hero, as well as from the author and audience. The gypsies, such as those in Pushkin's poem by that title, are of this type. They are depicted as alien or "other," definitely, categorically *not* Russian. The Cossacks of the myth, on the other hand, *are* Russian. In fact, they are both "other" and quintessentially "self." Geographically, they live distant from the main centers of Russia, and their overexuberant revelry and pillaging challenge all civilized decorum. Yet, and here we find the essence of the myth, the popular image would have the Cossacks as the principal upholders of the Russian Orthodox faith and preservers of the purity of Rus'. Rus' was the Kievan kingdom known as the origin of Russian civilization, a culture destroyed by the Mongol invasion, but whose "soul" remained somewhere alive. The Cossack heroes of literature repeatedly evoke this soul, the Russian origins in old Rus', and thus represent continuity through the disruptive period of Eastern domination.

The Cossack myth also helps define the Russian in contrast to the opposite geographic direction: the West. The Cossack heyday in pre-Petrine, pre-Nikonian Russia, represented a period in history that the Russian people would hope to reclaim for themselves. By the early eighteenth century, Peter the Great had reorganized the empire into a European-styled bureaucracy, subordinating even the Church to a government ministry, and had brought in advisers from Europe to reshape his society. Patriarch Nikon's reforms of the late seventeenth century had already "modernized" the Russian church to bring it more in line with the contemporary Greek church, causing many, in particular the so-called Old Believers (to whose doctrine many Cossacks continued to adhere years after the Bolshevik Revolution), to label the official clergy "agents of the Antichrist." Thus, the Cossacks of old, and the Cossacks who remained in the nineteenth century, signified an era that allegedly existed before dilution of the Russian people by the corrupt and corrupting West.

At this point, it would be instructive to compare the Cossack myth with another that also arose during the Romantic period: the myth of the Caucasus. Both literary myths helped establish the empire as a dominant and "masculine" entity, and both ultimately rested on a vision of Russians as inherently Asiatic *and* European.[13] Yet the differences are more vital than the similarities. Russian writers could establish their strength vis-à-vis the Caucasian tribes people or by contrasting their maleness to the "femininity" of Georgia, that is, by contrasting the stable center to the savage (albeit "noble") and shifty periphery. Even when writers stressed similarities between the Caucasus and Russia, they still did so in terms of a comparison and contrast of "us" versus "them."

The myth of the Cossack works in a more complex way, as I shall show in terms of the Cossack appropriation of, rather than contrast to, the female space of the expansive steppe. In large part, both myths are spatial, and both deal with a spatial issue less known in western European literature, but crucial to the myth of America: the ever-expanding frontier. In this sense, the Russian relationship to the Caucasus might be closer to that of Americans and the Wild West; as the subtitle of Susan Layton's study of empire and the Caucasus suggests, the question was one of *conquest* and civilization. The Cossacks of Russian literature, however, do not conquer and subdue the wide frontier. Rather they become one with it, absorbing its expanse and wildness. Created through a wealth of authors and genres, and in response to perceived or real threats from East and West, from within and without the empire, from past and future, the myth of the Cossack thus establishes stability on the inherently *un*stable frontier. It makes a positive from a negative by glorifying borderlessness and incorporating "female" space into the male community; it does so not by moving the center to the margins, but by "marrying" the border and giving birth to a new and freer version of self.

THE FEMALE THREAT

The time has come to turn our attention more directly to one of the Cossack hero's characteristics: his maleness. Nikolai Gogol provides us with the richest examples, from his fantastic stories of *Evenings on a Farm Near Dikan'ka* (*Vechera na khutore bliz Dikan'ki,* 1831–32), from his essays on Ukrainian history and folk songs in *Arabesques* (*Arabeski,* 1835), from the story "Vii," (1835) and, especially, from the short novel *Taras Bul'ba,* the most mythical of all nineteenth-century works featuring Cossack heroes.

Daniel Mordovtsev's nineteenth-century novel *Sagaidachny* (1882) suggests a typical Cossack expression of disbelief. We are told that warriors have gathered to witness the marvel of an aurochs dancing at the end of its tether. "Perhaps," speculates one Cossack, "the Muscovites have taught it to dance, as if it were a dancing bear." "Huh!" responds another skeptically. "Like you could teach a woman to be a Cossack!"[14]

The retort reflects a basic premise of mythic Cossackdom: women do not make Cossacks. Cossacks are male. No women, in fact, are allowed in the Cossack camp at all. (Here the direct reference is to the camp of the Zaporozhian Cossacks, the Sech, which was located beyond the rapids—*za porogami*—of the Dnieper River.) Even thoughts of women are dishonorable and must be excluded from the camp, often together with those who bore them. A good unit is one from which no Cossack has run off to marry;[15] as Gogol tells us, "a Cossack is not meant to hang around with womenfolk" (*Kazak ne na to, chtoby vozit'sia s babami*).[16] Mordovtsev repeats the precept in *Sagaidachny:* "The feminine sex, according to Zaporozhian custom, was not supposed to be in the Sech."[17]

In *The History of Pugachev* (*Istoriia Pugacheva,* 1833), Pushkin writes about the passionate belief in bachelorhood of the Cossacks of poetic tradition, and relates how some Cossacks proposed to murder their own children and abandon their wives. Support of the cultural myth was not Pushkin's primary purpose in the history, however;[18] he concludes in favor of civilization and ultimately praises the women for preventing the murder. Gogol and later glorifiers of the Cossack hero would not be so quick to condemn such counterdomesticity.

Repeatedly, literary Cossacks declare that the steppe or Sech is their mother, or the Dnieper River, or the Volga. For a bride, the men must take their sword, or their saber, or perhaps their horse, or again the steppe or the Sech. They wed their free and spontaneous warrior life and the great expanse that represents it. Characteristically, their fight itself is called a wedding, and to die is to marry:

> A Cossack has married, he took for himself a little woman,
> In the virgin field he took an earthen hut:
> And the free wind will not enter into there,
> And the sun of the world will not pour into there.
> There in a wine box an ox-cart driver of the steppe
> Has buried his brave bones in the earth.[19]

The motifs of marriage to the Cossack lifestyle and the motherhood of the Cossack land clearly originate in folk poetry.[20] The epithet "Mother Volga"

(*Volga-matushka*) is particularly prevalent in songs of the Cossack Sten'ka Razin, perhaps the most popular hero of Cossack folk poetry, and relates there to the traditional image of the Russian land itself as female: "Damp Mother Earth" (*Mat' syra zemlia*) and "Mother Russia."[21] Furthermore, the metaphor of battle as wedding has a long tradition in epics of all nations. The topos in literature about the Cossacks, however, goes further. Its pervasiveness and the variety of its forms beg us to look deeper to determine what the frequent repetitions might be saying about the Cossacks themselves.

It must be kept in mind that, in reality, Cossacks most certainly had relations with women, whether at home in their villages or on campaigns and raids. Women were taken as booty and frequently married to their captors. More important, many new recruits brought families with them, or married local women. These Cossacks produced heirs and created a nation that obviously included males *and* females. Folk poetry, as opposed to the myth of written literature, does not fail to glorify the Cossack women as well as the men. To be fair, Taras Bul'ba does have a wife. But she is immediately abandoned at the start of the novel in favor of horse and saber, and Taras becomes the nurturer (such as nurture might be in the camp and on raids) and educator of his two sons.

When relations between Cossack men and women are described in the literature of the nineteenth century, they almost always lead to disaster, betrayal and/or death. *Sagaidachny* again provides a pithy explanation. One Cossack is led to treasonous statements on account of his defense of having "acquired" a Tatar girl during the last campaign. The subsequent teasing by his fellow Cossacks takes the form of a proof that the girl cannot remain on the Sech: "She's a woman, a girlie. And women, according to Zaporozhian customary law, are not admitted to the Sech, no more than they are to the altar."[22] The unspoken premise is clear; as the altar is holy, so, too, is the Cossack community. Priests who serve at the altar are male; therefore males must be holy. Cossacks are male; therefore Cossacks must be holy. And women must therefore be unholy.

Implicitly or explicitly, several texts suggest that entrance into the Cossack community is, indeed, tonsure. In fact, certain initiation rituals among the historical Cossacks did bear a resemblance to holy vows. The hero of Vasily Narezhny's *The Zaporozhian* reminds us that a newcomer abandons all former titles and signs of distinction, takes on a new name, and shaves his head (except for the characteristic forelock of the Cossack). And, of course, "not one single woman crossed over the gates of their town." If we still have missed the association with monastery life, he continues, "And in no time at all, this layman becomes initiated into the Zaporozhian mysteries."[23] Not only do Cossack customs resemble those of the Church, but the Cossack community as a whole becomes associated with the unearthly atmosphere of those who have sanctified themselves to a life of God. Perhaps it is not surprising that the Cossacks reject women if we accept the implication that they form a holy Christian brotherhood.[24] Sexuality is problematic throughout the history of Christianity, and the attitude toward women in both the Eastern and Western church has not always been enlightened, despite the fact that Orthodoxy accepts married clergy. What is striking, however, is that the substitute for women should be in that case not the Church, nor ideal femininity embodied in the Mother of God or an abstract, theological Sophia, but, rather, the elemental earth and the regenerating violence of the Cossacks' relationship to it.

The frequent declarations of "Mother-Sech" and "Mother-Volga"—*Mat'-Sech', Mat' ty nasha Sech', Sich'-mati* (in Ukrainian), *Volga-mat' rodnaia*—are therefore significantly more than folk imitations. As a monk vows celibacy and marries the Church, the Cossack transcends established heterosexual, marital, and maternal bonds. He is born from and matures to unite instead with his fellow male Cossacks (Sech refers both to the physical camp and to the community that resides within it) and with nature herself. Furthermore, the union is sanctified. The warrior is a holy monk; when he dies he becomes a sainted martyr.

The Cossacks' exploits are repeatedly referred to as *podvigi,* the term for the deeds of saints, and Ostap Bul'ba, Taras's elder son, for one, prepares for his death like the martyrs of old. The narrator tells us that at his execution he did not bend in the face of torture, and "he was the first to have to drink this painful cup" (*etu tiazheluiu chashu*).[25] But "Ostap endured the agony and torment like a giant" (2:164). Significantly, his final cry is for his father, not his mother; the male bond is intact through death. By way of contrast, his traitorous brother Andrii's last cry "was the name of the beautiful Polish girl" with whom he had fallen in love, and for whom he forsook his land, the Orthodox church, and, most important, the Cossack brotherhood (2:144). In life and death, the true Cossack hero, unlike Andrii, does not need women.

The depiction of women in these texts of the nineteenth century brings into focus an interesting contrast between Cossack works on the western European Romantic model, based on Byron's *Mazeppa,* and less derivative Russian works. Byron includes a romantic element that is central to the poem; a girl discovers Mazepa, nurses him to health, and the two fall in love. Kondraty Ryleev, who was strongly influenced by Western models, repeats the motif in *Voinarovsky* (1823–25), where a Cossack maiden saves the hero from the brink of death. In most Russian texts, however, instead of acting as innocent saviors, women ally themselves with the devil. And insofar as they are mothers who hold their sons back from warrior life (as does Taras Bul'ba's wife)[26] or, more usually, sexually attractive young women who lure the Cossacks away from their comrades, they are a threat that must be kept from possessing the Cossack world.

CREATION WITHOUT REPRODUCTION

This topos of woman as evil, even deadly threat appears most explicitly in Gogol's fantastic stories from *Evenings on a Farm Near Dikan'ka* and in "Vii" from his next collection, *Mirgorod* (1835). The stepmother from "A May Night or the Drowned Girl" turns into a cat, a traditional symbol of black magic, and female witches test a Cossack at cards in "The Lost Letter," causing him to exclaim about their cheating: "What kind of devilry is this!" (2:189). "Christmas Eve" boasts a witch-seductress, and the Cossack Khoma in "Vii" mounts a maiden/old witch, only to precipitate his own torment and death. Associations between women and the devil are drawn quite clearly in typical exclamations such as "the devil sits in an old woman" (1:133) and, about Khoma's sexual attraction/revulsion toward the witch in "Vii": "He felt a devilishly sweet feeling" (2:187). Gogol's stories are notoriously full of references to the devil, many of which unite the images of sex, women, and evil powers, and we need not reiterate them all here.[27]

The strained nature of Gogol's own relationship to women and sex has been amply covered in Gogol scholarship; the Cossack myth seems tailored to justify his sexual attitudes. But psychological speculations aside, the treacherous females in Gogol's Cossack tales are symbols of the non-Cossack or the anti-ideal, and by no means unsuccessful attempts at realistic portrayals of women with whom Gogol may or may not have been able to sustain relationships. Female eroticism is significant; it endangers the Cossacks' mythic unity and their "holy marriage" to the female land.

Nowhere is this clearer than in *Taras Bul'ba,* to which we now turn. In this novel, the two Bul'ba boys arrive home from the (Western-oriented) seminary in Kiev, only to be met by their playfully combative father. Over the mother's objections, Bul'ba decides to take his sons the very next morning to the all-male Zaporozhian Sech, for "That's where learning is really learning. There's your school. That's where you'll get your smarts" (2:43).[28] Ostap and Andrii hone their physical skills on the Sech, but, according to Taras, still must be tempered in battle. To this end, Taras fabricates the need for a controversial raid (some of the more staid Cossacks feel the host should abide by treaties they had signed!), only to be upstaged by news of a real need for Cossack intervention in Poland. (N.B., the real or perceived threats are from both East and West.) Taras sets off with his two sons, both of whom prove to be excellent fighters, until Andrii learns that a Polish woman whom he had met while in school, and with whom he had fallen in love, is starving inside the beseiged fortress. He sneaks in, is again captivated by her beauty, and joins the Polish army. "What is a father to me, or a comrade or a fatherland?" Andrii now asks significantly, separating himself from the *male* community (2:106). "And a Cossack perished! He was lost for all of Cossack knighthood!" the narrator tells us (2:107). This symbolic death is soon followed by his actual death at the hands of his own grieving but steadfast father.

Ostap, by contrast, distinguishes himself in battle and is elected ataman (Cossack leader), although he is soon captured and executed by the Poles. To the last moment he remains a Cossack hero, never crying out from pain or fear. He dies with a call for his father on his lips, forever cementing his union with the male Cossack community. Taras had travelled to Warsaw to witness the execution, encased in a "tomb" of bricks. He ultimately emerges, however, with renewed strength. Although he, too, is finally caught and executed by the Poles, his men continue his fight. The ending sees them floating off, as it were, into the sunset:

> The Dniester is no small river, and many are its backwaters, thick river reeds, shallows and depths. The mirror of the river glistens, deafened by the ringing voices of swans. A proud goldeneye duck glides quickly along, and snipes, red-cropped sandpipers and birds of all sorts abound in the reeds and on the banks.[29] The Cossacks were vigorously rowing their narrow, double-ruddered boats, plying the oars in unison, carefully avoiding the shallows, startling the soaring birds, and speaking of their leader. (2:172)

Despite the predominance of male characters in this story of adolescent education, war, and revenge, and in contrast to the two clearly negative characters of the domestic Bul'ba mother and the sexually attractive Polish girl,[30] Gogol includes a strong and positive female throughout *Taras Bul'ba:* the expansive Cossack environment. The structure of the Russian language allows Gogol to refer to both the Sech (*sech'*) and the steppe (*step'*) using singular, feminine pronouns and endings. He can thus establish them as the partner of the singular, masculine Cossack group. Actual women play no part in the Cossack life; Gogol refers instead to the Cossack homeland as both mother and fiancée. When the Bul'bas ride into the steppe, "she" is called a "green, maidenly expanse" (2:58). Perhaps the best example of Gogol's personification of the steppe as the female counterpart to the Cossacks occurs immediately after the narrator relates Andrii's memories of his enchantment in the arms of the Polish girl. Gogol switches back to the narrative present and tells us: "But meanwhile the steppe had long since taken them all into her green embraces" (2:58). The contrast between the individual Polish girl who entraps the alienated Andrii, ensuring his total isolation (and eventual death), and the life-nurturing steppe that embraces but does not contain the group emphasizes the aspect of a wholesome, indeed holy, wedding of Gogol's Cossacks to their female environment.

An association between entrapment and enchantment reinforces the unholy quality of Andrii's unofficial betrothal to the Polish girl. On their initial meeting, her laugh turns Andrii to stone and her beauty, and specifically her eyes, are blinding, recalling the gnome of the title in the story "Vii," who destroys the Cossack Khoma once its eyelids are lifted and it can see. She "bewitches" Andrii again on their second meeting, but only after Andrii has walked through the eerie monastery crypt with its open caskets and exposed human bones, and then through the cathedral where "women knelt, resembling ghosts" (2:96). Andrii has entered the world of the dead. On the square Andrii meets a man about whom the narrator uses the word "mad" three times: (*besnuiushchiisia, beshenstvo, kak beshenaia sobaka*), a word derived in Russian from the root *bes*, or devil. When describing both the square and the girl's chamber, Gogol fills the pages with the verb "to seem" ("The square *seemed* dead"; "It *seemed* that she was still young"; "It *seemed* as though many had purposefully run out into the street, unable to bear the torment in their houses"; "[the woman] *seemed* to be frozen and petrified in the course of some kind of fast motion," and so forth), suggesting again the eerie, even evil quality of Andrii's encounter with the girl. Although merely metaphorically, the girl herself is witchlike enough to charm (literally, *pricharovat'*) Andrii; to cause him to offer to kill himself, to relinquish all, and finally to deny his Cossack blood.

In discussions of gender in Gogol's works, critics usually cite the confusion of male and female characters or symbols. The analyses often conclude that in the struggle between male and female values, men are stifled, overcome, and emasculated.[31] Yet *Taras Bul'ba* must then be relegated to the status of anomaly, for although Taras dies at the end, the Cossack spirit, in all its maleness, is clearly not suffocated.[32] The Cossack tradition endures through his disciples. As they leap off a cliff into the eternally flowing waters of the Dniester River, the Cossacks may exit any semblance of historical time or space, but they consequently enter fully into the reality of myth. The use of past imperfective verb forms (*plyli, grebli, minali, govorili*) in the last paragraph of the novel, cited above, further opens up the narrative beyond the bounds of simple past time; it suggests the opening of a story, not the ending. In general, imperfective verbs require some explanation or continuation, as in: "The Cossacks were rowing when suddenly . . ." To leave off narration at this point thus implies a continuation through time, or lack of closure on the past, historical event. A close reading of the text disallows any conclusion about suffocation of the Cossack hero.

Gogol worked on *Taras Bul'ba* throughout most of his creative career (1835–42), and references to Cossack topoi or inversions of them can be found in many of his other stories. The Cossack novel is not at all a total oddity, but rather is central to all of Gogol's oeuvre, as it is to the Cossack myth as a whole. The question of women and sexuality in relation to the Cossacks perhaps has another answer.

Sociological explanations can be ventured: the topos of the threatening woman in Cossack texts may express Russian gender biases, or more broadly, xenophobia, if women are symbolic of any aliens in the male-dominated Russian society. Psychological answers can and have been offered as well: Cossack characters give vent to sexual fantasies of male dominance and machismo.[33] An analysis of the Cossack as cultural myth, however, presents deeper options. Cossacks do not so much fear or reject women as they themselves represent self-sufficient and, most important, self-regenerating individuals. Their union with the feminine land—and, as has already been noted, Sech, steppe, and even saber are conveniently all feminine nouns in Russian—is an interpenetration of their own essence. Far from representing suppression of the male principle, the Cossacks of Russian literature recover the earth for men. They repossess the land (symbolically stabilizing the empire in the process) as they become one with free, boundless, and "female" space. They thus reconcile male and female qualities within themselves, and, like male Amazons, can further their own kind without recourse to women.

As Gogol informs us: "It seemed that this nation was eternal. Its size never diminished, for new [Cossacks] replaced those who left, were murdered, or drowned" (8:48). The reference to eternal existence is more telling than the historical fact of a constant supply of new recruits to swell the host. It emphasizes the mythic aspect and ignores the logical one; Gogol gives us perpetuity without female interference in the process of creation. In fact, Cossacks did marry, have intercourse, and, consequently, children, who themselves became Cossacks by birth rather than choice. It is the choice itself, however, that makes a Cossack hero authentic.

Cossack sexual power, instead, often transmogrifies into violence. This too is not unfamiliar to experienced readers; the warrior is male and his masculinity is tested in war. What is particularly interesting in terms of the Cossacks is the association between their violence and consequent resurrection. With amazing regularity, Cossack characters undergo some sort of death-in-life experience, whether by apparently dying themselves, or causing the death of another, from which they emerge renewed, refreshed, and reborn. We can find the topos of rebirth through violence particularly widespread in Cossack literature of the early twentieth century. The nineteenth-century antecedents, however, are equally compelling. The death of a Cossack repeatedly represents not an end, but a renewal of life. And the new life given to him derives not from a woman, but from the Cossack's own exuberant exploits within his free and boundless land.

Gogol's Cossack Petro in "St. John's Eve" falls into a "death-like sleep" only to awaken on the third day—unmistakable as a reference to Christ's resurrection; Vakula in "Christmas Eve" is rumored to have committed suicide, and to have been "resurrected" when he reappears; the monk in "A Terrible Vengeance" sleeps in a coffin; and Taras Bul'ba receives a mortal wound—"And he crashed to the ground like a felled oak. And mist covered his eyes"—

from which he could have "fallen asleep . . . perhaps forever" (2:146). He is, however, nursed back to life by companions, and resumes his Cossack role as though reborn. (N.B., in *Taras Bul'ba,* the most mythic of Cossack works, it is males who nurse.)

Later in the novel Taras undergoes a metaphoric death and resurrection as well. In order to see his son, he agrees to capitulate to the Jews and Poles, that is, to those who represent the opposite of his own Cossack essence. As already noted, he rides to Warsaw enclosed in a tomblike pile of bricks; he offers to make a contract with the Jews; he dresses in German clothes; he bribes the Polish guards at the prison where his son is incarcerated—all examples of "non-Cossack" behavior. As a consequence, his Cossack spirit seems to die: "He no longer resembled his former self, steadfast, unbending, as strong as an oak; he became cowardly and weak," until finally, "the heart of Taras stopped beating" (2:156). Taras recovers after this death of his Cossack heart, however, stronger than ever, and sets out to avenge the death of his son with more vigor than his younger compatriots. As the elevated figure of the Cossack leader presides over the end of the novel, with his hands nailed to a tree trunk that had been "cleaved at the top by thunder" (2:170), we are conditioned to see this "crucifixion" as an implication of Taras's "resurrection."

Interesting inversions of the motif occur in Gogol's story "A Terrible Vengeance," where corpses rise from their graves and the wizard opens his eyes after death, and in "Vii," with its female corpse that will not completely die. These figures represent life-in-death rather than death-in-life followed by reinvigoration or even resurrection. The inversion of the imagery parallels an inversion in the characters; both the wizard and his ancestors are demonic, decidedly unholy men. And the girl in "Vii" who refuses to sit still in her coffin is of course antithetical to the Cossacks: she is a sexual female. Vii itself, with the earth that still clings to it after its assent from underground, is an excellent symbol for life-in-death. And the gnome brings destruction, not vitality to the Cossack Khoma.

Typically, the tradition on the Sech that most fascinates Andrii, the son in *Taras Bul'ba* who is destined to betray his Cossack self and his comrades, is the punishment for murder. "They dug a pit, placed the living murderer into it, placed over him the coffin containing the victim's body, and then sprinkled earth over them both" (2:67–68). This practice again suggests a cruel life-in-death experience rather than the positive death-in-life/rebirth imagery associated with the Cossacks. It is fitting that Andrii, who will come to reject the Cossack ethos, singles out this particular custom.

Birth, or rebirth, out of violence is well known in myth; Dionysus is born from the flames of his mother's destruction. Creation is thus inextricably linked to death, and violence is not only destructive. Out of its ashes can emerge great heroes, as well as phoenixes. By insisting on the creative, and thus positive aspect of violence, moral structures are evaded. This is manifest in Gogol: though many readers express indignation at the Cossacks' wanton violence, Gogol himself does not judge. In fact, for him there seems to be something highly positive, even marvelous about the Cossacks. With no irony, their battle is a feast; their fight is music; their murdering is dance.

Gogol's admiration of the Cossacks' violent strength and activity can be seen in his vocabulary as a whole, particularly in the articles of the miscellany *Arabesques,* published the same year as *Mirgorod* and the first version of *Taras Bul'ba,* and which includes his articles on Ukrainian history and music. In describing the Middle Ages—the time, he claims, that transformed the world, united ancient and modern, and functions in history like the heart of the human body (8:14)—Gogol employs the terms variety (*pestrota*), lively activity (*zhivoe deistvie*), sharp contrasts (*rezkie protivopolozhnosti*), and strange brightness (*strannaia iarkost'*) (8:16), all of which he will use in *Taras Bul'ba* to describe the Cossacks. He claims that the Middle Ages possess a gigantic, almost miraculous colossal nature (*kolossal'nost' ispolinskaia, pochti chudesnaia,* 8:17). Gogol uses a similar image when he writes of what we must recognize as Cossack-like colossal grandeur (*kolossal'noe velichie*) of history (8:27), or again of the gigantic colossal nature (*ispolinskaia kolossal'nost'*) of subterranean geography (8:102). We must remember the Cossack Ostap, as he "endured the agony and torment [at his execution] like a giant (*ispolin*)" (2:164).

Even more telling is Gogol's article on "Sculpture, Painting and Music," published as the introductory piece to *Arabesques.* Gogol ranks these three art forms on various, and typically Romantic scales. He sees a Hegelian-like historical progression from pagan (sculpture)[34] to Christian (painting) to modern (music); from stasis to movement; and from passive reception by the viewer to actual participation, in fact, to the interpenetration of music and the human soul. Gogol's description of music, the highest stage, prefigures his Cossack heroes. All the vocabulary used to explain music evokes power and violence:

> But effervesce with more vigor, my third goblet! Resounding foam, sparkle more brightly and splash against the golden rim—you sparkle in honor of music. She is more effusive, more impetuous than her two sisters. She is a pure gust of energy. Suddenly and instantaneously she rips man from his earth, deafens him with the thunder of mighty sounds, and immediately plunges him back into his world. Commandingly, she strikes his nerves, as on a keyboard, and turns him trembling. He no longer simply enjoys [as he did with sculpture], no longer simply feels compassion [as with painting]. He is himself transformed into suffering itself. His soul does not passively contemplate incomprehensible phenomena, but lives itself, lives its own life, lives violently, crushingly, rebelliously. (8:11–12)

Gogol's aesthetic, we note from this passage, is generically feminine. His third goblet, music, is one of three sisters.[35] Yet her actions all derive from a stereotypical male pool. She rips, she thunders, she strikes powerfully. And, in turn, she causes the soul of the male viewer to act similarly: to live violently, crushingly, and rebelliously. In other words, through contact with music, the male companion is reborn in her vibrant, violent image. By her very presence, the highest form of artistic creativity produces Cossack-like heroes who are "not of woman born."

If we recall the frequent musical references used in conjunction with the Cossacks in *Taras Bul'ba,* and the contrasting static, pictorial descriptions of the enemy Poles, we can begin to recognize a relationship between violence, art, and our heroes. Thus, upon seeing a Cossack dance on the Sech, the narrator tells us: "Man has freedom in music alone. . . . He is willful only when he loses himself in wild dance, when his soul does not fear his body" (2:300 [1835 ed.]). Less directly: "Andrii immersed himself in the enchanting music of the bullets and swords" (2:85); and, on the steppe, the Cossacks' open home: "All the music which rang out during the day became quiet and was replaced with another music," so that "the steppe was deafened with whistles" (2:59–60). Finally, the watery infinity into which the Cossack men glide at the end of the novel is similarly musical: "The mirror of the river glistens, deafened by the ringing voices of swans" (2:172).

By contrast, Gogol uses static, visual imagery to characterize the enemy troops, along with their accoutrements and environment. He describes the Poles' clothes and armor in great detail, but does not show them in motion. Instead, he calls them a tableau vivant (*zhivaia kartina,* 2:114); they are no more than sculpture in flesh and bones. When Gogol describes the scene in Warsaw at the execution of Ostap, he again pays close attention to the pictorial aspects of the Polish crowd. He carefully describes their clothing and jewelry, and particularly concentrates on a young girl and her beau who are standing in the "foreground" (*na perednem plane,* 2:162), as though within the immobile frame of a picture. No reader has ever argued that the Poles, associated with static or, at best, immobile painting, are anything but false heroes. True art, like music, and true heroes, like the Cossacks, are active, even destructive. Yet they create. Cossacks destroy, yet through their violent community and their communion with a (female) musical land they participate in Gogol's creative aesthetic.

In "A Glance at the Composition of Little Russia," Gogol calls the Cossack era "a poetic time," marked by unity, activity, and growth, when "the saber and the plow made friends and could be found by the side of every peasant" (8:49). This formulation (of questionable historical truth) reads like a Gogolian transformation of the biblical passage: "And they shall beat their swords into plowshares, and their spears into pruning hooks"

(Isaiah 2:4, Micah 4:3). For Gogol, Cossack destruction is not transformed into domesticity; swords do not become farm tools. Rather, the violence of the saber and the productive potential of the earth exist in organic unity within the Cossacks' mythic aura; martial frontiersman and feminine land unite. And this is a way that the feminine principle has a place in the Cossack world: not reproduction by women, but rebirth from the union of violent male Cossack and the fertile earth.

Thus, Gogol does not simply ignore aggressive aspects of the world, the Cossacks included, but rather raises them to an aesthetic ideal. He does not condemn the Cossack violence, nor does he contrast it to their or others' potential for good. In fact, despite the ethical tenor of many Cossack stories, evil and good do not appear as a contradictory pair; the two are reconciled within the heroes. The Cossacks can destroy, and do so in a major key, because they can transcend traditional moral boundaries.[36] They unite with and are reborn by amoral music itself. Ethics in the Cossack myth gives way to aesthetics, just as individual female reproduction gives way to a self-sustaining, self-nurturing collective male brotherhood, at home on the free and creative steppe. Indeed, Gary Larson's Cossacks have nothing to fear *but* Mrs. Caldwell, whose fenced-in garden represents a segment of the earth to which they are not yet wed.

Alternative Histories

Jennifer J. Hixon

The Fall of Novgorod in Karamzin's Fiction and History

Лета к суровой прозе клонят (The years to austere prose incline)
—A.S. Pushkin, *Evgenii Onegin*, 6.43.5; Nabokov's translation

"But ah," Desire still cries, "give me some food."
—Sir Philip Sidney, *Astrophel and Stella*

NIKOLAI MIKHAILOVICH KARAMZIN's last work of fiction, completed the year before he devoted himself exclusively to his *History of the Russian State*, is the historical novella "Marfa Posadnitsa" (1803). The story narrates the fall of republican Novgorod to monarchical Moscow in 1478. Karamzin was, by his own and others' accounts, "a republican in his heart, but a monarchist in his head."[1] The fall of Novgorod allowed him to explore republican and monarchical principles in direct conflict. A "loyal subject of the Russian tsar"[2] and a saddened witness to the excesses of the French Revolution, Karamzin always makes clear his belief in the historical necessity of the monarchy's victory. But he also reveals his fascination not only with the republic, but with Novgorod and with Marfa Posadnitsa herself, in three separate treatments of the theme: the tale "Marfa Posadnitsa," the essay "On Marfa Posadnitsa" ("Izvestie o Marfe Posadnitse," 1803), and the pertinent chapters of the *History of the Russian State* (*Istoriia gosudarstva Rossiiskogo,* 1818–26). Of the many insightful studies of Karamzin's fictional and historical treatments of the fall of Novgorod, none has paid particular attention to a fact that seems to me of singular importance in Karamzin's creative biography: in the conflict between Novgorod and Moscow, the republic is represented by a woman, the monarchy by a man. I hope to show that the opposition between republic and monarchy was, for Karamzin, not only one between heart and mind, but between private and public, poetry and history, and ultimately, between mother and father.

Indeed, Karamzin's fictional and historical treatments of the fall of Novgorod can productively be viewed as pre-Oedipal and Oedipal versions of the same tale. The fictional and historical versions bear striking similarities to the pre-Oedipal "Foundling's" tale of lost utopia and the Oedipal "Bastard's" tale of worldly conquest that Marthe Robert finds at the core of all novelistic plots in spite of their superficial variety. I shall explore those similarities, and, relying on Peter Sack's Oedipal explication of the conventions of the elegy and Jessica Benjamin's examination of the ambivalent compromises in the Oedipal resolution, suggest ways in which Karamzin's repeated meditations on the fall of Novgorod may have reflected his psychological adjustment to traumatic events in his own history.

In the fifteenth century, Ivan III of Moscow united the many principalities of Russia into a state finally strong enough to throw off the 300-year-old Tatar yoke. A critical step in this unification was the subjugation of Novgorod. Although Novgorod had originally "invited" the Varangian princes to rule over Russia in 862, it had grown increasingly high-handed in its treatment of their descendants. It eventually enjoyed extensive autonomy from the rule both of the Riurikovian Great Princes and the Tatar Khans. Novgorod also boasted an elected civil government, with a governor (*posadnik*) at its head. Thus, Moscow's conquest of Novgorod in 1478 represented not only the triumph of one powerful city-state over another, but the triumph of the monarchical over a more-or-less republican principle. Moscow's victory was presided over by Ivan III; Novgorod's resistance was led by Marfa Posadnitsa, the widow of Isaak Boretskii, one of the last Novgorod posadniks. (The title "posadnitsa" means either a female posadnik, or the wife of the posadnik. In Marfa's case, it means both.)

Having been both the birthplace of Russian monarchy, and the stronghold of popular democracy, Novgorod became a touchstone in eighteenth- and nineteenth-century debate on the form of government proper to the Russian state. Sumarokov, Catherine the Great, Kniazhnin, Radishchev, Kheraskov, Derzhavin, the Decembrist poets, Pushkin, and Lermontov were all inspired to write about Novgorod, and their works were conceived and interpreted in the context of the contemporary political discussions.[3] Most of these authors focused on the ninth-century conflict between Riurik and Vadim the Brave, a Novgorod patriot put to death for his resistance to Varangian rule.

Karamzin, however, did not focus on the conflict at the beginning of the Riurik dynasty, but rather on the struggle that marked the end of Novgorod's independence. In the aftermath of the Terror in France, Karamzin subscribed to the increasingly popular notion that a nation's form of government must be decided as much by national tradition as by abstract philosophy.[4] Rapid changes and radical restructuring were seen as fatal to public order, which was, in the end, the guarantee of private freedom if not of political liberty.[5] The conflict between Riurik and Vadim pitted imported monarchy against native republic; the conflict between Ivan III and Marfa Posadnitsa was between two systems that could lay equal claim to the sanction of national custom. By examining this later conflict between monarchy and republic, Karamzin set himself the important task of explaining why one traditional system prevailed over another. Karamzin was not just contrasting two political systems, however, but two realms of human existence: a feminine, private world of artistic fantasy and a masculine, public world of historical action.

According to the chronicles, Marfa used her tremendous wealth to influence by no means unanimous public opinion. She led a party advocating alliance with Lithuania to preserve and enlarge Novgorod's power against Moscow. She herself planned to marry a prominent Lithuanian nobleman. Marfa's bribes roused the rabble, but many ordinary citizens were less than enthusiastic about defending the independence of their nominally republican, but in fact oligarchic, city.[6] Despite their superior numbers, Novgorod's forces were quickly conquered by Moscow's, and Novgorod was deprived of its historical freedoms in 1478.

In Karamzin's fictional portrayal, however, Marfa is far from a scheming plutocrat. She is a loyal, if misguided, patriot, who scorns the idea of alliance with Lithuania. Marfa confesses to her daughter and son-in-law that she has devoted herself to defending Novgorod's freedom not because of an advanced political consciousness but out of love for her husband, who just before he died made her vow to replace him as the champion of Novgorod's liberty. She recalls how her life used to be spent entirely within the domestic sphere, caring for her husband and children, only venturing out into public to go to church. Now, however, she presides at the elders' council, commands the multitudes, and calls for war and bloodshed, the very names of which used to horrify her. Here is how Marfa herself accounts for this transformation:

> Love! Love alone—for your father. . . . He perished along with my happiness . . . I don't know whether I shed tears on his grave: I wasn't thinking of tears, but, adoring my spouse, I burned with a passion to resurrect his spirit in myself. The wise legends of antiquity, languages of foreign lands, chronicles of free peoples, and experiences of past centuries enlightened my reason. I spoke—and the elders heeded my words with astonishment.[7]

I recommend special attention to this passage. Marfa explains to her children that she is assuming her late husband's civic struggles *in order to resurrect him.* To properly understand her public, "masculine" exploits, her children must understand them as expressions of a private, "feminine" desire to honor—and in part to recover—her lost domestic happiness. Stunned by grief, she moves from the realm of Sentiment to the realm of History. Karamzin himself was making a similar transition. At the very time he was working on "Marfa Posadnitsa," Karamzin's beloved first wife, Elizaveta Ivanovna, née Protasova, was dying. "Marfa Posadnitsa" was to become Karamzin's last work of fiction.

Although Karamzin had already immersed himself in historical reading, it was not until after his wife's death that he devoted himself exclusively to historical writings. Karamzin, founder of a sentimental style designed simultaneously to appeal to and educate the Russian female reader, was transforming himself into the father of a Russian history that he would present as ever more exclusively masculine. In adopting a masculine persona, Marfa assumed her dead husband's identity; Karamzin, on the other hand, made himself over not in the image of a dying wife and mother but in the image of a surviving father. This is one of the hallmarks of the Oedipal "resolution," whether it is a stage in child development or in adult mourning: seduced and threatened by the fantasy of an omnipotent mother[8] or by death's imagined promise of reunion with the beloved,[9] the child and the mourner alike cling to symbols of male potency as to totems that can protect a sorely tried confidence in independent survival. In "Marfa Posadnitsa," however, the Oedipal polarization of male (usually glorified) and female (usually denigrated) spheres is not complete: not only is the main character a woman with "masculine" qualities who bears a striking resemblance to the author with his "feminine" sympathies, but the setting and structure of the story conform to the pre-Oedipal "Foundling's" tale of lost paradise as explicated by Marthe Robert. Robert conceives of the novel as an elaboration of Freud's " 'family romance of the neurotic.' "[10] This family romance has a pre-Oedipal and an Oedipal phase that correspond to the two fundamental plots, one or the other of which, according to Robert, lies at the base of every novel. The first is the pre-Oedipal "Foundling's": when reality, in the persons of the child's mother and father, thwarts the child's sovereign will, he invents a tale in which he is a foundling and the people taking care of him are not his real parents. Rather, his real mother and father preside in regal splendor over a paradise in which, as royal scion, his own right to untrammeled rule would be recognized.[11] The Foundling's tale is one of escape from reality, of quixotic quest for this lost paradise. The Foundling has not yet understood the sexual difference between his parents, and therefore scorns both "impostor" parents, and worships both "real" parents, equally.

Karamzin invents a foundling for the tale "Marfa Posadnitsa." Miroslav is a handsome, brave, and noble youth who was found as a baby in Novgorod's public square. He was raised by the Novgorodians, distinguished himself in battle, and is now chosen by Marfa to marry her beloved daughter and to lead Novgorod in battle against Ivan III. Marfa refers to him as her son.

In battle, Miroslav comes face to face with his archenemy, Ivan III, but cannot bring himself to kill him. One of Ivan's knights is about to dispatch the youth when Ivan III protects Miroslav with his own shield. And finally, when the battle is over, Miroslav buried, and Novgorod defeated, Ivan is seen mourning at the grave of the brave youth. The secret of Miroslav's birth seems to be solved: he is in reality Ivan III's son.[12]

Thus, we have a foundling, and we have royal parents: noble Marfa, in addition to being Miroslav's mother-in-law, is called "the mother of Novgorod," and regal Ivan, apparently Miroslav's real father, becomes the "father of Novgorod" (*IS*, 1:722). We even have a paradise of sorts. Although Karamzin makes clear that "the people in Novgorod were at that stage of morality, 'at which Republics fall,' "[13] the very fact that Novgorod was subject to a fall confirms its Edenic status. Furthermore, in his writings of the 1790s, Karamzin repeatedly invoked the republic to stand for the kind of youthful dreams and artistic inspiration that could not survive harsh reality. For instance, in the 1794 poem "Poslanie k Dmitrievu v otvet na ego stikhi, v kotorykh on zhaluetsia na skorotechnost' schastlivoi molodosti" (Epistle to Dmitriev in reply to his verses, in which he complained of the fleetingness of happy youth), the republic represents the kind of ideal world a dreamy youth would try to build.

Но время, опыт разрушают
Воздушный замок юных лет;
Красы волшебства исчезают . . .
Теперь иной я вижу свет,—
И вижу ясно, что с Платоном
Республик нам не учредить,
. . . .
Гордец не любит наставленья,
Глупец не терпит просвещенья—
Итак, лампаду угасим,
Желая доброй ночи им.[14]

(But time and experience destroy
The castles in air of youthful years.
The charms of enchantment disappear . . .
Now I see a different world—
And I see clearly that Plato and I
Will found no republics,
. . . .
The proud man does not love instruction,
The stupid cannot bear enlightenment—
And so, we'll douse our lamp,
Bidding them good night.)

The image of the doused lamp recurs in "Marfa Posadnitsa," and with the same meaning. Marfa warns Novgorod's citizens: "When, in the depths of night, the lamp in my high tower goes out and no longer serves as a sign to you, that Marfa is thinking of the good of Novgorod by its light, then, then say: 'All is lost! . . .' " (*IS*, 1:715). Indeed, once the battle is lost, the people look toward her tower and see that "there the night lamp had gone out!" (*IS*, 1:722). The dousing of the lamp and the fall of the republic signal the end of humanitarian dreams and inspiration, and with it the end of the pre-Oedipal fantasy of utopia.

In the 1795 "Afinskaia zhizn' " (Athenian life), the narrator is painfully aware that the utopia he creates in his fantasy cannot survive outside it. In the story, the narrator transports himself in his imagination to the quintessential republican city in order to escape the horrible events reported in contemporary newspapers. In his dream, he finds himself in a land of childlike wonder and artistic ferment. He reflects:

> We are more learned than the Greeks, but the Greeks were—smarter than we are, just as children chasing after a many-colored butterfly in a spring meadow are smarter than adults, sailing to America or to India for spices. . . . Everywhere and in everything they sought—enjoyment; sought it with the ardor of passion, with the most intensely felt need, like a lover seeking his beloved—and their life was, so to speak, the very flower of Poetry.[15]

Karamzin ascribes to the Greeks an instinctive, emotional wisdom identical to that which he ascribes to women. Compare the following lines from his 1795 "Poslanie k zhenshchinam" (Epistle to women) to his praise of the Greeks above:

> . . . Хвалить ли в вас то чувство,
> Которым истину находите в вещах
> Скорее всех мужчин? Нам надобно искусство,
> Трудиться разумом, работать, размышлять,
> Чтоб истину сыскать;
> Для нас она живет в лесах, в вертепах темных
> И в кладезях подземных,—
> Для вас же птичкою летает на лугах
> (*PSS*, 175)

> (. . . Should I praise in you that feeling
> That discerns the truth in things
> More quickly than all men do? We need art,
> We need to labor with our reason, to work, to ponder,
> In order to find truth;
> For us it lives in forests and dark caves
> And in underground mines—
> For you it's a bird flying over the meadows)

For Karamzin, the same values prevail in feminine society as in the republican city, and, although he does not make an explicit reference to the republic in "Epistle to Women," he does suggest as ideal a form of government that would befit his imagined Athens:

> Велите мне избрать подсолнечной царя:
> Кого я изберу, усердием горя

Ко счастию людей? Того, кто всех страстнее
Умеет вас [женщин] любить,—и свет бы счастлив был!
(*PSS*, 173)

(Command me to choose a tsar of the universe:
Who would I choose, burning with zeal
For people's happiness? Him who more passionately than all others
Could love you [women]—and the world would be happy!)

On the one hand, for Karamzin the republic was a utopia that he knew could not survive the shocks of historical events. On the other, in the 1790s, he still dreamed of creating it, at least in a domestic sphere and among his female readers. In "Epistle to Women," he formulated his literary program, and revealed the motivation behind it:

О вы, которых мне любезна благосклонность
Любезнее всего! . . .
. . . .
Для коих после я . . .
. . . .
Взял в руки лист бумаги,
Чернильницу с пером,
Чтоб быть писателем, творцом,
Для вас, красавицы, приятным;
Чтоб слогом чистым, сердцу внятным,
Оттенки вам изображать
Страстей счастливых и несчастных,
То кротких, то ужасных;
Чтоб вы могли сказать:
«Он, право, мил и верно переводит
Всё темное в сердцах на ясный нам язык;
Слова для тонких чувств находит!»—
(*PSS*, 169–70)

(O, you whose delightful favor toward me
Is more delightful than anything! . . .
. . . .
For whom I later . . .
. . . .
Took paper,
Inkwell, pen in hand
So as to be a writer, a creator,
Pleasing for you beautiful women;
So as, in style pure and intelligible to the heart,
To depict for you the nuances
Of passions happy and unhappy,
Some mild, some horrible;

So that you could say:
"He really is sweet and truly translates
All that's dark in hearts into a language clear to us;
He finds words for subtle feelings!"—)

As Marfa's historic defense of Novgorod's freedom is motivated by her love for her late husband, so, in this poem, Karamzin's famous development of Russian sentimental literature and the language in which to write it are linked to his affection for women and desire for their approval. He links his craving for specifically feminine favor, and his seeking that favor through literary endeavors, to his infant deprivation of maternal care. When Karamzin was not yet three years old, his mother died, leaving his father to raise several small children. Karamzin's identification with his missing mother is illustrated in a passage from his unfinished "true story" (*byl'*) "A Knight of Our Time" ("Rytsar' nashego vremeni"), published in *Messenger of Europe* (*Vestnik Evropy*) in 1802 and 1803. Influenced by Sterne, Rousseau, and Wieland,[16] but widely acknowledged as semi-autobiographical, the story narrates the early years of Leon, son of a middle-aged provincial landowner and his beautiful young wife. This young woman dies when her son is seven years old, but bequeaths to her son her love of sentimental literature: "Soon they gave Leon the key to the yellow bookcase, in which his late mother's library was preserved, and where there were novels on two shelves and a few religious books on a third: an important epoch in the education of his mind and heart!" (*IS*, 1:764)

Seeing young Leon completely enthralled by the novels, his father muses, " 'Just like his mother! She wouldn't let a book out of her hand." (*IS*, 1:764). Again in "Epistle to Women," Karamzin invokes his missing mother and praises the woman who in some degree took her place. He calls this woman "Nanina" in the poem; many of his readers would have known that he referred to Anastasia Ivanovna Pleshcheeva, née Protasova.

Ах! я не знал тебя! . . . ты, дав мне жизнь сокрылась!
Среди весенних ясных дней
В жилище мрака преселилась!
Я в первый жизни час наказан был судьбой!
Не ног тебя ласкать, ласкаем быть тобой!
. . . .
Нанина! десять лет тот день благословляю,
Когда тебя, мой друг, увидел в первый раз;
Гармония сердец соединила нас
В единый миг навек. Что был я? Сиротою
В пространственном мире сем . . .
. . . .
Но знай, о верный друг! что дружбою твоей

Я более всего горжуся в жизни сей
. . . .
Что истина своей рукою
Напишет над моей могилой? *Он любил*:
Он нежной женщины нежнейшим другом был!
(*PSS*, 174–79)

(Ah! I didn't know you!. . . . you, having given me life, stole away!
In the clear days of spring
You withdrew to the dwelling of gloom!
In the first hour of life I was punished by fate!
I couldn't caress you, nor be caressed by you!
. . . .
Nanina! For ten years I have blessed the day
When I saw you, my friend, for the first time;
Harmony of hearts united us
Forever in a single instant. What was I? An orphan
In this wide world . . .
. . . .
But know, o faithful friend! that your friendship
Is what I prize most in this life
. . . .
What will truth inscribe with its hand over my grave? *He loved:*
He was the tenderest friend of a tender woman!)

Karamzin met Anastasia Ivanovna Pleshcheeva in 1785, when he was not yet twenty and she was in her early thirties. She was married to a man she considered incapable of the strength and tenderness of feeling that were natural to her.[17] Derzhavin, for one, considered Karamzin's public expressions of devotion to her somewhat scandalous.[18] But her friendship with Karamzin seemed to conform to an ideal of sentimental friendship in which men and women were equals and the difference in gender was not an essential ingredient, but rather acted as "a piquant spice."[19] This equality of the sexes recalls the undifferentiated adoration of both mother and father in the pre-Oedipal stage, although Karamzin's *later* fictional portrait of a friendship similar to his and Pleshcheeva's certainly has sexual and indeed Oedipal overtones. The portrayal, obviously colored by Rousseau's account of his relationship to Mme de Warens, appears in "A Knight of Our Time," published in 1803. A beautiful countess, married to a cold older man, becomes a "second Mama" to the eleven-year-old Leon. Unlike Rousseau, Karamzin did not enter into sexual relations with the woman who took his mother's place; it was, however, her younger sister Elizaveta Ivanovna who became his first wife in 1801, and who, dying shortly after delivering their first child in 1802, made him a widower and a father almost simultaneously.

The gentle worlds of sentimental friendship and innocent pleasure-seeking that Karamzin praises in "Epistle to Women" have much in common with the polite society Zhukovsky defines in his 1808 essay "The Writer in Society":

> It is a republic with its own laws, obedient to its own ideal ruler. . . . Imagine a multitude of people of both sexes, gifted by fortune with either wealth or nobility, joined together by a natural inclination toward polite sociability, ordaining pleasure alone as the aim of its association, pleasure consisting solely in appealing to one another—imagine this, and you will obtain a rather clear understanding of the "great world."[20]

But in 1795, it remained for Karamzin himself to create this society, or at least to create a Russian language in which it could express its concerns. As Lotman writes,

> When he appealed to ladies' taste in literature or to the language of polite society, he had in mind neither the real ladies nor the real society of his time: in society French was spoken, and the ladies of Karamzin's day did not read Russian books. . . .
>
> He had in mind a society that it remained to found through the efforts of literature, first of all by means of his, Karamzin's, own works.[21]

Karamzin's literary efforts, then, can be seen as an attempt to create a society that would be congenial toward the kind of tender friendship he shared with Anastasia Ivanovna Pleshcheeva, and toward the literary enthusiasms young Leon shares with his mother. By the 1790s, Karamzin knew that this society could not be created through political action. Disillusioned not only by the Terror in France, but also the persecution to which the aging Catherine, made paranoid by the fate of French royalty, subjected all but the most obsequious authors, Karamzin took refuge in the intimate society gathered at the Pleshcheevs' country estate Znamenskoe, and devoted himself to the production of a "private" literature.[22] Sometimes, this literature circulated no more widely than the albums and impromptu readings at Znamenskoe; sometimes, still in its domestic dress, it ventured out into the world in collections such as *Aonidi,* where "Epistle to Women" appeared, and *Aglaia,* where "Athenian Life" was published in 1795.

Thus, in his work of the 1790s, Karamzin associates the republic with youthful dreams, artistic imagination, and a feminine society in which reunion with his lost mother can be imagined and even approximated. In "Marfa Posadnitsa," the republic is again represented as a pre-Oedipal utopia. But it is not a perfect paradise: the royal parents cannot be reconciled and the republican city's liberty is sacrificed for the sake of the larger state's survival. Ivan's spokesman compares the blessed stability of monarchy to the pernicious license of democracy, but it is Marfa herself who rehearses a republic's need for extraordinary civic virtue. "If vile cupidity has indeed mastered the Novgorodians' souls, if we love treasures and leisure more than virtue and glory, then the last hour of our liberty will soon strike and the Veche bell, its ancient voice, will fall from Iaroslav's tower and never sound again!" (*IS*, 1:692)

In the heady atmosphere of Novgorod's final struggle for freedom, the virtue Marfa calls for seems attainable; in light of the commentary Karamzin had just published on current European events, however, his readers would know he did not consider such virtue sustainable, even in a country with a republican tradition. In an 1802 article on the fall of Switzerland, in terms markedly similar to those Marfa uses in warning her fellow citizens, Karamzin sadly reflected on the Swiss republic's loss of the stern virtues that had protected its freedom:

> This unfortunate land now presents all the horrors of civil war, which is the effect of personal passions, evil and insane selfishness. This is how public virtues disappear! Like people, they outlive their time in states; but without high public virtue a republic cannot stand. That is why the monarchical form of government is much more felicitous and reliable: it does not require extremes of its citizens and can prosper at the same level of morality, at which republics fall. . . . The mercantile spirit that in time possessed the Swiss filled their trunks with gold, but exhausted their proud and exclusive love for independence. (*IS*, 2:278–79)

By 1802, any hopes Karamzin may have cherished that a republic could survive as a political reality had been destroyed by the French Terror and Napoleon's reestablishment of autocratic order. Between 1799 and 1802, the Swiss republic, divided by regional rivalries, had gradually come under the control of Napoleon's forces. Ironically, more people were eligible for the privileges of citizenship under French influence than had been so in what was really the oligarchy of the native Swiss order; by 1802, Karamzin, and the Swiss themselves, mourned not so much the loss of the egalitarian *svoboda* (freedom) Karamzin had praised in a letter of 1789, but rather the disappearance of Swiss national *nezavisimost'* (independence). This distinction between freedom and independence would play an important role in Karamzin's discussion of the conflict between Novgorod and Moscow in his *History of the Russian State*. Indeed, as the *History* was at least in part intended as a didactic tool for the edification of the tsar Alexander I, to whom it was dedicated, so Karamzin's article on the fall of Switzerland, published within a year of Alexander's coronation, may have been an early attempt to restrain the young tsar's liberal tendencies and to emphasize the importance of national unity and sovereignty over almost all else. Unlike Marfa, he was not warning his fellow citizens, but his tsar. The regional rivalries that, in Karamzin's view, had made Switzerland vulnerable to foreign domination would have had a special significance for Alexander, one of whose tutors had been a revolutionary who agitated for the Vaud canton's independence from Bern's control.[23] Although "Marfa Posadnitsa" suggests a foundling's quest for a lost utopia in which mother, father, and child are united in harmony, its author knew that such a quest was in vain. His treatment of the fall of Novgorod in book 6 of the *History* would be fiercely Oedipal in its orientation toward reality, and in its polarization of genders.

His first nonfiction consideration of the Novgorod theme, however, does not yet emphasize this polarization. The essay "On Marfa Posadnitsa," published in 1803, is one of several meditations on the proper way to write history that he published around this time. In this essay, Marfa is described as a worthy subject for a historian's pen; her character is a wonder of nature: "However, nature sometimes loves extremes, departs from its usual law and gives women characters that bring them out of domestic anonymity onto the public stage" (*IS*, 2:227). Marfa is "an extraordinary, rare woman," (*IS*, 2:227) an "ardent woman" (*IS*, 2:228). At this point, Karamzin seemed to imagine women as the most likely subjects—and the most likely readers—of his historical writings. As he had developed a Russian style capable of expressing the formerly ineffable feelings of the heart, he now conceives of his task as understanding as much by intuition as by study the truths behind the reticent historical record: "It's true that the Russian chroniclers . . . are extremely stingy with details; however, a mind that is attentive and gifted with *historical conjecture*, can supply missing elements by its powers of conception, like the learned classicist who, deciphering . . . an old Greek inscription, by two letters divines the third, worn away by time, and does not err" (*IS*, 2:229–30). Karamzin seemed at this stage to imagine the Russian historical record as a collection of semi-intelligible hints, oriental and feminine.[24] He would divine its secrets using the same intuition that had enabled him to express in his fiction the finest shadings of sentiment. Indeed, he envisioned the result of his researches as an account of the historical exploits of Russian *women:* "In a word, *a gallery of glorious Russian women* could be a very pleasing composition, if the author, possessing talent and taste, were to depict such persons with the vivid colors of his love for the female sex and for the fatherland" (*IS*, 2:231).

"Glorious Russian women" such as Olga and Gorislava were also prominent in Karamzin's 1802 essay "O sluchaiakh i kharakterakh v rossiiskoi istorii, kotorye mogut byt' predmetom khudozhestv" (On events and characters in Russian history, suitable as subjects for the arts). He also calls for a picturesque Russian history in a letter from the Paris section of his *Letters of a Russian Traveler.* Although this letter is dated "May 1790" (and is often referred to as if it were actually written then), it, like his other letters "from Paris," was almost certainly not written before 1793 and not published until 1801.[25] In this letter, Karamzin advises the would-be Russian historian to follow the examples of

Tacitus, Hume, Robertson, and Gibbon and "select, animate and color" events from Russian history, abbreviating those that are "not important . . . as Hume did in his *English History*."[26]

But as Iurii Lotman points out,[27] Karamzin rejects his own earlier recommendations and to a certain extent his English models in the 1815 preface to the *History of the Russian State:*

> The Historian of Russia might, of course, . . . present the important, most memorable aspects of antiquity in a skillful *picture* and begin the *detailed* narration with Ivan's time or with the fifteenth century, when one of the greatest state formations in the world was accomplished; he could easily write 200 or 300 eloquent, pleasing pages, instead of many books, difficult for the Author, tedious for the Reader. But these *surveys*, these *pictures* do not take the place of chronicles, and someone who has read only Robertson's Introduction to the History of Karl V still lacks a detailed, accurate conception of medieval Europe.[28]

In this passage, Karamzin explicitly and dramatically disavows his earlier pronouncements, but he does something else as well: he declares the new goal of his historical labors, the new prize that will reward conscientious attention to still tedious detail. The historian should no longer aim for imaginative portraits of remarkable Russian women; rather, he should labor toward a true understanding of the glory and might of the very masculine Ivan III, "father of Novgorod," and of Russia. He no longer sees the Russian historical record as a collection of inarticulate fragments, but rather as the annals of one of the greatest state formations in the world.

It was only after Karamzin had struggled through the five volumes necessarily devoted to earlier Russian history, however, that he was able to turn his eager attention to the reign of Ivan III. Although they would later prove delightful to readers, those first five volumes really had been difficult for Karamzin. He wrote to Dmitriev on 9 August 1811, of his relief that they were now behind him: "I am working zealously, and getting ready to describe the period of Ivan Vasilievich. There's a real historical subject! Heretofore I've only dissembled and subtilized, extricating myself from difficulties. Behind me I see the sandy African plain, but in front of me majestic groves, beautiful meadows, rich fields, and so on. But poor Moses never entered the Promised Land!"[29] But Karamzin did enter his promised land. Karamzin's sixth volume, written between 1811 and 1812 and devoted to Ivan Vasilievich's reign, begins with the triumphant words: "Henceforth our history assumes a dignity truly befitting a state, no longer describing senseless Princely feuds, but the acts of a Kingdom that has achieved independence and greatness" (*IGR*, 6:5).

In the first chapter of the sixth volume, Karamzin describes two of "the celebrated triumphs of Ivan's reign." The first was a stunning defeat of the Tatars at Kazan, the beginning of Ivan's successful campaign to free Russia completely from the Tatar Yoke. But, writes Karamzin, "the second [triumph] had even more favorable consequences for the might of the Great Prince within Russia" (*IGR,* 6:16). That victory was the first in a series of battles that led to the conquest of the independent republic of Novgorod. To the Moscow troops, writes Karamzin, "the Novgorodian traitors seemed worse than Tatars" (*IGR,* 6:25). Perhaps it was Napoleon's looming threat to Russia's sovereignty that made any internal dissent seem so heinous to Karamzin, and the unity Ivan had imposed so necessary. Still, the harshness of Karamzin's condemnation of Novgorod and particularly of Marfa Posadnitsa is striking in light of his earlier enthusiasm for her. Where formerly her ardent character had been described as a worthy work of creative nature, now she is clearly an unnatural freak: "In spite of the ancient customs and mores of the Slavs, which removed the female sex from any participation in civil affairs, a proud, ambitious woman, the widow of the former Posadnik Isaak Boretskii, the mother of two grown sons, Marfa by name, undertook to decide the fate of her fatherland" (*IGR,* 6:18–19). Critics have remarked upon the difference between the fictional and historical portraits of Marfa, agreeing that Karamzin had to ignore historical evidence in order to create the idealized fictional version in the tale.[30] However, Caryl Emerson's observations that Karamzin deployed rhetoric skillfully and tendentiously in his historical account of Boris Godunov are pertinent here. In the fictional version of "Marfa Posadnitsa," as in his 1802 "Historical Reminiscences and Observations on the Road to Troitse," Karamzin justifies his departure from historical record by casting doubt on the chronicles. In his "Historical Reminiscences," Karamzin "deflects [a] rebuke . . . away from Boris and redirects it against the documents that condemned him,"[31] remarking that "history sometimes becomes the echo of slander."[32] In "Marfa Posadnitsa," Marfa herself foresees that she will be defamed in the historical record, musing, "Marfa will be the wonder of posterity, if slander doesn't darken her deeds in the chronicles!" (*IS,* 1:704).

There is indeed evidence that incriminates Marfa: in his notes to the *History,* for instance, Karamzin quotes a treaty of alliance between Novgorod and Lithuania (*IGR,* 6:12–14 n). But according to Likhachev and Dmitriev the only ancient Russian source that "gives Marfa Boretskaia an important place is the 'Slovesa izbranna,' in which Marfa is likened to biblical 'wicked wives' " such as Jezebel, and it is from this source that Karamzin drew his portrait.[33] In his *History,* however, Karamzin suppresses the biblical comparison and makes his condemnation seem scientific and inevitable.

Although he removes the biblical references, Karamzin does not erase the idea that Marfa is a fallen woman: she is a widow, and a mother of two grown sons, but still "this proud woman wanted to free Novgorod from Ivan's power, and, according to the chronicles, marry some Lithuanian grandee, in order to rule with him, in the name of Kazimir, over her fatherland"

(*IGR,* 6:19). Thus Marfa's infidelity to Ivan's legitimate rule is given an erotic element; she betrays her dead husband—and more important, Ivan—by a second marriage to another man. While in "Marfa Posadnitsa" Karamzin could still identify with his heroine even as both of them turned toward the masculine, in the *History* this identification with the feminine no longer seems permissible. Marfa's formerly admired political activity is now seen as contrary to "the ancient customs and mores of the Slavs," and her touching fidelity has been converted to a dangerously ambitious sexuality. Jessica Benjamin's discussion of the changes in a boy's psychic relation to his mother during the Oedipal stage casts an interesting light on the reversals in Karamzin's portrayal of Marfa:

> The Oedipal constellation is characterized by the polarization of object love and identification—the prohibition on having and being the same object. This prohibition prevents the boy from using the most common psychic method of dealing with loss and separation—trying to "be" the lost object, the mother. . . .
>
> Coupled with the loss of identification, the Oedipal experience of sexuality makes of the tantalizing mother a disturbing and dangerous figure, who could be as ferocious as the boy's unsatisfied desire.[34]

Karamzin, who had represented himself in fiction as reading novels in imitation of his lost mother, who created the language of sentimental fiction in order to please her surrogates, and who had at first imagined history as yet another way to appeal to and educate women, no longer uses his writings to express his identity with women nor to celebrate their activity. Instead, he glorifies Ivan for his epoch-making actions, while condemning Marfa for daring to participate "in civil affairs." This painting of history as an exclusively male domain suggests the polarization of genders characteristic of the Oedipal stage, and indeed the *History* has some striking similarities to the second possible plot that Marthe Robert discovers in the novel: the family romance of the Oedipal "Bastard." Having understood the sexual difference between his parents, Robert says, the child realizes that the uncertainty of his origin is really uncertainty about the identity of his father. In the new version of his family romance, the child

> [decides] to keep his real mother with all her familiar features and humdrum circumstances, . . . [and concentrates] his efforts on his father whose uncertain status has been revealed to him. . . . Thus, with an ordinary mother and an imaginary, noble father ever more distant as he rises in rank, the child assumes an illegitimacy that opens, for his pseudo-biography, new vistas with untold consequences.
>
> . . . [T]he child's asserted illegitimacy reveals his true motives and the orientation of his sexual desires. For he thus keeps his mother beside him, and such a proximity encourages a relationship which, being henceforth the only concrete one in the story, grows increasingly intimate; and furthermore—though the

> two operations are so intricately linked that [it] is hard to dissociate them—he relegates his father to an imaginary kingdom, beyond and above the family circle—a form of tribute, maybe, but in fact an exile, since this royal, unknown father who is forever absent might just as well not exist for all the part he plays in everyday life: he is a phantom, a corpse, who may be the object of a cult, but whose vacant place cries out nonetheless to be filled.[35]

In Robert's formulation, the boy child's denigration of the feminine serves to keep the mother within reach while his exaltation of the masculine serves to remove the powerful father to a safe distance. Thus, the boy can entertain a fantasy of replacing his father without actually sinning against him. The coldness that Karamzin ascribes to Ivan III in the *History* is reminiscent of the corpselike remoteness that Robert suggests we should expect in the Oedipal Bastard's ambivalent characterization of his father. Ivan III is quite unlike the ideal tsar that Karamzin imagined in "Epistle to Women," the one "who more passionately than all others / could love [women]." Rather, Ivan is hard and severe, for, as Karamzin says, "the founders of Monarchies are rarely famous for tender sensitivity, and the firmness, necessary for great works of state, borders on severity" (*IGR,* 6:115). Karamzin's definition of the qualities most needed in a leader may have changed, but, while Ivan's coldness helps qualify him as tsar, it simultaneously disqualifies him as most passionate lover of women. Ivan's kingdom is not "imaginary," to use Robert's terms above, but it *is* "beyond and above the family circle." Having recognized a reality harsher than his imagined pre-Oedipal utopia, the ambivalent Oedipal son sends the father off to found suitably severe monarchies, leaving the "tenderest friend of a tender woman" (*PSS,* 179) unchallenged ruler in the domestic world of sentiment.

Of the Bastard's tale, Robert writes: "Murder, revolt and usurpation, invariably justified in the plot, are what motivate the Romance even when it is ostentatiously moralistic."[36] Of course, Karamzin did not imagine the murder, revolt, and usurpation that necessarily formed the subject of his narrative of Russian history. But Russian history certainly captured his imagination, perhaps in part because in it were writ large the very conflicts of filial revolt and piety that obsess the Oedipal child. And, despite his complete repudiation of Marfa and his expressions of admiration for Ivan III, there is throughout book 6 a palpable ambivalence. Karamzin's eloquent arguments for the historical necessity of Novgorod's subjugation never quite conceal his regret for the human tragedy it represents. The historian Eidel'man sees in this the distinctive achievement of Karamzin's combined talents: "Thus, the historian glorifies Ivan III, . . . autocracy—and doesn't conceal his sympathy for Novgorod, . . . 'dear liberty.' Karamzin, possessing the gifts of both the scholar and the artist, gave free rein to both his talents and staged a 'duel' between the two principles—state and human, historical and artistic."[37]

Following Eidel'man, I argue that over the course of Karamzin's creative biography, the fall of Novgorod became emblematic for the tension between the two principles, historical and artistic. We have seen how the republic represented an ideal world of sentimental friendship and artistic inspiration, and how the poet became increasingly disillusioned about the possibility that such a realm could be anything other than imaginary. In the story "Chuvstvitel'nyi i Kholodnyi" (The Sensitive and the Cold), published in 1803, Karamzin had personified the principles of idealism and realism in two friends. The two friends possess the strengths and weaknesses that were traditionally assigned to such characters by European Sentimentalism,[38] but they also had a personal significance for Karamzin. "The Sensitive" with his sentimental, artistic nature clearly corresponds to the young Karamzin, while "the Cold" reminds us that Madame de Staël dismissed the mature Karamzin as "a dry Frenchman."[39] In the story, Karamzin shows that "the Sensitive," while much more susceptible to emotion and art, was in the end less reliable and less hardy than his stolid friend, "the Cold." But, in 1803, it is still "the Sensitive" who claims the reader's greater sympathy. "Indifferent people are more prudent in everything, live more quietly in the world, do less harm and disturb the harmony of society less frequently; but only sensitive people make great sacrifices for virtue, and surprise the world with great acts" (*IS,* 1:741).

In 1811, in the *History,* Karamzin would contrast Ivan and Novgorod in much the same way, and sometimes in the same words, as he had contrasted "the Cold" and "the Sensitive" characters. "Cold" Ivan is so cautious that admiration for him is likely to be grudging:

> But in the years of passionate youth he displayed a caution characteristic of mature and experienced minds, but for him inborn: neither at the beginning nor later did he care for audacious courage; . . . never rushing swiftly toward his goal, he rather approached it in measured steps, avoiding equally both frivolous ardor and injustice, respecting the general opinion and the rules of the age. (*IGR,* 6:6)

In "sensitive" Novgorod's rebellion, on the other hand, there is something that still appeals to the imagination: "The chronicles of republics usually present us with powerful motions of the human passions, with magnanimous impulses and often the moving triumph of virtue, amongst the rebellions and disorder characteristic of popular rule: thus the chronicles of Novgorod in their unaffected simplicity reveal qualities that captivate the imagination" (*IGR,* 6:84). In his poetry and fiction, Karamzin had celebrated the "sensitive character," with its capacity for self-sacrifice, its lively imagination, its susceptibility to love, and its disregard for social convention. Yet in the *History* he assigns "sensitivity" to the city whose subjugation was necessary for the survival and glory of the Russian state, and "coldness" to the prince whose destiny it was to achieve that glory. "Coldness" is now valorized and "sensitivity" represented as a luxury that a great nation can no longer afford.

In Marthe Robert's formulation, the child in the Oedipal stage is caught "between love [for his mother] and admiration [for his father], or between sexual desires and moral aspirations; or again, and to sum up the antithesis in an accepted formula, between what the heart desires and the mind dictates." For Karamzin, "a republican in his heart, but a monarchist in his head," this antithesis was symbolized by a conflict between the two forms of government. But in every Bastard's narrative, says Marthe Robert, the Foundling's dream of an undifferentiated paradise where mother, father, and child are united survives in one or another clandestine form: "the Foundling's myth . . . becomes as it were encysted in an isolated work where it bears witness to an irreducible survival of rebellion and nostalgia."[40] In the *History of the Russian State,* Novgorod itself plays this role. By describing Novgorod in the same terms as the "Sensitive" character, Karamzin gives Novgorod an almost subliminal appeal for readers familiar with his earlier work, and likewise takes away some of the luster from Ivan. Thus, in writing the *History,* Karamzin fixes for all time the magic of his beloved republic, land of his primary desire, even as he argues that the law of the father, which interrupts that desire, must be obeyed.

Sally Kux

Petr Andreevich Viazemsky: A Necessary Virtue

Many years and generations
Have I already survived,
And through my long peregrinations
Many events have I beheld.
Excessive talents have I not,
Nor pose as a great man
To be a *notebook* is my lot
Where life plays the role of scribe
—P. A. Viazemsky

SEVERAL FEATURES dominate the landscape of Golden Age culture in Russia: a growing interest in historical and memoir literature, particularly about Russia; a fascination with verbal and visual portraits of individuals; and the blossoming of a prose tradition. These three features come together in the historical and critical writings of Petr Andreevich Viazemsky (1792–1878).[1]

Viazemsky, a man of letters active in poetry, criticism, journalism, translation, and biography, had more than a passing interest in history. His critical essays and pioneering biography of Denis Fonvizin are informed by a spirit of historical inquiry that views words—written and oral—as cultural artifacts. His writings characterize Russian high culture of the late eighteenth and early nineteenth centuries as finding its truest self-expression in informal, but artful interaction, and in the cultivation of eccentricity and wit as much as of fashionable dress and comportment. To depict this cultural milieu, Viazemsky crafts a particular form of historical narrative, one based on anecdotes. Viazemsky contends that anecdotal narratives, brief and witty stories about notable people and events, adequately represent the recent Russian past. By telling its stories, Viazemsky tells the story of his age.

The purpose of this article is to reconstruct Viazemsky's model for this particular kind of historical narrative as it is expressed implicitly and explicitly across the body of his prose work. A rich source for understanding Viazemsky's views on this subject are his *Old Notebooks,* a series of notebooks (thirty-six in all), varied in content and purpose, that Viazemsky kept from 1813 until his death in 1878.[2] In these notebooks and in his critical articles,

Viazemsky uses anecdotes to construct a model for history drawn from social interactions—letters and oral stories. According to Viazemsky this is not a makeshift historical method, but, in fact, the most fitting way to represent the Russian culture of the late eighteenth and early nineteenth centuries.

Viazemsky delineates this anecdotal model for history in several ways. First, he perceives the anecdote to constitute a strategy for historical narrative that enables the historian to make use of limited material, rather than uncovering enough "facts" to create a seamless, linear, and objective narrative about the past. Second, he views anecdotes to be valuable sources for information about the recent past, a past that he does not restrict to tales of political and military developments on a grand scale. Third, he considers anecdotes themselves to be cultural and literary monuments, artful narratives that distill the essence of a passing era in portraits of unique individuals. According to Viazemsky, anecdotal strategy and material are necessary given the primitive state of Russian historical science. Viazemsky makes a virtue of this necessity, however, claiming that anecdotes convey a truer sense of the past than strictly factual history, because they bring the past to life. History based on anecdotes is especially suitable for depicting an era that, in Viazemsky's estimation, deserves to be remembered for the unique Russian characters that peopled it and the stories they inspired.

That Viazemsky turns to the anecdote is no accident: the form was extremely popular during the late eighteenth and early nineteenth centuries. As a historical genre, anecdotes functioned in Russia primarily to convey the lives and deeds of important military and political figures. Collections of brief stories about a wise general or enlightened monarch served to glorify that individual as an exemplary Russian.[3] Viazemsky shifts the emphasis from the symbolic expression of patriotism and civic virtue, returning to an older tradition in which the anecdote was regarded as an "unofficial" historical genre, originating in Procopius's *Private History* of the court of Justinian.[4] In this tradition the anecdote was a form that told previously unknown, frequently scandalous stories, often drawn from the private lives of public figures. Viazemsky uses the form to capture the characters of extraordinary Russians of his temporal and cultural environment that he fears will be lost from the historical record.

Viazemsky's childhood and youth contributed to his conviction that his cultural milieu needed to be documented, as well as to his assessment of what merited preservation. The theme of loss pervades Viazemsky's writings about this period; not only did Viazemsky lose most of his family at a young age, he outlived by many years such friends and colleagues in letters as Alexander Pushkin, Ivan Dmitriev, Denis Davydov, Evgeny Baratynsky, and Andrei Turgenev.[5] Viazemsky's acute experience of, and fierce protest against, the actual and potential loss of history prompted him in 1868 to remark that Moscow was becoming his Pompeii, where he must search deeply for remnants of life "already long covered over by the lava of the past."[6]

Viazemsky's keen perception of history and its losses was sharpened not only by the deaths of many friends and colleagues, but also by the experience of living in an era of Russian history characterized by immense and profound change on the political, social, and cultural fronts. According to one scholar, "he lived through several sharp 'breaks' in time—such conditions of society when it seems the recent past is irretrievably gone, and real history is beginning only now."[7] Spanning the reigns of four tsars (Paul I, Alexander I, Nicholas I, and Alexander II), Viazemsky's lifetime saw Russia grow to a significant international power and, domestically, fluctuate between reactionary and progressive regimes.

Just as loss and change conditioned Viazemsky's desire to arrest the flow of time, if only on paper, so did the informal education he received growing up shape his cultural values. His father's home, Ostaf'evo, was frequented by leading literary figures of the day. Here Viazemsky absorbed ideas and tastes of the French Enlightenment, while, after his sister's marriage to Karamzin, the tone of Ostaf'evo became more Russian. The literary figures who frequented Ostaf'evo included Vasily Pushkin, Vasily Zhukovsky, and Konstantin Batiushkov, as well as Davydov, Andrei Turgenev, and Dmitriev.

Critics, as did he himself, stress the importance of Viazemsky's early informal education for the development of his literary and cultural views. One critic suggests that Viazemsky was so deeply imprinted with a model of literature as an institution grounded in familial relations that he could accept no other: "When Viazemsky later speaks of 'our domestic circle of literature,' . . . this is not a metaphor for him. . . . The appearance of new names—from Pushkin to Gogol—is perceived by him . . . as the broadening and enrichment of the periphery of that circle which had taken the place of his family."[8] Hence Viazemsky's estrangement from the literary status quo of his later years and his emphasis on a model of cultural history based on intimate relations.[9]

Viazemsky articulates his historical mission as a redemptive one: to document a segment of early nineteenth-century Russian culture that will otherwise be lost. The historical model that emerges implicitly and explicitly from the *Old Notebooks,* as well as from writings, is based on the written documentation of an oral culture. The written word must mimic speech if it is to represent an older model of culture for which oral exchange not only conveyed information, but constituted a way of life. Viazemsky describes his own upbringing to illustrate how early exposure to the rich culture of salon society at Ostaf'evo infected him with curiosity about colorful personages that people his own later writings: "I have scant faith in that literature which is conceived of within and concentrated solely on itself—outside of the larger flow of life. Whatever you may say about the so-called salons, they often provided a fertile, fruitful soil" (*PSS*, 1:xxvii).

It is within this cultural hothouse that Viazemsky locates the germination of his own future historical efforts: first, it was the setting of his nonacademic education; second, as the scene of endless and endlessly fascinating conversations, it spurred his intellectual development and gave him a taste for listening to, remembering, and retelling other peoples' stories. Recalling his first efforts at history, Viazemsky describes a collaboration in eavesdropping:

> I loved to transmit snippets of conversations I had overheard from my father to my uncle Nikita, who subsequently became an awful drunkard and used to entertain Zhukovsky. Probably neither my uncle, nor I understood accurately or fully the meaning of these excerpts, but, even in this emerged hints of the powers of observation characteristic of me and of the development of my capabilities in these exercises as a literary detective and society gossip. (*PSS*, 1:ix–x)

In an article on national education ("Neskol'ko slov o narodnom obrazovanii,"1855), Viazemsky again refers to his childhood at Ostaf'evo as a school that was as important to his development as his formal instruction. He underscores the unconscious effects of his immersion in a constant flow of famous and colorful personages who appeared before his eyes as a series of portraits. Viazemsky re-creates these portraits as exemplary representatives of an extraordinary generation (*PSS*, 7:92).

Another significant consequence of this at once domestic and worldly education is the natural continuity it created between generations, beginning with Viazemsky's youthful observations of, and interactions with, his father's circle. Viazemsky perceives himself as belonging to a different time than they, yet they are familiar to him. He is sympathetic to and curious about them, and therefore feels neither an embittering sense of alienation from the older generation, nor the need to define himself strictly in opposition to it. He claims never to have lost the willingness to bridge the gap of time and sensibility learned as a young man: "In my youth I did not avoid conversations with old men; in my mature years and in my old age I was equally close to youth. This, so to say, broadened the circle of my life and enriched me with a multitude of impressions and reminiscences" (*PSS*, 7:101). In this essay, a portrait gallery of the characters and eccentrics who frequented his father's salon, Viazemsky attempts to pass on a legacy of curiosity and tolerance to a generation he finds lacking in these qualities.

HISTORICAL NARRATIVE

Viazemsky's views on historical narrative can be deduced from comments in his *Old Notebooks* and other essays. The picture that emerges, however, is not definitive, since the structure of an anecdotal narrative is not conducive to a closed philosophical statement. The question of overall unity is particularly formidable with regard to the *Old Notebooks,* which, composed over the course of some sixty-odd years, were authored by a Viazemsky who himself changes over time, even as he remains a constant organizing presence in the text. One quality that Viazemsky does not emphasize is objectivity; he masks neither affinity nor antipathy for certain historical and literary figures, certain tendencies and ideas. While he frequently censures, though, he rarely censors.[10] Ultimately, Viazemsky's intent is not to condemn that with which he does not sympathize, but rather to open a door into the past, to enable readers to catch more than a passing glimpse of noteworthy (to Viazemsky) events, attitudes, and faces.

Viazemsky's view of the need for full disclosure in historical narrative and his concern for lost stories are reflected in the importance he accords to memoir literature. He praises Ivan Dmitriev's memoirs, but with qualifications, claiming that their value lies in the "portraits of [Dmitriev's] contemporaries in the Ministry and Council," and in the often curious facts he relates (57). Viazemsky finds the *Notes'* weakness to be their incompleteness, which results from Dmitriev's sensitivity to his official position; in Viazemsky's words, Dmitriev wrote his memoirs "in full-dress uniform." He cites as an example Dmitriev's destruction of an entry harshly portraying Prince N. I. Saltykov, who presided over the State Council and the Committee of Ministers. Viazemsky "respects, but disapproves of this action," arguing that Dmitriev has violated the writer's duty to be dispassionate and has, by striking this entry from his notes, stricken it from the "book of posterity." Viazemsky contrasts Dmitriev's cautious memoirs to his frank oral style, suggesting that the memoirs would be more complete if supplemented with selections from his conversations.[11]

Another valuable source of stories about Russian political history is Prince Aleksei Orlov, soldier and statesmen, twice chief of the Russian delegation to the Ottoman Porte in the 1830s. Viazemsky introduces Orlov with an anecdote illustrating his characteristic blend of canniness and simplicity. A diplomatic incident is anticipated when the Russian delegation learns that the Turkish Grand Vizier plans to receive Orlov, in Constantinople on a diplomatic mission from Nicholas I, sitting. Orlov proposes to his functionaries that the matter will sort itself out:

> On the following day he proceeds to the Vizier, who in actual fact does not budge from his place at the entrance of our plenipotentiary ambassador. Aleksei Fedorovich was previously acquainted with him. As though he did not notice that he was sitting, he walks up to him, greets him amicably and, as though joking, with his mighty Orlovian arm, raises the old man out of his seat, lowering him back down onto his chair right away. That is what you call

> practical and positive diplomacy. Another man would have begun negotiations, written exchanges about empty questions of protocol. All of those negotiations, correspondences might not achieve the desired goal, while here, simply and directly, all was decided by a masterful arm. (129–30)

According to Viazemsky, Orlov, a veritable treasure-house of information about the reigns of Alexander I and Nicholas I, and of the Grand Duke Konstantin Pavlovich, was an accomplished and eager storyteller, but one unlikely to have kept a journal. Those stories not recorded by others are not likely to have survived.

Like Orlov, Natalia Kirilovna Zagriazhskaia, whose knowledge spans the reigns of three tsars, is both a historical subject to Viazemsky and a source of narratives of historical value. Like Orlov, Zagriazhskaia's stories were saved because others collected them. Zagriazhskaia's tales caught Pushkin's attention. He recorded them in *Table-talk:*

> She was, like those old family portraits, painted with the brush of a great artist that decorate the walls of the salons of the most recent generation. The costumes, many of the appurtenances of these representations have long ago gone out of fashion; but the facial features and the sympathetic expression of the physiognomy, the charm of these creations, which this representation created and transmitted to posterity, all of this together catches our attention and enchants us. With an exquisite and deferential sense of pleasure you gaze at these portraits; you lose yourself in contemplating them; you, so to say, listen to them, spellbound. Thus did Pushkin listen, spellbound, to the tales of Natalia Kirilovna. (131)

According to Viazemsky, Pushkin heard in Zagriazhskaia's stories echoes of times and generations past, as well as "an extraordinary historical and poetic charm, for even history contains much true and exalted poetry, and poetry contains its share of history." Viazemsky notes that Pushkin recorded only some of Zagriazhskaia's narratives; like shards of a mirror they sparkle and shine, but do not reflect an image of the whole. In Viazemsky's discussion of historical sources the common notes are loss, the brittle fragility of the past, the tenuous nature of our hold on it, and the utter irretrievability of days once they are lost from the individual and collective memory.[12]

LITERATURE AND HISTORY

Viazemsky's digression on poetry and history points to his conflation of literary and historical narratives; for Viazemsky both constitute the "material inheritance of our fathers." With the example of Zagriazhskaia, Viazemsky notes that his generation has squandered its historical legacy and, bereft of nearly all material traces, risks losing the intellectual baggage that accompanied it. Pleased to listen to stories of the past, people rarely recorded them and, thus, let slip between their fingers the "capital of oral literature." "Now we would be glad to record that daily life; but, to use a typographical expression, we lack the original, or lack the originals—in the everyday sense" (Teper' rady by my zapisyvat' tekushchuiu zhizn'; no, po vyrazheniiu tipograficheskomu, ne khvataet originalu, ili ne khvataet originalov—po zhiteiskomu znacheniiu.) (131). Viazemsky points to the loss of literary texts as equally impoverishing, because literary monuments are invaluable as gauges of times past; they are

> an expression of Russian intellectual activity, so to say, a barometric indication of the temperature of its contemporary society. Nowadays we look down on these toys of the elderly children of olden days; but there are toys and toys, and when a toy bears the imprint of thought and art, then it is fitting to preserve it in a museum, just as they preserve the smallest implements and knickknacks dug out from under the ruins of Pompeii. It is by these knickknacks that people are able to form an opinion about the social conditions of that time. (133)

Viazemsky's expansion of the boundaries of literature proper, as well as his conflation of literature and history, is evident in a category of historical material he terms oral or current literature (*khodiachaia literatura*), a social art form that tells a great deal about society. Viazemsky gives as an example the often humorous use and misuse among Russians of the French language, which leads to the telling and retelling of such incidents. Viazemsky calls these humorous distortions "a whole oral literature, an anecdotal literature" (273). Bearing witness to Russia's strange and incomplete integration of French language and culture, such tales, for Viazemsky, also demonstrate the centrality of gentle laughter to the culture of earlier days (274). Sometimes humor—"current wit, that wit *qui court la rue*"—emerges from deliberate mutilation of French by too literal a translation, as when "*bien-être général en Russie*" is rendered "it is good to be a general in Russia" (khorosho byt' generalom v Rossii) (164). For Viazemsky this anecdote exemplifies the oral nature of the Russian wit: "In Moscow and, in general, in Russia this wit not only runs through the streets, it is also well received in salons but, on the other hand, it somehow rarely visits books. We have more of an oral than a printed wit." In other instances informal literature denotes what is intended for informal performance rather than publication. As an example, Viazemsky quotes a poet's lament to the New Year that, compared to the gifts received by others—high rank and lucrative positions—he has been shabbily rewarded with only new patches for his old trousers. Viazemsky suggests that gathering such typically irreverent material would bring to light much that is unknown in Russian literature and would provide an invaluable source for "certain features of earlier social life" (59–60).[13]

Just as literary texts can serve the cause of history, so is the past a rich source of material for literature. Viazemsky argues that the most imaginative and fecund literature in Russia is molded from the material that life offers up—often connected with incongruities and anomalies that provoke guileless laughter. He contrasts this sort of writing to a dour, pedantic literature that attempts to subordinate life to "the laws and conditions of a Platonic academy and a Platonic republic" (270) and, in so doing, crowds out laughter, that "joyous and life-giving appurtenance of life and man." According to Viazemsky, this is the sort of literature which he would write:

> If I knew how to write comedies or novels, I would treasure the legacy of our olden days; without bitterness, without pompous ranting, I would bring onto the stage certain eccentrics, living for their own pleasure, but, by the way, not harming anyone. Our old everyday life possessed its own dramatic personifications, its own movement, its own diverse colors. Had I the necessary gift, I would dip my brush not in bile; not foaming at the mouth, but with a laughing smile I would mix for my picture the fresh and bright colors of a guileless joke. I would arouse in readers and viewers sympathetic laughter, because I would myself provide an example not of malicious, but of sincere and not hurtful laughter. I would run from, shun any tendentiousness, as evil inspiration. Thus, it would seem, did Gogol act. Where in art, in literature, in painting tendentiousness appears, with claims to instruct, there will be found neither nature, nor art. Realistic truth in creations of thought and the imagination cannot be a living truth: it is already a cold corpse under the doctor's knife, not in the theater of living people, but in the anatomical theater, as the French say. . . . Paint from nature, do not blacken it, do not slander it, and the pictures will emerge, amusing sketches, but pleasant, and with satirical tints. Literature must in no way be an institution parallel to the Criminal Department. But our literature loves always to punish. In truth, for those with the inclination, it is easier to be an apprentice to the executioner than a talented painter. (270–72)

Elsewhere Viazemsky maps out a similar historical project. Contemplating the "internal-moral constitution" peculiar to each nation, Viazemsky says he has considered writing his own "Rossiada," but the epic he envisions is not heroic, and, in fact, not an epic at all. He imagines an "everyday, domestic Rossiada," an encyclopedic collection of "everything that an exclusively Russian soil produces, as prepared and cultivated by time, history, customs, popular beliefs and mores that are exclusively Russian" (198–99).[14]

While advocating a richer notion of history and illustrating ways this might be achieved, Viazemsky also protests what he views as superficial attempts to popularize Russian historiography, among which he counts Polevoi's *History of the Russian People* (1833). Attacking Polevoi's endeavor as misguided and "poorly welded," Viazemsky places himself in the camp of the supporters of Karamzin's *History* (126–27). He does include criticisms of Karamzin, as well, but these appear ironic rather than serious.

For instance, in a portrait of the Princess Golitsyna, Viazemsky mentions that she criticizes Karamzin for his use of the word "however" (*odnako*).[15]

Viazemsky notes that this comment belies critics' patronizing claims that high society is not interested in philology and not connected to literature. Both of these comments are ironic; moreover, following Viazemsky's ambiguous comments regarding the female mind, any remark originating from a woman is of questionable authority.[16] Finally, Viazemsky's alleged discovery of an affinity in the literary tastes of the *beau monde* and "hack writers" hardly masks his intimation that society sorely lacks taste and discrimination.

From irony Viazemsky shifts into more weighty debates over the origins of the Russian people, which arose in the wake of Karamzin's *History*, and specifically, Mikhail Orlov's discontent with the plebeian and Philistine origins that Karamzin attributes to the Slavs.[17] Here, Viazemsky takes issue with a host of unnamed "patriots," who cannot bear a "prosaic and bourgeois" narrative about the birth of their nation.[18] As before, Viazemsky's own position is elusive. He alludes to schools of thought that arose long after Orlov, but mocks them simultaneously as he defends their existence, if not their convictions. Viazemsky quotes the governor's wife from *The Inspector General*, who argues that if someone wants to establish beyond a shadow of a doubt the hair color of his long-dead wet nurse, then there is no reason anyone should prevent him from such an innocent and harmless exercise. Use of a questionable authority once again leaves no doubt of Viazemsky's irony, but does not illuminate his own position.

From this digression, itself a deviation from an earlier narrative, Viazemsky turns to a more weighty issue. The debate over Karamzin's choice of conjunctions is obviously petty, and, by the time Viazemsky has finished, arguments about the origins of the Slavs appear frivolous and self-serving. The nature of truth is surely relevant, however, to a discussion of the historical science. Viazemsky contends that historical truth is neither absolute nor easily accessible. "Historical truth, like many other truths in our day, is not born fully robed, as was wisdom from the head of Jupiter" (220). Historical truth is not discovered or stumbled upon in some newly opened archive; for Viazemsky it is reached by the "labor-intensive reworking and smelting of refined delusions, outmoded errors, preconvictions, superstitious prejudices" (221).

Drawing back from this series of digressions, Viazemsky chides himself for straying from his original path, his portrait of the Princess Golitsyna, and takes the opportunity to restate his historical mission, which he juxtaposes starkly with the idle pursuits of those scholars sneezing their way amid the dust of days long past. His own goal is limited and concrete: "to place in a fixed frame a little corner of the life of our society and to personify it by the depiction of a personality that, in its time, occupied not the last place on the stage of our society" (221). Viazemsky renders Golitsyna concrete through the immediacy with which he depicts her remarkable nature, providing a sharp contrast to his archaeological digression on the origin of the Slavs. Taunting readers with

Golitsyna's nearness, Viazemsky closes his digression by drawing over it her "famous sarafan."

In a postscript to this entry, Viazemsky defends both his historical project and his age against potential derision by skeptical critics of the generation following him. "Necessity" moves Viazemsky to record the ghosts of his former acquaintances as they disturb his memory. He considers it his obligation to act as a guardian of the social memory that will otherwise disappear and hopes that his sketches will enable later historians or novelists to retrace a picture of the past, just as the famous naturalist, Cuvier, reconstructed organisms long since extinct on the basis of skeletal fragments. Viazemsky's reference to Cuvier suggests he anticipates that a "disinterested" history of the immediate past will not be written without a lengthy hiatus. This is in keeping with his appraisal of the lack of sympathy for and understanding of the recent past on the part of the generation following his:

> as a result of unintentional (we do not want even to think about intentional and premeditated) ignorance, they unconsciously and untruthfully depict this society from the most unsightly sides: they daub their picture with sharp, unpleasant and, what's more, fantastical colors. In a word, they cast aspersions on our society, so as not to say they slander it. According to their sketches it turns out that our society (it goes without saying that, both from their point of view and ours the discussion concerns high society) was, if not is today, colorless in the extreme, feeble, dry, and anemic. To believe them, its muscles are flabby; in it there is neither strength of will, nor the ability to act. The creatures that make up this society are not people, but some sort of painted, dressed-up dolls. (222)

Viazemsky contends that he is not whitewashing his generation's weaknesses. He argues that perceived weaknesses may also have positive aspects; superficiality and a dilletantish approach to education and outlook endowed his contemporaries with quickness, agility, and a broad-ranging sensitivity that their children and grandchildren lack.

HISTORICAL TRUTH AND ARTISTIC LIES

Despite Viazemsky's disdain for the younger generation's alleged historical distortions, he himself expresses ambivalence about historical truth. Distinguishing between the letter and the spirit of truth, he argues that factually inaccurate narratives may be psychologically true, just as factually accurate narratives may misrepresent the essence of a person or event. For instance, an anecdote recounts how, in the days preceding the French entrance into Moscow, Sergei Glinka rode through the streets shouting: "Dump your French wines and drink our Russian home-brew! It will bring you more relief!" Viazemsky concedes that this event may not have actually occurred, but claims that it nonetheless contributes to knowledge because it accurately depicts "the color" of the place, the time, and of Glinka's personality (208).

In an article about Vladislav Ozerov (1869), Viazemsky examines truth in the context of the genre of historical tragedy, asking; "Does the tragedian have the right to express in his own way personages whom he has borrowed from history, and can he be satisfied with that which history offers him?" Noting that the ancients permitted themselves to change the chronology of historical events and to mix actual events with legend, Viazemsky argues that contemporary tragedians may also take liberties with the particulars of historical truth, if in so doing, they are true to the spirit of history:

> It is permissible, for example, for a tragedian to alter history in its details and according to his desires to transport the hero twenty years forward or backward in his life, to forget about his family ties, but the character of the historical hero must remain a sacred object which he must not touch with a capricious hand. A tragedian who presents us a tyrant as a philanthropist to his subjects, or a friend of freedom as a groveling slave, is equally guilty before history and before tragedy. (*PSS*, 1:43–44)

In an article from the same year, Viazemsky accuses Tolstoy of such historical distortion in *War and Peace*, and, as one of a few remaining eyewitnesses to the war, offers to set the record straight (208). While praising Tolstoy's talent, Viazemsky claims Tolstoy uses history selectively, to the detriment of both the novel and the history. Viazemsky refers to a scene depicting Tsar Alexander that, he claims, is untrue to the essence of Alexander's character. In Tolstoy's scene, Alexander appears before the people eating a biscuit. When a chunk of the biscuit falls to the ground and the crowd fights over it, the emperor asks for a plate of biscuits, which he proceeds to toss to the people, provoking further fighting and jostling. Viazemsky writes of this scene:

> In relation to history, we can say positively that it is a fabrication; in relation to imagination, we can say that here is even more a lack of historical faithfulness and more incongruity. This story reveals a complete ignorance of Alexander I's personality. He was so measured, so careful in all His actions and smallest movements; He so avoided anything that might appear ridiculous or awkward; was in everything so deliberate, decorous, imposing, scrupulous about the smallest details, that probably, He would have sooner thrown himself into the sea than decide to appear before the people, particularly in such ceremonious and significant days, *finishing off a biscuit.* Not only that: He even amuses himself by tossing biscuits to the people from the balcony of the Kremlin Palace, —just as during the holidays the old-world landowner tosses gingerbread to village boys so they fight over it![19]

Although Viazemsky frames this discussion with his larger criticism of the novel, which he considers an attack on 1812, his most vociferous objection is to what he views as Tolstoy's frivolous and misleading use of historical character. He contrasts Tolstoy to Scott and Pushkin, whom he describes as writers who poeticized and romanticized history in their work, but remained true to the "moral force" of historical truth by remaining faithful to the essence of historical personages.[20]

In "Griboedov's Moscow" (1874–75), Viazemsky takes issue with indiscriminate use of historical material that, like Tolstoy's portrait of Alexander (he argues), distorts reality. The revelation of so-called historical truth, he contends, often provides occasion to point a finger at the misdeeds of a famous figure, without contributing to a more profound understanding of the past (*PSS,* 7:375). Viazemsky contends that in some cases historical tact is just as important as historical truth. He likens the historian to the chef whose refined sense of smell should enable him to sniff out anything of dubious quality:

> Those who go prospecting for old material must possess a similar sensitivity that, in the business of historical concoctions, is known as *tact,* and such tact is often lacking among us. I am not even speaking of those cooks who very likely possess sufficient sensitivity, but who, for personal profit, serve their table companions doubtful victuals, sometimes entirely unfit [for consumption] and by such contraband, ruin the entire meal. Moreover, there are some consumers who demand food with a spicy smell: their coarse and thick-skinned palates demand an oversalting, overpickling of what resembles carrion. An artful cook, educated in a good school and respectful of his own worth, would never agree to encourage their savage appetite. The culinary art also possesses its tact, its style, its measure. Likewise writers must not cater to all demands and all tastes. (*PSS,* 7:375–76)

Viazemsky nonetheless expresses admiration for the artistry of those who avoid or embroider the truth, since artful liars belong to the brotherhood of those who create, write, paint, or sculpt a model of some story, history, or reality. When lying is elevated into a high art form, Viazemsky pays unreserved tribute to the virtuoso. He compares artful liars (*lguny*) to poets and suggests that, in some cases, they surpass in their imagination many "sworn" poets. He praises their verbal swagger and declares that it is somehow unconscionable to degrade such poetry by referring to it as lies. An example of one such poet-liar is Prince Tsitsianov, who once arrived completely dry at the house of a friend during a rainstorm. His friend assumes he came by carriage, but Tsitsianov denies it: "No, I came on foot. . . . I know how to make my way very adroitly between the raindrops" (111). Another talented teller of tall tales, distinguished by his intricate narratives and the pleasure he takes from his improvisations, is Count Krasinsky. As Viazemsky tells it, Krasinsky manages to recover his footing even after slipping beyond the limits of credibility. Krasinsky recalls an exceptionally daring attack by the cavalry division under his command and Napoleon's reward of his bravery:

Napoleon galloped up to him on the field of battle and says, "Vincent, je te dois la couronne," [Vincent, I owe you my crown] and right there divested himself of the star of the Legion of Honor and put it on [Krasinsky]. "How is it that you never wear this star?" asked one ingenuous listener. Coming to his senses, Krasinsky said, "I returned it to the Emperor, because I did not deem my actions worthy of such a reward." (113)

Lying can get out of control, of course, as Viazemsky warns with an anecdote about a con man (à la Chichikov and Khlestakov) who travels from village to village passing himself off to the locals as a government official:

There are some who neither directly lie (*lgat'*), nor can they have the reputation of a liar (*lgun*), but know how to circumvent the truth masterfully. Sometimes a certain kind of circumvention is necessary for the most certain achievement of a goal; but it is dangerous to give oneself up too much to these circumventions: you end up getting lost in the small villages and never find your way back to the high road. (87)

In other instances, Viazemsky considers the possible inaccuracy of stories. Recounting two anecdotes from the time of the reign of Paul that he came across in a French journal concerning the writer Kop'ev's behavior toward that sovereign, Viazemsky claims the first (about Kop'ev pulling the emperor's hair on a dare) is known in Russia, although he contends that it was not Kop'ev who played this trick, but rather Alexander Nikolaevich Golitsyn. The second anecdote (how Kop'ev took a pinch of snuff from the emperor's snuff-box), Viazemsky calls implausible and blames the tale's French origins:

most likely [the anecdote] came to the French from Russia. They could not have thought it up. How could they know of Kop'ev? That Kop'ev was a great prankster was well known. That he was not too timid to play such a trick is also not beyond a shadow of a doubt, but was he ever in a position, where such a trick was within his reach? That is the question. As far as we know, Kop'ev was never a page, nor ever in service anywhere near the Court. (116)

In another instance Viazemsky questions the veracity of an anecdote from a native source, A. A. Naryshkin. According to this story, in the confusion preceding Catherine's coronation, no one had prepared a proclamation to be delivered before her oath. While members of Catherine's suite fretted, a man came forth from the crowd and offered to present a proclamation. The stranger pulled a blank sheet of paper from his pocket and, as if reading, presented an impromptu discourse. According to the story, this man, the actor Volkov, so impressed Catherine that she bestowed a considerable pension on him and his descendants.[21] Viazemsky expresses his own doubt about the accuracy of this tale:

It is necessary to make sure of the truth of this story. I am a great doubting Thomas in relation to anecdotes. I love to listen to and hear them when they

> are well told, but I do not trust them before a lawful testing. Anecdotes, even genuine ones, are often not without base metal and a false stamp. Anecdoteers, even when they do not lie, rarely hold to literal and mathematical faithfulness. (126)[22]

While aware of the problems of relying on potentially unreliable material, Viazemsky still advocates anecdotal history over the self-proclaimed democratic history of historians such as Polevoi.

Elsewhere, Viazemsky suggests that the problem of accuracy is deeply rooted in Russia with its low level of literacy and lack of proper accounting. Likening Russian statistics (*statistiki*) to the mute performance of mimes (*statisty*), Viazemsky despairs of monitoring anything in such an immense and underdeveloped nation. He illustrates with an anecdote about the introduction of statistical surveys at the beginning of the century. A regional official requests certain statistics from a lower administrative division. The local constabulary chief responds as if to counter an accusation of the basest sort:

> In the course of the last two years, that is, from the very beginning of my appointment to the post I currently occupy, there has been, by the grace of God, no word of any sort of statistical occurrences in our region. Should such rumors have reached the authorities, then it is singularly due to the malevolence of envious persons and my enemies, who wish to sabotage me in the eyes of the authorities, and I most humbly ask for protection against such statistical slander. (207)

Related to issues of truth and accuracy is the question of the reliability of memoir literature. In the *Old Notebooks* (themselves a form of personal historical narrative), Viazemsky characterizes Filipp Vigel's notes as uneven and permeated with "rancor and malicious anger." As an example, he cites Vigel's comment about a certain Kozodavlev who "was a kind man and even not a bad Christian, but it was apparent from his behavior and deeds that he was relying more on God's mercy than on justice" (268).[23] Viazemsky contends that Vigel's malevolence adds color, but detracts from the credibility of his stories. Viazemsky also claims Vigel's notes contain inconsistencies and criticizes him for relying on rumor without troubling to discern its reliability. Nevertheless, Viazemsky speaks favorably of Vigel's historical contribution, emphasizing that the value of the *Notes* often lies in capturing the spirit, if not the letter, of his times: "these notes are very interesting and they reflect Russia with all of its nuances: political, governmental, literary, social, including the capitals and the provinces, as well as characters, quite completely, although perhaps, not always faultlessly or infallibly faithfully" (268).

Viazemsky does not find historical value only in the salon gossip reported by the likes of Vigel. Observing the rumors and gossip that inundated Moscow's lower social echelons during the outbreak of cholera, Viazemsky contends that, particularly in times of crisis, hearsay and distortions that gain currency among the common people offer material for a social history of the masses. Viazemsky once again conflates notions of literature and history: "it is said: 'la littérature est l'expression de la société . . . ,' even more [is this true of] gossip, especially in our country; we have no literature, our literature comes by word of mouth. There should be a stenographer to gather it. Society is not merely expressed in gossip, it is, more precisely, spat up. Bring on a spittoon" (94).[24]

WHOSE STORY: ECCENTRICS AND ORIGINALS

Although Viazemsky alludes to historical projects that would encompass all of Russia, he writes most frequently and convincingly about its upper social echelons. This is the uniquely Russian culture and character whose essence Viazemsky best knows and most effectively preserves in his writing. The figures that attract him, however, are not statesmen, or at least what Viazemsky chooses to record about them are not their civic merits. Rather, Viazemsky highlights the artfulness with which they lived their lives. The most prominent type of "typically Russian" character to emerge from Viazemsky's history is that of the eccentric or original. These individuals—as subjects of stories and as talented storytellers—are, indeed, the essence of Viazemsky's history.

Strong or eccentric character and life lived artfully and wittily—these are the essential ingredients for Viazemsky's historical recipe. Society cannot consist solely of giants; Viazemsky's landscape requires rolling hills to create a backdrop against which the mountain summits stand out. In Viazemsky's eyes, however, it is the summits that render the landscape worth regarding and painting.[25] Consequently, it is not surprising that Viazemsky often visualizes people as portraits, and society and history as a portrait gallery. While approaching his subjects through their social interactions, he frames them individually. He draws attention to their comical qualities or to aspects of the comic to which they themselves, by wit and eccentricity, draw attention. He includes such figures not just to elicit laughter, but to promote eccentricity as a socially beneficial quality: "Originality, when it is not affected, not studied, not counterfeit, not touched up, is always more or less a sign of independence of character; and such independence represents a kind of courage, a kind of valor. Don Quixote, perhaps, is laughable, but first of all he is chivalrously noble. Sometimes the mere fact that you are not like others can be regarded as a virtue" (154).

Eccentricity manifests itself in different ways, but all of Viazemsky's eccentrics are nonconformists. Irreverence toward the niceties of social discourse is found in some of Viazemsky's eccentrics, such as Vasily Apraksin, who appears as a kind of "natural man." His talents for music and drawing exist alongside a total lack of education, his essentially good heart with an instinctive amorality, and these seeming contradictions, Viazemsky contends, made Apraksin "a fundamental and exemplary child of Russian nature and Russian society" (73). Viazemsky tells how Apraksin complained about not being promoted to the rank of general. When told that the occasion for promotions would arrive with the birth of the grand duchess's child, Apraksin, unsatisfied, demands, "And if she miscarries?" (72)

Another example of an impetuous eccentric who disregards social rules is P. F. Balk-Pol'ev, Russian ambassador to the Brazilian court. Having received an incongruous bill from a shoemaker, Balk-Pol'ev requests an audience with the (Brazilian) emperor, and asks the emperor himself to examine the bill. When the emperor refuses, the ambassador tosses it at his feet and walks out. He was subsequently recalled to Russia and dismissed from diplomatic service. (108)

Another original, Alexander Pavlovich Ofrosimov, distinguished himself in society by giving voice to its absurd and amusing aspects. Viazemsky cites as one example an episode relating to the delay with which new European fashions (in his words, "the revolution in male dress") arrived in Russia in the early nineteenth century:

> Short breeches worn with buckled shoes were abolished, as were narrow, close-fitting trousers with boots worn over the trousers; introduced into usage and lawfully confirmed were liberally wide-legged trousers, with a flap in the front, worn above boots or with shoes at balls. This beneficial reform had not yet reached Moscow at this time. The newly arrived NN was the first to appear in such inexpressibles at M. I. Korsakova's ball. Ofrosimov, noticing him, came running up to him and said, "Hey, what sort of a trick are you trying to play? You were invited to a ball to dance, not to clamber up a mast; yet you took it into your head to dress up as a sailor." (152)

Ofrosimov's talent did not stop at exposing potential absurdities; he also had a gift for recounting episodes he had overseen, overheard, or in which he had taken part. According to Viazemsky, Ofrosimov's stories would form an excellent repertoire of comedies of manners (153).

Alexander Pavlovich's mother is portrayed by Viazemsky to exemplify a particular kind of female eccentric. Viazemsky likens Nastasia Dmitrievna Ofrosimova to an old-style military commander. Highly respected for her strong character, frankness, her sober-mindedness, and "congenital sharp-wittedness," Ofrosimova served as a powerful social arbiter, resolving disputes and conferring her blessing and protection on young women (151).

Natalia Kirilovna Zagriazhskaia, another woman whom Viazemsky cites as a particular type of female eccentric common to Russia in an earlier era, gained both respect and social notoriety through her strength of character and disregard for convention (130). The integrity of her character enables

Zagriazhskaia to remain a monument to older days; according to Viazemsky she is a rare example of someone not diminished by "social transformations and . . . that which is called enlightenment." Endowed with a stubborn personality, she possessed "adequate force and tenaciousness to stand through and save her inner character from the requirements and despotic demands of that which is called the new order or simply fashion" (130–31).

Another original is Alexander Turgenev, whose character Viazemsky describes as broad, sometimes contradictory, and uniquely Russian. Referring to Turgenev as a "typical native character" as well as an "intellectual cosmopolitan," Viazemsky finds "he was of an eclectic, mixed or selected nature" (174–75). Viazemsky contends that eclecticism is, indeed, characteristic of anyone, who "is not a bronze statue, which is cast at once fully formed" (190) Viazemsky believes Turgenev's nature embraces seeming contradictions: strengths accompanied by weaknesses, Germanic pedantism coexisting with French frivolity; "he was not at home, as they say, in any one sphere of human knowledge, nor was he in any sphere out of place" (175).[26]

Viazemsky draws parallels between the eclectic, dilletantish, sharp-minded, sensitive and somewhat childish character of Turgenev and the (former) character of Russian society—or with that spirit which animated at least a part of it (190). He contrasts this spirit to the spirit of the successor generation, which he views as marked by a serious single-mindedness tending toward intellectual despotism on the one hand, and tedium on the other (178). Viazemsky concludes by denouncing one form intellectual despotism assumes: false liberalism. Unlike the flexible, non-pedantic Turgenev, Viazemsky claims that the so-called liberals of this day build systems that bear little relation to life around them. They are "journalistic Nestors who, craftily gazing and repeating sophistries, write the social chronicle of a society they do not know, about people who are completely alien to them, to whom they are not close, could never be even friendly, about events, which reach them third- or fourth-hand" (192–93). Viazemsky implicitly contrasts the resulting historical legacy to his own project, which—characteristically for an anecdotal history—relies on firsthand information and does not attempt to build a system out of it. He suggests that the current development of Russian letters, characterized in his mind by the complete rejection of its predecessors, dooms posterity to a distorted picture of the past.

Across the body of his critical work Viazemsky endorses and attempts to exemplify a particular kind of historical narrative based on what he views as the idiosyncrasies of the Russian situation. Drawing on weaknesses (lack of a deeply rooted tradition of historical narrative and a resulting lack of resources for the would-be historian) as well as strengths (an abundance of colorful and eccentric personalities, a rich oral literary and social tradition)

Viazemsky proposes a kind of historical narrative that depicts the social and cultural life of Russia of the late eighteenth and early nineteenth centuries by capitalizing on Russia's rich anecdotal tradition. Such a narrative uses anecdotes as the raw material for history, creating a nonlinear, patchwork structure, and contends that a small incident can convey the truth about the whole. Viazemsky emphasizes the value of individuals whose colorful and unusual characters brighten the social canvas. This emphasis, central to Viazemsky's historiographic position, reflects his use of nontraditional historical sources as well as his conviction that it is eccentrics and people of unusual character who make—literally and figuratively—Russian history.

Over his long life, Viazemsky occupied different positions in the stream of Russian political, social, and cultural thought. The burden of loss, nostalgia, and his own marginality increased over time, feeding his desire to create a historical narrative that would serve as a bridge to the past for future generations. But this increasing burden alone does not account for Viazemsky's historical strategy. His innovations were also a product of his desire to preserve a distinct era of Russia's past in a form he saw as not only befitting but also necessary.

Stephen Baehr

Is Moscow Burning? Fire in Griboedov's *Woe from Wit*

And Moscow is burning up.
The black smoke spreads and curls.
And, behold, the brilliant head of Moscow
Stops gleaming.
Poor Moscow is ablaze,
Moscow has been burning for 12 days . . .
—N. M. Shatrov, "The Fire of Moscow: To the Year 1812"

IN A. S. GRIBOEDOV's comedy *Woe from Wit* (*Gore ot uma,* completed 1824),[1] fire imagery plays a central structural role. Fire is polysemous in the play, summarizing many essential themes and conflicts, connecting and capsuling major events and themes, and serving as a "master image" for the play as a whole. Through frequent references to fire, flame, fumes, and smoke, the idea is implicit that both Moscow and its inhabitants are "burning" with several very different fires. In this essay I shall attempt to uncover the meanings of this essential (but largely unnoticed) fire imagery in Griboedov's play, which provides a fitting frame for the period portrayed, beginning with the 1812 burning of Moscow that saved the city from Napoleon and ending just before the revolutionary "fire" of the 1825 Decembrist uprising.[2] As I shall argue, Griboedov in this play parodically reverses the apocalyptic fire imagery of post-1812 Russian chauvinistic literature (which was often based on the oxymoron of a destructive conflagration that *saved* the nation), replacing it with a satiric vision of a hellish Moscow, burning with the prejudices of its post-Petrine past and scorching anyone trying to "rebuild" the city with new ideas.[3]

Much of Griboedov's comedy is structured on the punning interplay between words formed from two similar-sounding (and etymologically linked) roots: *goret'* (to burn) and *gore* (woe—one of the two key words of the title).[4] Even several character names reflect this interplay. In the original draft of the play, for example, the main character (called Chatsky in later drafts) was named Chadsky, reflecting immediately a connection with *chad* (fumes, smoke), and thus with fire, that became somewhat more oblique in the published version of the play.[5] His "woe" is caused in part by the gossip, liar, and cardsharp Zagoretsky, whose name derives from *zagoret'sia* (to catch fire)—a name justified when he fans the flames of rumor that Chatsky "has gone out of his mind" (a rumor begun at the ball by Sophia as vengeance against Chatsky's caustic tongue, 3.438–44).[6] The only other character besides Chatsky who feels "woe" in and is "burned" by fiery Moscow is Chatsky's old friend Platon Mikhailovich *Gorich,* whose name comes from *gorech'* (bitterness), which derives from *gore* (woe).[7]

As in much world literature, fire is connected with change on one level of Griboedov's play. Indeed, the play can be read as being about the impossibility of change in Moscow, a city that even "fire" (both the historical fire of 1812 and the symbolic fire of "intelligent" ["umnye"] critics like Chatsky) cannot change.[8] In this article, I shall explore three distinct layers of fire imagery in *Woe from Wit* and their interaction: the fire of passion associated with Chatsky; the portrayal of Moscow as a hellish "burning city"; and the attempt of the Moscow upper classes to extinguish the "fire" of revolution and, with it, any form of "enlightenment."

THE FIRE OF PASSION: CHATSKY

Throughout Griboedov's play, Chatsky is associated with passion, heat, and fire. He is described by himself and others through nouns like *zhar* (heat), *pylkost'* (ardor [etymologically: "burning"]), *dym* (smoke), and *chad* (fumes). This "fire" with which Chatsky is linked has at least three distinct meanings: love, choler, and enlightenment. In the first part of the play, much of the fire imagery is commonplace, reflecting the "sacred fire of love" felt by Chatsky for Sophia.[9] At Chatsky's first entrance, the stage directions indicate that he immediately kisses Sophia's hand "with passion" (*s zharom;* literally, "with heat"). When Chatsky realizes that a similar "fire" is no longer burning in Sophia, he says to her that he would not even wish on an enemy what is now "*boiling,* agitating, raging (*kipit, volnuet, besit)*" in him (3.52).[10] Indeed, he criticizes his rival Molchalin for *lacking* this fiery passion.[11] He explicitly uses imagery of fire in stressing his love for her: "Order me to walk through *fire,* and I'll go as if to dinner (*Velite zh mne v ogon': poidu, kak na obed*) (1.445). Sophia's caustic retort—"*All well and good if you burn up,* but what will happen if you don't?" (*Da, khorosho sgorite,* esli zh net? 1.446)—unwittingly portends a later truth: that Chatsky will be "burned" by the "fire" raging in Moscow society. Sophia's father, Famusov, also identifies Chatsky with fire when he says (after realizing that not simply one but two "undesirable" suitors—his clerk Molchalin and now Chatsky—are in love with his daughter): "Now, *out of the fire and into the flame*" (*v polmia iz ognia,* 1.482 [the equivalent of "out of the frying-pan and into the fire"]).

On a second level, Chatsky's connection with fire may also be explained through the famous theory of "humors" that saw the healthy body—paralleling the universe—as containing a balance between four fluids or "humors," each of which corresponded to one of the elements: black bile (earth), blood (air), phlegm (water), and yellow bile/choler (fire).[12] According to this theory, a person's character could be explained by the prominence of one humor. In Chatsky's case, the dominant humor is clearly yellow bile (*zhelch'*), giving him his "fiery" character.[13] Chatsky's link with yellow bile is made explicit several times during the play. As Sophia says to him, "It is obvious that you are ready to pour your bile (*zhelch' . . . izlit'*) on everyone" (3.30–31). And in his last speech in act 4, Chatsky states:

Теперь не худо б было сряду
На дочь и на отца
И на любовника глупца,
И на весь нир *излить всю желчь* и всю досаду.
(4.503–6)

(Now it's not a bad idea
To vent all my bile and fury
On the daughter, on the father,
On the stupid lover, and on all the world.)

Chatsky's "yellow bile"/fire is implicitly opposed to the "phlegm"/water of his foil and rival, the "stupid lover" Molchalin, whose name derives from the root for "silence" (*molch—*), recalling the widespread Russian idea that a life without trouble is possible only by being "*quieter* than *water,* lower than grass" (*tishe vody, nizhe travy*).[14]

Chatsky's fiery choler is directed largely against the servile spirit of self-advancement among Moscow's bureaucrats and the virulent hatred of change among its decrepit doyens. Already in his first appearance on stage, he sarcastically expresses his certainty that no change has occurred there during the three years he has been absent:

Что нового покажет мне Москва?
Вчера был бал, а завтра будет два.
Тот сватался—успел, а тот дал промах
Всё тот же толк, и те ж стихи в альбомах.
(1.353–56)

(What new things can Moscow show me?
There was a ball yesterday and there will be two tomorrow.
One man has managed to get engaged, and one man has failed.
The conversations are the same, as are the verses in the albums.)

Throughout the play, this unchanging Moscow is associated with "the old," metonymically represented by its "gerontocracy" (the malicious old aristocracy who dominate the city); for the young Chatsky "what is older is worse" (*Chto staree, to khuzhe,* 2.345–46). This Moscow gerontocracy is so hateful to Griboedov and his fiery hero that Simon Karlinsky has fairly stated that one of the main themes of the play is "gerontophobia."[15] The attempts of this gerontocracy, and of the bureaucracy with which it is linked, to thwart change and to retain the standards of the past (specifically those of the epoch of Catherine II) are symbolically prefigured in the first scene of the play when the servant Liza sets a clock forward at daybreak so that it will chime the hour and signal Molchalin to leave Sophia's room. But Liza is caught by Famusov, who stops the clock—an emblem for his actions in the rest of the play.

In Griboedov's play, the Moscow gerontocracy fights the fire of change, challenge, and nonconformity in Chatsky and tries to "extinguish" it, declaring Chatsky mad and thus trying to eliminate the harm that his fire can bring;[16] in Moscow, only those who *lack* fire (like Molchalin) can be successful. As Chatsky states:

Теперь пускай из нас один,
Из молодых людей, найдется—враг исканий,
Не требуя ни мест, ни повышенья в чин,
В науки он вперит ум, алчущий познаний.
Или в душе его сам бог возбудит *жар*
К искусствам творческим, высоким и прекрасным,—
Они тотчас: разбой! *пожар*!
И прослывет у них мечтателем! опасным!!
(2.376–83)

(Now, let's suppose that one of us,
One of the younger people, could be found who was an enemy of self-advancement,
Who did not demand a position or promotion to a higher rank,
Who would focus his mind on scholarship, in quest of knowledge.
If God himself should awaken a *passion* in his soul
For the creative arts, sublime and lofty,
These people would immediately yell: "Robbery!" "*Fire!*"
And among them he would gain the reputation as a dreamer and a danger.)

As this speech reflects, the fire burning in Chatsky is, on another level, the fire of "enlightenment" and learning—a "passion" (*zhar*) that challenges the obscurantist upper classes, who cry "fire" at any sign of deviation from their unchanging bureaucratic norm. In an earlier draft of this speech, the clash between Chatsky and these groups is even stronger, with Chatsky emphasizing their intolerance of anyone "who *burns with a different fire*" (*inym ognem goriashchii:* Griboedov, *Gore ot uma,* 1969, 164). As is clear from this version, even at an early stage of writing, Griboedov was opposing two very different fires: one raging in Chatsky and one burning in Moscow.

THE BURNING CITY

From Chatsky's first scene in the play (act 1, scene 7) through his last (act 4, scene 14), he describes Moscow society through imagery of fire and smoke. When he returns to the city after his three-year absence, he is even prepared to forget its foibles, although he well remembers the repulsive and ridiculous characters who have peopled it. His desire to see Sophia has even created a degree of homesickness in him, expressed through a Latin proverb about smoke:

Опять увидеть их мне суждено судьбой!
Жить ними надоест, и в ком не сыщем пятен?
Когда ж постранствуем, воротимся домой,
И дым отечества нам сладок и приятен!
(1.383–86; emphasis in original)

(I am again fated to see them all again!
I'll be bored by living among them, but in whom can one not find fault?
When you have been traveling, and you finally return home
Even the smoke of one's Fatherland is sweet and pleasant.)

The expression used by Chatsky about the "smoke of one's Fatherland" being "sweet and pleasant" comes from a Latin proverb (Et fumus patriae est dulcis), taken from Ovid, which had its ultimate origin in Homer's *Odyssey.*[17] As Griboedov's play develops, this expression acquires clear irony: the play becomes a kind of "anti-*Odyssey*," where the hero, who (like Odysseus) had pined for the "smoke of his fatherland," cannot tolerate the place for even a single day.

Within Griboedov's play, the "*smoke* of the fatherland" is linked, on one level, with the Moscow *fire* of 1812—that "pyric victory" that saved the city from Napoleon, destroying more than 6,000 of its 9,000 buildings. In Russian literature and culture in the years after 1812, this "great fire" was a symbol of hope and salvation. As Tsar Alexander I proclaimed after the burning of Moscow: "God has chosen the venerable capital of Russia to save not just Russia but all of Europe through her sufferings. Her fire was the *conflagration of freedom* for all the kingdoms of the earth."[18] In literature like N. M. Shatrov's panegyric "The Fire of Moscow: To the Year 1812" ("Pozhar Moskvy: 1812 godu," 1813 or 1814), this fire had been similarly praised as a savior of Europe from Napoleon. As Shatrov describes the fire:

И *загорается* Москва.
Дым черный стелется, клубится,
И се перестает светиться
Москвы блестящая глава.

Москва несчастная *пылает*
Москва *горит* двенадцать дней.
(Lotman and Al'tshuller, *Poety,* 589)

(And Moscow is *burning up.*
The black *smoke* spreads and curls
And, behold, the brilliant head of Moscow
Stops gleaming.

Poor Moscow is *ablaze,*
Moscow has been *burning* for 12 days.)

I would argue that Griboedov takes fire imagery like that in much chauvinistic literature and rhetoric appearing after the "Great Patriotic War" of 1812—imagery of an apocalyptic, purgative fire creating the "new earth" foreseen in Revelation—and uses it ironically to challenge, rather than to praise, contemporary Russia.

The fire of 1812 is discussed explicitly in act 2 in a conversation among Famusov, Skalozub, and Chatsky. Skalozub describes the massive rebuilding project that has taken place in Moscow: "In my judgment, / The *fire* greatly helped improve its looks" (*Po moemu suzhdeniiu / Pozhar sposobstvoval ei mnogo k ukrasheniiu,* 2.319–20).[19] To this, Famusov responds in agreement: "Since then the roads, the sidewalks, / The houses, and everything has been built anew" (*na novyi lad;* 2.322–23). But Chatsky immediately rejoins:

Дома новы, но предрассудки стары.
Порадуйтесь, не истребят
Ни годы их, ни моды, ни *пожары.*
(2.324–26)

(The houses are new, but the prejudices old.
Rejoice, that neither years
Nor modes, nor *fires* will wipe them out.")

Thus, while Skalozub sees the fire as purgative—the current commonplace—Chatsky argues that even "fire" cannot change Moscow, a city that has, paradoxically, been "captured" by the customs and language of the defeated French.

Chatsky prays for a "spark" that will start a different fire—one that would consume Russia's habit of blindly imitating foreign customs and ignoring its own native traditions:

Я одаль воссылал желанья
Смиренные, однако вслух,
Чтоб истребил господь нечистый этот дух
Пустого, рабского, слепого подражанья;
Чтоб искру заронил он в ком-нибудь с душой,
Кто мог бы словом и примером
Нас удержать, как крепкою вожжой,
От жалкой тошноты по стороне чужой.
(3.592–99)

(I, at a distance, sent up my wishes,
Which were humble but said aloud,
That God should destroy that unclean spirit
Of empty, slavish, blind imitation;
That He should place a *spark* in someone with a soul
Who could by his example and his word
Restrain us, as with strong reins,
From pitiful yearning for some foreign land.)

Chatsky's words (in a speech that at points prefigures views of the later Slavophiles) describe a prayer to God ("desires sent upward") to "destroy the unclean spirit / . . . / of empty, slavish, blind imitation" in Moscow.[20] The use of the phrase "the *unclean* spirit" ("*nechistyi* dukh") links Moscow's "spirit of imitation" with the devil, who was often called "the *unclean* force" ("*nechistaia* sila") in Russian culture; it thus creates an implicit comparison of Moscow to hell.

I would argue that this implicit image of Moscow as hell assumes three different but related forms in Griboedov's play: a generic "burning city"; Babylon; and Sodom. This Muscovite "inferno" is described by Chatsky (in almost Dantean terms) as populated by:

. . . Мучителей толпа,
В любви предателей, в вражде неутомимых,
Рассказчиков неукротимых,
Нескладных умников, лукавых простяков,
Старух зловещих, стариков,
Дряхлеющих над выдумками, вздором.
(4.508–13)

(. . . A crowd of torturers,
Of betrayers of love who are indefatigable in hatred,
Of indomitable tellers of false tales,
Unsuccessful wits, cunning simpletons,
Malicious old ladies and old men,
Who are growing senile over their made-up tales and nonsense.)[21]

Immediately following this description of upper-class Muscovites, Chatsky describes their Moscow through the implicit metaphor of a burning city in his last speech in the play:

Безумным вы меня прославили всем хором.
Вы правы: из *огня* тот выйдет невредим,
Кто с вами день пробыть успеет,
Подышит воздухом одним
И в нем рассудок уцелеет.
(4.514–18)[22]

(You have pronounced me mad in a single chorus.
Correct you are. Any person will escape from *fire* unscathed

> Who succeeds in spending a day with you,
> Who breathes the same air that you do,
> And whose reason remains intact.)

Here Chatsky compares Moscow society to a fire that chars any reasonable person who comes into contact with it; he leaves Moscow, having been "burned" by its senseless fire of malice, rumor, lies, and servile self-advancement.

On a second level, Moscow is implicitly compared to the burning city of Babylon—a symbol of a "fallen and corrupt existence, the *opposite* of the Heavenly Jerusalem and of Paradise."[23] Indeed, this comparison may help explain the important interplay between grief and burning (between *gore* and *goret'*) that runs throughout the play. In Revelation 18, the burning of Babylon by God in retribution for the sins of the city is described in the Russian Bible through several famous verses intertwining imagery of grief and fire:

> . . . *горе, горе* тебе, великий город Вавилон, город крепкий! Ибо в один час пришел суд твой. . . . И видя *дым* от *пожара* ее, возопили, говоря: какой город подобен городу великому! (Откровение 18:10 and 18)

Since the King James version of the English Bible does not correspond exactly to the Russian Bible here, I shall translate into literal English:

> *Woe, woe* unto you, o great city of Babylon, o mighty city. For in one hour your judgment has come. . . . And when [the merchants and ship captains] saw the *smoke* from its *fire,* they cried out, What city is like this great city? (Revelation, 18:10 and 18)[24]

In originally naming his play *Gore umu* (Woe to wit)—a phrase that creates a direct parallel to the first phrase of this biblical quotation with its use of the word *Gore* plus the dative case—and in strongly emphasizing fire imagery throughout his drafts, Griboedov was, I argue, making an implicit comparison between the "great city" of Moscow and the burning city of Babylon.

Within the play there is also an implicit comparison of Moscow to Sodom, where God "*rain[ed] brimstone and fire*" (*dozhdem seru i ogon'*) and "the *smoke* [*dym*] was rising from the earth like smoke from a furnace" (Gen. 19:24, 28). The word *sodom* (with a small "s," meaning "disorder," "chaos," or "noise" in early nineteenth-century Russia) is used explicitly in act 2 of the play. After Chatsky criticizes fawning courtiers like Famusov's late uncle Maksim Petrovich (who was promoted for the fact that after once accidentally falling while bowing to Empress Catherine the Great, he purposefully fell a second and a third time upon seeing her amusement; 2.78ff.), Famusov chastises Chatsky and his "radical" ideas: "Well, I expect disorder from this" ("Nu, tak i zhdu *sodoma,*" 2.155–56). To an audience that is watching (as opposed to reading) the play, the word *sodom* is clearly ambiguous ("disorder" or "Sodom" itself).[25] Given this hint, it may not be coincidental that Chatsky says in his last speech, "Von iz Moskvy! Siuda ia bol'she ne ezdok / Begu, *ne oglianus*'" (I'm leaving Moscow! I won't come here again. / I rush and *won't look back*," 4.519–20). The overtones of the words *ne oglianus'* recall the warning of one of the angels to Lot as they were leading them out of Sodom: "Save your soul; don't look back" (*ne ogliadyvaisia nazad*) (Gen. 19:17). Like Lot, Chatsky dares not look back on the "burning city" of Moscow.

Griboedov's play in effect reverses a cultural tradition that had been frequent in Russia from the mid-fifteenth through the late eighteenth century and had arisen, once again, after the Russian victory over Napoleon in 1812: that of depicting Moscow, or Russia as a whole, as the Third Rome, paradise, heaven-on-earth, or New Jerusalem. This tradition was graphically represented in a famous mid-sixteenth-century icon called "The Church Militant" (*Tserkov' voinstvuiushchaia*), which celebrated Ivan IV's victory over the Tartar horde and his capture of the city of Kazan by depicting the Archangel Michael leading troops from the burning city of Sodom (Kazan), to a paradise or holy city, a "city on a hill" (Moscow), where the Mother of God sits enthroned.[26] In depicting *Moscow* as the burning city, Griboedov joined a number of other important writers of Russia's Golden Age (including, at times, Pushkin and Lermontov) who were *reversing* such traditions, portraying Moscow and/or Russia not as paradise but as hell.[27]

THE FIRE OF REVOLUTION

A third layer of pyric imagery in Griboedov's play centers around the symbolic "fire" of revolution. As the French Revolutionary writer Sylvain Maréchal wrote in his 1799 *Voyages of Pythagoras* (the six volumes of which were translated into Russian from 1804 to 1809 and achieved great popularity): "with the smallest *spark* a *great fire* can be ignited."[28] This image of the fire of revolution spread throughout nineteenth- and twentieth-century Russian literature and culture, used by writers as diverse as Petr Viazemsky, Aleksandr Odoevsky, Dostoevsky, and Blok, among others, and provided the title for several journals advocating revolution (including Lenin's *Iskra* [The Spark]).

The connection of fire with revolution in original Russian literature and culture goes back at least to Count Rostopchin's anti-Napoleonic placards and brochures. In one 1807 brochure, for example, he stated about the French Revolution: "*The Revolution is a fire* (*pozhar*), the French are pieces of *smoldering wood* (*goloveshki*), and Napoleon is the *stoker* (*kochegar*)."[29] This link of fire with revolution is also implied in Petr Viazemsky's fable "The Conflagration" ("Pozhar," 1820), which was not printed at the time because of its Aesopian fire imagery. The poem tells of a conversation between the owner of a house that is burning and a "councillor" (*sovetnik*). The councillor tells the owner that he himself avoids such risks by not using fire to light his house at night or to heat it in winter. The owner, however, retorts that "man was not born to go numb in the dark" (*kostenet' vpot'makh*): "*Fire can be a danger but more often brings use to us.* And your tomblike house is suitable only to make wolves freeze to death (*chtob v nem morit' volkov*) and for owls to weave their nests" (*gnezda vit' sycham*).[30] As V. S. Nechaeva notes in her commentary to this poem: "Conflagration (*pozhar*) is often a symbol of revolt, of revolution, the reason for which is fire (*ogon'*)—a symbol of knowledge and enlightenment, both of which are opposed to the 'tomblike house' of Russia, in which reactionaries suppressed knowledge out of fear of revolutionary activity"[31] Imagery of revolutionary fire was also used by Aleksandr Odoevsky in his response to some verses sent by Pushkin in 1827 to the Decembrists imprisoned in Siberia:

Наш скорбный труд не пропадет:
Из искры возгорится пламя,
. . . .
И *пламя* вновь зажжем *свободы*.[32]

(Our mournful labors won't be in vain,
From a spark there will flash a flame
. . . .
And once again we will light the *fire of freedom.*)

In short, it was not without precedent when Dostoevsky in his famous antirevolutionary novel *The Possessed* (*Besy*, 1872) had his provincial governor, Lembke, say about the fires being set by revolutionaries: "The *conflagration* is in people's minds, and not on the roofs of houses" ("*Pozhar* v umakh, a ne na kryshakh domov"); or when Aleksandr Blok wrote in his notebooks about the "terrible tongues of the revolutionary flame" ("strashnykh iazykov *revoliutsionogo plameni*").[33]

In Griboedov's play, "fire" is often a symbol of enlightenment, education, or new ideas, which obscurantist, upper-class Muscovites frequently mistook for revolution. Thus, *Woe from Wit* attacks the crusade against enlightenment that often accompanied the chauvinism arising after the war of 1812. As Anatole Mazour has written:

> The war of 1812–14 . . . and especially the burning of Moscow, greatly stimulated the chauvinistic sentiment. It was a call to die-hard conservatives to raise their banner . . . and declare open warfare against the . . . "Jacobin spirit." . . . Fighting political windmills everywhere, the authorities saw revolution in the most timorous opposition. . . . The government . . . considered all societies potential *Carbonari* and forbade them entirely, except those sponsored by itself. Hence the crusade against revolution in Russia turned into a petty persecution of various developments of national life, destroying thus the finest elements within the state.[34]

Griboedov's play depicts just such "petty persecution," portraying Famusov, his friends and colleagues as what contemporaries like the future

Decembrist N. I. Turgenev dubbed "gasil'niki" (Extinguishers)—people who, in the conservative reaction occurring after the fire of 1812, tried to "extinguish" the fires of change and enlightenment within Russian society by opposing any new ideas.[35] Famusov embodies typical views of these *gasil'niki* when he states:

> Ученье—вот чума, ученость—вот причина,
> Что нынче, пуще, чем когда,
> Безумных развелось людей, и дел, и мнений.
> (3.522–24)
>
> (Learning—that's the plague; erudition—that's the reason
> That now, more than ever,
> There are more mad people, mad deeds, and mad opinions.)[36]

Others at the ball support this attack on learning, justifying their "noms parlants" as they blame education for all contemporary evils: Khlestova (Famusov's sister-in-law, whose name comes from the word "to whip") blames schooling of all kinds, especially the Lancaster System "of mutual education" (a system associated with liberal ideas and freethinking at the time, which, in the manner of Mrs. Malaprop in Sheridan's *The Rivals*, she mistakenly calls the "Landcart [= map] system"); Princess Tugoukhovskaya ("Princess Hard-of-Hearing") blames the Pedagogical Institute (where "they give exercises in schism and atheism"—reflecting the fact that four professors had recently been fired for godlessness and other subversive activities); and Colonel Skalozub (whose name comes from the phrase *skalit' zuby* ["to bare one's teeth," "to laugh in a threatening way"]) advocates an Arakcheev-type project for education:

> Я вас обрадую: всеобщая молва,
> Что есть проект насчет лицеев, школ, гимназий;
> Там будут лишь учить по-нашему: раз, два;
> А книги сохранят так, для больших оказий.
> (3.535–39)
>
> (I've got good news: there's a rumor circulating
> That there is a plan for lycées, schools, gymnasia,
> Where they will only teach in our own Russian way—left, right, left—
> And books will be reserved for special occasions.)

This interpretation of the society surrounding Famusov as a group of "Extinguishers" is further justified when Famusov urges an obscurantist "auto-da-fé": "[I]f you want to stop all evil / Gather all the books, and *burn* them all at once" (Uzh koli zlo presech'; / Zabrat' vse knigi by, da *szhech'*, 3.540–41).

Griboedov establishes a context of absurd suspicions by upper-class Muscovites of any intelligent nonconformist or critic, who is immediately taken for a revolutionary. Thus, Famusov declares Chatsky a "Carbonarist"

(2.121)—a member of the revolutionary group striving for a constitutional system of government in countries throughout Europe[37]—after he hears Chatsky decry Famusov's beloved ideal, the age of Catherine, as "a regiment of jesters" (*polk shutov*, 2.124) and listens to him disparage Famusov's favorite role model, his uncle Maksim Petrovich:

> Хоть есть охотники поподличать везде,
> Да нынче смех страшит и держит стыд в узде;
> Недаром жалуют их скупо государи.
> (2.118–20)
>
> (Although there still are people who would grovel everywhere,
> Now laughter frightens them, and shame holds them in check.
> It is not in vain that rulers now reward them poorly.)

Famusov concludes that with statements like this Chatsky will "inevitably be dragged into court" (*upekut pod sud*) and calls him "a dangerous man" (2.152–53, 123). Indeed, Famusov is so convinced of Chatsky's revolutionary intentions that when a servant comes in announcing the arrival of Skalozub, Famusov—in one of the classic Freudian slips in Russian literature—is too upset to understand, taking Chatsky's words "Vas zovut" (You are being called) for the words "A? bunt?" (What? A rebellion?) and declaiming (as was discussed above): "Indeed, I expect disorder" (*sodom*) (2.155–56).

The supposed connection of Chatsky with the "fire" of subversive groups—specifically the Masons and the Carbonarists—is humorously asserted again at the ball, when Zagoretsky (who "burns" with the fire of rumor) spreads the word that Chatsky is mad, even though he at first cannot remember who Chatsky is. In trying to tell this rumor to the old Countess Khriumina (a hard-of-hearing dotard, whose name combines the well-known noble name Riumina with the sound made by a grunting pig [*khriuk*]), Zagoretsky is asked by her: "What's going on? What's going on? Is there a *fire* here ("uzh net li zdes' *poshara*" [*sic*])?" (3.478) After being told by Zagoretsky that Chatsky "was wounded in the forehead while in the mountains (*v gorakh izranen v lob*) and went crazy from his wound," the countess says, "What? He's joined the club of Freemasons (*k farmazonam v klob*)? He's become a heathen!" (3.482).[38] This same Khriumina later spreads a rumor to Prince Tugoukhovsky (Prince "Hard-of-Hearing," who can understand even less than she) that the chief of police has come to jail Chatsky and will conscript him into the army as a private because he broke the law and is, to boot, a heathen and "a damned freethinker" (*okaiannyi vol'ter'ianets*); later the Prince's wife says of Chatsky: "[I]t's even dangerous to speak with him / He should have been locked up long ago / . . . / I think that he's simply a Jacobin" (4.252–56, with omissions). In short, Griboedov is satirizing the tendency of upper-class Russian society after the burning of Moscow to confuse the frequently distinct "fires" of enlightenment and revolution.[39]

Those actually trying to light the "fire" of revolution are portrayed as absurd or comical in Griboedov's play (which was completed in May 1824, about nineteen months before the Decembrist revolt). Although Griboedov was friendly with such future Decembrists as Kiukhel'beker, Ryleev, and Bestuzhev, their influence (despite some pre- and post-revolutionary Russian interpretations) seems minimal here.[40] Indeed, the only "revolutionary" in the play is the ludicrous Repetilov, who describes his "most secret union" (*sekretneishii soiuz*) in act 4 using several images of fire. In Repetilov's words his unit consists of "a dozen *hot*heads" (*Goriachikh* diuzhina golov") (4.96, 116), whose leader, "when he speaks about high honor" has "eyes [that] turn bloodshot" and a face that "is on *fire*" (*gorit*), "as though he was possessed by a demon" (4.156–58). Given the inanity of this "most secret union," it is most unlikely that Griboedov intended this group as a portrait of the future Decembrists (as some commentators have proposed); conversely, it is unlikely that Griboedov is portraying Chatsky as a future Decembrist (as others have argued, beginning with Herzen and continuing with Dostoevsky, Goncharov, and Grigor'ev, among others). It is more likely, I would argue, that the imagery of revolutionary "fire" in Griboedov's play is used more as a portrait of the Moscow "Extinguishers" and their intolerance of any new ideas than as a serious portrait of the revolutionary movement itself.[41]

In sum, I have argued that through the imagery of fire Griboedov is describing the obscurantist Moscow of the upper classes (including both bureaucrats like Famusov and army officers like Skalozub), who opposed any change in Russia after the war of 1812 yet continued to borrow their language, conduct, and clothing from the French whom they had defeated. Griboedov depicts a stagnant Moscow that is burning with servility and malice, a city that has become a modern Babylon or Sodom and that, in turn, "burns" any idealist who hopes for change. The imagery of fire connects and capsulizes several of the main events and themes of the play: the return to Moscow of Chatsky, burning with love for Sophia; the lack of change in Moscow after its rebuilding (indicating that the fire of 1812 was not the fire of purification that many had hoped for); and the absurdity of the *gasil'niki* of Moscow high society, who saw the fire of revolution in every act of nonconformity and individuality.

Chatsky's hopes at his return to Moscow are charred by a single day there. As he states in a speech at the beginning of act 4, which makes his original name (Chadskii) into another of the many *noms parlants* in the play:

Ну вот и день прошел, и с ним
Все призраки, весь *чад и дым*
Надежд, которые мне душу наполняли.
. . . .
В повозке так-то на пути
Необозримою равниной, сидя праздно,

Всё что-то видно впереди
Светло, синё, разнообразно.
И едешь час, и два, день целый, вот резво,
Домчались к отдыху, ночлег: куда ни взглянешь,
Всё та же гласъ и степь, и пусто и мертво! . . .
Досадно, мочи нет, чем больше думать станешь.
(4.24–37, with omissions)

(Well, the day has passed, and with it
All the ghosts, all the *fume and smoke*
Of hope which filled my soul.
. . . .
In just this way, you drive in your carriage along the road,
Sitting idly across the boundless plain.
All the time something is visible ahead,
Bright, blue, and varied.
You drive an hour, two, and then a day,
And finally you've reached your rest, your lodging place, but wherever you look
There's the same old plain and steppe, and it's empty and dead.
The more you begin to think, the more maddening it becomes.)

Chatsky's emphasis on the "extinguishing" of the "smoke of hope" in him by Moscow society uses the image of *chad* (the hazardous smoke of a coal that has almost—but not fully—burned out) to imply that the "fire" that had burned in him in the morning has been virtually extinguished by the end of the night and that Moscow has "burned him out."[42] His bitter comparison of Moscow (the "lodging place," to which he has been looking forward and "rushing" on his long trip) to a mirage—a place that from a distance looks "bright, blue, and varied" but in reality is as dull, "dead," and "empty" as the Russian steppe—represents the essence of the city as depicted in the play.[43] By act 4, Chatsky says about his native land, which he had praised earlier by stating that even its smoke is "sweet and pleasant": "And this is my native land. . . . No, for this trip, / I see that I will soon have taken all that I can" (*Net, v nyneshnii priezd, / Ia vizhu, chto ona mne skoro nadoest*) (4.287–88). It is fitting that the stage directions for this scene state that the speech takes place when "the last light is extinguished" (*posledniaia lampa gasnet*) (act 4, scene 10). For the *gasil'niki* of Moscow society have fully "extinguished" the fire of hope that had fueled Chatsky's return to this "burning city"—a hellish place that is "empty" and "dead," a place that even fire cannot change.

Irina Reyfman

Alexander Bestuzhev-Marlinsky: *Bretteur* and Apologist of the Duel

DUELING ARRIVED in Russia later and also stopped later than in other European countries except Germany. Furthermore, it was transplanted at the time when complex social changes that shaped post-Petrine Russia were taking place. Most important, the assimilation of dueling paralleled the incorporation of the Russian nobility as a privileged class striving for autonomy from the central government. This was a two-sided process, the initiative coming both from the nobility itself and from Russian monarchs—the latter needing the incorporated nobility as much as the nobility longed to be independent and privileged. Ideally, the monarchs wanted a noble class that would be loyal to the monarchy and the state, serving them willingly and honestly. For these purposes, they promoted the idea of honor as corporate devotion to service. The unintended by-products, however, were the notions of gentleman's honor, which defined not only the corporate but also the personal integrity of a gentleman, and the duel of honor, which regulated relations between individuals within the privileged class without the state's interference.

The duel was an appropriate vehicle for the formation of the independent Russian noble class, because of its inherent capacity to serve as a weapon in the power play between the monarch and the nobility. As François Billacois points out regarding the French situation, "[s]uch was the political meaning of duels: both a violent challenge to the man in power, a refusal to submit to his orders, and a refusal to take power or to participate in his power. The duel is an injunction to the King to be the King and a warning to the monarch to behave as a gentleman."[1] With amendments, Billacois's observation also applies to Russia. However, while the French duel for the most part played a balancing, stabilizing role in the struggle between the monarch and the nobility, in Russia its function as a statement of the nobility's emancipation from and even opposition to the government was far more prominent. Moreover, in going to a duel, a Russian gentleman claimed not only his independence from the state, but also his right to defend his personal integrity—both against his peers and against central authority. In a state that for centuries had tended to curtail the autonomy of the individual, such behavior not only registered the nobility's protest against the monarch's excessive power, but, most important, served as a powerful means of safeguarding personal rights.

Alexander Bestuzhev-Marlinsky belonged to the generation of the most passionate duelists in the history of the Russian duel—the generation that was particularly sensitive both to the duel's political symbolism and to its ability to define and defend personal space. Accordingly, he was an ardent apologist and a prolific portrayer of dueling: in the years between the early 1820s, his literary debut, and 1833, when his interest in literary duels diminished, he portrayed in detail ten conflicts of honor and mentioned scores more. Moreover, he established the framework of dueling discourse in Russian literature. He was the first to discuss the technicalities of dueling, as well as the philosophical and psychological questions pertaining to dueling behavior. He examined the duel's capacity to protect an individual's private space and pointed out its limitations. He was the first to pay attention to the duel's capacity to deprive a person of free will. He also probed the controversial question—later taken up by Dostoevsky—of how to refuse a duel.

As a Romantic writer, Bestuzhev preached what he lived and lived what he preached. His life was rich in adventures and his talents were remarkably versatile. His extraordinary personality fostered rumors and legends both about his life in the Caucasus and especially about his death. The legends portrayed him as a man who enjoyed exceptional success with women, and as a soldier of uncommon courage who, due to his linguistic facility and exotic appearance, could go live among the enemy either as an intelligence agent or a supporter of their cause. After Bestuzhev's death in action in June 1837, he became one of those figures in Russian cultural memory who, despite clear evidence to the contrary, were presumed to have survived death and continued a posthumous existence full of adventures. Posthumously Bestuzhev was credited with both passionate love affairs and amazing military exploits.[2]

Bestuzhev's death came less than six months after Pushkin's, and in the popular consciousness the two writers' tragic ends intertwined. One contemporary mourned the deaths of "three great Alexanders": Alexander I, Alexander Pushkin, and Alexander Bestuzhev-Marlinsky.[3] Bestuzhev himself interpreted Pushkin's death as a foreboding of his own: "Yes, I sense that my own death will also be violent and unusual, that it is already close; I have too much hot blood, blood that boils in my veins, too much for old age to freeze it. I beg for one thing: not to die on a bed of suffering or in a duel" (2:674). Nonetheless, Bestuzhev considered challenging D'Anthès, Pushkin's killer, in order to avenge the death of Russia's national poet: "Let him know

(God is my witness, I am not joking) that after our very first meeting one of us will not return alive" (2:674). Bestuzhev's legendary persona thus naturally incorporated the idea of dueling.

One of the legends about Bestuzhev's death (although by far not the most popular) maintained that he was killed in a duel with a jealous husband.[4] While the legend was false, it seemed fitting for a person who not only frequently depicted duels in his fiction but also participated in several actual duels, either as the principal or as a second. Bestuzhev's first duel occurred in the early years of his military career, while he was serving in the Light Dragoon Regiment of the Guards. In his memoir, Bestuzhev's younger brother, Mikhail, tells that Bestuzhev's first duel was over his caricature portraits of fellow officers: "Everyone laughed as they recognized themselves. Only one officer, who was portrayed as a turkey-cock, took offense at the joke, and they fought."[5] In his addendum to the memoir, Mikhail Bestuzhev mentions two other duels that his brother fought: "His second duel was over dancing. The third was with an engineer staff-officer who was with the duke of Württemberg. [M]y brother and the engineer were among his suite and my brother was challenged for some word that had been considered insulting."[6] Bestuzhev's sister, Elena, reports that Alexander shot into the air all three times.[7] In his memoir of their older brother, Nikolai Bestuzhev, Mikhail also mentions Alexander's near duel with Pavel Katenin, whose translation of Racine's *Esther* he had criticized.[8] Finally, Bestuzhev tried but failed to gain a duel with a certain von Dezin, Nikolai's fellow officer, who, as Mikhail reports "became jealous of my brother Alexander, but, instead of getting even with my brother, spoke rudely to our mother as they left church. My brother challenged him to a duel, but he refused."[9] Kondraty Ryleev helped Bestuzhev to teach the reluctant duelist a lesson: "Ryleev met him by chance and, in response to his impertinent talk, lashed his stupid mug with a whip that he had in his hand."[10]

In fact, Ryleev and Bestuzhev often participated in conflicts of honor together. Bestuzhev was Ryleev's second in his February 1824 duel with Prince Konstantin Shakhovskoi, the lover of Ryleev's unmarried half-sister. The conditions of this duel were extremely harsh: there was no barrier (that is, the minimal distance between the opponents was not determined) and the duelists had to shoot simultaneously, at a second's command. The opponents agreed to shoot as many times as it would take to wound seriously or kill one of them. They exchanged two shots at a distance of three paces. By sheer luck both times the bullets hit the opponents' pistols. One of the bullets ricocheted and wounded Ryleev in the heel. The seconds then ended the duel.[11] Significantly, it was Ryleev who had insisted on these brutal conditions, despite the fact that by this time he was a married man and the father of a young daughter. Initially, Shakhovskoi was reluctant to fight. According to

Bestuzhev, "[a]t first, [Shakhovskoi] refused, but after Ryleev had spat in his face, he made up his mind."[12] Ryleev, however, resolved to engage his opponent in a deadly duel neither because of a quarrelsome disposition, nor because of brotherly love for his sister. He did it as a matter of principle. He felt it necessary both to hold the insolent aristocrat responsible for his actions toward a young woman without social prominence and to demonstrate that Prince Shakhovskoi and the insignificant nobleman Ryleev were equals under the honor code.

Bestuzhev shared Ryleev's sentiments concerning all noblemen's equality under the honor code, regardless of their social status, wealth, or rank. Like Ryleev, he believed this cause to be important enough to risk his or his friends' lives. Both Bestuzhev and Ryleev participated in another conflict of honor that had distinct social undertones and that shocked contemporaries as a reckless and cruel affair: the 10 September 1825 duel between a young aristocrat, Vladimir Novosil'tsev, an aide-de-camp of Alexander I, and a petty noble, Lieutenant of the Guards Konstantin Chernov, a member of the Decembrist conspiracy. While Ryleev, who was Chernov's cousin, served as his second, Bestuzhev participated informally: Chernov's deathbed letter, explaining the duel's significance, is in Bestuzhev's handwriting and displays the idiosyncrasies of his style.

The duel was fought over Novosil'tsev's treatment of Chernov's sister: he had proposed to her, but backed out because of his mother's objections to a socially inferior daughter-in-law. As in the Ryleev-Shakhovskoi duel, the conditions were severe: the distance was set at eight paces (at one point, Chernov suggested three), and the opponents were to shoot simultaneously. Furthermore, if Konstantin were to be killed, three of his brothers and, finally, his father planned to challenge Novosil'tsev one by one. Both Novosil'tsev and Chernov were mortally wounded and died soon after. Chernov's funeral attracted a large crowd of supporters, which his friends interpreted as the first political rally in Russian history.[13] In this case also, the Chernovs and their friends perceived the duel as a matter of principle. They wanted Novosil'tsev to recognize the Chernovs as his social peers. After the duel, Ryleev praised Chernov precisely for insisting on his equality with Novosil'tsev under the honor code: "[He] showered Chernov's family with enthusiastic praise, claimed that this duel—between a man of the middle class and an aristocrat and aide-de-camp—was a notable phenomenon, and it demonstrated that there were people among the middle class who highly valued their honor and their good name."[14] Chernov's sentiments, as expressed in the letter written by Bestuzhev in his name about the impending duel, were similar: "Let me die, but let him also die, as a lesson to miserable prideful fellows and in order that neither gold, nor noble origin should sneer at innocence and nobility of the soul."[15] According to a contemporary, Bestuzhev greeted the rally at Chernov's funeral as a "democratic celebration."[16]

Bestuzhev thus viewed the duel as a means to formulate the notions of the individual and his rights. He and his contemporaries often behaved as *bretteurs*—a special type of reckless duelist, ready to fight at any provocation—and this behavior represented the Russian nobility's response to the failure of the Russian legal system to guarantee their individual rights. Together with Ryleev and other like-minded people of his generation, Bestuzhev attempted to shape the honor code into an institution protecting the individual in the absence of legal safeguards. They did so as part of their confrontation with the wealthy and powerful wing of the Russian nobility created by and loyal to the central government. Casting themselves as representatives of the Russian "middle" class and champions of the Russian national tradition, the early nineteenth-century *bretteurs* succeeded in formulating their conflict with the new aristocracy in populist terms. Although they were motivated by class interests in their hostility against the aristocrats, in the long run their egalitarian stance helped establish the general idea of innate individual rights.

Bestuzhev and his comrades were especially anxious about the absence of firm guarantees of physical inviolability. This anxiety reflected the fear of physical violation that arose among the Russian nobility at the turn of the eighteenth century, after their hopes for legal protection offered by the 1785 Charter to the Nobility proved futile. This fear powerfully promoted the duel's popularity in Russia.[17] Corporal punishment is an act of violence by a superior (either the state or an individual acting in the name of the state) against a subordinate. Dueling is an act of violence between equals. The nobility used dueling to signal their refusal to accept the state's authority over their bodies. Their campaign was fairly successful. In the mid-eighteenth century, Mavra Shuvalova held a church service every time her husband, Count Petr Shuvalov, came home from a hunting trip with Elizabeth's favorite, A. G. Razumovsky, without having been flogged by the latter. By the turn of the century, however, a commanding officer could no longer strike a subordinate officer without facing an imminent duel.[18] Nonetheless, rumors about noblemen flogged or tortured persisted into the second half of the nineteenth century, reflecting the abiding need for reliable legal guarantees of physical inviolability.

In trying to secure their rights, the Russian *bretteurs* frequently endowed duels with political significance. In extreme cases, the duel was seen to function as a political assassination or a tyrant's execution. Alexander Iakubovich attempted to frame his planned assassination of Alexander I as a duel. A well-known *bretteur,* Iakubovich was sent to serve in the Caucasus for his role as a second in the 1817 duel between Vasily Sheremetev and Alexander Zavadovsky, in which Sheremetev was killed. In 1825, while in St. Petersburg on a leave of absence, Iakubovich offered to assassinate the tsar for the Decembrist leaders. For him personally the proposed regicide was a means to avenge his "unjust transfer" to the Caucasus, which he interpreted as an insult to his honor.[19] Mikhail Lunin's attempts to challenge Grand Duke

Constantine, as well as the group of officers' 1822 demand for "satisfaction" from Grand Duke Nicholas for threatening a fellow officer with physical violence, evidence similar reasoning.[20]

Bestuzhev's stories about dueling reflect this historical context and the view that the duel was a means to affirm an individual's rights as well as to promote a political cause. However, his fiction also shows Bestuzhev's awareness of the duel's deficiencies. His support for the duel is never unequivocal and never without reservations. Significantly, this ambivalence is least evident when the conflict of honor arises over a physical assault. In other cases, Bestuzhev's stories, while teaching the reader how to behave in dueling situations, always point out the duel's shortcomings as a means of resolving personal conflicts.

Bestuzhev's ambivalence about dueling was fed by the European and nascent Russian literary tradition (stories like the anonymous 1802 "A New Sentimental Traveler, or My Excursion to A***," which contains the first full-scale—and very negative—description of a conflict of honor in Russian literature). However, his ambivalence also drew on his and his contemporaries' own dueling experiences. Early nineteenth-century Russian duelists engaged in brutally harsh duels and thus faced a high probability of killing an opponent or of being killed themselves. They witnessed duelists dying and they knew duelists who had killed. Witnesses of the Zavadovsky-Sheremetev duel vividly recalled Sheremetev's agony at the dueling site even decades later.[21] The Decembrist Evgeny Obolensky, who had taken the place of his younger cousin in a duel and killed his opponent, could never forgive himself. One contemporary compared his mental anguish to the sufferings experienced by Orestes: "This unfortunate man fought a duel—and killed. From that time on, like Orestes pursued by Furies, he could not find peace."[22] Early nineteenth-century duelists thus understood the duel's violent nature and knew its power to traumatize a victorious duelist for life. And yet they not only accepted the duel but cultivated its most brutal forms. It was in literature that they allowed themselves to explore the duel's limitations and sometimes to argue eloquently against dueling.

Bestuzhev examined duels in two genres: historical tales and society tales. He wrote two types of historical tales: about ancient Russia (his so-called Russian cycle) and about the medieval Baltic area (his so-called Livonian cycle). Only one of his Russian tales, the 1831 "The Raids: A Tale of the Year 1613," set in Poland, features dueling.[23] In contrast, Bestuzhev's Livonian tales, cast in the Middle Ages and populated with German knights, abound in conflicts of honor. All of these tales condone a person's right to a duel regardless of his social status. I shall focus on two tales that specifically address the question of physical inviolability: the 1821 "Castle Wenden" and the 1825 "Castle Eisen."[24]

Bestuzhev's very first Livonian tale, "Castle Wenden," features a conflict between two opponents of unequal social standing: the powerful Magister, Winno von Rohrbach, and a knight, Sir Wigbert von Serrat. Rohrbach disregards Serrat's claim to independence and denies his right to protect his vassals. When Serrat protests, Rohrbach lashes him with a whip. Rohrbach clearly wants to establish his opponent's inferior status: " 'A scoundrel!' he exclaimed in fury, 'For your insolence, for your opinions you deserve punishment befitting a slave.' With these words he struck the unarmed Wigbert with a whip" (1:41).

To restore his honor, Serrat seeks a duel, but Rohrbach refuses to accept his challenge, citing Serrat's inferior status and alluding to the lashing that he has endured as a proof of his inferiority. Having anticipated Rohrbach's refusal, Serrat warns him in his challenge: "Beware of rejecting an honest fight: the one who offends and does not give satisfaction with his lance deserves to be killed as a thug. In case of rejection—I swear on my knightly honor—the last drop of Rohrbach's blood will dry on my dagger" (1:41). Bestuzhev's narrator is not blind to the fact that Serrat's intention is criminal (at one point, he calls Serrat's dagger "murderous"), but he seems to share Serrat's conviction that it is a lesser dishonor to kill and be executed than not to avenge the offense and thus accept inferior status. Serrat then sneaks into Rohrbach's castle at night, kills the offender with a dagger, is caught and executed.

Serrat carefully stages his murder to resemble a duel: he challenges Rohrbach, warns him about his intention to kill him, uses the so-called noble weapon in his assault, and wakes him up before assaulting him, thus giving him a chance to defend himself (1:44–45).[25] In presenting Serrat's attack as a surrogate duel, Bestuzhev protects his character's reputation as a man of honor: while some nineteenth-century duelists felt that an opponent who had dishonored himself (as Rohrbach did when he rejected Serrat's challenge) was not worthy of a duel and could be killed "like a dog,"[26] the prevailing view condemned such assaults. When, in 1832, Konstantin Chernov's brother Alexander, instead of challenging Alexander Shishkov over a slap in the face, slew him on the spot, public indignation against him was unanimous.[27] However, contemporaries were more lenient toward Nikolai Pavlov who, in 1836, mortally wounded Alexander Aprelev on the steps of the church, after first challenging him several times over his sister's honor and then staging his assault as a surrogate duel in a fashion very similar to that of Serrat.[28]

Furthermore, Bestuzhev adds the flavor of political execution to this killing by inserting the phrase "Rohrbach's blood irrigated the scaffold" (1:45). "Scaffold" (*pomost*) among other things denotes the platform where executions take place. Its appearance in the story is unmotivated, making it a probable transmitter of a political message. The story's political overtone is further enhanced as Serrat dies as a political criminal, an assassin, rather than a common murderer: "The Magister ceased to exist, but his power remained, and the lawless [*samosudnyi*] murderer, mauled by torture, died broken on the wheel" (1:45).

A conflict over the right to physical inviolability also occurs in Bestuzhev's last Livonian tale, "Castle Eisen," where the offender is again socially superior. In this work, the evil Baron Bruno von Eisen oppresses everyone around him, including his nephew Reginald. Bruno takes from Reginald his bride, Louise, and marries her himself. Later Bruno orders his nephew to commit an act of cruelty; when Reginald refuses, Bruno threatens his nephew with violence. His threat refers both to a glove, an attribute of a knightly duel, and straps, an instrument of corporal punishment: "Be quiet, you brat, or I shall order this iron glove to be stuffed into your mouth. . . . Go away, or I will flog you with straps, as if you were the lowest among stablemen" (1:161). Furious, Reginald prepares to shoot an arrow at Bruno but is restrained and locked up in a dungeon. While Bruno is away, Louise frees Reginald and the two have an affair. Upon his return, Bruno discovers them kissing in the woods and attacks Reginald. Reginald defeats Bruno, ties him up, and slays him, despite Bruno's entreaties and Louise's intercession.

In contrast to the "Castle Wenden," in which Serrat imitates a duel, Reginald kills a defenseless man. This difference is crucial; the narrator censures Reginald's egotistical motives and in his case rejects the idea of punishment without trial (*samosud*). Accordingly, Reginald and Louise are punished for their transgression: when they come to the altar to be married, Bruno's ghost (actually Bruno's long-lost twin brother) arrives in the church on a black horse, tramples Reginald to death, kidnaps Louise, and buries her alive.[29]

Bestuzhev's historical tales, although cast in foreign lands and in past historical epochs, reflected the contemporary Russian situation. The conflicts of honor that Bestuzhev examined were thinly disguised allusions to the early nineteenth-century antagonism between the independent-minded and politically weak lower nobility who tried to assert their personal rights by means of dueling and the powerful high nobility who tended to disregard those rights. Bestuzhev never seriously aspired to reenact history, but used it as a backdrop for the unfolding of what he presented as a timeless human conflict, and what in fact was a contemporary controversy for which he sought historical precedents.[30] The conflict between Winno von Rohrbach and Wigbert von Serrat portrayed in "Castle Wenden" bears little resemblance to the story of the quarrel between Magister Wenno and Wickbert von Soest as described in contemporary sources.[31] In "Castle Eisen," Bestuzhev did not even attempt to reconstruct a concrete historical epoch, he merely created a vaguely medieval Livonian setting. In "Castle Neihausen" and "Tournament in Revel," plots and characters are pure inventions.

Bestuzhev's tales foreshadowed reality as often as they reflected it. Serrat's plight, in "Castle Wenden," anticipated the plights of Ryleev, Konstantin Chernov, and Bestuzhev himself, who, in order to be taken seriously by their socially superior opponents, felt it necessary to behave like *bretteurs*, overreacting in response to perceived offenses and, if necessary, using brutal force to persuade their opponents to accept their challenges. Pavlov's and Alexander Chernov's assaults on their offenders resemble, respectively, Serrat's and Reginald's murders of their opponents. In "Tournament at Revel," Bernhard von Burtneck's reluctance to accept Edwin, a commoner, as his son-in-law anticipates Novosil'tsev's unwillingness to marry a social inferior.

Bestuzhev expected his tales to be interpreted in an early nineteenth-century context and signaled his wish to his readers. One effective clue was Bestuzhev's use of a narrator who was not just a contemporary of the story's readers, but also their peer and an expert on the honor code. Bestuzhev's narrator in "Castle Wenden" is a Guards officer, a person very much like himself and many of his friends. This narrator not only recounts events, but also passes judgment on the characters' conduct, particularly on their actions in situations involving honor. For example, he instructs readers how to interpret Serrat's behavior: "I hate the villain in Serrat; but how can I totally refuse to empathize with the unfortunate man who was carried away by the spirit of the barbaric time and by the force of despair that possessed him?" (1:45) Similarly, in "Castle Eisen," a first-person voice that Bestuzhev's readers recognized as their contemporary's pronounces judgment on the characters' actions, thereby making the ancient story topical.

Bestuzhev's readers picked up his clues and deftly uncovered allusions to contemporary circumstances in his historical tales. The first readers of "Castle Eisen" not only interpreted it as a work about tyrannicide, but also identified a likely prototype for Reginald—Iakubovich, the famous *bretteur* and self-appointed would-be-assassin of Alexander I. Stepan Nechaev, a Decembrist and minor poet, wrote to Bestuzhev in November 1825: "[Vasily] Davydov correctly guesses that 'Blood for Blood' originated in the Caucasus. Iakubovich was your muse. Shake his heroic hand for me."[32] Interestingly, Bestuzhev's readers approved Reginald's killing of the cruel tyrant more enthusiastically than Bestuzhev himself, who, in the voice of his narrator, questioned his character's (and, by extension, Iakubovich's) selfish motives.

Readers identified the theme of the duel in its medieval guises all the more easily in that the writer also examined dueling in society tales cast in their own time. The earliest society tale dealing with a duel is the 1823 "Evening at a Bivouac," the latest, the 1832 "The Frigate Hope." Bestuzhev's society tales provide a far more complex and even contradictory view of the duel. By offering detailed descriptions of the dueling ritual, Bestuzhev teaches his readers how to fight a proper duel. At the same time, he examines the duel's negative aspects and even suggests that there could be—and should be—honorable ways out of dueling situations. I shall concentrate on three of Bestuzhev's society tales, in which the contradictory treatment of the duel is the most evident: "A Novel in Seven Letters" (1824), "The Test" (1830), and "The Terrible Divination" (1830; published in 1831).

While all of Bestuzhev's society tales are ambivalent about dueling, "A Novel in Seven Letters" judges the duel the most harshly, pointing out its uselessness in mitigating complex psychological conflicts and especially its dangerous capacity to induce a puppetlike state in duelists and make them act against their principles. The hero of the story, who is in love with the beautiful and virtuous Adèle, challenges his fortunate rival, Erast, and kills him, despite his earlier resolve not to shoot at all. He describes the strange inertia that overcame him during the duel:

> We approached each other from twenty paces. I advanced firmly—three bullets had flown past my head [in previous duels] — I advanced firmly, but without any thought, any intention: the feelings buried in my soul completely darkened my mind. At six paces, I do not know why and do not know how, I pulled the fateful trigger—and the shot echoed in my heart![33]

The rest of the tale dwells on the hero's painful memory of his terrible deed, which is likely to haunt him forever and which makes him desire death. The tale also underscores the irony that killing a rival exacerbates the hopelessness of a successful duelist's position, turning him into his beloved's enemy.

The remorseful hero of "A Novel in Seven Letters" cites a "false sense of honor" as the power that drove him to the duel and murder.[34] Bestuzhev's condemnation of the duel echoes Rousseau's argument, in *La nouvelle Héloïse,* that duels spring from a false sense of honor and that truly honorable behavior requires the avoidance of dueling altogether. Julie develops these ideas in her letters to Saint-Preux and Milord Edouard mitigating their conflict over her honor. She supports her criticism of the duel with a vivid description of her father's tormenting memories of the friend he had killed in a duel.[35]

In Rousseau's novel, Julie's intercession works: convinced by her arguments, the rivals reconcile. Common in the European literary tradition, this device was never popular with Russians who, in real life as well as in literature, remained hostile to the idea of backing out of a duel. Rousseau's solution posed special problems for them due to the Russian duel's status as a safeguard against abuses of individual rights. To make the duel protect an individual and his private space, Russian duelists had to be belligerent in their insistence on strict adherence to the honor code.[36] Hence spitting in the face, "lashing [one's] stupid mug with a whip," threatening to kill (and actually killing) were used as "arguments" to force an opponent to accept a challenge. At the same time, Russians agreed that in principle Rousseau was right and that the duel was sustained by social convention and a falsely understood sense of honor.[37] Hence the ambivalence in their treatment of the duel in fiction and, at the very time when dueling was at its peak, their search for honorable ways for their fictitious characters to avoid dueling.

Bestuzhev, in "A Novel in Seven Letters," implies that it suffices to recognize the duel's evil nature in order to stop it. Pushkin, in *Eugene Onegin,* both develops Bestuzhev's thesis regarding the duel's evil power over a duelist and, at the same time, disagrees with his simplistic solution. Similarities in plot and style between the dueling scenes in "A Novel" and *Eugene Onegin* mark this polemic.[38] Notably, Onegin is even more aware of the duel's evil nature than is Bestuzhev's character. He knows that he should not accept Lensky's challenge; he is aware that he is driven by a false sense of honor. Onegin's failure to act on his convictions demonstrates the difficulty, even the impossibility, of extracting oneself from a dueling situation. In Pushkin's view, once initiated, a duel is likely to run its course.[39]

In his turn, Bestuzhev took issue with Pushkin's acceptance of the honor code's tyranny. After having read the novel's sixth chapter, he wrote to his brothers that the duel in *Eugene Onegin* "is described quite perfectly, but one can see everywhere the old school and bad logic."[40] Accordingly, in "The Test," Bestuzhev explores the means of regaining one's free will and escaping a duel without compromising one's honor. He suggests a new way to halt the duel's inertial force: the interference of a person who by virtue of her special status is free from social conventions. In this tale, Prince Gremin, commander of a hussar squadron, asks his friend, Major Strelinsky—who is traveling to St. Petersburg to spend a leave of absence with his younger sister, Olga—to test the feelings of the rich and beautiful young widow, Countess Alina Zvezdich, with whom Gremin had had a brief platonic love affair while her husband was still alive. Since Strelinsky himself had also been attracted to Alina, he is reluctant to accept the commission, but Gremin assures him that he will not mind if Strelinsky and Alina fall in love: he just needs to know whether she still is interested in him.

Strelinsky and Alina indeed fall in love, while Gremin realizes that he has feelings for Alina and hurries to St. Petersburg. Once there, he learns about Strelinsky's and Alina's imminent marriage and decides to challenge Strelinsky. Gremin goes to Strelinsky's house, discovers that he is out, and instead spends some time with Strelinsky's sister, Olga, who has been in love with Gremin since childhood. Gremin is moved by her love, but nonetheless challenges Strelinsky, who accepts. Olga suspects a duel in the making and secretly listens in on the seconds' negotiations. She then arrives at the dueling site in time to stop the duel. Thanks to Olga, the two opponents reconcile, Gremin proposes to her, Strelinsky gets Alina, and a double wedding is planned. The happy ending signifies that the spell of the duel can be broken.

Curiously, "The Test" offers its readers two contradictory sets of advice: on the one hand, its lengthy passages on the dueling ritual instruct them how to fight a duel; on the other, it teaches how not to fight one. The instructions on the particulars of the dueling ritual are extensive and detailed: they contain precise descriptions of how bullets are made, dueling sites are prepared, and seconds conduct their negotiations. The seconds and other characters involved in the prearrangements discuss pistols, bullets, gunpowder, and types of wounds. These discussions frequently become technical, offering advice on a duelist's diet on the morning of a duel, indicating the preferred type of carriage, and reminding readers that preparations have to remain secret, lest the police find out and prevent the duel. These discussions neither move the plot, nor add to the personages' characterizations. They serve primarily as an instruction manual and thus promote dueling.

And yet "The Test" also contains the opposite message. The story suggests that it is proper to stop an arranged duel and offers advice on how to do so. The author indicates from the outset that the Gremin-Strelinsky duel does not have a serious cause, and thus should not be undertaken. Even the seconds consider the duel frivolous: "How stubborn they are! If they at least would fight over some serious matter, not over a woman's caprice and their own whims" (1:222). They nonetheless proceed with the duel. Gremin too knows that he is wrong in challenging his friend because of a woman he does not even love. Furthermore, Gremin now realizes that he likes Olga and that he will lose her, regardless of the duel's outcome. Even so, fear of public opinion pushes him forward:

> But the voice of prejudice sounded like a trumpet and drowned all gentle, all kind sentiments. "Now it is too late to hesitate," [Gremin] said [to himself] with a sigh that tore his heart apart. "What is done cannot be undone and it is shameful to change my decision. I do not want to be the talk of the town and my regiment, if I agree to make peace in front of the pistol's barrel. People more easily believe in cowardice than in noble inspirations. I would still shoot at Strelinsky even if more gratifying hopes and more precious existence were placed in my barrel." (1:226)

Strelinsky, being the challenged party, is not in a position to offer peace. Besides, he wants to die, since he mistakenly believes that Alina has abandoned him. Thus, under the honor code's spell, everyone proceeds with the duel.

Olga, however, breaks this spell. Disregarding all rules of proper behavior, she goes to the tavern where both parties are assembled and pleads with Gremin to make peace with her brother, threatening her own death: "Beware, Prince Gremin! If the word of truth and nature is not accessible to souls who have been brought up in bloody prejudices, you can reach my brother only though this heart. I have not spared my reputation, and I will not spare my life" (1:229). Gremin's prejudices and Olga's reputation are mentioned here with a purpose: Olga succeeds precisely because she is bound neither by the conventions of the honor code ("bloody prejudices"), nor by the conventions of social decorum. She escapes the requirements of the dueling ritual by virtue of being a woman; and she can dispense with proper behavior because she is an *institutka,* that is, a graduate of the Smolny Monastery.

Founded by Catherine the Great as the first educational institution for girls in Russia and charged with the task of creating a new kind of noblewoman—well versed in foreign languages and fine arts, yet natural and pure—Smolny Monastery produced an educated female that in the Russian tradition received the names *smolianka* and *monastyrka* (from Smolny Monastery) or *institutka* (from the school's other name, Smolny Institute). A student of Russian cultural history offers a brief description of an *institutka* as a peculiar and paradoxical creature: "Some education and worldly naïveté; strictly ceremonious manners and childish spontaneity in expressing their feelings; thirst for a merry and free life and timidity, fear of life; dreaminess and acceptance of one's fate—such were the main features of this sociopsychological type."[41] *Institutki* markedly differed from other women of their time, and contemporaries' opinions about them varied: some admired them as ideal, pure, and natural creatures, whereas others ridiculed their ignorance of real life and their belated infantilism.[42]

"The Test" portrays Olga as an *institutka* in a decidedly positive light:

> Brought up in Smolny Monastery, she, as her other girlfriends, has paid with ignorance of society life's trifles for the beneficial ignorance of vice's early impressions and of passions' untimely riot. In society, she was charming as a paragon of lofty simplicity and childish frankness. It was delightful to settle one's eyes on her bright face, on which neither the play of passions, nor the hypocrisy of manners had left their prints yet, had cast their shadows. It was delightful to warm one's heart with her gaiety, since gaiety is the bloom of innocence. In the muddy sea of societal prejudices, gilded depravity, and vain triviality, she towered like a green island, where the tired swimmer could find repose. (1:200–201)

Olga's naïveté, while sometimes amusing, makes her capable of distinguishing between true values and prejudices fostered by social conventions and permits her to act in a truly noble manner. Because of her special status, she violates decorum with impunity. Moreover, she can help others do the same. When she defies the rules and goes to the dueling site, the dueling convention collapses. Her actions free others to act in accordance with their true beliefs and feelings. Gremin forgets that it is shameful to reconcile under the pistol's barrel and asks Strelinsky's forgiveness. Strelinsky gladly accepts his apology and offers his own. Their seconds also shake free from the ritual's inertia and voice their support, praising the opponents' decision to reconcile. Strelinsky momentarily falters, fearing that Olga's intervention will stain his reputation as a duelist. However, Olga's natural behavior again forces him to change his attitude:

> Valerian entered the other room, hand in hand with the prince, merrily and light-heartedly, but his face darkened [*chelo ego podernulos' kak zarevom*] when he saw his sister there. "What does this mean?!" he exclaimed wrathfully. But when his sister, with the joyful greeting "You will not remain enemies, you will not fight!" fell senseless on his bosom, his voice softened. (1:230)

Although Strelinsky is still concerned about his sister's reputation, Gremin's marriage proposal dissolves this concern.

Olga is able to interfere successfully with the dueling ritual thanks to her special status as an *institutka*—a person who is different, innocent, and thus free to act on her convictions. No one else is allowed to do so: what for Olga is right and good, for Gremin, Strelinsky, and their comrades would be wrong and dishonorable. Unless someone like Olga helps them, duelists have to follow the honor code. Hence the detailed dueling instructions offered in the story. The story's double message thus reflects a double standard in respect to dueling: while it is far from perfect and often wrong, the honor code is obligatory for the majority of people. Only special people are exempt from its tyranny because they have an intuitive sense of true justice.[43]

Olga is a woman, which makes it easier for her to defy the honor code. Bestuzhev's tale "The Terrible Divination" explores the possibility that a man can also come to understand true values, thereby gaining his freedom from the honor code. This can happen, however, only by way of an extraordinary experience, such as contact with the supernatural. An anonymous hero, a young officer, is in love with a married woman, Polina, who returns his love. In order to preserve Polina's virtue and reputation, the lovers decide to part without consummating their affair. The hero struggles to stay away from his beloved, but on New Year's eve he goes to see her. On his way, he gets lost in a snowstorm and finds himself in a peasant's hut, where the local youth have gathered to divine and tell Yuletide stories. There the hero meets a mysterious stranger, in whom the reader, but not the hero, easily recognizes the devil. On a dare, the hero goes to the graveyard to practice divination. After the divination's apparent failure, the stranger shows up and drives the hero to the ball. Once there, the hero, at the stranger's urging, elopes with Polina. Her husband catches up with them and confronts the hero who is ready to give him satisfaction. The husband attempts to slap him in the face instead, and the hero reacts with fury. In retrospect, he describes his response as a reflex reaction, caused by a deeply ingrained sense of personal dignity: "Who among us was not from infancy nourished by notions of a gentleman's inviolability, of a well-born person's honor, of human dignity?" (1:338). Like Reginald in "Castle Eisen," the hero kills his defenseless opponent, and the stranger helps him push the body into the ice-covered river. Polina is horrified and, although the lovers continue their flight, the hero realizes that he has ruined their chance for happiness. He also recognizes the duel as an immoral and cruel act of "bloody vengeance" (1:342). The narrator has learned the lesson offered to him on this terrible evening through a supernatural experience—which turns out to be a Yuletide dream.[44] He makes good use of this lesson and, upon waking up, decides never to see Polina again.

Significantly, Bestuzhev's ambivalent treatment of the duel, evident in "The Test," can be detected in "The Terrible Divination" as well. The hero speaks against dueling, yet retains a reflex reaction to any threat to his physical inviolability: "A lot of time has passed since then in my head; [time] has cooled it, my ardent heart beats slower, but until now, given all my philosophical principles and all my experience, I cannot vouch for myself, and even the touch of a finger would blow up both me and my offender" (1:338). Despite its flaws, the honor code helps define and defend a person's private space, and Bestuzhev's character is not ready to forfeit it altogether.

The ultimate lesson about dueling offered in Bestuzhev's tales is that while *point d'honneur* has limitations, it is still indispensable. Bestuzhev's duelists recognize the duel's weak sides: the vanity and egotism that frequently underlay duelists' behavior (especially evident in his society tales), the duel's cruelty as an act of violence against human life, and its uselessness in avenging certain kinds of offenses (such as marital infidelity, which the duel cannot undo even if the transgressor is killed). Nonetheless, Bestuzhev's characters feel obliged to answer any perceived threat to their honor with a challenge. This readiness to fight serves a useful purpose: it guards against violations of a person's private space and defends his individual rights, physical inviolability in particular.

While Bestuzhev's treatment of the duel in his fiction was never fully positive, the very attention that he paid to it promoted it as a popular literary topic. His dueling tales profoundly influenced the contemporary and subsequent Russian literary tradition. Bestuzhev formulated many questions concerning the duel, which continued to be discussed and reexamined throughout the nineteenth century. His literary descendants made use of his discoveries not only when his fiction was still popular, but also long after his name had disappeared from the rosters of read and admired Russian writers.

David M. Bethea

Slavic Gift-Giving, The Poet in History, and Pushkin's *The Captain's Daughter*

> . . . several things dovetailed in my mind, & at once it struck me, what quality went to form a Man of Achievment especially in Literature & which Shakespeare posessed so enormously —I mean *Negative Capability*, that is when man is capable of being in uncertainties, Mysteries, doubts, without any irritable reaching after fact & reason—Coleridge, for instance, would let go by a fine isolated verisimilitude caught from the Penetralium of mystery, from being incapable of remaining content with half knowledge. This pursued through Volumes would perhaps take us no further than this, that with a great poet the sense of Beauty overcomes every other consideration, or rather obliterates all considerations.
>
> —letter of John Keats to George and Tom Keats, 21, 27 [?] December 1817

PRELIMINARY REMARKS

Like the bread and salt that are their folk embodiments, the values of generosity and hospitality are very old in the Russian mentality. And no writer is considered more "Russian" in this sense of spiritual generosity and inexhaustible "giftedness" than Alexander Pushkin. But what exactly does this mean, once one leaves the porous level of cultural myth? "There should not be any free gifts," writes the social anthropologist Mary Douglas, since each gift and each personality donating and receiving each gift belongs to a larger system of ongoing and mutually implicating relations. "Gift cycles engage persons in permanent commitments that articulate the dominant institutions."[1] How can one precisely and usefully apply the notions of donor, recipient, and gift to Pushkin's works and to the life he fashioned for himself in the interplay of his epoch's social and aesthetic codes?

Normally when one invokes the economy of gift-giving in the context of Pushkin there is, following Nabokov, a slight shift *upward* in stylistic register: from the concrete *podarok*, which seems too pedestrian for the riches of

Pushkin's language and thought, to the lofty *dar*, with its implication of high calling (the Ur-text being "Prorok") and high (read "Western") literary values.[2] This almost unconscious adjustment may be unfortunate; as I shall demonstrate, Pushkin was himself exquisitely sensitive to the necessary concrete "containers" and quotidian psychological subtleties that gifts and gift-giving require. In this essay I shall be examining, inter alia, Petr Grinev's famous present of a very Russian, very concrete hareskin coat (*zaiachii tulup*) to a chance peasant (Pugachev) as Pushkin's last and greatest expression of the gift-giving economy, in *The Captain's Daughter*.

It will be my argument that the Pushkin of the 1830s moved back in time, especially to the eighteenth century, to work his way free of the salon mentality of the 1810s and 1820s and to get closer to a sense of history that was more authentic, less "Karamzinian"—Karamzin being the author of the great "salon"[3] history that stood squarely in Pushkin's path.[4] Pushkin wanted to find a "poetry" in history that more closely reflected his view of reality, that was less moralizing, less harmonizing, less "sentimental." And as Pushkin moved back into the eighteenth century, he became increasingly interested in the historical situation where an individual's spiritual "charge" or *darovanie* (a component of character) encounters a concrete situation requiring a gesture of outward generosity or *podarok* (a component of action or plot). Pushkin wanted to isolate the energy-releasing (or "inspiring") *move-outside-oneself* that redefines everything that has come before, from aspects of genre (one's art) to aspects of psychology (one's life). This latter has been described by Iurii Lotman in one of his last and most adventuresome works as the moment of unanticipated *vzryv* (breakthrough), when the rules of a predefined "plot" (in life or in history) or the *predskazuemost'* (predictability) of established behavioral patterns are suspended and the future opens up as something full of multifarious potential: "The moment of breakthrough is simultaneously a place of sharp increase in the informativeness of the whole system. Here the developmental curve jumps onto a completely new, unpredictable, and more complex path. . . . The moment of exhaustion in the breakthrough is the turning-point of the process. In the sphere of history it is not only the point of departure for future development but the place of self-knowledge as well."[5] Pushkin's unparalleled ability to link this moment of *vzryv* both with the *sluchainost'* (chance) of history and the notion of gift goes to the heart of his later works and his growing sense of himself as the *poet in history*.

In the following study I shall bring these various ruminations into focus by dwelling on three related concepts in the later Pushkin: (1) the gift-giving economy, particularly in its Slavic variety; (2) inspiration, or what I call "the poet in history" sensibility; and (3) the structure of reciprocal relationships in *The Captain's Daughter*. My hypothesis is that these three seemingly loose ideational threads form in fact a surprisingly dense, evocative weave in the

Pushkin of the 1830s—a weave that constitutes, one might say, a kind of pattern in the poet's magic carpet and thus a unique vantage from which to investigate his last works. This relation between gift-giving and poetic inspiration has significant theoretical implications for how Pushkin narrated the subject of history and the subject in history.

PUSHKIN AND SLAVIC GIFT-GIVING

In an important article entitled " 'Agreement'[6] and 'Self-Giving' as Archetypal Models of Culture" (" 'Dogovor' i 'Vruchenie sebia' kak arkhetipicheskie modeli kul'tury"), Iurii Lotman advanced the thesis, primarily from within a Russian Orthodox worldview, that "a religious act has as its basis an unconditional act of self-giving" (*bezogovorochnoe vruchenie sebia vo vlast'*) (125).[7] Lotman cites numerous examples to make his case that for Slavs religiously inspired behavior is essentially *one-sided* and *noncompulsory;* that is, it must bear no signs of an implied quid pro quo. In this regard, the Slavic model differs radically from the Western, largely Roman model for such behavior:

> In the West the sense of agreement, though having its remote origin in magic, had the authority of the Roman secular tradition and held a position equal to the authority of religion: in Russia, on the other hand, it was felt to be pagan in character. . . . It is significant that in the Western tradition an agreement as such was ethically neutral. It could be drawn up with the Devil . . . but one might also make agreements with the forces of holiness and goodness. . . . [In the Russian context, however,] an agreement may only be made with a Satanic power or its pagan counterpart. (Lotman, *The Semiotics of Russian Culture,* 126–27)

What Lotman is suggesting is that the sense of measurement, portioning-out, and calculated atonement that is part and parcel of the sin-and-redemption economy of the Roman Church (that is, one's activities on earth, such as prayers, donations, and so forth, can affect one's relative placement on the terraces of Purgatory or in the rings of Hell in the other world) is essentially antipathetic to the Slavic religious mentality. The notion of agreement (quid pro quo) or of "supererogation" cannot coexist with the notion of genuine, free giving of one's self.[8] The Slav[9] enters into a religious transaction not as a "negotiating partner" (*dogovarivaiushchaisia storona*) but precisely as the immeasurable—"a drop flowing into a sea" (*kaplia, vlivaiushchaiasia v more*). All that is required of the recipient of a gift or sacrifice in this case is that it acknowledge itself as the source of a higher power.

Lotman's arguments here compare and contrast in provocative ways with work done in the West on potlatch economies in archaic societies. The French social anthropologist Marcel Mauss has made the point, for example, that "the potlatch is an example of a total system of giving . . . each gift is part of a system of reciprocity in which the honour of giver and recipient are engaged. It is a total system in that every item of status or of spiritual or material possession is implicated for everyone in the whole community" (Mary Douglas, in Mauss, *The Gift*, viii). The system can incorporate rivalry (the Haida and Tlingit of the American Northwest), so that a gift must be returned "with interest," or it can be stable (Polynesia), so that exchanges are fixed within a hierarchy. But what is interesting is that Mauss's concept of sacrifice—"a gift that compels the deity to make a return: *Do ut des*" (*The Gift*, ix)—does not accord with Lotman's concept of one-sided, noncompulsory giving among Slavs. Above all, for Mauss and his Durkheimian tradition the potlatch seems to be about the notion of power, even when deities are involved, for humans and among humans. Even "voluntary" acts of destruction of wealth or lives are not necessarily self-abnegating but in fact can be self-asserting. "In certain kinds of potlatch one must expend all that one has, keeping nothing back . . . it is not even a question of giving and returning gifts, but of destroying, so as not to give the slightest hint of desiring your gift to be reciprocated. . . . Such trade is noble, replete with etiquette and generosity" (*The Gift*, 37).

Hence regardless of whether the end result is acquisition or destruction of riches, the dispensing of precious items becomes a way of gaining and keeping prestige and control: presents are intended to challenge and obligate rivals in a continuously operating three-part system (to give, to receive, to reciprocate). The one who is afraid to or cannot reciprocate in kind becomes emotionally enslaved ("flattened") by his debtor status (cf. the Roman *nexum*) (*The Gift*, 39, 42). However, in the conclusion to his study, even as he emphasizes the total and totalizing system of social relationships that is the potlatch—"All these phenomena are at the same time juridical, economic, religious . . ."—Mauss admits to one potentially important lacuna: "these institutions [that is, potlatch, clans, tribes, and so forth] have an important aesthetic aspect that we have deliberately omitted from this study" (*The Gift*, 79). It is the expenditure or destruction of an item of value that, qua gesture, is beautiful for its own sake and that cannot be completely subsumed under the desire for prestige and power within one's own group that leaves what Bakhtin would call a loophole (*lazeika*) in Mauss's otherwise elegant analysis.

It is this *lazeika* that was then seized upon and amplified by the French writer Georges Bataille in his 1933 essay "The Notion of Expenditure."[10] Here Bataille makes the distinction between a "restricted economy" and an "economy of loss" as the latter two relate to the expenditure of energy by human organisms. Weaving together a provocative tapestry of discourses (the Dostoevsky of the Underground Man, Nietzschean will to power, Freudian "excremental fantasy," Marxist disgust at bourgeois values, French anti-utilitarianism and anti-individualism) that both tellingly anticipates poststructuralism and is itself culturally conditioned, Bataille sets out to create a space in the potlatch and indeed in all gift-giving situations for *the self-destructive gesture that is beautiful.* Applying Mauss, Bataille explains most potlatch situations through their application of the principle of the restricted economy: any surplus of energy left over from a transaction is controlled or reinvested, but in any event it is eventually accounted for. In some situations marked by "unproductive expenditure," however, such as those involving "luxury, mourning, war, cults, the construction of sumptuary monuments, games, spectacles, arts, perverse sexual activity (i.e., deflected from genital finality)" (*Visions of Excess,* 118), simple notions of production and acquisition cannot explain the seemingly extravagant expenditure of energy. These activities "have no end beyond themselves," meaning that an economy of loss has set in: here the requirement to receive a gift and then reciprocate is deliberately, and one assumes somehow *aesthetically,* preempted. What rises to the fore is the idea that the greatest gift is the one proffered without thought of remuneration or return on investment (in fact quite the opposite), so that, in a characteristically Bataillean move, power in its purest form becomes the "power to lose" and "glory and honor are linked to wealth" *through loss* (*Visions of Excess,* 122).[11]

Bataille's thoughts about poetry and the poet as vehicles for unconditional expenditure will be useful to us in the context of Pushkin and his tradition, since many of the Frenchman's concerns about the lack of beauty in an increasingly dreary and utilitarian age were shared by the Pushkin who used the term *meshchanin* ironically to define himself (that is to say, this is what he, with his aristocratic roots, was not) in his polemics with Bulgarin in the 1830s, and who, following Tocqueville, expressed dismay at democratic "leveling" in the John Tanner essay (1836). As Bataille writes,

> The term poetry, applied to the least degraded and least intellectualized forms of the expression of the state of loss, can be considered synonymous with expenditure; it in fact signifies, in the most precise way, creation by means of loss. Its meaning is therefore close to that of *sacrifice.* . . . [F]or the rare human beings who have this at their disposal, poetic expenditure ceases to be symbolic in its consequences; thus, to a certain extent, the function of representation engages the very life of the one who assumes it. (*Visions of Excess,* 120)

Lotman's interpretation of Slavic gift-giving and Mauss's and especially Bataille's analyses of the potlatch psychology have some fascinating implications for the later Pushkin. The difference between Bataille and Lotman on the act of giving that is potentially destructive of the self is subtle and shows to what extent these matters are culturally determined and perhaps deeply embedded in ancient East-West binaries: the Dionysian gesture of unconditional expenditure in Bataille still focuses on *the self* (its honor, glory, nobility) even as that self is consumed, whereas in Lotman the emphasis—consider the traditional example of the beauty of the Russian Orthodox service—is on *the higher power* of the sea the drop of "I" is poured into. It is my working hypothesis, to be tested below, that Pushkin, while more than any other Russian author before and probably since was aware of the subtle differences in a culture's gift-giving economy, finally comes closer to the Lotmanian than to the Bataillean model.

As Pushkin approached the historical theme, he seemed to become aroused, aesthetically and even as it were *erotically,* by the increased proximity to genuine risk, potential chaos, violent death, the lack of prefabricated literary plot. He was interested above all in the palpable seam separating legend and brute historical fact. He wanted to feel what was not his, what was not under his control. Yet Pushkin came to history and historiography not as a prose writer but, first and foremost, as a poet.[12] His *dominant,* his episteme, his way of organizing the world, was not the notion of "plot" or tellable *mythos* but the poetic or logosemantic *simultaneity* of sound's play with sense: the rhyme pair, paranomasia, the internal pun. This is why the "metahistorical" theories of Hayden White or Arthur Danto, based as they are on notions of *emplotment,*[13] will not suffice to explain the internal mechanisms of Pushkin's historical thinking.[14] Like two poles in an electromagnetic field, the ontological rhyme pair *volia/dolia* (liberty, freedom/lot, fate) is at the center of the poet's consciousness.[15] Plot does not come first; what comes first is one's *dolia,* which fixes one within certain untransgressible conventions (honor, for example, or social class), and what comes second is the *volia* one exercises given those constraints. To express the verbal equivalent of unencumbered movement within a fixed rhyme scheme or to try one's fate while keeping one's honor intact are not identical (life does not "equal" art), but they are isomorphic statements: both go right to the heart of Pushkin's understanding of true creative risk. Moreover, the sense of arousal that plays at the edges of literary structure and takes pleasure in its transgressive potential has a name—"inspiration," about which I shall have more to say below. But what is striking about this gradual evolution from various poetic genres through a novel-in-verse to artistic prose and ultimately to historiography is that Pushkin repeatedly imagined the seam between legend and fact as a liminal gift-giving situation. Inspiration, the creative process itself, gift-giving, the threat of death, punishment, and historical judgment are all telescoped, all point to that energy which gives of itself while asking nothing in return.

Let us examine now a few examples before returning to *The Captain's Daughter.* Pushkin's poetic cycle "Pesni o Sten'ke Razine" (Songs About Sten'ka Razin, 1826) celebrates the legendary leader of the Don Cossacks who fomented a major peasant rebellion in the towns along the Volga in 1670–71 (during the reign of Aleksei Mikhailovich).[16] The personality and activities of Sten'ka fascinated Pushkin in a way that suggests unmistakably a dress rehearsal for the later Pugachev studies. Indeed, in fall 1824 while in exile in Mikhailovskoe, Pushkin wrote his brother asking for a biography of Pugachev (*Zhizn' Emel'ki Pugacheva*) and then, virtually simultaneously, asked for information about Sten'ka, the "edinstvennoe poeticheskoe litso russkoi istorii" (the one and only poetical character in Russian history) (*PSS*, 10:84, 86). Clearly, the fates of Sten'ka and Pugachev were linked in Pushkin's mind, as were the notions of poetry and history.

The three-poem cycle revolves around different gift-giving situations, all important for what they do and do not say about the treatment of Pugachev in *The Captain's Daughter* and *History of Pugachev*. In the first poem, realizing that he is in debt to his "mother" the Volga and that in his love for the captive Persian princess he has betrayed his greater love for the motherland, Sten'ka voluntarily drowns the beautiful *foreign* tsarevna and bows obediently to the *native* river.[17] In other words, Sten'ka gives the ultimate gift—something falling into the marked "exorbitant" categories of both beautiful and beloved—in a Slavic/Russian expression of quintessential *udal'stvo* (daring, boldness), or what Bataille would call an "economy of loss."[18] What is more, because Pushkin, according to Sergei Fomichev ("Pesni," 17) composed the first and third poems of the cycle in spring 1825, under the influence of folk songs sung to him by his nanny Arina Rodionovna, his Russian popular hero is making this spiritually generous gesture at a time of maximal introspection for his author: recall that just months earlier, on the cusp of the move from Odessa to internal exile at Mikhailovskoe (late summer/early fall 1824), Pushkin had turned away from the two greatest representatives of Western high literary values and historical drama—Byron and Napoleon—in another poem entitled, significantly, "K moriu" (To the sea).

The second poem is a mirror image of the first and, because of its probable *later* dating (between 12 September 1826 and 20 July 1827; see Fomichev, "Pesni," 19), a post hoc turning point inserted into the cycle to give it shape and meaning.[19] Here Sten'ka, who has gone to Astrakhan to barter goods at the market (a potential conflict of the gift and market economies),[20] is confronted by a *voevoda*. Not only does the *voevoda* break the rules of gift-giving by first demanding presents ("Stal voevoda / Trebovat' podarkov"), he then refuses the valuable damasks and brocades Sten'ka does offer ("Podnes Sten'ka Razin / Kamki khrushchatye, / Kamki khrushchatye— / Parchi zolotye") (*PSS*, 2:300–301). What the *voevoda* wants is for Sten'ka to *give* him (*otdat'*) the fur coat (*shuba*) off his back; if he does not the more powerful nobleman will hang the peasant from the nearest tree. This is an instance of a *forced gift*,[21] which in the Slavic mentality is no gift at all; moreover, since the *voevoda* is demanding it from the peasant, it is a shorthand for official oppression and a veiled explanation for the revolt.[22] Indeed, as Dmitrii Blagoi has argued from evidence outside the poem that Pushkin presumably could have known, the *voevoda* in question eventually paid for the extorted gift with his life,[23] an implication apparently not lost on the censors and thus an important reason why the cycle was not published until 1881 (Blagoi, *Tvorcheskii put'*, 525; see also Fomichev, "Pesni," 4). When Sten'ka finally says to the *voevoda:* "Voz'mi sebe shubu, / Da ne bylo b shumu" (*PSS*, 2:301), he has shifted the center of gravity of the exchange situation from his *giving* (*otdat'*) to the stronger man's *taking* (*vziat'*), a move that, significantly, leaves no room for spiritual beauty.

In the third poem a personified Russian nature calls out to Sten'ka and, in an expression of folkloric wishful thinking and pure desire, returns all that has been lost and more to the peasant prince: in the first boat there is gold, in the second, silver, and in the third (the folklorically most "magnetized"), a beautiful maiden (*dusha-devitsa*), a replacement for the original sacrifice. Note that Sten'ka made his gift with no thought of recompense and note that nature's gifts, coming after history's trials, are *more* than was originally sacrificed. This amounts to a kind of potlatch, but what is important is that there is no rivalry (the urge for power) and that Sten'ka has not attempted to arrange this outcome with a force greater than himself. Note further what is most important: that the forced gift of the fur coat to the nobleman in the second poem will be reworked *through inversion* by Pushkin in the famous gift-giving scene of *The Captain's Daughter,* where the nobleman (Grinev) will give, freely and generously, the hareskin coat to the peasant (Pugachev)—the first in a series of spontaneous overpayments that will constitute the salient links in the plot of the historical novel and that will bring the worlds of the nobleman and peasant together. And finally, note how the concept of gift-giving is linked with the theme of history (Sten'ka's uprising), violence (the death of the princess), and hints of possible betrayal (Sten'ka's initial guilt toward the Volga).

Pushkin never returned to the story of Sten'ka Razin. Instead, his interest turned to the Pugachev rebellion. One reason, we might hypothesize, is that Sten'ka's exploits were too thickly covered with the patina of legend, too removed to the distant and irretrievable past, not sufficiently complicated by the real carnage and chaos of the revolt, so that Pushkin could no longer feel that seam between myth and actual historical personage.[24] Pugachev, on the other hand, could still be recollected by eyewitnesses interviewed by the historian in fall 1833. Pushkin could put his hand right on the very seam, and this gesture both aroused and inspired him.

THE CAPTAIN'S DAUGHTER, HISTORY OF PUGACHEV, AND THE POET IN HISTORY

Now, in the last part of my essay I shall apply the notions of Slavic gift-giving and inspiration/arousal to the elements of fictional plot in *The Captain's*

Daughter and to the factual account of events in *History of Pugachev.* I shall begin with a scene of terrible cruelty in the history, a scene that shows without the slightest doubt that Pushkin understood implicitly how blind *sluchainost'* (chance) and violence take over in real life when an oppressive government pushes the peasant masses beyond the breaking point. Recall that Pushkin had begun the history with a retelling of the sources of the conflict: the Iaik Cossacks of the Loginov faction had been complaining about the oppressive measures taken by the chancery officials whom the government had imposed on the Host (withholding of allotted wages, arbitrary taxes, infringement on fishing rights) (*PSS,* 8:113–14).[25] And when the Cossacks attempted to send their own men on a secret mission to the Empress to explain their position, they were found out, arrested, and further humiliated and antagonized (head-shavings). In any event, Pushkin understood that this violence had a cause and, moreover, when it erupted, it would have no fictional plot involving miraculous salvation—indeed, quite the opposite. This is how Pushkin describes the murder of Colonel Elagin and his family in the *History* (Elagin is the commander of the fortress at Tatishchev that Pugachev's forces overran on 27 September 1773):

> The wounded Elagin [. . .] put up a desperate fight. At last the rebels charged into the fort's smoking ruins. The commanders were captured. Bulow was beheaded. Elagin, a corpulent man, was skinned [*S Elagina, cheloveka tuchnogo, sodrali kozhu*]; the scoundrels cut his fat out and rubbed it on their wounds. His wife was hacked to pieces. Their daughter, Kharlov's wife, widowed the day before, was led before the victor who presided over the execution of her parents. Pugachev was struck by her beauty and decided to make the poor woman his concubine [*i vzial neschastnuiu k sebe v nalozhnitsy*], sparing her seven-year old brother for her sake. . . . [Then, somewhat later,] the young Kharlova had the misfortune of winning the pretender's affections. He kept her at his camp below Orenburg. She was the only person allowed to enter his covered wagon at any time, and at her request he gave orders to bury the bodies of all those hanged at Ozernaia at the time the fort was taken. She became suspect in the eyes of the jealous villains and Pugachev, yielding to their demand, gave his concubine up to them. Kharlova and her seven-year-old brother were shot. Wounded, they crawled up to each other and embraced. Their bodies, thrown into the bushes, remained there in each other's arms for a long time. (*PSS,* 8:123, 132; *Complete Prose,* 376, 385)

What we see here in the history is, first of all, not the absence of an organizing intelligence[26]—after all, Pushkin is giving a narrative account of first why and then how the violence took place—but the absence of any positive source of energy (all urges and angers are immediately acted upon, nothing is stored up or left over) and of any sense of *siuzhet* as "happy ending" or deus ex machina. If one wishes, here is a straight and brutal quid pro quo: these victims, who are not recognized by Pugachev's men for their individuality or beauty or honor or rectitude, are the payment due for prior oppression. Note that here too are all the elements for Pushkin's fictional plot in *The Captain's Daughter:* the commander of the fortress, who fights bravely and who refuses to declare an oath to the impostor, is savagely murdered along with his wife, while his daughter becomes Pugachev's concubine. But Pushkin leaves room for excess energy and a positive gift-giving economy in the novel: Mironov is quickly hanged (not skinned alive), his wife is struck down with one blow, and his daughter, importantly, is only threatened with the possibility of concubinage. There is violence to be sure, but the child is spared, and the body lying grotesquely unattended is that of Vasilisa Egorovna and not that of Kharlova (a potential Masha) or that of her little brother. If Sten'ka had been too legendary for Pushkin, not real enough, then the Pugachev of the *History* is exactly the opposite: he is, in Bibikov's words, a "puppet" (*chuchelo* [*PSS*, 8:151]) in the hands of his lieutenants, he quickly yields to their demands, he arrives drunk in battle, and so on. In the *History* there is no seam separating man from myth because there is no room for myth.

Now, if we look at an analogous crisis moment in the novel, one fraught with the specter of execution, a different principle exists. After Grinev has been spared the first time and is preparing to return to Orenburg, the meddling Savel'ich appears and demands recompense from Pugachev for the losses to his master's household incurred at the hands of the rebel forces.[27] According to the logic of the Slavic gift-giving mentality, Savel'ich's inventory is not only dangerously stupid, it is ungrateful, for it does not allow the other side the possibility of a *non-compulsory, unidirectional* gesture of generosity. Coming to the end of the inventory, Savel'ich exclaims, "And finally a hareskin coat given to Your Grace at the wayside inn, fifteen rubles." To which the angry Pugachev responds, "Hareskin coat! I'll give you a hareskin coat! Before you know it, I'll have you flayed alive and a coat made of your skin!" ("Ia-te dam zaiachii tulup! Da znaesh' li ty, chto ia s tebia zhivogo kozhu veliu sodrat' na tulupy?") (*PSS*, 6:319; *Complete Prose*, 321). These words resonate with the first song of the Western Slavs ("Videnie korolia"), a cycle that Pushkin composed at the time he was working on the history and the novel: here the betraying brother Radivoi (a potential Shvabrin), who bows down before the sultan (that is, he does the equivalent of swearing allegiance to Pugachev), is made the ghastly gift of a caftan stitched together from the flayed skin of his Orthodox brother (a potential Grinev) (*PSS*, 3:266–68). Violence, gift-giving, and betrayal are again telescoped. With Savel'ich, however, Pushkin has taken the terrible circumstances of Colonel Elagin's death (the flaying) and worked them into the fictional text only as threat. As any reader of a novel in Pushkin's time knew, to skin the good Savel'ich alive (or to hang his master, for that matter) would be to cross an impossible line composed of genre, taste, and psychology. Instead of carrying through with his threat, the fictionalized Pugachev does the opposite: "in a fit of generosity," he gives the departing duo a horse, the fur coat (*shuba*) off his back (cf. Sten'ka), and a *poltina* (half-ruble) (*PSS*, 6:320). Again, he overpays, and the historical plot-cum-potlatch continues.

But the question remains, Is this a potlatch in the Maussian sense that Pugachev and Grinev are involved in an elaborate system that obligates and challenges the rival? Or is the overpayment a symbol of something else? I suggest, using Lotman's terminology, that the intersection (*peresechenie*) of events that first brought Pugachev and Grinev together in the snowstorm created an explosion (*vzryv*) in the fixed patterns of response typical of peasant and nobleman in their dealings with one another (*Kul'tura i vzryv*, 26–30). This explosion is full of potential energy; it forces each subject *out of itself* and into an intermediate space that is open, vulnerable, and no longer—at least no longer in the same way—"emplotted."[28] It is also, significantly, tied to the wonder or *chudo* of folk logic, which is crucial to understanding the "deep structure" of the novel and which serves, through the barge haulers' song ("Ne shumi, mati zelenaia dubrovushka"), the Kalmyk tale, and the chapter epigraphs taken from folk songs, to counterbalance the Western plots and high literary values of the salon culture (cf. *The Belkin Tales*).[29] Pushkin is not saying that there is no meaning or communication in this space—in fact, quite the opposite—but what he is saying is that this communication is maximally dangerous, "archaic," or unmediated by the veneer of civilization, very close (at least on Pugachev's end) to the subconscious urge for complete "barrierlessness," and, like the eagle of the Kalmyk *skazka* that would rather drink fresh blood and die than eat carrion and live three hundred years, both dark and intoxicating.[30]

For Pushkin, the *sluchainost'* that underwrote the potlatch between Grinev and Pugachev lies at the heart of all history but especially of *Russian* history. Only the Grinev who lived to tell of his encounter with Pugachev can call this intersection the work of Providence (*Providenie);* to the young Petrusha at the time it is rather the work of *sluchai.* Indeed, the two words are joined in Grinev's mind as that very seam and energy source where what is private and anecdotally Russian becomes History: "A strange thought entered my mind: it seemed to me that providence [*providenie*], bringing me face to face with Pugachev for the second time, was presenting [*podavalo* (N.B., the notion of "giving" or "serving up")] me with an opportunity [*sluchai*] to execute my plans" (*PSS*, 6:332; *Complete Prose*, 332). As epigraph to the *History* Pushkin took the words of Archimandrite Platon Liubarskii, which made sense of the impostor's military exploits not in terms of "rational considerations or military precepts," but in terms of "daring, happenstance [*sluchai*], and luck" (*PSS*, 8:110; *Complete Prose*, 362). And in his 1830 review of Polevoi's *History of the Russian People* Pushkin was critical of Guizot's lack of appreciation of *sluchainost'* in historical events and insisted that it was precisely this possibility of chance and this avoidance of Western emplotment that made Russian history different:

> Understand as well that Russia never had anything in common with the rest of Europe, that her history requires another way of thinking, another formula, than the thinking and formulas adduced by Guizot from the history of the Christian West. Don't say *it was impossible otherwise.* If that were true, then the historian would be an astronomer and the events in the life of mankind would be predicted, like solar eclipses, in calendars. But Providence is not algebra. The human mind, according to the popular expression, is not a prophet but a guesser; it sees the general course of things and can extrapolate from the latter profound assumptions, which are then often justified by time, but what it can't do is predict chance, the powerful instantaneous tool of Providence. (*PSS,* 7:100).

In conclusion, the better Grinev gets to know Pugachev, the more articulate and even *inspired* become his answers to the risk-laden questions put to him by this human symbol of the historical id.[31] Pushkin gives to Grinev, who is no poet in terms of his artistic talent, that very quality of inspiration which distinguishes, in the author's own words, not the "prophet" but the fate-"guesser," the poet in history: "a disposition of the soul toward the most vivid reception of impressions, and thus to the rapid apprehension of ideas, which process also promotes the clarification of these latter" ("raspolozhenie dushi k zhiveishemu priniatiiu vpechatlenii, sled[stvenno] k bystromu soobrazheniiu poniatii, chto i sposobstvuet ob"iasneniiu onykh") (*PSS,* 7:29; see also Terts, *Progulki,* 63). When asked by Pugachev during one of their several tête-à-têtes, "Don't you believe that I am your Sovereign Majesty? Give me a straight answer," Grinev hesitates before this particular riddle of survival and then answers in a way that shows he has broken through the irreconcilable binaries (*muzhik/barin*) of his historical situation. He answers both directly, in that he answers sincerely, *and* indirectly, in that he does not respond with a binary "yes" or "no." Like Ivan Kuzmich (Captain Mironov), the military man Grinev *père* would have said, "You're not our sovereign, you, fellow, are an impostor and pretender," which is, from *within that individual's system,* undoubtedly correct (*PSS,* 6:308; *Complete Prose,* 311). But the son answers by not embracing the strict judgmental code of the father and by, as it were, seeing that code from the outside, as a range of potentials. He *tells Pugachev the truth* ("Listen, let me tell you the honest truth" [*PSS,* 6:315]) by telling him that *God only knows* who he is and that his game, regardless of who he is, is a dangerous one. At the same time, Grinev again makes explicit his refusal to serve as one of Pugachev's officers, even adding that, if given his freedom, he cannot promise not to fight against his present benefactor.

In other words, Grinev is able to take in the impressions of his risky situation, quickly to understand their potential ramifications, and then to present them to his interlocutor so that, again, a breakthrough in communication takes place. The categories of public and private, peasant and nobleman, dissolve as each is forced to see the inherent rightness and necessity of the other's position.[32] Grinev is "inspired," as it were, to speak the truth in precisely this way. This is not a moment to lose oneself (the Kiukhelbekerian/Derzhavinian *vostorg* [rapture]) but to find oneself. The hero's multivalent "sincerity" stuns Pugachev ("Moia iskrennost' porazila Pugacheva" [*PSS*, 6:316]) because, like the gift that initiated their relationship, it is more than it needs to be. Grinev could fall on his knees before Pugachev in order to save his life (as Shvabrin will soon do), but then he will have lost his honor. He could also tell Pugachev the state's truth, that the latter is a *samozvanets* (impostor), but by so doing he will have kept his honor by losing his life. He finds instead a third way. And after telling the truth, he puts the decision back in Pugachev's hands: "My life is in your hands: if you let me go, I'll be grateful; if you execute me, God shall be your judge; in any case, I've told you the whole truth" (*PSS*, 6:316; *Complete Prose*, 318). Pugachev of course answers in kind, with his own brand of peasant generosity: "Be it so. . . . Hang him or spare him: don't do things by halves" ("Kaznit' tak kaznit', milovat' tak milovat' ").

At least one recent scholar has made a point of the "intergeneric dialogue" between *The Captain's Daughter* and *History of Pugachev*, the implication being that for Pushkin each genre had its inherent rules and limitations and that the "truth" (the difference between the *vozvyshaiushchii obman* and the *t'my nizkikh istin* of the famous "Geroi" poem) should be sought in some extratextual vectoring of the two.[33] Details from the history can migrate, becoming tied to the fates of individual lives, into the novel, while the novel, again for reasons of genre, might refer the reader back to the history (with its broader, more impersonal sweep), as when Grinev demurs at describing the siege of the fortress: "I will not describe the siege of Orenburg, which belongs to history rather than to a family chronicle" (*PSS*, 6:325; *Complete Prose*, 326; see Ungurianu, "Fiction and History," 6). Both genres have their unique "observation points" (Ungurianu, "Fiction and History," 5), and the dialogue that ensues takes place between and around, but not exactly *in* them. Thus Tsvetaeva's arch-Romantic hierarchy of values is not necessarily Pushkin's: "In *The Captain's Daughter* Pushkin the historiographer is beaten by Pushkin the poet" ("Pushkin i Pugachev," 300).

Yet this approach, while true enough, does not adequately account for how Pushkin energizes his verbal material from within, giving the gift of his own special brand of generosity to his own words. I claimed at the outset of my remarks that Pushkin came to every verbal structure, even those describing history, with the sensibility of the poet. I have suggested here that this sensibility operated on two levels *simultaneously:* that of sound and that of sense. The gift-giving moment that generates so much creative potential in *The Captain's Daughter,* Grinev's present of the hareskin coat, is, as Sergei Davydov first elegantly demonstrated, organized paranomastically or logosemantically: the $p + l + t$ sounds in *tulup* are repeated in the thematically magnetized popular sayings (*poslovitsy*) in the text: "beregi *plat'*e snovu" and "dolg *plat*ezhom krasen."[34] What is more, this principle of phonetic similarity makes perfect semantic sense, inasmuch as these sayings bring together the theme of dress (*plat'e*) and the theme of (over)payment (the *platezh* is *krasen* because it is more than the initial investment), both crucial to the overall meaning of the novel.

Hence the *tulup* that existed in historical reality as an item of the pretender's clothing becomes "poeticized" as it passes into the novel. It does so not only because Pushkin has chosen to insert it into preexisting plots or structures (Walter Scott's "wavering" heroes, the trapped wolf-turned-friend of folklore, the anecdote about how Pugachev freed the pastor who had earlier shown him kindness [*PSS,* 8:178]), but because he has illuminated it from within with his own special genius, or "giftedness." Grinev gives the coat because he cannot give money; his gambling losses have forced him to cede control of his purse to Savel'ich, and he must honor his word.[35] The literal seams of the *detskii tulup,* now bursting with the body of the mysterious *vozhatyi,* become, as it were, the metaphorical seams of *sluchai* and *Providenie.* The very uselessness of the gift makes its expression more aesthetically marked, more "beautiful." Pugachev and Grinev instinctively understand this; that is their bond. Generosity of spirit, the essence of gift-giving, means that one should be willing to give the shirt off one's back, especially if that move, here taken by a nobleman to repay a peasant for his help, will create an alternative economy of mutual understanding. Perhaps it was wishful thinking or poetic desire, but Pushkin understood that by bringing these implacable enemies (*barin/muzhik*) together and by creating a flexible middle space where they could step outside their historical roles, one might undo the work of the *voevoda* in the earlier Sten'ka Razin poem and actually think one's way beyond the tragic alternative of revolt: "May God preserve us from a Russian revolt" (*PSS,* 6:370). Likewise, the notion of payment becomes altered when what is at stake is not justice but mercy and forgiveness ("one good turn deserves [more than] another" rather than "an eye for an eye and a tooth for a tooth").

I shall close, therefore, with two thoughts: first, it is fitting that Catherine's debt to the daughter of Captain Mironov should be repaid by the state in a coin—the generosity of *milost'*—that pleasurably echoes the (read *novelistically*) fatidic potlatch involving Grinev and the peasant tsar. Second, it is proper that Catherine, the threat to the state eliminated and her matriarchy safely restored, should be wearing a *dushegreika* (literally, "soul-warmer"; that is, her sleeveless version of Pugachev's *tulup*) when Masha happens upon her in the park at Tsarskoe Selo. After all, this was the article of clothing that Vasilisa Egorovna was wearing when the rebels seized the fortress and she and her husband were so brutally murdered. With his remarkable sense of compositional symmetry, Pushkin now offsets the bearded Cossack who had dressed himself in a simulation of imperial regalia (red caftan with gold tassles) with the empress who impersonates a simple woman.[36] Let Catherine the matriarch, who had her own way of using men, beware, says Pushkin, for a fate such as Vasilisa Egorovna's awaits her and her family if Russia's historical id, here portrayed as male, is too long repressed or, in political terms, oppressed.[37] Likewise, it is to be expected that the opposing parent figure in the novel, the peasant tsar himself and Catherine's mortal foe (because as long as he is alive as Peter III her legitimacy is in question), is brought to justice, that is, *payment for his crimes,* with variations on the same clothing motifs. The words, ironically, are from Dmitriev's memoirs and the place is the conclusion to Pushkin's *History,* but even so it is difficult to imagine a stronger contrast to the notion of soul-warming and mercy:

> At this moment the executioner gave a signal, and the headsmen rushed on Pugachev to undress him: they pulled off his white sheepskin coat [*sorvali belyi baranii tulup*] and started tearing at the sleeves of his crimson silk caftan [*stali razdirat' rukava shelkovogo malinovogo polukaftan'ia*]. He clasped his hands and fell backwards, and a minute later a head dripping with blood was raised high. (*PSS,* 8:248; *Complete Prose,* 437)

The stripping or figurative flaying that accompanies Dmitriev's description of Pugachev's here at the end of *History of Pugachev* will become, through the poet's own spiritual giftedness, the bestowal of the shirt off one's back that initiates the plot of *The Captain's Daughter.* How well Pushkin understood the laws of Clio and the laws of Calliope!

Encroaching Modernity: The Public and the Subject

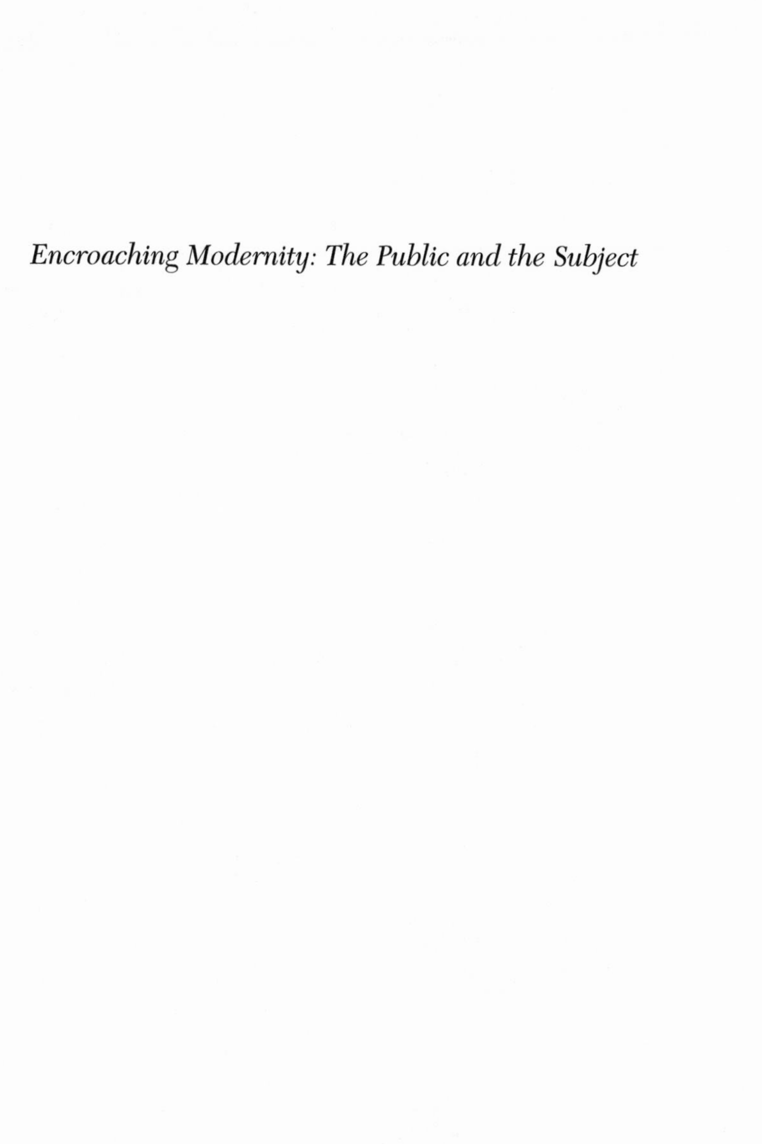

Melissa Frazier

Arabesques, Architecture, and Printing

WHEN GOGOL PUBLISHED his collected works in 1842, he did not republish quite everything. From *Arabesques* (*Arabeski*), his 1835 collection of thirteen articles, three short stories, and two novel fragments, he took only the short stories, and one of them, "The Portrait," he published in a significantly revised version. Among the changes Gogol made in the 1842 version, one appears particularly interesting. Toward the end of the story we find a new passage in which a character remembers a speech supposedly made by Catherine II on the relationship of art and empire:

> Her Majesty noted that it is not under monarchic government that lofty, noble movements of the soul are oppressed, it is not there that creations of the mind, of poetry and the arts are despised and persecuted; that, on the contrary, monarchs alone have been their patrons; that the Shakespeares, the Molières blossomed under their generous protection while Dante could find no corner to call his own in his republican homeland; that true geniuses arise in the time of the brilliance and might of sovereigns and states, and not in the time of the chaotic political phenomena and republican terrorisms that to this day have not given to the world a single poet . . . that scholars, poets, and all creators of art are the pearls and diamonds in the imperial crown: by their means the epoch of a great sovereign is beautified and receives still more brilliance.

The way in which Gogol intended this speech to be understood is perhaps indicated by the character's final summing-up: " 'In a word, her Majesty, pronouncing these words, was in that minute divinely beautiful.' "[1]

This open praise of empire and of the system of patronage by which empire rewards its artists did not appear in "The Portrait" of 1835. That it did not reveals Gogol's aims not just in the original "Portrait" but in *Arabesques* as a whole. Gogol always had a leaning toward wholes, wholes in the form of political and also religious autocracies; in 1835, however, with the writing of *Arabesques* that tendency was countered by a very strong interest in parts, the parts that together make up the nation. Along with that interest in the nation came a hesitant admiration, not for the patronage system, but for the literary free market and for the agent of its existence, the printing press. In *Imagined Communities: Reflections on the Origin and Spread of Nationalism* Benedict Anderson tells us that nation and the printing press, or, to use his term, "print-capitalism," go hand in hand: it is "print-capitalism" that creates a sense of community not through kinship or common religion or even subjugation to a common ruler, but through the common reading of the printed vernacular in two particular genres, the novel and the newspaper.[2] We might add to Anderson's list one more: the genre of the arabesque.

The arabesque belongs alongside the novel because in the context of Romantic aesthetics, particularly Romantic aesthetics as expounded in the very first years of the nineteenth century by Friedrich Schlegel, both terms refer to the same phenomenon.[3] In his efforts to reconcile epistemology with ontology, re-creation and creation, Schlegel imagines a part that is simultaneously a whole, one genre that is to be all of poetry and that he calls variously the Romantic genre, the *Roman* or novel, and the arabesque. As poetry ever in the process of becoming, the arabesque is to be finite art in its infinite potential, the seemingly impossible combination of the beautiful and the sublime.[4] Needless to say, the actual realization of an ever-becoming genre is no easy task, and as Schlegel strives to create divisions that are not divisions, lines that blur, a vaguely delineated space where art and science, poetry and criticism can co-exist as individual parts that yet make up a whole, he does indeed resort to that agent Anderson describes: the printing press. Schlegel very deliberately defines the novel as "a Romantic book" (*ein Romantisches Buch*), for publication is an important means of re-opening the closed work, returning the whole of the work to a part in a much greater whole. In Schlegel's view, the finality that is writing is endlessly reiterated by printing.[5]

As its title would suggest, Gogol's seemingly chaotic collection of art and science, poetry and criticism, is, in Susanne Fusso's words, permeated by Schlegel's theory of genre.[6] And yet, *Arabesques* is not an arabesque, in part because of Gogol's ambivalent feelings toward the printing press. Contrary to what we might expect, Gogol is not bothered—or is bothered only a little—by the connection of the printing press to the commercialization of literature. What truly disturbs him is the notion that the arrival of the printing press signals the end of architecture, a notion he seems to derive from Hugo's *Notre-Dame de Paris* (1831). As Gogol counters Hugo's printing press with what we ultimately see is Peter Chaadaev's Gothic architecture, it becomes increasingly difficult to determine just what sort of community he hopes to create with his writing. For if in 1842 he seems solidly on the side of empire, in 1835 he wavers, torn between the community of empire and of theocracy (which he represents by means of the Gothic church) and the community of nation he imagines through the printing press. And as he lurches back and forth between the two, Gogol in the end creates very much his own genre:

not Schlegel's arabesque, that impossible balancing of part and whole, but a deeply contradictory *Arabesques.*

In Schlegel's theory of the arabesque, the printing press serves as a sort of backup. As the fragment that implies the whole, the arabesque is in a sense already intended to be *self*-(re)producing. This point becomes especially clear when the arabesque appears in the form of the *Charakteristik,* for example in Schlegel's 1801 collection of articles *Charakteristiken und Kritiken.* In "On the Essence of Criticism" ("Vom Wesen der Kritik," 1804) Schlegel explains that the *Charakteristik* identifies the essence of the work, isolates the fundamental idea or germ from which the work can be reconstructed again and again by every new reader.[7] And by *reader* not by writer: once the essential idea of the work has been captured, whether by critic or by poet, any and all authors—of *Charakteristiken* or original works—exit the scene, and there is no more creation to be done; only infinite re-creation is possible. In this germinal form, the work becomes apparently self-(re)producing and infinitely repeats what Schlegel calls its "movement and formation" with the help of every new audience it encounters.

If Schlegel conceived the printing press as a fail-safe device to ensure that the process of re-creation would take place, mechanical reproduction proved to complicate notions of the Romantic genre. The combination of beauty and sublimity is not an easy one to achieve, and the printing press is at best a problematic means to this end. Just as the printing press offers the potential for infinite reiteration, the literary marketplace provides that vaguely delineated space where product is transformed back into process, where the chaos that was the unfinished work is re-created, only on a drastically larger scale. But, whatever the sublimity thus suggested, the printing press and its companion, the literary marketplace, are often perceived as lacking what Schlegel, after Kant, would call "free beauty." In fact, the beauty of the printing press is not "free" at all; it is tainted with the hint of an inner purpose, and a very sordid one at that: money.

Novalis enacts both sides of the debate over the printing press in the first of his unpublished dialogues written sometime between 1797 and 1799 and originally intended for the *Athenäum.* The dialogue between A. and B. begins when A. finds B. reading the latest book catalogue. A.'s first disdainful query sets the tone for the anti-printing press party: "You don't then want to make of yourself the eulogist of this book epidemic."[8] A. certainly grants the infinite potential of book publishing, but he characterizes this infinity as an epidemic, a "Bücherseuche," as something that presumably should be stamped out. Further on he also firmly rejects the idea that some sort of whole could be made of the ever-increasing numbers of books, saying, "A whole from miserable parts is itself a miserable whole, or rather no whole at all" (2:661). He bemoans the waste of money spent on books, asking why a man should not be contented with a single book, as he is with a few good friends.

B., who represents the pro-printing press party, responds boldly to his friend's complaints. Not a bit afraid to call books "merchandise" (*Handlungsartikels*), B. gleefully compares the wealth of the German printing presses to that of the Peruvian silver mines. To A.'s rejection of the wholeness of the great mass of printed books, B. answers by attacking A.'s notion of system (or structure) as altogether too narrow and confining, as coming from without rather than within. Coincidence is the basis of any system, claims B.: "Individual facts are accidents—the combination of accidents—their meeting is no longer accident, but law—the result of the most profound, most systematic wisdom" (2:662). As for A.'s plea that we should hold to just one book, B. answers: "You speak like a devout—unfortunately, you meet a pantheist in me—for whom the immeasurable world is hardly wide enough" (2:664). One book could not hold all his gods, says B., and nor can it hold all his spirit. He would like "to see before me a whole collection of books from all arts and fields of knowledge as the work of my spirit" (2:664). What B. envisions, courtesy of the printed press, is a whole of infinite, irreducible parts in which the parts are the completed works, and the whole is the unfinished and unfinishable collection of all books of all times.

No doubt Gogol would have easily grasped the positions in Novalis's dialogue, since some thirty-five years later, at the time he was writing *Arabesques*, what William Mills Todd III calls the "debate over literary commerce" in Russia was just under way.[9] The would-be literary professional of the time faced numerous obstacles, from the unpredictable behavior of the tsarist government to the competition of older literary institutions, many of which questioned the morality of commercializing high literature. The debate over uniting literature with commerce approached these issues somewhat indirectly, however. The first concern of its participants was not to discuss abstract principles, but to respond to the enormously successful journal *Library for Reading* first published in 1834, and to the often unscrupulous tactics of its editor, Osip Senkovsky. The bold and provocative stances taken by Senkovsky further muddied the debate, and his attackers found themselves addressing in their polemics a number of issues not really related to the problems of commerce: for example, Senkovsky's tendency to alter submissions without their authors' permission.

Gogol's personal loyalties and general conservatism might lead us to expect that he would take the part of A. against the printing press in the Russian discussion of literary commercialization. In fact, he does not, although there are certainly those who do. Most notable in this regard is Stepan Shevyrev, who in his 1835 article "Literature and Commerce" ("Slovesnost' i torgovlia") not only adopts an extreme anticommerce position, but also makes it clear that in taking this position against the literary trade, he at the same time takes a stand against the novel; in other words, throughout the article, Shevyrev makes the connection between trade and the novel, (that is, the Romantic genre) and rejects both simultaneously.

Where Novalis's B. calmly accepts the analogy between literature and money, printing presses and silver mines, Shevyrev apparently assumes that any right-minded reader would be shocked at such a comparison, and he uses it repeatedly and scornfully throughout his article. "*The Library for Reading* is just a stack of banknotes turned into articles," he cries.[10] "Here comes a *littérateur* in his sleigh," he tells us somewhat later. "You think it's a sleigh. But no, it's an article for the *Library for Reading* taking the form of a sleigh covered with a bear skin with rich silver claws" (8). With heavy-handed sarcasm Shevyrev asks what his reader sees in a novel. Most probably, suggests Shevyrev, you look at a novel with the desire to "guess at the meaning of the features of contemporary life in it, to read the soul and character of our epoch through the transparent picture of a distant life which it seems to represent." Shevyrev himself has a very different approach. With, as it were, a sad shake of his head, he tells us: "I look entirely differently at that Novel. You see in it something abstract, but I see in it something much more concrete—to be precise, the village into which the author turned it" (8).

The mention of the novel here is not accidental. In fact, Shevyrev refers to the novel and its miniature partner in crime, the *povest'* or short story, again and again throughout the article, connecting both with the evils of commerce. Shevyrev is forthright in his attack. "You think," he writes, "that the Novel and its miniature, the Short Story, is the type that corresponds to our epoch—and therefore it dominates in our literature. But I think that the greater part of Novels and Short Stories appear among us because they pay better" (11). After all, authors are now paid by the page, so the longer the better, not only in terms of genre, but also in terms of style. It is commerce, according to Shevyrev, that is responsible for the length and long-windedness of contemporary literature. Trade and the novel are in, and poetry, unfortunately is out, for "Poetry alone does not submit to speculation" (19). Shevyrev pleads to turn back the clock with regard to both literary commerce and literary genre. His linking of the two is perfectly logical, especially the context of Romanticism where the process of publishing is interpreted as the necessary infinitization of the Romantic genre, the novel or *Roman.* And Shevyrev wants none of it.

Gogol, on the other hand, at least at the time of the writing of *Arabesques,* is very engaged with the notion of a Romantic genre, and so he does support the commercialization of literature, if a little cautiously. *Arabesques* nowhere directly addresses the issue of literary trade, although we do find references, both positive and negative, to trade in general. For an open expression of Gogol's stance in the debate over literary commerce we must look rather at his 1836 article "On the Movement of Periodical Literature in 1834 and 1835" ("O dvizhenii zhurnal'noi literatury v 1834 i 1835 godu") and here we find something that sounds a good deal like Novalis's B. Unlike Shevyrev, Gogol makes an important distinction, warmly supporting the commercialization of literature on the one hand, while violently attacking Senkovsky on the other. Senkovsky's flaws are easily summarized. He, and accordingly *The Library for Reading,* lack any kind of unifying idea that would draw together the diverse ideas and articles into a single whole. The journal is just too chaotic, and not productively so.

But this failure to elicit structure, Gogol hastens to assure us, in no way reflects on the journal's publisher, Smirdin. Smirdin in general received high marks for his honesty and reliability from the participants in this debate, even from Shevyrev. With no exception, Gogol repeatedly praises the man whom he refers to each time as "the bookseller Smirdin," even twice in the same sentence. Smirdin apparently does have the ability to draw chaos into structure, as Gogol suggests in his description of Smirdin's decision to start the *Library for Reading:*

> At that time the bookseller Smirdin, already long known for his activity and conscientiousness, the only one who, to the shame of his other, less farsighted colleagues, showed enterprise and by his efforts gave momentum to the book trade, the bookseller Smirdin decided to publish an extensive, encyclopedic magazine, to win over all the littérateurs, however many there may be in Russia, and make them participate in his undertaking. (8:156)

As this sentence would indicate, Gogol is no more afraid than was B. of contaminating literature through the consideration of its commercial aspect, and in fact seems to go out of his way to use a sort of business terminology. Not content with his constant reminders of Smirdin's role specifically as a seller of books, Gogol further emphasizes the business aspect of literature when he describes the source of a journal's "credit." A strong editorial presence is essential to a journal, Gogol tells us, for "[t]he entire credit of the journal is based on him, on the originality of his opinions, on the liveliness of his style, on the general clarity and engagingness of his language, on his constant fresh activity" (8:168). And the free market, according to Gogol, is a wonderful thing, especially in the realm of journalism. "The more competition, the greater the gain for readers and for littérateurs"(8:167). "Literature had to turn into commerce," he adds, "because readers and the demand for reading increased" (8:168). Finally, Gogol also mentions the actual organ of literary commerce, the printing press. If the printed novel makes a good candidate for the Romantic genre, infinite in its finitude, what about journalistic literature, especially as described by Gogol here, as a genre that:

> moves with the taste of the crowd, turns about and gets out into the literary world all the news that otherwise would be in both senses dead capital. It is the rapid, capricious exchange of general opinions, the living conversation of everything stamped out by the printing presses; its voice is the true representative of the opinions of the whole epoch and age, opinions that, without it, would disappear unvoiced. (8:156)

Given some kind of guiding thought, that very thought which Senkovsky so conspicuously lacks, what structure could be more perfect than the chaos of the competing voices of the press, more alive than the rapid-fire dialogue of journals?

If *Arabesques* doesn't respond directly to the issue of the commercialization of literature along the lines of "On the Movement of Periodical Literature in 1834 and 1835," it does include mention of the printing press, and such mention as would again suggest Novalis. Explicit references to the printing press appear only twice in *Arabesques,* on both occasions, however, with the same vision of creative chaos breaking open the confines of sterile structure of which Novalis wrote. The main difference is that where Novalis presents the printing press as exploding the limitations of the written word, or traditional genre, Gogol shows it as exploding the limitations of the pope.

The pope makes a rather dramatic appearance in *Arabesques* as a force of that negative structure which would suppress all chaos. In "A Glance at the Making of Little Russia" ("Vzgliad na sostavlenie Malorossii") Gogol compares Ukraine of the thirteenth century to the West of that time, "where the autocratic pope entangled all of Europe with his religious power as if with an invisible spider's web, where his powerful word ended conflict or ignited it, where the threat of terrible damnation curbed passions and half-wild nations" (8:41). The pope is regularly presented in this vein, and it would seem that one force could best counter his overwhelming order: the printing press. In "On the Teaching of Universal History" ("O prepodavanii vseobshchei istorii") Gogol describes the fall of the pope at the hands of Luther. Gogol would explain:

> How the thought formed in the mind of the humble monk, how strongly and stubbornly he defended his position! How, during his fall, the pope became more threatening and inventive: he introduced the terrible Inquisition and, frightening in its invisible strength, the Jesuit order which suddenly deployed in all the world, penetrated into everything, went everywhere and communicated secretly from two different ends of the earth. But the more threatening the pope became, the more strongly the printing presses worked against him. (8:34)

In "On the Middle Ages" ("O srednikh vekakh") Gogol describes that same moment in more detail as he tries to summarize the effects of the Middle Ages:

> The power of the Pope crumbles and he falls, the power of ignorance crumbles, the treasures and international trade of Venice crumble, and when the general chaos of revolution is purified and clarified, before amazed eyes appear monarchs who hold in their powerful hands their own scepters; ships which in a broad stroke skim along the waves of the unembraceable ocean beyond the Mediterranean Sea; instead of powerless weapons, in their hands Europeans hold—the gun; printed sheets fly to all ends of the earth; and all this is the result of the Middle Ages. (8:25)

Here printing seems less a cause than an effect, but again it is the infinite nature of the printed word that is emphasized, as it flies to all corners of the earth.

That the confines of traditional genre are replaced here by the confines of the pope is due to the tremendous impact made on the Russian literary world by the publication in 1831 of Victor Hugo's *Notre-Dame de Paris.* Although there is no direct evidence of Gogol's having read *Notre-Dame de Paris,*[11] commentators have long noted the striking resemblance between two of the articles in *Arabesques,* "On the Middle Ages" and "On the Architecture of the Present Day" ("Ob arkhitekture nyneshnego veka") and the ideas expressed by Hugo in his novel, starting with Senkovsky who sneered that *Arabesques*' views on Gothic architecture reveal only that "the author read Victor Hugo's novel to great advantage."[12] Of course, Gogol's foreign languages were notoriously bad and the novel was translated into Russian only in 1862; still, Gogol could have grasped the main points of *Notre-Dame de Paris* from the translation of the second chapter of the fifth book, "This Will Kill That" ("Ceci tuera cela"), which appeared in the *Moscow Telegraph* in 1833 as the main part of an article entitled "Architecture and Printing" ("Zodchestvoi knigopechatanie").

"Architecture and Printing" starts with a brief introduction from the editor accounting for the appearance of this chapter in the pages of his journal. He explains that to the eighth edition of his tremendously successful novel Hugo had added three chapters, and quotes Hugo to the effect that these chapters were not new, but had simply been mislaid until recently, and so had unfortunately not been included in any earlier editions. While it may seem strange that Hugo would lose part of his book, the editor takes this explanation at face value; later commentators have tended to doubt Hugo on that score, suggesting that the chapters may have originally been excluded due to an editorial conflict, or perhaps under the encouragement of Lamennais, who may have disliked the predictions offered therein for the future of the church.[13] In any case, these three chapters, the sixth chapter of book 4 and both chapters of book 5, were added to the edition that appeared in December 1832, along with the preface from which "Architecture and Printing" liberally quotes.

The *Moscow Telegraph* publishes only the last-mentioned chapter, "This Will Kill That," and a brief summary of the chapter preceding it. There Claude Frollo is visited in his cell high up in Notre-Dame by Jacques Coictier, the doctor to the king, and by an unknown man whom Frollo eventually recognizes as Louis XII himself. They come for consultation, as the archdeacon of Notre-Dame was well known for his learning, not so much in matters of theology as in alchemy and astronomy. Frollo speaks with his usual bitterness on science and the pursuit of knowledge, finishing with the reminder that while books made of paper are useful, there are other books still more important. In response to his unknown visitor's lack of comprehension, Frollo opens his window and points to the enormous building of Notre-Dame itself:

> For some time the archdeacon contemplated the gigantic edifice in silence; then, with a sigh, stretching out his right hand towards the printed book opened on his table and his left hand towards Notre-Dame, and casting a sad glance from book to church:
>
> —Alas! he said, this will kill that. (4:135)

Neither Coictier nor the king understands the import of these words, and the narrator seems concerned that the reader may not as well; the next chapter, "This Will Kill That," is an attempt to explain their meaning.

In this chapter the narrator offers two ultimately related interpretations to Frollo's words. One is that Frollo, as a member of the church, senses the dire effects printing, the Gutenberg Bible, and Luther will have on the power of the Catholic church, a thought Hugo summarizes as "the press will kill the church" (4:143). Here we find Gogol's opposition of the printing press and the pope, specifically in the *Moscow Telegraph*'s translation: "Printing will kill the power of the Vatican."[14] The second interpretation suggested by the narrator is that Frollo's comment contains also the idea that "printing will kill architecture" (4:136), an idea that requires further explanation. Essentially, Hugo's point is that until the fifteenth century, humanity wrote in stone, its ideas were expressed in architecture. With the invention of the printing press all that changed, and the Middle Ages marked the greatest and the last achievement of stone. Now architecture is made obsolete, as humanity writes with the printed word, and it is the printed word that gives form to its thought: "The great poem, the great edifice, the great work of humanity will no longer be built; it will be printed" (4:143).

There is certainly a degree of regret expressed in this passage, and indeed in the novel as a whole, for the passing of architecture. *Notre-Dame de Paris* is a paean to just that, Notre-Dame of Paris, and to the precious relics of Gothic architecture still remaining in the Paris of Hugo's day. If Hugo particularly admires the Gothic, however, it is because the Gothic is the end of architecture, an end already lit by the rays of the rising sun of printing. It is the printed book that best gives form to man's thought, the printed book that, with all its apparent frailty, is truly omnipotent and eternal. We must ever wonder at the book, written by architecture, and yet we must also give the greatness of the building built by printing its due:

> That edifice is colossal. . . . And all of humanity works on it without rest, and its monstrous head is lost in the deep abysses of the future. . . . In that building there are thousands of floors. Here and there on its ramps the openings of the dark caverns of Knowledge which intersect in the cellars, in the interior of the foundations, can be seen. Everywhere on its surface Art luxuriates for the eyes with its Arabesques, its colors, its lacework. Here every separate work, no matter how whimsical or isolated it may seem, has its place, its expression. From the whole comes harmony. From the Gothic edifice of Shakespeare to Byron's mosque, thousands of turrets and bell towers crowd together pell-mell in this metropolis of universal thought. . . . On the left from the entrance is set the bas-relief of Homer, cut from white marble; on the right the old polyglot translation of the great Book raises its seven heads. . . . ("Architecture and Printing," 33)

In Hugo's description of the edifice that is the printed word, we find sublimity combined with beauty as a colossal and, indeed, truly infinite structure made into a work of art by a frame of arabesques, flowers, and lace.[15] We find, too, Novalis's praise for its wholeness made from diverse parts. This wholeness, Hugo says, very much in the spirit of Jena, will remain ever unfinished, and unfinished because it is being built every day, by every member of humanity. As Hugo concludes:

> Indeed, here is a construction which increases and which piles up in spirals without end; here there is a confusion of languages, incessant activity, untiring labor, the furious competition of all of humanity, a promised refuge for the intellect against a new flood, against a submersion of the barbarians. It is the second tower of Babel of the human race. (4:144)

Hugo's conclusion suggests both the power of the printed word and its possible dangers. With the book, it would seem, man again aspires to God's level, and this time with greater hope of success, as the languages that became many in the destruction of the finite tower of stone unite once more in their very diversity to build an infinite tower of words.[16]

The similarity to the ideas expressed by Gogol in *Arabesques* and especially in the entries "On the Middle Ages" and "On the Architecture of the Present Day" is indeed very marked. In "This Will Kill That," Hugo develops the idea of structure as some kind of order that incorporates but does not overcome chaos, either as a multiplicity in singularity or as a singularity in multiplicity, and he offers as models for this structure the Gothic church and the printed word. Gogol, in turn, would add one more example, the history of the Middle Ages, a structure that, if not explicitly stated, is certainly not absent from Hugo's novel as a whole. As Hugo's ideas resemble Gogol's, so does his very language. Such a structure must be "colossal" in Hugo as in Gogol; what is more, the terminology that would become *Arabesques'*—including "formation [obrazovanie]," "chaos" and even "arabesque" itself—is particularly prominent in the *Moscow Telegraph*'s translation.[17]

Like Gogol, Hugo presents architecture and the book as analogous to one other, as two types of ideal structures, two genres, two epistemological forms. Both Hugo and Gogol use one term metaphorically for the other. For example, in "On the Architecture of the Present Day" Gogol writes: "Architecture is also a chronicle of the world. It speaks when songs and legends have already fallen silent and when no one any longer speaks of a perished nation" (8:73). Similarly, Hugo describes architecture as the original "great book of humanity":

> When the memory of the first peoples became overloaded, when the baggage of remembrances of the human race became so heavy and confused that the word, naked and flying, risked being lost along the way, mankind transcribed them on the ground in the most visible, the most durable and at the same time the most natural way. Each tradition was sealed under a monument. (4:136)

Both writers repeat this comparison when they equate the creation of architecture with the creation of literature. In the Middle Ages, Hugo wrote, an individual "born a poet became an architect" (4:139), just as Gogol insisted that any great architect must be both "creator and poet" (8:75).

Still, if in *Notre-Dame de Paris* architecture is compared to a book, it is nonetheless set in contrast to the printed word; while this point is not immediately evident in *Arabesques,* it emerges more distinctly when we read Gogol's work in light of Hugo's. For Gogol, the only clear opposition to the printed word is that offered by the pope; but this opposition is Hugo's, too, and it is one that Hugo encompasses in the opposition of printing and architecture. We recall that "the press will kill the church" (or, as the *Moscow Telegraph* translation would have it, "Printing will kill the power of the Vatican") was the first explanation given by Hugo's narrator to account for Frollo's strange words. This, in turn, was ultimately connected to the other assertion, "printing will kill architecture." Indeed, the two ideas run parallel and might both be reduced to the following: democracy succeeds theocracy.

Hugo offers a general rule, borrowed from Auguste Comte: "Every civilization begins as a theocracy and ends as a democracy. This law of liberty succeeding unity is written in architecture" (4:138). This law, Hugo argues, holds true for all eras, a claim he proceeds to illustrate with the example of the Middle Ages, in his description of which we find many of the elements later used by Gogol in "On the Middle Ages." According to Hugo, the Middle Ages began under the tight control of the pope and with Romanesque architecture, "the inalterable emblem of pure Catholicism, the immutable hieroglyph of papal unity" (4:138), and passed through the tumult of the Crusades to develop an architecture, as Hugo calls it, of the people, the wonderful chaos of Gothic architecture, just in time for Gutenburg's Bible and the Reformation.

The invention of the printing press both interrupted this cycle and re-created it on a larger scale. Architecture may have gone through its phases of being more or less democratic, but never could it hope to be of the people in the same way as is the printed word, infinitely cheaper and less time-consuming to produce, as Hugo never tires of pointing out. Architecture and the Church ended together, for it was the printing press that made Martin Luther's attack on the pope the revolution it was. By comparison with the printed word, architecture and the pope are both phenomena of too much order, of a theocracy, and so must give way to democracy. After Gutenberg, mankind's way of thinking changed once and for all: "In the time of architecture, it became a mountain and powerfully seized an age and a place. Now it has become a flock of birds, scattering to the four winds and occupying at the same time all the points of air and space" (4:141). The thoughts of man now become a flock of birds, like Gogol's printed pages that fly to all corners of the earth.

If we observe Hugo's scheme, we can see that Gogol, in opposing the printed word to the pope, by analogy also opposes the printed word to architecture. If he supports the chaos of the printed word against the structure of the pope, it should follow, then, that he supports the chaos of the printed word against the structure that is architecture. But at this point Gogol balks. Gogol's *Arabesques,* itself a creation of the printing press, is filled rather with Gogol's admiration for Gothic architecture, an admiration that he expresses in ideas and words lifted straight from Hugo, but without Hugo's recognition that the Gothic, and architecture as a whole, has gone forever; Gogol makes clear his refusal to make this transition in the opening lines of "On the Architecture of the Present Day": "Has the age of architecture truly gone, never to return?" (8:56).

Gogol's unwillingness to surrender architecture to the passing of time probably has something to do with the pretensions of Romanticism, pretensions with which he was never entirely comfortable. When the edifice that is the printed word loses its "monstrous head" somewhere in the "deep abysses of the future," the writer's re-production threatens to supplant the actual production of God. It is this usurping of divine power that Romantic aesthetics pursued all along. Schlegel's idea of the fragment that implies the whole in fact blurs the line between creation and re-creation. The writer of the *Charakteristik* covertly appropriates a prerogative of the divinity: the isolation of the germ of the work, after all, is really no different from the creation of what Plato calls essential forms.[18] The notion of the self-(re)production of the work then proves more than a little deceptive; in the end the writer is absent from his *Charakteristik* only in the sense that God is absent from his essential forms: he is unseen, unheard, but omnipresent.

When re-creation elides into creation, the democracy that Hugo advocates becomes one in which all men are not only equal among themselves, but are also equal with God. If this process of democratization held a certain fascination for Gogol, its ultimate leveling of man and God frightened him. His anxiety over the role of writer-God is most evident in another entry in *Arabesques*, "Nevsky Prospect." In "Nevsky Prospect" Gogol fits *Charakteristiken* one inside the other like so many Chinese boxes: he attempts, for example, to grasp the essence of St. Petersburg in Nevsky Prospect and then the essence of Nevsky Prospect in its appearance at different times of day, making more and more specific distinctions that ever promise the reader essential forms while failing to provide them. At the story's end the reason for this failure becomes clear. Gogol explains that the shapes we meet along Nevsky Prospect are but illusions illuminated by lamps lighted not by God, but by the devil; and that devil is the writer, Gogol himself. After all, Piskarev and Pirogov are to be met not on the real Nevsky Prospect, but only in the imaginary one, and, with his reference to infernal powers, Gogol makes sure we understand the distinction. "Nevsky Prospect," Gogol warns, is not Nevsky Prospect: re-creation is not creation but only a lie.

As Gogol shrinks from the democratic implications of the printing press, however, he may have more pragmatic concerns in mind as well. Gogol, seemingly devoted to the idea of the Russian nation in works like "Taras Bulba" (1835; 1842) and *Dead Souls* (1842), nevertheless had a very personal reason to feel ambivalent about the means of its formation, "print-capitalism." While Gogol was among the first real wave of professional writers in Russia who attempted to live off their writing, his attempt cannot be said to have been completely successful. Despite his best efforts Gogol was unable to benefit fully from the purposiveness of his art because the sales of his works never brought in sufficient income. Often nearly penniless, Gogol faced the unhappy truth, as he wrote Zhukovsky in 1837, that "writers in our time can die of hunger" (11:97).

That Gogol postponed that fate as long as he did was not because his championing of the literary free market in "On the Movement of Periodical Literature in 1834 and 1835" in any way cleared the path for his professional activity, but because, as Fanger puts it, if his income came "only from being a writer," it was yet "not exclusively from writing itself."[19] In other words, Gogol survived because in the Russia of his day the traditional patronage system had not yet been fully supplanted by "print-capitalism," which allowed him to receive a number of grants and "loans" from the Tsar and other wealthy admirers of his talent. This coexistence of "print-capitalism" and the patronage system in Russia of the 1830s—not to mention in the making of Gogol's income—helps account for the juxtaposition of the printing press and architecture in the pages of *Arabesques.* This connection offers another explanation why Gogol is both drawn to the printing press and repelled by it. He may have wished to earn money from his works themselves, but the fact was that such income was insufficient. In particular, the 1842 version of "The Portrait" suggests that Gogol, perhaps understandably, grew to prefer the support of gifts and patronage.

That second version of "The Portrait," however, is just that, a new version and not a new story. As he had earlier in *Arabesques,* Gogol compares the community of common readership with an older and equally, if not more, attractive community of common religion. For Gogol that community is represented by its meeting place, in particular the Gothic cathedral. In his image of architecture Gogol responds to both spiritual and material hesitations at the Romantic enterprise. In its sublimity his Gothic cathedral is less important as a seemingly infinite work of man than as a symbol of the truly infinite God. Gogol finds an ally in this vision of the sublime in a new and different voice: the voice of Peter Chaadaev.

Chaadaev enters *Arabesques* as a counterweight to Hugo, and as a response to that aspect of Hugo's argument which perhaps made Gogol a little uncomfortable. Where Novalis in his support for the printing press is pantheistic, Hugo is openly atheistic. No matter how interested Gogol may be in the downfall of the Catholic pope, it is difficult to imagine that he is not bothered by the broader anti-Church and anti-Christian bent of "This Will Kill That" that allegedly disturbed Lamennais. Any such religious inclinations on Gogol's part would find support in the writings of Chaadaev, where Gogol could encounter ideas diametrically opposed to those of Hugo. Most important in this regard are Chaadaev's first and second philosophical letters and his so-called fourth letter,[20] published in 1832 in *Telescope* as "Something from the Correspondence of N.N." ("Nechto iz perepiski N.N.")

The main section of "Something from the Correspondence of N.N." purports to be part of a letter written to a lady in response to her suggestion that some kind of connection might exist between Egyptian and Gothic architecture.[21] It is followed by six short fragments or aphorisms with no explicit addressee, all comments on death and immortality. Attached to the whole is a brief note addressed to the editor of *Telescope,* where the seven fragments are described as translations from the French of selections from a Russian gentleman's correspondence. The entire correspondence, as the author of this note assures the editor, represents the development of "a single, complete, profoundly thought-out system,"[22] and if these selections seem very diverse, he continues, there yet exists among them an inner connection that the reader will have to divine in answering the question, What do architecture and the immortality of the soul have in common?

The question is largely answered by the longest fragment, the letter on architecture. The similarity between Egyptian and Gothic architecture lies, according to N.N., in their basic dependence on one geometrical shape, the triangle, in their emphasis on height, on monumentality and on utter uselessness for this world. That they are useless for this world, however, does not mean that they serve no purpose at all: for N.N., the overall effect of these awesomely tall, monumental creations is to lift man's thoughts upward, toward God, and toward a spiritual world. N.N. contrasts this effect with that produced by Greek architecture, where he sees an emphasis on the material world. As he says, "[t]he Greek style is a shelter, a residence, a home; the Egyptian and Gothic styles are a monument, poetry, a thought. The former relates to a man's material needs, the latter to his moral needs" (2:21). Ultimately for N.N. the connection between architecture and the immortality of the soul lies in the fact that the right sort of architecture, of which the Gothic is the best example, can instill in man the sense of the greatness of God, and of his own humility. N.N. asks rhetorically:

> When you, while strolling along the banks of the Rhine on an autumn night, approach one of the ancient local cities humbly spreading out at the foot of its tall cathedral, just as the moon hangs above the summit of that majestic giant: why is this giant presented to your gaze? But maybe it instills in you feelings of piety, maybe it inclines your brow down into the outpouring of your feelings before God, the source of this lofty poetry, and makes you pronounce your evening prayer with an unusual ardor of faith, one new to you: this is why this giant stands before you! (2:23).

Chaadaev seems to be describing a species of the sublime, but not the man-made, Romantic variety. Certainly it is not Hugo's, for nothing could be further from Hugo's *Notre-Dame de Paris* than N.N.'s vision of the Gothic cathedral as an awe-inspiring agent of God. Humility in general is not espoused by Hugo nor, despite the looming presence of Notre-Dame, is Christianity. For Hugo, the Gothic has little to do with Christianity, even when it comes in the form of Gothic cathedrals. Hugo views the Middle Ages, as he would any era, as consisting of two phases, first theocracy, then democracy, each of which finds its representation in an architectural style, the first in the Romanesque and the second in the Gothic. It is Hugo's Romanesque that more closely approximates Chaadaev's Gothic, for Hugo's Gothic, as the creation of democracy—of the people and not of the pope—is so antithetical to Christianity as to actually produce entirely heretical buildings: "Sometimes a portal, a facade, even an entire church offer a symbolic meaning absolutely alien to worship, even hostile to the church. Guillaume de Paris in the thirteenth century and Nicolas Flamel in the fifteenth wrote such seditious pages. Saint-Jacques-de-la-Boucherie was entirely a church of opposition" (Hugo, *Oeuvres complètes,* 4:139). The sublimity of Hugo's Gothic cathedral does not refer to God. What Notre-Dame represents for Frollo is the cumulative knowledge of man, and what makes the tower of words more sublime than the tower of stone is that the knowledge expressed in the tower of words is ever-growing and more truly infinite, more infinite even than the God whom Frollo purports to serve.

It is the sublimity of man's infinite power to name and so create, that Schlegel would join with beauty in his arabesque. But it is precisely this sublimity that Gogol fears. If in his *Arabesques* he borrows much from Hugo, when it comes to the relationship of the Gothic to Christianity he sounds a great deal more like Chaadaev. Gogol shares N.N.'s emphasis on height in architecture, as he indicates in "On the Architecture of the Present Day" when he explains his preference for Gothic architecture above all others. Not only is the Gothic the style native to Europe, but its emphasis on height over breadth gives the greatest scope to the artist:

> The imagination strives toward height more ardently and in a more lively fashion than it does toward width. And therefore Gothic architecture should be used only in churches and other structures which rise up high. . . . Raise it as it should be: so that its walls rise higher, higher, as high as possible, so that the uncounted corner pillars surround them more thickly, like shafts, like poplars, like pines! . . . Let the windows be more immense, their form more varied, their height more colossal! Let the steeple be airier, lighter! . . . And remember the most important: let there be no comparison of height with width. The word width should disappear. Here there is one fundamental idea—height (8:65).

Gogol, too, makes the distinction between architecture of the spirit and that of the body when he reminds his reader that "[t]he majestic temple is as . . . great before the ordinary residences of people as the demands of our soul are great before the demands of the body" (8:57). As for what style of architecture would produce that "majestic temple," Gogol concurs with Chaadaev: "Anyone would agree that there is no more majestic, more lofty or more appropriate architecture for a building dedicated to the Christian god than the Gothic . . . [because of] . . . [i]ts majesty, its colossalness at whose sight all thoughts strive to one thing and tear the petitioner away from his lowly hut" (8:65).

As the poor petitioner would agree, there is something in Gogol's Gothic cathedral far greater than the mind of man, something in fact that he directly tells us "the audacious mind of man dares not even touch"(8:56). Where Hugo's infinite tower of words lifts man to the level of the divine, Gogol's finite tower of stone, at least in part, serves to measure the distance between the two, and, as the gathering place of the religious community, his Gothic cathedral is a symbol not of Romantic chaos but of religious unity. It is precisely religious unity that forms Chaadaev's concern, most evidently in his first and second philosophical letters. The first letter was published in 1836, again in *Telescope;* the second letter, in consequence of the unfortunate results of the publication of the first, was published only much later, in Gagarin's *Oeuvres choisies de Pierre Tchadaïf* of 1862.[23] Still, it is more than likely that Gogol was familiar with the letters that were written somewhere between 1829 and 1831, and that he recognized in them the theocracy of which Hugo wrote, now cast in a positive light (Chaadaev, *Sochineniia,* 1:369).

In the first letter, for example, Chaadaev notes, as did Hugo, the power of religion to unite. However, where for Hugo this power was portrayed negatively, as the ponderous immutability of theocracy, for Chaadaev it is that which gives the Christian idea its beauty. "See," he asks his reader, "what a diversity of natures, what a multiplicity of forces . . . [the revealed thought] . . . has made move; that the different powers make up but one thing; that the hearts constructed differently beat for but one idea!" (1:92). Gogol, for all his attacks on the pope as a figure of too much order, something like a spider lurking in the center of his web, shares this admiration for the unifying force of religion, and especially of Christianity. In "A Glance at the Making of Little Russia," for example, he regrets the lack of well-organized religion in thirteenth century Ukraine since religion "more than anything binds and forms a nation" (8:40).

Chaadaev values this unity to such an extent that, in the second letter, he launches an angry attack on the Reformation. The Reformation, he argues,

> has put the world back into the *disunity* of paganism; it has once more reestablished the great individualistic ethics, the isolation of souls and of spirits which the Savior came to destroy. If it has accelerated the movement of the human spirit, it has also removed from the conscience of the intelligent being the fecund and sublime idea of universality! The actual deed of any schism in the Christian world is the breaking of that mysterious *unity* in which is comprised all the divine thought of Christianity and all its power (1:117).

Here, however, Chaadaev goes too far for Gogol, who, as we saw above, perceived the Reformation rather as the glorious restoration of creative chaos, of a potential rather than a finished product. In fact, Gogol never does go quite as far as Chaadaev, at least not in *Arabesques.* Instead, he seems to lunge from one side to the other; turning now to Hugo and now to Chaadaev, he oscillates between creative chaos and unifying structure, democracy and theocracy, printing and architecture.

Gogol has never been known for his consistency, and on one level his combination in *Arabesques* of contradictory bits and pieces of both Hugo and

Chaadaev derives simply from his own personal idiosyncrasies. Gogol's words are ever marked by insufferable arrogance and equally insufferable humility, as he was drawn simultaneously to both the fragment and the whole. While he ever tended toward the chaotic, in the untidiness of his mind, the creative disorder of his work and especially in his inability to achieve completion, he yet had a fundamentally religious aspect, one that grew with time, as if unity—and total unity—were what he increasingly desired, though chaos remained somehow more natural to him.[24] With the passing of years Gogol may have tried to suppress the more arrogant and fragmentary sides of his personality, for example in his selective republication of *Arabesques* in the collected works of 1842, but his refashioning of himself cannot be said to have been entirely successful. Gogol started as a writer and ended only as a would-be prophet. Works like *Arabesques* gave way to the second version of "Taras Bulba" and finally to the second part of *Dead Souls,* his ultimately unrealizable prophetic word—unrealizable because, despite his aspirations toward unity, Gogol was still caught in the incompleteness of chaos, and the impossible balancing of part and whole that Schlegel imagined became for Gogol the terrible tensions of his own reality.

If Gogol made use of both Hugo and Chaadaev in the expression of the opposing sides of his personality, however, it is only because both were ready at hand, important voices in Gogol's contemporary context. That both were already there on the outside of *Arabesques* suggests another reason for their appearance on the inside. Russia of the 1830s was in a time of transition, not least from the patronage system to "print-capitalism" and, correspondingly, from empire to something at least colored by the notions of nationality. In this sense the contradictions of *Arabesques* could be said accurately to reflect the contradictions of Gogol's actual community. This community was one defined not exclusively by subjugation to a common ruler or religion, nor yet by its common reading of the printed vernacular, but rather by a combination of the various possibilities. We should note that Gogol was not the only one to produce an odd hybrid in the effort to describe its contours; in 1832, Uvarov, former Arzamassian and then minister of education, offered his own version in his famous slogan: "Orthodoxy, Autocracy and Nationalism."

Benedict Anderson tells us that Uvarov carefully grafts old onto new in the hope of at least slowing the clock down, if not stopping it. This same hesitation marks Gogol's representation of this community in the genre of *Arabesques.*[25] That Gogol's world was characterized by the same tensions as his genre does not mean that Gogol was comfortable with either, and, while Gogol moved in new directions with the times, he did so with his gaze fixed ever more firmly backward and with the nostalgia felt both in the passage quoted above from the 1842 version of "The Portrait" and in the despairing cry "Has the age of architecture truly gone, never to return?" Indeed, 1835 and *Arabesques* were a long way from 1800 and Schlegel's arabesque. Many hopes that were in the air at that earlier time had dissipated by the 1830s, and for many printing no longer looked quite so promising, nor architecture quite so limiting.

Where the 1842 edition of his collected works contained only the short stories from *Arabesques,* the edition Gogol was working on at the time of his death in 1852 was supposed to include the articles as well, albeit in a separate volume, along with parts of *Selected Passages from Correspondence with Friends* (1846). Apparently influenced by Gogol's own intentions, later editors have never republished *Arabesques* in its entirety and proper order with the exception of an illustrated edition put out by *Molodaia gvardiia* in 1990.[26] Transition, by definition, doesn't last, and neither did *Arabesques,* which quickly disintegrated into its separate pieces. Even fragmented, though, *Arabesques* is still not fragmentary, at least not in the sense of Schlegel's arabesque. Where Schlegel strove deliberately for incompletion, an incompletion that could be accomplished through the printing press's reopening of the work, Gogol achieved incompletion despite a gaze that looked beyond to some not-quite-attainable whole just over the horizon. On some level, Gogol was always bent upon producing a true whole, even at the expense of the part. It is only that he failed in his aim; try as he might, the whole where printing and architecture, Hugo and Chaadaev would co-exist lay just beyond his grasp.

David Powelstock

Living into Language: Mikhail Lermontov and the Manufacturing of Intimacy

> Becoming human is becoming individual, and we become individual under the guidance of cultural patterns, historically created systems of meaning in terms of which we give form, order, point, and direction to our lives.
>
> —Clifford Geertz, *The Interpretation of Cultures*

PERHAPS NO Russian writer's rise to prominence has been so dramatic as that of Mikhail Lermontov. While many a writer achieves fame by being "discovered," Lermontov stands apart in that his meteoric rise, a consequence of his fiery elegiac ode on the death of Pushkin ("Smert' poeta," 1837), was accompanied by a no less remarkable transformation of his poetics. Apart from a handful of relatively successful early poems, it is Lermontov's work after "Smert' poeta" upon which his literary reputation rests. The conclusion I draw is that Lermontov's consciousness of his own poetic career should be understood as an integral component of his poetic practice. It is important to remember that Lermontov, like many of his ambitious contemporaries of noble birth, felt that his identity as a human being depended on traveling one of the avenues of public success open to him. In very general terms, this meant a career in one (or more) of three spheres: cultural life, military service, or government service. As we shall see, as a child of Romantic culture, Lermontov aimed very high indeed: he aspired to the status of cultural hero.

A fourth sphere of public success occupied a special place in the lives of young men like Lermontov. This sphere, that of "high society," stood apart, because it both cut across the other spheres and played the role of ultimate judge of one's cultural success within them. If one earned one's right to respect in literature, the military, or government, it was in society that these accomplishments were rewarded. To speak specifically in terms of literature, the recognition of the writer meant his acceptance into the elite of Petersburg or Moscow society. Ultimately, then, entrance into human community, albeit tinged with a concern for hierarchical status, was the highest form of success. What is important to note at this point, is the manner in which the writer's sense of community had changed between the 1820s and the 1830s. While Pushkin and his peers—the Golden Age poets—had written from the context of an already established community of gentry camaraderie, this system of intimate literary relations had broken down by the next generation. Numerical increases in readership and the expansion of the audience to include newly literate non-noble classes were accompanied by increasingly commercial journalistic and publishing institutions, as well as a new breed of cultural actors: professional critics. The intimate literary society of Pushkin's age, where friends wrote for friends and evaluated one another's work consensually, was increasingly supplanted by the relative impersonality of the literary marketplace.[1]

The period of Lermontov's literary apprenticeship coincided with these developments. Although as a poet of the gentry class he was heir to the Golden Age legacy, as a member of the new generation he was also acutely aware that the Golden Age poetic code, whose basis in aristocratic social intimacy distanced it from the new readerships, could no longer fit the needs of a young man bent on a literary career. Nevertheless, Lermontov—out of nostalgia for the lost age, no doubt, coupled with a deeper human urge for communion—valued intimacy with the reader as the sine qua non of successful lyric poetry. In Lermontov's case, the longing for the lost intimacy of Golden Age polite society was redoubled by his own status as a relative outsider to what remained of that society. Although his maternal line of fairly well-to-do landowners, ensured him a certain access to Moscow society, his father's family was impoverished and obscure provincial gentry. The name Lermontov meant nothing in society. Intimacy and social success were not guaranteed him. They would have to be fought for and won. Lermontov's outsider status was particularly marked in St. Petersburg, the literary capital at the time, where his Moscow-based family had very few connections.[2]

Despite, or perhaps because of, his relative social disadvantage, Lermontov was from his earliest years possessed by the wishful premonition that he himself might turn out to be an extraordinary individual, a great man after the models of Napoleon and Byron.[3] In the 1830s, of course, such Romantic aspirations were hardly unique to Lermontov, or to Russians in general, but one is struck by the obsessive concern with heroic personal fate in the young poet's work. One early lyric clearly illustrates Lermontov's yearning after the role of *homme de destin:*

Нет, я не Байрон, я другой;
Еще неведомый избранник,
Как он гонимый миром странник,
Но только с русскою душой.
Я раньше начал, кончу ране,

Мой ум не много совершит,
В душе моей, как в океане,
Надежд разбитых груз лежит.
Кто может, океан угрюмый,
Твои изведать тайны? кто
Толпе мои расскажет думы?
Я—или [Б]ог—или никто!
(1832, 2:32)[4]

(No, I am not Byron, I am another
As yet unknown favorite,
Like he, a wanderer, persecuted by the world,
But with a Russian soul.
I began earlier, and earlier shall I finish,
My mind will not accomplish much,
In my soul, as in the ocean,
Lies the cargo of shattered hopes.
Who can, o gloomy ocean,
Fathom your mysteries? Who
Shall narrate my thoughts to the crowd?
I myself—or God—or no one!)

Along with the dream of heroic greatness, this poem illustrates the other pervasive theme of Lermontov's early verse: his acute sense of the rift between the inner world of the poet's experience and the outer world of his audience, coupled with a fervent desire to bridge this gap, to achieve communicative intimacy through lyric expression.[5] The lyrics Lermontov wrote in the years 1828 to 1832 constitute an ongoing diary or confession in verse, an attempt to pour out the "natural self" as a means of achieving human connection. Lermontov was not, however, unconscious of the problems such a project posed. Indeed, almost every such naive effusion is accompanied by a lamentation of the insufficiency of established poetic language for conveying the "true" self. It is easy to see how Lermontov could have felt this way. The poetic language of the Golden Age had never borne the burden of linguistic intimacy, since its sense of intimacy—reflected in, but not achieved through language—stemmed from extraliterary personal acquaintance rather than poetic work and thus, from the standpoint of poetic creation, was a given.

It is a measure of Lermontov's desperation in confronting this crisis of poetic faith that he employs the frequently encountered Romantic trope of self-sacrifice as a solution to it. In one poem, for example, his lyric I declares himself to be "prepared to sacrifice myself, in order somehow to pour out at least the shade [of my lofty passions] into another's breast."[6] Lermontov's distinction in this respect is that he, unlike poets such as Adam Mickiewicz and Byron who felt that poetry might have to be offered up as a sacrifice to a life of action, still sees the act of self-sacrifice not only as falling within the boundaries of poetry, but even as necessary for the sake of lyric expression: the sacrifice occurs in order to achieve *poetic intimacy.* Despite this urgent willingness to give up life for the sake of poetic effect, the young Lermontov frequently succumbed to doubts that his dual goals of heroic glory and intimate lyric communication—each in itself a distant ideal—were reconcilable. When in 1832, at the age of eighteen, he entered the St. Petersburg Junker Guard School, he envisioned his new career as a military officer (a career that might perhaps bring with it the heroic glory he sought, à la Napoleon) as displacing his poetic ambitions. Upon his arrival in St. Petersburg from Moscow, he wrote to his friend Mariia Lopukhina:

> I cannot imagine what effect my great news will have upon you; I, who have until now lived for a literary career, after having sacrificed so much for my ungrateful idol, now I am becoming a soldier; perhaps it is the peculiar will of Providence! Perhaps this road is the shortest; and if perhaps it does not suit my original end, it will perhaps suit the final end of all. To die with a bullet in one's heart is after all far better than the slow agony of old age; what is more, if there is war, I swear to you in God's name that I will be first among all [the ranks]. (6:418–19)

It is significant also that from this time until 1837, Lermontov ceased almost entirely to write lyric poems, although he continued to compose action-packed narrative poems filled with heroic military exploits. Still, the seed of Lermontov's ultimate success in uniting his two ends, heroic fame and lyric intimacy, can already be seen in his early, immature lyrics, themselves efforts to find an alternative to the alien poetic code of the Golden Age, to achieve lyric intimacy with his projected audience.

One of the conditions of Lermontov's ultimate success was his rejection of the Golden Age faith in *le mot juste.* He framed the word as a necessary, but deeply flawed vehicle for the expression of the mysteries of personal experience. When it came to such matters, there was no such thing as "the right word." Instead of emphasizing the denotative meanings of the words themselves, he dwelt on the emotional meaning contained in speech *as an act in and of itself.* Over and over again among the early lyrics we find poems in the form of miniature speeches, complete with a speaker and addressee. The speeches are set in recognizable emotional contexts: scenes of parting, meeting and death, prayers, confessions of love, or personal disagreements. These poems are immediately distinguishable from the Golden Age's intimate genre, the familiar verse epistle, by their abandonment of polite convention and limitations on content.[7] Lermontov was not a part of the intimate social world of the Golden Age poets, which had, in any case, receded into the past. The initial audience for poetry had shifted from tightly bound groups of social peers to the broader, socially more heterogeneous readerships of popular journals. As a consequence, the moderated understatement of the Golden Age poet addressing his peers, for whom the poet's identity is unproblematic, gives way in Lermontov to an exhibitionist self-portrayal, designed to establish and dramatize the poet's identity and experience by emphasizing the *emotive and affective* qualities of language, the emotional impact of words that derive their power from a posited universality of certain human situations:

Итак, прощай! Впервые этот звук
Тревожит так жестоко грудь мою.
Прощай!—шесть букв приносят столько мук!
Уносят всё, что я теперь люблю!
Я встречу взор ее прекрасных глаз,
И, может быть, как знать . . . впоследний раз!
(1830, 1:168)

(And so, farewell! For the first time does this sound
So cruelly trouble my breast.
Farewell!—eight letters [six in Russian] bring so many torments!
They bear away all that I now love!
I shall meet the gaze of her beautiful eyes,
Perhaps, who can know . . . for the last time!)

Here a single word serves as a focal point for the impact of the concrete emotional drama. The word "farewell," which is in Russian unequivocally imperative in grammatical form (*prosti* or *proshchai*), and therefore colored with the presence of both speaker and listener, absorbs its meaning from its implied context (the universal experience of parting) and thus (and only thus) becomes capable of influencing emotional outcomes through the medium of sound. The emotional impact is, typically for the early Lermontov, substantiated in a metaphor of physical response, emphasizing the corporeal presence of the lyric hero. By framing the poetic utterance within such recognizable dramatic social situations, Lermontov draws upon reservoirs of meaning beyond the boundaries of the utterance proper, thus disburdening poetic language of some of its semantic load, deferring that load onto the situational frame. The utterance thus becomes the response of the speaker to an a priori antecedent (the speech context) in dialogue with an (implied or explicit) interlocutory other. The lyric is no longer a monologic meditation on a fixed and distant object, but a dramatic scene, whose lines are meant to have the immediacy of theater.[8]

This dramatization of the lyric speech act implies the creation, or representation, of a concrete world within lyric discourse. In a great many of Lermontov's early lyrics, the "I" of the poem does not merely speak as a subject; it becomes, in addition, the *object* of speech, a "he." Recurring themes in such poems are society's slandering of the lyric I; his inscription in the memory and discourse of the love object, or else of society at large; and the poet's death and return to the love object as a ghost. In this way, the lyric I is objectified and made concrete within the poetic world. It becomes more than a speaker; it becomes a character in a narrative. This tendency again reflects, this time in lyric form, in a projection onto the lyric hero, Lermontov's desire to become a meaningful figure inscribed in his culture: a Romantic hero. It is worth pointing out once again, that such a strategy became necessary for Lermontov because he himself did not "exist" for his readership beyond the boundaries of his poetry in the way that Pushkin, for example, existed as a human subject for his own (initially very intimate) audience of social and intellectual peers. Lermontov's poetry had to create its own speaker.

Lermontov graduated from the Junker School in 1834 at the age of twenty and was commissioned with the Guard Regiment of the Hussars in Tsarskoe Selo. The primary functions of this elite corps consisted of parades and balls.[9] For the next three years, Lermontov engaged in a few amorous intrigues, wrote almost no lyric poems, and grew increasingly dissatisfied with his prospects for future greatness. In late 1834 he wrote the following to Mariia Lopukhina:

> My dear friend! Whatever may come I shall never refer to you in any other way, for to do so would be to sever the last bond that links me to the past; and I would not wish this for anything in the world; for my future, so brilliant to the eye, is empty and dull; I must confess to you that each day I perceive more and more clearly that I will never amount to anything, with all my beautiful dreams and my failed endeavors along life's road . . . for either the opportunity is wanting, or else I lack nerve. . . . They tell me: the opportunity will one day come! Experience will give you the nerve! . . . And who knows whether, when all that comes, I shall still retain something of that ardent, young soul with which God so inappropriately endowed me? (6:426–27)

As it turned out, Lermontov did not have to wait very long for his opportunity, nor did he lack the nerve to seize it when it arose.

On 27 January 1837 (old style), Russia's greatest poet, Alexander Sergeevich Pushkin was fatally wounded in a duel with Georges D'Anthès, a Frenchman who had been adopted by a Dutch diplomat stationed in Russia. This event set in motion the cultural processes that were to elevate Lermontov to the status of Romantic poet-hero. There had already been a great deal of talk in St. Petersburg to the effect that Pushkin had been provoked by D'Anthès as part of a conspiracy by Tsar Nicholas I's repressive regime to eliminate the troublesome poet. Pushkin, after all, for many represented a holdover from the politically freethinking gentry of the second and third decades of the nineteenth century. Various interpretations of the duel and its causes were and have been proposed. Some adhered to the aforementioned state-conspiracy theory, while others blamed Pushkin's "blind jealousy, suspiciousness, or rash temperament."[10] Lermontov's poem played an important role in generating a mythology of the event that eulogized Pushkin as an innocent victim of pernicious social forces. His version of the affair became a touchstone for the cultural myth not only of Pushkin, but of the Russian poet in general as archetypal outsider. Most important for the present study, it was in this poetic response to Pushkin's death that the mythology of Lermontov himself as poet-hero was born into the cultural consciousness.

Lermontov's initial response to the duel's outcome was immediate, the first draft of the poem "Death of the Poet"("Smert' poeta"). The title of the poem and its very first words, "Pogib poet!" (Dead is the poet!), already betray Lermontov's mythopoetic interpretation of the event. The title presents the "death of Pushkin" as an archetypal "death of the Poet," a gesture amplified by the absence of the poet's name in the text. The stylistically elevated inversion of subject (*poet*) and verb (*pogib*) in the first line reinforces the effect by equalizing and heightening the first two stresses of the line. The uninverted variant, "Poet pogib!" (The poet is dead!) would by contrast have rendered the second stress intonationally stronger, while potentially reducing the word "poet" to the position of automatic theme.[11] The inversion has the intonational effect of bonding the two words into a single verbal monolith, a unitary epic event of great cultural import.

Having established a mythic frame for Pushkin's death, Lermontov proceeds to ramify the image of the poet. This portrayal fuses multiple markers familiar both from Lermontov's early depictions of heroes and from depictions of the Romantic hero in general: social outsider, Christ figure, embodiment of national character, and tragic victim of fate.

From this depiction, and from Lermontov's interpretation of the poet's murder "in cold blood," derives the image of the poet's apotheosis as Christ figure: "I prezhnii sniav venok—oni venets ternovyi, / Uvityi lavrami, nadeli na nego" (And stripping off his former crown—a crown of thorns / Wound with laurels did they place upon him"). This trajectory reflects one possibility for achieving the status of Romantic hero: the transmogrification of the extraordinary individual through a suffering that underscores precisely the *heavenly*, and thus exceptional, nature of the gift of genius that is incompatible with *earthly* existence. The sources of this suffering in "Death of the Poet" are familiar to any reader of Lermontov's early verse: society's treacherous calumny, the failure of the "other" (in this case a Frenchman) to appreciate greatness,[12] and the hostility of "fate."

Nevertheless, beneath the surface of Lermontov's attribution to Pushkin of all the trappings of greatness, and his mythologization of the poet through the language of his poem, there lurk undercurrents of jealousy, Oedipal desire, and a self-serving mythopoetic strategy. If we dig more deeply into the poem, aided by an understanding of the young Lermontov's mythology of heroic status, we soon find ourselves on the "dark and daemonic ground" governed by the "anxiety of influence."[13]

The treatment of the hero in Lermontov's early verse is characterized by an alternation between two modes of depiction.[14] The first mode, passive and iconic, emphasizes the heavenly and immanent aspect of the hero's image and is derived from elegiac poetry. The iconic image does not allow for earthly action; its realm is the sacred sphere of emotional reflection. Frequently, this type of hero is portrayed as a passive victim of fate. Lermontov's early poem about the poet Dmitry Venevitinov, "Epitafiia" (Epitaph, 1830), offers the purest example of this mode. Its final line forms a transparent summary of the tragic fate of this type of hero: "On ne byl sozdan dlia liudei" (He was not created for people [1:122]). The passive image is the product of others' perceptions and representations of the hero. The second mode is active and dynamic. This type of image focuses on the hero's will as a vital force opposed to the finalizing forces of the external world. This hero *acts* in the world of men and historical events, and his natural generic environment is, therefore, the narrative. The tension between these two modes is one of the dominant themes of Lermontov's works, as the heavenly (spiritual) and earthly (social) valences frame a landscape of eternal paradox, inhabited by the hero. Lermontov's poetic practice shows that he considered both aspects equally necessary to the depiction of the hero, although neither was sufficient. One consequence of this double requirement, of course, is the conventional image of the narrative hero posed on a cliff, halting the swirl of events for one ekphrastic moment. A more interesting and original consequence, however, is the striving of the heroes in Lermontov's lyric poems to break out of the static, iconic frame typical of the elegiac tradition: the passive elegiac hero, criticized by Kiukhel'beker, becomes narrativized. Lermontov's 1829 poem, "Napoleon," provides an interesting example of this: when the typical elegiac *pevets* (bard or singer) appears to pronounce his iconizing words over Napoleon's grave, Napoleon's ghost rises up to silence him, breaking the static frame of the elegy, saying,

> «Умолкни, о певец!—спеши отсюда прочь,—
> . . . .
> Пускай историю страстей
> И дел моих хранят далекие потомки:
> Я презрю песнопенья громки;—
> Я выше и похвал, и славы, и людей!»
>
> (1:45–47)

> ("Be silent, o bard!—Hurry you hence!
> . . . .
> Let the history of my passions
> And my deeds be kept by distant descendants:

I despise loud singing of songs;
I am above all praise and glory and men!")

Characteristically for Lermontov, the immortal (sacred) spirit of Napoleon's passions and *deeds* will be perpetuated as an active and dynamic force in the historical discourse of legend, not merely as a static image sketched by the elegiac bard. The historical hero resists the finalization of the bard's elegiac discourse. This active and earthly aspect of the heroic legend is a necessary component of Lermontov's mythology of an immortality that can be achieved by inhabiting the landscape of discourse. At the same time, of course, the discursive frame would have to expand to accommodate the active hero.

What first strikes a reader familiar with the early Lermontov's usual technique of heroic mythopoeisis is the omnipresence in "Death of the Poet" of images of death with no explicit mention *whatsoever* of transcendent immortality.[15] Indeed, Lermontov uses verbs and participles connoting death eleven times: *pogib, pal, ubit* (three times), *ugas, uvial, vziat mogiloi, srazhennyi, umer, zamolkli* (perished, fallen, killed, extinguished, withered, taken by the grave, slain, died, fallen silent). While death had always been a prerequisite for the immortal hero in Lermontov's early poetics, so had a redemptive memorialization. The closest Lermontov comes to granting Pushkin eternal life is in the metaphor of "crown of thorns," evoking the Christological subtext. Even here, however, neither Resurrection nor Ascension is directly evoked, only the Passion. At the same time, the reference to Christ is somewhat muted by the introduction in the next line of "laurels" woven into the crown of thorns. The implication is that society flattered Pushkin into his ultimate role as their victim. The result is a subtle undercutting of the Christological parallel, as well as a less than flattering portrayal of Pushkin's own complicity in the matter.

Another striking silence is revealed in the almost total absence of *activity* in the portrayal. Lermontov's image of Pushkin is that of a man utterly defeated and humiliated by society. Pushkin is "fallen, defamed by rumor . . . having bowed down his head"; "he could not bear the final torments: extinguished, like a lamp, is the wondrous genius, withered is his festive crown"; "the secret needles harshly stung his glorious brow; his last instants were poisoned by the insidious whispers of mocking churls." The "wondrous genius" with the "free, bold gift" has "rebelled against society's opinions, alone as before," but, "slandered by rumor," overwhelmed by the "shame of petty offenses" and "torments," he has ultimately "bowed down his head" in defeat.[16] Throughout the poem the great poet is seen as a passive victim of *others'* actions. This portrayal is compounded in the grammatical texture of the poem by the number of times Pushkin appears as the direct object of transitive verbs or the subject of sentences whose predicate implies actions done to Pushkin by others (ten times). The one instance of Pushkin's active resistance to fate ("He rebelled against society's opinions") apparently refers to his effort to exact revenge on D'Anthès (who had implied Pushkin's wife's infidelity, thus giving rise to rumors, "society's opinions") by engaging him in a duel, an effort that is thwarted tragically and *absolutely.*[17] Otherwise, when Pushkin appears as grammatical subject, it is usually of a verb or participle synonymous with "to die" (eight times). In a section describing Pushkin's trusting participation in society ("Why from peaceful comforts and openhearted friendship did he depart into society, envious and constrictive for the free heart and fiery passions?") he is the subject of three verbs, but taken together they denote actions characterized by Lermontov's poem as naively complicit, if not utterly foolish.

In his passivity, Lermontov's Pushkin is compared to another guileless sacrificial poet: Pushkin's own character, Vladimir Lensky, killed in a duel by Eugene at the end of chapter 6 of *Eugene Onegin.* The comparison with Lensky, who is depicted by Pushkin as the victim of his own naïveté and Onegin's fatal boredom, is in itself no compliment, but even Pushkin's sacrificial lamb is granted, in chapter 7 of *Onegin,* the spatial and verbal locus required for an afterlife in discourse: an elegiac gravesite, complete with epitaph, and a lengthy eulogy. Thus, Lermontov, apart from the ambivalent eulogy represented by the poem itself, does not even grant Pushkin the complete last rites afforded Pushkin's fictional *pevets.* It can be argued that Pushkin's cultural immortality required no boost from Lermontov. However, the lack of need for such memorialization had never before stopped Lermontov from providing it (in his poems about Napoleon and Venevitinov, for example, both objects of powerful personality cults at the time).

As a poet, of course, Lermontov could not possibly avoid Pushkin's legacy, as evidenced by the numerous reminiscences of the latter's verse in this poem (primarily recalling the Lensky episode, as well as Pushkin's lyrics "Poet" and "André Chénier").[18] And yet, even though the poem is presumably devoted to defending Pushkin's reputation, the references to the great poet's verse are assimilated into Lermontov's own discourse of self-creation as a poet, which in turn paints Pushkin as a decidedly *passive* Romantic hero, and thus no threat to Lermontov's own concupiscent claim to the title of *active* poet-hero, a claim he buttresses by depicting himself as Pushkin's avenger. Lermontov could have made reference to the fiercely anti-tyrannical ode "Vol'nost'," which had contributed to Pushkin's exile to the Caucasus in 1820. Instead, the theme of the *political* (rather than social) repression of Pushkin, a theme much celebrated in Soviet scholarship, is conspicuously absent. In connection with this absence, it is interesting to note that an earlier draft of "Death of the Poet" had included a line calling Pushkin the "bard of the Caucasus," but Lermontov excised it, one suspects out of a sense of territoriality.[19]

Lermontov's image of Pushkin as a passive figure is reinforced by the double use of the epithet *pevets,* a conventional cognomen for the passive elegiac hero (as in "Napoleon," cited above), to which Lermontov opposed the *active* hero. This complex of meanings is further associated with the idealized community of poets, Lermontov's mythologized conception of the Golden Age society as a lost Eden, an intimate environment of "peaceful comforts and openhearted friendship," hospitable to the elegiac *pevets.* Times have changed, Lermontov implies, and the poet raised in the supportive environment of consensual literary salons has no chance of surviving in the treacherous landscape of contemporary society. There is more than a tinge of nostalgic jealousy in this passage, especially in its final line, which describes Pushkin as "having understood people from an early age" ("s iunykh let postignuvshii liudei"). The subtle implication is that Pushkin, by succumbing to the flattery of society, squandered a "free and bold" poetic gift, one that Lermontov, as a struggling poet in a hostile landscape, would have eagerly treasured.

Lermontov's admiringly jealous and egocentric view of Pushkin provides an example of what Harold Bloom has called poetic influence "in the sense—amazing, agonizing, delighting—of *other poets,* as felt in the depths of the all but perfect solipsist, the potentially strong poet."[20] Lermontov's eagerness, which some might call perverse, to pound the nails into Pushkin's coffin becomes comprehensible when viewed in terms of his own passionate desire to take Pushkin's place as a "strong" or "active" poet, a poet-hero.[21]

Lermontov's desire to assume the mantle of poet-hero is especially evident in the patricidal urge to *silence* the great predecessor, expressed in "Death of the Poet." Lermontov seems overanxious to extinguish discourse *about* Pushkin: "What use now the sobbings, the useless choir of empty praise, the pitiful babble of justification?" ("K chemu teper' rydan'ia, / Pustykh pokhval nenuzhnyi chor, / I zhalkii lepet opravdan'ia"). On the surface these lines can be read as pure elegiac lament (What use is there in speaking about the poet, since he is now dead and gone? We cannot bring him back) or even subtle reproach (Where were you when he needed you?). I argue, however, that Lermontov's somewhat conventional grieving tone (the "what use?" trope is frequently encountered in the Russian popular genre of the *plach,* or funeral lament) is on at least one level rather disingenuous. The Russian interrogative idiom used in this passage is ambiguous: *K chemu?,* (what use? or to what end?). It is apparent from examining Lermontov's discourse of immortality that he saw a very great use and perceived a very clear end in discourse about the individual, at least when the individual in question was a worthy Romantic hero, such as Napoleon or Byron, or, most frequently, *himself.* Moreover, Lermontov's poem does not explicitly frame the uselessness of discourse about Pushkin in terms of a desire to bring the poet back. Against this background, Lermontov's ostensibly laudatory eulogy can be seen to conceal a hidden resentment born of the anxiety of influence. To be sure, Lermontov's poem *itself* speaks about Pushkin. And yet, as Vladimir Solov'ev observed in 1899, "with Lermontov, even when he speaks about someone else, one can feel that his thought, even from an enormous distance, is striving to return to himself."[22] Here Lermontov's reflexive discourse is refracted through the intervening medium of Lermontov's own stake in the game of cultural mythopoeisis: the crown of the archetypal poet-hero.

Whatever his mixed feelings regarding the value of speech *about* Pushkin, Lermontov is unequivocal when it comes to the speech *of* Pushkin. The last four lines of this first draft of "Death of the Poet" contain the clearest indication of Lermontov's anxious ambivalence about Pushkin's legacy. The grammatical predicates in these lines go about the business of silencing Pushkin with relentless finality. The "sounds" of Pushkin's "wondrous songs have fallen silent," "never to ring out again." (This last image is particularly revealing, since the poet's *songs*—that is, his poems—had most decidedly *not* fallen silent, a nuance that could not possibly have been lost on the mythopoetically aware Lermontov.) The poet's mouth has been closed with a "seal." Finally, the figure of the "gloomy and cramped" grave into which Lermontov crams Pushkin toward the end of the poem shrinks the great poet's image in a vividly physical sense.

The foregoing argument is by no means intended to imply that Lermontov was unmoved by Pushkin's poetry. On the contrary, the point is that he was moved all too greatly. While the younger poet's poem does not explicitly imagine the echoes of Pushkin's lyric sounds, the poem itself constitutes such an echo. The citations of and allusions to Pushkin's verse clearly betray Lermontov's appreciation of Pushkin's work. The imaginative process at work here *uses* Pushkinian material, while attempting to *suppress* Pushkin himself. Pushkin the man is wishfully consigned to the alien landscape of discourse that formed the mythological background for Lermontov's own struggle for heroic identity. This poem, masquerading as a mere eulogy of *Pushkin,* has as its less recognized agenda the preparation of a mythological role for *Lermontov* as the avenger of poetry and the poet. Thus, for the first time, Lermontov's lyric discourse succeeds in spanning the gap between established poetic discourse (with Pushkin as its founding center) and his own ambition.

This first draft of the poem was widely circulated in handwritten copies throughout Petersburg society, where liberal circles received it with great enthusiasm.[23] In the meantime, however, loyalists at court were circulating versions of the affair defending D'Anthès, saying that Pushkin had behaved improperly and that D'Anthès could not have acted otherwise. When Lermontov, already emboldened by the success of the first draft of "Death of the Poet," caught wind of this talk, he responded by adding to the poem a rage-filled sixteen-line coda directly addressing Nicholas's court and condemning it to eternal cultural damnation.[24] Here are the added lines (I include the last four lines of the original version in order to highlight the dynamic gesture described by the addition of the coda):

Замолкли звуки чудных песен,
Не раздаваться им опять:
Приют певца угрюм и тесен,
И на устах его печать.

    А вы, надменные потомки
Известной подлостью прославленных отцов,
Пятою рабскою поправшие обломки
Игрою счастия обиженных родов!
Вы, жадною толпой стоящие у трона,
Свободы, Гения и Славы палачи!
    Таитесь вы под сению закона,
    Пред вами суд и правда—всё молчи! . . .

Но есть и Божий суд, наперсники разврата!
Есть грозный суд: он ждет;
    Он недоступен звону злата,
И мысли и дела он знает наперед.
Тогда напрасно вы прибегните к злословию—
    Оно вам не поможет вновь,
И вы не смоете всей вашей черной кровью
    Поэта праведную кровь!

(2:85–86)

(The sounds of his wondrous songs have fallen silent,
Never to ring out again:
The bard's refuge is gloomy and close,
And on his lips there is a seal.

    But you, haughty descendants
Of fathers famous for their well-known baseness,
You fragments, trampled by the heel of slavery,
Of races condemned by the play of fortune!
You, executioners of Freedom, Genius and Glory,
Standing in a greedy mob by the throne!
    You hide beneath the canopy of the law,
    Before you justice and truth are silenced!

But there is Divine justice, confidants of depravity!
There is a terrible justice: it awaits:
    It is inaccessible to the ring of gold,
And it knows thoughts and deeds beforehand.

Then in vain will you resort to slander—
    It will not help you this time,
And with all of your black blood you will not wash away
    The poet's righteous blood!)

This expanded version circulated rapidly throughout Petersburg society, meeting with even greater success than the first draft.[25] The liberal gentry perceived Lermontov's voice as that of a hero, someone willing to say what they themselves could not. It was the final lines, constituting an act of brazen sociocultural defiance, more than the original poem itself, that marked Lermontov's progress toward his goal of casting *poetic discourse* as *heroic action.*

The two-stage composition of the poem is of great importance to its interpretation. A careful examination of the relation of the added lines to the original version illustrates the process by which Lermontov used the occasion of his great predecessor's death to forward his own mythology of self as poet-hero. Following the line "*I na ustakh ego pechat'* " (And on his lips there is a seal), the emphatically *final* image that concludes the first version of the poem, Lermontov's use of the contrastive Russian conjunction *a* to introduce the added coda marks a sharp break in tone and voice. The poem shifts from a *description* of the silencing of Pushkin's voice to a *manifestation* of Lermontov's newly discovered public voice, playing on the simultaneous presence of two semantic levels in the poem as a speech act. While the topic shifts from Pushkin to his tormentors, one semantic field (that of Pushkin as silenced poet) shifts from explicit to implicit. As we move into the coda, an *explicit* first proposition ("On Pushkin's lips there is a seal") is transformed into an *implicit* second proposition ("On *my* lips there is *not* a seal"), invoked by the heightened personal involvement of the speaker of the poem. Pushkin's silenced voice (which the poem's first part *describes*) is in this way supplanted by Lermontov's own living heroic voice (which the poem's coda *is*).

Thus, the addition of the coda brings about a semantic doubling. The lexical line of the poem (the *content* of the speech event: poetry, with Pushkin's as silenced speaker) continues onward: Pushkin is dead, and you deceitful courtiers are to blame. But another semantic line springs into being, a field constituting the *context* of the speech event (the poem, with Lermontov as speaker). When we follow this second, contextual line, the poem's performative gesture— Lermontov's entrance onto the cultural stage—comes into view. This second, contextual field of meaning opens up into Lermontov's self-conscious meditation on his own poetic career: Lermontov as a *doer* of poetry, the poem as an action. Whereas in the first version of the poem Lermontov is closer to the elegiac *pevets,* a witness to the cultural spectacle of the poet's death, in the coda he becomes an actor: Pushkin's avenger and successor. Accordingly, the poet's voice shifts modes from elegiac description to imprecatory direct address, as this new poet-hero is born into the world of his culture.

These lines, and their author's subsequent banishment to active military service in the Caucasus, elevated Lermontov overnight to the status of poet-hero among the cultural opposition. In the process, Lermontov gave voice to the emotional response of a significant portion of society to a highly conspicuous and controversial public event in culture. "Death of the Poet" expands the frame of the lyric to encompass the very notion of the poet's position in contemporary society. It frames Pushkin as the archetypal poet of its title, and as the victim of a mercenary and reactionary court, composed in large part of European imports, hostile not only to Pushkin in particular, but to poetry as a whole. The poem's enthusiastic reception is thus hardly surprising, given that the hereditary Russian gentry, sensitive to their displacement by foreigners and other parvenus at court and in culture at large, felt itself marginalized and stripped of its natural rights as aristocrats.[26] Lermontov thus transformed a shared cultural experience into an emotive speech act—a condemnation and a curse—and the speech act into a poem. These lines marked a symbolic rite of passage in Lermontov's perception of the mythopoetic process: the moment when, suddenly finding himself on center stage, he not only found his voice as a poet, but also his role as a cultural figure. Poetic discourse had succeeded in projecting the image of the poet into the contemporary cultural mythology as an active hero.

Having become the most famous living poet in Russia, the toast of literary St. Petersburg, Lermontov acquired a new authority, derived from several sources. His exile for "Death of the Poet" made him a political hero to the liberal gentry, but also broadened the appeal of his image beyond liberal gentry circles to the new Romantic readership. In the mythological system of Russian Romanticism, the Caucasus played a role analogous to the "Orient" in the corresponding European system. Exile to this dangerous exotic locale, especially as an *active* participant in battle, placed a real-life frame around Lermontov that coincided with the situation familiar to the Romantic imagination from works of fiction popular in Russia at the time. To the readers of such fiction, Lermontov was born into the cultural consciousness of his day as a literary hero come to life. What is more, in defining himself as the successor of Pushkin, for many the symbol of Russian cultural achievement, Lermontov acquired an image as poet-avenger that tapped into the reservoir of popular national meaning associated with his great predecessor.

The new frame around Lermontov resonated with the cultural situation of the time. As in his earlier speech act poems, this poetic utterance did not rely solely on an established literary code. Rather, its meaning now emerged in large part from its situation in a recognizable context. What is more, the contextual frame of the utterance had expanded to accommodate not only the response of the thinking, feeling individual to personal experience, but also a metacultural myth regarding the status of poetry and the poet.

Lermontov clearly saw the opportunity for fame presented by the enormous popularity of "Death of the Poet." When the official proceedings began against Lermontov for his poem (which Nicholas's chief censor Alexander Benckendorf called in a note to the tsar an example of "shameless freethinking"),[27] Lermontov's close friend Sviatoslav Raevsky was called to testify, inasmuch as he had been instrumental in distributing the poem. In his testimony Raevsky strives to show that Lermontov had intended no political "thoughts" in writing the poem, and that its success had nothing to do with politics and everything to do with the young poet's literary aspirations, which Raevsky implies were perfectly natural for a man of Lermontov's age and position. In explaining why he and Lermontov had circulated the poem, he gives a telling account of Lermontov's reaction to the success of the first version:

> This success gladdened me out of love for Lermontov, and it turned Lermontov's head, so to speak—because of his *desire for fame*. . . . Being indebted to Lermontov for friendship and favors, and seeing that *his joy was great from the realization that at the age of 22 he had become known to everyone,* I was pleased to listen to the salutations with which he was showered on account of the copies [of the poem].[28]

On 25 February 1837, as a punishment for his poem, Lermontov was officially transferred from Petersburg duty in the prestigious Hussar Regiment to active duty in the Caucasus with the Nizhgorod Dragoon Regiment. Lermontov's own enthusiasm at the prospect of forging a heroic reputation in battle is echoed in a letter to Raevsky written in early March while under house arrest. He can scarcely contain his excitement at the thought of returning to his beloved Caucasus, even under such ostensibly dire circumstances, and evokes no less a hero than Napoleon: "Farewell, my friend. I shall write you about the land of wonders—the East. I am comforted by the words of Napoleon: the great names are made in the Orient" (6:438). Despite his subsequent undercutting of these heroic-mythological images with a self-dismissive comment—"You see: nothing but idiocies" (*Vidish': vsë gluposti*), Lermontov's thrill at finally embarking on the Romantic adventure of his youthful dreams (and at further establishing a *name* for himself) shines through.

During the period of Lermontov's exile in the Caucasus the value of his cultural stock increased. Upon his return to Petersburg from this first exile at the end of January 1838, he was greeted with social and literary invitations from every quarter. Fortunately for his Romantic reputation, his behavior brought him new troubles, as his friend the poet Evdokiia Rostopchina recalled in an 1858 letter to Alexandre Dumas *père:*

> In 1838 he received permission to return to Petersburg, and since his talent, as well as his exile, had erected for him a pedestal, society rushed to receive him well.
>
> Several successes with the women, several episodes of lady-killing in the salons, provoked the men's enmity against him; a disagreement about the death of Pushkin was the reason for a clash between him and M. de Barante, the son of the French envoy; the disagreement led to a duel—the second between a Russian and a Frenchman in a very short time; several women let the cat out of the bag, and [the authorities] found out about the duel before it was to occur; in order to put an end to this international enmity, Lermontov was exiled to the Caucasus for the second time.[29]

Thus Lermontov's behavior subsequent to his first success reinforced the image his readers desired of him. Lermontov had acquired the fame he had sought. The location of his exile in the Caucasus and his active participation in warfare there coincided perfectly with the heroic dreams he had projected before his first exile. The fact of Lermontov's exile lent his words the context of heroic actuality that captured readers' imaginations. But if Lermontov's poetry had not changed in response to this sudden fame, if his writing had not progressed beyond the Romantic eclecticism of his youthful verse, he most certainly would not have retained the poetic reputation he enjoys today.

The success of "Death of the Poet," enhanced by Lermontov's exile, ignited a chain reaction of changes in the poet's poetic practice. Suddenly empowered with the ability to influence cultural values, Lermontov began to streamline radically his use of poetic language, exploiting the "unspoken" level of text, carefully preserving the possibility of myth in his every utterance and action, and framing the words and image of the poet in terms of the poet's (mythologized) context. In the four years between Pushkin's death and his own death in a duel, Lermontov wrote the poems upon which his reputation as a great Russian poet rests, as well as his one completed novel, *Hero of Our Time,* to which he owes his international fame. The revolution in Lermontov's poetics produced a second Lermontov, one that contained the former self within it as a substratum. And because Lermontov's earlier self had been shaped in conformity with the Romantic mythologies of his age, only the merest hint was necessary on his part to evoke the entire constellation of Romantic associations in the mind of the contemporary reader. Such a reader would have experienced the sensation of familiarity with every nuance of the history of this poet's soul, because this poet represented *the* Romantic hero.

As we have seen, Lermontov's aspirations for his poetic career had been double. He desired not only fame, which the events surrounding "Death of the Poet" had brought him, but also a type of lyric connection through poetry, a projection of his own unique "I" into discourse. He was to find out that fame posed certain obstacles to the projection of that "I" at the same time that it served as its prerequisite. Even in his early verse, of course, Lermontov had found poetic language lacking when it came to the expression of the inner world of the poet. Now, even though events had conspired to erect for him the cultural "pedestal" he had sought, the original problem of unique self-expression, far from being alleviated, was in fact worsened. As the *object* of cultural discourse, he was all the more subjected to the "slander" and "rumors" of society, which, even when positive, conspired to trap the poet in an iconic, static frame. Much of Lermontov's later poetry is shaped by his desire to reach beyond this frame (to the "sacred" realms of nature and the inner psyche) or else to break or appropriate it (through lyric gestures that narrativize or reframe the lyric I within the poet's own depiction of the landscape of culture). At the center of this new aesthetic lay Lermontov's discovery, in the very process that brought him fame, of the means by which the personality of the poet, poetic discourse, and the social discourse of culture could be brought into a relationship that projected the poet's individual voice into culture. Whereas in his early verse Lermontov had viewed the spiritual experience of the poet as an essence, whose expression, or transmission to the reader, was impeded by the alien materiality of preexisting poetic language, he now began to discover the poetic means to re-create himself in poetry, to navigate the signs of culture, to *live into* language.

To a large degree, Lermontov's accomplishments as a poet and his success on the stage of Russian culture depended (and continue to depend) on his development of a coherent mythology of the poet's place in culture. The themes of this mythology of the poet's place run through Lermontov's poetic discourse like threads, lending it continuity and historical concreteness, passion and authenticity. Lermontov wove together his ever-present twin desires to be both intimate lyric poet and famous Romantic hero by projecting his two careers as writer and warrior in such a way that each framed the other. As he resumed writing lyric poetry in 1837 after nearly five years, his voice acquired the pathos of the sensitive poet confronting mortal fate in perilous battle. His thoughts and feelings as a tender individual were framed by his status as an eyewitness to the death and savagery of war, a mode of experience he starkly privileges over the superficial life of Petersburg society.

The clearest example of Lermontov's contrasting military battle experience to the superficial life of high society is his long lyric poem, conventionally known as "Valerik" (1840). The title, given the poem by editors for convenience of reference, is Chechen for "river of death" and derives from a stream in the Caucasus where Lermontov participated in a Russian defeat of the native Chechens on 11 July 1840.[30] The poem gives a detailed account of the battle itself, including descriptions of the emotional states of the participants and a graphic death scene. But at least as remarkable as Lermontov's eyewitness testimony to the battle is the generic framework within which he sets his account. The poem is composed as an epistle addressed to a former love object of the lyric I, whom he claims he still cannot forget. The lyric I associates the woman in question with the most tender love of which he is capable and thus, inevitably, with the suffering he has experienced as a consequence of love's loss. This alienation of the speaker from the addressee both reflects Lermontov's personal sense of lost intimacy (echoing the loss of Golden Age poetic culture) and expresses his sense of separation from "our age," where "all feelings are merely temporary." Accordingly, although the lyric I mouths words indicating that he no longer loves her, it is apparent that she remains in his memory because of the strong emotional experience (love and suffering) she continues to represent. The lyric I's strong recollection of the woman is a source of continuing torment that he bears with a fatalistic resignation he associates simultaneously with Christian sacrifice and the Islamic notion of predestination.

The lyric I traces this turn of mind to his contact with Muslim peoples in the South, the nomadic lifestyle of the army, and, finally, firsthand experience of both nature and battle. In the passage forming the transition from these considerations to the description of the actual battle at Valerik, the lyric I strategically plays down the emotional impact of small military skirmishes. This strategy of understatement makes it very clear that such battles are commonplace for the officer, that he faces danger so frequently that it ceases to affect him. The last three lines of the transition heighten the effect by alluding ironically to the night life of St. Petersburg society, preparing a dramatic contrast between high society and the ensuing description of a battle so bloody that it is sure to make an impression on the addressee (and the reader):

Но в этих сшибках удалых
Забавы много, толку мало;
Прохладным вечером, бывало,
Мы любовалися на них,
Без кровожадного волненья,
Как на трагический балет;
За то видал я представленья,
Каких у вас на сцене нет . . .
(2:169)

(But in these bold clashes
There is much entertainment, but little sense;
At times, of a cold evening,
We took them in
Without bloodthirsty agitation,
As if at a tragic ballet;
Although I have seen performances
That you will not find on your stages . . .)

The battle scene matter-of-factly describes lethal hand-to-hand combat, heaps of bodies, and the death of a commander witnessed by his own shocked troops. The self-consciously neutral tone of the lyric I's testimony in painting the aftermath of the battle is almost journalistic (in the modern sense), as he emphasizes his own equanimity (once again, a consequence of the everyday nature of such experiences for the officer in war):

Но не нашел в душе моей
Я сожаленья, не печали.
Уже затихло всё; тела
Стащили вкучу; кровь текла
Струею дымной по каменьям,
Ее тяжелым испареньям
Был полон воздух.

(2:172)

(But I found in my soul
Neither sympathy, nor grief.
All had already fallen silent; the bodies
Were dragged together into a pile. Blood flowed
In a smoky stream upon the rocks,
Its heavy miasma
Filled the air.)

After the description of the battle and its aftermath, the poem concludes with a passage contrasting his battle experience with the life of polite society. The ostensibly self-dismissive tone here intentionally fails to veil the poet's derisive sarcasm:

Но я боюсь вам наскучить,
В забавах света вам смешны
Тревоги дикие войны;
Свой ум вы не привыкли мучить
Тяжелой думой о конце;
На вашем молодом лице
Следов заботы и печали
Не отыскать, и вы едва ли
Вблизи когда-нибудь видали,
Как умирают. Дай вам [Б]ог
И не видать иных тревог
Довольно есть. В самозабвеньи
Не лучше ль кончить жизни путь?
И беспробудным сном заснуть
С мечтой о близком пробужденьи?

Теперь прощайте: если вас
Мой безыскуственный рассказ

Развеселит, займет хоть малость,
Я буду счастлив. А не так?—
Простите мне его как шалость
И тихо молвите: чудак!
(2:173)

(But I fear that I will bore you,
Amid society's amusements the savage anguishes
Of war must seem ridiculous;
You are not accustomed to tormenting your mind
With heavy thought about the end;
On your young face
The traces of cares and grief
Cannot be found, and scarcely can you have
Seen sometime up close
How men die: there are enough
Of other cares. Is it not better to end
The path of life in self-oblivion?
And fall into unwaking sleep
With a dream of quick awakening?

And now farewell: if my artless story
Should give you cheer,
Amuse you, though it be a trifle,
I will be happy. And if not?
Forgive it me as you would a prank
And quietly say: odd fellow!)

Lermontov's dismissal of his own experience is, of course, a ploy. By assuming the stance of the indifferent, unruffled officer while describing a scene of enormous human destruction, Lermontov magnifies the attributes of courage and proud independence in his lyric hero. At the same time, by means of the mock-gallant tone he uses to compare his encounter with death to the empty glitter of society life, he succeeds in elevating himself vis-à-vis that same society by virtue of what he has witnessed. The stoic pathos of this position is heightened by his allusion, earlier in the poem, to his suffering born of his lost love for the addressee. By resigning himself to the double threats of love lost and violent death, the lyric I draws an implicit parallel between the two spheres. The life of the poet-hero in society is war, and society's coldness is the enemy.

This new lyric I, the poet as officer, stoically suppresses his emotional response to tragic fate. Lermontov builds this stoic facade around the sensitive, emotive poet of the early period. In doing so, however, he does not erase his young Romantic self. On the contrary, the sensitive youth within gains authority by the bravery embodied in the very act of repression. Repressed pathos turns out to be heightened pathos. At the same time Lermontov detaches himself from and rises above the *marchands de pathos et les faiseurs d'emphase* Auguste Barbier criticized (in lines Lermontov used as the epigraph to his 1839 lyric "Ne ver' sebe"), thus creating a new, superior *literary* self.

"Valerik" frames the poetic utterance in terms of its speaker's battle experience, thus lending poetry (and the poet) an authority that comes from a more sacred experiential realm than that of society (more sacred, because it involves a direct confrontation with the metaphysically privileged categories of "fate" and "death"). Conversely, Lermontov casts the act of lyric utterance as the defense of the poetic values of individual feeling, sacred experience, and sincerity, against the hostile onslaughts of an increasingly commercial, superficial society, indifferent to the pathos of individual fate—and to lyric poetry as the expression of that pathos. Thus, the battle metaphor is carried over into society, where poetry represents a sincere discourse of the soul, and the enemies of poetry are framed as the enemies of all that is sacred. By mythologizing (magnifying and reifying) the obstacles posed to the poet and poetry by the hostility of contemporary culture, Lermontov heroicizes the act of poetic self-expression as such. A startling consequence of this strategy is that it manages to revive the chivalric code of courtly love in an altered, Romantic form, by aligning two opposed impulses: that of tender feeling and that of relentless warfare. This uniquely Lermontovian paradox finds vivid expression in the 1838 lyric "Kinzhal" (Dagger). The poem apostrophizes the dagger of its title, which, in addition to symbolizing hardness in battle, here acquires more surprising associations with a most tender love. The cold steel weapon, forged in the Caucasus for the purposes of vengeance, has been given to the lyric I by a beautiful woman in a passionate moment of parting. The blood in which the personified dagger is usually bathed is replaced in this instance by a "bright tear, the pearl of suffering." The glitter of the steel is likened to the emotional vitality of the woman's eyes. In the poem's final stanza, the hardness of the dagger is metaphorically extended into the sphere of spiritual stoicism by the hero's vow to be "as hard in soul as you, as you, my friend of steel."

These paradoxical pairings—love/combat, tenderness/hardness, expressiveness/stoicism—reveal an aspect of Lermontov's Romantic aesthetic that can be called "Militant Sentimentalism." Like the Sentimentalism of Rousseau, Sterne and, in Russia, Nikolai Karamzin, Lermontov's worldview highly values sincerity and openness of feeling. It is easy to imagine Lermontov agreeing, up to a point, with Karamzin's 1793 assertion that the writer requires a "good, tender heart, if he wants to be the friend and favorite of our soul; if he wants his gifts to shine forth with undying light; if he wants to write for eternity and garner the blessings of the peoples."[31] The spirit of Karamzin, its concern with the "goodness" and "tenderness" of heart, by means of which the author is able to reach out in empathy to both his characters and readers, remains evident in Russian letters well into the 1820s, although in increasingly weakened form. Even as cultural pressures began to demand more of poetry—that it occupy itself with the culturally relevant issues of national identity, societal mores, philosophy, and spirituality—the Sentimental mood never completely disappeared. Instead, it became the cliché scaffold upon which any number of briefly popular epigones of the Golden Age, such as Vladimir Benediktov, hung their verse. Very few of them, however, were capable of even the bold, albeit somewhat strained formal originality of Benediktov. For most, as Wilhelm Kiukhel'beker had long complained, the formulae of Sentimental-elegiac verse remained an opaque cloak through which it was impossible to transmit any previously unexpressed thought or feeling, or any glimmer of individual personality.[32]

Lermontov, who remained fully aware of the inertia of elegiac poetic language, but at the same time fully intent on the expression of his own emotional experience, sought to give sentiment a new edge, the power to break through the curtain of conventional poetic language. So it happened that, by inhabiting the metaphoric spaces of battle and social opposition, of officer and exile, he found a way to turn emotional expression into an active, incisive *cri de guerre.* By mythologizing the repressive forces arrayed against emotionality as an enemy—the hostility and indifference of which reverberated with both sociopolitical repression in general and his own particular fate as an exile and front-line combatant—Lermontov created an image of himself as poet-hero that drew on the energy of the contemporary cultural situation. The eminently plausible (perhaps even true) story of his own social alienation and political persecution lent the emotions he expressed historical justification, and thus authority in a new cultural atmosphere where contemporary relevance was highly valued, while the image of his militant opposition to the hostility of the enemy acquired an aura of bravery. By framing poetry as an act of war, Lermontov raised its stakes: culture was a battlefield, and the poet was a warrior. The Sentimental poet had turned militant as a means of reestablishing his role in Russian culture.

In Lermontov's mature aesthetic mythology, poetic discourse serves as a bridge between privileged, sacred experience (that of the poet) and the pure souls trapped in the profanity of social existence (his sympathetic readers). The heroism of the poet consists in his confrontation of both the (sacred) mysteries of death and fate and the (profane) obstacles posed by the hostility of society and its ulterior discourses. The poet is thus doubly framed as hero, both in the perceptual act of experience and in the speech act of literary production. The crucial aspect of this double framing is that it creates a role of transcendent value for poetic vision at the same time that it participates in the very real field of cultural signs. With this revelation, Lermontov salvages what he saw (or chose to see) as the immanent value of lyric poetry by justifying it in terms of the contemporary cultural landscape.

To illustrate Lermontov's exploitation of self-framing to create the effect of intimacy with his readers, I now turn to one of his most well known and influential poems, the untitled lyric beginning "Vykhozhu odin ia na dorogu" (I go out alone on the road), which he wrote in 1841, less than a month before his death in a duel:

Выхожу один я на дорогу;
Сквозь туман кремнистый путь блестит.
Ночь тиха. Пустыня внемлет Богу,
И звезда с звездою говорит.

В небесах торжественно и чудно!
Спит земля в сиянье голубом . . .
Что же мне так больно и так трудно?
Жду ль чего? Жалею ли о чем?

Уж не жду от жизни ничего я,
И не жаль мне прошлого ничуть.
Я ищу свободы и покоя!
Я б хотел забыться и заснуть!

Но не тем холодным сном могилы . . .
Я б желал навеки так заснуть,
Чтоб в груди дремали жизни силы,
Чтоб, дыша, вздымалась тихо грудь,

Чтоб, всю ночь, весь день мой слух лелея,
Про любовь мне сладкий голос пел,
Надо мной чтоб, вечно зеленея,
Темный дуб склонялся и шумел.
(1841, 2:208–9)

(I go out alone on the road;
Through the mist shines the rocky path.
The night is quiet. The wilderness hearkens to God,
And star speaks with star.

The heavens are festive and full of marvels!
The earth sleeps in her azure glow . . .
Why do I feel such pain and difficulty?
Do I expect something? Is there something I regret?

Nothing more do I expect from life,
And the past I regret not a bit.
It is freedom and peace I seek!
I would forget myself and go to sleep!

But not that cold sleep of the grave do I desire . . .
I wish for such a sleep eternal
That life's forces might slumber in my breast,
That my breast might gently swell in breathing,

Such that, delighting my ear, all night, all day,
A sweet voice might sing to me of love,
And over me, greening for eternity,
A dark oak bend and rustle.)

In this poem Lermontov does not explicitly rely on his mythology of the militant poet-hero, and yet, for the knowledgeable reader of Lermontov, and in particular for his contemporaries, this mythology is implicitly present, framing the utterance, inhering in the poem's stoic refusal to indulge in the direct and plaintive discourse of elegiac lament. At the same time, Lermontov exploits the Romantic code of images as a frame, within which he manufactures the effect of a new lyric intimacy.

The poem opens with the image of a recognizable lyric hero, the Romantic wanderer, emerging into an equally recognizable Romantic landscape. Everything about the framed landscape suggests a space of potential, a space waiting to be filled by the lyric I: the poet is alone, no other living being is around; mist occludes the surroundings; the path leads off through the mist toward an unnamed destination; the night is quiet; the wilderness is conscious of God, but of no other being; the stars speak only with themselves, not with man. The imagery is peaceful, but, when read against the Romantic code, clearly suggestive of a mood of melancholy in its indifference to the lyric hero, its mists and distant stars. With these images, Lermontov quite consciously evokes the elegiac frame familiar to every Romantic reader. This frame brings with it a set of expectations: that this wanderer will now recount the unhappy experiences of his past, meditate on his lack of prospects in the future, or both. Lermontov shows his consciousness of these readerly expectations by anticipating them in the form of questions (at the end of stanza 2) assigned to an invisible interlocutor, who is congruent with a reader nourished on a diet of Romantic clichés. By referring to the conventional Romantic image of the hero, Lermontov draws the reader into the poem, engaging him in an intimate dialogue in the idiom of contemporary Romantic culture. At the same time, while relating the lyric I of this poem to the conventional hero, Lermontov makes it clear that the conventional Romantic expectations expressed in the questions are part of the framing of the poet from *without,* part of the cultural context of the Russian 1830s.

It is in the third stanza that Lermontov deviates from the external frame of the elegiac lyric hero, opening a new space, a frame within a frame, into which he can now project the "truer" image of the poet, one that reflects the poet's "genuine" inner world. This image is defined differentially with respect to the frame of conventional expectations manipulated by the poet in the first half of the poem. As the poem progresses, the reader is first engaged on the level of the contemporary cultural paradigm of the Romantic hero. From the standpoint of the lyric hero, the conventional image is inaccurate and constraining, and he rejects it for a less conventional one. While for Lermontov this move is an escape from an imposed conventional self, from the standpoint of the contemporary reader the conventional image appears a point of entry and its rejection draws the reader inward.

The lyric hero serves as a frame that both mediates between the outer and inner images of the hero and separates the two images, distinguishing the "real Lermontov" from the cultural model of the conventional Romantic hero, on which it nevertheless continues to feed. Thus, the positive image placed in the end of the poem—in fact substantially borrowed from a lyric by Heinrich Heine ("Der Tod, das ist die kühle Nacht . . .")[33]—seems to provide the contemporary Russian reader with privileged, intimate acquaintance with a real, live Russian Romantic hero, and has continued to present subsequent Russian readers with a real, live Russian poet, immortalized in discourse.[34] Through the negation of extant conventions, Lermontov creates the illusion of a positive, although not wholly finalizable presence.

One way to summarize Lermontov's contribution to the Russian poetic tradition would be to say that he introduced into lyric discourse the idea of the poet's personal stake in engaging in lyric discourse. This is no small matter. It would seem to go without saying that every poet must have a reason for writing poetry, whether it be a matter of value to the writer or value to culture. But to place this value so firmly at the center of one's poetics is to posit an utter transformation of the cultural potential of poetic discourse itself. Poetry becomes more than one discourse among many; it becomes a means, the only means, of envisioning the existence of the individual in an imperfect society and cosmos, a mythology for understanding (or creating) personal meanings. It is no doubt this sense of poetry's role in culture that Boris Pasternak had in mind when he wrote: "I dedicated *My Sister Life* not to the memory of Lermontov but to the poet himself as though he were living in our midst—to his spirit still effectual in our literature. What was he to me, you ask, in the summer of 1917? —The personification of creative adventure and discovery, the principle of everyday free poetical statement."[35]

In Lermontov's poetic world, the lyric word is charged with a compelling urgency. First and foremost, Lermontov desired to become a unique and meaningful node in the cultural web without allowing his individual identity to be subsumed into, and homogenized by, cultural conventions. In other words, he sought to be the hero of cultural discourse, simultaneously a passive object of desire and an active agent. This desire encountered a whole array of contemporary cultural forces: the potential for self-presentation offered by lyric poetry; the new possibilities for literary audiences; the cultural forces aligned against lyric discourse; the chilling atmosphere of political reaction. Against this background, Lermontov's search for an identity in poetic discourse could not be undertaken in isolation. Lermontov not only had to justify himself in poetry's traditional terms, he had to justify the role of the poet and his calling in the broader terms of contemporary culture at large.

When seen in this light, Lermontov's emergence from Pushkin's shadow becomes more understandable; we see how he succeeded as a public lyric poet where Pushkin failed.[36] Graced from the outset with a "free, bold gift," recognized and embraced at the age of fifteen by the self-contained society of Golden Age men of letters, Pushkin was provided with a beginning to his career that helped establish his proud credo of poetic independence: "The goal of poetry is poetry" (*Tsel' poezii—poeziia*).[37] As Pushkin matured, and the Golden Age society of poets disintegrated, he felt increasingly isolated and abused by uninformed and vicious critics (see, for example, his poem "The Poet and the Crowd" ["Poet i tolpa," 1828]). Nevertheless, perhaps because Pushkin's poetics had been so powerfully shaped by the sophisticated and insular socioliterary milieu from which he emerged, his perceptions of a hostile cultural landscape were never distilled into a single, focused mythology that placed the poet's unique and unchanging identity at the center of poetic practice. Pushkin's legendarily protean lyric hero seems somehow less concerned with establishing a fixed identity for himself than with the creative process itself (inspiration) and its concrete fruits (literary artifacts). The poet himself merges with the great poets of the past, freely exchanging identities, and participating in one great historical progression, external to the poet's "personality" and objectified in a line of literary texts. As Solov'ev observed, while Lermontov's attention is forever returning to himself, "Pushkin, even when speaking about himself, speaks as if about someone else."[38]

When we interrogate what is left of Lermontov, his literary legacy, posing the question, What is the goal of poetry? we receive a bundle of insistent answers: the defense of individual feeling; social criticism; the confrontation of death; the definition of fate; the examination of the problems of good and evil, the meaning of love, and the power of speech; and recognition of the divine. Thus Lermontov's poetry seeks to justify itself in social, philosophical, and even religious terms. It poses precisely the types of questions that not only concerned his cultural peers, but to varying degrees have always served as themes of lyric poetry. In this respect, apart from the particular views he holds (but rarely divulges) regarding these issues, he differs little from Pushkin, or any other poet of his or any age.

But Lermontov's obsession with selfhood, his constant refraction of all other issues through the prism of self, is what marks him as different from Pushkin and as a predecessor of the anguished poetics of self represented in the twentieth century by poets such as Blok and Mayakovsky. The question that gives birth to all others in Lermontov's work is, Who am I, and what is my place in all of this? It is a question to which he can give no final answer; and so his poems ask it over and over again, each time giving a different answer, none of them fully satisfying. Yet he goes on asking, and in the process becomes more and more present in his texts. The paradox in this is the very one that defines the notion of identity in the modern age: while one cannot give a final answer to the question "Who am I?" the urgency and manner of this self-questioning, which takes place in the flux of cultural signs, help define what makes one individual. If for Pushkin (arguably) identity was a process of continual kaleidoscopic discovery without seeming to search, for Lermontov it was an impassioned search for a unitary self, without hope of final discovery. Lermontov threw himself into this questioning and, like Hamlet, threw the entire reflexive dialogue onto the public stage. In doing so, he created a self that lives on in his texts, one that cannot be finalized, because the condition for its existence is that of perpetual search: each of its self-defining gestures differentiates it from the category into which the reader might try to force it. This lyric hero came into being (or, better, is continually coming into being) in the space between specific personal desires and specific cultural expectations—perhaps the only space where identity is possible—and it continues to flicker in these interstices, the delicate, ultimately indefinable flame of the individual human life in culture.

Stephen Moeller-Sally

0000; or, The Sign of the Subject in Gogol's Petersburg

NIKOLAI GOGOL came into being as an author under a name not his own. Having arrived in Petersburg in December 1828, he set about publishing "Hanz Kiukhel'garten," a derivative narrative poem in the romantic style, which appeared in June 1829 as the work of V. Alov. Such masks were not uncommon in Russian literary life at this time, nor is it surprising that a young man just arrived from the provinces and unsure of his vocation would want to take the precaution of hiding his identity.[1] The pseudonym provided a convenient screen from behind which Gogol could, and indeed would, escape: after the embarrassingly poor reception of his poem, Gogol bought up all the available copies and consigned both them and V. Alov to the fire. The fiasco of "Hanz" would dampen Gogol's literary ardor briefly, but he soon returned to writing and would generate several other surrogates during a fresh assault on the Petersburg literary scene in 1830–31. Almost every genre he essayed was accompanied by the creation of a new name: a chapter from his tale "The Terrible Boar" gave birth to the author P. Glechik, "Some Thoughts on Teaching Geography to Children" begot G. Ianov, and his first true literary success, *Evenings on a Farm Near Dikan'ka,* was populated by a hive of storytellers and tended by Gogol's stand-in, Rudyi Pan'ko, the garrulous Ukrainian beekeeper.[2]

Surely the oddest authorial designation Gogol chose at this time had to be "0000," the enigmatic pseudonym under which a chapter from his historical novel *The Hetman* appeared in early 1831. A widely cited hypothesis based on the testimony of Viktor Petrovich Gaevsky decodes the puzzle with the aid of Gogol's own name, interpreting the signature as the four "o"s found in Nik*o*lai G*o*g*o*l-Ian*o*vsky.[3] This solution has the comforting advantage of simplicity and directness, since it locates the signature quite literally within the author's name. However, it also obscures troubling ambiguities. Why should the four round figures necessarily be letters? Why not four zeroes instead of four o's? In fact, Gogol himself described the signature just this way in a letter to his mother. Reporting that he had sent her a "little book" in which an "article" of his had appeared, he informed her: "It is signed with four zeroes: *0000.*"[4] When critics have bothered to pause over this peculiar autograph, they have only gestured at its possible meaning. Here, for example, is Vladimir Nabokov's account: "The selection of the void and its multiplication for concealing his identity is very significant on Gogol's part."[5] Although he offers us more than a simple choice between letters or numbers, Nabokov nonetheless leaves the sense of the signature floating and obscured in a murky sea of possibilities.

My task in this paper is to plumb the significance of the four round figures Gogol used to identify himself at the end of 1830. In order to coax Gogol's signature into yielding a specific meaning, we might first reconsider the terms of Nabokov's aperçu. Nabokov seems most taken with how the multiple void *concealed* Gogol's identity. Perhaps he had in mind what Robert Maguire has called Gogol's "games of indirection, feint, and evasion"[6] and the consequent difficulty of grasping anything that could be definitively described as "Gogol's identity." Such a focus is not surprising for Nabokov, who expertly stage-managed his own elusive public persona (which, by the way, may also explain his reluctance to pursue the implications of Gogol's signature). However, if we succumb to Nabokov's defensive posturing, we cannot even begin to approach a solution to the riddle of "0000." Instead, we must assume that signature *reveals* something about Gogol's identity, indeed, something that would become obscured when he began to sign his works using his own name.

In order to unpack its meaning, I propose to examine "0000" in light of the multiple social causes and effects of the signature. After all, Gogol signed the void not as a joke in private correspondence, but as a public autograph appended to a literary text. In her provocative book *Signature Pieces,* Peggy Kamuf has called attention to the "conventional systems" that support the mode of writing we call a signature and has observed the dependency of social institutions on the process of identification accomplished by it.[7] Through an analysis of the literary signature in particular, she aims to remove the mask of convention from the act of signing and thus to reveal the frailty and ephemerality of the bond between the signature and "the subject named." The "disruptive implications" of the signature, she argues, inhere in the internal dividedness of the sign, "an always divisible limit" that is masked by institutions. Since the disruption of language and its normal functioning is a hallmark Gogolian trait, this insight can likely assist the interpretation of "0000." However, in pursuit of her deconstructive punchline, Kamuf passes over a crucial point: that is, the semiotic economies of modern social institutions themselves destabilize the link between the signature and "the subject named" by constituting the subject in diverse, and sometimes conflicting, ways. This, I believe, is the insight suggested by "0000," which we should read not as a mask Gogol used to conceal himself, but as his discovery about the nature of subjectivity in Petersburg, as a void he uncovered within his own name when he arrived in Russia's modern capital. Combining an analysis of his letters with readings of his Petersburg tales, this paper will show that the signature both distilled the trials and tribulations of Gogol's first two years in the capital and crystallized a crisis of subjectivity that he would work out at length in his mature fiction. In short, "0000" became for him a sign of the Petersburg subject.

COMMERCE

Gogol's "Chapter from a Historical Novel" appeared in a commercial literary publication, Baron Delvig's almanac, *Northern Flowers for 1831.* The signature "0000" thus marked a trace of its author's participation in Russia's rapidly developing profession of letters. If literary almanacs had provided the principal vehicle for Russian literature during the 1820s, by 1830 they were already in decline.[8] Pushkin, who had declared their leading position in literary affairs a scant four years earlier, now looked upon almanacs almost exclusively as an economic enterprise.[9] Even the novice Gogol seemed unimpressed with his publication, for at this time he was plying the literary trade mainly in order to supplement a paltry civil service income. "In salary I receive a mere trifle," he wrote to his mother in February 1830, "My entire earnings consist in the fact that I sometimes write or translate a little article for Messrs. Journalists" (10:166). And when he sent a copy of *Northern Flowers* home, he effectively disowned the "Chapter" with a trademark mystification: "The little book will be pleasant for you, since in it you will find an article of mine, which I wrote while at the Nezhin Gymnasium. I simply can't understand how it got there. The publishers say that they received it a long time ago with a letter from a stranger and that, if they had known it was mine, they wouldn't have placed it without asking me first, and so I ask you not to tell anyone that it is mine; keep it for yourself" (10:205–206). There is no evidence to support Gogol's dating of the text or his story about its mysterious submission to the almanac's editors.

Gogol's keenness to dissociate himself from the "Chapter" not only speaks of the pride that so often caused him to dismiss his latest work as outdated, but also reflects an ambivalence about the enterprise of literary commerce. Gogol had displayed an antagonistic attitude to the urban market economy from the moment he arrived in Petersburg. His first recorded impressions of the capital revolved almost exclusively around the cost of living: "I'll say also that Petersburg appears to me not at all as I thought; I imagined it to be much more beautiful, grander, and the rumors that others have spread about it are also false. To live here not entirely like a pig, that is to have cabbage soup and porridge once a day, is incomparably more expensive than we thought" (10:137). No doubt Gogol was softening up his mother for a handout, but the litany of prices for housing, food, clothes, and services contained in this letter also suggests an underlying connection between the importunities of the market and Gogol's disappointment with the capital. Before long he would also note the peculiar leveling effect of Petersburg life on the city's inhabitants: "In general every capital is characterized by its people, who impart to it the stamp of nationality, but Petersburg bears no character at all: foreigners who have moved here have accustomed themselves and are not at all like foreigners, and the Russians in their turn have foreignized [*ob"inostranilis'*] and become neither one nor the other" (10:139). The underlying connection between the undifferentiated mass of the urban population and the money economy has perhaps been best argued by the sociologist Georg Simmel. His essay "The Metropolis and Mental Life" demonstrates how the mental habits of the market—punctuality, calculability, exactness—affect the social forms of city life and pose a threat to individuality. "Money," he writes, "is concerned only with what is common to all, i.e., with the exchange value which reduces all quality and individuality to a purely quantitative level."[10] Against this background, we can discern in the reductive signature "0000" Gogol's ironic self-presentation as a commercial subject, *homo economicus.*[11]

The grip of the money economy on the capital serves as the pretext for the interweaving narrative strands of "Nevsky Prospect." In his opening encomium the narrator confirms its pervasive influence on Petersburg's inhabitants by distinguishing Nevsky as the only space in the city that has escaped its capacious embrace.

> Here is the only place where people do not show themselves out of necessity, where need and the mercantile interest that envelops all of Petersburg do not drive them. It seems, a person encountered on Nevsky Prospect is less of an egoist than in Morskaia, Gorokhovaia, Liteinaia, Meshchanskaia and other streets, where greed and selfishness and need are expressed on those who walk and those who fly along in carriages and droshkies. (3:9)

The narrator introduces the motor force of the story and defines the field of conflict through a logic of opposition.[12] If the market governs a space of coercion and necessity, which goad the residents of the capital and impress a legible stamp on them, then, as the narrator will reveal explicitly at the end of the tale, Nevsky delineates the realm of desire. But the desire that initiates the tale will ultimately be thwarted, and three narratives of deceit will emerge: beguiled by her beauty, the artist Piskarev believes a prostitute to be a virtuous maiden; deluded by his experience, Pirogov expects a German housewife to display a sexual desire equal to the appetite she shows for baubles and finery; and, finally, the narrator, who believed that there was nothing better than Nevsky Prospect, discovers in it a place of peril and sometimes tragedy. The root of deception, as we will see, is fed by the market economy.

A closer look at the beginning of "Nevsky Prospect" reveals that the disruptive force of the economy is already internalized in the style and substance of the narrator's discourse. His description of a generic day on the avenue belies his claim that Nevsky is free of mercantile interest.

> Let's begin with the earliest hours of the morning. . . . Then Nevsky Prospect is empty: hearty shopowners and their commission agents are still sleeping in their holland shirts, or they are soaping their noble cheek and drinking coffee; beggars gather at the doors of sweet shops, where a sleepy Ganymede, who had only the day before been darting about like a fly with chocolate, crawls out with a broom in hand, no tie, and flings to them stale pies and scraps. (3:10)

This juxtaposition of absent merchants and congregating scavengers figures Nevsky as an ontological threshold between the final annihilation of yesterday's refuse and the rosy anticipation of today's profits. Almost in spite of himself, it seems, the narrator confirms that the market stands as the ghostly origin of the allegedly free promenade he describes later.

> Here you will meet singular sidewhiskers let down underneath the tie with unusual and amazing art, velvet sidewhiskers, silken ones, sidewhiskers black like sable or coal, but, alas, belonging only to members of the foreign service. . . . Thousands of kinds of hats, dresses, sheer, multicolored kerchiefs that sometimes for two whole days sustain the affections of their owners will blind anyone on Nevsky Prospect. . . . And what ladies' sleeves you will meet on Nevsky Prospect! (3:12–13)

The satire of vanity and fickle human affections ventriloquized through the narrator's naively expressed wonder at the many things that can be seen on Nevsky is tied explicitly to a ballooning rhetoric of accumulation that resembles nothing if not a sales pitch. Gogol's generous use of metonymy contributes to this effect: it not only gives rise to an image of the city as fragmented and kaleidoscopic but also suggests a kind of economic relation to the body that is reinforced by the description of the "exhibition" that takes place on the avenue every day.

> One is showing off his foppish frock-coat with the best beaver, another a Greek beautiful nose, a third is *wearing* superb *sidewhiskers,* a fourth *a pair of pretty little eyes* and a surprising hat, a fifth a ring with a talisman on his foppish pinky, a sixth *a foot* in a charming little boot, a seventh a necktie arousing surprise, an eighth a moustache causing astonishment. (3:14; emphasis added)

Gogol's peculiar use of sidewhiskers, eyes, and a foot as direct objects of the verb "to wear" draws an equivalence between common commodities and the body. It is as if the market were the very force that animated the residents of Petersburg.

Piskarev's misadventure hinges on what might be described as the *anaesthetic* effect of the money economy. As a representative of the Petersburg artist, he cuts a parodic figure. The narrator lavishly describes the poverty, timidity, and grayness that characterize this type and expands particularly on the incongruous fact that, although his art relies on his eye, he is not particularly observant.

> [The Petersburg artist] never looks you straight in the eye; if he does look, then it is somehow vague and undefined; he does not pierce you with the eagle eye of an observer or with the falcon's eye of the cavalry officer. This happens because at one and the same time he sees both your features and the features of some plaster Hercules that stands in his room; or he imagines a picture of his own he is thinking about producing. (3:17–18)

With the turn of a brunette's head, this heightened, almost obsessive, aesthetic sensibility is drawn into a conflict with the commercialization of beauty and sexual desire. When Piskarev crosses the stranger's threshold, the space of her apartment reveals to him her professional calling. If she had been an ethereal beauty—a virtual goddess of love—out on the street, here she "was transformed into some kind of strange ambiguous being, where together with purity of soul she had lost everything feminine and repulsively appropriated the craftiness and insolence of a man and had already ceased to be that weak, that beautiful being so distinguished from us" (3:21). The ambiguity of the prostitute's gender metaphorically expresses the contamination of the aesthetic by the economic. As a representative of that peculiar class, "the Petersburg artist," Piskarev has no doubt engaged in some commercial art dealing, albeit ineptly. ("[Petersburg artists] are in general very timid," the narrator informs us, "a star or a thick epaulette brings them into such a state of confusion that they involuntarily lower the prices on their works" [3:17].) In the scene with the prostitute, however, Gogol makes clear that Piskarev internally resists the marriage of art and commerce and considers them incompatible sign systems. The disturbing effect of their coincidence is emphasized by the prostitute's smile: "[T]he beauty . . . smiled significantly, looking him straight in the eye. But this smile was full of some sort of pitiful insolence: it was so strange and suited her face just as an expression of piety suits a bribe-taker or an account book a poet" (3:21). This smile and answering gaze not only confirm the split in her own subjectivity, but also reveal the dividedness of Piskarev's. Just as Piskarev's aesthetic eye confounds her economically constituted being, so her economic gaze and expression of desire threatens his identity. And just as the prostitute's expression of desire disrupts her gender identity, so it renders Piskarev sexless too: in response he is "laughable and simple like a child" (*ditia*). The grammatically neuter "*ditia*" aptly expresses Piskarev's sexual enervation.

The ironic overtones of this scene become clear when we acknowledge that the prostitute is, in fact, a figure of the artist's predicament in a commercially driven society. She represents the subordination of beauty to economic gain. Piskarev is blind to this realization, yet his incomprehension derives not from the shock of the encounter, but rather from a faulty aesthetic philosophy. As Robert Maguire has recently explained, "for Gogol, the true subject [of art] is present from the beginning, but is veiled or hidden. The artist's job is not so much to call it to memory (*anamnesis* in Greek) as to bring it out of hiding—what the Greeks call *aletheia,* whose general meaning is 'truth,' but whose more literal sense is not letting lie concealed or forgotten (*lethe*)."[13] In light of this observation, we can see that Piskarev's confrontation with the economy feeds a negative aesthetic. His efforts to recapture the woman's idealized image through sleep and opium—provided, significantly, by a purveyor of veils—only obscure the reality of her being with successive layers of fantasy and thus lead him ever further from *aletheia.* Gogol structures the culmination of this an-aesthetic as an inversion of the Pygmalion myth. If Pygmalion's love for his art brought it to life, Piskarev's love for his fantasies of the prostitute drives him to desire her metamorphosis into art: "It would be better if you did not exist at all! if you did not live in the world, but were the creation of an inspired artist! I would not stray from the canvas, I would look at you endlessly and kiss you!" (3:29–30). The bankruptcy of Piskarev's aesthetic is shown in his last, desperate attempt to make reality conform to his fantasies. When the prostitute rejects both his proposal of marriage and his offer of a conjugal life of simplicity, hard work, and purity, Piskarev is forced to confront the complete separation of his ideals from reality. The distance between them can be overcome only in death. As we might expect, Piskarev's hand is as faulty as his eye: "A bloody razor languished on the floor. By his convulsively spread arms and his terribly distorted look it was possible to conclude that his hand had been *untrue* and that he suffered for a long time before his sinful soul left his body" (3:33; emphasis added).

If in Piskarev Gogol demonstrates that an aesthetic of purity is untenable in Petersburg, then through Pirogov's story he explores the opposite extreme: the complete surrender of art to the money economy. Pirogov himself is an avid reader of the *Northern Bee,* indiscriminately attends public lectures, and frequents the theater, where he can enjoy a good satirical verse comedy, but draws the line at vaudevilles. Though invested with a fair share of pretensions, Pirogov is not, as was Piskarev, interested in pursuing the true coin of culture. Rather, he uses cultural forms as a medium of social exchange, the only apparent goal of which is to move up the Table of Ranks and into a rich family. He loves to quote verses and discuss literature, but, like the money that drives the cultural market, he is indifferent to quality and individuality. For example, in his praise he does not discriminate among Bulgarin, Grech, and Pushkin, and displays an equal talent at reciting snatches of *Woe from Wit* and the joke about "how a cannon is one thing and a unicorn is another" (3:36).[14] In short, Pirogov exemplifies the consumer of the kind of low- to middlebrow culture that the market sustained in early nineteenth-century Russia.

To complement this image of the money economy's "ideal" reader, Gogol creates a figure of the commercial author. Pirogov's pursuit of the blonde he spots on Nevsky leads him to the merchant district of Petersburg and an encounter with two German tradesmen. Gogol gives them the names Schiller and Hoffmann: "Before him sat Schiller, not the Schiller who wrote *William Tell* and the *History of the Thirty Years' War*, but the well-known Schiller, the tinsmith on Meshchansky Street. Next to Schiller stood Hoffmann, not the writer Hoffmann, but the rather good cobbler from Ofitsersky Street, a great friend of Schiller" (3:37). By effectively transforming two of the best-known German authors of the early nineteenth century into tradesmen, Gogol emphasizes the leveling effect of literary commerce. And, as in the episode with Piskarev, the conflict between art and the economy finds expression in an image of sexual ambiguity. "Schiller sat, exhibiting his rather fat nose and raising his head up; and Hoffman held him by this nose with two fingers and brandished the blade of his cobbler's knife over its very surface" (3:37). Although Pirogov himself remains ignorant of the motivation for this scene because he knows no German, the narrator reveals it to the reader:

> I don't want, I don't need a nose! . . . Three pounds of tobacco go on my nose alone every month. And I pay in the Russian nasty store . . . 40 kopecks for every pound; that would be a ruble and twenty kopecks—that would be fourteen rubles forty kopecks. Do you hear, friend Hoffman? fourteen rubles forty kopecks on my nose alone. . . . It's robbery, I ask you, my friend Hoffman, isn't that so? (3:37)

The logic of financial calculation to which Schiller subjects his body not only constrains his activities (remember that as a rule he kisses his wife only twice a day), but drives him to the very edge of symbolic castration. He is prepared to sacrifice all sensual—and, therefore, aesthetic—pleasure to the profit motive. Through the character of Schiller, then, Gogol shows that the hyperrationality of the money economy is as destructive to art as the purely ideal aesthetic of Piskarev.

The images of the consumer-reader and the tradesman-writer can be incorporated into a larger parodic structure, for "Nevsky Prospect" is, in part, a self-parody, an ironic allegory of Gogol's earliest Petersburg experiences.[15] In the figure of Piskarev we have the idealistic young author of "Hanz

Kiukhel'garten," who was, if we are to believe Gogol's letters, smitten by a divine, angelic woman at about the time his poem failed. The rhetorical verve with which Gogol described his beloved strikingly anticipates Piskarev's thoughts: "I saw her . . . no, I will not name her . . . she is too exalted for any man, not only for me. I would call her an angel, but that expression is low and does not suit her. . . . It is a divinity, but lightly clothed in human passions. A face, whose striking brilliance is impressed on the heart in a moment; eyes which quickly pierce the soul. But not a single man can bear their radiance, which burns and passes through anything" (10:146). If we extend the association of Piskarev with the author of "Hanz Kiukhel'garten," further parallels unfold. Unbeknownst to the starry-eyed young artist, his companion (that is, his reader) had tastes that led in a completely different direction. He preferred a blonde to the artist's "divine" brunette; that is, he read the *Northern Bee,* one of two journals to pan Gogol's poem. The incompatibility of a pure aesthetic and the market economy drives the ideal artist (V. Alov) to his death. He is subsequently resurrected and newly incarnated as the commercial author, who identifies himself only with the indifferent, an-aesthetic sign of the money economy, 0000.

SUBSTITUTION

The fashion for pseudonyms in the early nineteenth century shaped the signature as a space of substitution. Readers constantly confronted the possibility that the sign identifying the author of a work in fact only pointed to another proper name, the "proper" origin of the text. David Kropf has recently argued that pseudonyms liberated the writer (the one who writes the text) from the author (the increasingly reified social subject constituted by the hermeneutic conventions of literary criticism and legal conventions such as censorship and copyright). They made "it possible for a writer to nurture the author's existence (in order, say, to increase sales), while simultaneously living separately from it so as to engage in different kinds of writing."[16] Or, as we have observed in Gogol's early literary efforts, pseudonyms could give writers the opportunity to conduct a diagnostic exercise in self-presentation and thus to seek out the optimum point of departure for their authorial selves. However, the practice of publishing under pseudonyms (or anonymously, for that matter) reflected a deep anxiety about the status of the creative individual within the modern social institution of authorship. The commercial, legal, and social forces applied to the literary signature bore with them the constant threat to the individual person: to use Kropf's terminology, where the author appeared, the writer began to disappear. Against this background, we can perceive in Gogol's signature of four zeroes an understanding of the wages of social subjectivity.

Compounding the impact of the economy and the institutions of literature on the young Gogol was the state bureaucracy. Before he made his way to Petersburg, Gogol had dreamed of making himself socially useful through a career in the civil service.[17] Not long after his arrival, however, he noted the dire effects the bureaucracy appeared to have on its officials: "There is an unusual quiet in [the capital], no spark of spirit in the people; it's all civil servants and functionaries, they all talk about their departments and colleges, everything is suppressed, everything is bogged down in the useless, petty labors in which their lives are fruitlessly spent" (10:139). Gogol resisted a career in the civil service for several months, but, when his literary aspirations fell into abeyance as a result of the bitter disappointment with "Hanz," he resigned himself to finding a place in the bureaucratic machine. The same characteristics that make the money economy hostile to individuality—punctuality, calculability, exactness—obtain also in the bureaucratic organization. As Max Weber phrased it: "The objective discharge of [bureaucratic] business primarily means a discharge of business according to *calculable rules* and 'without regard for persons.'"[18] Because bureaucracy privileges offices and functions over persons, signs of individual identity such as proper names, are subordinated to generic forms of identification like titles and honorifics. At the time Gogol signed "A Chapter from a Historical Novel" he was employed in the Department of Crown Lands at the lowest civil service rank, collegiate registrar. We might also suppose, then, that Gogol's experience of bureaucratic subjectivity intersects with the signature "0000."

The struggle to find a sense of self while enmeshed in the web of state bureaucracy forms a fundamental theme in "Diary of a Madman." On one level, the story can be construed as a typical instance of love impeded by social hierarchy: a poor government clerk, Aksenty Poprishchin, has fallen for his departmental director's daughter, who is, by virtue of her family status, hopelessly beyond his reach; the obstruction of his desire leads him to madness and eventual incarceration in an insane asylum. A familiar critique of social divisions can easily be elicited from this rudimentary plot, but Gogol directs the reader's attention elsewhere. As a first-person narrative (and, significantly, Gogol's only one), the story enacts a satire of social structures through a drama of self-fashioning. Poprishchin's diary details his attempts to find a valid form for his desire, or rather, to find a form for his self that will legitimate his desire.[19]

Poprishchin's desire is stymied and his subjectivity imperiled by his bureaucratic identity as titular councilor. Not only does it set him at a distance from the director's daughter that he desperately yearns to overcome, but, as the department head makes explicit when he calls Poprishchin on the carpet for stalking Sophie, his position defines him as worthless and empty: "What do you imagine yourself? You think that I don't know all your pranks? You're tailing after the director's daughter. Well, look at yourself and think only, what are you? You're *zero* and nothing more" (3:197–98; emphasis added). The department head puts Poprishchin in his place: neither the clerk's rank, nor age, nor economic position sanction his desire for the director's daughter. Indeed, he *is* the bureacratic equivalent of the number zero: he simply marks an available space without himself having any value.

The tension between Poprishchin's desire and his position takes the form of an acute status anxiety. The level of his insecurity can be measured, first of all, by the numerous allusions to his class identity. "Yes, I admit," he says, "if it weren't for the nobility of service, I would have left the department long ago" (3:194). By the conventions of the Table of Ranks, Poprishchin would have gained noble status already with his promotion to grade 12 (titular councilor was grade 9).[20] However, his claim to membership in the gentry is tenuous, for his position has neither past nor future that extends beyond himself: only beginning with the next rank higher, collegiate assessor, did civil servants become entitled to hereditary nobility. All the more reason, then, for Poprishchin, like many other of Gogol's status-conscious bureaucrats, to make frequent reference to himself as a nobleman (*dvorianin*). For example, he mentally defends himself against the department head's insult in just this way: "Do I come from some kind of *raznochintsy,* or tailors, or the children of noncommissioned officers? I am a nobleman" (3:198). Yet, while upholding the class status of his rank, which he uses to validate his amorous pretensions, Poprishchin must still struggle with the paradigmatics of his place, the ever-present possibility of substitution by any other titular councilor. In order to guard his individuality, Poprishchin develops a cultural identity that, he believes, sets him apart from the crowd. "I love to go to the theater. As soon as a half-kopeck appears in my pocket, there is no way you can stand not to go. But among our brother clerks there are such swine: he will decidedly not go to the theater, the peasant, even if you give him a ticket for free" (3:199). Through such judgments of his fellow clerks and his earnest attention to the literary style of the *Northern Bee,* Poprishchin endeavors to fashion a cultural self commensurate with his gentry status. In the end, his cultural pretensions are as laughable as his bureaucratic ambitions, since he dedicates himself to the earnest and discriminating evaluation of thoroughly lowbrow culture.

Most important for Poprishchin, however, is to differentiate his feelings for Sophie from the run-of-the-mill erotic impulse experienced by others. This need is evident already in the first entry, when he describes meeting a colleague on the street: "As soon as I saw him, I said to myself: aha! no, my dear, you're not going to the department, you're hurrying after the one running in front of you and looking at her little legs. What a rogue [*bestiia*], our brother the clerk" (3:194). Poprishchin's diary bears the traces of his efforts to raise his feelings above lust and to give them a form to suit the exalted object of his desire. First, the self-censoring refrain, "nothing, nothing . . . silence" punctuates his narrative with the suppression of his erotic fantasies. He also summons his culturally constituted self for assistance, for example in the entry for 4 October: "At home for the most part I lay on the bed. Then I copied out some very nice little verse: 'My love for one hour I did not see, and a whole year it seemed to me; My life is now a hated task, How can I live this life, I ask.' Must be Pushkin's work" (3:197).[21] Through the discipline of copying these pathetically sentimental lines—and by giving them no less than Pushkin's imprimatur—Poprishchin tries to redirect his tormenting physical desires into respectable, "poetic"emotions.

Although Poprishchin attempts to suppress it through self-censorship and cultural airs, the identity he shares with his fellow titular councilors asserts itself in the form of a symbolic substitution. The first intimation of this inverted sublimation comes at the end of the first diary entry, when Poprishchin follows the dog home: "I know this house, I said in myself (*sam v sebe*). This is the Zverkov house. It's enormous! What kind of people don't live there: so many cooks, so many Poles! and our brother clerks sit one on top of the other like dogs" (3:196). The associative bridge between clerks and dogs is constructed by the name of the house: the root of "Zverkov," *zver'*, means "wild animal." For Gogol, the origin of this symbolic substitution might have gone back as far as the early 1830s; he lived in Zverkov house while he was working in the civil service from the end of 1829 until May 1831.[22] The unusual phrasing "said in myself" suggests an incipient attempt on Poprishchin's part to distinguish his "true" internal self from any external similarity between himself and his brother clerks, or, dogs. In future entries, the dog will serve as the image that melds together those parts of Poprishchin's social subjectivity that he would prefer to suppress: animal appetites, promiscuous sociability, and low rank. With this in mind, we can read the canine correspondence between Madgie and Fidele as a field in which Poprishchin's ideal ego confronts his illegitimate desires.

As with his fellow clerks, Poprishchin strives to maintain a psychological distance from Madgie's letters by subjecting them to his rigorous cultural judgments. After beginning the first letter, he is pleasantly surprised by the dog's style: "The letter is written quite properly. The punctuation and even the letter *yat'* is everywhere in its place. After all, even our department head simply can't write like this, though he says he studied somewhere at the university" (3:202). But much as Poprishchin's exclamations of desire—"ay, ay, ay"—disrupt the surface of his own diary, Madgie appears unable to uphold the proper tone: she repeatedly slips into digressions about food. Poprishchin vigorously protests such "nonsense," but the correspondence subsequently takes a crucial turn that breaks down the distance between himself and the dogs. In an undated letter, which anticipates the subsequent chronological disorder of Poprishchin's diary, Madgie describes to Fidele the parade of suitors that has appeared outside her window with the coming of spring:

> I will reveal to you that I have many courtesans [*mnogo kurtizanov*]. I often look them over while sitting on the window sill. Ah, if you only knew what ugly mugs there are among them. Some ever so tasteless mongrel [*dvorniaga*]—awfully stupid, stupidity is written on his face—ever so importantly walks along the street and imagines that he is an ever so exalted personage and thinks that everyone is looking at him. Not in the least. (3:203)

Two words converge to reveal this passage as an allegorical moment of self-recognition. Both of them play on the idea of *dvor,* or court, and thus recall Poprishchin's frequent self-identifications as a nobleman (*dvorianin*). The unexpected "kurtizan" reveals the sexual impulse that lies behind Poprishchin's social and cultural pretensions: the "high" French borrowing refers not to one who pays court (which appears to be Madgie's meaning), but to a prostitute. Furthermore, in a situation familiar from "Nevsky Prospect," the creation of a highly unusual masculine form reverses the conventional gender roles associated with the courtesan. Here it is the females—Madgie and, allegorically, Sophie—with all the advantages of rank, wealth, and class on their side, who "keep" the males. The other part of this associative cluster further debases Poprishchin's self-image. A paronomastic transformation reveals the truth of Poprishchin's position: our "dvorianin" is, in fact, a "dvorniaga." He is no more exalted than any of his brother clerks; he does not have the breeding to aspire to Sophie's hand; the only court he can hope to attend is the courtyard (*dvor*) of Sophie's house.

It is at this moment, when Poprishchin's group identity has prevailed and rendered him a dog like any other, that he attempts to turn the perilous logic of substitution to his own advantage. If, as he discovers through the allegory of the dogs, his body and his physical desires cannot be distinguished from those of other clerks, what then differentiates the chamberlain who is engaged to Sophie from Poprishchin himself? "What of it that he's a chamberlain? After all, that's nothing more than a rank (*dostoinstvo*); not some sort of visible thing that you can take in your hands. After all, from the fact that he's a chamberlain a third eye isn't added to his forehead. After all, his nose isn't made of gold, but is just like mine, like anyone's; after all, he smells with it not eats, sneezes not coughs" (3:205–6). The pun here on the word "dostoinstvo," which means both "rank" and "worth," reinforces Poprishchin's discovery that, in terms of social identity, the body has no value. It is, we might say, the subject degree zero—the empty screen onto which the signs of subjectivity are projected. The indifference of the body, its ability to occupy any place in the social hierarchy, opens up the possibility for him to become the king of Spain. His own hollowed-out subjectivity forms a perfect fit with the empty space on the

Spanish throne. Thus, from the very principles of the bureaucratic system, Poprishchin wrests the aristocratic privilege not to coincide with himself.[23] The remainder of the narrative will show, however, that this freedom is available only in the realm of the imagination. Poprishchin's heroic efforts to sustain his new identity in the face of adversity only isolate him further from the society he desires, this time behind the walls of the insane asylum.

Poprishchin's accession to the Spanish throne is as much a conquest of time as of space. At the moment he declares his pretensions, the temporal sequence of the diary undergoes a radical shift: 8 December is followed by 43 April 2000. But we would be mistaken to consider the temporal disorder of subsequent entries merely as another symptom of Poprishchin's madness. Rather, his manipulation of the calendar reveals the link between time and subjectivity: in order for Poprishchin to become Ferdinand VIII, time must begin again. That no readily discernible coherence can be found in these entries does not undermine this point.[24] Whether he is awaiting the deputation in his apartment or being tortured by the "inquisitors," Poprishchin is never fully recognized as the king of Spain. Therefore, in hopes of finding the beginning of the temporal sequence that will lead to the throne, he must restart time with each entry. Indeed, his earliest attempts to create a self commensurate with his desires rely on the very same strategy. When the department head calls him a zero, Poprishchin retorts in his diary with a reference not only to his status as a nobleman, but also to the possibilities for the future: "Why, I, too, can reach the top. I'm only forty-two years old—such a time when, in reality, the service is only beginning"(3:198). With this herculean effort to wrench his biological clock into line with his aspirations, Poprishchin creates for himself a future that is unburdened by the past, an empty temporal space in which a new self can take shape. The manipulation of time returns us, finally, to the signature "0000." Poprishchin's model suggests the possibility of reading in Gogol's pseudonym not a name, but a date: the four zeroes marking the beginning of a new calendar year, and thus a new authorial identity. After the failure of "Hanz," Gogol was, like Poprishchin, seeking a future unburdened by the past. What better sign of a new beginning than zero?

FROM CREATION EX NIHILO TO CREATION METABOLLO

The opening of "A Chapter from a Historical Novel" begets its hero in medias res: "*Meanwhile* our wanderer crossed the border separating the Piriatin district from the Lubny."[25] The "wanderer," a Polish envoy named Lapchinsky, is roaming the Ukrainian countryside on a mission from his king to a "distant ally" known as the "Mirgorod colonel." As John Mersereau has neatly summarized, this fragment of Lapchinsky's journeys bears the unmistakable marks of Walter Scott's influence:

> a central figure travels on a dangerous mission; he encounters an enigmatic person who later is revealed to be someone of importance; the countryside is described through the eyes of the protagonist; there are auctorial digressions commenting on the changes between the past and present; a local legend is interpolated; the apparel of the people is detailed, the habitations fully described with emphasis on furnishings, decorations, utensils, weapons, arrangement.[26]

If Gogol hewed to the conventions of the fashionable historical novel, he nonetheless used them to articulate the creative interests that would shape his work over the next several years: the seeds of *Taras Bul'ba* can be found in the seventeenth-century Ukrainian setting; the legend of the Orthodox deacon who is fantastically avenged on a Polish *pan* anticipates the tales of *Evenings on a Farm Near Dikan'ka;* the detailed and sometimes quirky description of setting would mature into a characteristic Gogolian trait. Gogol bound these various pieces together with a recurrent figure: as in the beginning of the narrative, every transition is accomplished via an empty or undifferentiated space. Perhaps the most striking of these moments occurs at the end of the "Chapter," when the old man Lapchinsky met while lost in the forest complains of his poor memory: "So who is it, sir, . . . you're going to see? With old age my head is like a bucket full of holes: no matter how much water you pour into it, it's always empty."[27] Having baited the envoy into repeating the name of the Mirgorod colonel, the peasant reveals himself to be the very man. So the chapter concludes as it began, with a new persona suddenly conjured in an empty space.

Set against its signature, the "Chapter" itself appears as a conjuring, or creation ex nihilo. "0000" presents to the reader the same kind of enigma that challenged Lapchinsky and suggests that we might interpret Gogol's text as an ironic allegory of the reader's experience during the early 1830s, when the vogue for pseudonyms was at its height. After all, it describes an encounter between an auditor and an anonymous storyteller, whose narrative is framed by the contemplation and then disclosure of his mysterious personality. What is more, Gogol planted in the "Chapter" a clue to his own identity. He christened the Mirgorod colonel Glechik, a name he used to sign his first publication of 1831, an excerpt from "The Terrible Boar." Through Lapchinsky's musings over his mission, then, Gogol can be seen to ventriloquize a hypothetical reader's reaction to this earlier tale: "It was the first time he was to fulfill such a mission: to ride, God knows where, into the unpopulated steppe of Ukraine! and who was this Glechik? . . . He had not been told anything satisfactory either about his character, or about his power; what connections did he have and with whom?"[28] Thus, when the anonymous peasant finally reveals himself as Glechik, the Mirgorod colonel, Gogol effectively announces that the author of the "Chapter" and the author of "The Terrible Boar" are one and the same.[29] However, this double disclosure is more a provocation than a solution to the riddle of the author's identity. Like Lapchinsky, the reader is left with sneaking suspicions: "And his eyes fixed motionless on his host, as if wishing to be assured of the falseness of what his ear had caught."[30]

Perhaps more than any other of Gogol's tales, "The Nose" shows that the mutability granted to the authorial subject by the powers of the literary pseudonym was, in fact, emblematic of the Petersburg subject in general. It strikingly dramatizes the power of Petersburg's constituent sign systems—the bureaucracy, the economy, cultural institutions—to generate subjectivity ex nihilo and "without regard to persons." The "unusually strange occurrence" recounted in the first part of the tale, the barber Ivan Iakovlevich's discovery of a nose in his breakfast roll, anticipates the metamorphosis of that same body part into a full-fledged member of Petersburg society. What would otherwise be only dead, inert matter—indeed, only the merest fraction of a body—gains the integrity of a subject when it enters into the capital's sign systems. Even Kovalev cannot get past the signs of subjectivity when he confronts his own nose in the Kazan' Cathedral.

> "How should I approach him?" thought Kovalev, "By all accounts, by his uniform and his hat, it is evident that he is a state councillor. The devil only knows how to do it!" . . .
>
> "Sir . . . ," said Kovalev, internally compelling himself to take courage, "Sir . . ." (3:55)

Despite his surprise and indignation, Kovalev resolves to approach the nose as a superior, with all the attendant honorifics, tact, and indirection required of such a conversation. Thus acknowledging the rank signified by the uniform and hat, he *himself* confers subjectivity on the nose and validates its claim to autonomy. Kovalev's own reactions explain why the others in the cathedral do not respond to the nose with surprise or alarm: no one looks beyond the signs of subjectivity.

The interlocking layers of "The Nose" emerged gradually. The initial inspiration occurred in 1832, when Gogol roughed out the opening scene, evidently under the strong influence of the "noseological themes" prevalent in contemporary literature.[31] It was not until 1833–34, however, that Gogol wrote the first full draft, which included the nose's adventures abroad in Petersburg and Kovalev's hapless attempts to recover it. The metaliterary stratum of the story, which has occupied the most perceptive of its recent critics,[32] was brought into relief only when "The Nose" took on its final form in early 1835. At this time, the Russian cultural elite were thoroughly preoccupied with the journal *Library for Reading*, which had burst onto the literary scene the previous year and, thanks to Osip Senkovsky's unscrupulous editorial practices and pandering to the lowest possible taste, quickly realized all the worst fears about literary commerce.[33] Anxiety over the *Library* grew steadily along with its readership. Members of the literary "aristocracy" soon began in earnest to fear its deleterious impact on the quality of literary life. Among the journals that were undertaken to combat this "elephant among petty quadrupeds" was the *Moscow Observer.*[34] The opportunity to join the *Moscow Observer* in its struggle against Senkovsky seems to have inspired Gogol to return to "The Nose," which he had not worked on for at least four months, perhaps even longer. Evidently, he now saw in it an original contribution to the debate over the state of contemporary letters. "I can't give you anything from *Evenings,*" Gogol wrote to Mikhail Pogodin, a friend and collaborator on the journal, in February 1835, "because *Evenings* is coming out in a few days. But for *M[oscow] O[bserver]* I am writing *a special tale*" (10:352; emphasis added).[35]

How to reconcile spiritual, or intellectual, values with material values? This was the question posed by Stepan Shevyrev's lead article, "Literature and Commerce," in the first issue of the *Moscow Observer.* In a doggedly materialist survey of the contemporary scene, Shevyrev laid the blame for the decline of letters at the feet of the literary "capitalists." He presented a world in which literature had acquired the easy liquidity and exchangeability of money: "*The Library for Reading* is simply a bundle of banknotes turned into articles. . . . There goes a writer in a new sleigh: you think that's a sleigh. No, that is an article from *The Library for Reading* that has taken the form of a sleigh."[36] There remained only one refuge from this commercial assault—poetry. "In vain does the bookseller pour before the Poet's eyes jingling and gleaming ten-ruble pieces—his eyes will not light up with inspiration, Phoebus does not heed the ring of metal."[37] However, as Shevyrev himself admitted, in the commercial environment true poetry did not get much press. The article closed with the timidly expressed hope that, with time and education, the reading public would eventually tire of lifeless and false prose and demand of their writers something more.

If we compare the various redactions of "The Nose," it becomes clear that Gogol took up the terms of Shevyrev's essay in his final revisions.[38] Through certain small but significant alterations, he interpolated new layers of meaning that specifically responded to the ongoing debate. Naturally enough, Gogol revised the scene in the newspaper office. Among the changes was an elaboration of the clerk's reasons for refusing Kovalev's announcement about the loss of his nose:

> "And in what way is this affair absurd?" [asked Kovalev.] "There is nothing of that sort here."

> "So it might seem to you that there isn't. But last week we had the same sort of episode. A civil servant came in the very same way you did just now, he brought a note, by my reckoning the money came to 2 rubles and 73 kopecks, and the whole announcement consisted in the fact that a black poodle had run away. What is there to that, you'd think? Well, it turned out a pasquinade: this poodle was a treasurer, I don't remember from which office."

The story of a black poodle metamorphosing into a man brings to mind the figure of Mephistopheles, as it must have done for Gogol's contemporary readers. In Goethe's play, Mephistopheles makes his appearance as if in response to a conversation between Faust and his assistant Wagner about the relative merits of physical experience of the world and abstract knowledge. The pedantic Wagner exclusively favors the pleasures of the mind:

> One quickly gets his fill of seeing woods and fields,
> and I shall never envy any bird its wings.
> How different is the way the pleasures of the mind
> transport us from book to book, from page to page!
> Then winter nights are pleasant and congenial,
> a vital happiness gives warmth to your whole being,
> and if you do unroll some precious manuscript
> celestial joy is yours on earth.[39]

Faust, on the other hand, is not so complacent:

> You know only one driving force,
> and may you never seek to know the other!
> Two souls, alas! reside within my breast,
> and each is eager for a separation:
> in throes of coarse desire, one grips
> the earth with all its senses;
> the other struggles from the dust
> to rise to high ancestral spheres.[40]

This exchange, which Gogol had at one time read in Dmitry Venevitinov's translation,[41] deftly frames the complexities of the Russian literary scene as a Faustian predicament. The cozy, familiar, and autonomous world of the literary "aristocracy" was giving way to a struggle between material and intellectual desires in the public realm of literary commerce. Thus unraveled, the allusion to *Faust* suggests an encoded polemic with the program of the *Moscow Observer.* Against Shevyrev's Wagner-like desire to retreat to the refuge of "pure" poetry and scholarship while the gradual improvement of the reading public takes place, Gogol asserts the desirability of a Faustian striving to comprehend contradictory impulses.

In this context, Mephistopheles aptly figures the role of commercial literary periodicals. On the pretense of enabling Faust to extend his knowledge and experience of the world, Mephistopheles in fact plots to lull him into a state of contentment through material pleasures and so to win his soul. Like Mephistopheles, the *Library for Reading* and the *Northern Bee* represented the material principle in literary life. Not only did they subordinate the quality of writing to financial gain; they also cultivated in their public a demand that was not so much intellectual as it was physical. Gogol himself noted this about the readers of "The Son of the Fatherland": "These readers and subscribers were respectable and elderly people living in the provinces for whom having something to read is just as essential as napping for an hour after dinner or shaving twice a week" (8:164). (Note, by the way, that shaving and napping are both prominent activities in "The Nose.") In other words, under the influence of commercial journalism reading was becoming just another form of consumption, an idea the allusion to Mephistopheles also insinuates through a paronomastic association. While the metamorphosis of poodle into man in Gogol's story takes place via the newspaper—perhaps Bulgarin's *Northern Bee* (*Pchelka*)—in *Faust* it occurs behind a stove (*pechka*). The parallel between the oven and the newspaper puts into play two related metaphors: it equates reading with eating and bread with commercial literature. Shevyrev had appealed to this same cluster of images in his own essay. Complaining of the prolix style that reigned at this time, he remarked: "From such a style the article grows, the printer's sheets grow fat, and the book itself rises like a roll. . . . Forgive me that my simile smells of the bakery; but it fully describes my thought."[42]

The *Faust* subtext, which embraces the problems of literary commerce, the tension between the spiritual and the material, and the image of bread, ultimately leads us back to the first appearance of the nose.

> Ivan Iakovlevich out of politeness put on a frock coat over his shirt and, having seated himself at the table, poured some salt, prepared two onions, took a knife in hand and, making a significant face, set to cutting the bread. Having cut the bread into two halves, he looked into the middle and to his surprise saw something white. Ivan Iakovlevich poked carefully with his knife and pinched with his finger: "Something solid?" [*Plotnoe?*] he said to himself, "what could it be?" He stuck in his fingers and pulled out—a nose! (3:49–50)

The donning of a "ritual" garment, the high seriousness with which the barber addresses his meal, the breaking of bread, and, finally, the emergence from it of flesh all betoken the Christian sacrament of the Eucharist and transform the barber's breakfast into a mock ritual of transubstantiation—creation metabollo.[43] Gogol, in fact, strengthened this association in the final revisions of the text, adding the word "plotnoe," which has as its root *plot'*, or flesh.[44] The reference here, reinforced by the fact that the action takes place on the Feast of the Annunciation, is to the quintessential reconciliation of the material and the spiritual: the incarnation of Christ. If we recall from the example of Shevyrev's article that the printed (*pechatannoe*) and the baked (*pechenoe*) were freely exchanged in the minds of Russia's writers at this time, the appearance of a nose in a breakfast roll would seem to signify something about Gogol's story itself. Indeed, through the barber's bewilderment Gogol anticipates his readers' reaction to the appearance of "The Nose" amid their usual literary fare; to paraphrase Ivan Iakovlevich: "Prose is a baked thing, but "The Nose" is not at all" (3:50). In offering up a modern variation of the evangelist John's "word made flesh," Gogol announces his own story as the solution to the seemingly irreconcilable difficulties of the current literary situation. To Shevyrev's complaint that contemporary prose was lifeless and false Gogol responds with a Faustian creative achievement that synthesized both material and spiritual values; that is, it endowed prose with the artistic value of poetry.

"GOGOL"

In 1835 Gogol began regularly to don the mantle of his own name.[45] With the publication of *Mirgorod,* "the continuation of *Evenings on a Farm Near Dikan'ka,*" he at last peeked out from behind the mask of Rudyi Pan'ko for all to see. The almost simultaneous appearance of *Arabesques,* which incorporated his early prose pieces including "A Chapter from a Historical Novel," solved the various riddles of his debut. By the end of the year, Gogol had not just arrived, he had all but taken over. In the first extended treatment of his work, Vissarion Belinsky placed Gogol at the head of Russian literature.[46] No doubt it was this newly acquired prominence that motivated Gogol to make his first programmatic statement about literature. Whereas "The Nose" devoted attention to the reconciliation of spiritual and material values in literature, "On the Movement of Periodical Literature in 1834 and 1835" focuses on the question of integrity. Gogol complained about how current literary practices seemed to isolate Russian literature both from its European counterparts and, more important, from its own past: "Almost never do the names of Derzhavin, Lomonosov, Fonvizin, Bogdanovich, Batiushkov stand on the pages of periodicals. . . . Never have they been brought into comparison with the current epoch and so our epoch seems cut off from its roots, as if it had no beginning whatsoever, as if previous history does not exist for us" (8:174). The key to a literature of integrity was, according to Gogol, an institution of authorship with integrity. Five years earlier, when making his debut as a prose writer, Gogol had reveled in the mobility of the literary masquerade; he had taken full advantage of the opportunity to create both literary works and authorial selves ex nihilo. Now, however, he took Osip Senkovsky to task for the very same behavior: "Mr. Senkovsky appears in his own journal as a critic, a storyteller, a scholar, a satirist, a herald of news, etc. etc., he appears in the guise of Brambeus, Morozov, Tiutiundzhu-Oglu,

A. Belkin, and finally in his own guise. . . . [H]e never cares about what he says and in the next article no longer remembers at all what he had written in the previous one" (8:159–160). Gogol found it necessary to reject a fluid authorial subjectivity because authorship had finally become for him a vocation.

It would not be long, however, before Gogol would feel the pinch of his established vocation. The deaths of Pushkin in 1837 and of Lermontov in 1841 concentrated the entire weight of Russian readers' hopes on his shoulders. He acknowledged the burden of these expectations in a lyrical flight that burst through the fabric of the last chapter of *Dead Souls:* "Russia! What wouldst thou of me, then? What incomprehensible bond is there between us? Wherefore dost thou gaze at me thus, and wherefore has all that is in thee and of thee turned its eyes, filled with such expectancy, upon me?"[47] Although the interrogative mode points to the future of the novel, distinct tremors of anxiety nonetheless filter through this apostrophe. What the conclusion of *Dead Souls* frames in a major-epic key, "The Overcoat"—a text from the same period—treats in a minor-ironic key. Its hero, the lowly copy clerk Akaky Akakievich, emblematizes the perils of a subjectivity that is invested entirely in writing. What begins as a vocation ends in a solipsism so complete that it erases not only the world, but the writer.

> It would be too little to say that he served zealously, no, he served with love. There, in his copying, his own sort of diverse and pleasant world appeared to him. Delight would express itself on his face; certain letters were his favorites, such that when he reached them, he was beside himself; he would chuckle and wink and help them along with his lips, so it seemed that in his face you could read every letter that his pen traced out. (3:144)

The mirror reflection of the letters in Akaky Akakievich's face suggests not only a mutually constitutive relationship between writer and writing—as we have seen in the example of Gogol's debut, this in itself was not a discovery for Gogol—but also an emptiness and stasis that are the product of endless repetition and reproduction. Perhaps the most significant detail in this regard is Akaky Akakievich's failure to do so little as change first-person forms in a text to the third-person. It speaks of a textually grounded identity so all-encompassing as to prevent the possibility of improvising a new self.

The struggles of Gogol's last decade resulted in part from the realization of Gogol's anxiety of authorship. The debates aroused by the first volume of *Dead Souls* polarized Russian intellectuals, who both further elevated and further objectified his status as an author.[48] The novel's success only intensified the expectant gaze of the reading public as they now awaited the second volume. Paradoxically, at the very moment Gogol seems to have most completely fulfilled his vocation, he had already became convinced of the need for a new persona. His efforts to answer this need put him on a collision course with the Russian public. In the foreword to the second edition of *Dead Souls,* released in 1846, Gogol took the astonishing step of inviting his readers to collaborate with him in the fashioning of his new authorial self (6:587–90). However, the fiasco of *Selected Passages from Correspondence with Friends* a year later starkly pointed out how far Gogol's imagined audience and his real audience had diverged. Nor could it have impressed upon him more deeply that he had failed to jar himself loose from the previous authorial incarnation that was lodged in the minds of his readers. This quandary would generate the terrible silence of the last five years of his life: his creative design compelled him to find a new persona, yet his obligations to his public would not allow it. Gogol had become trapped in his own name.

Notes

MONIKA GREENLEAF AND STEPHEN MOELLER-SALLY, "INTRODUCTION"

1. On the "romance of the classical" during Russia's Golden Age, see Monika Greenleaf, *Pushkin and Romantic Fashion: Fragment, Elegy, Orient, Irony* (Stanford: Stanford University Press, 1994), 29–36, 54–85.

2. Boris Gasparov, Robert Hughes, and Irina Paperno, eds., *The Cultural Mythologies of Russian Modernism: From the Golden Age to the Silver Age,* California Slavic Studies, vol. 15 (Berkeley and Los Angeles: University of California Press, 1992). Concerning the retrospective application of the phrase "Golden Age" see Boris Gasparov, "The 'Golden Age' and Its Role in the Cultural Mythology of Russian Modernism," in *Cultural Mythologies.*

3. The importance of print culture—particularly the novel and the newspaper—for the spread of linguistic nationalism has been argued by Benedict Anderson, *Imagined Communities: Reflections on the Origin and Spread of Nationalism,* rev. ed. (London: Verso, 1991), 67–82.

4. Johann Gottfried Herder, *Briefe zur Beförderung der Humanität,* in his *Sämtliche Werke* (Berlin: Bernhard Suphan, 1877–1913), 17:151.

5. See Liah Greenfeld's discussion of the transmission of cultural leadership in *Nationalism: Five Roads to Modernity* (Cambridge: Harvard University Press, 1992), 99–100.

6. Richard S. Wortman, *Scenarios of Power: Myth and Ceremony in Russian Monarchy* (Princeton: Princeton University Press, 1995), 1:13. We should note, however, that the sixteenth-century "Tale of the Vladimir Princes" traces the lineage of the Muscovite grand princes to Prus, a mythical brother of Augustus Caesar. See "Skazanie o kniaz'iakh vladimirskikh," in *Pamiatniki literatury drevnei Rusi. Konets XV—pervaia polovina XVI veka,* ed. L. A. Dmitriev and D. S. Likhachev (Moscow: Khudozhestvennaia literatura, 1984), 422–35. We are grateful to William Mills Todd III for bringing this precedent to our attention.

7. Stephen Lessing Baehr, *The Paradise Myth in Eighteenth-Century Russia: Utopian Patterns in Early Secular Russian Literature and Culture* (Stanford: Stanford University Press, 1991), 14–16, 41–68.

8. Wortman, *Scenarios of Power*, 82.

9. See David Bethea's synopsis of the *eques* tradition, in "Remarks on the Horse as Space-Time Image from the Golden to Silver Ages of Russian Literature," in *Cultural Mythologies*, 110–17; as well as Karen Rasmussen, "Catherine II and the Image of Peter I," *Slavic Review* 1 (1978): 60.

10. See V. M. Zhivov, "Gosudarstvennyi mif v epokhu Prosveshcheniia i ego razrushenie v Rossii kontsa XVIII veka," in *Vek Prosveshcheniia; Rossiia i Frantsiia, Vipperovskie chteniia* (Moscow, 1989); and Andrew Kahn, "Readings of Imperial Rome from Lomonosov to Pushkin," *Slavic Review* 4 (1993): 745–68.

11. Baehr, *Paradise Myth*, 23; see also Brian Baer, "Towards a Chronotope of the Nation: Derzhavin's 'Zhizn' Zvanskaia,'" in "National Figures: Writng the Modern Nation" (Ph.D. diss., Yale University, forthcoming).

12. Letters to A. A. Bestuzhev and A. A. Del'vig, beginning of June 1825, from Mikhailovskoe. In *Pushkin on Literature*, ed. and trans. Tatiana Wolff (Stanford: Stanford University Press, 1986), 147, 149.

13. The impulse that prompted the seventeen-year-old Pushkin to elude Derzhavin's embrace at the famous passing-of-the-baton ceremony at Alexander's Lycée expressed itself in his and later historians' ambivalent assessments of the Catherine epoch's legacy. This topic has recently begun to be discussed in print (see, for example, James Cracraft, "Great Catherine," *Slavic Review* [Spring1993]: 107–15) and will receive more extensive consideration in a future forum.

14. On displacement and absorption, see Stephen J. Greenblatt, *Renaissance Self-Fashioning: From More to Shakespeare* (Chicago: University of Chicago Press, 1980), 7–8.

15. See Terry Castle's synthesizing discussion in *Masquerade and Civilization: The Carnivalesque in Eighteenth-Century English Culture and Fiction* (Stanford: Stanford University Press, 1986). Furthermore, Russian Structuralists have long been sensitive to the semiotics of court and aristocratic life in the post-Petrine period. See "The Theater and Theatricality as Components of Early Nineteenth-Century Culture" and other classic articles by Iurii Lotman and Boris Uspensky in *The Semiotics of Russian Culture*, ed. Ann Shukman, Michigan Slavic Contributions, No. 11 (Ann Arbor: University of Michigan Press, 1984).

16. See Jacques Lacan's formulation in *Le Séminaire: Livre I* (Paris: Editions du Seuil, 1975), 267. Stephen Greenblatt illuminates an analogous dynamic in "Power, Sexuality and Inwardness in Wyatt's Poetry," in *Renaissance Self-Fashioning*, 115–56.

17. See Greenfeld's discussion of this chip-on-the-shoulder stance in *Nationalism,* 252–57. Whether the Nietzschean concept *ressentiment* provides a sufficient explanatory paradigm for the formation of Russian national identity remains open to discussion.

18. On LeSage's influence in Russia, see Ronald D. LeBlanc, *The Russianization of Gil Blas* (Columbus, Ohio: Slavica, 1986). On *Joseph Andrews* see Iu. D. Levin, "Translations of Henry Fielding's Works in Eighteenth-Century Russia," *Slavonic and East European Review* 2 (1990): 217–33.

19. V. K. Kiukhel'beker, "O napravlenii nashei poezii, osobenno liricheskoi, v poslednee desiatiletie, " in *Puteshestvie. Dnevnik. Stati'i* (Leningrad: Nauka, 1979), 456.

20. Letter to N. N. Raevsky, July 1825, in *The Letters of Alexander Pushkin,* trans. J. Thomas Shaw (Madison: University of Wisconsin Press, 1967), 183–84.

21. William Mills Todd III, *Fiction and Society in the Age of Pushkin* (Cambridge: Harvard University Press, 1986).

22. On the ties between the European nobility and the land, see J. G. A. Pocock, *Virtue, Commerce, and History: Essays on Political Thought and History, Chiefly in the Eighteenth Century* (Cambridge: Cambridge University Press, 1985), 103–7.

23. Traces of this specifically Russian and long-lasting genre are still observable in the modern urban *intelligent*'s "dacha sensibility," with its obligatory naming of local species.

24. For a stimulating analysis of Tatiana and her "cult" among Russian writers and thinkers, see Caryl Emerson, "Tatiana," in *A Plot of Her Own: The Female Protagonist in Russian Literature,* ed. Sona Stephan Hoisington (Evanston: Northwestern University Press, 1995), 6–20.

25. See Greenfeld's provocative discussion in *Nationalism,* 250–60.

26. N. M. Karamzin, *History of the Russian State,* 12 vols. (St. Petersburg, 1816–29); N. A. Polevoi, *History of the Russian People,* 6 vols. (Moscow, 1829–30).

27. The concept was established by Alexander Welsh in *The Hero of the Waverley Novels* (New Haven: Yale University Press, 1963).

28. Caryl Emerson, *Boris Godunov: Transpositions of a Russian Theme* (Bloomington: Indiana University Press, 1986).

29. See Lynn Hunt, *The Family Romance of the French Revolution* (Berkeley and Los Angeles: University of California Press, 1992).

30. Stephanie Sandler, *Distant Pleasures: Aleksandr Pushkin and the Writing of Exile* (Stanford: Stanford University Press, 1989).

31. Charles Ruud, *Fighting Words: Imperial Censorship and the Russian Press, 1804–1906* (Toronto: University of Toronto Press, 1982), 7–23.

32. On the network of familiar associations in early nineteenth-century Russia see William Mills Todd III, *The Familiar Letter as a Literary Genre in the Age of Pushkin* (Princeton: Princeton University Press, 1976); on the transformation of literary institutions at this time see his *Fiction and Society in the Age of Pushkin.*

33. Donald Fanger, "Gogol and His Reader," in *Literature and Society in Imperial Russia, 1800–1914,* ed. William Mills Todd III (Stanford: Stanford University Press, 1978), 68–69.

34. For a contemporary analysis of the "crisis" of poetry see Stepan Shevyrev, "Slovesnost' i torgovlia," *Moskovskii nabliudatel'* 1 (1835): 7–9.

35. Donald Fanger offers an elegant extended analysis of the mutually constitutive relationship between Gogol and his audience in *The Creation of Nikolai Gogol* (Cambridge: Harvard University Press, 1979).

36. We have in mind here aesthetic, as opposed to social, aspects of aristocratic identity. See Domna C. Stanton, *The Aristocrat as Art* (New York: Columbia University Press, 1979).

37. Marcus C. Levitt, *Russian Literary Politics and the Pushkin Celebration of 1880* (Ithaca: Cornell University Press, 1986); and "Pushkin in 1899," in *Cultural Mythologies of Russian Modernism,* 183–203.

HARSHA RAM, "RUSSIAN POETRY AND THE IMPERIAL SUBLIME"

1. Aleksandr Pushkin, *Kavkazskii plennik,* in *Sobranie sochinenii v desiati tomakh* (Moscow: Khudozhestvennaia literatura, 1960), 3:90; hereafter, citations from this edition of Pushkin's works will be provided in the text.

2. While often historically and philologically informed, Russian criticism on the Caucasian theme in Russian literature has been most typically marked by a "life and works" approach, whereby the Caucasus is examined principally as the lived experience of exile and as the locus and occasion for poetic inspiration. As Agil Gadzhiev observes, with few exceptions, Soviet critics have chosen to examine the Caucasian theme in "this or that concrete writer," for which reason "monographs of a more general theoretical or historico-literary character" are "still lacking" in Soviet literary studies (*Kavkaz v russkoi literature pervoi poloviny XIX veka* [Baku: Iazychy, 1982], 6). The narrative model of exile and homecoming might seem inevitable in biographies proper (see most recently Iu. M. Lotman, *Aleksandr Segeevich Pushkin, Biografiia pisatelia* [Leningrad: Prosveshcheniia, 1983]). Yet this tendency is in fact more widespread, resurfacing in the otherwise fascinating book by N. Ia. Eidelman, *Byt' mozhet za khrebtom Kavkaza (Russkaia literatura i obshchestvennaia mysl' pervoi poloviny XIX v. Kavkazskii kontekst)* (Moscow: Nauka, 1990). Earlier Soviet critical writing typifying this episodic and biographical

approach with respect to Pushkin includes Valerii Briusov, "Pushkin v Krymu," in *Moi Pushkin* (Moscow: GIZ, 1929); L. P. Semenov, *Pushkin na Kavkaze* (Piatigorsk: Severo-Kavkazskoe kraevoe gosudarstvennoe izdatel'stvo, 1937); I. K. Enikopolov, *Pushkin na Kavkaze* (Tbilisi: Zaria vostoka, 1938); K. G. Chernyi, *Pushkin i Kavkaz* (Stavropol': Kraiizdat, 1950); L. A. Cherneiskii, *Pushkin i severnyi Kavkaz* (Stavropol': Stavropol'skoe knizhnoe izdatel'stvo, 1986). A rare book that links biography to cultural history is Vano Shaduri's *Pushkin i gruzinskaia obshchestvennost'* (Tbilisi: Izdatel'stvo "Literatura de Khelovneba," 1966).

There is, of course, a considerably wider body of Russian criticism devoted to Russian literary orientalism, primarily of the Romantic period. Given the ideological constraints of the Soviet period, the most informed approach was often the narrowly philological, for example: V. Zhirmunskii, *Bairon i Pushkin. Iz istorii romanticheskoi poemy* (Leningrad: Academia, 1924); V. L. Komarovich, "K voprosu o zhanre 'Puteshestviia v Arzrum'," *Vremennik pushkinskoi komissii* 3 (1937); Leonid Grossman in "Lermontov i kul'tura vostoka," *Literaturnoe nasledstvo* (1941): 43–45; and N. N. Kholmukhamedova's recent "Vostok v russkoi poezii 30-kh godov XIX v.," *Izvestiia Akademii nauk*, Seriia literatury i iazyka, 1 (1985): 57–67. Ideologically sophisticated readings are rarer in the Soviet tradition. An interesting example of early Soviet anti-imperialism is S. Vel'tman's *Vostok v khudozhestvennoi literature* (Moscow: GIZ, 1928). Vel'tman's critique of imperialism is tied to a realist aesthetic that demands a "correct reproduction of daily life in the Orient." Even in the better Soviet criticism of recent times, frequent insights are vitiated by the customary narrativization of Russian literature as the growth of realism: see R. F. Iusufov, *Dagestan v russkoi literature kontsa XVIII i pervoi poloviny XIX v.* (Moscow: Nauka, 1964); S. L. Kaganovich, *Russkii romantizm i vostok* (Tashkent: Izdatel'stvo FAN, 1984); and the collection *Russkaia literatura i vostok (osobennosti khudozhestvennoi orientalistiki XIX-XX vv.)* (Tashkent: Izdatel'stvo "FAN" Uzbeksoi SSR, 1988). Most Russian and Soviet evaluations of orientalism seem thus to vacillate between a Marxism that is in fact little more than official Soviet literary history and a reconciliatory hypostasis of culture that, however philologically suggestive, seems entirely remote from the upheavals of real history; for the latter trend see, for example, V. N. Toporov, "Prostranstvo kul'tury i vstrechi v nem," *Vostok-Zapad. Issledovania, Perevody, Publikatsii* (Moscow: Nauka, 1989), 4: 6–17. The subtlest interventions in the Soviet tradition have successfully combined formal readings with historical generalization, for example: Iu. N. Tynianov, "O 'Puteshestvie v Arzrum'" (1936), in *Pushkin i ego sovremenniki* (Moscow: Nauka, 1969), 192–208; B. Tomashevskii's study of Pushkin's creative evolution *Pushkin*, 2 vols. (Moscow-Leningrad: AN SSSR, 1956, 1961); G. A. Gukovskii, *Pushkin i russkie romantiki* (1946; Moscow: Khudozhestvennaia literatura, 1965); and in part R. F. Iusufov, *Russkii romantizm nachala XIX veka i natsional'nye kul'tury* (Moscow: Nauka, 1970).

3. Susan Layton, *Russian Literature and Empire: Conquest of the Caucasus from Pushkin to Tolstoi* (Cambridge: Cambridge University Press, 1994). In her earlier article, "The Creation of an Imaginative Caucasian Geography," which reappears with some modifications as a chapter in the subsequent book, Layton in fact nuances this chronology significantly: "What Belinskii termed Pushkin's 'discovery' of the Caucasus thus was predicated to a significant extent on the writer's discovery of a native tradition of mountain poetry, which was itself indebted to Alpine motifs long present in European literature. . . . The rhetoric of sublimity and patterns of imagery that interconnect the poetry of Pushkin with that of Derzhavin, Zhukovskii, and Byron produced a highly literary landscape in *Kavkazskii plennik*" (*Slavic Review* 3 [1986]: 472–73, 477). Layton's article thus decisively links the Caucasian topography of the above Russian poets to the eighteenth-century European sublime as it became localized in the Alps. The present article will seek to extend and deepen this insight, which in many ways remains undeveloped in Layton's own work. Layton invokes Derzhavin and Zhukovsky principally as Pushkin's predecessors rather than as participants in an established and evolving tradition; her suggestion that Derzhavin stands only "in contrast" to the Lomonosovian sublime (473n9) indicates the extent to which the continuities of this tradition, in its aesthetic and political dimensions, fall outside her purview. Layton's book is nonetheless the most systematic attempt in western criticism, following in the wake of Edward Said's *Orientalism* (New York: Vintage, 1979), to link Russian literature to the imperial project. More conscientious in linking (and contrasting) Romanticism to eighteenth-century and pre-Petrine literary cultures as Paul M. Austin in "The Exotic Prisoner in Russian Romanticism," *Russian Literature* 16 (1984): 217–74, which provides a thorough genealogy of the topos. Other examples of post-Saidian or methodologically innovative western criticism on this topic include Stephanie Sandler, *Distant Pleasures: Alexander Pushkin and the Writing of Exile* (Stanford: Stanford University Press, 1989), esp. Chapter 4; Peter Scotto, "Prisoners of the Caucasus: Ideologies of Imperialism in Lermontov's 'Bela'," *PMLA* 2 (1992): 246–60; Robert Reid, "Ethnotope in Lermontov's Caucasian Poèmy," *Russian Literature* 4 (1992): 555–73; Monika Greenleaf, *Pushkin and Romantic Fashion: Fragment, Elegy, Orient, Irony* (Stanford: Stanford University Press, 1994); and a collection of three articles appearing in *Russian Review* 3 (1994) with an introductory essay by Alfred J. Rieber, "Russian Imperialism: Popular, Emblematic, Ambiguous." Of these last, the most relevant article for our purposes is Katya Hokanson's "Literary Imperialism, *Narodnost'* and Pushkin's Invention of the Caucasus" (336–52). Hokanson's article, despite its insights, dismisses Pushkin's own acknowledgment of the

prior tradition in the notes to *Prisoner of the Caucasus* as a "fabricated context of intelligibility," thereby foreclosing what will be the subject of this article.

4. Longinus, *On The Sublime*, trans. James A. Arieti and John M. Crossett (New York: Edwin Mellen, 1985), 1.3.

5. The principal theoreticians of the sublime in modern times have been from western Europe. Anglo-American culture has provided the richest reflections on the problem in the wake of Burke and the English Romantics, while in France Jean-François Lyotard has recently called the Kantian aesthetic of the sublime the germ of the modernist avant-garde; see his "Le sublime et l'avant-garde," in *L'inhumain: Causeries sur le temps* (Paris: Editions Galilée, 1988), 110. Recent Anglo-American critics include Samuel H. Monk, *The Sublime: A Study of Critical Theories in XVIII-Century England* (1935; Ann Arbor: University of Michigan Press, 1960); M. H. Abrams, *The Mirror and the Lamp: Romantic Theory and the Critical Tradition* (New York: Oxford University Press, 1953), 72ff.; Thomas Weiskel, *The Romantic Sublime: Studies in the Structure and Psychology of Transcendence* (Baltimore: The Johns Hopkins University Press, 1976); Paul Fry, *The Reach of Criticism: Method and Perception in Literary Theory* (New Haven: Yale University Press, 1983), 47–86; Neil Hertz, "A Reading of Longinus," in *The End of the Line: Essays on Psychoanalysis and the Sublime* (New York: Columbia University Press, 1985), 1–21; Suzanne Guerlac, "Longinus and the Subject of the Sublime," *New Literary History* 16 (1985): 275–89; Harold Bloom, *Ruin the Sacred Truths. Poetry and Belief from the Bible to the Present* (Cambridge: Harvard University Press, 1989), 117–41; Frances Ferguson, *Solitude and the Sublime: Romanticism and the Aesthetics of Individuation* (New York: Routledge, 1992) and Paul Fry, *A Defense of Poetry: Reflections on the Occasion of Writing* (Stanford: Stanford University Press, 1995), 133–56.

6. Edmund Burke, *A Philosophical Enquiry into the Origin of our Ideas of the Sublime and the Beautiful*, ed. James T. Boulton (1757; London: Routledge and Kegan Paul, 1958), part 2, sec. 5.

7. G. W. F. Hegel, *Aesthetics: Lectures on Fine Art*, trans. T. M. Knox (Oxford: Clarendon Press, 1975), 1:365, 371, 372, 376; for the notion of oriental despotism as the secular political equivalent to the religious sublime in Hegel, these pages must be read alongside Hegel's discussion of the Orient in *The Philosophy of History*, trans. J. Sibree (1899; New York: Dover Publications, 1956), 116–222. See also Peter Szondi, "Hegels Lehre von der Dichtung," *Poetik und Geschichtsphilosophie* (Frankfurt: Suhrkamp, 1974). For a history of the *imperial* aesthetics of the sublime and the picturesque, see Partha Mitter, *Much Maligned Monsters: A History of European Reactions to Indian Art*, 2d ed. (Chicago: University of Chicago Press, 1992), 120–40; Sara Suleri, *The Rhetoric of English India* (Chicago: University of Chicago

Press, 1992), in particular 65–66. More generally see Raymond Schwab, *The Oriental Renaissance: Europe's Rediscovery of India and the East, 1680–1880,* trans. Gene Patterson Black and Victor Reinking (New York: Columbia University Press, 1984), and Simon Schama, *Landscape and Memory* (New York: Vintage, 1996), particularly the chapter "Vertical Empires, Cerebral Chasms" (447–78), which posits a link between eighteenth-century accounts of Alpine crossing and "the fate of the British Atlantic Empire" (461). The analogy with Russia's conquest of the Caucasus wll shortly become evident.

8. Immanuel Kant, *Critique of Judgment,* trans. Werner S. Pluhar (Indianapolis: Hackett, 1987), sec. 25 (106).

9. Kant, sec. 29 (135). An interesting chapter between Kant and Hegel is Schiller's "On the Sublime" ("Über das Erhabene," in *Schillers Sämtliche Werke* [Leipzig: Insel, 1924], 5:354–70), which opens up the sublime's moral imperative (which Schiller, like Kant, derives from the Old Testament) to the experience of history, thus preparing the way for Hegel.

10. Lomonosov read Boileau's rendition of Longinus in 1738: his notes are preserved in TsGADA (Moscow), F.17, ed.khr. 9, lines 2–7; see also the notes to his *Polnoe sobranie sochinenii* (Moscow: Akademiia nauk, 1959), 8:871; and E. Ia. Dan'ko, "Iz neizdannykh materialov o Lomonosove," *XVIII vek.* (Moscow: Akademiia nauk, 1940), 2:248–75 for the history of the manuscript and its context. In these notes we see Lomonosov quote Longinus quoting: if his notes seem indecisive on the level of content—"La sublimité vient ou de la grandeur de l'âme ou de l'imagination, ou de l'imitation"—his pattern of attention to the original text bespeaks a constant attempt to verify judgment through citation, as if to guarantee the adequacy of literature to its critical model. Yet this search for stylistic norms also bespeaks a relation between Longinus and Lomonosov that is itself sublime: each citation allows Lomonosov a fictive identification with the source of utterance as a norm-giving authority. As Suzanne Guerlac observes in "Longinus and the Subject of the Sublime": "the structure of citation appears embedded in the very operation of sublimity" (275–76).

11. M. V. Lomonosov, "Predislovie o pol'ze knig tser'kovnykh v rossiiskom iazyke," in *Biblioteka poeta: Izbrannye proizvedeniia* (Moscow: Sovetskii pisatel', 1965), 497: "Sim shtilem sostavliat'sia dolzhny geroicheskie poemy, ody, prozaicheskie rechi o vazhnykh materiiakh, kotorye oni ot obyknovennoi prostoty k vazhnomu velikolepiiu vozvyshaiutsia. Sim shtilem preimushchestvuet rossiiskii iazyk pered mnogimi nyneshnimi evropeiskimi, pol'zuias' iazykom slavenskim iz knig tserkovnykh." Compare Boileau's statement that "ainsi c'est la simplicité même de ce mot qui en fait la grandeur," "Traité du sublime ou du Merveilleux dans le Discours, traduit du Grec de Longin," *Oeuvres complètes de Boileau-Despréaux* (Paris: Chez Léfèvre, 1858), 1:350.

12. Viazemsky mentions Longinus in passing in "Vmesto predisloviia [k 'Bakhchisaraiskomy fontanu']. Razgovor mezhdu izdatelem i klassikom s vyborgskoi storony ili s Vasil'evskogo ostrova," in *Estetika i literaturnaia kritika* (Moscow: Iskusstvo, 1984), 50. For a brief account of the Russian reception and translation history of Longinus's work, see N. A. Chistiakova, "Traktat 'O vozvyshennom,' ego avtor, vremia i soderzhanie," in Longinus, *O vozvyshennom,* trans. N. A. Chistiakova (Moscow: Nauka, 1966), 116–17.

13. For Boileau's "Discours sur l'ode" and the accompanying poem, see his *Oeuvres complètes,* 1:248–55. Other critics and poets also loom large here. The German rhetorician Gottsched had quoted Boileau's very same ode in his *Versuch einer Critischen Dichtkunst* (1733; Leipzig: Verlegts Bernhard Christoph Breitkopf, 1751), 371–72, a known point of reference for the student Lomonosov. In Gottsched's work, as in Lomonosov's, Boileau's poem is discussed in purely metrical terms, but in Gottsched this moment is preceded by an explicit discussion of the Longinian sublime:

> This [pathetic] style is the reckoned place of the so-called sublime [*das sogennante Hohe*], about which Longinus has written an entire book. . . . This pathetic style is to be found firstly in odes, where the poet, on becoming agitated, finds release in fiery expression. One example of this is Günther's ode to Eugen, which displays this character almost throughout.

Johann Christian Günther's poem of 1718, "Auf den Zwischen Ihro Kaiserl. Majestät und der Pforte an. 1718 geschlossenen Frieden" (see *Günthers Werke* [Weimar: Volksverlag, 1958], 97) is yet another mirror to Lomonosov's "Ode on the Taking of Khotin": composed in four-foot iambs, it commemorates an earlier European victory over Ottoman Turkey. Metrically and ideologically, then, it functions as part of a chain of literary antecedents that ground Lomonosov's intervention of 1738 in a broadly European revival of the Longinian sublime. These antecedents often contain analogous arguments that throw further light on Lomonosov's critical strategy in linking together problems of form and content.

14. "*Son style impetueux souvent marche au hazard, / Chés elle, un beau désordre est un effet de l'art.* . . . Sego pravila nikto na Frantsusskom iazyke, kak mnitsia, ne upotrebil luchshe samogo Avtora Depreó, kotoroe on samym delom sovershenno vsem pokazal v preizriadnoi svoei Ode, sochinennoi po sluchaiu vziatogo goroda Namura ot Frantsusskogo voiska. . . . kotoroi moia est' Podrazhenie." "Rassuzhdenie ob Ode vobshche" (1752), in *Sochineniia Trediakovskogo* (St. Petersburg: Tipografiia Voenno-Uchebnykh Zavedenii, 1849), 279–81. In these lines Trediakovsky also mentions the biblical Psalms as a source of the sublime: their importance will become clearer later. The two redactions of the ode on Gdansk can be conveniently compared in V. K. Trediakovskii, *Izbrannye proizvedeniia* (Moscow: Sovetskii pisatel', 1963),

129–34, 453–58; while both editions of Trediakovsky's "Novyi i kratkii sposob k slozheniiu rossiiskikh stikhov" can be found in the English anthology *Russian Versification: The Theories of Trediakovskij, Lomonosov, and Kantemir,* ed. Rimvydas Silbajoris (New York: Columbia University Press, 1968), 36–67 and 100–127. Trediakovsky's strategy appears to be one of yielding on most points to his politically and poetically stronger enemy while insisting on his own chronological precedence. Nonetheless, Trediakovsky was capable of disagreeing with Lomonosov on specific counts: while Lomonosov had insisted on the superiority of the iamb over the trochee, Trediakovsky argued (again in 1752) that neither was intrinsically more sublime (see his "K chitateliu," in *Sochineniia Trediakovskogo,* xvi—xx). Lomonosov is not mentioned here, not only because his relevant works had not been officially published, but also because of his political influence. The other link between Trediakovsky's ode on Gdansk (1734) and Lomonosov's ode on Khotin (1739) is historical: both mark links in what was effectively a complex chain of events in the Eurasian imperial theatre of the time.

15. Lomonosov, "Pis'mo o pravilakh rossiiskogo stikhotvorstva," in *Izbrannye proizvedeniia,* 491: "Chistye iambicheskie stikhi khotia i trudnovato sochiniat', odnako podnimaiasia tikho vverkh, materii blagorodstvo, velikolepie i vysotu umnozhaiiut. Onykh nigde ne mozhno luchshe upotrebliat', kak v torzhestvennykh odakh, chto ia v moei nyneshnei i uchinil."

16. Lomonosov, "Oda na vziatie Khotina," in *Polnoe sobranie sochinenii,* 7:17. All future citations of Lomonosov's poetry are from this volume and are provided in parentheses after their translation.

17. Iurii Tynianov, "Oda kak oratorskii zhanr," in *Arkhaisty i novatory* (1929; Munich: Wilhelm Fink, 1967), 75.

18. G. R. Derzhavin, "Vodopad," in *Stikhotvoreniia: Biblioteka poeta* (Leningrad: Izdatel'stvo pisatelei v Leningrade, 1933), 163. All future citations of Derzhavin's poetry are from this volume and are provided in parentheses after their translation. We need not be concerned that the waterfall referred to in Derzhavin's poem is not located in the "South": while less of an abstraction than Lomonosov's Parnassus, it serves chiefly to generate a sublime verticality that will quickly shift its focus to beyond what is visible as empirical topography.

19. G. R. Derzhavin, "Rassuzhdeniia o liricheskoi poezii ili ob ode (1811–1815)," in *Sochineniia* (St. Petersburg: Tipografiia Imperskoi akademii nauk, 1878), 7:550.

20. G. R. Derzhavin, "Poslanie indeiskogo [*sic*] bramina k tsarevichu Khloru," from *Poslanie indeiskogo [sic] bramina k tsarevichu Khloru i gimn Solntsu* (St. Petersburg: Imperatorskaia tipografiia, 1803), 3–6.

21. M. V. Lomonosov, "Drevniaia rossiiskaia istoriia. Vstuplenie," written in 1758, in *Polnoe sobranie sochinenii,* 6:171: "raznomyslennoiu vol'nostiiu

Rossiia edva ne doshla do krainego razrusheniia; samoderzhavstvom kak snachala usililas', tak i posle neschastlivykh vremen umnozhilas', ukrepilas', proslavilas'. Blagonadezhnoe imeem uverenie o blagosostoianii nashego otechestva, vidia v edinonachal'nom vladenii zalog nashego blazhenstva." On the eighteenth century and its historical debates see Anatole Mazour, *Modern Russian Historiography* (Princeton: D. Van Nostrand, 1958), 9–49; Hans Rogger, *National Consciousness in Eighteenth-Century Russia* (Cambridge: Harvard University Press, 1960), particularly 186–252; Il'ia Serman, "Russian National Consciousness and its Development in the Eighteenth Century," in *Russia in the Age of Enlightenment: Essays for Isabel de Madariaga,* ed. Roger Bartlett and Janet M. Hartley (London: Macmillan, 1990); and P. Miliukov, *Glavnye techeniia russkoi istoricheskoi mysli,* 2d. ed. (Moscow: Kushnerev, 1898), 17: "With the historians of the eighteenth century to these two tendencies of thought [the Orthodox idea based on Russia's evangelization and the national idea based on the Battle of Kulikovo] a third is added: that of the state and the monarchy."

22. Montesquieu, *De l'Esprit des lois,* vols. 1–2 (1748; Paris: Société les Belles Lettres, 1950), 2:book 5, chap. 14, 120–21: "Voyez, je vous pris, avec quelle industrie le gouvernement moscovite cherche à sortir du despotisme, qui lui est plus pesant qu'aux peuples même. On a cassé les grands corps de troupes; on a diminué les peines des crimes; on a établi des tribunaux; on a commencé à connoître les loix, on a instruit les peuples. Mais il y a des causes particulières, qui le rarnèneront peut-être au malheur qu'il vouloit fuir." On Montesquieu see Louis Althusser, *Montesquieu: La politique et l'histoire* (Paris: Presses universitaires de France, 1974): 83, 91–92: "Le despotisme est bien une *idée* politique, . . . l'idée de la limite même du politique comme tel. . . . Il est trop clair que Montesquieu a voulu représenter dans cette figure du despotisme tout autre chose que l'Etat des régimes orientaux: *l'abdication du politique même* . . . le despotisme n'est illusion géographique que parce qu'il est allusion historique." Althusser's essay contains some precious insights on the time and space of despotism—"espace sans lieu, temps sans durée" (87)—and on the constitutive gap between ruler and the ruled: "Le paradoxe du despotisme est de si bien s'acharner sur les grands . . . que le peuple en est comme épargné." For a genealogy of the term *despotism* from Greek antiquity to the Enlightenment, see R. Koebner's "Despot and Despotism: Vicissitudes of a Political Term," *Journal of the Warburg and Courtauld Institutes* 14 (1951), while Franco Venturi's "Despotismo orientale," *Rivista storica italiana* 72 (1960) is useful in showing how Montesquieu's ideas were contested by the early oriental philologists such as Anquetil-Duperron. A more recent Marxist summary of this earlier debate is Bryan S. Turner's "Orientalism and the Problem of Civil Society in Islam," in *Orientalism, Islam, and Islamists,* ed. Asaf Hussain, Robert Olson, and Jamil Qureishi (Brattleboro: Amana

Books, 1984), 23–42. The debate has been revived in our time by Karl A. Wittfogel's *Oriental Despotism: A Comparative Study in Total Power* (New Haven: Yale University Press, 1957), a book deeply traumatized by a Stalinism for which it seeks to provide an Asiatic ancestry and morphology. In the case of both Montesquieu and Wittfogel "historical allusion" is decisive, threatening to empty the term *despotism* of any referential status with respect to the East. Perry Anderson seeks to rebut Wittfogel in *Lineages of the Absolutist State,* 3d ed. (London: NLB, 1977), 463. One of the most startling recent contributions to the debate on despotism is Gilles Deleuze and Félix Guattari's *L'Anti-Oedipe: Capitalisme et schizophrénie* (1972; Paris: Editions de Minuit, 1980), 217–57, for whom despotism also spills over well beyond the Orient to embrace the imperial dimensions of culture in general.

23. Catherine II, "Nakaz kommissii o sostavlenii proekta novogo ulozheniia," in *Sochineniia imperatritsy Ekateriny II* (St. Petersburg: Tipografiia Imperatorskoi Akademii Nauk, 1849), 4–5: "6. Rossiia est' Evropeiskaiia derzhava. . . . 9. Gosudar' est samoderzhavnyi; ibo nikakaia drugaia, kak tol'ko soedinennaia v ego osobe, vlast' ne mozhet deistvovati skhodno s prostranstvom tol' velikogo gosudarstva. 10. Prostrannoe gosudarstvo predpologaet samoderzhavnuiu vlast' v toi osobe, kotoraia onym pravit. Nadlezhit, chtoby skorost' v reshenii del, iz dal'nikh stran prisylaemykh, nagrazhdala medlenie otdalennostiiu mest prichiniaemoe." (The "Skazka o tsareviche Khlore" [see below] is from the same volume, 279–96.) Montesquieu's citation is from *De l'Esprit des lois,* 1:book 8, chap. 17–19, 222–24: "Un Etat monarchique doit être d'une grandeur médiocre. . . . Un grand empire suppose une autorité despotique dans celui qui gouverne. Il faut que la promptitude des résolutions supplée à la distance des lieux où elles sont envoyées; que la crainte empêche la negligence du gouverneur ou du magistrat éloigné; que la loi soit dans une seule tête." The two texts correspond right down to grammatical structure and lexical choice. That Catherine's text is based on Montesquieu and Cesare Beccaria is well known (these and other correspondences have also been noted by W. F. Reddaway, editor of the English version *Documents of Catherine the Great* [Cambridge: Cambridge University Press, 1931], 322ff.), but the question of *specific* semantic slippages and their import remains open to discussion.

24. Gregory Nagy, *Pindar's Homer: The Lyric Possession of an Epic Past* (Baltimore: Johns Hopkins University Press, 1990), 153–59; my thanks to Kevin Crotty for the reference.

25. Cf. V. V. Barthold, *La Découverte de l'Asie: Histoire de l'orientalisme en Europe et en Russie* (Paris: Payot, 1947), 249–50; Alan W. Fisher, "Enlightened Despotism and Islam Under Catherine II," *Slavic Review* 4 (1968): 552–53; and more generally, Elizabeth E. Bacon, *Central Asia under Russian*

Rule. A Study in Cultural Change (Ithaca: Cornell University Press, 1966); Alexandre Benningsen and Chantal Lemercier-Quelquejay, *Islam in the Soviet Union,* trans. Geoffrey E. Wheeler and Hubert Evans (London: Pall Mall Press, 1967); the collection *Central Asia: A Century of Russian Rule,* ed. Edward Allworth (New York: Columbia University Press, 1967); the collection *The Nationality Question in Soviet Central Asia,* ed. Edward Allworth, (New York: Praeger, 1973); the collection *Russian Imperialism from Ivan the Great to the Revolution,* ed. Taras Hunczak (New Brunswick: Rutgers University Press, 1974), particularly Emanuel Sarkisyanz, "Russian Imperialism Reconsidered," 45–81; N. S. Kiniapina, M. M. Bliev, and V. V. Degoev, *Kavkaz i sredniaia Aziia vo vneshnei politike Rossii: Vtoraia polovina XVIII-80-e gody XIX v.* (Moscow: Izdatel'stvo Moskovskogo universiteta, 1984); the collection *Russian Colonial Expansion to 1917,* ed. Michael Rywkin (London: Mansell, 1988), particularly Muriel Atkin, "Russian Expansion in the Caucasus to 1813," 139–87; Milan Hauner, *What Is Asia to Us? Russia's Asian Hinterland Yesterday and Today* (Boston: Unwin Hyman, 1990); *Geographic Perspectives on Soviet Central Asia,* ed. Robert A. Lewis (London: Routledge, 1992), particularly Ralph S. Clem, "The Frontier and Colonialism in Russian and Soviet Central Asia," 19–34, and Lee Schwartz, "The Political Geography of Soviet Central Asia: Integrating the Central Asian Frontier," 37–69.

26. F. M. Dostoevskii, "Goek-Tepe. Chto takoe Aziia dlia nas?" in *Polnoe sobranie sochinenii* (St. Petersburg: Samoobrazovanie, 1896), 21:513.

27. Prince Viazemsky's negative reaction, never publicly aired, can be found in his letter to A. I. Turgenev, dated 27 September 1822, cited in the notes to P. A. Viazemskii, *Estetika i literaturnaia kritika* (Moscow: Iskusstvo, 1984), 393.

28. Boris Tomashevskii, *Pushkin, Kniga pervaia (1813–1824)* (Moscow: AN SSSR, 1956), 405.

29. Pushkin's "imperialist apologia" is in fact repeatedly postponed, and even rendered a mere possibility: "Byt' mozhet, povtorit ona . . ." (Perhaps she [the muse] will repeat . . .). Pushkin never did fulfill his promise, as we know from the controversy surrounding his later work "Puteshestvie v Arzrum," yet another celebration of empire that never quite eventuated, being, not unlike *Prisoner of the Caucasus,* fundamentally concerned with deflecting the problem of empire onto the plane of psychological response.

30. The genre sources of *Prisoner of the Caucasus,* from the elegy to Byron's "Turkish tales," have been widely discussed, but their relationship to the sublime merits further consideration. The elegiac reworking of the imperial theme impinges equally on other Pushkin texts: the epilogue to *The Gypsies,* for example, is rhetorically identical to *Prisoner of the Caucasus,* if less stridently so.

MONIKA GREENLEAF, "FOUND IN TRANSLATION: THE SUBJECT OF BATIUSHKOV'S POETRY"

I borrow the title and its underlying concept from Eva Hoffman's innovative autobiography, *Lost in Translation: A Life in a New Language* (New York: Dutton, 1989). All translations in the text except where otherwise noted are mine.

I wish to take this opportunity to thank Caryl Emerson, William Mills Todd III, Gregory Freidin, Lazar Fleishman, and Andrei Zorin for their acute and helpful criticisms and additions, and above all, Stephen Moeller-Sally, without whose lucid compositional advice and perfectly attuned insights this essay would not have found its final form.

1. See Jean Kim's analysis of nineteenth-century Russian translation practices in "Making Another's Voice Mine: Pushkin and the Poetics of Translation" (Ph.D diss., Yale University, 1992), esp. chap. 3.

2. V. K. Kiukhel'beker, "O napravlenii nashei poezii, osobenno liricheskoi, v poslednee desiatiletie," in *Puteshestvie. Dnevnik. Stat'i* (Leningrad: Nauka, 1979), 453–58.

3. Lidiia Ginzburg, *O lirike* (Leningrad: Sovetskii pisatel', 1974), 20–47; B. M. Tomashevskii, "Pushkin i Batiushkov," in *Batiushkov K. N. Stikhotvorenia,* ed. I. Medvedeva (Moscow: Sovetskii pisatel', 1936), 5–49. The formal analyses I have found most useful are: Efim Etkind, *Russkie poety-perevodchiki ot Trediakovskogo do Pushkina* (Leningrad: Nauka, 1973), 116–54, and *Mastera russkogo stikhotvornogo perevoda* (Leningrad: Sovetskii pisatel', 1968); Lazar Fleishman, "Iz istorii elegii v Pushkinskuiu epokhu," in *Pushkinskii sbornik* (Riga: Redaktsionno-izdatel'skii otdel LGU, 1968); G. A. Gukovskii, *Pushkin i russkie romantiki* (Moscow: Khudozhestvennia literatura, 1965), 63–103; V. B. Sandomirskaia, "Iz istorii Pushkinskogo tsikla 'Podrazhania drevnim' (Pushkin i Batiushkov)," in *Pushkinskii vremennik,* 1975 (Leningrad: Nauka, 1978), 15–30; Ilya S. Serman, *Konstantin Batyushkov* (New York: Twayne, 1974); V. Toporov, "Istochnik Batiushkova v sviazi s 'Le Torrent' Parny," in *Uchenye zapiski Tartuskogo gos. univiversiteta 236, Trudy po znakovym sistemama IV* (Tartu: Izdatel'stvo Tartuskogo gosudarstvennogo universiteta, 1969), 306–35; V. V. Vinogradov, *Stil' Pushkina* (Leningrad: Ogiz, Gosudarstvennoe izdatel'stvo khudozhestvennoi literatury, 1941), 147–51, 179–85, 287–307, 317–29. For comprehensive commentary see L. N. Maikov, "O zhizni i sochineniiakh K.N. Batiushkova," in *Sochineniia K.N. Batiushkova,* ed. P. N. Batiushkov (St. Petersburg: Tipografiia B. S. Balasheva, 1885–87), 1:1–360; Erica Brendel, "The Poetry of Konstantin Batiushkov" (Ph.D diss., University of California at Berkeley, 1969); N. V. Fridman, *Poeziia Batiushkova* (Moscow: Nauka, 1971), and *Proza Batiushkova* (Moscow: Nauka, 1965); K. N. Batiushkov, *Opyty v stikhakh*

i proze, ed. Irina Semenko (Moscow: Nauka, 1977), 433–600; as well as Semenko's chapter on Batiushkov in *Poety Pushkinskoi pory* (Moscow: Khudozhesvennia literatura, 1970); N. Zubkov, "Opyty na puti k slave," in *Sud'by knig: Svoi podvig svershiv . . . ,* by A. Zorin, A. Nemzer, and N. Zubkov (Moscow: Kniga, 1987), 265–350.

4. Batiushkov, *Opyty,* 447.

5. Walter Benjamin, "The Task of the Translator," in *Illuminations,* trans. Harry Zohn (New York: Schocken, 1969), 69–82. See also Paul de Man, "Conclusions: Walter Benjamin's 'The Task of the Translator,'" in *The Resistance to Theory,* Theory and History of Literature, vol. 33 (Minneapolis: University of Minnesota Press, 1989), 73–105.

6. D. P. Iakubovich, "Antichnost' v tvorchestve Pushkina," *Pushkinskii vremennik* 6 (Moscow: Nauka, 1941), 72–159. "Cultural semiotics" and the concept of *stroenie lichnosti* have bridged the gap between a contextual study locked in positivism, and a formal study locked in ahistoricity. See Svetlana Boym's interesting discussion of precisely this problem in *Death in Quotation Marks* (Cambridge: Harvard University Press, 1991), 1–27. Particularly useful studies for Batiushkov's period are Mario Praz, *On Neoclassicism,* trans. Angus Davidson (Evanston: Northwestern University Press, 1969); Iu. M. Lotman, "Teatr i teatral'nost' v stroe kul'tury nachala XIX veka," and "Stsena i zhivopis' kak kodiruiushchie ustroistva kul'turnogo povedeniia cheloveka XIX stoletiia," in *Stat'i po tipologii kul'tury* (Tartu: Izdatel'stvo Tartuskogo gosudarstvennogo universiteta, 1973), 42–73 and 74–89; and Iu. M. Lotman and Boris A. Uspensky, "Binary Models in the Dynamics of Russian Culture (to the End of the Eighteenth Century)," in *The Semiotics of Russian Cultural History,* ed. Alexander D. Nakhimovsky and Alice Stone Nakhimovsky (Ithaca: Cornell University Press, 1985), 30–66. See also Harold Segel, "Classicist and Classical Antiquity in Eighteenth- and Early Nineteenth-Century Russian Literature," in *Eighteenth-Century Russia,* ed. J. Garrard (Oxford: Oxford University Press, 1973); and G. M. Fridlender, "Batiushkov i antichnost'," *Russkaia literatura,* 1 (1988): 44–49. I explore this topic more fully in *Pushkin and Romantic Fashion: Fragment, Elegy, Orient, Irony* (Stanford: Stanford University Press, 1994).

7. Richard S. Wortman, *Scenarios of Power: Myth and Ceremony in Russian Monarchy,* vol. 1. (Princeton: Princeton University Press, 1995). See also Stephen Lessing Baehr, *The Paradise Myth in Eighteenth Century Russia: Utopian Patterns in Early Secular Russian Literature and Culture* (Stanford: Stanford University Press, 1991).

8. Batiushkov's letter of request for a diplomatic post in Italy, composed by Zhukovsky and addressed to Alexander I in June 1818, contains a complete account of his war record. See Maikov, "O zhizni," 1:261–62. N. V. Fridman,

Poeziia Batushkova, pays serious attention to Batiushkov's "battle poetry," 152–99.

9. For a detailed publication history, see Zubkov, "Opyty na puti k slave," 307–34.

10. Kiukhel'beker, "O napravlenii."

11. See Philippe Lacoue-Labarthe and Jean-Luc Nancy, *The Literary Absolute: The Theory of Literature in German Romanticism*, trans. Philip Barnard and Cheryl Lester (Albany: State University of New York Press, 1988); Hugh Lloyd-Jones, *Blood for the Ghosts: Classical Influences in the 19th and 20th Centuries* (Baltimore: Johns Hopkins University Press, 1982); and Richard Jenkyns, *The Victorians and Ancient Greece* (Cambridge: Harvard University Press, 1980).

12. Wortman, *Scenarios of* Power, 229.

13. Robert Gildea, *Borders and Barricades: Europe, 1800–1914* (Oxford: Oxford University Press, 1987), 54, 35–56. See also Alan Palmer, *Alexander I: Tsar of War and Peace* (London: Weidenfeld and Nicolson, 1974), 132–215.

14. Terry Castle, "Phantasmagoria and the Metaphorics of Modern Reverie," in *The Female Thermometer: Eighteenth-Century Culture and the Invention of the Uncanny* (New York: Oxford University Press, 1995), 155, 140–67.

15. Ibid.

16. Gildea, *Borders and Barricades*, 55.

17. "Rech' o vlianii legkoi poezii na iazyk," in *Sochinenia,* 2:237–49.

18. Letter to N. I. Gnedich, 5 December 1811, *Sochineniia,* 3:164–65.

19. Dmitri N. Bludov uses a characteristically bloody metaphor to characterize his friend's work: "Batiushkov's style can be compared with the inner organs of a sacrifice in the hands of a shaman: they still palpitate and glow with its life." Quoted by Maikov, *Sochineniia,* 1:235.

20. Letter to N. I. Gnedich, mid-February 1810. *Sochineniia,* 3:78: "Posylaiu tebe malen'kuiu pi'esku, kotoruiu vzial u Parny, to-est', zavoeval. Ideiia original'naia. . . . V nei *kakoe-to osoblivoe nechto melankholicheskoe,* chto mne nravitsia." Zubkov shows that this characterization and the first lines of the translation echo Zhukovsky, in what might be seen as a challenge to his supremacy in the spiritualist genre. Zubkov, "Opyty na puti k slave," 275–76. See also Etkind, *Russkie poety-perevodchiki,* 121–24, on the relationship between the two poems. The text for "Le Revenant" can be found in Evariste Désiré de Forges, vicomte de Parny, *Oeuvres d'Evariste Parny* (Paris: Chez Debray, 1808), 1:24–27.

21. Terry Castle, "The Spectralization of the Other in *The Mysteries of Udolpho,*" 136, 123, 120–39, and "Spectral Politics: Apparition Belief and the Romantic Imagination," 168–89, in *The Female Thermometer.* Castle

cites (172), among many other contemporary studies, Christoph Friedrich Nicolai's "Memoir on the Appearance of Specters or Phantoms Occasioned by Disease, with Psychological Remarks," published in German in 1799, in English in 1803. See also Kristin Pfefferkorn, *Novalis: A Romantic's Theory of Language and Poetry* (New Haven: Yale University Press, 1988), esp. "Translation as a Linguistic and Metaphysical Method of Raising," 48–59.

22. Norman Bryson, *Word and Image: French Painting of the Ancien Régime* (Cambridge: Harvard University Press, 1983), 98.

23. P. A. Viazemskii, *Ostaf'evskii arkhiv kniazei Viazemskikh,* 2:382, quoted in Batiushkov, *Opyty,* 442.

24. "The absence of the speaker from his speech" rather than an idiosyncratic subjective voice constituted the ideal Romantic self-transcendence for other nineteenth-century poets as well. See especially Geoffrey Hartman, "Romanticism and 'Anti-Self-consciousness,'" in *Romanticism and Consciousness,* ed. Harold Bloom (New York: Norton, 1970), 47.

25. Castle, *Female Thermometer,* 137.

26. Letters to P. A. Viazemskii and to N. I. Gnedich, October 1812, from Nizhnii Novgorod, in *Sochineniia,* 3:205–10.

27. Letters in *Sochineniia,* 3:251–52, 234–35, and 258, quoted in Maikov, "O zhizni," 1:171–72. See his account of the Paris experience, 168–79. "Eto ne mramor—Bog!" exclaimed Batiushkov in a letter to Dashkov about his frequent visits to the Apollo Belvedere. *Sochineniia,* 3:262–63.

28. Henri Troyat, *Alexander of Russia: Napoleon's Conqueror,* trans. Joan Pinkham (New York: Dutton, 1982), 121, 114, 187–226.

29. Wortman, *Scenarios of Power,* 229.

30. *Tibullus: Elegies,* ed. Guy Lee (Liverpool: Francis Cairns, 1982), 2d ed., 35–41.

31. The relationship between the "work of mourning" in elegiac poetry and the Oedipal dynamics of linguistic substitution is lucidly presented by Peter Sacks in *The English Elegy: Studies in the Genre from Spenser to Yeats* (Baltimore: Johns Hopkins University Press, 1985), 1–37.

32. Ibid., 229, 236.

33. Letter to V. A. Zhukovskii, 3 November 1814, *Sochineniia,* 3:303.

34. Friedrich Schiller, "Odysseus," *Schillers Werke* (Weimar: H. Bohlaus, 1943), 227.

35. Friedrich Schiller, "On Naive and Sentimental Poetry," in *German Aesthetic and Literary Criticism: Winckelmann, Lessing, Hamann, Herder, Schiller and Goethe,* ed. H. B. Nisbet (Cambridge: Cambridge University Press, 1985), 189–90.

36. French, with its analytical, sequential syntax, was regarded as a historically late and quintessentially prosaic langauge, incapable of rendering

the instantaneity and complexity of the poetic impulse, which was supposedly closer to the "origins of language." A famous articulation of this idea is the passage from Diderot's "Lettre sur les sourds et muets": "Notre âme est un tableau mouvant, d'après lequel nous peignons sans cesse . . . ce que le grec et le latin rendent par un seul mot. A, Monsieur! combien notre entendement est modifié par les signes," in *Diderot Studies VII*, ed. Otis Fellows (Syracuse: Syracuse University Press, 1952), 64.

37. See Brendel, "Poetry of Konstantin Batiushkov," for a good discussion of this topic.

38. Benjamin, "The Task of the Translator," 81–82.

39. Zubkov, "Opyty na puti k slave," 317. Zubkov gives a meticulous and psychologically acute account of Batiushkov's process of revision and textual self-fashioning.

40. Batiushkov, *Opyty*. See Zubkov, "Opyty na puti k slave," 302, 288–329, for a detailed autobiographical and textological account of its composition.

41. Batiushkov, "Nechto o poete i poezii," in *Opyty*, 22.

42. Denis Diderot's *Entretiens entre D'Alembert et Diderot* is a well-known example. On Diderot's prose genres, including the peripatetic art criticism in *Les Salons*, see Jack Undank and Herbert Josephs, eds., *Diderot: Digression and Dispersion* (Lexington: French Forum Publishers, 1984), as well as *Diderot et l'Art de Boucher à David: Les Salons: 1759–1781* (Paris: Editions de la Réunion des Musées nationaux, 1984); and on Winckelmann's rhapsodic style, "Winckelmann," in Praz, 406–9.

43. Batiushkov, "Vecher u Kantemira," "Progulka v Akademiiu khudozhestv," in *Opyty*, 34–51 and 71–94.

44. See Francis Haskell and Nicholas Penny, *Taste and the Antique: The Lure of Classical Sculpture, 1500–1900* (New Haven: Yale University Press, 1981), 88–90, 211–21, 254–55, 277.

45. Batiushkov, "O kharaktere Lomonosova," in *Opyty*, 29, 33.

46. Batiushkov, "Pis'mo k I. M. Murav'evu-Apostolu," in *Opty*, 57, 62, 64.

47. Batiushkov, "Chuzhoe—moe sokrovishche," in *Opyty*, 410–12.

48. *Sochineniia*, 3:447–48.

49. Ibid., 416, quoted in Maikov, "O zhizni," 1:246.

50. Batiushkov, "Nechto o poete i poezii," 22.

51. I have used the English translation of W. R. Paton (Cambridge: Harvard University Press, 1980), 4 vols. See my *Pushkin and Romantic Fashion*, 36–38, 62–85, 206–16 for a more extensive discussion of the Greek Anthology, the fragment, and the formation of national identity.

52. Johann Gottfried Herder, "Letters in Defense of Humanism" (1793–1795), *Briefe zu Beorderung der Humanität* in his *Sämtliche Werke* (Berlin:

Bernard Suphan, 1877–1913), 251. Friedrich Schlegel, "On Incomprehensibility," in *German Aesthetic and Literary Criticism: The Romantic Ironists and Goethe,* ed. Kathleen M. Wheeler (Cambridge: Cambridge University Press, 1984), 32–39.

53. Friedrich Schlegel, Fragment 24 from "Athenaeum Fragments," in *Lucinde and the Fragments,* ed. Peter Firchow (Minneapolis: University of Minnesota Press, 1971), 164.

54. S. S. Uvarov, preface to "The Greek Anthology," in Batiushkov, *Sochinenia,* 3:423–29. Batiushkov translated Uvarov's interlinear French prose translations of the Greek originals into Russian verse; although Uvarov also "competed" with his own French verse translations. See Etkind, *Russkie poety-perevodchiki,* 129–39.

55. That Greek antiquity was a preoccupation of certain nineteenth-century homosexual circles, indeed, almost a codeword, is suggested by Jenkyns, *Victorians and Ancient* Greece, 132–54. This certainly seems to apply to Uvarov, whose homosexual circle, according to Simon Karlinsky, was well known. See his *The Sexual Labyrinth of Nikolai Gogol* (Chicago: University of Chicago Press, 1976), 56–58.

56. See Lacoue-Labarthe and Nancy, *Literary Absolute,* 39–48; and Efim Etkind, "'Liricheskaia epigramma' kak zhanrovaia forma," in *Forma kak soderzhanie* (Wurzburg: JAL-Verlag, 1977), 53–61.

57. See Marjorie Levinson, *The Romantic Fragment Poem* (Chapel Hill: University of North Carolina Press, 1986); Anne F. Janowitz, *England's Ruins* (Cambridge: Blackwell, 1990); Paul de Man, "Shelley Disfigured," in *The Rhetoric of Romanticism* (New York: Columbia University Press, 1984), 93–123; and my *Pushkin and Romantic Fashion* for a more complete discussion and bibliography.

58. Batiushkov diary entry of 1817, in *Sochineniia* 2:340, quoted by Maikov, "O zhizni," 1:236.

59. Zubkov, "Opyty na puti k slave," 330.

60. Maikov gives a detailed account of Batiushkov's sojourn in Italy, in Batiushkov, *Sochineniia,* 1:259–91.

61. Letter to S. S. Uvarov, May 1819, in *Sochineniia,* 3:781. Rome was also experienced by Batiushkov as an assault on his intellectual coherence: "I always felt my ignorance, always had an inner awareness of my small talents, bad upbringing, weak knowledge, but here I became horrified. . . . Rome is a book: who will ever read it through?" (1:271).

62. See Iu. M. Lotman's formal analysis in "Batiushkov," in *Analiz poeticheskogo teksta* (Leningrad, 1972), 137–43.

63. Horace, *Odes and Epodes,* trans. C. E. Bennett (Cambridge: Harvard University Press, 1978), book II, ode XVIII, 156–59.

64. Troyat, *Alexander of Russia,* 248, 240–60; Palmer, 362–417.

65. Wortman, *Scenarios of Power,* 229. The Russian word traditionally used for enumerating serfs on a property was *dusha* or "soul"; while the word *rab* or "slave" was used by the nobility in its transactions with the monarchy as a mark of obeisance.

66. Lazar Fleishman and Andrei Zorin inform me that the date of the poem is still undecided: as late as 1824 or as early as 1821.

67. S. A. Kibal'nik, "Ob istochnikakh poslednego stikhotvoreniia Batiushkova," *Izvestiia Akademii nauk, Seria literatury* i *iazyka,* vol. 47, no. 4 (1988): 379–382.

LESLIE O'BELL, "KRYLOV, LA FONTAINE, AND AESOP"

References to memoir material about Krylov are to the edition *I. A. Krylov v vospominaniiakh sovremennikov* (Moscow: Khudozhestvennaia literatura, 1982) (K). References to La Fontaine's career are drawn from Marie-Odile Sweetser, *La Fontaine* (Boston: Twayne, 1987) (S). All translations are my own.

1. See discussion of Vigel below.

2. The prime example in Russian scholarship is Vladislav Kenevich, *Primechaniia k basniam Krylova,* 2d ed. (St. Petersburg: Glazunov, 1878).

3. I. A. Krylov, *Sochineniia* (Moscow: Khudozhestvennaia literatura, 1969), 2:437.

4. For a table of borrowings from La Fontaine, see Maurice Colin, *Krylov fabuliste* (Paris: Publications orientalistes de France, 1975), 563–64.

5. For other relatively recent treatments of this comparison, see A. Tseitlin, "Krylov i La Fonten," in *I. A. Krylov: Issledovaniia i materialy,* ed. D. D. Blagoi and N. L. Brodskii (Moscow: GosIzdKhudLit, 1947), 187–208 and Colin, "Krylov et La Fontaine" in his *Krylov fabuliste,* 547–66.

6. Colin tends to see the contrast between the two as stemming from a class difference (La Fontaine the patrician versus Krylov the plebian), while I take a less political approach.

7. See Mark Al'tshuller, "Krylov v literaturnykh ob"edineniiakh 1800–1810 godov" in *I. A. Krylov: Problemy tvorchestva* (Leningrad: Nauka, 1975), 154–95). Revised reprint in his *Predtechi slavianofil'stva v russkoi literature: Beseda liubitelei russkogo slova* (Ann Arbor, Mich.: Ardis, 1984), 210–248.

8. Tomashevsky points out that Pushkin was mainly interested in La Fontaine's verse tales, the *contes,* rather than his fables, and that his remarks about the French poet were commonplaces. See B. V. Tomashevskii, "Pushkin i Lafonten," *Pushkin: Vremennik pushkinskoi komissii,* 3 (1937): 242–43.

9. The quotation is from the conclusion of Krylov's fable "The Mouse Council" "Sovet myshei." Krylov, *Sochineniia,* 2:139.

10. A. S. Pushkin, *Polnoe sobranie sochinenii v desiati tomakh* (*PSS*) (Moscow: Nauka, 1966), 10:189 [1825].

11. Pushkin, *PSS,* 10:83 [1824].

12. I am extending the concept of *smekhovoi mir* developed by Dmitrii Likhachev and derived from Bakhtin's exploration of the comic world-vision of the Middle Ages. See D. S. Likhachev and A. M. Panchenko, "*Smekhovoi mir" drevnei Rusi* (Leningrad: Nauka, 1976), 3–4.

13. On Olenin and his circle, see Mary Stuart, "Olenin and Russian Culture," in her *Aristocrat-Librarian in Service of the Tsar: Aleksei Nikolaevich Olenin and the Imperial Library* (Boulder, Colo.: East European Monographs, 1986), 39–59; and L.V. Timofeev, *V krugu druzei i muz: dom A. N. Olenina* (Leningrad: Leninzdat, 1983). The N. A. L'vov circle where the poet Khemnitser had read his fables was the prototype for Olenin's.

14. See Al'tshuller, *Predtechi slavianofil'stva.* Others portray Krylov as positioned between the two camps. See N. L. Stepanov, "Evoliutsiia i teoriia basni v 1790–1810 godakh," in *I. A. Krylov: Problemy tvorchestva* (Leningrad: Nauka, 1975), 196–200.

15. This is the argument of Ol'ga Freidenberg (among others). See especially "Teoriia antichnogo fol'klora" in her *Mif i literatura drevnosti* (Moscow: Nauka, 1978).

16. It is interesting that one tradition of illustrating the fables depicts the characters as human torsos wearing animal masks on their heads. See Anne Stevenson Hobbs, ed., *Fables* (London: Victoria and Albert Museum, 1986), 60.

17. David Lee Rubin writes: "So it was that La Fontaine replaced the folk wisdom of Aesopic and Indic fable-writing with his personal adaptation of philosophical principles derived from a literary model." See *A Pact with Silence: Art and Thought in the Fables of La Fontaine* (Columbus: Ohio State University Press, 1991), 77.

18. Jean de La Fontaine, *Fables, contes et nouvelles* (Paris: Librairie Gallimard, 1954), 283.

19. See A. M. Bassy, *Les fables de La Fontaine: Quatre siècles d'illustration* (Paris: Promodis, 1986). La Fontaine was immediately illustrated by Chauveau, in what became the standard baroque edition, followed by Oudry's rococo designs (which have been called a masterpiece of book illustration), several neoclassical editions by different artists, and Grandville's famous 1835 edition, to name only the versions that Krylov might have seen with his direct access to the Imperial Library. By contrast, though the publisher Smirdin brought out an illustrated edition with prints by the minor Russian painter Sapozhnikov (reprint, Leningrad: Khudozhestvennaia literatura, 1983), Krylov had to wait until the turn of the twentieth century to be illustrated by artists of the first rank like Serov and Chagall.

20. Hobbs, ed., *Fables,* 60.

21. This was the natural in the eighteenth-century sense where nature is "a regulating principle, not a liberating one," and "human virtue consists in 'following Nature.'" See Basil Wiley, *The Eighteenth-Century Background: Studies on the Idea of Nature in the Thought of the Period* (1940; London: Chatto and Windus, 1980), 16, 70.

22. Philippe Destouches (pseud. Néricault), *Le glorieux* (1732), act III, scene 5. See *Dictionnaire de citations françaises* (Paris: Robert, 1978), 433.

23. I. Z. Serman, "Literaturnaia sud'ba Krylova," *Russkaia literatura* 4 (1970): 29.

24. Berkov, as quoted in Serman, "Literaturnaia sud'ba Krylova," 22.

25. Serman, "Literaturnaia sud'ba Krylova," 21.

26. Krylov, *Sochineniia,* 2:225.

27. Ibid., 2:64 ("Ogorodnik i filosof").

28. G. A. Gukovskii, "Lirika Krylova," in *I. A. Krylov: Issledovaniia i materialy* (Moscow: GosIzdKhudLit, 1947), 209–24.

29. Krylov, *Sochineniia,* 2:203.

30. I. Z. Serman, "Krylov-basnopisets," in *Krylov: Problemy tvorchestva* (Leningrad: Nauka, 1975), 222.

31. See Leslie O'Bell, "The Spirit of Derzhavin's Anacreontic Verse," *Welt der Slaven* 29, no. 1, n.s., 8, no. 1 (1984): 62–87.

32. After the work of Iurii Tynianov in *Arkhaisty i novatory* (1929; Ann Arbor, Mich.: Ardis, 1985) it is apparent that the Karamzinian "middle style" was only the basis for a much richer, expanded literary diction that took shape when writers like Pushkin assimilated certain extremes still represented in the party of the opponents, or "archaisers," both high Slavonic diction and low speech or *prostorechie.* It seems to me that the argument about Krylov is whether he worked parallel with Pushkin or was one of the "archaisers" from whom Pushkin learned. Vinogradov was of the first opinion (see note 36). I am of the second, supported also by scholars like Al'tshuller. I think that the touchstone in Krylov's case is not low or folk diction from which he *was* able to create a special poetic idiom, but high diction, for which he did not have the taste or the poetic range.

33. Hans Georg Beck, *Geschichte der byzantinischen Volksliteratur,* part II, vol. 3 (Munich: Beck, 1971), 29–30.

34. N. K. Gudzii, *Istoriia drevnei russkoi literatury,* 7th ed. (Moscow: Prosveshchenie, 966), 169.

35. Ibid., 43–44.

36. V. V. Vinogradov, *Izbrannye trudy: Iazyk i stil' russkikh pisatelei ot Karamzina do Gogolia* (Moscow: Nauka, 1990), 161.

37. D. S. Likhachev, ed., *Istoriia russkoi literatury X–XVII vekov* (Moscow: Prosveshchenie, 1980), 415–16, 423.

38. Gudzii, *Istoriia,* 469–70. See also V. P. Adrianova-Perets, "Basni Èzopa v russkoi iumoristicheskoi literature XVIII veka," in *Izvestiia po russkomu iazyku i slovesnosti* (Moscow: AN SSSR, 1929), vol. 2, part 2, 377–400.

39. See P. B. Tarkovskii, "Gosudarev tolmach Fedor Govzinskii i ego perevod basen Èzopa,"in *Vestnik Leningradskogo universiteta,* Seriia istorii iazyka i literatury (1966), 3:104–15.

40. I. Z. Serman, "Spor o basne," in his *Russkii klassitsizm* (Leningrad: Nauka, 1973), 189.

41. See Serman, "Spor o basne."

42. I do not mean that Krylov's "originality" is greater; he is simply a different kind of poet. Those who preferred La Fontaine might see more value in his stylistic innovations than in Krylov's powers of invention. As did Zhukovsky; see note 45.

43. The classic commentary is Kenevich.

44. La Fontaine, *Fables, contes et nouvelles,* 247.

45. Iu. M. Prozorov, ed., *V. A. Zhukovskii-Kritik* (Moscow: Sovetskaia Rossiia, 1985), 54.

46. Ibid., 56.

47. Ibid., 57–58.

48. Ibid., 58.

49. M. A. Gasparov, *Antichnaia literaturnaia basnia (Fedr i Babrii)* (Moscow: Nauka, 1971), 22–23.

50. F. A. Petrovskii, "Krylov i antichnaia basnia," In *Iazyk i stil' antichnykh pisatelei* (Leningrad: Izdatel'stvo leningradskogo universiteta, 1966), 144–54.

51. The definitive textual history of the Aesopic tradition is B. E. Perry, *Studies in the Text History of the Life and Fables of Aesop* (1936; Chico, Calif.: Scholars Press, 1981).

52. Josef Matl, "Antike Gestalten in der slawischen literarischen und Volksuberlieferung," *Saeculum* 6, no. 4 (1955): 428.

53. See Tarkovskii, "Gosudarev tolmach." The life of Aesop (*Zhitie*) also appeared in the oft-reprinted Russian translation of Roger Lestrange's fable collection. See P. B. Tarkovskii, "Basnia v Rossii XVII—nachala XIX v," *Filologicheskie nauki* 3 (1966): 97–109 and Adrianova-Petets, "Basni Ezopa."

54. Lloyd W. Daly, trans. and ed., *Aesop without Morals* (New York: Yoseloff, 1961), 19–20.

55. See Todd Compton, "The Trial of the Satirist: Poetic *Vitae* (Aesop, Archilochus, Homer) as Background for Plato's *Apology,*" *American Journal of Philology* 3, no. 3 (1990): 330–47. The legend of Aesop's trial and death at Delphi predates the Socratic dialogues, although the Hellenistic romance that is the Life of Aesop of course postdates them. Thus the argument in Compton

is not an anachronism. He specifically states, "Socrates' trial returns us to the Aesopic tradition" (338). "[Socrates] is being assimilated to Aesop by Plato" (341). See also Niklas Holzberg, ed., *Der Äsop-Roman: Motivgeschichte und Erzählstruktur,* Classica Monacensia, Münchener Studien zur Klassischen Philologie, vol. 6 (Tübingen: Gunter Narr, 1992). Philosophical schools and ancient biographers had a tendency to "invent associations between famous men," like all popular historical tradition, according to Janet Fairweather ("Fiction in the Biographies of Ancient Writers," *Ancient Society,* 5 [1974]: 248). It is not excluded that great men may, in fact, have imitated their models.

56. Francisco R. Adrados, "The 'Life of Aesop' and the Origins of the Novel in Antiquity," *Quaderni Urbinati di Cultura Classica,* n.s. 1 (1979): 93.

57. Krylov, *Sochineniia,* 2:78 ("Volk i lisitsa").

58. Adrados, "The 'Life of Aesop,'" 96.

59. John J. Winkler, *Auctor and Actor: A Narratological Reading of Apuleius' Golden Ass* (Berkeley and Los Angeles: University of California Press, 1985), 282, 288.

60. See Compton, "Trial of the Satirist," 346.

61. See Marie-Christine Bellosta, " 'La Vie d'Esope le Phrygien' de La Fontaine ou les ruses de la vérité," *Revue d'histoire littéraire de la France* 1 (1979): 3–13.

62. Sloth was more a part of Krylov's self-created legend than his own character. S. M. Babintsev has documented the very real editorial and bibliographic work that Krylov did in the study *I. A. Krylov: Ocherk ego izdatel'skoi i bibliotechnoi deiatel'nosti* (Moscow: Izdatel'stvo vseisoiuznoi knizhnoi palaty, 1955). However, the gluttony is amply attested to.

63. Hobbs, ed., *Fables,* 46.

64. Pushkin, *PSS* (1964), 5:487. The "Golden Cockerel" was published in 1835.

65. Krylov, *Sochineniia,* 2:189.

66. Gasparov, *Antichnaia literaturnaia basnia,* 17.

67. This apologue reuses a topos of fable literature that can be found in both La Fontaine and the life of Aesop. See La Fontaine: "The Donkey Laden with Sponges and the Donkey Laden with Salt" ("L'Ane chargé d'éponges et l'âne chargé de sel," *Fables, contes et nouvelles,* 59–60). While the heavy load of salt melts away as one animal fords a stream, what seems light—the sponges—becomes heavy and nearly drowns the second animal as well as his stupid driver. This compares with an episode from Aesop's life when Aesop has to choose which basket to carry and decides on the heavy one with the bread, since it will soon be emptied by the hungry party. See Daly, *Aesop without Morals,* 38–39.

68. A. A. Potebnia, "Iz lektsii po teorii slovesnosti. Basnia, poslovitsa, pogovorka" [1894], in *Teoreticheskaia poetika* (Moscow: Vysshaia shkola,

1990), 55–132. See especially 90: "The role of the fable, and more generally, of poetry in human life is a synthesizing one: it aids us in coming to generalizations, not in proving these generalizations logically." Potebnia goes still further and compares the structure of the fable with the fundamental, bipartite structure of the proposition or sentence: theme and rheme (59–60).

69. Ibid., 80.

RONALD D. LEBLANC, "A LA RECHERCHE DU GENRE PERDU: FIELDING, GOGOL, AND BAKHTIN'S GENRE MEMORY"

An earlier version of this essay was presented at the Seventh International Bakhtin Conference held at the Moscow State Pedagogical University in June 1995.

1. For an intelligent discussion of Bakhtin's notion of genre, see Clive Thomson, "Bakhtin's 'Theory' of Genre," *Studies in Twentieth Century Literature* 9 (1984): 29–40. "Although genre is a matter (directly or indirectly) for discussion in most of Bakhtin's works," Thomson notes, "we find nothing like an attempt to develop a systematic theory" (30).

2. Gary Saul Morson and Caryl Emerson, *Mikhail Bakhtin: Creation of a Prosaics* (Stanford: Stanford University Press, 1990), 278. For their discussion of Bakhtin's theory of genres, see 271–305.

3. Mikhail Bakhtin, *Problems of Dostoevsky's Poetics,* trans. Caryl Emerson (Minneapolis: University of Minnesota Press, 1984), 106.

4. K. Skipina, "O chuvstvitel'noi povesti," in *Russkaia proza,* ed. Boris Eikhenbaum and Iurii Tynianov (1926; The Hague: Mouton, 1963), 13–41. "The sentimental tale," Skipina writes, "constitutes a complete negation of the principles which determine the language and plot of the adventure novel" (36).

5. Skipina, "O chuvstvitel'noi povesti," 30. I am quoting here from the English translation provided in *Russian Prose,* ed. and trans. Ray Parrott (Ann Arbor: Ardis, 1985), 35.

6. A. G. Tseitlin, "Iz istorii russkogo obshchestvenno-psikhologicheskogo romana," in his *Masterstvo Turgeneva-romanista* (Moscow: Sovetskii pisatel', 1958), 7. I am indebted to Donald Fanger for this reference. See his essay, "Influence and Tradition in the Russian Novel," in *The Russian Novel from Pushkin to Pasternak,* ed. John Garrard (New Haven: Yale University Press, 1983), 30.

7. John Garrard, "Introduction: The Rise of the Novel in Russia," in *The Russian Novel from Pushkin to Pasternak,* 11.

8. V. G. Belinskii, *Polnoe sobranie sochinenii,* 10 vols. (Moscow: Akademiia nauk, 1954–55), 9:643.

9. See William Mills Todd III's thorough and intelligent treatment of these issues in *Fiction and Society in the Age of Pushkin: Ideology, Institutions, and Narrative* (Cambridge: Harvard University Press, 1986), especially chap. 2, "Institutions of Literature," 45–105. N. N. Akimova addresses the issue of the clash between elite culture and mass culture in Russia during the 1830s in her article, "Bulgarin i Gogol' (massovoe i elitarnoe v russkoi literature: problema avtora i chitatelia)," *Russkaia literatura* 2 (1996): 3–22.

10. V. F. Pereverzev asserts that Pushkin felt impelled to turn to prose mainly due to the commercial successes that were being enjoyed by Bulgarin, Senkovsky, and other literary philistines in Russia during the 1830s. "A broad reading audience had appeared," Pereverzev explains, "an audience that demanded prose and that could be influenced only by artistic prose. Not to meet these needs would have meant locking oneself away in aristocratic exclusiveness, losing a broad audience, and in the end foresaking a role as a serious factor in the cultural development of society. In order to preserve this role, in order to counter the successes of a vulgar, bourgeois prose that lacked any aesthetic refinement, it was necessary to democratize artistically, to lower oneself to 'contemptible' prose and to create one's own prose, a prose that would maintain a high cultural and aesthetic value." See Pereverzev, *U istokov russkogo real'nogo romana* (Moscow: Khudozhestvennaia literatura, 1937), 48.

11. A. S. Pushkin, *Polnoe sobranie sochinenii* (Moscow: Akademiia nauk, 1937–49), 6:135.

12. For a study of Gogol's *Dead Souls* as a response to Bulgarin's *Ivan Vyzhigin,* see my article, "Gogol's Chichikov: Russian Picaro or Real Vyzhigin?" *Canadian-American Slavic Studies* 23, no. 4 (1989): 409–28. For Gogol's relationship to Cervantes and Dante respectively, see Ludmilla B. Turkevich, *Cervantes in Russia* (Princeton: Princeton University Press, 1950) and Marianne Shapiro, "Gogol and Dante," *Modern Language Studies* 17 (1987): 37–54.

13. See, for example, Susan Layton, *Russian Literature and Empire: The Conquest of the Caucasus from Pushkin to Tolstoy* (Cambridge: Cambridge University Press, 1994); Peter Scotto, "Prisoners of the Caucasus: Ideologies of Imperialism in Lermontov's 'Bela,'" *PMLA* 107 (1992): 246–60; Anthony Anemone, "Gender, Genre, and the Discourse of Imperialism in Tolstoy's Cossacks," *Tolstoy Studies Journal* 6 (1993): 47–63; and Katya Hokanson, "Literary Imperialism, *Narodnost'*, and Pushkin's Invention of the Caucasus," *Russian Review* 53 (1994): 336–52. The introductory essay to the present volume itself suggests that "empire" and "nation" serve as two of the defining concepts for Russian literature during the Golden Age.

14. N. Belozerskaia explores the scope of this indebtedness, and demonstrates how a slavish imitation of foreign works retarded the development of original novels in Russia, in her essay, "Vliianie perevodnogo romana i zapadnoi tsivilizatsii na russkoe obshchestvo XVIII veka," *Russkaia starina* 83 (1995): 125–56.

15. C. L. Drage, *Russian Literature in the Eighteenth Century* (London: Drage, 1978), 215. "In the 1760s, emboldened by the translated novels' success, native Russian novelists began to emerge," Drage explains, "but the west European masterpieces in the genre, which were translated into Russian in the 1770s, 1780s, and 1790s, so outshone the native productions that the latter tended to circulate only among children and adolescents and in the less educated sectors of Russian society. At the end of the eighteenth century the educated Russian reader preferred to read Richardson, Sterne, Fielding, Goldsmith, Swift, and Rousseau, among the classics, and Miss Burney, Mme de Genlis, and Kotzebue, among the popular novelists: he seems to have generally ignored the native Russian novelists, perhaps not always justifiably in view of the merits of certain of them" (215).

16. T. Grits, V. Trenin, and M. Nikitin, *Slovesnost' i kommertsiia (knizhnaia lavka A. F. Smirdina)*, ed. V. Shklovskii and B. Eikhenbaum (Moscow: Federatsiia, 1929), 177. Elsewhere in their study the authors refer to "foreign dominance" and "foreign intervention" in eighteenth-century Russian literature (181). In his "Peterburgskie zapiski 1836 goda," Gogol refers to the Russian capital as "a European-American colony." See Gogol, *Polnoe sobranie sochinenii* (Moscow: Akademiia nauk, 1937–52), 8:179–80.

17. See, for example, Iurii Stennik, "Preemstvennost' traditsii i literaturnyi protsess (russkaia literatura na rubezhe XVIII-XIX vekov)," *Russkaia literatura* 4 (1969): 89–95. Rufus Mathewson observes that we find in Pushkin "not only an incomparable Russian poet but a European man of letters of great learning and flawless judgment who took exactly what he and Russia needed from Rousseau, Byron, Shakespeare, and all the others . . . his practice of selecting, rejecting, combining, altering, and finally going beyond his models is one of his greatest gifts to the Russian tradition." See "Russian Literature and the West," *Slavic Review* 21 (1962): 414.

18. Edward Said, *Culture and Imperialism* (New York: Knopf, 1993), 217. For a study that examines cultural imperialism—as distinct from imperialism of a predominantly economic or political nature—see John Tomlinson, *Cultural Imperialism: A Critical Introduction* (Baltimore: Johns Hopkins University Press, 1991).

19. Liah Greenfeld, *Nationalism: Five Roads to Modernity* (Cambridge: Harvard University Press, 1992). See especially chap. 3, "The Scythian Rome: Russia," 189–274. In *Atlantic Double-Cross: American Literature and British Influence in the Age of Emerson* (Chicago: University of Chicago Press, 1986),

Robert Weisbuch examines how American literary nationalism likewise arose largely as a self-conscious effort to resist—and, ultimately, to overcome—foreign influence: in this case, the tyranny of British literary models.

20. *Poliarnaia zvezda, izdannaia A. Bestuzhevym i K. Ryleevym,* ed. V. G. Bazanov (Moscow: Akademiia nauk, 1960), 488.

21. David Gasperetti discusses the literary patriotism manifested by some of these eighteenth-century Russian writers in his forthcoming book, *The Rise of the Russian Novel: Carnival, Stylization, and Mockery of the West.* I am very grateful to Professor Gasperetti for allowing me to read portions of his manuscript.

22. See my *The Russianization of Gil Blas: A Study in Literary Appropriation* (Columbus, Ohio: Slavica, 1986).

23. For a discussion of the "English" psychological-family novel and its reception in Russia, see part 1 of V. V. Sipovskii's monumental study, *Ocherki iz istorii russkogo romana* (St. Petersburg, 1909–10). The high regard in which Russian critics held the English novel is evident from the following passage taken from an essay, "O povestiakh i romanakh," that appeared in the journal *Avrora* in 1806: "When undertaking to write a novel, the author should set himself the goal of portraying people such as they are in reality. He should depict the human heart with all its strengths and weaknesses; with the passions that possess it; with its dominant habits; with the virtues that beautify it and the mores that disfigure it. For this he should choose as his models: Wieland's Agathon, the novels of Lesage, Fielding, Sterne, Lafontaine and others." Quoted in Sipovskii, *Iz istorii russkogo romana i povesti (Materialy po bibliografii, istorii i teorii russkogo romana)* (St. Petersburg, 1903), 252.

24. Ernest J. Simmons, *English Literature and Culture in Russia (1553–1840)* (1935; New York: Octagon Books, 1964), 137.

25. For a study that examines Fielding's reception in Russia, see—in addition to the aforementioned works by Sipovsky and Simmons—M. P. Alekseev, "Fielding in the Russian Language," *VOKS Bulletin* 5 (1954): 88–92.

26. Alekseev, "Fielding in the Russian Language," 89.

27. In his encyclopedic study of the novel (both translated and original) on eighteenth-century Russian soil, Sipovsky makes the highly questionable assertion that no Russian novelists during that period imitated Fielding. See *Ocherki iz istorii russkogo romana,* 1:892.

28. D. S. Mirsky, *A History of Russian Literature: From Its Beginnings to 1900* (New York: Vintage Books, 1958), 119–20.

29. "Here is a Ukrainian Gil Blas!" exclaimed one contemporary critic about Narezhny's Neon. "One sees it in his juvenile, romantic, comic and tragic adventures." The reviewer proceeds to call the author a "Russian Lesage." See *Damskii zhurnal* 3 (1825): 114. John Mersereau Jr., who finds

that both Narezhny and his hero share "a quite healthy, unneurotic attitude towards life, a gusto which is also evident in the story's inventories about food and drink," sees closer affinities with Fielding than with Lesage. "Neon is something of a Ukrainian Tom Jones," Mersereau observes, "and like his progenitor is prone to err, not from any innate wickedness but simply because he is thoughtless and very human." See *Russian Romantic Fiction* (Ann Arbor, Mich.: Ardis, 1983), 70, 71.

30. The affinities between Bulgarin's *Ivan Vyzhigin* and Fielding's *Tom Jones* are discussed in my book, *The Russianization of Gil Blas* (168–69).

31. For studies on *Dead Souls* as a picaresque novel, see Iurii Mann, "*Mertvye dushi* Gogolia i traditsii zapadnoevropeiskogo romana," *Slavianskie literatury,* ed. M. P. Alekseev (Moscow: Nauka, 1978), 235–55; I. V. Egorov, "*Mertvye dushi* i zhanr plutovskogo romana," *Izvestiia Akademii nauk SSSR.* Seriia literatury i iazyka 37 (1978): 31–36; T. E. Little, "*Dead Souls,*" in *Knaves and Swindlers: Essays on the Picaresque Novel in Europe,* ed. Christine J. Whitbourne (London: Oxford University Press, 1974), 112–38; Karl Selig, "Concerning Gogol's *Dead Souls* and *Lazarillo de Tormes,*" *Symposium* 8 (1954): 138–40; and Olga Markof-Belaeff, "*Dead Souls* and the Picaresque Tradition: A Study in the Definition of Genre," (Ph.D. diss., University of California at Berkeley, 1982).

32. Two of my articles examine these so-called Flemish tendencies that critics have perceived in Gogol's prose style. See "Teniersism: Seventeenth-Century Flemish Art and Early Nineteenth-Century Russian Prose," *Russian Review* 49 (1990): 19–41, and "Teniers, Flemish Art, and the Natural School Debate," *Slavic Review* 50 (1991): 576–89.

33. See the section entitled "The Two Stylistic Lines of Development in the European Novel" in Bakhtin's essay, "Discourse in the Novel," in *The Dialogic Imagination,* ed. Michael Holquist (Austin: University of Texas Press, 1981), 366–422.

34. See Gogol's posthumous essay, "Uchebnaia kniga slovesnosti dlia russkogo iunoshestva," in his *Polnoe sobranie sochinenii,* 8:478–79. In his analysis of *Dead Souls,* D. E. Tamarchenko argues that—like Gogol's "epic poem"—the novels of both Lesage and Fielding deserve to qualify as "minor epics" since they successfully fuse together the picaresque tradition with elements from the new family novel in order to create the "epos of family life." See "*Mertvye dushi,*" in *Istoriia russkogo romana,* ed. G. M. Fridlender (Moscow: Akademiia nauk, 1962), 1:324–58. John Garrard, meanwhile, notes that "Henry Fielding's definition of the novel as a 'comic epic in prose' in the preface to *Joseph Andrews* is suggestive as a description of *Dead Souls.*" See "Introduction: The Rise of the Novel in Russia," 18. For a thorough discussion of Gogol's *Dead Souls* as a modern "epic," see Frederick Griffiths and

Stanley Rabinowitz, *Novel Epics: Gogol, Dostoevsky, and National Literature* (Evanston: Northwestern University Press, 1990).

35. See Gogol, *Polnoe sobranie sochinenii,* 6:553, 644. As Fanger points out, however, we have no real evidence that Gogol actually had any firsthand knowledge of these foreign writers from whom he claims he drew inspiration. "Save for Pushkin," Fanger notes, "neither the letters nor the essays betray signs of direct acquaintance with works by any of them. . . . His correspondence gives us little notion of his reading, knowledge, tastes, or even specific awareness of literature in the forms he himself cultivated." See *The Creation of Nikolai Gogol* (Cambridge: Harvard University Press, 1979), 12–13.

36. Pushkin, *Polnoe sobranie sochinenii,* 11:216.

37. Richard Freeborn, *The Rise of the Russian Novel: Studies in the Russian Novel from "Eugene Onegin" to "War and Peace"* (Cambridge: Cambridge University Press, 1973), 76 n. 3.

38. Fanger, *Creation of Nikolai Gogol,* 88. "Virtually all of Gogol's works show such borrowing," Fanger notes, "though most often transformed beyond recognition in the crucible of his genius" (50).

39. M. P. Alekseev provides a synoptic account of Russian familiarity with the English language during the eighteenth and nineteenth centuries in his essay, "Angliiskii iazyk v Rossii i russkii iazyk v Anglii," *Uchenye zapiski Leningradskogo gos. universiteta.* Seriia filologicheskikh nauk 9 (1944): 77–137. According to Iurii Levin, one of Fielding's own Russian translators (Vladimir Zolotnitskii, 1741–97) apparently did not even know English. See "Translations of Henry Fielding's Works in Eighteenth-Century Russia," *Slavonic and East European Review* 68 (1990): 222.

40. For Gogol's poor command of foreign languages, see Mark Altshuller, "The Walter Scott Motifs in Nikolay Gogol's Story 'The Lost Letter,'" *Oxford Slavonic Papers* 22 (1989): 84. According to one of his friends (P. A. Kulish), Gogol could hardly understand a book in French without the help of a dictionary. See V. V. Veresaev, *Gogol v zhizni* (1933; Moscow: Moskovskii rabochii, 1990), 89. In G. I. Chudakov's essay on Gogol's relationship to West European literatures, meanwhile, the author provides a list indicating that all of Fielding's novels were readily available to Gogol in Russian translation in the private library of Troshchinskii, a library that the young gymnasium student used frequently during his school years. See "Otnoshenie tvorchestva Gogolia k zapadnoevropeiskim literaturam," *Universitetskie izvestiia* (Kiev) 48 (1908): 101–26.

41. See I. M. Levidova, *Genri Fil'ding: Bio-bibliograficheskii ukazatel' k dvukhsotletiiu so dnia smerti* (Moscow: Vsesoiuznaia gosudarstvennaia biblioteka inostrannoi literatury, 1954), 22.

42. See, for example, D. P. Iakubovich, "Rol' Frantsii v znakomstve Rossii s romanami V. Skotta," *Iazyk i literatura* 25 (1930): 137–84; and P. R.

Zaborov, " 'Literatura-posrednik' v istorii russko-zapadnykh literaturnykh sviazei XVIII—XIX vv.," in *Mezhdunarodnye sviazi russkoi literatury,* ed. M. P. Alekseev (Moscow: Akademiia nauk, 1963), 64–85.

43. Rachel May examines the role of translations in the flow of literary influence out of—rather than into—Russian literature. See *The Translator in the Text: On Reading Russian Literature in English* (Evanston: Northwestern University Press, 1994).

44. Harry Sieber, *The Picaresque* (London: Methuen, 1977), 59. Noting that "these translations are historically of cardinal importance," Alexander A. Parker asserts that they "can alone explain the changes that the picaresque tradition underwent as it moved into the eighteenth century." See *Literature and the Delinquent: The Picaresque Novel in Spain and Europe, 1599–1753* (Edinburgh: Edinburgh University Press, 1967), 111.

45. Hendrik van Gorp, "Translation and Literary Genre: The European Picaresque Novel in the Seventeenth and Eighteenth Centuries," in *The Manipulation of Literature: Studies in Literary Translation,* ed. Theo Hermans (London: Croom Helm, 1985), 136–48.

46. Jurij Striedter provides a thorough reception study of European picaresque fiction in late eighteenth-century and early nineteenth-century Russia in *Der Schelmenroman in Russland: Ein Beitrag zur Geschichte der russischen Romans vor Gogol'* (Berlin: Erich Blaschker, 1961).

47. Alekseev, "Fielding in the Russian Language," 91.

48. As an example of just how scrupulously faithful Kharlamov is to La Place's French translation of Fielding's novel, consider how at one point in his own Russian translation he includes the following: "The English author of this story provides a great and very lengthy description of the beauty of the person, morals and traits of our Heroine; but, in order to spare our French readers [*sic*]—who are less patient than our neighbors—the boredom that is always connected with length, I will say quite simply that Sophia was beautiful and worthy of love." I am quoting here from the second edition of Kharlamov's translation, *Povest' o Tomase Ionese, ili Naidenyshe* (Moscow, 1787), 1:94.

49. See especially Harold Wade Streeter, *The Eighteenth-Century English Novel in French Translation* (New York: Benjamin Blom, 1970), 23–36, and Constance B. West, "La théorie de la traduction au XVIIIe siècle," *Revue de littérature comparée* 12 (1932): 330–55.

50. Streeter, *The Eighteenth-Century English Novel in French Translation,* 27.

51. The situation was hardly different, of course, in eighteenth-century Russia, where liberal translation likewise was the rule. As Caryl Emerson observes, "Translators were expected to adapt and alter the text, bearing as they did a moral responsibility to transmit, via received texts, the values

appropriate to their society." See *Boris Godunov: Transpositions of a Russian Theme* (Bloomington: Indiana University Press, 1986), 22.

52. L'abbé Prévost, "Préface du traducteur," *Nouvelles lettres anglaises ou Histoire du chevalier de Grandisson, par l'auteur de "Paméla" et de "Clarisse"* (Amsterdam, 1755–58), as cited in Streeter, *The Eighteenth-Century English Novel in French Translation,* 28. In a recent deconstructionist study that examines French and German translations of Richardson's *Clarissa,* Thomas O. Beebee argues that, by their very perversity, loose translations such as the one by Prévost actually allowed the larger meanings of Richardson's novel to emerge. Indeed, translations (and even mistranslations), Beebee asserts, can show a deeper truth that lies behind the original text. See *Clarissa on the Continent: Translation and Seduction* (University Park: Pennsylvania State University Press, 1990), 4.

53. For Desfontaines's activity as a translator of Swift and Fielding, see Thelma Morris, "L'Abbé Desfontaines et son rôle dans la littérature de son temps," *Studies on Voltaire and the Eighteenth Century* 19 (1961): 266–323.

54. Quoted in Sybil Goulding, *Swift en France* (Paris: Champion, 1924), 76.

55. Pierre Clément, *Cinq années littéraires ou Nouvelles littéraires des années 1748 à 1752* (Berlin, 1755), 1:286, as cited in West, "La théorie de la traduction au XVIIIè siècle," 338.

56. Elie Fréron, *Lettres sur quelques écrits de ce temps* (1751), 4:4–6, as cited in Streeter, *The Eighteenth-Century English Novel in French Translation,* 78.

57. Henry Fielding, *Tom Jones,* ed. Sheridan Baker (New York: Norton, 1973), 190, and Pierre Antoine de La Place, *Tom Jones, ou L'Enfant trouvé* (Paris, 1832), 1:166. All further references to Fielding's *Tom Jones,* as well as to La Place's French version of it, come from these two later (but more readily accessible) editions of those works; they will be cited parenthetically in the text by volume and page number.

58. For a thorough treatment of this issue, see Robert L. Chibka, "Taking the SERIOUS Seriously: The Introductory Chapters of Tom Jones," *Eighteenth Century: Theory and Interpretation* 31 (1990): 23–45.

59. Scott's essay on Fielding, part of his *Lives of the Novelists* (1827), can be found in *Sir Walter Scott on Novelists and Fiction,* ed. Ioan Williams (New York: Barnes & Noble, 1968), 46–56.

60. Fred Kaplan, for instance, argues that the reader-directed prefaces in *Tom Jones* constitute a second plot in Fielding's novel, "whose major theme is how and why the author writes this novel as he does." See "Fielding's Novel About Novels: The 'Prefaces' and the 'Plot' of Tom Jones," *Studies in English Literature, 1500–1900* 13 (1973): 536.

61. Chibka, "Taking the SERIOUS Seriously," 30. Michael Bliss concurs with this view. "The introductory chapters of Tom Jones," he writes, "are indeed an integral and organically functional part of the novel." See "Fielding's Bill of Fare in Tom Jones," *ELH* 30 (1963): 237.

62. John J. Burke Jr., "History without History: Fielding's Theory of Fiction," in *A Provision of Human Nature: Essays on Fielding and Others in Honor of Miriam Austin Locke,* ed. Donald Kay (Birmingham: University of Alabama Press, 1977), 59.

63. Fanger, *Creation of Nikolai Gogol,* 260. Elsewhere in his book, Fanger explains that Gogol's "best works are self-reflexive and ultimately 'about' the nature of their own literary being" (23).

64. Ibid., 152.

65. See, for example, Richard Freeborn, *The Rise of the Russian Novel,* 2. "He [Gogol] may have found a precedent for his own narrative digressions in Sterne and Fielding," Fanger writes, "but the native precedent for the passages in Dead Souls that are traditionally called lyrical digressions could only have come from Pushkin." See *Creation of Nikolai Gogol,* 152.

66. Vasily Gippius, *Gogol,* ed. and trans. Robert A. Maguire (Durham: Duke University Press, 1989), 116–17.

67. *Gogol i problemy zapadnoevropeiskogo romana* (Moscow: Nauka, 1972), 45–46. I am quoting here from the English translation of Elistratova's book. See *Nikolai Gogol and the West European Novel,* trans. Christopher English (Moscow: Raduga Publishers, 1984), 41–42.

68. *Nikolai Gogol and the West European Novel,* 42.

69. Alekseev, "Fielding in the Russian Language," 89.

70. Levin, "Translations of Henry Fielding's Works in Eighteenth-Century Russia," 228.

71. *Travels in Various Countries of Europe, Asia, and Africa* (London, 1810), 72, as cited in A. G. Cross, " 'S aglinskago': Books of English Origin in Russian Translation in Late Eighteenth-Century Russia," *Oxford Slavonic Papers* 19 (1986): 74–75.

72. See *Nikolai Gogol and the West European Novel,* 26, and Gippius, *Gogol,* 117.

73. Bernard McGuirk's "On Misreading Mallarmé: Rubén Darío and the Anxiety of Influence," for example, invokes Bloom's theories as a way to explain the influence of the French Symbolist poet on a Nicaraguan writer. See *Nottingham French Studies* 26 (1987): 52–67. George J. Zytaruk, meanwhile, in "D. H. Lawrence's *The Rainbow* and Leo Tolstoy's *Anna Karenina:* An Instance of Literary 'Clinamen,' " argues that Lawrence's wrestling with the famous Russian novelist provides an instance that effectively proves Bloom's theory about the need to "misread" a strong precursor. See Zytaruk's essay in *Tolstoi and Britain,* ed. W. Gareth Jones (Oxford: Berg, 1995), 225–38.

74. Harold Bloom, *The Anxiety of Influence: A Theory of Poetry* (New York: Oxford University Press, 1973), 9–10.

75. Bloom, *A Map of Misreading* (New York: Oxford University Press, 1975), 69.

76. The felicitous term *influence de rebours* is one used by Claudio Guillén in "Genre and Countergenre: The Discovery of the Picaresque," in his *Literature as System: Essays Toward the Theory of Literary History* (Princeton: Princeton University Press, 1971), 135–58.

77. It is entirely possible, of course, that Fielding's style may have been communicated to Gogol in an indirect artistic manner as well: that is, through the works and discussions of the French Romantics from the 1820s and 1830s who were in the process of rejecting their own native neoclassical tradition in favor of the English style.

78. Bakhtin, *Problems of Dostoevsky's Poetics,* 157.

79. Morson and Emerson, *Mikhail Bakhtin: Creation of a Prosaics,* 296.

80. Bakhtin, *Problems of Dostoevsky's Poetics,* 121.

81. Bakhtin, "Response to a Question from the *Novyi Mir* Editorial Staff," *Speech Genres and Other Late Essays,* ed. Caryl Emerson and Michael Holquist, trans. Vern W. McGee (Austin: University of Texas Press, 1986), 5–7.

82. I am quoting here from the newly revised edition of Bernard Guilbert Guerney's translation of *Dead Souls* prepared by Susanne Fusso (New Haven: Yale University Press, 1996). All subsequent quotations from *Dead Souls* will come from this edition and will be cited parenthetically in the text, following the volume and page number from the *Polnoe sobranie sochinenii.*

83. I am quoting here from the anonymous review of La Place's *Histoire de Tom Jones, ou L'Enfant trouvé* that appeared in the 20 March 1750 issue of the *Gentleman's Magazine.* See Fielding, *Tom Jones,* 782. La Place proceeds to explain that the French reader "becomes impatient under all sorts of digressions, dissertations, or moral touches, and regards all such ornaments, however fine, as obstacles to the pleasure which he is in haste to enjoy. I have done no more than what the author himself would have done" (782).

84. In his review of Martin Battestin's biography of Fielding, Derek Jarrett notes that the English novelist "had always been excessively fond of eating and drinking" and that "the best known and most popular of his compositions during his lifetime was neither a novel nor a political satire but a song called 'The Roast Beef of Old England,' which it soon became customary for theater audiences to sing before and after and even during performances." See "Rogue Genius," *New York Review of Books,* 22 November 1990, 40.

85. Vladimir Nabokov, *Nikolai Gogol* (New York: New Directions, 1944), 98. For studies that examine the use of food imagery in Gogol's

novel, see Alexander Obolensky, *Food-Notes on Gogol* (Winnipeg: Trident, 1972), Natalia M. Kolb-Seletski, "Gastronomy, Gogol, and His Fiction," *Slavic Review* 29 (1970): 35–57; and Ronald LeBlanc, "Dinner with Chichikov: The Fictional Meal as Narrative Device in Gogol's *Dead Souls*," *Modern Fiction Studies* 18 (1988): 68–80.

86. Andrei Belyi, *Masterstvo Gogolia* (1934; Ann Arbor, Mich.: Ardis, 1982), 155.

87. Sergei Aksakov asserted that "if fate had not made Gogol a great poet, then he would most certainly have become an *artiste-chef*." See *Istoriia moego znakomstva s Gogolem* (Moscow: Akademiia nauk, 1960), 35. Gogol himself makes use of the "author-as-chef" metaphor when he writes to a friend for a critique of *Dead Souls*, phrasing his request in the following manner: "Imagine that I am an innkeeper in some European hotel and I have a table for everyone or a *table d'hôte*. There are twenty dishes on my table and perhaps more. Naturally, not all these dishes are identically good or, at least, it goes without saying that everyone will choose for himself and eat only the dishes he likes. . . . So I am only asking you to say this: 'This is what is more to my taste in your work, these places here' " (12:81).

88. *Moskvitianin* 8 (1842): 375–76.

89. Bakhtin, *Dialogic Imagination*, 293.

90. See Bakhtin's essay, "Epic and Novel," in *Dialogic Imagination*, especially 5–7.

91. It should be noted that Gogol's *Dead Souls*, in its turn, would be held "captive" in Fielding's homeland during the second half of the nineteenth century, not terribly unlike the way *Tom Jones* had been held prisoner in Russia during the first half of the century. In the spurious English translation that appeared in London in 1854 under the distorted title *Home Life in Russia. By a Russian Noble*, Gogol's text was stripped of many of its lyrical digressions, including the impassioned address to Russia, metaphorized as a speeding troika, with which the first part of the novel comes to a memorable close. Instead of the famous apostrophe to Russia as a speeding troika, this English version of *Dead Souls* ends with Chichikov being arrested by tsarist officials soon after he leaves town and being sent immediately into Siberian exile. See *Home Life in Russia. By a Russian Noble*, revised by the editor of "Revelations of Siberia" (London, 1854), 2:314. Elistratova briefly discusses this "crudely falsified" English translation of *Dead Souls* in her essay, "Gogol' i prosveshchenie (*Mertvye dushi* i angliiskii prosvetitel'skii roman)," in *Problemy Prosveshcheniia v mirovoi literature* (Moscow: Nauka, 1970), 216–34; see 218. Commenting upon this corruption of *Dead Souls* in English translation, Vladimir Nabokov remarks wryly that "Gogol's book has had a most Gogolian fate" (*Nikolai Gogol*, 63).

92. For a discussion of the Spanish roots in Narezhny's picaresque novel, see my "Making Gil Blas Russian," *Slavic and East European Journal* 30 (1986): 340–54.

93. Markof-Belaeff seems to observe a similar pattern (of looking "through" absences) in Gogol's appropriation of European picaresque fiction. She writes that "Gogol' has more in common with the earlier Spanish picaresque forms—which he did not know—than with the later French and Russian forms to which he had access." In *Dead Souls,* she notes, we witness "the reappearance of genre potentialities that had long been forgotten." See "*Dead Souls* and the Picaresque Tradition," 254.

KATYA HOKANSON, "PUSHKIN'S CAPTIVE CRIMEA: IMPERIALISM IN 'THE FOUNTAIN OF BAKHCHISARAI'"

1. I have also discussed this elsewhere, albeit in a different vein, in "Literary Imperialism, *Narodnost'*, and Pushkin's Invention of the Caucasus," *Russian Review* 53 (1994): 336–52. See also the first chapter of "Empire of the Imagination: Orientalism and the Construction of Russian National Identity in Pushkin, Marlinskii, Lermontov, and Tolstoi (Ph.D. diss., Stanford University, 1994).

2. See the sources referred to in note 1.

3. The polemical article led to a long debate with M. A. Dmitriev. See discussions in B. Tomashevskii, *Pushkin: Kniga vtoraia* (Moscow: Akademiia nauk, 1961), 126–27, and *Pushkin: Kniga pervaia* (Moscow: Akademiia nauk, 1956), 516–19, and in Lauren Leighton, *Russian Romantic Criticism* (Westport, Conn.: Greenwood, 1987).

4. P. A. Viazemskii, *Sochineniia v dvukh tomakh* (Moscow: Khudozhestvennaia literatura, 1982), 2:96. All translations are mine unless otherwise indicated.

5. Ibid., 98–99.

6. Leonid Grossman, "U istokov *Bakhchisaraiskogo fontana,*" in *Pushkin: Issledovaniia i materialy* (Moscow: Akademiia nauk, 1960), 3:89.

7. See A. S. Pushkin, *Polnoe sobranie sochinenii* (*PSS*) (Leningrad: Akademiia nauk, 1977–79), 4:149. All subsequent citations from "Bakhchisaraiskii fontan" and its appendices refer to this edition and will appear in parentheses within the body of the article.

8. See N. M. Karamzin, *Istoriia gosudarstva rossiskago* (Mouton: Slavistic Printings and Reprintings, 1969), 6:192.

9. See discussion of Pushkin's technique of presenting mutually conflicting points of view of historical events and facts in Boris Gasparov's "*Graf Nulin*" in *Text and Context: Essays to Honor Nils Åke Nilsson,* ed. Peter Alberg

Jensen et al. (Stockholm: Almquist and Wiksell International, 1987), as well as in Andrew Wachtel, *An Obsession with History: Russian Writers Confront the Past* (Stanford: Stanford University Press, 1994).

10. See Stephanie Sandler's *Distant Pleasures: Alexander Pushkin and the Writing of Exile* (Stanford: Stanford University Press, 1989). See also Susan Layton, *Russian Literature and Empire: Conquest of the Caucasus from Pushkin to Tolstoy* (Cambridge: Cambridge University Press, 1994), 196–200.

11. Monika Greenleaf, *Pushkin and Romantic Fashion: Fragment, Elegy, Orient, Irony* (Stanford: Stanford University Press, 1994), 125–38. Greenleaf's excellent analysis of *Bakhchisarai* also engages gender issues.

12. See, among others, Greenleaf, *Pushkin and Romantic Fashion,* V. M. Zhirmunskii, *Bairon i Pushkin* (Leningrad: Nauka, 1978), B. Tomashevskii, *Pushkin. Kniga pervaia* (Moscow: Akademiia nauk, 1956), G. A. Gukovskii, *Pushkin i russkie romantiki* (Moscow: Khudozhestvennaia literatura, 1965).

13. A later traveler even claims that Lalla Rookh describes Bakhchisarai (William Elery Curtis, *Around the Black Sea* (New York: Hodder and Stoughton, 1911), 274–75.

14. Greenleaf, *Pushkin and Romantic Fashion,* 127–29.

15. Greenleaf's discussion of the poem reminds us that Maria, who venerates her culture's sacred texts and whose special privileges result from the khan's recognition of her cultural "superiority," ultimately "continues to give rise to legend, art, culture, while Zarema's passion reverted to nature, leaving no trace" (*Pushkin and Romantic Fashion,* 133). One could argue, however, that because Pushkin uses the poem to show a connection to both "Oriental" and European roots, Zarema also retains her power to inspire cultural artifacts.

16. See Simon Karlinsky, "Two Pushkin Studies: I. Pushkin, Chateaubriand, and the Romantic Pose; II. The Amber Beads of Crimea (Pushkin and Mickiewicz), *California Slavic Studies* 2 (1963): 96–120. See in particular 108–20.

17. Pushkin uses a variation of the quotation again in the fifty-first stanza of chapter 8 of *Eugene Onegin.*

18. Saadi wrote poetry in both Persian and Arabic.

19. Tomashevsky states that Pushkin took his quotation from a translation of the piece by the French translator Amedé Pichot, who also translated Byron. Tomashevskii, *Pushkin. Kniga pervaia,* 505–06. See also the textual annotations to the narrative poem, in Pushkin, *PSS,* 4:418.

20. Thomas Moore, *Lalla Rookh* (Philadelphia: Henry Altemus, 1895), 120.

21. B. Tomashevskii, *Pushkin. Kniga pervaia,* 505–7.

22. Interestingly, when Pushkin uses a variation of the same quotation

in the fifty-first stanza of chapter 8 of *Eugene Onegin*—"Inykh uzh net, a te daleche / Kak Sadi nekogda skazal" (Some are no longer, and the others are far away / As Saadi once said)—there is no ambiguity whatsoever. Whether the friends are dead or in exile, the meaning is ominous. Moreover, the quotation, rather than forming an epigraph as it does in "Bakhchisarai," appears in the final, rather melancholy stanza of the novel in verse. Though the two quotations are used in rather different ways, when Pushkin alludes to Saadi in *Eugene Onegin,* his allusion is rich with texture: he refers to his former narrative poem, written before the Decembrist uprising; to the "fountain of tears;" to the Russian south, where so many Decembrists were exiled; and to the notion of poets' work outlasting any physical monument. To most Russians, a more immortal monument than *Eugene Onegin* can hardly be imagined.

23. Recent scholarship has suggested that a 1796 translation of Saadi into Russian did exist and that Pushkin may have known it (M. L. Nol'man, "Saadi ili Tsitseron?" from *Tvorchestvo Pushkina i zarubezhnyi Vostok* [Moscow: Nauka, 1991]: 219–28). However, other aspects of Moore's *Lalla Rookh* indicate that Pushkin encountered the quotation in Moore. A prose passage introducing the framed poem "The Light of the Haram" contains a number of motifs that correspond to motifs in "Bakhchisarai." Eyes that had created a garden, but were now now longer there to see it, recalls the Saadi epigraph; Moore's Sultana Nourmahal fed fishes in marble basins, a detail very similar to the description of the khan's wives dropping earrings to fishes in marble basins. Most strikingly, Lalla Rookh's visit to the Royal Gardens called forth a poem about the woman, Nourmahal, who was memorialized by the gardens and basins, just as the poet-narrator's visit to Bakhchisarai called forth a poem about Maria and Zarema (Moore, *Lalla Rookh,* 237).

24. *Morals Pointed and Tales Adorned: The Bustan of Sa'di,* trans. G. M. Wickens (Leiden: E. J. Brill, 1974), Persian heritage series 17:30; emphasis added.

25. See *Encyclopaedia Britannica* (Chicago: Wm. Benton, 1965), 2:184–85. See also G. M. Wickens, "Persian Literature" in *Encyclopedia Americana,* International Edition (Danbury, Conn.: Grolier, 1988), 21:753, and Edward G. Browne, *A Literary History of Persia: From Firdawsi to Sa'di* (New York: Scribner, 1906), 17–34.

26. Browne, *A Literary History of Persia,* 528.

27. This move is in some sense an adoption of a Byronic mask, since Byron also molded himself as the latest successor to oriental poets, but it is noteworthy that Pushkin was in fact called "our young Saadi" by a delighted critic who wrote a short review in the *Damskii zhurnal* (referred to by Tomashevskii in *Pushkin: Kniga pervaia,* 521).

28. Iu. M. Lotman, "Problema Vostoka i Zapada v tvorchestve pozdnego Lermontova," in *Lermontovskii sbornik* (Leningrad: Nauka, 1985): 5–22; see in particular 16–17.

29. See Greenleaf, *Pushkin and Romantic Fashion,* Layton, *Russian Literature and Empire,* and Peter Scotto, "Prisoners of the Caucasus: Ideologies of Imperialism in Lermontov's 'Bela,'" *PMLA* 107 (1992): 246–60.

30. See Mark Bassin, "Russia between Europe and Asia: The Ideological Construction of Geography," *Slavic Review* 50 (1991) 1–17.

31. Here, and elsewhere in the essay, in discussing the uses of the doubled time frame of "Fountain," I am indebted to Andrew Wachtel's insightful commentary.

32. Tomashevskii, *Pushkin: Kniga pervaia,* 503–4.

33. Jeremiah Curtin, *The Mongols in Russia* (Boston: Little, Brown, 1908), 453.

34. Alan Fisher, *The Crimean Tatars* (Stanford, Calif.: Hoover Institution Press, 1978), and George Lantzeff and Richard Pierce, *Eastward to Empire: Exploration and Conquest on the Russian Open Frontier to 1750.* (Montreal: McGill-Queen's University Press, 1973).

35. Tomashevskii, *Pushkin: Kniga pervaia,* 496.

36. For an explanation of the functioning of the term "north" to denote Russia, see Lotman, "Problema Vostoka i Zapada v tvorchestve pozdnego Lermontova."

37. George Gordon, Lord Byron, "The Giaour," from *Poetical Works* (Oxford: Oxford University Press, 1987), lines 723–28, p. 259.

38. Ibid., lines 1329–34, p. 264.

39. See "O romanticheskoi poezii" in Orest Somov, *Selected Prose in Russian,* ed. John Mersereau and George Harjan (Ann Arbor: University of Michigan, 1974), as well as the first chapter of my "Empire of the Imagination."

40. Iurii Lotman, *Aleksandr Sergeevich Pushkin: Biografiia pisatelia* (Leningrad: Prosveshchenie, 1983). See chapter 3, "Iug," 52–110. For additional discussion of this issue, see Monika Greenleaf, "Pushkin's Byronic Apprenticeship: A Problem in Cultural Syncretism," *Russian Review* 53 (1994): 382–98. See also her *Pushkin and Romantic Fashion.*

41. See Sandler, *Distant Pleasures,* 165–66. See also Grossman, "U istokov 'Bakhchisaraiskogo fontana,'" in *Pushkin: Issledovaniia i materialy* (Moscow: Akademiia nauk, 1960), vol. 3, 49–100.

42. Sandler, *Distant Pleasures,* 180–81.

STEPHANIE SANDLER AND JUDITH VOWLES, "BEGINNING TO BE A POET: BARATYNSKY AND PAVLOVA"

We note with gratitude the astute readings offered by Catherine Ciepiela, Sarah Pratt, Monika Greenleaf, and Stephen Moeller-Sally of earlier versions of this essay.

1. For a fine analysis of Pushkin's poetic debut, see David Bethea, "Where to Begin: Pushkin, Derzhavin, and the Poetic Use of Filiation," *Rereading Russian Poetry,* ed. Stephanie Sandler (New Haven: Yale University Press, forthcoming). Mikhail Lermontov's "Death of a Poet" ("Smert' poeta," 1837) similarly drew public attention to an emerging poetic voice able to speak a nation's anger and grief at the death of Pushkin.

2. For an insightful study of Pushkin's lifelong friendship with Zhukovsky, see R. V. Iezuitova, "Zhukovskii i Pushkin (K probleme literaturnogo nastavnichestva)," in *Zhukovskii i russkaia kul'tura,* ed. D. S. Likhachev, R. V. Iezuitova, and F. Z. Kanunova (Leningrad: Nauka, 1987), 229–43.

3. It might seem to us, from the vantage point of late twentieth-century American poetry, that the publication of a first book of poetry would have this status. But that appears not to have been the most important symbolic element in a poet's biography in Pushkin's lifetime, though the details of book publication were themselves quite symbolic. Sometimes the first publications were handled entirely by others; it was common among Pushkin's contemporaries to have collections of verse discreetly assembled by friends who also solicited subscriptions. For examples of such arrangements, as well as an analysis of how the practice stemmed from typical self-mythologizations by gentlemen-poets, see William Mills Todd III, *Fiction and Society in the Age of Pushkin* (Cambridge: Harvard University Press, 1986), 82.

4. In an illuminating study of Pushkin's ways of shaping his career, Monika Greenleaf considers such seemingly "minor" genres as love elegies and anthology poems. See her *Pushkin and Romantic Fashion: Fragment, Elegy, Orient, Irony* (Stanford: Stanford University Press, 1994), 56–107.

5. Many early poems by these and other poets contain invocations of enabling friendships; such references document the cult of friendship described in William Mills Todd III, *The Familiar Letter as a Literary Genre in the Age of Pushkin* (Princeton: Princeton University Press, 1976), esp. 40–42.

6. E. A. Baratynskii, *Polnoe sobranie stikhotvorenii* (*PSS*) (Leningrad: Sovetskii pisatel', 1989), 58 (all subsequent Baratynsky quotations come from this source). A. N. Krenitsyn (1801–65) was a close friend from the *pazheskii korpus,* also a poet.

7. For a discussion of Baratynsky's early misadventures in the *pazheskii korpus,* resulting in his being banned from all government service save being a soldier in the military, see Geir Khetso (= Geir Kjetsaa), *Evgenii Baratynskii: Zhizn' i tvorchestvo* (Oslo: Universitets Forlaget, 1973), 16–37.

8. "K Evgeniiu" (1819) in A. A. Del'vig, *Polnoe sobranie stikhotvorenii* (Leningrad: Sovetskii pisatel', 1959), 129–30. As we know, Baratynsky's army service took him to Finland, a separation that enabled his pose as a "Finnish

exile" and helped along his emerging poetic fame; Delvig's poem offers reassurances that predate this successful Romantic self-fashioning.

9. For a brief, clear account of the epicurean, erotic aspect of Baratynsky's early poetry, see M. L. Gofman, *Poeziia Boratynskago* (Petrograd: Gosudarstvennaia Tipografiia, 1915), 7–15.

10. The parody "Soiuz poetov" by Boris Fedorov was part of the attack launched by the "izmailovtsy" on the pages of *Blagonamerenyi* and *Vestnik Evropy:* it refers to Baratynsky as Barabinsky, and contains palpable references to the 1819 epistle to Delvig. Reprinted in *Poetry 1820–1830-kh godov,* 2 vols. (Leningrad: Sovetskii pisatel', 1972), 1:202–4.

11. The role of familiar letters exchanged among Arzamasians and others played perhaps an even greater role in the formation of literary tastes and habits, as William Mills Todd III has shown in *The Familiar Letter.*

12. Lidiia Ginzburg, *O lirike,* 2d ed. (Leningrad: Sovetskii pisatel', 1974), 39–41. See also V. A. Grekhnev, *Lirika pushkina: O poetike zhanrov* (Gor'kii: Volgo-Viatskoe knizhnoe izdatel'stvo, 1985), 18–86.

13. Ironically, Mikhail Saltykov-Shchedrin's denunciation later in the century pegged her as a representative of this very aspect of early nineteenth-century Russian poetry: he cast her as the author of verse epistles, and saw her within the culture of the salon. See his 1863 review of *Stikhotvoreniia K. Pavlovoi* in his *Polnoe sobranie sochinenii,* 20 vols. (Moscow: Khudozhestvennaia literatura, 1966), 5:362–67. He singles out for criticism some of the same early poems about the image of the poet that are discussed below.

14. Karolina Pavlova, *Polnoe sobranie stikhotvorenii* (*PSS*) (Moscow: Sovetskii pisatel', 1964), 80. (Subsequent quotations from Pavlova come from this source.)

15. The poem also recalls the elegiac tradition, as in Pushkin's "Arion" (1827), which begins "We were many in the boat" ("Nas bylo mnogo na chelne") and ends by delineating its poet/speaker from all the others. Pavlova's domestic and feminine narrative contrasts sharply with Pushkin's shipwreck imagery and his civic pathos in referring to the Decembrists, however; thus she stands in the same self-consciously unsure position toward the elegy as toward the genres we discuss more fully in this essay.

16. In a brief reference to this poem, Barbara Heldt also stresses its "theme of being a stranger to one's former self" and suggests that this theme was productive for later women poets, her example being Anna Akhmatova. See Heldt, *Terrible Perfection: Women and Russian Literature* (Bloomington: Indiana University Press, 1987), 112.

17. Sarah Pratt has delineated five Romantic images of the poet in Russia in this period. See her *Russian Metaphysical Romanticism: The Poetry of Tiutchev and Boratynskii* (Stanford: Stanford University Press, 1984), 95–104. Only one of these self-images, the poet as outsider, appears to have been

immediately useful to Pavlova; a second, poet as mystic, occurs in some lyrics, for example "Poet" (discussed below), but its presented warily, as if Pavlova foregrounds her own uncertainty about appearing in this guise.

18. Pavlova reinforced this sense of isolation when revising the poem in 1863; there she excised an earlier third verse in which another human figure appears. See Pavlova, *PSS*, 550.

19. We shall cite a third instance of the image of wildness, Pavlova's poem to E. Milkeev, in a moment. The idea of Pavlova herself as uncivilized became the basis for an epigram against her by S. Sobolevsky, cited in *A History of Russian Women's Writing, 1820–1992,* by Catriona Kelly (Oxford: Oxford University Press, 1994), 96. Kelly comments on the poem's image of a "she-wolf" as implying that Sobolevsky saw Pavlova as "a woman whose unmusical rampages are unfit for civilized society."

20. This phrase is all the odder since at the time a girl was more often represented as a stranger to thought. See Baratynsky's poem "Flit from pleasure to pleasure' ("Pereletai k vesel'iu ot vesel'ia") discussed below and Khomiakov's "Meditations" ("Dumy," 1831), in A. S. Khomiakov, *Stikhotvoreniia i dramy* (Leningrad: Sovetskii pisatel', 1969), 95–96. Pavlova, reaching for the image of the poet found in Baratynsky, wants to write philosophical poetry (see her later phrasing "deva-duma" in "To N. M. Ia . . . v" ["N. M. Ia[zyko]vu" 1844], 119).

21. Compare Rostopchina's poem "How Women Should Write" ("Kak dolzhny pisat' zhenshchiny," 1840), in Rostopchina, *Stikhotvoreniia. Proza. Pis'ma,* ed. Boris Romanov (Moscow: Sovetskaia Rossiia, 1986), 133–34, which develops explicitly the feminine aspect of this imagery, something contemporary readers would have sensed.

22. Her notions of poetry, as Mikhail Fainshtein has observed, were formed under the aegis of Romanticism. See M. Sh. Fainshtein, *Pisatel'nitsy pushkinskoi pory: Istoriko-literaturnye ocherki* (Leningrad: Nauka, 1985), 109.

23. Such poet-outsiders were fashionable in the Romantic period and their fates were often tragic. Compare the life history of John Clare.

24. Milkeev stayed in Pavlova's imagination long beyond this poem. He is commonly assumed to be the model for the poet who uncomfortably declaims his verse in the opening pages of her novel *Dvoinaia zhizn'* (1848), and Pavlova was to write a poem in memory of him in 1855 that recounts all the more starkly the cruel indifference with which Moscow society treated him, and imagines the scene of his suicide. See "In Memory of E. M." ("Pamiati E. M[il'keeva]"), in Pavlova, *PSS,* 185.

25. Khomiakov, *Stikhotvoreniia i dramy,* 110. Khomiakov's ending with the word *priiut* aggressively corrects Pavlova's beginning with this image (in

her poem, as cited above, it refers to Siberian open spaces, which are the only true haven Milkeev can expect to find).

26. For an account of the reception of Pavlova's mature poetry, most of it infused by the ideological struggles of the later 1840s and by the hostility directed against Pavlova after her husband's arrest and her having left Moscow without attending her father's funeral (both in 1853), see Barbara Heldt's introduction to Pavlova, *A Double Life,* trans. Barbara Heldt Monter (Ann Arbor, Mich.: Ardis, 1978), i-xxii.

27. The penultimate stanza in the poem to Milkeev nicely images this preference for dangerous natural sounds over tame social chatter:

> Не гул там разговоров скучных,
> Там бури бешеный набег,
> И глас лесов седых и звучных,
> И шум твоих сибирских рек.
>
> (76)
>
> (No droning there of dull conversation,
> There the storm's frenzied assault,
> And the voice of gray, echoing forests,
> And the noise of your Siberian rivers.)

28. One vivid example of her self-consciousness with the genre (the opposite of others' natural-seeming ease) emerges in the opening lines of her first verse epistle, to N. M. Iazykov in 1840. She subtitles the poem "Reply" ("Otvet"), as if wishing to clarify that she has not initiated this poetic correspondence, and beginning "Improbable and unexpected, / The poet's greeting song winged its way to me" (Neveroiatnyi i nezhdannyi / Sletel ko mne pevtsa privet," 88). The poem is also interesting for its offering her the occason of self-definition as a poet, again so self-consciously as to seem clumsy; "Here I write Russian poems / To the noise of Russian rain" ("Stikhi zdes' russkie pishu ia / Pri shume russkogo dozhdia").

29. A letter from Baratynsky, apparently written shortly after their acquaintance, apologizes in gallent French for canceling a planned outing, and it is this document that lets us date their acquaintance. See Khetso, *Evgenii Baratynskii,* 589–90 for the brief text in full.

30. Pavlova's first published book was *Das Nordlicht: Proben der neueren russischen Literatur* (Dresden: In der Arnoldischen Buchhandlung, 1833), and included translations of Pushkin, Baratynsky, Zhukovsky, Iazykov, and others into German. Her next book, *Les Préludes,* appeared in Paris (Typographie de Firmin Didot Frères, 1839), and included Mickiewicz's work along with translations from the Russian. Later in her life she continued to publish translations, in part to earn a living. For a listing, see Munir Sendich, "The Life and Works of Karolina Pavlova" (Ph.D. diss., New York University,

1968), 284–85. The translations let her experiment with poetic identities, and her original poems in German and French also offered opportunities for impersonation or ventriloquism. See Catriona Kelly's comment, in the beginning of her discussion of Pavlova, that Pavlova's having been born into linguistic and genetic difference from her Russian surroundings was a salutary source of identity for her as she moved through a society that believed that "the composition of poetry was anomalous for women" (*History of Russian Women's Writing,* 93).

31. See his letter to I. V. Kireevsky from May 1832, cited in E. A. Baratynskii, *Razuma velikolepnyi pir: O literature i iskusstve,* ed. E. N. Lebedev (Moscow: Sovremennik, 1981), 139.

32. We exclude her final poem to Iazykov from 1846, the sad result of their political and personal dispute (Pavlova, *PSS,* 88–89, 113–14, 119–21; and for the 1846 poem, 133–34). On Pavlova's relationship with Iazykov, see Sendich, "The Life and Works of Karolina Pavlova," 32–36.

33. Sendich, "The Life and Works of Karolina Pavlova," 31.

34. Munir Sendich, "Moscow Literary Salons: Thursdays at Karolina Pavlova's," *Die Welt der Slaven* 17 (1972): 341–57. On the eighteenth-century salons and the serious endeavors of women who headed them, see Dena Goodman, *The Republic of Letters: A Cultural History of the French Enlightenment* (Ithaca: Cornell University Press, 1994). Goodman traces the transformation of attitudes toward such salons and the history of the ways in which their gatherings were slowly discredited and their work presented as frivolous. Such views found their way to Russia, for example, in Pushkin's criticisms of how the presence of women trivialized the intellectual work undertaken there. See "O predislovii g-na Lemonte k perevodu basen I. A. Krylova," in Pushkin, *Polnoe sobranie sochinenii,* 10 vols. (Leningrad: Nauka, 1977–79), 7:19–24, esp. 22. Recent scholarship on Russian women's salons in this period includes Lina Bernstein, "Women on the Verge of a New Language: Russian Salon Hostesses in the First Half of the Nineteenth Century," in *Russia—Women—Culture,* ed. Helena Goscilo and Beth Holmgren (Bloomington: Indiana University Press, 1996), 209–24; and Bernstein, "Avdotia Petrovna Elagina and Her Contribution to Russian Letters," *Slavic and East European Journal* 40, no. 2 (1996): 215–35.

35. See also her poem "Strangely we met" ("My stranno soshlis'," 1854) for a still later poem that similarly characterizes the true and false languages of conversation (153–54).

36. These poems ask repeatedly whether one should make deeply held emotions or convictions public at all, and more than once they resolve in favor of preserving the heart's secrets. In this mistrust of words, Pavlova comes close to the sentiments of Tiutchev's "Silentium" (1829/early 1830s). Her views

also recall those of Rostopchina's poem "How Women Should Write," where silence is linked to femininity (see note 21).

37. For the history of albums, the various kinds, and the range of inscriptions, see M. P. Alekseev, "Iz istorii russkikh rukopisnykh sobranii," in *Neizdannye pis'ma inostrannykh pisatelei XVII-XIX vekov iz leningradskikh rukopisnykh sobranii,* ed. M. P. Alekseev (Moscow: AN SSSR, 1960), 1–122, esp. 1–28; and V. E. Vatsuro, "Literaturnye al'bomy v sobranii Pushkinskogo doma (1750–1840-e gody)," in *Ezhegodnik rukopisnogo otdela Pushkinskogo doma na 1977 god* (Leningrad: Nauka, 1979), 3–56. See also Vatsuro, *S. D. P.: Iz istorii literaturnogo byta pushkinskoi pory* (Moscow: Kniga, 1989) and Gitta Hammarberg, "Flirting with Words: Domestic Albums, 1770–1840," in *Russia—Women—Culture,* ed. Goscilo and Holmgren, 297–320. Lotman has suggested that albums were like "manuscript almanacs," continuing the traditions of handmade books and joining the cultural contexts of family and literary circle in their creation and circulation: see Iu. M. Lotman, *Roman A. S. Pushkina 'Evgenii Onegin': Kommentarii* (Leningrad: Prosveshchenie, 1980), 241. Perhaps the best-known characterization of albums is in *Eugene Onegin:* see Pushkin, *Polnoe sobranie sochinenii,* 5:77 (*Evgenii Onegin,* chap. 4, lines 27–30).

38. See, for example, the later poem "A piece of a page in this album" ("Stranitsy chast'v al'bome etom," 1861). Pavlova also wrote erotic poems, much like men's album verse, in connection with her ill-fated encounter with Adam Mickiewicz. But they seem to have been possible for her only *after* she had established her readiness to write at all in the first place. She did not publish her two poems about Mickiewicz at the time ("November 10, 1840" ["10 noiabria 1840"] appeared in 1863; "On the Tenth of November" ["Na 10 noiabria"], not at all in her lifetime), further suggesting that these were not meant as public poems of initiation in the way that Baratynsky's erotic verse could function. We discuss Pavlova's relationship with Mickiewicz more fully in "Abandoned Meditation," forthcoming in a collection of essays on Pavlova edited by Susanne Fusso and Alexander Lehrman (Northwestern University Press).

39. This distance from album verse marks an important difference between Pavlova and the other reasonably well known woman poet of her generation, Countess Evdokiia Rostopchina. Rostopchina made varied use of album poetry conventions—for example, "The Empty Album" ("Pustoi al'bom," 1841), "In an Album to Sofia N. Karamzina" ("V al'bom Sof'e N[ikolaevn]e Karamzinoi," 1843)—and she placed herself squarely within various social settings, like the ballroom, even to the point of self-irony, as in "Temptation" (Iskushen'e," 1839). See Rostopchina, *Stikhotvoreniia,* 99–101, 152–56, 171.

40. This poem is addressed to Baratynsky's sister-in-law, A. D. Baratynskaia, herself a translator and poet of some note.

41. On gender and poetic identity in the Romantic period, see Margaret Homans, *Women Writers and Poetic Identity: Dorothy Wordsworth, Emily Brontë, and Emily Dickinson* (Princeton: Princeton University Press, 1980), 12–40; Anne K. Mellor, *Romanticism and Gender* (New York: Routledge, 1993), 13–29; and Karen Swann, "Harassing the Muse," in *Romanticism and Feminism,* ed. Anne K. Mellor (Bloomington: Indiana University Press, 1988), 81–92.

42. Another example is "Delightful as the Graces, and modest" ("Mila, kak gratsiia, skromna," 1824) to A. V. Lutkovskaia, but originally written to S. D. Ponomareva; see also "May I paint your image, can your image be captured?" ("Tebia l' izobrazit' i ty l' izobrazima?" 1819, 1823–24), first written to Varvara Kuchina and finally inscribed in Lutkovskaia's album (Baratynskii, *PSS,* 59, 125).

43. Vatsuro, *S. D. P.,* 289–90. Igor' Phil'shchikov observes a similar pattern of shifting addressees in Baratynsky's epigrams in his essay "Debilitata venus (Dva stikhotvoreniia E. A. Baratynskogo o starostii krasote)," in *V Chest '70-letiia professora Iu. M. Lotman,* ed. V. Besprozvannyi et al. (Tartu: Eidos, 1992), 108–21, esp. 118 n. 8.

44. Vatsuro, *S. D. P.,* 65–69, 177–202; see also Khetso, *Evgenii Baratynskii,* 76–78. For example, "We separated; a moment's enchantment," sometimes entitled "Parting" ("Rasstalis' my, na mig ocharovan'em," "Razluka," 1820, 1826); "Disillusionment" ("Razuverenie," 1821); "Do not demand feigned tenderness from me," sometimes entitled "Declaration" ("Pritvornoi nezhnosti ne trebui ot menia," "Priznanie," 1823, 1832); "We drink sweet poison in love" ("My p'em v liubvi otravu sladkuiu," 1824); and "How much in how few days you [lived]" ("Kak mnogo ty v nemnogo dnei," 1824–25).

45. On Baratynsky's passion for Zakrevskaia, see Khetso, *Evgenii Baratynskii,* 98–106, passim; and, in considerable and absorbing detail, P. P. Filippovich, *Zhizn' i tvorchestvo E. A. Boratynskago* (Kiev: Tipografiia Universiteta Sv. Vkladimira, 1917), 82–99.

46. For a condensed account of the history of interpretations of the poem, see Baratynskii, *PSS,* 407.

47. In *Pushkin and Romantic Fashion,* Monika Greenleaf uses Pushkin's erotic elegies as material for assessing his characteristic self-portraitures. The argument runs throughout the book, but see, for example, 92–107, 287–348.

48. See especially a poem bidding farewell to Sh. Shlaktinsky (a friend from Smolensk) in Baratynskii, *PSS,* 65.

49. As established by V. Fridkin, "Al'bomy Karoliny Pavlovoi," *Nauka i zhizn',* no. 12 (1987): 140–48; see 144, where Fridkin reproduces the autograph of the poem as it appeared in Pavlova's album, and 146–47, where he discusses the textological history of this poem, which exists in several versions.

50. Pavlova's salon acquaintances in the mid-1820s generally knew that she wrote original poetry and translated as well; see Fainshtein, *Pisatel'nitsy pushkinskoi pory,* 105, and Sendich, "The Life and Works of Karolina Pavlova," 29.

51. In that sense, Pavlova is like the serious "Corinne" of Baratynsky's album poem discussed above, rather than like its flighty addressee.

52. The term *filosof* would not yet primarily connote the contemporary sense of a professional scholar devoted to writing philosophical discourse. This usage came into currency in the nineteenth century, to be sure, but we rarely find it so early in the century. Rather, it was a contested term in ways that relate far more to eighteenth-century cultural debates influenced by French thought, when a *philosophe* was the term for the kind of cultural equivalent of the Renaissance man—someone who thought and wrote in a wide variety of ways (they would not yet have been separate disciplines), from the natural sciences to poetry to essays classifying human experience. The separate disciplines of thought began to emerge in the nineteenth century, a process we have come to understand better largely through the work of Michel Foucault (in *The Order of Things: An Archaeology of the Human Sciences* [New York: Random House, 1973]), and the term *philosopher* grew to have a narrower meaning.

53. The examples of usage from *Eugene Onegin*'s description of Lensky are well known; for a fuller sense of the word's meanings in Pushkin's oeuvre, see *Slovar' iazyka Pushkina,* 4 vols. (Moscow: Gosudarstvennoe izdatel'stvo inostrannykh i natsional'nykh slovarei, 1961), 4:786.

54. In a sense, Pavlova's true "genre" was the nineteenth-century novel. This surprising insight was first suggested by Vladislav Khodasevich, who meant to criticize Pavlova by arguing that "Pavlova's poetry is like prose." See Vladislav Khodasevich, "Odna iz zabytykh," *Sobranie sochinenii,* ed. John Malmstad and Robert Hughes, projected 5 vols. (Ann Arbor, Mich.: Ardis, 1990-) 2:216–19, cited from 217. His review appeared in 1916 and polemicizes with Bely's praise for Pavlova's rhythmic innovations. But the interesting issue here is not so much the music of verse (Khodasevich's concern) as the fashioning of a self in a web of relationships to others. Identity emerges as a problem, an open-ended project for endless exploration in Pavlova's poetry—and in the poetry of Baratynsky. He, too, was to move beyond the formulae of friendly epistle, album verse, and madrigal to produce lyrics of incomparable psychological subtlety. Even more than in Pavlova's work, Baratynsky's poetry explores the theme of disillusionment, a psychological structure that also characterizes the best early novelistic achievements of the nineteenth century, including Balzac and Stendhal. For a much fuller discussion of the relationship between Russian psychological lyric verse and the emergence of the novel, see Ginzburg, *O lirike.*

JUDITH DEUTSCH KORNBLATT, "COSSACKS AND WOMEN: CREATION WITHOUT REPRODUCTION IN GOGOL'S COSSACK MYTH"

This paper is an expanded revision of "Death Transcended and the Female Threat" from my study of the Cossack in *The Cossack Hero in Russian Literature: A Study in Cultural Mythology* © 1992. Reprinted by permission of the University of Wisconsin Press.

1. Unfortunately, the post-Soviet crisis in Chechnya summons up similar images. The hostility between the Chechens and Caucasian Cossacks forms the background for Tolstoy's short novel, *The Cossacks.*

2. A fascinating example can be found in Edward T. Heald's account of his travels through the nascent Soviet Union. "I met an interesting Ural Cossack on the train," he writes in a letter of 27 May 1919. Heald then puts into the Cossack's mouth much of the inflated rhetoric of the Cossack myth concerning superhuman size, strength, freedom, and glory: "We have a rich country," says the Cossack:

> We have fertile land and big crops. We have wonderful cattle and horses. And the rivers abound in the most tasteful fish, which have no bones. And watermelons that weigh from forty to eighty pounds, not like the little Petrograd melons which really aren't melons; everything that the heart can desire, except forests. For we live in the steppes, the broad level glorious steppes. But the crowning creation of all are the Ural Cossacks. We're the flower of creation. We have souls, and we fight, live, love, and die for glory, for freedom, for honor, for our rights.

Heald concludes the entry: "I jot this down because it is typical of the Cossack spirit and is the first time that I have had a Cossack open up to me so freely." *Witness to Revolution: Letters from Russia, 1916–1919,* ed. James B. Gidney (Ohio: Kent State University Press, 1972), 352–53.

3. Much good scholarship in American Studies has recently been devoted to debunking the myth of the cowboy, as well as the larger Turnerian myth of the American frontier. See, for example, *New Essays on the Literature of the American West,* ed. Michael Kowalewski (Cambridge: Cambridge University Press, 1996). Similar skeptical studies of the Cossack by Russian scholars are not yet in vogue.

4. See Kornblatt, *The Cossack Hero in Russian Literature,* 5–13 and 99–101, as well as the endnotes to chapter 1 for a brief account of Cossack history and biographies of several Cossack leaders. For the English-language sources of my own account, see: W. E. D. Allen, *The Ukraine: A History* (Cambridge, 1940); Paul Avrich, *Russian Rebels:1600–1800* (New York: Schocken, 1972); Linda Gordon, *Cossack Rebellions: Social Turmoil in the Sixteenth-Century Ukraine* (Albany: State University of New York Press, 1983); Philip Longworth, *The Cossacks* (New York: Holt, Rinehart and Winston, 1969);

Ivan L. Rudnytsky, "A Study of Cossack History," review of Longworth's book in *Slavic Review* 31 (December 1972): 870–75; and Longworth's response to Rudnytsky's review and Rudnytsky's counterresponse in *Slavic Review* 33 (June 1974): 411–16; and Albert Seaton, *The Horsemen of the Steppes: The Story of the Cossacks* (London: Bodley Head, 1985). Research into Cossack history, as well as ethnographic and sociological studies of Cossack communities, are experiencing something of a boom in recent years, and a number of books are currently in progress.

5. Although myth in common parlance means a fiction, or made-up story, as Mark Schorer cogently wrote many years ago, myths are "the instruments by which we continually struggle to make our experience intelligible to ourselves. A myth is a large, controlling image that gives philosophical meaning to the facts of ordinary life; that is, which has an organizing value for experience" ("The Necessity of Myth," *Daedalus* 88, no. 2 [Spring 1959]: 360, excerpted from *William Blake* [New York: Henry Holt, 1946]). For the present study, this understanding of myth is complemented by the somewhat more political view of the early Roland Barthes (see below).

6. Roland Barthes, "Myth Today," in *Mythologies,* trans. Annette Lavers (London: Jonathan Cape, 1972): 129.

7. "Little Russia," "Malorossiia," or "Malaia Rossiia" was the official term in the nineteenth century for the area called the Ukrainian Soviet Socialist Republic under the Communists, and now called Ukraine. It was the location of ancient Kiev, Kievan Rus' as a whole, as well as of the powerful Zaporozhian Sech in the seventeenth and eighteenth centuries. The borderland ("Ukraina" literally means at the border) that was "Little Russia" held a particular fascination for the Russian Romantics of the first half of the nineteenth. The fascination was not without its political dimension, however, and later Ukrainian nationalists bristled under the connotations of "little." Ukrainians today usually object to the russifying tendency of the early Romantic writers. For a definition of the names of Russia and the Ukraine, see George W. Simpson, "The Names 'Rus',' 'Russia,' 'Ukraine,' and their Historical Background," *Slavistica* 10 (1951): 5–18. See also "Ukraina," in *Entsiklopedicheskii slovar',* eds. F. A. Brokgauz and I. A. Efron (St. Petersburg, 1897), 68:633–35.

8. The idea that peoples create their history from these three processes is persuasively argued by Bernard Lewis in *History Remembered, Recovered, Invented* (Princeton: Princeton University Press, 1975).

9. Here, perhaps, is the place to recognize that scholars of Ukrainian literature and history insist on the integrity of the Zaporozhian Cossacks, and consider Cossacks a purely Ukrainian phenomenon. Without denying the vital role that the Zaporozh'e played in Ukrainian history and society, this study purposely views the Ukrainian Cossacks through the eyes of Russian

literature, written in Russian for a Russian audience. The myth in Russian literature incorporates Ukrainian, Tatar, Caucasian, and Siberian Cossacks into its own idealized hero.

10. Lev Tolstoi, *Polnoe sobranie sochinenii* (Moscow: Gosudarstvennoe izdatel'stvo, 1952), 48:123. Also quoted in P. B. Bekedin, "Drevnerusskie motivy v *Tikhom Done* M. A. Sholokhova (k postanovke voprosa)," in *Russkaia literatura* 2 (1980): 96.

11. *Slovo o polku Igoreve* tells the story of Igor's unsuccessful campaign against the neighboring Polovtsy people during the Kievan period. As such, it glorifies the patriotism of a prince of Rus', not Russia, and cannot technically be called a "Russian" epic, if "Russian" refers to the Russian empire centered in Moscow. Russians, however, often associate Rus' with their own political and cultural origins. When the manuscript of the tale was rediscovered in the eighteenth century, Russian writers accepted it as a story about their own past.

12. For an analysis of these poems, see Hubert Babinsky, *The Mazeppa Legend in European Romanticism* (New York: Columbia University Press, 1974). Examples of Slavic works that most closely fit the Western paradigm would be Kondratii Ryleev's poem, "Voinarovskii," and Juliusz Slowacki's play, *Mazeppa.*

13. See the excellent study of the literary Caucasus by Susan Layton, *Russian Literature and Empire: Conquest of the Caucasus from Pushkin to Tolstoy* (Cambridge: Cambridge University Press, 1994).

14. Daniel Mordovtsev, in *Polnoe sobranie istoricheskikh romanov, povestei i razskazov* (St. Petersburg: Izdatel'stvo P. P. Soikina, n.d.), 1:80. The term *tur* (aurochs) refers to a now almost extinct breed of wild bison that is much beloved in Russian folk literature. It may also signify a type of Caucasian goat, but a reference earlier to *buitur* (1:67), reminiscent of the "valiant aurochs" of *The Lay of Igor's Campaign,* clearly suggests the former, more "mythic" definition.

15. See the boast of one chief that his unit has known no deserters to marriage in Nestor Kukol'nik, *Zaporozhtsy,* in *Istoricheskie povesti* (St. Petersburg: Izdanie A.S. Suvorina, 1902), 5:1.

16. N. V. Gogol', *Polnoe sobranie sochinenii* (Moscow: Izdatel'stvo Akademii Nauk SSSR, 1937–52), 2:43. Henceforth all references to Gogol will be indicated by volume and page number in the text.

17. Mordovtsev, 1:12.

18. On the other hand, myth-making was not entirely beyond his scope, and we can find points of comparison between the Pugachev of the history and that of his more "romantic" novel, *Captain's Daughter.* Similarly, in his narrative poem about Mazepa, "Poltava," Pushkin does not so much reject mythologizing, as he manipulates its connotations. His heroine is thus carried

away by her mythic "mental picture" of the Cossack hero, only to go mad when confronted by his treacherous reality:

> I took you for another,
> Old man. Leave me.
> Your gaze is mocking and horrible.
> You are ugly. He is beautiful:
> In his eyes shines love,
> Langour in his speech!
> His moustache is whiter than snow,
> But yours is dried with blood! . . .

(A. S. Pushkin, *Polnoe sobranie sochinenii,* 16 vols. [Moscow: Izdatel'stvo Akademii Nauk SSSR, 1937–49], 5:62, lines 399–406). Still, Pushkin ends his poem with the evocation of an epic bard who will continue to sing the mythic songs written, presumably, by Mazepa himself. For more on Pushkin, see Kornblatt, *The Cossack Hero in Russian Literature,* 30–38.

19. G. P. Danilevskii, "Pesnia bandurista," in *Sochineniia G.P. Danilevskogo v 24-kh tomakh* (St. Petersburg: Izdanie A.F. Marksa, 1901), 8:162.

20. Indeed, many aspects of the myth show similarities to pagan and quasi-Christian folk motifs. Unfortunately, this approach cannot be explored here in any depth.

21. For a sometimes provocative, but not always convincing study of the association of Russia with the feminine, see Joanna Hubbs, *Mother Russia: The Feminine Myth in Russian Culture* (Bloomington: Indiana University Press, 1988).

22. Mordovtsev, 1:197. The Eastern captive whose relations with a Cossack provokes consternation among the men is an echo of the story of Razin and his Persian princess. When confronted by the Cossack brotherhood, Razin drowns his female booty. Tellingly, it is another woman, in fact a wife in some versions of the story, who betrays Razin and leads to his capture and death.

23. Vasilii Narezhnyi, *Zaporozhets, Romany i povesti Vasiliia Narezhnago,* 2d ed. (St. Petersburg: Tipografiia Aleksandra Smirdina, 1836), 8:184–85.

24. This, of course, is a rather large "if." Rape and pillage clash somewhat with our "mental picture" of monastic life.

25. Cf. Ezekiel 23:31–34; Matthew 20:22 and 30:39; John 18:11.

26. Here we can see yet another contrast between the Russian and American myths of the frontier. In the latter, separation from the mother leads to greater individuation, a positive ideal in the American myth. In Russian literature about the Cossack, however, it leads to participation in the collective.

27. See Dmitrii Merezhkovskii, *Gogol': Tvorchestvo, zhizn', religiia* (St. Petersburg: Panteon, 1909) for a more in-depth study of Gogol's depiction of the devil. James B. Woodward, among others, discusses the association of women and the devil in *The Symbolic Art of Gogol: Essays on his Short Fiction* (Columbus, Ohio: Slavica, 1981), 39.

28. Palei in Faddei Bulgarin's novel *Mazepa* reminds us that the "learning" characteristic of the Sech protects Cossacks from female influence: "If only I had brought you up in the Zaporozhian camp and not given you over to the accursed Poles for your education, then you wouldn't now be running after girls like a madman and you'd know nothing but Cossacks affairs!" (*Sochineniia* [St. Petersburg, 1827–34], 2:12.

29. Gogol inserts himself into this timeless and abundant setting as well, since a goldeneye duck in Russian is a *gogol'*.

30. We should perhaps add the Tatar maidservant who leads Andrii into the beseiged city of Dubno, and into the arms of his love.

31. See, for example, Donald Fanger, *The Creation of Nikolai Gogol* (Cambridge: Belknap Press of Harvard University Press, 1979), 100; Gary Cox, "Geographic, Sociological, and Sexual Tensions in Gogol''s Dikan'ka Stories," *Slavic and East European Journal* 24 (1980): 219–32; George C. Grabowicz, "The Myth of the Ukraine in Gogol'," unpublished lecture, Columbia University, 1980, and his dissertation, "The History and Myth of the Cossack Ukraine" (Harvard University, 1975); James B. Woodward, *The Symbolic Art of Gogol: Essays on his Short Fiction* (Columbus, Ohio: Slavica, 1981), 12; and Simon Karlinsky, *The Sexual Labyrinth of Nikolai Gogol* (Cambridge: Harvard University Press, 1976), 36, 59.

32. In an effort to place *Taras Bul'ba* in the context of the pathos of most of Gogol's other stories, many critics have incorrectly interpreted the death of Taras Bul'ba at the end of the story as an indication of the disappearance of Cossackdom. In a typical statement, Alex de Jonge writes: "When [Taras Bul'ba] is finally hunted down his world dies with him. . . . Thus negative values triumph on every level. Bul'ba pursues a downward path till he has outlived his sons and practically outlived *kazachestvo.* One feels that with the end of the book one witnesses the end of the Cossacks' golden age" (A. de Jonge, "Gogol'," in *Nineteenth-Century Russian Literature: Studies of Ten Russian Writers,* ed. John Fennell [Berkeley and Los Angeles: University of California Press, 1973], 81).

33. An interesting comparison of cowboy and Cossack texts can be made on this score. See John G. Cawelti, *The Six-Gun Mystique* (Bowling Green: Bowling Green University Popular Press, n.d.), 62, 82.

34. That sculpture should be "pagan" corresponds to Orthodox condemnation of three-dimensional art.

35. Gogol borrows this convention from an article of the same title by D. V. Venevitinov in *Severnaia lira* of 1827. Venevitinov in turn borrowed it from Wilhelm Wackenroder. Gogol's explicit aesthetic statements are by no means original and have usually been dismissed by scholars, but the hidden assumptions revealed in his choice of vocabulary deserve a second look. For more on sculpture, painting, and music in this article and in *Mirgorod,* see my "Gogol' and the Muses of *Mirgorod,*" *Slavic Review* 50, no. 2 (Summer 1991): 309–16.

36. For an analysis of Tolstoy's ambivalent look at the Cossack, with a decidedly ethical tenor, see *The Cossack Hero in Russian Literature,* 91–96.

JENNIFER J. HIXON, "THE FALL OF NOVGOROD IN KARAMZIN'S FICTION AND HISTORY"

1. P. A. Viazemskii, quoted in L. G. Kisliagina, *Formirovanie obshchestvenno-politicheskikh vzgliadov N. M. Karamzina (1785–1803 gg)* (Moscow: Izd. Moskovskogo Universiteta, 1976), 152.

2. Unless otherwise noted, all translations from the Russian are mine, with help, in this as in everything, from Timothy Sergay.

3. N. M. Karamzin, *Pis'ma N. M. Karamzina k I. I Dmitrievu* (St. Petersburg: Imperatorskaia Akademiia Nauk, 1866), 249.

4. For more on literary treatments of Novgorod, see I. I. Zamotin, "Predanie o Vadime Novgorodskom v russkoi literature," *Filologicheskie zapiski,* 1899–1900; F. Ia. Priima, "Tema 'novgorodskoi svobody' v russkoi literature kontsa XVIII—nachala XIX v.," in *Na putiakh k romantizmu* (Leningrad: Nauka, 1984); and Andrew Baruch Wachtel, *An Obsession with History* (Stanford: Stanford University Press, 1994).

4. Richard Pipes, "The Background and Growth of Karamzin's Political Ideas Down to 1810," in *Karamzin's Memoir on Ancient and Modern Russia: A Translation and Analysis* (New York: Atheneum, 1986), 3.

5. Ibid., 90.

6. S. V. Bushuev and G. E. Mironov, *Istoriia gosudarstva Rossiiskogo* (Moscow: Knizhnaia palata, 1991), 242–44.

7. N. M. Karamzin, *Izbrannye sochineniia* (Moscow: Khudozhestvennaia literatura, 1964), 1:703–4. Subsequent references to this edition will be indicated parenthetically in the text by the abbreviation *IS,* followed by volume number and page number.

8. Jessica Benjamin, *Like Subjects, Love Objects: Essays on Recognition and Sexual Difference* (New Haven: Yale University Press, 1995), 81ff.

9. Peter Sacks, *The English Elegy* (Baltimore: The Johns Hopkins University Press, 1985), 15–16.

10. Marthe Robert, *Origins of the Novel,* trans. Sacha Rabinovitch (Bloomington: Indiana University Press, 1980; originally published as *Roman des Origines et Origines du Roman* [Paris: Editions Bernard Grasset, 1972]), 22.

11. Ibid., 24.

12. Caryl Emerson (personal communication, July 1996) points out that the conqueror's sudden encounter with his half-forgotten illegitimate child in the defeated enemy camp is "a Romantic topos" and "not an historical fact as much as a genre." She notes a particularly telling parallel with the later nineteenth century work *Pskovitianka* (The Maid of Pskov). Originally published in 1860 as a drama by L. A. Mei, later adopted by N. A. Rimsky-Korsakov for his opera (first performed in 1873), *Pskovitianka* explains the conquering Ivan IV's unexpected leniency toward Pskov by imagining that Ivan (Ivan III's grandson, popularly known as "the Terrible") had fathered a daughter on a youthful visit to the city, and that by chance he now meets that daughter and recognizes her as his own. The daughter, Olga, her loyalty divided between the tsar and her invaded city, kills herself in Mei's version and is literally caught in the crossfire in Rimsky-Korsakov's version. As Richard Taruskin writes,

> Olga's tragic situation—torn between the tsar, her father, toward whom she feels a strange and inexplicable attraction, and her lover Tucha, the leader of the abortive insurrection—is the predicament of Pskov itself, torn between its independent republican traditions and the historical necessity of submission to Moscow. ("Russian Opera and Russian Historiography, ca. 1870," in *Russian and Soviet Music: Essays for Boris Schwarz,* ed. Malcolm Hamrick Brown [Ann Arbor, Mich.: UMI Research Press, 1984], 96)

13. Iu. M. Lotman, "Evoliutsia mirovozzreniia Karamzina (1789–1803)," *Uchenye zapiski Tartuskogo gosudarstvennogo universiteta,* 1957, 51:159.

14. N. M. Karamzin, *Polnoe sobranie stikhotvorenii,* Vstup. stat'ia, podgotovka teksta i primechaniia Iu. M. Lotmana (Moscow: Sovetskii pisatel', 1966), 137–38. Subsequent references to this edition will be indicated parenthetically in the text by the abbreviation *PSS,* followed by the page number.

15. N. M. Karamzin, *Sochineniia Karamzina,* vol. 1–9 (Moscow, 1820), 63–64.

16. Dan E. Davidson, "Christoph Martin Wieland in Russia: On the Role of Nikolai Mikhailovich Karamzin (1766–1826)," in *Lessing Yearbook XV* (Detroit: Wayne State University Press, 1983), 228.

17. L. V. Krestova, "A. I. Pleshcheeva v zhizni i tvorchestve Karamzina," in *XVIII vek.* Sb. 10: "Russkaia literatura i ee mezhdunarodnye sviazi." (Leningrad: Nauka, 1975), 266.

18. Ibid., 268.

19. Iu. M. Lotman, *Sotvorenie Karamzina* (Moscow: Kniga, 1987), 270.

20. Translated and quoted by William Mills Todd III in his *Fiction and Society in the Age of Pushkin* (Cambridge: Harvard University Press, 1986), 17; ellipsis mine.

21. Lotman, *Sotvorenie Karamzina,* 274.

22. Ibid., 245–49.

23. *Encyclopedia Brittanica: Macropedia,* 15th ed. s.v. "Switzerland, History of."

24. In her recent book, *Pushkin and Romantic Fashion: Fragment, Elegy, Orient, Irony* (Stanford: Stanford University Press, 1994), Monika Greenleaf discusses the Russian variant of orientalism. Following Edward Said (*Orientalism* [New York: Vintage Books, 1979], she treats representations of the East as the West's Other, paying particular attention to the way in which Russian literature assigned to the Orient qualities of femininity, passivity, inarticulateness, and isolation from history. Her examination of the bifurcation of human traits enforced by orientalism strongly influenced my reading of Karamzin's early historical writings, in which he seems intent on disrupting the intellectual construct that exiled women from the historical realm. Indeed, Greenleaf's insights on orientalism, as well on the elegy, and on the mature author's artistic allusion to his youthful work, are all fundamental to my understanding of the changing distribution of binary values throughout Karamzin's writings.

25. N. A. Marchenko, "Istoriia teksta *Pisem russkogo puteshestvennika,*" in *Pis'ma russkogo puteshestvennika,* ed. N. M. Karamzin (Leningrad: Nauka, 1987), 608, 610.

26. N. M. Karamzin, *Pis'ma russkogo puteshestvennika* (Leningrad: Nauka, 1987) 252–53.

27. Iu. M. Lotman, "Puti razvitiia russkoi prozy 1800–1810-kh godov, " *Uchenye zapiski Tartuskogo gosudarstvennogo universiteta,* 1961 (*Trudy po russkoi i slavianskoi fililogii* IV), 104:42.

28. N. M. Karamzin, *Istoriia gosudarstva Rossiiskogo* (1842–44; reprint, Moscow: Kniga, 1988–89), Predislovie:xi. Subsequent references to this edition will be indicated parenthetically in the text by the abbreviation *IGR,* followed by volume number and page number.

29. Karamzin, *Pis'ma N. M. Karamzina k I. I. Dmitrievu,* 154

30. See F. Z. Kanunova, *Iz istorii russkoi povesti—istoriko-literaturnoe znachenie povestei N. M. Karamzina* (Tomsk: Izdatel'stvo Tomskogo universiteta, 1967) and P. A. Orlov, "Povest' N. M. Karamzina 'Marfa Posadnitsa'," *Russkaia literatura,* no. 2 (1968): 192–201.

31. Caryl Emerson, *Boris Godunov: Transpositions of a Russian Theme* (Bloomington: Indiana University Press, 1986), 58.

32. Karamzin, translated and quoted by Emerson in *Boris Godunov,* 58.

33. D. S. Likhachev and L. A. Dmitriev, "Kommentarii," in *Pamiatniki literatury drevnei Rusi, vtoraia polovina XV veka* (Moscow: Khudozhestvennaia literatura, 1982), 628–29.

34. Benjamin, *Like Subjects, Love Objects,* 99–100.

35. Robert, *Origins of the Novel,* 26.

36. Ibid., 30.

37. N. Eidel'man, *Poslednii letopisets* (Moscow: Kniga, 1983), 75.

38. A. G. Cross, *N. M. Karamzin: A Study of his Literary Career, 1783–1803* (Carbondale: Southern Illinois University Press; London: Feffer & Simons, 1971), 127.

39. Quoted in Lotman, *Sotvorenie Karamzina,* 278.

40. Robert, *Origins of the Novel,* 144.

SALLY KUX, "PETR ANDREEVICH VIAZEMSKY: A NECESSARY VIRTUE"

1. The edition of Viazemsky's works used is *Polnoe sobranie sochineniia v dvenadtsati tomakh* (St. Petersburg, 1878–96); henceforth cited in the text as *PSS.*

2. See V. C. Nechaeva, ed., *P. A. Viazemskii: Zapisnye knizhki (1813–1848)* (Moscow: Literaturnye pamiatniki, 1963); L. Ia. Ginzburg, ed., *P. A. Viazemskii: Staraia Zapisnaia Knizhka* (Leningrad, 1929); E. Ia. Kurganov, "Iz istorii sobraniia i osmysleniia russkogo literaturnogo anekdota kontsa XVIII—nachala XIX vekov" (O "Staroi zapisnoi knizhke" P. A. Viazemskogo), in *Uchebnyi material po teorii literatury, zhanry slovesnogo teksta: anekdot,* ed. A. F. Belousov (Tallinn, 1989).

3. For more on the anecdote as a historical and literary form, see Sally Kux, "On the Boundary of Life and Literature: The Anecdote in Early Nineteenth-Century Russia" (Ph.D. diss., Stanford University, 1994).

4. See Averil Cameron, *Procopius and the Sixth Century* (Berkeley and Los Angeles: University of California Press, 1985).

5. See Victor Terras, ed., *Handbook of Russian Literature* (New Haven: Yale University Press, 1985); M. I. Gillel'son, *P. A. Viazemskii: Zhizn' i tvorchestvo* (Leningrad, 1969); Nechaeva, *Viazemskii.* Viazemsky lost his mother in 1802, his father in 1807, and his elder sister in 1810. Born seven years before Pushkin (1799–1837), Viazemsky survived him by forty-one years. The same year brought the death of another friend, the poet and writer, Ivan Dmitriev (1760–1837). Two years later the poet and soldier, Denis Davydov (1784–1839), died. Eight years older than Evgeny Baratynsky (1800–1844), Viazemsky outlived him by thirty-one years. The following year saw the

death of A. I. Turgenev (1784–1845), Viazemsky's close friend and partner in a voluminous correspondence. Viazemsky outlived Vasily Zhukovsky (1783–1852) and Nikolai Gogol (1809–52) by twenty-six years. He lived twenty-three years past the death of Konstantin Batiushkov (1787–1852) (born five years before Viazemsky, Batiushkov "died" for literature and society in 1822, succumbing to mental illness).

6. *Vospominaniia o Bulgakovykh kniazia P. A. Viazemskogo* (Moscow, 1868), 23.

7. L. V. Deriugina, ed., *P. A. Viazemskii: Estetika i literaturnaia kritika* (Moscow, 1984), introductory article, 7.

8. Ibid.

9. See the "Autobiographical Introduction," written for Viazemsky's collected works: "I feel somehow alone in our contemporary literature. My former fellow-travelers are already gone, my contemporaries, so to say, my fellow-believers. There is no longer that full sympathy, which grew and strengthened itself in the native soil of comradeship, common habits, understanding, disposition, tendencies. Now, when I write something that I am myself satisfied with and which seems successful to me, I do not feel the urge, the interest to read the freshly written [text] to my friends. Those friends are no longer. Rejoicing for myself, I am sad to rejoice alone. I cannot run to Batiushkov, Zhukovsky, Pushkin, to share with them the fruit of my thoughts, my inspiration, just ripened, just torn from the branch. Their appraisal would have been my own final appraisal; their approval would have been the illumination of my joy. This loneliness, perhaps, is the cause of a certain cooling toward my very self and, perhaps, of my meager sympathy and often indifference toward what is written in our country" (*PSS*, 1:xlvii).

10. A good example is a discussion of freedom of the press, politics, and poetry, in which Viazemsky expresses his disapproval of certain political verse of Pushkin and Zhukovsky. See L. Ia. Ginzburg, ed., *P. A. Viazemskii: Staraia Zapisnaia Knizhka* (Leningrad, 1929), 96–100. Hereafter citations from the *Notebooks* will be made parenthetically in the text. Since Viazemsky's *Polnoe sobranie sochinenii* is a bibliographic rarity and Nechaeva's edition (though it has the best scholarly apparatus) covers only 1813–48, I have chosen to cite Ginzburg's as the most complete and readily available edition of the *Notebooks*.

11. In a letter to A. I. Turgenev, just three years earlier, Viazemsky comments: "God grant that Dmitriev begin to write his memoirs: I have repeated this to him several times. That is his real business: a survey of an observant Russian mind should be quite curious. Every nation looks at the world in a particular way; all the more should a seeing man in a nation of blind and nearsighted men have his own particular view. From the literary side his memoirs are precious: he really has something to recollect. A whole

generation of [our] literary forebears passed before him and a new one has partly matured, partly matures. Let him sometimes, as an old man, regret the old days and reproach the present: it is nice. Everyone must settle his own affairs and play his own role" (Deriugina, *Viazemskii: Estetika i literaturnaia kritika,* 376–77).

12. The fragmentary quality of Zagriazhskaia's legacy in this case is not seen by Viazemsky as a vehicle for avoiding a final or closing statement about the past, rather he sees it as a tragic loss of the material of history.

13. The poem, by G. G. Politkovskii, reads:

Не прав ты, новый год, в раздаче благостыни;
Ты своенравнее и счастия богини.
Иным ты дал чины,
Другим места богаты,
А мне—лишь новые заплаты
На старые мои штаны.

14. Viazemsky echoes his plans for a new "Rossiada" in his 1865 article, "Dopotopnaia ili dopozharnaia Moskva," in a discussion of the nature of Russian wit. In this article the emphasis of the project is different; it is meant to showcase in particular this characteristic wit and, moreover, includes a defense of the fact that "Russianness" is as characteristic of the higher classes as it is of the "simple folk." Viazemskii writes: "I have often wanted to put together a new "Rossiada" from jokes, sayings, witty utterings which are stamped with a particular Russicism. There is a particular mentality, a certain kind of buffoonery, of pretty-talk that really smells of Rus', and that scent is noticeable not only in that which we call the people . . . no, this mentality, this capriciousness of the Russian mind is not only found in the hut, on the squares, at peasant gatherings, but also in the glittering salons, furnished and imbued with appurtenances, the air, the inspiration of the West" (*PSS,* 7:97).

15. This criticism is in fact only attributed to Golitsyna. Viazemsky cites Pushkin (in the context of revealing the dual nature of Pushkin's feelings for Golitsyna, with whom he was enamored in his youth): "One could hardly not attribute to the Princess the following remark on the subject of the appearance of the eighth volume of *The History of the Russian State:* 'A certain lady, in fact quite respected [in the first variant the text reads: nice], in my presence, opening the second part [of the *History*], read aloud: Vladimir adopted Sviatopolk, *however* he did not love him . . .' However! Why not *but?* However! How stupid! Do you feel the paltriness of your Karamzin?" (219–20; emphasis added). The citation from Pushkin can be found in his *Otryvki iz pisem, mysli, i zamechaniia* (*Polnoe sobranie sochinenia v 10 tomakh* [Leningrad, 1978], 7:44).

16. "Was the Princess wise or not? Knowing her fairly briefly, it is not without some confusion that we pose this difficult and ticklish question. But

we will not presume to give a definitive answer. First, the mind is such an elusive and slippery component, that it is impossible to measure, weigh, and positively define it. It seems that in Spain they do not say of someone that he is brave, they say, he was brave on such a day, in such an affair. This caution could also be applied to people's minds. The female mind is particularly difficult to evaluate definitively. The mind of a woman is sometimes limited, but also seduces and prevails, because it is sensitive to what other people are thinking. The female mind is often hospitable; it willingly invites and welcomes wise guests, carefully and gracefully making them at home: thus a perceptive and experienced hostess does not promote herself in front of her guests, but does not contradict them, does not rush to cross their path, but on the contrary, seems to hide herself in order to give only them space and freedom. A woman, gifted with these qualities, will all but win over to her side the dominion of a woman endowed with sharper and more power-loving capabilities. This passivity of the female mind is often an attracting charm and force" (216–17).

17. As with "however," this comes via Pushkin who, notably, accuses Orlov of confusing history with literature: "He (that is, Orlov) reproached Karamzin for not having placed in the beginning of the *History* some sort of brilliant hypothesis about the origins of the Slavs, that is, he demanded a novel in the history" (220).

18. Andrew Wachtel has pointed out that Catherine makes a similarly ironic thrust at those who felt her interpretation of the founding of the Russian state to be pedestrian. See his reference to an ironic letter attributed to a reader, but penned by Catherine and included with the third installment of her *Notes,* which reads: "what a dry and insignificant account you give of the ancestry of the Russians! Could you really not have given such a glorious people a more miraculous cradle than this?" (*An Obsession with History: Russian Writers Confront the Past* [Stanford: Stanford University Press, 1994], 26.)

19. P. A. Viazemskii, *Pominki po Borodinskoi Bitve i Vospominaniia o 1812 gode* (Moscow, 1869), 34.

20. Viazemsky does not provide a formula for determining the validity of accounts of historical figures. In the case of Tolstoy, Viazemsky believes himself justified as a contemporary and eyewitness of events; theoretically, the anecdotal approach works from the ground up, building a picture from small units of eyewitness testimony. This approach is opposed here to that of Tolstoy, who starts with an image of the whole and finds or creates material to support it. Viazemsky does not address the question of who arbitrates between conflicting "eyewitness" accounts.

21. F. G. Volkov from a family of Iaroslavl merchants, was a well-known actor and founder of one of the most successful provincial amateur

theatrical troupes; he was brought to Petersburg by Empress Elizabeth in the mid-eighteenth century and remained to become one of the founders of a public theater in the capitol (Simon Karlinsky, *Russian Drama from its Beginnings to the Age of Pushkin* [Berkeley and Los Angeles: University of California Press, 1985], 63–64).

22. In *PSS* (8:172–74) this is attributed to Prince Ivan Golitsyn, who overheard it from Prince Pavel Zubov; this could reflect sloppy editing on Ginzburg's part, since in her edition this entry begins: "Here is another story from the same source" and the preceding entry ends with a story by Naryshkin.

23. See also *PSS*, 10:247 (1863–64), where Viazemsky recommends Vigel's *Notes* for their chronological accuracy, but comments that in their essence they may be questionable to people familiar with Vigel's "character and passions" (*pristrastiia*).

24. See also Bartenev's *XIX Vek*, 2:225–26, for the published version of this anecdote, which is expressed more delicately.

25. In one entry, Viazemsky makes a connection between these towering figures and the nonegalitarian nature of society: "In society it is necessary for things to be subordinated to something and to someone. Many people talk about equality, which exists neither in nature, nor in human nature. There is nothing more boring and tedious than flat valleys: the eye absolutely requires that something—a hillock, tree—be set off from the visual monotony and to some degree rise above it" (151).

26. Placing a premium on eclecticism of character is described by William M. Todd III as typical of the *honnête homme* during the Pushkin period: "Russian life of the period, with its whirl of activities, ever-changing fashions, abundant foreign models, and orientation toward talk, developed this multiplication of selves to an extraordinary degree, largely because the subject that the ideology of polite society constituted was an insistently composite . . . a person of balanced humors, emotions, and interests, capable of playing a variety of roles" (*Fiction and Society in the Age of Pushkin: Ideology, Institutions, and Narrative* [Cambridge: Harvard University Press, 1986], 34).

STEPHEN BAEHR, "IS MOSCOW BURNING? FIRE IN GRIBOEDOV'S *WOE FROM WIT*"

For helpful comments on previous versions of this article, I am grateful to Caryl Emerson, Monika Greenleaf, Irina Mess-Baehr, and Stephen Moeller-Sally.

1. The play was first published posthumously, with cuts, in 1833 but not published in full until 1861. Unless indicated otherwise, all emphases in quotations from the play are my addition.

2. The importance of the events of 1812 to Griboedov during the mid-1820s is reflected not only by the overt references to the fire of 1812 in the play but also by the fact that in 1824 (the year that he completed *Gore ot uma*) he even began a tragedy about 1812 (which he never completed). In the surviving sections of this latter play, fire imagery also plays an important role. In the second part, Griboedov planned to show the destruction wrought by the 1812 fire and to depict the burning houses of Moscow; in his sketches, he notes that the events of 1812 will arouse in later generations "an *inextinguishable flame* (*ogn' neugasimyi*), a zeal for the glory and freedom of their fatherland" (A. S. Griboedov, *Sochineniia v stikhakh,* ed. I. N. Medvedeva [Leningrad: Sovetskii pisatel', 1967], 328).

3. My argument about Griboedov's parody of the apocalyptic fire imagery in contemporary chauvinistic literature is not intended to challenge the well-known fact that Griboedov was himself a nationalist. Indeed, much of his criticism of upper-class Moscow society reflects his feeling that Russia was ignoring its own native traditions and favoring those of the France it had defeated; he implicitly blames the reforms of Peter the Great for this blind imitation of the West. Indeed, as will be noted below, some of Chatsky's speeches prefigure ideas of the Slavophiles and other nationalists.

Models for this apocalyptic fire imagery had already appeared in Russian literature before the conflagration of 1812. For example, M. A. Dmitriev-Mamonov's 1811 ode to fire called "Ogon'" (Fire) uses the biblical image of creation of "a new heaven and a new earth" out of the apocalyptic destruction of the old as "an allegory for the moral and political rebirth of Russia" (Iu. M. Lotman and M. G. Al'tshuller, eds., *Poety 1790–1810-x godov* [Leningrad: Sovetskii pisatel', 1971], 872). As Dmitriev-Mamonov wrote: "Fire, you devour the impure, / And can beautify the pure / And embrace everything in yourself" (Lotman and Al'tshuller, *Poety,* 721). As David Bethea has observed, this work uses the image of an apocalyptic "great fire" (*ekpyrosis*) resulting in the creation of a new world (*The Shape of Apocalypse in Modern Russian Fiction* [Princeton: Princeton University Press, 1989], 29 n). Works like Dmitriev-Mamonov's to some extent justify Frank Kermode's overbroad generalization that "the mythology of Empire and of Apocalypse are very closely related" (*The Sense of an Ending* [Oxford: Oxford University Press, 1967], 10).

4. Words formed from *gore* and *goret'* in turn interact with the other major word in the title, *um* ("mind," "wit"), to punningly show how the "intelligent" (*um-nyi*) Chatsky is "burned" and receives "woe" (*gore*) when he comes into contact with Moscow's idle, rumormongering high society. As I shall show later in discussing the problems of Moscow, Griboedov's witty punning throughout the play reflects the truth of A. W. Schlegel's observation in his *Lectures on Dramatic Art and Literature* that "indignation makes a man witty."

Several critics have observed that during Griboedov's time, the word *um* often connoted freethinkers, members of secret societies, and other independent citizens. See Vladimir Orlov, *Griboedov: Ocherk zhizni i tvorchestva* (Moscow: Gosudarstvennoe izdanie khudozhestvennoi literatury, 1954), 127; and Wladimir Troubetzkoy, "Tchatski, ou la Répétition," in *Le Misanthrope au Théâtre: Ménandre, Molière, Griboiedov,* ed. Daniel-Henri Pageaux (Mugron, France: Editions José Feijóo 1990), 281–83. On the role of *umniki* in Russian comedies of Griboedov's time, see Jean Bonamour, *A. S. Griboedov et la vie littéraire de son temps* (Paris: Presses universitaires de France, 1965), 278. On Griboedov's text as a "long conceit or pun on the meaning of the word *um,*" see J. Douglas Clayton, " 'Tis folly to be wise: The Semantics of *um-* in Griboedov's *Gore ot uma,*" in *Text and Context: Essays to Honor Nils Åke Nilsson,* ed. Peter Alberg Jensen et al. (Stockholm: Almqvist and Wiksell International, 1987), 8ff.

Clayton argues quite convincingly that the title summarizes the main problems of the play, which he sees as a clash between two opposing types of *um:* the "common wisdom" of Moscow society that demands conformity with its values of "nepotism, corruption, [and] foreign fashions" and declares anyone mad who does not share these values; and the *um* of Chatsky, which "criticizes the hypocrisy of Famusov's [i.e. Moscow high society's] *um*" and is often associated with education and enlightenment. As Clayton has suggested, Griboedov's switch from his original title *Gore umu* ("Woe to Wit") to *Gore ot uma* allowed purposeful ambiguity (7 and 9).

5. There has been major controversy surrounding Griboedov's naming of his "Chadsky"/Chatsky. Although Piksanov sees the name as "purely invented" and views the derivation of Chatsky from *chad* as "artificial," Medvedeva argues that this derivation is likely (reflecting Chatsky's tendency to live in "the fumes—*chad*—of ideas and enthusiasm"). Karlinsky sees the name "Chadsky" as suggesting "both that the young man fumes a lot and that his head is in a daze," but El'zon proposes that "Chatsky" is linked with *chaiushchii* (thinking, hoping), recalling the proverb "Zhdut Fomu, chaiut, byt' umu" (which means, very roughly, "They are waiting for Foma, hoping for brains"). Tynianov even suggests that the name reflects a link with that of the philosopher Chaadaev (which was occasionally written as "Chadaev"). As I shall argue below, I believe that the text explains Chatsky's name in act 4, associating it with the "burning" of the hopes with which Chatsky had returned to Moscow in act 1. On this controversy, see V. I. Korovin, commentary to Griboedov, *Gore ot uma* (Moscow: Russkii iazyk, 1984), 132–33; Simon Karlinsky, *Russian Drama from Its Beginnings to the Age of Pushkin* (Berkeley and Los Angeles: University of California Press, 1985), 288; M. D. El'zon, " 'Chad' " ili 'chaiat'? O smysle familii 'Chatskii,'" *Russkaia literatura* 24, no. 2 (1981): 182–83; Iu. N. Tynianov, "Siuzhet 'Goria ot uma'," in *Pushkin*

i ego sovremenniki, ed. V. A. Kaverin and Z. A. Nikitina (Moscow: Nauka, 1968), 360–68.

6. All quotes throughout this article are from A. S. Griboedov, *Gore ot uma,* ed. N. K. Piksanov and A. L. Grishulin (Moscow: Nauka, 1969). References will be given to act and line number. Thus, "3.52" is act 3, line 52.

7. Gorich is tied to Moscow because of his wife, Natal'ia Dmitrievna, who, unlike him, loves Moscow's balls, social life, and style. Her constant henpecking reflects the broader theme of misogyny in the play, which Simon Karlinsky has identified as one of its two main themes (the other, "gerontophobia," will be discussed below). As Karlinsky argues: "What is really wrong with Moscow is that it is run by corrupt old men ('the older the worse') and by domineering women of all ages" (292).

It is significant that Gorich longs to leave Moscow and return to the country. Thus, a second theme raised by Gorich and Chatsky (the only two male characters who can be seen as positive) is the opposition between the negative Moscow and the positive rural areas (the home of what Chatsky calls "our bold, intelligent folk" [*umnyi, bodryi nash narod,* 3.615]). Griboedov, therefore, is probably being ironic when he has Famusov threaten to punish Sophia by sending her "to the country (*v derevniu*), to your aunt's, to the backwoods (*glush'*)," where (in her father's words) she will "grieve *woe*" ("*Tam budesh' gore gorevat'*)."

8. On fire and change, see Gaston Bachelard, *The Psychoanalysis of Fire,* trans. Alan C. M. Ross (Boston: Beacon, 1964), 7, 16.

One early indication that change/lack of change will be central to Griboedov's play is the repeated emphasis in the early scenes on clocks and time. The words *chasy* (clock" and *chas* (hour) are repeated four times in the first scene (21 lines) and six times in the first 75 lines. Indeed, the first prop mentioned in the stage directions to act 1, scene 1 is the "large clock."

9. The commonplace image of love as a "sacred fire" was rather frequently used in Russia during the Golden Age—especially by Romantic writers. For example Lermontov in the "Princess Mary" section of *Hero of our Time* (*Geroi nashego vremeni,* 1840) has Pechorin write in his diary for 3 June: "[A]n electric *spark* ran from my hand to hers; almost all passions begin this way, and we often deceive ourselves greatly in thinking that a woman loves us for our physical or moral qualities. Of course, these qualities prepare and incline their hearts for the reception of the *sacred fire,* but nevertheless it is the first contact that decides the matter" (M. Iu. Lermontov, *Sobranie sochinenii v chetyrekh tomakh* [Moscow: Izdatel'stvo Akademii nauk, 1958–59], 4:406–7).

10. Chatsky's search for a passion that will match his own is reflected in the use of fire imagery for women whom he finds attractive. For example, in an early manuscript for the play, Griboedov had Sophia respond to Chatsky's

accusations of Molchalin by "hotly" (*goriacho*) defending the latter, presenting a clear parallelism between her and Chatsky (Griboedov, *Gore ot uma,* 1969, 182). After his rejection by Sophia, Chatsky is attracted to Natal'ia Dmitrievna at the ball: "[Y]ou're such a lot prettier / You've become younger, fresher; / There's *fire,* color, laughter, play in all your features" ("[P]okhorosheli strakh; / Molozhe vy, svezhee stali; / *Ogon',* rumianets, smekh, igra vo vsekh chertakh," 3.233–35).

11. In this speech about his "boiling" love, Chatsky pretends to admire Molchalin, saying to Sophia: "Let's grant him a lively wit, a bold genius. / But is there that passion in him? That feeling? That *ardor* (*pylkost'*) / That would make all the world except for you / Seem just vanity and dust?" (3.43–46). In an earlier draft, Griboedov had emphasized the phlegmatic Molchalin's *lack* of fire even more explicitly, continuing after the penultimate line just quoted: "Seem just laughter and dust? Just *smoke* and trivia and vanity?" (*dym,* meloch' i tshcheta) (Griboedov, *Gore ot uma,* 1969, 181).

12. On the theory of humors, which predominated in medicine from Galen through the medieval period and was a frequent source of metaphors in literature from the Renaissance through the early nineteenth century, see E. M. W. Tillyard, *The Elizabethan World Picture* (New York: Vintage Books, n.d), 69–79.

13. The term "fiery" (*ognennyi*) was used for Chatsky by critics from the first appearance of the play. For example, Pushkin in 1825 called Chatsky "fervent" (*pylkii,* etymologically "flaming"), and one 1833 commentary said he was "animated by fiery passions" and "fervid." On such criticism, see A. M. Gordin, ed., *A. S. Griboedov v russkoi kritike* (Moscow: Gosudarstvennoe izdatel'stvo khudozhestvennoi literatury, 1958), 40. According to Orlov, passion and "zeal" (*goriachnost',* etymologically "hotness") were frequent characteristics of the liberal youth of the 1810s—1820s (*Griboedov,* 121).

14. In the theory of humors, the "cold and moist" phlegmatic type opposes the "warm and dry" choleric type (Tillyard, *Elizabethan World Picture,* 69). Molchalin has some of the typical characteristics of the "phlegmatic" individual: unemotional, even-tempered, calm. His name may also reflect the saying that "silence is a mark of assent" (*molchanie—znak soglasiia*), which originated with Pope Boniface VIII but was popular in Russia (N. S. Ashukin and M. G. Ashukina. *Krylatye slova: Literaturnye tsitaty, obraznye vyrazheniia,* 2d ed. [Moscow: Gosudarstvennoe izdatel'stvo khudozhestvennoi literatury, 1960], 370–71). I am grateful to Monika Greenleaf and Stephen Moeller-Sally for suggesting Molchalin's possible connection with the phlegmatic personality.

15. Karlinsky argues that "all of Chatsky's speeches that identify old age with corruption—beginning with his famous Act II monologue 'And who are the judges'—are quite specifically aimed at the situation in Moscow." He goes

on to say that "the trouble with the aged" in this play is that "they shut out the modern world and still see things in eighteenth-century terms" (*Russian Drama,* 292).

16. In a famous January 1825 letter to Katenin, Griboedov himself stressed the opposition between the "intelligent" Chatsky and Moscow society as a whole. As he wrote: "[I]n my comedy there are 25 fools (*gluptsov*) for one intelligent (*zdravomysliashchego*) person. And this person, of course, contradicts the society which surrounds him" (quoted in Tynianov, "Siuzhet 'Goria ot uma'," 348). Pushkin, in a letter to Bestuzhev of the same month, disagreed with Griboedov, stating that the only "intelligent" (*umnoe*) character in the comedy is Griboedov himself; he criticized Chatsky by noting that "the first sign of an intelligent man is to know from the first glance with whom he is dealing and not to cast pearls before Repetilovs"—perhaps an unwitting draft of his own future lines to his muse in "Exegi monumentum" (1836); "And do not contradict the fool" (*I ne osparivai gluptsa*) (letter excerpted in Gordin, *A. S. Griboedov v russkoi kritike,* 40).

17. The image of the "smoke of the fatherland" probably first occurs in Homer's *Odyssey* (book 1, lines 57–59), in a prayer by Athena to Cronus asking him to release Odysseus from the spell of Calypso, who "charms him to forget Ithaca." As Athena states: "Odysseus, however, wanting to catch sight even of *smoke* leaping up from his fatherland, is longing to die" (*The Odyssey,* trans. and ed. Albert Cook [New York: Norton, 1974], 5). The phrase was later used by Ovid (*Epistulae ex Ponto,* 1.3.33), from whom the Latin proverb came (Ashukin and Ashukina, *Krylatye slova,* 243).

In Russia, this phrase had been used as an epigraph for the journal *Rossiiskii muzeum* (The Russian museum, 1792–94) and was quoted in a number of poems at the turn of the century, including Derzhavin's poem "The Harp" ("Arfa," 1798)—the probable immediate source of Chatsky's quote. Griboedov has Chatsky quote the last line of Derzhavin's poem in the version that appeared in the journal *Aonidy* (1798–99, book 3, p. 14) (V. I. Korovin, commentary to Griboedov, *Gore ot uma,* 1984, 135). For an interesting short history of this phrase in Russian literature from Derzhavin through Mayakovsky, see Ashukin and Ashukina, *Krylatye slova,* 242–43.

18. Quoted in Ernst Benz, *The Eastern Orthodox Church: Its Thought and Life,* trans. Richard and Clara Winston (New York: Anchor Books, 1963), 188.

19. In an early manuscript of the play, Skalozub made even stronger comments about the effects of the Moscow fire: "In my judgment, the fire flamed as if someone ordered it (*Pozhar kak na zakaz pylal*). It helped to beautify the city. And the style of life has improved." But Chatsky responds, "It was a gloomy year (*chernyi god*) for us and served no purpose" (Griboedov, *Gore ot uma,* 1969, 161).

20. Given the association of Chatsky with fire (as discussed earlier), it would at first appear that Griboedov has Chatsky in mind as the person "with a soul" in whom a "spark" would be placed to destroy the "spirit of . . . blind imitation" in Russia. But as the speech progresses, Griboedov uses imagery implying that such changes could be made in Russia only by a powerful monarch. Indeed, the image of restraint "with strong reins" recalls the iconographic tradition—used in the West since Roman times and in Russia since the eighteenth century—of the emperor as horseman, controlling the "horse" of his empire with strong "reins." This tradition was used, for example, by the sculptor Falconet some fifty years before *Woe from Wit* when he depicted Peter the Great as "the Bronze Horseman." On the symbolism of horsemanship in Russian literature and culture of the eighteenth century, see Stephen Baehr, *The Paradise Myth in Eighteenth-Century Russia: Utopian Patterns in Early Secular Russian Literature and Culture* (Stanford: Stanford University Press, 1991), 50, 58, 213.

The need for a monarch who could eliminate the "harm" caused by Peter's westernizing reforms is implied several lines after this speech when Chatsky says that "for me our North [Russia] has become a hundred times worse" since Peter's reforms, requiring Russians to change their ways and imitate the West: "he gave everything away for a new style— / Our morals and our language and our holy past— / And changed our majestic clothing for another, / Which was like that of a jester (*po shutovskomu obraztsu*)" (3.602–5). Chatsky makes a clear opposition in his speeches between "copies" (*spiski*) or "imitations" (*podrazhan'ia*) and "originals" (*originaly*) (for example, 3.323–24; 3.595), and stresses that Russia should be returned to its own original path and should stop copying the foreign.

21. Since completing this section, I have seen Apollon Grigor'ev's 1862 comment that "Griboedov's comedy is a true *divina commedia*" (Gordin, *A. S. Griboedov* 225).

22. It is probably not coincidental that this last speech (act 4, scene 14) is pronounced on a stage lit with a large number of lanterns and candles—the "fire" illuminating the truth. Famusov at the beginning of the scene explicitly calls for "more candles, more lanterns" (4.420). Indeed, Griboedov seems to have designed the play to move from darkness (the play begins at the first sign of dawn) to light (the "exposure scene" that we are discussing, where Famusov discovers the rendezvous between Sophia and her lover, Sophia realizes the truth about Molchalin, and Chatsky, finally, realizes that Sophia loves Molchalin). The candles and lanterns reveal Moscow's old aristocrats as liars, cheaters, double-dealers, and so forth. On one level, Chatsky is like the raisonneur of eighteenth-century Russian drama, "illuminating" society for what it is.

23. J. E. Cirlot, *A Dictionary of Symbols,* trans. Jack Sage (New York: Philosophical Library, 1962), 21.

24. These verses were (and still are) extremely well known in Russia. Ivan Bunin even used Revelation 18:10 as an epigraph to one edition of his 1915 "The Gentleman from San Francisco."

Chapter 18 of Revelation may provide a clue to the overall meaning of Griboedov's play, uniting the major themes of "fire" and "woe" with the theme of judgment, which is also central to the play (as reflected in important speeches like "A sud'i kto? [Who are the Judges], 2.340ff.). Indeed, like the *gor-* roots (fire, woe) and the *um-* roots (intelligence, mind, wit), the *sud-* root (judgment) is extremely important in the play, reflecting, once again, Griboedov's tendency to stress central themes through a repetition of roots.

25. According to Dal', the phrase "u nikh Sodom i Gomorra" meant "the epitome of disorder." Compare also the proverb "Takoi sodom, chto dym koromyslom" (There is such disorder that all hell is breaking loose; literally, There is such a Sodom that smoke is like a yoke). See Vladimir Dal', *Tolkovyi slovar' zhivogo velikorusskogo iazyka,* 4 vols. (Moscow: Gosudarstvennoe izdatel'stvo inostrannykh i natsional'nikh slovarei, 1956), 4.260; 1.506.

26. In this icon, the victory of Ivan IV at Kazan is allegorically depicted as the victory of Christianity over Islam. As Olga Dacenko has observed, "Christ's armed horsemen advancing in triple rank toward the Heavenly City symbolize the Russian people, God's chosen ones, the 'new Israel.' " See M. W. Alpatov and Olga Dacenko, *Art Treasures of Russia,* trans. Norbert Guterman (New York: Abrams, 1967), 142. I am grateful to Michael Flier of Harvard University for pointing out the possible relevance of this icon in a March 1995 discussion.

27. For a discussion of this tradition of Russia as paradise, third Rome, or a place enjoying the Golden Age, see Baehr, *The Paradise Myth.* On the reversal of this tradition in the early nineteenth century, see ibid., 162–67.

28. James H. Billington, *Fire in the Minds of Men: Origins of the Revolutionary Faith* (New York: Basic Books, 1980), 104.

29. F. V. Rostopchin, *Okh, Frantsuzy!* ed. G. D. Ovchinnikov (Moscow: Russkaia kniga, 1992), 151; Irina Mess-Baehr, " 'Soldattskaia' satira i allegoriia v neizdannykh antinapoleonovskikh stikhakh Derzhavina," *Study Group on Eighteenth-Century Russia Newsletter* 8 (1980): 82 n.

30. P. A. Viazemskii, *Stikhotvoreniia,* ed. L. Ia. Ginzburg and K. A. Kumpan (Leningrad: Sovetskii pisatel', 1986), 142.

31. P. A. Viazemskii, *Izbrannye stikhotvoreniia,* ed. V. S. Nechaeva (Moscow: Academia, 1935), 540. Viazemskii, in a letter of 22 March 1820 to A. I. Turgenev that included this poem, encouraged such political readings of the poem, stating that he wondered if this fable would pass the censors

because of its allusions (Viazemskii, *Stikhotvoreniia,* 472). His fears proved justified when the censors rejected its publication.

32. Aleksandr Odoevskii, "Strun veshchikh plamennye zvuki," cited in A. S. Pushkin, *Stikhotvoreniia,* ed. B. V. Tomashevskii (Leningrad: Sovetskii pisatel', 1955), 3:819. Odoevskii's acknowledgment of receipt of the "*flaming* sounds of prophetic strings" of Pushkin's poetic lyre (that is, the 1827 poem Pushkin sent to the Decembrists, entitled "Vo glubine sibirskikh rud") in its very first line already signals the relevance of revolutionary fire symbolism. The last four lines of the poem affirm this, stating that the Decembrists (and, implicitly, other freedom fighters) will "forge swords from chains / And once again light the *fire* of freedom / And with this freedom we will pounce upon rulers (*grianem na tsarei*), / And nations (*narody*) will sigh with joy." For Pushkin's text and additional commentary, see 392 and 819.

33. F. M. Dostoevskii, *Polnoe sobranie sochinenii,* 30 vols., ed. B. G. Bazanov et al. (Leningrad: Nauka, 1972–90), 10:395; Aleksandr Blok, *Sobranie sochinenii,* 8 vols. (Moscow: Gosudarstvennoe izdatel'stvo khudozhestvennoi literatury, 1960–63), 7:279. The theme of revolutionary fire in Dostoevsky already begins in *Crime and Punishment,* when Raskol'nikov goes to a tavern to read newspaper accounts about the murder that he has committed and can find only material on (revolutionary) fires being set throughout Petersburg (and, as Luzhin notes, throughout the country); see Dostoevsky, 6:117, 124–25.

34. Anatole Mazour, *The First Russian Revolution, 1825: The Decembrist Movement* (Stanford: Stanford University Press, 1961), 29.

35. See N. I. Turgenev, *Dekabrist N. I. Turgenev,* ed. N. G. Svirin (Moscow: Izdatel'stvo Akademii nauk SSSR, 1936), 396 n. The term "Extinguisher" came from a liberal French newspaper, *Nain Jaune,* which satirized the Old Regime (Turgenev, *Dekabrist,* 387 n). In the 5 January 1815 issue there appeared "The Organic Statutes of the Order of Extinguisher," providing the bylaws of this "group," supposedly created on the order of Mizofan the 2367th: "Wishing to restrain 'the oppressive progress of enlightenment,' Mizofan announces the founding of this order, [which] consists of a grand master, judges or grand extinguisher, commanders, and knights of the double extinguisher." According to these bylaws, "every person entering this order must take a vow of hatred for philosophy, for liberal ideas, and for any constitutional charter" (quoted in Turgenev, *Dekabrist,* 396 n). In his letters, Turgenev sometimes used two cone-shaped candlesnuffers instead of the word "extinguisher" to signify this group (e.g. Turgenev, *Dekabrist,* 193, letter 76); at least once he called the movement by the French equivalent name, describing contemporary Russia as being dominated by "egoism, laziness, and in addition a lack of trust of anything good, a coarse mysticism, and

éteignorisme (*eten'uarizm*)" (288). I am grateful to Savely Senderovich for giving me the reference to this volume.

36. I. Medvedeva notes that the "learned committee" (*uchenyi komitet*) satirized by Chatsky in his first diatribe against Moscow—a committee on which Sophia's "tubercular relative, an enemy of books" served, and which "demanded with a shout that no one should be literate or should learn" (1.379–82)—was effectively under the control of the "extinguisher of enlightenment M. L. Magnitskii" (*Gore ot uma A. S. Griboedova,* 2d ed. [Moscow: Khudozhestvennaia literatura, 1974], 32).

37. The Carbonarists, faithful to their name (which meant "charcoal-burners"), used imagery of fire throughout their ritual: new members were referred to as sticks or pieces of wood who were to be transformed into "the purer, more useful form of charcoal." Meetings were depicted as "a ritual purification by fire in the furnaces of a secret grotto." Guards standing at the door where the Grand Master entered were called "flames," and two sabers "like flames of fire," were placed on either side of the door (Billington, *Fire in the Minds of Men,* 133).

38. As a Mason (an active member of the lodge *Soedinennye druz'ia* / "Des Amis Réunis" from 1816), Griboedov would have known from Masonic songs that Freemasonry was often called a "sacred fire" by its members. So the old countess's error had an element of truth. This association of Freemasonry with a "sacred fire" appears in Russian Masonic songs as early as the reign of Empress Elizabeth. One song, for example, says that James Keith (the founder of Freemasonry in Russia) *"lit* the *sacred fire"* of Freemasonry in Russia (*Pesni,* n.p., n.d., 66). Within the Masonic lodge fire imagery (especially images of "sparks" and of burning) was frequent.

It may (or may not) be coincidental that the first question asked by Sophia to Liza in act 1 and repeated by Repetilov in act 4—"What time is it? (*Kotoryi chas?*, 1.15, 17; 4.69)—was also a question asked at the opening of the initiation ceremony into Freemasonry (asked by the grand master to the officers of the lodge). (In the opening of the lodge, the answer is "five minutes to seven"; in the play Liza answers "seven, eight, nine.") Both in the play and in the lodge, the question reflects the important theme of time and of change. See, for example, Harry B. Weber, "*Pikovaia dama:* A Case for Freemasonry in Russian Literature," *Slavic and East European Journal* 12 (1968): 438.

39. It is likely that in this play the Mason Griboedov is reacting against the popular contamination of the Masonic quest for enlightenment and moral change with the revolutionary quest for violent political change.

40. On Griboedov's friendship with future Decembrists, see Karlinsky, *Russian Drama,* 284; Harold B. Segel, "Griboedov, Aleksandr Sergeevich," in *Handbook of Russian Literature,* ed. Victor Terras (New Haven: Yale

University Press, 1985), 184–85; and M. Nechkina, *Griboedov i dekabristy,* 3d ed. (Moscow: Khudozhestvennaia literatura, 1977).

41. For a summary of the views of Dostoevsky, Goncharov, and Grigor'ev on this "most secret union," see: A. V. Arkhipova, "Dvorianskaia revoliutsionnost' v vospriiatii F. M. Dostoevskogo," in *Literaturnoe nasledie dekabristov,* ed. V. G. Bazanov and V. E. Vatsuro (Leningrad: Nauka, 1975), 221–24; Bonamour, *A. S. Griboedov,* 318; Medvedeva introduction to Griboedov, *Sochineniia v stikhakh,* 45.

D. P. Costello has suggested that this "most secret union" is a parody of Arzamas (the "mock-secret" society to which Pushkin, Zhukovsky, Batiushkov, and other important literary figures belonged), a group that Griboedov had previously parodied in his 1817 comedy *The Student* and that, like Repetilov's, also met "on Thursdays" (4.96), discussed Byron, and at points created impromptu vaudevilles (4.167); see his argument in his edition of *Gore ot uma* (Oxford: Clarendon Press, 1951), 192.

Simon Karlinsky, on the other hand, sees the "most secret union" as a parody of the secret societies that prepared for the Decembrist rebellion; he argues on the basis of the satire in act 4—including the discussion of themes like legislative chambers (implying constitutional government) and juries (4.101–2)—that Griboedov "must have been aware of the . . . societies that fomented the [Decembrist] rebellion," even though he did not know of their specific plans for rebellion, as an investigation disclosed after Griboedov was arrested (284–85). Following V. Filippov, Karlinsky argues that "Griboedov's familiarity with the inner workings of the Decembrist societies extends even to having Repetilov cite a phrase from Baldassare Galuppi's opera *Didone abbandonata* 'A! non lasciar mi, no, no, no,' which was used by the Decembrists as a password" (295).

For additional material on the supposed Decembrist references in act 4 to Byron and his revolutionary activities, as well as to chambers of deputies (parliamentary systems) and the jury system, see V. I. Korovin's notes to his edition of *Gore ot uma,* 153. For an exhaustive analysis of possible Decembrist connections, see Nechkina, *Griboedov i dekabristy.*

42. The harmfulness of *chad* is expressed in Russian through such proverbs as "S khudoi golovoi, ne suisia v chad" (If you have a headache, stay away from the fumes), and "Zharko topit', ne boiat'sia chadu" (Those who heat a place warmly are not afraid of the fumes) (Dal', *Tolkovyi slovar',* 4.580).

43. Another emblem for the unchanging city is the ball, where (as the stage directions state at the end of act 3), "everyone goes round and round" (*vse kruzhatsia*). As I have mentioned, several stage props in the play are also implicit metaphors. See the discussions of the clock (above and note 8) and of the candles and lanterns in the "discovery" scene (note 22).

IRINA REYFMAN, "ALEXANDER BESTUZHEV-MARLINSKY: *BRETTEUR* AND APOLOGIST OF THE DUEL"

1. François Billacois, *The Duel: Its Rise and Fall in Early Modern France,* ed. and trans. Trista Selous (New Haven: Yale University Press, 1990), 233.

2. About Bestuzhev's life and his legendary biographies, see Lewis Bagby, *Alexander Bestuzhev-Marlinsky and Russian Byronism* (University Park: Pennsylvania State University Press, 1995), especially chapters 2 and 4 and the conclusion; Lauren G. Leighton, *Alexander Bestuzhev-Marlinsky* (Boston: Twayne, 1975), chap. 1, 13–36; Iu. Levin, "Ob obstoiatel'stvakh smerti A. A. Bestuzheva-Marlinskogo," *Russkaia literatura* 2 (1962): 219–22; M. P. Alekseev, "Legenda o Marlinskom," in his *Etiudy o Marlinskom: Sbornik trudov Irkutskogo universiteta* 25 (1928): 113–41; P. V. Bykov, "Zagadka (Iz legend o Bestuzheve-Marlinskom)," *Niva* 52 (1912): 1039–40; repr. in Bykov, *Siluety dalekogo proshlogo* (Moscow: Zemlia I fabrika, 1930), 28–34.

3. See Iv. Abramov, "K kharakteristike chitatelia Pushkinskogo vremeni," *Pushkin i ego sovremenniki* 16 (1913): 104. It should be noted that a fourth Alexander, Griboedov, was murdered in 1828 in Teheran. Bestuzhev considered this a significant coincidence: the morning after receiving the news about Pushkin's death, he went to Griboedov's grave in the monastery of Saint David, ordered a mass to be served at the site of his burial, and wept through the service. See his 23 February 1837 letter to P. A. Bestuzhev, in *Sochineniia v dvukh tomakh,* 2 vols. (Moscow: Gosudarstvennoe izdatel'stvo khudozhestvennoi literatury, 1958), 2:673–74. Unless otherwise noted, all citations to Bestuzhev's writings are taken from this edition and will appear in parentheses in the body of the article.

4. This version of Bestuzhev's death is mentioned as one of the wild rumors in F. D. K . . . , "Smert' Aleksandra Aleksandrovicha Bestuzheva," in *Pisateli-dekabristy v vospominaniiakh sovremennikov,* 2 vols. (Moscow: Khudozhestvennaia literatura, 1980), 2:176.

5. M. A. Bestuzhev, "Detstvo i iunost' A. A. Bestuzheva," in *Pisateli-dekabristy,* 2:124. See also *Vospominaniia Bestuzhevykh,* ed. M. K. Azadovskii (Moscow: Izdatel'stvo Akademii nauk SSSR, 1951), 210.

6. M. A. Bestuzhev, "Melkie zametki ob A. A. Bestuzheve," in *Pisateli-dekabristy,* 2:135; *Vospominaniia Bestuzhevykh,* 222.

7. "Rasskazy E. A. Bestuzhevoi," in *Vospominaniia Bestuzhevykh,* 413.

8. M. A. Bestuzhev, "Iz 'Vospominanii o N. A. Bestuzheve,' " in *Pisateli-dekabristy,* 2:207; *Vospominaniia Bestuzhevykh,* 284.

9. M. A. Bestuzhev, "Moi tiur'my," in *Pisateli-dekabristy,* 1:53; *Vospominaniia Bestuzhevykh,* 55.

10. Ibid. Mikhail Bestuzhev also refers to this episode in his "Vospominaniia o N. A. Bestuzheve," in *Vospominaniia Bestuzhevykh*, 269. Mikhail believed that von Dezin was behind Alexander Bestuzhev's 1831 transfer to active duty from Tiflis, a relatively safe and pleasant place to serve. See also Nikolai Bestuzhev's account of the confrontation, in his "Vospominanie o Ryleeve," *Pisateli-dekabristy*, 2:75; *Vospominaniia Bestuzhevykh*, 22.

11. For a description of the duel, see Bestuzhev's letter to Iakov Tolstoy, first published in *Russkaia starina* 11 (1889): 375–76; M. A. Bestuzhev, "Melkie zametki ob A. A. Bestuzheve," in *Pisateli-dekabristy*, 2:135 and *Vospominaniia Bestuzhevykh*, 222; Dm. Kropotov, "Neskol'ko svedenii o Ryleeve. Po povodu zapisok Grecha," in *Pisateli-dekabristy*, 2:17–18.

12. A. A. Bestuzhev, letter to Tolstoy, in *Pisateli-dekabristy*, 2:376.

13. For descriptions of the conflict see "Bumagi o poedinke Novosil'tseva i Chernova," in P. I. Bartenev, ed., *Deviatnadtsatyi vek: Sbornik* 1 (1872): 333–37; *Pisateli-dekabristy*, 1:291 n; 2:18–19, 53, and 321–22; T. I. Ornatskaia, ed., *Rasskazy babushki. Iz vospominanii piati pokolenii. Zapisannye i sobrannye ee vnukom D. Blagovo* (Leningrad: Nauka, 1989), 289, 291. The memory of this duel is still alive in Russia: in 1992, a monument was erected at the site of the encounter.

14. P. P. Karatygin, "P. A. Katenin," in *Pisateli-dekabristy*, 1:291 n.

15. "Bumagi o poedinke Novosil'tseva s Chernovym," 334.

16. "Iz bumag Baten'kova," in *Memuary dekabristov*, ed. M. V. Dovnar-Zapol'sky (Kiev: Izdatel'stvo knizhnogo magazina S. I. Ivanova, 1906), 165.

17. On the link between the nobility's anxiety about the absence of firm guarantees of physical inviolability and the growth of the duel in Russia, see my "The Emergence of the Duel of Honor in Russia: Corporal Punishment and the Honor Code," *Russian Review* 54 (1995): 26–43.

18. For a report on Mavra's plight, see "Semeistvo Razumovskogo," in Petr Bartenev, ed., *Os'mnadtsatyi vek. Istoricheskii sbornik*, 2 (1869); quoted in A. Romanovich-Slavatinskii's *Dvorianstvo v Rossii ot nachala XVIII veka do otmeny krepostnogo prava. Svod materialov i prigotovitel'nye etiudy dlia istoricheskogo issledovaniia* (St. Petersburg: Tipografiia ministerstva vnutrennikh del. 1870), 20. The 1803 duel between A. P. Kushelev and N. N. Bakhmet'ev over Bakhmet'ev's having hit Kushelev with a walking stick during military training in 1797 exemplifies the nobility's newly acquired intolerance of physical abuse. I discuss this duel in my "Emergence of the Duel," 41–42.

19. Iakubovich's fellow Decembrists testified that he formulated his proposal to assassinate Alexander I in terms of a duel of honor; see *Vosstanie dekabristov*, vol. 2 (Moscow: Gospolitizdat,1926), 293–94, 296; "Iz pokazanii Kondratiia Fedorovicha Ryleeva," in *Iz pisem i pokazanii dekabristov: Kritika sovremennogo sostoianiia Rossii i plany budushchego ustroistva*, ed. A. K. Borozdin (St. Petersburg: Izdanie M. V. Pirozhkova, 1906), 182; M. V.

Nechkina, *Dvizhenie dekabristov,* 2 vols. (Moscow: Izdanie Akademii nauk SSSR, 1955), 2:108–9.

20. The date and circumstances of this episode vary in different accounts. V. N. Zvegintsov, in *Kavalergardy dekabristy: Dopolnenie k sborniku biografii kavalergardov. 1801–1826* (Paris: [n.p.], 1977), 74, places it in 1808; A. E. Rozen, in *Zapiski dekabrista* (St. Petersburg: Tipografiia tovarishchestva "Obshchestvennaia pol'za," 1907), 30, after 1812. S. Komovskii, in "Zametki" (*Russkii arkhiv* [1868], col. 1034–35) and Natan Eidelman, in his *Lunin* (Moscow: "Molodaia gvardiia," 1970), 29, cite two other versions of the incident. See the discussion of Lunin's actions as a political statement in Iakov Gordin, *Pravo na poedinok* ([Leningrad]: "Sovetskii pisatel'," 1989), 408–10. On the officers' clash with Nicholas, see Gordin, *Pravo na poedinok,* 409–10. Herzen, in *Byloe i dumy,* relates yet another story about an officer's conflict of honor with Nicholas; see his *Sobranie sochinenii v 30-ti tomakh,* 30 vols. (Moscow: Izdatel'stvo Akademii nauk SSSR, 1954–64), 8:58.

21. See D. A. Smirnov, "Rasskazy o A. S. Griboedove, zapisannye so slov ego druzei," in *A. S. Griboedov v vospominaniiakh sovremennikov* (Moscow: Khudozhestvennaia literatura, 1980), 213, 242. Smirnov recorded S. N. Begichev's and I. G. Ion's accounts in the early 1840s.

22. V. A. Olenina, "Pis'ma k P. I. Bartenevu, 1869," in *Dekabristy: Letopisi gosudarstvennogo literaturnogo muzeia* (1938), 3:488; see also 3:491.

23. I cannot discuss here how the tradition of dueling in Poland, which was very strong, influenced the Russian duel. I point out, however, that Russians consistently mocked Polish duelists as both hotheaded and not serious enough. The beginning of this attitude can be traced at least back to Petr Tolstoy's account of his stay in Warsaw in 1697 (see *Puteshestvie stol'nika P. A. Tolstogo po Evrope. 1697–1699* [Moscow: Nauka, 1992], 25, 28). Bestuzhev's tale contributes to this view.

24. "Castle Wenden (A Fragment from a Guard Officer's Diary)" was first published in 1823. "Castle Eisen" initially was to appear in Ryleev's and Bestuzhev's almanach *The Little Star* under the title "Blood for Blood." After 14 December 1825, the whole edition of the almanac was confiscated and released only in 1861. The tale was published in 1827 as "Castle Eisen." The original version was recently published in *Faksimil'noe vosproizvedenie piati listov (80 stranits) almanakha A. Bestuzheva I K. Ryleeva ZVEZDOCHKA, otpechatannikh v 1825 godu* (Moscow: Kniga, 1981), 1–36. Two other Livonian tales are "Castle Neihausen: a Tale of Chivalry" (1824) and "Tournament at Revel" (1825). In light of Bestuzhev's populist treatment of the duel, it is noteworthy that "Tournament at Revel" upholds a commoner's right to a duel.

25. Serrat's historical prototype used an ax in his assault. See *The Chronicle of Henry of Livonia: A Translation with Introduction and Notes* by James A. Brundage (Madison: University of Wisconsin Press, 1961), 88–89.

26. A. N. Vul'f, *Dnevniki* (Moscow: Izdanie "Federatsiia," 1929), 246.

27. For contemporary reactions, see *Pis'ma P. V. Kireevskogo k N. M. Iazykovu,* ed. M. K. Azadovskii (Moscow: Izdatel'stvo Akademii nauk SSSR, 1935), 26 (published as volume 1, issue 4 of *Trudy Instituta antropologii, etnografii i arkheologii*); V. Vrasskaia, "Pushkin v perepiske rodstvennikov," *Literaturnoe nasledstvo* 16–18 (1934): 781. For a more recent publication of this letter, see *Famil'nye bumagi Pushkinykh-Gannibalov,* vol. 1, *Pis'ma Sergeia L'vovicha i Nadezhdy Osipovny Pushkinykh k ikh docheri Ol'ge Sergeevne Pavlishchevoi. 1828–1835* (St. Petersburg: "Pushkinskii fond," 1993), 122.

28. On Pavlov's case, see the report in a contemporary newspaper *Severnaia pchela,* no. 124 (1836), June 3; A. S. Pushkin, letter to N. N. Pushkina, 18 May 1836, in his *Polnoe sobranie sochinenii v 16-ti tomakh* (Leningrad: Izdanie Akademii nauk SSSR, 1946), 16:117; A. V. Nikitenko, *Dnevnik* (Leningrad: Gosudarstvennoe izdatel'stvo Khudozhestvennaia literatura, 1955), 1:183–84; N. Makarov, *Kaleidoskop v dopolnenie k "Moim semidesiatiletnim vospominaniiam"* (St. Petersburg: Tipografiia V. V. Komarova, 1883), 164–66; *Russkii arkhiv* (1906), cols. 433–34.

29. The narrator justifies her horrible execution with a peculiar reasoning that indirectly endorses the duel: "It seems that Louise was least of all guilty, and she suffered most of all. But God knows what He does. Blood upon man often washes away past stains, but upon woman it is almost always worse than Cain's mark" (1:168).

30. Leighton, in his *Alexander Bestuzhev-Marlinsky* (71–74), argues that Bestuzhev's historical tales were more accurate than most Romantic works about past events. While this might be true, Bestuzhev never seriously intended historical allusions to be more than a disguise for the discussion of contemporary issues. The 1820s censors intuited Bestuzhev's intentions and caused him difficulties in publishing his tales. The publication of "Wenden Castle" was initially banned by Moscow censors; see Sergei Isakov, "O 'livonskikh' povestiakh dekabristov (K voprosu o stanovlenii dekabrskogo istorizma)," *Uchenye zapiski Tartuskogo gosudarstvennogo universiteta* 167 (1965): 37. In his essay, which is devoted to the problem of historical accuracy in the Decembrists' works about the Baltic area, Isakov points out that Bestuzhev's knowledge of Livonian history was superficial and derived not from authentic historical sources or serious scholarly works, but from popular textbooks, which he used uncritically (38–40, 50–51). For example, Bestuzhev picked up a typo from one such source, F. G. de Bray, *Essai critique sur l'histoire de la Livonie,* vol. 1 (Dorpat: 1817), naming the character in his "Castle Wenden" Serrat instead of the historically correct Soest. For an analysis of Bestuzhev's "Livonian tales" as historical fiction see also Mark Altshuller, *Epokha Val'tera Skotta v Rossii (Istoricheskii roman 1830-kh*

godov) (St. Petersburg: Gumanitarnoe agenstvo "Akademicheskii proekt," 1996), 50–53. Both Altshuller and Leighton point out Scott's influence on Bestuzhev.

31. See *The Chronicle of Henry of Livonia,* 88–89.

32. Nechaev's letter is published in *Russkaia starina* 61 (1889): 320.

33. Bestuzhev, "Roman v semi pis'makh," in his *Vtoroe polnoe sobranie sochinenii,* 4th ed. (St. Petersburg: Ministerstvo gosudarstvennogo imushchestva, 1847), vol. 2, part 4, 126–27. Lotman, in his essay "Duel'," published in his *Besedy o russkoi kul'ture: Byt i traditsii russkogo dvorianstva (XVIII—nachalo XIX veka)* (St. Petersburg: Iskusstvo—SPB, 1994), briefly discusses the duel's capacity to deprive a person of free will (175). This aspect of the duel was later examined by Pushkin in *Eugene Onegin* and by Tolstoy in *War and Peace.*

34. Bestuzhev, "Roman v semi pis'makh," 126.

35. Jean-Jacques Rousseau, *La nouvelle Héloïse,* part 1, letters 57 and 60.

36. This is not to say that everyone in Russia shared this attitude and that reluctant duelists did not exist (this essay mentions at least two: Shakhovskoi and von Dezin). I am talking about a small group of like-minded people trying to establish the duel as a deterrent against personal abuses. Their cultural prestige, however—and therefore their influence—were significant.

37. Besides "A Novel in Seven Letters," this idea can be seen in "A New Sentimental Traveler" and in an anonymous 1809 "Ode on Duels" ("Oda na poedinki"). *Eugene Onegin* and, later, Dostoevsky's *Notes from Underground* are examples of polemical responses to Rousseau's argument. "Ode on Duels," which was first published in *Vestnik Evropy,* no. 16 (August 1809): 279–82, and signed G-v, can be found in A. S. Griboedov, *Sochineniia* (Moscow: Khudozhestvennaia literatura, 1988), 377–79, among the works ascribed to him. The influence of Rousseau is suggested in the commentary, 696. S. A. Fomichev argues that the ode was written by the adolescent Griboedov; see Fomichev, "Spornye voprosy griboedovskoi tekstologii," *Russkaia literatura* 2 (1977): 72–74.

38. Onegin's shooting at Lensky while still on his way to the barrier and without intent to kill follows the dueling scenario in Bestuzhev's story. The description of Erast's dying in the snow stylistically reverberates in Onegin's later recollection of Lensky's death.

39. Pushkin also rejects the solution offered by the European literary tradition: unlike Julie and other Sentimental heroines, Tatiana cannot prevent the duel because the male characters, in accordance with the honor code, keep her in the dark about the upcoming duel. William Mills Todd III, in his *Fiction and Society in the Age of Pushkin: Ideology, Institutions, and*

Narrative (Cambridge: Harvard University Press, 1986), 128, briefly discusses Pushkin's disagreement with literary convention.

40. Quoted in V. G. Bazanov, "Tvorchestvo Aleksandra Bestuzheva-Marlinskogo," in his *Ocherki dekabristskoi literatury. Publitsistika. Proza. Kritika* (Moscow: Gosudarstvennoe izdatel'stvo khudozhestvennoi literatury, 1953), 408. Bazanov argues (409–18) that "The Test" was written in response to the first six chapters of *Eugene Onegin.*

41. A. F. Belousov, "Institutka: sotsial'no-psikhologicheskii tip i kul'turnyi simvol "peterburgskogo" perioda russkoi istorii," in *Antsiferovskie chteniia: Materialy i tezisy konferentsii (20–22 dekabria 1989 g.)* (Leningrad: Leningradskoe otdelenie Sovetskogo fonda kul'tury, 1989), 181.

42. On the treatment of *institutki* throughout the nineteenth century and on presentations of this type in Russian literary works, see ibid., 181–84.

43. Dostoevsky later developed this idea in *The Idiot:* Prince Myshkin is exempt from the honor code due to his special status.

44. Yelena Dushechkina, in her *Russkii sviatochnyi rasskaz: stanovlenie zhanra* (St. Petersburg: Izdatel'stvo Sankt-Peterburgskogo gosudarstvennogo universiteta, 1995), analyzes traditional and literary Yuletide stories as a genre offering instruction on proper behavior. In chapter 3, 102, she discusses "The Terrible Divination" as a Yuletide story.

DAVID M. BETHEA, "SLAVIC GIFT-GIVING, THE POET IN HISTORY, AND PUSHKIN'S *THE CAPTAIN'S DAUGHTER*"

1. In Marcel Mauss, *The Gift: The Form and Reason for Exchange in Archaic Societies,* trans. W. D. Halls, with a foreword by Mary Douglas (New York: Norton, 1990), vii, ix; hereafter cited in the text.

2. On the frequency and possible levels of meaning of the word *dar* in Pushkin (in contrast to Mickiewicz), see Lawrence L. Thomas, "Toward a Contrastive Study of Word-Usage: Mickiewicz and Pushkin," in *Studies in Slavic Linguistics and Poetics,* ed. Robert Magidoff et al. (New York: New York University Press, 1968), 261–69. It turns out, curiously, that *dar* is not used at all in *The Captain's Daughter,* while *podarok,* in the sense of concrete gift, is used twice: once in reference to the gift of the *zaiachii tulup* and once as incriminating evidence at Grinev's trial (i.e., reference is made to Pugachev's various "presents" to the hero), see A. S. Pushkin, *Polnoe sobranie sochinenii,* ed. B. V. Tomashevskii, 10 vols. (Leningrad: Nauka, 1977–79), 272, 362; hereafter cited in the text as *PSS.* My thanks to J. Thomas Shaw for drawing this to my attention and in general for his careful reading of the present study in draft form. I also thank Gary Rosenshield, Caryl Emerson,

Sergei Davydov, William Mills Todd III, and Dan Ungurianu for their helpful suggestions and corrections.

3. I use the term *salon* here merely as a shorthand. The intentional deployment of archaisms for dramatic effect in Karamzin's text as well as his massive agglutination of notes and scholarly apparatus would not have been emulated by Voltaire the historian, for example.

4. Recent scholarship has placed particular emphasis on the powerful connecting links between the aestheticizing ("harmonizing") codes of (largely French-dominated) polite society and salon culture, on the one hand, and the special self-awareness and insider status of Pushkin's literary language, on the other. See, for example, William Mills Todd III, *Fiction and Society in the Age of Pushkin* (Cambridge: Harvard University Press, 1986), which applies the ideas of such social theorists and critics as Erving Goffman (theatrical metaphors of the self), Clifford Geertz (culture as text), and Iurii Lotman (culture as interpenetrating "semiospheres"). Also helpful for understanding the shifts in mythopoetic valences in Pushkin's language before and after 1825 (the Decembrist uprising) is B. M. Gasparov, *Poeticheskii iazyk Pushkina kak fakt istorii russkogo literaturnogo iazyka* (Vienna: Wiener Slawistischer Almanach/Sonderband 27, 1992). Finally, let it be said that Pushkin's attitude toward Karamzin and his monumental history was exceedingly complex, especially after Karamzin died in 1826 and was "misremembered" in the various official eulogies: in his own statements and historical research Pushkin had to find some authentic middle ground where he could (1) praise Karamzin for the man's "honorable deed" (the famous phrase *podvig chestnogo cheloveka*) and reasoned independence in the face of ideological pressures from all sides, (2) write the kind of history that both built on Karamzin's scholarly scrupulosity and yet implicitly went beyond his Enlightenment chronotope, and (3) serve Russia and its monarch (the office if not always the man) without debasing his own honor (*his* "honorable deed"). *History of Pugachev* is Pushkin's most explicit response to that challenge.

5. Iurii Lotman, *Kul'tura i vzryv* (Moscow, 1992), 28, 30; hereafter cited in the text.

6. "Agreement" is not a totally satisfactory translation for the Russian *dogovor,* which really means something akin to a "verbally agreed upon *contract.*" But I have left Shukman's rendering both in order to avoid confusion and because the root of "agreement" does go back both etymologically and psychologically to the notion of two different voices haggling over something and finally coming to rest at a mutually arrived upon spot ("*do*govorit'sia"). Conversely, the Russian borrowing *kontrakt* is more recent and gives off resonances that are strictly legalistic.

7. Iurii Lotman, " 'Agreement' and 'Self-Giving' as Archetypal Models of Culture," in *The Semiotics of Russian Culture,* ed. Ann Shukman (Ann

Arbor: Michigan Slavic Publications, 1984), 124–40; hereafter cited in the text.

8. As "supererogation" refers to good deeds performed by a saint that are *over and above* what is strictly needed for one's salvation, we see that the notion of "overpayment" is interpreted in a legal manner here as well. See, for example, Ernst Benz, *The Eastern Orthodox Church: Its Thought and Life* (Garden City, N.Y.: Anchor Books, 1963), 43–53: "From the beginning the West has understood the fundamental relationship between God and man primarily as a *legal* relationship" (43), while the focus in Orthodoxy has been on mysticism, apotheosis, and the primacy of love.

9. It should be stressed that I am not using the word "Slav" here in an ethnically precise way; a more rigorous scholarly treatment of the issue of *Slavic* gift-giving would need to make distinctions among such nonorthodox (or non-Orthodox) peoples as Slovenes, Czechs, and Poles.

10. Georges Bataille, "The Notion of Expenditure," in *Visions of Excess: Selected Writings, 1927–1939,* ed. and intro. Allan Stoekl (Minneapolis: University of Minnesota Press, 1985), 116–29; hereafter cited in the text.

11. Lest we forget, Pushkin lived in a period when Russian nobles were willing to gamble away not only entire fortunes but even, in one notorious example (A. N. Golitsyn's "Cosa-rara"), one's spouse! With regard to the biographical (as opposed to textual) Pushkin, one could say that "glory and honor are linked to wealth through loss" in his case by citing the famous episode when he lost the manuscript of his poems in a card game.

12. On the links between the "poetic" in Pushkin's prose and the "prosaic" in his poetry, see Wolf Schmidt, *Proza kak poeziia: Stat'i o povestvovanii v russkoi literature,* (St. Petersburg: Akademicheskii prospekt, 1994), 9–34.

13. It can of course be argued that the "poetic" aspects (say the link between sound and sense) of Pushkin's prose, even his historiography, only beg the question of their "origins." Are they not too "metahistorical" in the Whitean sense? Here it can only be answered that Pushkin, who tried his best to be a meticulous historian in the wake of Karamzin, did not suffer anxiety about his language's ability to "tell the facts." What Pushkin associated with the falsely "poetic" and "contrived" (*vydumannoe*) at the time of the writing of *History of Pugachev* was the notion of *literary* emplotment, of a storyline borrowed (perhaps unconsciously) from a novel and used to explain historical occurrences —something his own history writing could not be accused of. See his "Ob 'Istorii Pugachevskogo bunta' " in *PSS,* 8:263–78. To reiterate: that Pushkin *arranged* the order of narration (the notion of *siuzhet*) even in his history writing goes without saying, but that he himself viewed this arrangement as an aspect of novelistic fantasy and the *vydumannoe* is more open to question.

14. As Hayden White, for example, has argued in *The Content of Form: Narrative Discourse and Historical Representation* (Baltimore: Johns Hopkins University Press, 1987), the "value attached to narrativity in the representation of real events arises out of a desire to have the real events display the coherence, integrity, fullness, and closure of an image of life that is and can only be imaginary" (24). Furthermore, this very impulse toward narrativity is, according to White, profoundly "moralizing": in its attempt to locate a "legal subject" (the Hegelian "State cognizant of Laws") and to address such topics as "law, legality, legitimacy, or more generally, authority" (*The Content of Form,* 13), historiography can be distinguished from the "subject-less" writing of annals or chronicles. It is the argument of this essay that in Pushkin the "moralizing" aspect of narrativity underlying historiography is never prior to the "poetic" principle of sacrifice, generosity, and gift-giving. To repeat, Pushkin came to the genres of fiction and history through the genres of poetry.

15. As Abram Terts (Andrei Siniavskii) says in *Progulki s Pushkinym* (London: Overseas Publications Interchange/Collins, 1975), "Nesmotria na razdory i mery predostorozhnosti, u Pushkina bylo chuvstvo loktia s sud'boi, osvobozhdaiushchee ot strakha, stradaniia i suety. 'Volia' i 'dolia' rifmuiutsia u nego kak sinonimy. Chem bol'she my vveriaemsia promyslu, tem vol'gotnee nam zhivetsia, i polnaia pokornost' bespechal'na, kak ptichka" (48; cited hereafter in the text). Strictly speaking, the actual frequency of the *volia/dolia* pair in Pushkin's texts does not appear to bear out Siniavskii-Terts's provocative formulation: in all his basic texts the poet used the *volia/dolia* rhyme only twice and *voliu/doliu* once. In addition, the only time *volia/dolia* actually refers to Pushkin, or his lyrical I, as speaker is in "Pora, moi drug, pora," which as it turns out Pushkin did not publish in his lifetime. Even so, as a means of understanding Pushkin's psychology of creation and his somewhat superstitious tendency to see freedom as an inevitable extension of constraint, Terts's formulation strikes one as having much to recommend it. In a poet as subtle and self-concealing as Pushkin, frequency of usage may not be the only issue.

16. For discussion of the historical and folkloric material serving as background to the cycle, see Dmitrii Blagoi, *Tvorcheskii put' Pushkina (1813–1826)* (Moscow: Izd. AN SSSR, 1950), esp. 515–31; hereafter cited in the text.

17. Pushkin obtained his information about Sten'ka's drowning of the Persian princess from the travel account of the Dutch sailmaker Jan Jansen Struys who was in Astrakhan in 1669 and who witnessed Sten'ka after the latter's return from his "Persian campaign." Struys's book, entitled in Russian *Puteshestvie Striuisa,* existed in an 1827 French translation in Pushkin's library

as catalogued by Modzalevskii (one may assume in this instance Pushkin had access to an earlier copy of Struys, since the writing of "Pesni" dates to 1826). See Sergei Fomichev, "'Pesni o Sten'ke Razine' Pushkina: istoriia sozdaniia, kompozitsiia i problematika tsikla," in *Pushkin: Issledovaniia i materialy* 13 (1989): 4–20, esp. 6 and 10; cited hereafter as "Pesni."

18. It is curious, though presumably fortuitous, that Sten'ka makes his sacrifice in a virtual literalization of the "drop in the sea" metaphor offered above by Lotman.

19. For more on the structures of meaning in Pushkin's lyric cycles, see Fomichev, "Liricheskie tsikly v tvorcheskoi evoliutsii Pushkina," *Boldinskie chteniia* (Gorky, 1986).

20. "In being more directly cued to public esteem, the distributions of honour, and the sanctions of religion, the gift economy is more visible than the market" (Douglas, in Mauss, *The Gift,* iv).

21. The point here is that not only is a "forced gift" no gift at all, it is simply a tribute, a tax. The highly negative implications of "tax" (*nalogi,* that which is laid upon) in Russian culture, with its resonances of military extortion, as opposed to cooperative funding of social services, is, in its way, a polar opposite to *dar/podarok.* I would like to thank Caryl Emerson for bringing this point to my attention.

22. The fact that Pushkin uses tonic or accentual (non-metered) verse in the first and third poems of the cycle but a kind of *raeshnyi stikh* (lines loosely dominated by trochaic clausulae) in the second is also possibly significant on the thematic level: the latter is often used for satiric or humorous purposes (thus emphasizing the crudity and lack of generosity in the *voevoda*'s behavior), while the former, typical of the folk lyric, suggests Sten'ka large-spiritedness and *udal'stvo.* My thanks to Jennifer Ryan, a graduate student in Slavic Languages and Literatures at the University of Wisconsin-Madison, for first bringing this to my attention.

23. "V etikh vzveshennykh i netoroplivykh slovakh, kotorymi i zakanchivaetsia pesnia, iavstvenno slyshitsia zakipaiushchaia iarost', proiznositsia produmanno-groznyi i neotvratimyi prigovor nad bessovestnym i korystnym tsarskim voevodoi: deistvitel'no, v sleduiushchem 1670 g. Astrakhan' byla vziata Razinym i voevoda ubit" (Blagoi, *Tvorcheskii put',* 524).

24. It is also true in this context that Pushkin presumably felt the Pugachev uprising offered a richer source of parallels to his own 1830s (violent unrest in the military colonies, Polish uprising, war with Turkey, cholera epidemic, etc.) than did the case of Sten'ka. My thanks to William Mills Todd III for this suggestion.

25. See also A. S. Pushkin, *The Complete Prose Fiction,* trans., intro., and notes by Paul Debreczeny (Stanford: Stanford University Press, 1983), 366; hereafter cited in the text as *Complete Prose.*

26. The metahistorical critics who consider the organizing intelligence of a work like *History of Pugachev* isomorphic with the imposition of a literary *siuzhet* on an otherwise straightforward *fabula* are, in my judgment, overstating the case and extending quite different cognitive responses to reality over a broad and rather amorphous continuum.

27. Savel'ich's list was based on a similar petition submitted by a certain Court Councillor Butkevich to the government. What is ironic is that Pushkin has a servant rather than a nobleman submit the *reestr* of lost or stolen items in the novel. He avoids the incident entirely in the *History*. See Iu. G. Oksman, "Pushkin v rabote nad romanom *Kapitanskaia dochka*," in *Kapitanskaia dochka*, by A. S. Pushkin (Moscow: Nauka, 1984), 94–100; and Paul Debreczeny, *The Other Pushkin: A Study of Alexander Pushkin's Prose Fiction* (Stanford: Stanford University Press, 1983), 255.

28. Here Lotman's semiotic description of a paradigm shift has interesting links to what chaos theorists in the West term a "fractal": a system that appears to behave unpredictably but nevertheless displays some order. Also close to Lotman's distinction between *predskazuemost'* and *nepredskazuemost'* in the *Kul'tura i vzryv* book is Arthur Danto's notion of "narrative predicates" in *Narration and Knowledge* (New York: Columbia University Press, 1985): those statements made by a historian (as opposed to fiction writer) which, when applied to objects, "do so only on the assumption that a future event occurs," and which are seen as "retrospectively *false* . . . if the future required by the meaning rules of these predicates fails to materialize" (349–50).

29. On the role of folk logic in *Kapitanskaia dochka*, see especially I. P. Smirnov, "Ot skazki k romanu," in *Istoriia zhanrov v russkoi literature X–XVII vv.* (Leningrad: Nauka, 1972), 305–20. The use of the Aesopian fable to read the Kalmyk *skazka* is treated in Michael Finke, "Puskin, Pugacev, and Aesop," *Slavic and East European Journal* 35, no. 2 (1991): 179–92. Others who have touched on folkloric aspects in the novel include Iu. P. Fesenko, "Dve zametki ob A.S. Pushkine i V.I. Dale," *Vremennik Pushkinskoi komissii* 25 (1993): 154–61; Marina Tsvetaeva, "Pushkin i Pugachev" in *Izbrannaia proza v dvukh tomakh,* with a preface by J. Brodsky (New York: Russica, 1979), 2:280–302; Debreczeny, *The Other Pushkin* 258, 267–68; Viktor Shklovskii, *Gamburgskii schet* (Leningrad, 1928), 31; and V. D. Skvoznikov, "Stil' Pushkina," *Teoriia literatury* 3 (1965): 60–97, esp. 79–81. Fesenko makes the interesting point, for example, that Grinev withstands the four trials set to him in his meetings with Pugachev like the *dobryi molodets* of the barge haulers' song.

30. Lotman has no doubts about where Pushkin's sympathies lie in the confrontation between the two camps (peasant/nobleman) when he writes in "Ideinaia struktura *Kapitanskoi dochki*," *Pushkinskii sbornik* (Pskov: Pskovskii Gos. Ped. Inst., 1962), 3–20: "Bylo by zabluzhdeniem schitat', chto

Pushkin, vidia ogranichennost' (no i istoricheskuiu opravdannost') oboikh lagerei—dvorianskogo i krest'ianskogo—priravnival ikh eticheski. Krest'ianskii lager' i ego rukovoditeli privlekali Pushkina svoei *poetichnost'iu* [emphasis added], kotoroi on, konechno, ne chuvstvoval ni v orenburgskom komendante, ni vo dvore Ekateriny. Poetichnost' zhe byla dlia Pushkina sviazana ne tol'ko s koloritnost'iu iarkikh chelovecheskikh lichnostei, no i s samoi prirodoi narodnoi 'vlasti', chuzhdoi biurokratii i mertviashchego formalizma" (19).

31. For the psychological aspects of Petrusha's efforts to define himself against the various parent figures in the novel, see Caryl Emerson, "Grinev's Dream," *Slavic Review* 40, no. 1 (1981): 60–76; and Debreczeny, *The Other Pushkin*, 257–73. Pugachev is clearly a liminal figure, thus his eerie oneiric status to the hero, because he combines the role of "proxy father" (*posazhennyi otets*) and rebellious peasant son rising up against an authoritarian state symbolized by Catherine. See below.

32. Each feels, in Fomichev's formulation, a "korennoe dukhovnoe rodstvo pri vsei protivopolozhnosti svoikh klassovykh interesov" (*Poeziia Pushkina: Tvorcheskaia evoliutsiia* [Leningrad: Nauka, 1986], 265). This is what Lotman calls their ability to see the "*chelovecheskaia* pravota" of a foil's position ("Ideinaia struktura," 14).

33. In *An Obsession with History: Russian Writers Confront the Past* (Stanford: Stanford University Press, 1994), Andrew Wachtel writes, "The view of the Pugachev rebellion and the attitude toward history displayed in the novel are in no way meant to supersede the very different point of view of the history. Rather, Pushkin implies that the two works are meant to be read in tandem. The clash of their separate monologic narratives leads to an intergeneric dialogue that emphasizes the multiplicity of possible historical interpretations. Each belongs firmly to its own genre, but the two are linked to each other, and to all of Pushkin's work on historical themes by his conception of history as a series of possible stories" (83). My only reservation about this otherwise insightful argument is that it is a considerable impoverishment to describe a text as complex and cognitively challenging as *The Captain's Daughter* as a "monologic narrative." (One questions whether this is all Bakhtin meant by the term.) A similar but more nuanced approach is found in Dan Ungurianu's manuscript "Fiction and History in Pushkin's Portrayal of Pugachevshchina"; Ungurianu divides the reception history of *The Captain's Daughter* into two basic groups: the genres as "separate but equal" (Sollogub, Strakhov, Emerson, Debreczeny) versus a "hierarchy of truths" (Viazemskii, Katkov, Kliuchevskii, Iakubovich, Bliumenfel'd, and, most vividly, Tsvetaeva). There is also a third "middle ground" group that, while acknowledging the rules of each genre, see *The Captain's Daughter* as a "continuation of the author's historical research (or search for the truth) but this time through artistic means which compensate for the lacunas in

the documents": Annenkov, Cherniaev, Petrunina (Ungurianu, 1–5; cited hereafter in the text).

34. Sergei Davydov, "The Sound and Theme in the Prose of A. S. Pushkin: A Logo-Semantic Study of Paronomasia," *Slavic and East European Journal* 27, no. 1 (1983): 1–18, esp. 13.

35. Virtually all the gift-giving situations in the novel arise as a *combination* of chance and honor. At another point, for example, Grinev, who has escaped from a skirmish with the rebels, goes back to save his faithful servant Savel'ich. Ironically, it is Savel'ich, whom Grinev would have allowed to stay behind in Orenburg and keep half of his money, who now, out of his own sense of duty, follows too slowly and thus gets his master caught. Grinev's decision to return, which in the *History* would most certainly have resulted in his death, is his moral obligation to carry out. But then all these "chance" circumstances translate into a new meeting with Pugachev and a new opportunity for extravagant gift-giving (the rescue of Masha and Pugachev's role as matchmaker and "proxy father").

36. For more on the compositional symmetries in *The Captain's Daughter,* see Lotman, "Ideinaia struktura," 12–13.

37. "Pushkin iasno vidit, chto, khotia 'krest'ianskii tsar'' zaimstvuet vneshnie priznaki vlasti u dvorianskoi gosudarstvennosti, soderzhanie ee—inoe. Krest'ianskaia vlast' patriarkhal'nee, priamee sviazana s upravliaemoi massoi, lishena chinovnikov i okrashena v tona semeinogo demokratizma" (Lotman, "Ideinaia struktura," 9).

MELISSA FRAZIER, "*ARABESQUES*, ARCHITECTURE, AND PRINTING"

1. N. V. Gogol, *Polnoe sobranie sochinenii,* ed. N. L. Meshcheriakov, 14 vols. (Leningrad: Nauka, 1940), 3:123. Hereafter all citations of Gogol will be from this edition and will be given parenthetically in the text by volume and page number; this and all subsequent translations in the article are mine.

2. See Benedict Anderson, *Imagined Communities: Reflections on the Origin and Spread of Nationalism,* rev. ed. (London: Verso, 1991).

3. The main points of Schlegel's theory of genre can be found in *Gespräch über die Poesie* (1800) and the famous *Athenäums-Fragment* 116; my interpretation of these and other of Schlegel's works derives from Phillipe Lacoue-Labarthe and Jean-Luc Nancy's *The Literary Absolute,* trans. Philip Barnard and Cheryl Lester (Albany: State University of New York Press, 1988).

4. It is partly because Schlegel wants to create the apparently impossible combination of beauty and sublimity that he calls his Romantic genre the "arabesque." As Karl Konrad Polheim points out in his *Die Arabeske,* Schlegel

derives his term most probably from Kant's *Kritik der Urteilskraft* (1789), and in Kant we find the arabesque mentioned twice, once as an example of free beauty (under the name "delineations *à la grecque*"), and once as the product of a sublime commandment of God. See Polheim, *Die Arabeske* (Paderborn: Ferdinand Schöningh, 1966) and also sections 16 and 29 of Kant's *Kritik der Urteilskraft.*

5. Friedrich Schlegel, *Kritische Schriften* (Munich: Carl Hanser, 1964), 515. I should note that in *Geschichte der alten und neuen Literatur* (1815) the ever-inconsistent Schlegel reverses himself on the value of the printing press; of course, by that time Schlegel had reversed himself on a number of issues. Protestant and political progressive in 1800, in 1809 Schlegel converts to Catholicism and goes to work for Metternich; in 1815 he petitions to add a "von" to his name, as the advocate of parts and of nations becomes once and for all a devoted supporter of wholes and of empires.

6. Susanne Fusso, *Designing "Dead Souls": An Anatomy of Disorder in Gogol* (Stanford: Stanford University Press, 1993), 114. The extent to which Gogol actually knew of Schlegel's theory of genres is not clear, although the connection between *Arabesques* and Schlegel's arabesque has been made, for example by Joan Nabseth Stevenson in her Ph.D. dissertation, "Literary and Cultural Patterns in Gogol's 'Arabesques' " (Stanford University, 1984). Gogol does mention Schlegel's name in *Arabesques* in a note to the penultimate entry, "On the Movement of Peoples at End of the Fifth Century," but apparently with reference to *Über die Spräche und Weisheit der Indier* (1808). Still *Arabesques* must be considered in the context of Schlegel's arabesque; while Gogol could and probably did encounter arabesques elsewhere, for example in Hugo, Sir Walter Scott, and most important in Kant and in Goethe, these other arabesques, in particular the last two, all bear some sort of relation to Schlegel's. For more on this topic please see my "Frames of the Imagination: "Arabeski" and the Romantic Question of Genre" (Ph.D. diss, University of California at Berkeley, 1995).

7. In "On the Essence of Criticism" Schlegel offers the following explanation of his term: "And so one can only then say that one understands a work, a spirit, when one can reconstruct its movement and formation [*Gang und Gliederbau*]. Now this fundamental understanding which, if it were to be expressed in a particular word, is called characterization [*Charakterisieren*], is the true calling and inner being of criticism. Now, one could gather together the pure results of a historical mass into a concept, or rather not determine a concept to pure differentiation, but construct it in its becoming, from the first origin to the last perfection, giving the inner history of the concept together with the concept: both together are a *Charakteristik,* the highest task of criticism and the most inner wedding of history and philosophy" (400). My

interpretation of this typically difficult passage again derives from Lacoue-Labarthe and Nancy; see *The Literary Absolute,* 114–15.

8. Novalis, *Schriften,* ed. Richard Samuel, 2 vols. (Stuttgart: Kohlhammer, 1981), 2:661. Subsequent citations to Novalis's work will refer to this edition and will be given parenthetically in the text by volume and page number.

9. See William Mills Todd III, *Fiction and Society in the Age of Pushkin* (Cambridge: Harvard University Press, 1986).

10. S. P. Shevyrev, "Slovesnost' i torgovlia," *Moskovskii nabliudatel'* 1 (March 1835): 7. Subsequent citations to this article will be given parenthetically in the text.

11. According to Gerda Achinger in *Victor Hugo in der Literatur der Puskinzeit* (Cologne: Böhlau, 1990) Hugo's name is found only once in Gogol's writing, in a letter to Pushkin on 21 August 1831, where he makes a rather mocking remark about "Victor Hugo, unembraced by his own greatness"; see 10:204. He also mentions Hugo in one of the drafts of "On the Movement of Periodical Literature in 1834 and 1835"; see 8:528. Still, Achinger has no doubt that Gogol did know Hugo, and especially *Notre-Dame de Paris;* she cites M. P. Alekseev and in particular A. A. Nazarevskii in support of this claim.

12. O. I. Senkovskii, "Arabeski. Raznye sochineniia N. Gogolia," in *Russkaia kriticheskaia literatura o proizvedeniiakh N. V. Gogolia,* ed. V. Zelinskii (Moscow: Baladin, 1900), 25.

13. See note in Victor Hugo, *Oeuvres complètes,* ed. Jean Massin, 18 vols. (Paris: Le club français du livre, 1967–70), 4:22. Subsequent citations to this edition will be made parenthetically in the text.

14. "Zodchestvo i knigopechatanie," *Moskovskii telegraf,* part 52 (July 1833): 8. Anonymous translations in *Moskovskii telegraf* were usually the work of the editor, N. A. Polevoi.

15 In *The Truth in Painting* Derrida makes the argument that it is Kant, almost despite himself, who first suggests the possible combination of beauty and sublimity in colossally large buildings that are "framed," for example, by columns. See Jacques Derrida, *The Truth in Painting,* trans. Geoff Bennington and Ian McLeod (Chicago: University of Chicago Press, 1987), 15–147. I should note, by the way, as this reference to Kant would suggest, that real stone and not just paper Gothic churches also appear in Romanticism as a symbol of the combination of beauty and sublimity, for example in Schlegel's *Athenäums-Fragment* 389; for Schlegel, however, as for Hugo, this real building must give way to the imaginary and more truly infinite one; it is because Gogol refuses to make this transition that the Gothic churches in *Arabesques* begin to symbolize beauty combined with sublimity of a different kind.

16. In connection with the relationship of architecture and the word, God and man, it is worth mentioning Louis Marin's very interesting discussion "On a Tower of Babel," in *Of the Sublime: Presence in Question,* trans. Jeffrey S. Librett (Albany: State University of New York Press, 1993).

17. "Colossal" is truly the word for both *Notre-Dame de Paris* and *Arabesques;* it is no surprise that when Apollon Grigor'ev remembers the tremendous success achieved by the former, he speaks of "Hugo's colossal novel." See his *Vospominaniia* (Leningrad: Nauka, 1980), 6.

18. See Plato, *The Republic,* trans. H. D. P. Lee (Baltimore: Penguin Books, 1955), 373.

19. Donald Fanger, *The Creation of Nikolai Gogol* (Cambridge: Harvard University Press, 1979), 15. I should note, as does Fanger, that Gogol did find employment other than as a writer in the early part of his career: as a government clerk from 1829 to 1831, and as a teacher of history first at the Young Ladies' Institute and then at the university in 1834–35. Gogol, however, remained convinced that he should not have to work merely for the sake of money and he put this principle into practice for the main part of his career.

20. Gershenzon apparently mistakenly calls this work a "fourth" letter in his edition; later commentators no longer group this letter in the series of philosophical letters. See Raymond T. McNally, *Chaadaev and His Friends* (Tallahassee, Fla.: The Diplomatic Press, 1971).

21. Chaadaev was not the only one to link Gothic and Egyptian architecture. The comparison appears rather frequently in Paul Frankl's *The Gothic: Literary Sources and Interpretations through Eight Centuries* (Princeton: Princeton University Press, 1960), for example in the writings of James Cavanagh Murphy (1760–1840). In the association of the Gothic with Egypt (and in the wider association of the Gothic with the Saracens as well as in F. Schlegel's association of the Gothic with India) we find a hint of Romantic orientalism. While India, due to the efforts of the Germans, became the dominant locale of the Orient in Romanticism, Egypt was prominent earlier (think of Napoleon) and later specifically for the French (think of Napoleon again). See Raymond Schwab, *The Oriental Renaissance,* trans. Gene Patterson-Black and Victor Reinking (New York: Columbia University Press, 1984). Egypt as the Orient shows up in *Arabesques* in connection with monumentality.

22. P. Ia. Chaadaev, *Sochineniia i pis'ma,* ed. M. Gershenzon, 2 vols. (Moscow: A. I. Mamontov, 1913) 1:378. Subsequent citations to this edition will be made parenthetically in the text.

23. Ibid., 2:iii.

24. Gogol is at his most unendurable combination of arrogance and humility in his prefaces, or at least, so his contemporary critics seem to have thought. See the comments on the prefaces to *Arabesques* and to *Ganz*

Kiukhel'garten in the reviews of both works included in *Russkaia kriticheskaia literatura o proizvedeniiakh N. V. Gogolia,* ed. V. Zelinskii (Moscow: Baladin, 1900).

25. Anderson doesn't actually mention this example but he does mention others as he illustrates how even the most die-hard proponents of empire felt the power of the new "imagined" community of nation.

26. I see in a footnote to Susanne Fusso's *Designing "Dead Souls,"* 172, that a new and complete edition of *Arabesques* is in the works; while as a scholar I am pleased at the resurrection of Gogol's original intention, as a Romantic I can't help regretting the return of too much wholeness to Gogol's fragmentary work.

DAVID POWELSTOCK, "LIVING INTO LANGUAGE: MIKHAIL LERMONTOV AND THE MANUFACTURING OF INTIMACY"

1. The best overall account of the changing landscape of socioliterary institutions, and the responses of major Russian writers to these changes, remains William Mills Todd III's *Fiction and Society in the Age of Pushkin: Ideology, Institutions, and Narrative* (Cambridge: Harvard University Press, 1986).

2. Lermontov arrived in Petersburg in 1832, to attend military school. His letters from that time clearly depict his sense of Petersburg as alien to a young Moscovite. The two-city theme (friendly and sincere Moscow versus cold and venal Petersburg) is very sharply etched in Lermontov's unfinished novel, *Kniaginia Ligovskaia.*

3. According to P. A. Viskovatov's 1891 biography of Lermontov, in his teens the young poet bridled at his maternal relatives' disparagement of his father's lineage. P. A. Viskovatov, *Mikhail Iur'evich Lermontov: Zhizn' i tvorchestvo* (Moscow: Sovremennik, 1987), 68, 72. Although Viskovatov's biography does not always support its points with scholarly evidence (much of its material is based on interviews with people close to Lermontov's family who were still alive in the 1880s), such an attitude on Lermontov's part seems quite likely given (1) the poet's own attempts to investigate the Romantic possibilities in Lermontov family legends and (2) the signal value attached to the idea of *un grand nom* by both Lermontov himself and the society in which he circulated.

4. Here, and in all subsequent references to Lermontov's poems, notes, and letters, I cite volume and page number according to the six-volume Academic edition of Lermontov's works, *Sochineniia v shesti tomakh* (Moscow, 1954–57).

5. In many of his early poems, Lermontov locates this rift precisely in the conventionalized, unresponsive language he inherited from the Golden Age poetic. In one 1831 lyric, for example, he states that "With the cold letter it is difficult to explain / The struggling of thoughts" (Kholodnoi bukvoi trudno ob"iasnit' / Boren'e dum," from "1831-go iiunia 11 dnia" (1:177–78).

6. "I v etot mig gotov / Pozhertvovat' soboi, chtob kak-nibud' / Khot' ten' ikh [= vozvyshennykh strastei] perelit' v druguiu grud'," from "1831-go iiunia 11 dnia" (1:177–78).

7. See Lermontov's bitter and sarcastic lyric response to E. A. Sushkova's condescending reception of the young poet's declaration of love in "Blagodariu!" (1830, 1:148). This lyric is another fine example of Lermontov's use of implied context to imbue a single word with heightened emotional resonance.

8. It is worth noting that dramatic genres were of great importance to Lermontov in his early years. Of the five plays he completed in his lifetime, three were written in the years 1830–31 (*Ispantsy, Menschen und Leidenschaften,* and *Strannyi chelovek*). In addition, the preponderance of future projects sketched by Lermontov in his notebooks are plays; see the section in *Sochineniia v shesti tomakh,* "Plany. Nabroski. Siuzhety." (6: 374–85).

9. For an interesting discussion of the role of military service—and its competing modes of "parade" and "battle"—in the biography of the Russian nobleman of the early nineteenth century from the standpoint of behavioral semiotics, see Jurij Lotman, "The Theater and Theatricality as Components of Early Nineteenth-Century Culture," in *The Semiotics of Russian Culture,* by Ju. M. Lotman and B. A. Uspenskij, ed. Ann Shukman, Michigan Slavic Contributions, vol. 11 (Ann Arbor, Mich.: Department of Slavic Languages and Literatures, University of Michigan, 1984), 141–64.

10. See Iu. M. Lotman, "O dueli Pushkina bez 'tain' i 'zagadok,'" in his *Pushkin* (St. Petersburg, 1995), 375–88, esp. 380. Lotman's article was a review of the first edition of Stella Abramovich's balanced, sober treatment of this often mythologized and sensationalized topic; Stella Abramovich, *Pushkin v 1836 godu: predystoriia poslednei dueli* (Leningrad, 1984). Lotman's article is also reprinted as an epilogue to the second, expanded edition of Abramovich's *Predystoriia poslednei dueli Pushkina: Ianvar' 1836—ianvar' 1837* (St. Petersburg, 1994). See also V. V. Kunin, *Poslednii god zhizni Pushkina: perepiska, vospominaniia, dnevniki* (Moscow, 1988), and Ia. A. Gordin, *Pravo na poedinok: roman v dokumentakh i rassuzhdeniiakh* (Moscow, 1989).

11. Compare the almost comically mundane "On umer. Zdes' ego mogila" (He died. Here is his grave) of Lermontov's 1830 poem about the poet D. V. Venevitinov, "Epitafiia" (1:122).

12. In an earlier draft of the poem Lermontov had included the following lines about Pushkin's killer:

Его душа в заботах света
Ни разу не была согрета
Восторгом русского поэта
Глубоким пламенным стихом.
(2:273)

(Amidst the cares of society his soul
Was not once warmed with rapture
By the deep and fiery verse
of the Russian poet.)

13. Harold Bloom's insightful formulation in *The Anxiety of Influence: A Theory of Poetry* (London: Oxford University Press, 1973), 25.

14. I have analyzed this alternation in more detail in my "The Poet As Officer and Oracle: Mikhail Lermontov's Aesthetic Mythology" (Ph.D. diss., University of California at Berkeley, 1994), esp. chaps. 1 and 2.

15. Robert P. Hughes has remarked upon the manner in which Mikhail Kuzmin's poem "Pushkin" (1921) polemicizes with Lermontov's image of a dead Pushkin by emphatically repeating forms of the lexeme "life/live." "Pushkin in Petrograd, February 1921" in *Cultural Mythologies of Russian Modernism: From the Golden Age to the Silver Age,* ed. Boris Gasparov, Robert P. Hughes, and Irina Paperno (Berkeley and Los Angeles: University of California Press, 1992), 204–13.

16. The image of the poet "bowing down his head" is an inverted reference to Pushkin's poem "Poet" (1827). In Pushkin's lyric, the poet, inspired by "the divine word," "does *not* bow his proud head at the feet of the people's idol" ("K nogam narodnogo kumira / Ne klonit gordoi golovoi"). Pushkin, *Sobranie sochinenii v desiati tomakh* (Moscow, 1959–62), 2:179.

17. While it is possible to argue that line 7 should be interpreted in a broader, political sense, I find such an interpretation extremely tenuous. Against the background of bold, mythologizing strokes in the poem, line 7, if intended more generally as a eulogy of Pushkin's politics, seems jarringly timid. Any argument relying on censorship, or self-censorship, also seems strained, given that the poem could not possibly have been intended for publication. Finally, it is worth remembering that Pushkin, despite Soviet attempts to claim otherwise, was not a political activist.

18. A number of these reminiscences are traced by E. E. Naidich in his note to "Smert' poeta" in Lermontov, *Polnoe sobraniie stikhotvorenii v dvukh tomakh* (Leningrad, 1989), 2:601.

19. The line was "No chas nastal—i net pevtsa Kavkaza!" (But the hour has struck, and the bard of the Caucasus is gone! [2:273]). The latter half of this line can also be understood in the sense, "there is no poet of the Caucasus," which interpretation even more directly conflicts with Lermontov's own claim to that title. For a discussion of Lermontov's claim to the Caucasus

as his spiritual and poetic "home," see Powelstock, "The Poet As Officer and Oracle," esp. chap. 4.

20. See Bloom, *The Anxiety of Influence,* 26.

21. Unlike Bloom, I see the "strong poet" not merely as a category of inborn talent, but in some cases, and especially in Lermontov's, as the object of desire. As a psychological *and cultural* concept, Bloom's notion of the strong poet—which certainly owes a debt to the Romantic poetic culture it purports to describe—calls for a good deal of semiotic unpacking that I shall not undertake here.

22. See Vladimir Solov'ev, "Lermontov" (1899), in his *Literaturnaia kritika* (Moscow, 1990), 274–91, esp. 279.

23. Numerous accounts of the splash made by "Smert' poeta" can be found in M. I. Gillel'son, ed., *M.Iu. Lermontov v vospominaniiakh sovremennikov* (Moscow, 1989). This volume is usefully indexed by names of persons and of poems.

24. The story is recounted in the official testimony given by Lermontov's close friend Sviatoslav Afanas'evich Raevsky to the tsarist authorities investigating the incident. See Gillel'son, ed., *Lermontov v vospominaniiakh sovremennikov,* 483–85.

25. See G. A. Lapkina's note to "Smert' poeta" in Lermontov's *Sochineniia v shesti tomakh* (2:330).

26. In the poem "Moia rodoslovnaia" ("My Genealogy," 1830), Pushkin himself drew an ironic distinction between the old hereditary nobility and the so-called new aristocracy (*novaia znat'*), who earned their positions by service to the tsar.

27. The note is printed in *Lermontov v vospominaniiakh sovremennikov,* 486.

28. Ibid., 484; emphasis mine.

29. Ibid., 362. Although the original language of this letter was French, Gillel'son gives only a Russian translation, which I have translated into English. According to his note, the letter was first published in Dumas's *Le Caucase: Journal de voyages et romans* (Paris, 1859), 147–50. The book, unfortunately, is quite rare.

30. Lermontov was awarded the Order of Saint Vladimir, Third Degree, for his part in this battle. The announcement of the citation in the *Journal of Military Actions* stated that Lermontov, "heedless of any dangers, fulfilled the mission entrusted him with excellent courage and composure and burst through the enemy barricades with the first ranks of the very bravest." Quoted in G. A. Lapkina's note to the poem in *Sochineniia v shesti tomakh* (2:352).

31. N. M. Karamzin, "Chto nuzhno avtoru?" (1793), in *An XVIIIth Century Russian Reader,* ed. C. L. Drage and W. N. Vickery (Oxford: Clarendon Press, 1969), 162–63.

32. See Kiukhel'beker's article, widely discussed in the wake of its publication, "O napravlenii nashei poezii, osobenno liricheskoi, v poslednee desiatiletie," *Mnemozina: Chast' II* (Moscow, 1824), 29–44.

33. See E. E. Naidich's note to the poem in Lermontov, *Polnoe sobranie stikhotvorenii v dvukh tomakh,* 2:625.

34. It should be pointed out that in my use of the term "lyric hero," I depart slightly from Lidiia Ginzburg who, following Tynianov, uses "liricheskii geroi" to denote an already Romantic "lyric double" of the poet, his "ideal personality," which plays a central role in a given poet's poetics. While attributing this "double" to the poet's creation, Ginzburg simultaneously suggests that it belongs already to the semioticized sphere of cultural reception. It seems as if Ginzburg is playing on the double meaning of the Russian word *geroi,* which can mean a genuinely heroic "hero" or simply the axiologically neutral "protagonist." The ambiguity of her usage points to, but also slightly occludes the Romantic phenomenon by which the "I" of the lyric came to be identified by readers with a personality that was in some moral and psychological sense real. I prefer to use "lyric hero" as a synonym for "lyric I" or "speaker of the poem," thus keeping it rooted in poetics proper, while understanding that readers, in a secondary process, formed certain expectations about "lyric heroes." Maintaining this distinction between the poet's and reader's perceptions of the "lyric hero" allows me to explore the subtle slippage between the two frames. Lermontov's continual exploitation of this slippage to assert his independence from a homogenized, culturally defined lyric identity is crucial, I believe, to understanding the role that selfhood plays in his mature poetics. In referring to Lermontov's specifically Romantic desire to be seen (and desired) as a poet with heroic personality, I have used the term "poet-hero." See Ginzburg's *O lirike,* 2d ed. (Leningrad, 1974), esp. 160–62.

35. Letter to Eugene M. Kayden, 22 August 1958, written in English. Quoted in the preface to *Boris Pasternak: Poems,* ed. and trans. E. M. Kayden (Ann Arbor: University of Michigan Press, 1959), ix.

36. Very few of Pushkin's lyrics of the 1830s were published at the time, although today they are among his most admired. It is possible, I think, to attribute the withdrawal of Pushkin's lyric voice from the public sphere in part to the public's growing desire for a unified Romantic poet-hero, whose biography would conform to the personality projected in his poetry. Ginzburg brilliantly evokes this atmosphere by showing how Lermontov the dueling exile succeeded in this respect, where Vladimir Benediktov, a pockmarked *chinovnik,* failed. See her *O lirike,* esp. the chapter "Problema lichnosti."

37. Letter to V. A. Zhukovsky, 20 April 1825; Pushkin, *Sobranie sochinenii v desiati tomakh,* 9:155.

38. Solov'ev, "Lermontov," 279.

STEPHEN MOELLER-SALLY, "0000; OR, THE SIGN OF THE SUBJECT IN GOGOL'S PETERSBURG"

The ideas for this article evolved and took their final form under the stimulating influence of a sustained conversation with Monika Greenleaf. I express my gratitude to her, as well as to Caryl Emerson, William Mills Todd III, Edyta Bojanowska, and Betsy Moeller-Sally, for invaluable insights, suggestions, and corrections.

1. Contemporary examples of this practice are numerous in both Russian and other European literatures. Among the most prominent are James Macpherson's Ossian; Walter Scott, who was long known only as the author of *Waverley;* Stendhal, the pseudonym of Henri Beyle; Aleksandr Bestuzhev, who wrote under the pen name Marlinskii; Pushkin's *Tales of Ivan Petrovich Belkin.* An indispensable key to Russian literary pseudonyms is: I. F. Masanov, *Slovar' psevdonimov russkikh pisatelei,* 4 vols. (Moscow, 1956–60).

2. The first work to appear under Gogol's own name (and the only one before 1834) was the article "Woman," which was published in *Literaturnaia* gazeta, no. 4 (1831). Two others—a second chapter of "The Terrible Boar" and an early version of the tale "St. John's Eve"—appeared anonymously.

3. See Panteleimon Kulish, *Opyt biografii N. V. Gogolia* (St. Petersburg, 1854), 43.

4. N. V. Gogol, *Polnoe sobranie sochinenii,* 14 vols. (Moscow: AN SSSR, 1937–52), 10:206. All subsequent references to Gogol's work will refer to the Academy edition and will be made parenthetically in the text. Unless otherwise indicated, all translations of Gogol's works are my own.

5. Vladimir Nabokov, *Nikolay Gogol* (London: Weidenfeld and Nicolson, 1973), 27.

6. Robert A. Maguire, *Exploring Gogol* (Stanford: Stanford University Press, 1994), xi.

7. Peggy Kamuf, *Signature Pieces: On the Institution of Authorship* (Ithaca: Cornell University Press, 1988), viii–x.

8. For a definitive description of the professionalization of letters in early nineteenth-century Russia, see William Mills Todd III, *Fiction and Society in the Age of Pushkin* (Cambridge: Harvard University Press, 1986), 72–105.

9. Ibid., 81–82.

10. Georg Simmel, "The Metropolis and Mental Life," in *On Individuality and Social Form,* ed. Donald N. Levine (Chicago: University of Chicago Press, 1971), 326.

11. My thinking about zero, its potential meanings, and its link with the economy was influenced considerably by Brian Rotman's ingenious book

Signifying Nothing: The Semiotics of Zero (Stanford: Stanford University Press, 1987).

12. Robert Maguire has described the technique Gogol employs in the opening of the story as "retardation" (Maguire, 204–6). For another skillful formal analysis of the beginning of "Nevsky Prospect" see Donald Fanger, *Dostoevsky and Romantic Realism* (Cambridge: Harvard University Press, 1967), 110–13, 121–22.

13. Maguire, *Exploring Gogol,* 263.

14. Unicorn (*edinorog*) was the nickname of a howitzer cannon.

15. For a reading of Gogol's self-parody in "Nevsky Prospect" that accentuates composition and structure, see V. Sh. Krivonos, "Samoparodiia u Gogolia," *Izvestiia Akademii Nauk,* Seriia literatury i iazyka, vol. 52, no. 1 (1993): 25–34.

16. David Glenn Kropf, *Authorship as Alchemy: Subversive Writing in Pushkin, Scott, Hoffmann* (Stanford: Stanford University Press, 1994), 75.

17. See Gogol's letter of 3 October 1827 to his uncle Petr Petrovich Kosiarovskii, *PSS,* 10:111–13.

18. H. H. Gerth and C. Wright Mills, eds., *From Max Weber: Essays in Sociology* (New York: Oxford University Press, 1958), 215.

19. The inspiration for my analysis of substitution in "Diary of a Madman" came in part from Robert Maguire's reading of the story as a problem of place, particularly of disorder and displacement. See Maguire, *Exploring Gogol,* 49–66.

20. Ibid., 51.

21. I have taken the translation of the verses from Nikolai Gogol, *The Complete Tales,* trans. and ed. Leonard J. Kent (Chicago: University of Chicago Press, 1985), 1:243.

22. M.I. Gillel'son et al., *Gogol' v Peterburge* (Leningrad: Lenizdat, 1961), 34–35, 307.

23. On aristocratic self-fashioning see Domna Stanton, *The Aristocrat as Art: A Study of the "Honnête Homme" and the Dandy in Seventeenth- and Nineteenth-Century French Literature* (New York: Columbia University Press, 1980).

24. In a remarkably clever reading Richard Gustafson has shown that the dates in the latter part of the diary do betray a coherence: they are veiled references to the unlucky number thirteen. Poprishchin's attempts to escape reality, then, in fact represent a growing fixation on the one day, 13 November, when the truth of his situation is allegorically revealed to him in the dog's correspondence. Though this formula does not involve the number zero, it nevertheless can be seen to support the idea that Poprishchin is attempting—and failing—to restart time and thus a new persona. See "The Suffering

Usurper: Gogol's *Diary of a Madman*," *Slavic and East European Journal* 3 (1965): 268–80, esp. 273–74.

25. N. V. Gogol, "Glava iz istoricheskogo romana," *Severnye tsvety na 1831 g.* (St. Petersburg, 1831): 225 (emphasis added).

26. John Mersereau Jr., *Baron Del'vig's "Northern Flowers," 1825–1832* (Carbondale: Southern Illinois University Press, 1967), 197.

27. "Glava," 255.

28. Ibid., 227.

29. It is conceivable that Gogol also intended "Some Thoughts on Teaching Geography to Children" as another link in this chain. The segment of "The Terrible Boar" published in *Literaturnaia gazeta,* no. 1 (1831) was entitled "The Teacher."

30. "Glava," 256.

31. For the complete textual history, see *PSS,* 3:649–56. On noseological themes, see V. V. Vinogradov, *Evolutsiia russkogo naturalizma* (Leningrad, 1929), 7–88.

32. Donald Fanger has emphasized the narrative's claim to "pure instrumentality" (*Creation,* 122); Michael Holquist has argued that "the nose in Gogol's story is a part of the body that can only be appropriated as a part of speech," that "it *must* be read metaphorically" ("From Body-Talk to Biography: The Chronobiological Bases of Narrative," *Yale Journal of Criticism* 1 [1989]: 23); Gary Saul Morson has treated the story as a piece of "absolute nonsense" that serves as an illuminating "parable of explanation" ("Gogol's Parables of Explanation: Nonsense and Prosaics," in *Essays on Gogol: Logos and the Russian Word,* ed. Susanne Fussio and Priscilla Meyer [Evanston: Northwestern University Press, 1992], 226–33); finally, Thomas Seifrid has tied the text and its title character to a historically conditioned problem of finding an autonomous cultural discourse for Russia ("Suspicion Toward Narrative: The Nose and the Problem of Autonomy in Gogol's 'Nos,'" *Russian Review* 3 [1993]: 382–96). In its interpretation of "The Nose" as a response to Gogol's contemporary literary situation, my own reading builds on Fanger's and Seifrid's.

33. For a succinct and insightful summary of the controversy over *The Library for Reading* see Todd, *Fiction and Society,* 93–105.

34. The phrase is Gogol's in "O dvizhenii zhurnal'noi literatury v 1834 i 1835 godu" (8:165).

35. Gogol's tale was never published in the *Moscow Observer.* According to Belinsky, the editors rejected it for its "*poshlost'* and triviality." Gogol finally published "The Nose" more than a year later in Pushkin's *Contemporary.*

36. Stepan Shevyrev, "Slovesnost' i torgovlia," *Moskovskii nabliudatel'* 1 (1835): 7–9.

37. Ibid., 19.

38. "The Nose" had already been completed when "Literature and Commerce" appeared, but since Mikhail Pogodin seems to have kept him informed about the launching of the journal, Gogol would almost certainly have known at least the outlines of Shevyrev's position. See *PSS*, 10:341–42, 351–54.

39. Johann Wolfgang von Goethe, *Faust I & II*, ed. and trans. Stuart Atkins (Princeton: Princeton University Press, 1984), 30.

40. Ibid.

41. Gogol quotes the last two lines of Wagner's passage in a letter to Mikhail Pogodin dated 25 November 1832 (10:246). Venevitinov's translation appeared in his posthumous collected works in 1829.

42. Shevyrev, "Slovesnost' i torgovlia," 19. Also, Thomas Seifrid has suggested that "The Nose" may allude to an 1832 story by Senkovsky in which Satan munches on biscuits that turn out to be books. See Seifrid, "Suspicion Toward Narrative," 393.

43. *Metabollo* is Greek for "change," "alteration," or "turnabout." It is the term originally used in the Orthodox Church to describe the transformation of the bread and wine of the Eucharist into the Body and Blood of Christ. See Timothy Ware, *The Orthodox Church* (London: Penguin Books, 1963), 290.

44. In the earlier redaction of the text, which dates to 1833–34, Ivan Iakovlevich said "*Kholodnoe!*" not "*Plotnoe?*" (3:382).

45. I should note here two articles that address Gogol's complicated attitude toward his own original name (Gogol'-Ianovsky) in the context of "The Nose": Leon Stilman, "Nikolaj Gogol and Ostap Hohol," in *Orbis Scriptus: Dmitrij Tschizewskij zum 70. Geburtstag*, ed. Dietrich Gerhardt et al. (Munich: Wilhelm Fink, 1966), 811–25; Richard Gregg, "A la recherche du nez perdu: An Inquiry into the Genealogical and Onomastic Origins of "The Nose," *Russian Review* 4 (1980): 365–77.

46. Vissarion Belinskii, "O russkoi povesti i povestiakh g. Gogolia," in *Polnoe sobranie sochinenii* (Moscow: AN SSSR, 1953), 1:306.

47. Nikolai Gogol, *Dead Souls*, trans. B. G. Guerney (New York: Holt, Rinehart and Winston, 1966), 270–71.

48. For a useful summary of the reception of *Dead Souls*, see Paul Debreczeny, "Nikolay Gogol and His Contemporary Critics," *Transactions of the American Philosophical Society*, 56, no. 3 (1966): 29–50.

Index